Sodus Point

East Bay

Fair Haven

Sodus

Red Creek

Wolcott

CAYUGA

Marion

Cato

Clyde

Savannah

Port Byron

lmyra   Lyons

Newark

Montezuma

Weedsport

Clifton Sprs.

SENECA

rtsville   Phelps

Seneca Falls

Cayuga   Auburn

Fleming

igua   Geneva

Waterloo

Owasco

Stanley

Union Springs

ville

Scipio Center

YATES

Romulus

Aurora

Moravia

Penn Yan

Ovid

King Ferry

Genoa

Interlaken

TOMPKINS

Groton

Ludlowville

Dundee

Trumansburg

burg

Cayuga Hts.   Dryden

dsport

SCHUYLER

Ithaca

dford

Watkins Glen

Odessa

CHEMUNG

TIOGA

Campbell

Van Etten

Newark Valley

ted Post   Corning

Horseheads

Catatonk

Elmira Hts.

Elmira

Owego

Apalachin

Waverly

Nichols

N

The Diocese of Rochester
in America

1868 - 1993

FULTON JOHN SHEEN
(1895-1979)
Sixth Bishop of Rochester
1966-1969
Titular Archbishop of Newport
1969-1979

THE

Diocese of Rochester in America

SECOND EDITION
Emended and Updated

1868-1993

by ROBERT F. McNAMARA

With a Foreword by
Most Rev. Fulton J. Sheen, Ph.D., D.D.

Published by THE ROMAN CATHOLIC DIOCESE
OF ROCHESTER, NEW YORK 1998

The Diocese of Rochester in America, 1868-1993, printed by Upstate Litho, Rochester, New York, is published by The Diocese of Rochester, New York (1150 Buffalo Road, Rochester, NY, 14624; Phone: 716-328-3210; Fax: 716-328-3149). Address communications: "Attention, Book Orders."

Library of Congress Catalog Card number : 98-73870
International Standard Book Number : 0-9668610-0-0

Printed and bound in the United States of America

DEDICATED

TO THE MEMORY OF

THE DIOCESAN PIONEERS.

MAY WE BE WORTHY

OF THEIR GIFT

"Pioneers are those who work in the sun, so that those that come after them will have shady spots to enjoy."

✠ *James E. Kearney*
Bishop of Rochester
1937-1966

FOREWORD

WE ARE the heirs of the past. As a man cannot think without going back into the storehouse of his memory, so neither can a Church think and grow without a memory, which is Tradition and History. He who would ignore the history of his diocese or his Church, is like a man with amnesia, or a flower without roots.

The Church is both a Rock and a River. The Church was founded on a Rock—something immovable and fixed. But Scripture depicts waters coming from the Rock. Moses struck the Rock and waters came forth. The Christ, who is called the Rock, is the one from whose side John saw flow the waters of regeneration. Those who see only the Rock miss the dynamic unfolding of the Spirit in the Church; those who see only the waters pouring in the desert of the world, sometimes forget Christ Who is the Source of all grace.

History is not something wholly in the past. God invaded history; He established a beachhead in Bethlehem, rooted Himself in its soil on Calvary, and then gave the cosmos itself the only serious wound it ever received—the wound of an empty tomb. The past is in the present, and the future is, to some extent, in the present.

In this book we have the history of our diocese. In one sense it is a cameo of the history of the whole Church, in which we see forever God's arm outstretched in our fall—to lift us up. Every area and parish of the earth is under His Providence and not a cruel, relentless fate. Though none of the leaders of the Church, in the past, knew the issues of their struggles even in the darkest day, they nevertheless lifted up their hearts.

> The men of the East may spell the stars,
> And times and triumphs mark,
> But the men signed with the sign of the Cross
> Go daily in the dark.
>
> —Chesterton.

This history of the Diocese makes amends for those who have not lived through its one hundred years. Thanks to the "News of the Hour on the Hour", everyone knows what has happened all over the world the last twenty-four hours, but few know what has happened in the last fifty or one hundred years. The advantage of a history such as this, is that it enables the young people to be old without the afflictions of age, and the old to be young without ever being exclusively what Horace called *Laudator temporis acti*—"the singers of praise to things gone by". Christianity is a historical religion. Hence, it differs from all other religions. Boris Pasternak makes a good reason: "The ancients lacked the idea of a free personality and the idea of sacrifice. That is why they had no history".

All dioceses grow by cell expansion from a biological nucleus rather than by fission or splitting as in the atomic order. Rochester was first part of the New York Archdiocese; then a part of Buffalo; and finally in 1868 it became a diocese under Bishop McQuaid whose ministry was only nine years short of half the centennial existence of the Diocese. The *New York Herald* at the time of his consecration said: "The Right Reverend Gentleman was baptized by Bishop Connollly, the first Bishop of New York; confirmed by Bishop Dubois, the second Bishop of New York; ordained by Bishop Hughes, the third Bishop of New York, and consecrated Bishop by Archbishop McCloskey of New York".

That the Diocese has made material progress in the last hundred years can be measured in terms of population, buildings and personnel. But the true historian looks to the spiritual values as seen from an upper window.

As W. H. Auden put it:

> Let us honor if we can
> The vertical man
> Though we value none
> But the horizontal one.

We know how long a field is, but how far is it from the sky? This is the intangible of every history: Two men in a bed; two women at a mill, doing exactly the same things, but one is taken, the other lost.

The historian, therefore, must not only tell what "happened", but give also the vertical dimensions, such as the story of the good woman who carried her infant girl from Rochester to New York to have her baptized.

Father McNamara belongs to the school of documentation. His imagination and romanticism are locked up, and rarely does he allow them to play. He writes history as Thomas Aquinas wrote philosophy, rather than Augustine who broke out into ejaculations. He digs up the bones of those who have gone before, and in his hands, they are dry, but "their works do follow them". There is no Ezekiel vision of the dry bones taking on flesh and blood in his history, but there is rather the genealogy of a Matthew and a Luke describing an "event"—the revelation of the Diocese in its hundred years. In the clenched fists of the dead, which he opens, he has found their deeds and their words, and made them our heritage.

Bultmann demythologized the Gospel and forgot the historical Christ, but Father McNamara, while allowing no mythology, nevertheless, gives us a historical diocese. Who can number the dusty files, the old newspaper clippings, the forgotten desiccated books in the back shelves of libraries, the musty Baptismal records, the palimpsests, hieroglyphics, that he had to finger through to give us just a line. But somehow or other, characters emerge and we know them to be other Adams or other Christs like ourselves.

Mankind will not perish for want of information, but only for want of inspiration. This history contains both, the first overt; the second covert.

Strong and weak find their portraits here, and both have become the warp and woof of the Diocese. The weak and the strong are bound to the eternal, and both have shaped the Mystical Body we have before us now. In a sense, the history of a diocese is an eternal history, because all the participants rightly believed they were working to that order.

We thank Father McNamara for not allowing our history to be a *Hortus Conclusus;* or a *Fons Signata,* but for opening up its fruits and swirling fountains to our gaze. By his honesty and scholarship, he has made us realize that though we fear we live in an age of corruption, nevertheless, to some extent, all ages are corrupt, but we must not despair.

God is cleaning house; today, to those who will not accept His Truth, He asks: "Will you also go away?" He presses us to see that our mission in the face of a world that would be non-Christian, is to remain Christian, and thus, save the world from suicide. The "Finger of the God of Love" is in our diocesan history; and God in the history of the Diocese is not a joker in a pack of cards, to be banged down on the table for one important play. God is in our history as the soul in the body, for "in Him we live and move and have our being". May His protecting Hand continue to be over us to make us a holy people, a sanctified clergy and religious, and an area of the earth where all men live in peace in an ecumenism which is a foretaste of the joys of heaven.

✠ *Fulton J. Sheen*
Bishop of Rochester

PREFACE

IN 1958, His Excellency, the Most Reverend James E. Kearney, then Bishop of Rochester, requested the present writer to prepare a history of the Rochester Diocese in time for the diocesan centenary, 1968. The publication of this volume represents—how successfully we shall let others decide—the accomplishment of that commission.

A few words of explanation are in order. *The Diocese of Rochester* is a history of the Diocese rather than of its separate parishes and institutions. It is not, strictly speaking, a series of biographies of successive bishops. Division into episcopates is logical in the historiography of a hierarchical Church, and is most convenient. But the bishops themselves (whose *acta* since 1937 do not pretend to be more than a chronology) would be the first to declare that what is attributed to their regimes is in major part the result of the loyal collaboration of their priests, religious and laity.

The ideal diocesan historian would be one intimately acquainted with the past of every parish and every foundation. This writer falls short of such a requirement. He has had to content himself with giving a general and sketchy picture of diocesan growth. The spotlight naturally comes to rest most often upon the see city because it *is* the see city and because it is the largest Catholic center in the Diocese. But the Diocese comprises twelve counties, not one county. It is to be hoped that our effort to convey this wider impression has not failed.

Another tendency which we have tried to avoid is to represent the diocesan story as something occurring in a vacuum. It is becoming more and more clear nowadays that American Catholicism in the past was often too content to move along its own channel. But at no time has this been completely true, or completely possible. Furthermore, even the most stay-at-home Catholic cannot remain untouched by the great movements and tragedies of world history. *The Diocese of Rochester* makes some attempt to set the events of each epoch against their related national and international background.

Of one thing we are fairly confident. The reader will find in these pages the picture of a typical elderly American diocese of middling size and distinction. All the main matters are here: the pioneers, the

first and second immigrations, trusteeism, nativism, the school controversy, labor problems, secret societies, the great battles between bishops,
organized charities, catechetics, church-state issues, Catholic Action, inner-city problems. Of added and more particular interest is the episode
of the Jesuit missions among the local Iroquois in the seventeenth and
eighteenth centuries. As a fascinating chapter in the pre-history of the
Diocese, this noble episode could not in justice be omitted.

Regarding our sources. Especially for the later episcopates we have
had to lean heavily on newspapers. While the McQuaid archives have
come down to us, the files of his successors up to 1937 were unfortunately largely destroyed when the Chancery moved in that year. Items
about individual parishes and institutions are often drawn from questionnaires sent out in 1959 and thereafter, to the pastors and institutional directors of the Diocese. We have also drawn at times on the
parochial and institutional data collected during the Great Depression
by a committee of federal WPA investigators, and handed over to the
Diocese in typescript form before World War II. Where our notes mention no specific source of information in these matters, the information
generally comes from either the historical questionnaires or the WPA
reports.

Because of its thoroughness, *The Life and Times of Bishop Mc-
Quaid* by Father Frederick J. Zwierlein (Louvain and Rochester, 1925-
1927), has been taken, on competent advice, as the basis of the chapters on the first four decades of the Diocese. What we have added to
Zwierlein's study is certain newer items of information and other data
that often temper—we feel—the rather harsh features of the Zwierlein
portrait of the founding Bishop. A controversialist himself, Dr. Zwierlein seems to have preferred McQuaid at his most belligerent. The
Bishop was indeed a stalwart; but there were also several more winning
aspects of his character.

Another Rochester writer to whom this book is indebted is Dr.
Blake McKelvey. Even though not often cited in our notes, his four-
volume history of Rochester and his articles in *Rochester History* have
contributed much background material. His personal counsel has also
been very helpful.

Most of those who have furnished data or pictures are given recognition in the appropriate place. Here we wish to give a nod of gratitude
to several particular individuals.

For archival assistance, we are beholden: to Miss Emma Swift, past director of the Local History Department, Rochester Public Library, and to all the staff of that department; to Mrs. Edith M. Fox and the staff of the Collection of Regional History, Cornell University; to Sister Alma Joseph Bauman of the Rochester Sisters of St. Joseph; and to Sister M. Florence Sullivan of the Rochester Sisters of Mercy.

For assistance in production, we are especially grateful to: Father Joseph M. Dailey and the staff of the diocesan Pastoral Office; to Msgr. John S. Randall, Fathers Henry Atwell and Robert Kanka, and Thomas H. O'Connor of the staff of the Catholic Courier Journal; to Mr. Martin Q. Moll, Mr. James J. Lane, Mr. Melvin R. Quinn and the staff of the Christopher Press, Inc. All these have shown not only a technical but a genuinely personal interest in our project. But nobody has been so long and so deeply involved as Rt. Rev. Msgr. Wilfred T. Craugh, Rector Emeritus of St. Bernard's Seminary, who has patiently and critically read the whole manuscript and helped correct the proofs. For this aid we are most thankful.

Finally, the author must express abiding gratitude to three bishops. To Most Reverend Lawrence B. Casey, Bishop of Paterson, who, while Auxiliary Bishop of Rochester, first proposed the project of a centennial diocesan history. To Most Reverend James E. Kearney, who assigned the task. Both have followed its progress with kindly encouragement. And lastly, to the present Bishop of Rochester, Most Reverend Fulton J. Sheen. Shortly after his arrival, Bishop Sheen generously offered to read the manuscript. We are deeply indebted to him for his suggestions and for the meditative Foreword which he so graciously contributed.

It goes without saying, however, that no person who has assisted us is in any way responsible for the statements made in the following pages. That responsibility belongs solely to the writer.

So much with regard to our purpose and those who have helped us to achieve it.

The last word is addressed to our readers. Instead of framing a special admonition, we shall quote, as expressive of our own sentiments, the afterword of Sir Geoffrey Chaucer's *Canterbury Tales*.

Now preye I to hem alle that herkne this litel tretys or rede, that if ther be any thyng in it that liketh hem, that thereof they thanken our Lord Jhesu Crist, of whom procedeth al wit and al goodnesse. And if ther be any thyng that displease hem, I preye hem also that they arrette it to the defaute of myn unkonnynge, and nat to my wyl, that wolde ful fayn have seyd bettre if I hadde had konnynge . . . Wherfore I biseke yow mekely, for the mercy of God, that ye preye for me that Crist have mercy on me and foryeve me my giltes . . . so that I may been oon of hem at the day of doom that shulle be saved. *Qui cum patre et Spiritu Sancto vivit et regnat Deus per omnia saecula saeculorum. Amen.*

—*Robert F. McNamara*

St. Bernard's Seminary
Rochester, New York
January 1, 1968

PREFACE TO THE SECOND EDITION

The first edition of *The Diocese of Rochester, 1868-1968* has been out of print for several years. An increasing request for copies has prompted this reissue. While an ideal second edition would contain an ample updating of the intervening years, idealism must yield to reality. What we present herewith is a corrected version of the original centennial text. Lest the eventful recent past seem slighted, however, we have added a new chapter summarizing the annals of the Diocese's fifth quarter-century, 1968-1993.

Sincere thanks to those who have assisted us in producing this new edition, especially Father William E. Graf, Kathleen Urbanic, and our faithful typist Virginia Stevens.

—*Robert F. McNamara*
Archivist

November 3, 1998
Archives,
Diocese of Rochester

CONTENTS

PHOTO CREDITS

12. Daughters of Charity, Emmitsburg, Md. 19. Msgr. Charles O'C. Sloane, Mt. Vernon, N.Y. 10, 21. Mr. Warnick J. Kernan, Utica, N.Y. 24. Mr. Louis A. Langie, Sr. 25. Mr. Peter Barry. 43. Mrs. Mary LeBeau Weber, 50, 51, 52. William G. Bland photos. 53, 54, 64, 81, 82, 133. Martin J. Wahl photos. 63, 78. Eastman Kodak Company photos. 79. Msgr. Francis B. Burns. 95. Carbone photos, Syracuse. 102. Mr. Joseph H. Gervais. 103. Mr. Jeremiah G. Hickey, Jr. 107, 110. Hal Campbell photos. 111. U.S. Navy photo. 115, 123, Gannett Papers photo. 116. Bruno del Priore, photo, Rome,. 117. Varden Studio photo. 134. Paul L. and Sally L. Gordon photo. 135. Rowe photo. 137. Venard Chanski photo. 140, 143, 144. Lou Ouzer, photos. 148. Varden Studios photo. (Most of the other photographs come from the churches or institutions with which the subjects are connected, or from the Archives of the Rochester Diocese.)

CHAPTER ONE

THE FIRST SOWING : 1615-1763

TWELVE COUNTIES in western New York State constitute the present Catholic diocese of "Rochester-in-America." They are: Monroe (of which Rochester is the county seat), Livingston, Wayne, Ontario, Seneca, Cayuga, Tompkins, Yates, Steuben, Chemung, Schuyler, and Tioga. The territory which they occupy is bounded on the north by Lake Ontario and on the south by the New York-Pennsylvania border. Flat in the north and a sandy prairie where it basins the Lake, the terrain rises as it moves southward into the Appalachian Upland to become a highland furrowed by deep, broad valleys. Some of the valleys are watered by the leisurely streams of the Genesee and upper Susquehanna river systems. Others have bedded from time immemorial the placid "Finger Lakes." The soil is fertile; the climate is relatively temperate; and the scenery, combining as it does nice proportions of land and water, hill and plain, has a gentle charm which does not easily pall.

In the seventeenth century the district which we are considering was Indian territory. The Chemung River (formerly called the Tioga, or the Cayuga Branch of the Susquehanna) was under the sway of the Andastes or Susquehannock Indians. In the early years of that century their capital stood at Carantouan, near Athens, Pennsylvania, just across the state border from Waverly, New York. From this center they exercised a wide control down along the route of the Susquehanna River. Ruling the northern section of west-central New York were the Senecas and Cayugas, the two westernmost nations of the Five Nations of Iroquois. The Seneca villages were somewhat east of the Genesee River, in Monroe, Livingston, and Ontario Counties. The Cayuga villages were in Cayuga County, near the foot of the finger lake which still bears their name.

By the time this nation was established and American settlers began to move into western New York, the Andastes had long since been dispersed by the Iroquois, and the Iroquois themselves had largely scattered. But the hardy American farmers of both yesterday and today have often turned up with their plows or spades Indian graves containing religious medals, crucifixes, and rings bearing the monogram of Jesus. These point to only one conclusion: there was a time when

3

Catholic Christianity was current among the Senecas and Cayugas.

Catholics in western New York State became members of the Diocese of Baltimore in 1789; of the Diocese of New York in 1808; of the Diocese of Buffalo in 1847; and a portion of them were embraced, after 1868, in the Diocese of Rochester. Their Catholicism sprang up from a second sowing. Nevertheless, in writing a history of the Diocese of Rochester, we cannot ignore the earlier chapter of the epic, the story of the missions conducted among the Iroquois by the Jesuits of New France.

1. THE VISIT OF STEPHEN BRULE (1615-1616).

Historians may yet uncover evidence of Christian European contacts with the western Iroquois homeland before 1615. The first known contact was the journey made across western New York State in 1615 by Etienne [Stephen] Brulé, an emissary of the intrepid founder of New France, Samuel de Champlain (1567?-1635).[1]

Brulé's journey was undertaken in connection with a French war against the Iroquois. In 1609, one year after he founded Quebec, Champlain had established friendly relations with the Algonquin and Huron Indians of Canada. The alliance was almost an automatic declaration of war upon the Iroquois, who were implacable economic rivals of both of these Indian peoples. When in the same year Champlain, with threescore Canadian Indians, invaded New York and routed, near Ticonderoga, a force of two hundred Mohawk Iroquois, the lines became fairly drawn between the Iroquois and these Europeans-who-shot-with-fire.

In 1615, Champlain consented to invade New York State once more in collaboration with the Huron and Andaste Indians, who were at the same time kinsmen and economic enemies of the Iroquois. As the result of talks with the Hurons, who dwelt near Georgian Bay in the present Province of Ontario, the French leader agreed to lead an attack upon an important Iroquois citadel—apparently among the Onondagas—with the collaboration of an Andaste force to be summoned north from Carantouan. The agreement reached, Champlain sent this Frenchman, Etienne Brulé, to bear notice of the rendezvous to the Andaste capital.

Brulé, an adventurous young man, had come to New France in 1608. In the seven years that followed, he had acquired a considerable knowledge of Indian languages and ways. Mettle and experience therefore qualified him for the embassy. Still it was no easy journey that he and his twelve Huron companions undertook on September 8, 1615, for the road to Carantouan lay across the lands of the enemy. The trip could have been made safely if time had not been so short. The "Grand Détour" along Lake Erie, Chautauqua Lake, the Allegheny River, the upper Genesee, and the Cayuga Branch of the Susquehanna would have reduced greatly the chance of Iroquois confrontation. However, since the rendezvous had been set for barely a month off, Brulé's party was evidently obliged to take the shorter and riskier road. This means they would most likely have left Lake Erie at Tonawanda Creek, moved cautiously over the Genesee River south of Avon, in Livingston County, and then followed the Canisteo or Conhocton Rivers into the Cayuga Branch or Chemung, which flowed down past Carantouan. Despite their care, they encountered a band of hostile savages near the Genesee River. Fortunately for Brulé, his party was able to conquer them.

Reaching Carantouan, Brulé delivered his message, and the Andastes began their military preparations, taking their own good time. On account of their tardiness, when Champlain and his force arrived at the objective on October 10th, there was not an Andaste in sight.[2] Andastes or no, the French leader started the siege. But everything went wrong. The Iroquois put up a better resistance than he had anticipated, and he himself was wounded. By the 18th, the Andastes still had not put in an appearance, so Champlain finally ordered a retreat. Disabled by his wound, he had to be carried away from the scene of his frustration, lashed to a frame like a great papoose. The Andastes, who had finally left Carantouan on the 15th, reached the rendezvous two days after the forces from Canada had departed.

Brulé could do nothing but return with the "relief corps" to Carantouan and winter in their country, for they could give him no guides for his trip back to Huronia until the following spring. He busied himself during the intervening months by exploring the Susquehanna River, perhaps as far down as Chesapeake Bay.

In spring, 1616, the Andastes appointed the guides, and Brulé set out for Huronia. The return trip was less lucky than the original journey. At one point his party came upon some Senecas, and scattered for protection. Stephen thus became permanently separated from his guides, and hopelessly lost in the hostile wilderness. Half-starved and half-frozen by the chill of April, he finally decided to cast himself on the mercy of three Iroquois whom he sighted on the trail. The trio took temporary pity upon him and led him to their village (which was probably in the vicinity of East Avon or Lima, New York).

The villagers at first gave food to this lost soul. But after he had eaten they accused him of being a French aggressor, and began to torture him according to the cruel ritual in which they were specialists.

This was a poor beginning, but things turned out better than the victim could have expected. It so happened that he was wearing an *Agnus Dei* about his neck. An *Agnus Dei* is a medallion of wax, stamped with a religious symbol, and blessed by the Pope. These medallions, or portions of them, sewn into a small decorative sack, are often worn on a cord or chain around the throat, as one would wear a medal. Now, when one of the tormentors saw this, he asked Stephen what it was. Stephen, who had lost his freedom but not his wits, answered with a threat which was sounder psychologically than it was theologically: "If you take it and put me to death, you will find that immediately after you will suddenly die, and all those of your house."

The Seneca hesitated for a moment. Then, ignoring the warning, he ripped off the medallion. As soon as he did, strange to say, something quite marvelous happened. According to Brulé's account, the blue sky suddenly clouded over and a fierce electrical storm broke out. Frightened by the phenomenon, the torturers had second thoughts. Forthwith their captain ordered that the prisoner be released. He bound up Stephen's wounds and told him that until he was ready to depart he would be his guest. Thereafter the Frenchman was given every honor, and when he left the village Senecas were detailed to guide him.

Etienne Brulé finally got back to the country of the Hurons, and thereafter engaged in the fur trade among them, first as agent of Champlain, then on his own. In 1632 he became involved in a dispute with some Hurons, and met a tragic death, killed and *eaten* by his antagonists.

Brulé appears to have been the first of those adventurous French emigrants who went to live the rough life of the savages and became all but savages themselves. He emerges from the chronicles more as sinner than saint. But that is not why we have told his story.

We have told his story for two reasons. In the first place, he was the first white man and the first Catholic Christian on record as having traveled athwart the present diocese of Rochester. And in the second place, he came as the first representative of that French nation which forty years later was to bring the Christian faith among the Indians of western New York.

2. THE BLACKROBES ARRIVE.

If the Iroquois hated the Hurons, it is not surprising that they had no special love for the French Jesuit missioners who were laboring among the Hurons. If the Iroquois were intent upon destroying the Huron nation, it is not surprising that they were also ready to destroy the fruitful missions which the Jesuits had begun in Huronia as early as

1630. This was a setback which distressed the missionaries, but by no means discouraged them. With true Christian persistence, they became all the more interested in the Iroquois themselves, and all the more desirous of carrying the gospel into their strongholds. And by strange coincidence—if not by obvious Providence—it was the Iroquois themselves who made the acceptance of the missionaries inevitable. For the Iroquois, in keeping with their usual policy, brought back with them as captives a large number of Christian Hurons. Consequently, when the Jesuits finally came into the Iroquois country, they found a Huron Christian nucleus in every village.

The Five Nations of the Iroquois, united in a loose confederation, inhabited central and west-central New York State. We have already mentioned the location of the two westerly nations, the Senecas and Cayugas. The central nation, the Onondagas, lived in Onondaga County not far from the present Syracuse. Their capital was on "Indian Hill," south of Manlius, in the township of Pompey. The Oneidas inhabited Oneida County, east of Oneida Lake. The Mohawks had their villages on the Mohawk River, near Auriesville and Fonda in Montgomery County. Although in Champlain's time the population of the whole confederation was perhaps less than six thousand, their war parties had so skillfully developed the tactics of *blitzkrieg* that they could visit sudden fright, enslavement and death upon white and red man alike in regions supposedly remote from the Iroquois headquarters.

The Jesuits who had cast their lot with the enemies of the Hurons could scarcely escape the toils of the Iroquois-Huron war. In August, 1642, one of these missionaries, Father Isaac Jogues, was captured by a band of Mohawks as he and his party were returning from Quebec to Huronia. Jogues and companions were taken to the village of Ossernenon on the Mohawk and brutally tortured. His mission auxiliary, René Goupil, was killed for teaching an Indian boy to make the sign of the cross. Jogues himself was held as a slave for several months, but eventually escaped, aided by the Dutch at Albany. Four years later, after the French and the Mohawks had made peace, Father Jogues and a lay helper named Jean Lalande, returned to the Mohawk country to begin a mission. But the superstitious Bear Clan rose against them, and on October 18, 1646, its members murdered Jogues, and a day later, Lalande.

Five more Jesuits were to suffer death in Huronia proper during the course of Iroquois-Huron hostilities, which reached their peak in the years 1645-1649. The noble Jean de Brébeuf, head of the Huron missions, was executed along with gentle Father Gabriel Lalemant. The other victims were Fathers Antoine Daniel, Charles Garnier, and Noel Chabanel. In 1930, Pope Pius XI canonized these five, along with Jogues, Goupil and Lalande, as the North American Jesuit Martyrs.

Although the Huron nation was scattered by 1649, a large number of the Hurons, including many Christians, were brought, as we have stated, to live among the Iroquois nations. Indeed, during the course of the war, two whole Huron villages, called by the missionaries St. Michel and St. Jean Baptiste, reached an agreement with the Senecas to move down, bag and baggage, into the Seneca country and establish a village of their own.

By 1653, the Iroquois felt themselves in a position to propose peace to the French. The Canadian officials, wary about the proposal, sent down a former missionary to the Hurons to test the disposition of the Five Nations. This ambassador, Jesuit Father Simon LeMoyne (1604-1665), arrived at the Onondaga capital on August 5, 1654. Here leaders of the Onondagas, Cayugas and Senecas greeted him cordially. They not only insisted on their peaceful intentions, but instructed him to ask that a French colony be established in their midst. Although the Jesuit had come on a diplomatic mission, the feasibility of a subsequent spiritual mission to the Five Nations did not escape him. In fact, the first Indian he met on entering the Onondaga country was a captive Huron whom he himself had received into the Church more than a decade before. He came upon many another exiled Indian Christian during his brief stay, and had the consolation of hearing the confessions of some of them and baptizing their children.[3]

The French authorities accepted Father LeMoyne's report when he returned, but deferred immediate action. However, when a delegation of Onondagas came to Canada in September, 1655, to ask for resident blackrobes, the superior did send down two missionaries to survey the field. One was Father Joseph Chaumonot (1611-1693), a veteran of the Huron missions and an expert in the Indian mode of oratory. The other was Father Claude Dablon (1618-1697). Father Dablon had just arrived from France, and this was his first assignment.

When the chieftains gathered in council at Onondaga to hear from the newcomers, they were duly impressed by the unction and eloquence of Chaumonot. In fact, Saonchiogwa, a venerable Cayuga chief, adopted him as his brother—a high honor. One of the Fathers celebrated Mass in a cabin of the village on November 14, 1655. This Mass on Indian Hill was the first recorded Mass offered in New York State. On the 18th, the Onondagas built for the missionaries a little bark chapel. Dedicated to St. Jean Baptiste (St. John the Baptist), this was the first known Catholic church in the State.⁴ Soon the two missioners were busy with instructions and sacramental ministrations.

But the Indians had not given up their desire to have a French colony settled among them. Therefore, in March, 1656, Father Dablon made the long wintry trek back to Canada to reiterate their request. While the civil authorities still suspected treachery, they decided that it was now necessary to take the risk. Ten soldiers and some thirty or forty colonists were selected, outfitted, and dispatched in two large shallops and a number of canoes. On July 11, 1656, they arrived at the place selected for the settlement. It was not the Onondaga capital but a site on the east shore of Onondaga Lake, at the present Liverpool, New York, just north of Syracuse. (In 1933 the little palisaded fort of the French settlers was reconstructed at the original site.)

The chapel in the fort, called Ste. Marie de Ganentaa, was intended to be the mission center for all the Iroquois missions. For Father Dablon had not returned alone but with a whole contingent of missionaries. Superior of the undertaking was Father François LeMercier (1604-1690). Twenty years before, he and St. Charles Garnier, then working in Huronia, had baptized a Seneca Indian whom the Hurons had captured near Irondequoit Bay and brought back for execution.⁵ Since that summer day, LeMercier had had an intense interest in the possibility of a mission to the Iroquois. His two priest-companions were to distinguish themselves among the western Iroquois. They were René Ménard (1605-1661) and Jacques Frémin (1628-1691). Ambrose Brouet and Joseph Boursier, Jesuit lay brothers, and a few lay volunteers completed the mission band.

Early in August the Cayugas requested the Superior to send them a missionary of their own. Towards the end of the month Chaumonot and Ménard set out westward, intending to visit not only the Cayugas but the Senecas beyond them. They thus became the pioneer missionaries and pioneer white men to reside in the present diocese of Rochester.

The two Jesuits traveled the Great Middle Trail which traversed western New York along a route now largely identical with highways No. 5 and No. 20. A two-day journey brought them to the Cayuga capital Goyogouen, located, it seems, on the present John Gans farm, a quarter-mile west of Mapleton, Cayuga County.

They were not given the warmest possible reception. Pagan Huron captives, playing upon the superstition of the Iroquois, had already prejudiced many of the rank and file Iroquois against the preachers of Christianity. But the chieftains who had extended the invitation stood by their word, and Saonchiogwa assumed personal responsibility for their safety. Four days after the Fathers' arrival, the Cayugas began to build them a chapel. Dedicated to St. Joseph, this little bark structure was the first Catholic church within the present Rochester Diocese.

When St. Joseph's Chapel was completed around September 6, 1656, Father Ménard carpeted it with "the finest mats," and hung upon its walls pictures of Christ and the Blessed Virgin Mary. The Indians were so astonished by the pictures that they came in crowds to examine them and inquire about them. Before long their curiosity impelled them to attend the daily catechism classes which Ménard inaugurated. The attendance was so large that the missionary had to conduct classes in tandem from morning to night—at least at the beginning of his stay. Within a few days several of the Hurons and other slaves, and even some of the Iroquois themselves, had formally enrolled as neophytes of the congregation.

The second adult whom Father Ménard baptized was a Cayuga afflicted with an ugly facial cancer. In the course of his instruction the Indian revealed to his instructor that he had witnessed the martyrdom of Saints Jean de Brébeuf and Gabriel Lalemant. He had pitied them, he said, and tried to ransom them from their Mohawk captors. The Mohawks had first accepted the offer, then reneged. Ménard baptized the Indian "Lazarus"; and Lazarus, on becoming a Christian, won many others to the Faith. The missionary concluded that this Cayuga's kindness to the saintly martyrs had merited his rich graces.[6]

Work among the Cayugas was not always so easy. Pagan Huron gossips continued to whisper to the Iroquois that baptism was the seal of death. The Iroquois "jugglers" or medicine men sowed other dark suspicions in the fertile imaginations of their tribesmen. Frenzied savages now and again threatened the Jesuit's life. In spite of all this, Father Ménard's sojourn was quite productive. After only a few months he was able to report the conversion of over four hundred souls in the villages of the Cayugas.[7]

Most likely Father Chaumonot had not left Father Ménard at Goyogouen until the little chapel was finished. At all events, he soon set out for Gandagan (also called Gannagaro), the principal village of the eastern Senecas. At Gannagaro—which was not far from Victor, New York—he addressed the Indian leaders in solemn council assembled. Rising in the council chamber at the appropriate moment, he proclaimed, in traditional Indian rhetoric and with the traditional offering of presents, the missionary aim of his visit.

"I give myself with these presents as a warranty of the truths that I preach to you," he said. "And," he continued, "if my life, which I devote to you, do not seem sufficient to you, I offer you those of so many French who have followed me to Ganentaa, to bear witness to the Faith that I preach to you. Will you not trust those living presents, and such bravery and courage? And will you be simple enough to think that so clever a band of men would have left their native country—the finest and most agreeable in the world—and endured such fatigue, in order to bring a falsehood so far?"

Words like these evidenced the holiness, wit and patriotism of the speaker. They could hardly fail to impress his canny auditors. After a consultation the chieftains announced to Father Chaumonot that they would gladly give ear to his teachings, and they invited him to prolong his stay among them.

One of the earliest converts was Annonkenritaoui, the principal Seneca leader. He had a disabling ulcer; but after his reception into the Church, the ulcer mended. Hurons living in the Seneca district welcomed their former missioner with open arms. This was especially true of those who lived in their own village of St. Michel (Gandougarae), not far from Gannagaro. The Christians among them flocked about him to seek absolution for themselves and baptism for their children. And not a few of the pagan Hurons, happy to see one of their former blackrobes, showed a greater interest in Christianity than they had shown in Huronia.

Joseph Chaumonot spent only two months among the Senecas. He probably made the rounds of all the east and west Seneca settlements during these weeks. The records do not mention the building of a chapel, but it is most unlikely that he omitted celebrating Mass, especially among the Christians of St. Michel. At the end of eight weeks, apparently by prearrangement, he returned to the missionary center on Lake Onondaga. He was accompanied on the journey by David Le-Moyne, a young layman about twenty years old who had been his assistant through the whole mission trip. David was apparently frail in constitution, and the rigors of missionary life had hastened his decline in health. He died and was buried on the northern shore of Lake Cayuga, after breathing his last "with the gentleness and resignation of one of the elect."[8] In our own day an increasing number of laymen of the Diocese of Rochester have volunteered to serve on the foreign missions. David LeMoyne may be considered their forerunner.

The Jesuits, meeting at Ste. Marie de Ganentaa, held consultations with their Superior. It was to be the usual policy of the Jesuit superiors to leave no missionary in one nation overly long, but to circulate them for shorter terms among the various Iroquois peoples. On this occasion, Chaumonot was assigned elsewhere, and never returned to the Seneca nation. Ménard, on the other hand, was sent back to the Cayugas because of the insistence of their leaders.

Although he was back in Goyogouen long before the end of 1656, Father Ménard was recalled to Lake Onondaga in the early weeks of 1658. The French colonists had lately learned that the Onondagas were now contemplating what had been so long feared—a general massacre of the French. Father LeMercier therefore summoned all the Jesuits back to headquarters. By means of a brilliant strategy, the whole establishment—missionaries, soldiers, and settlers—fled the Onondaga country together on March 20, 1658. They were well on their way to Canada before the Iroquois recovered from their astonishment.[9]

The departure of the colony marked the end of the first phase of the Iroquois mission. The war which followed delayed for several years the return of the Jesuits.

In 1660, when Iroquois-French relations were for the nonce peaceable, Saonchiogwa, dispatched to Canada by the Onondaga chieftain Garakontié, asked that the blackrobes return at once and that the colonists subsequently follow them, this time accompanied by nuns to teach and nurse the Iroquois. The Canadian officials were quite unwilling to comply with the latter request. But they did depute Father Simon LeMoyne to go back with Saonchiogwa. The two left Montreal on July 21, 1661, and had reached their destination by August 11th.[10]

Father LeMoyne remained in New York State until the summer of 1662. He spent most of his time among the Mohawks, but passed a month in the Cayuga country. While he worked to heal Iroquois souls, a French surgeon who had come down with him did much to heal their bodies.[11] The Jesuit does not seem to have visited the Senecas on this trip. On August 31, 1662, he arrived in Montreal, bringing a number of French captives whom the Iroquois had released.[12]

Not until 1666 did the French and Iroquois achieve a durable peace. And it was two years more before the Jesuits could reestablish missions among the Senecas and Cayugas.

3. The Later Missions: Restoration and Recall.

Blackrobes were able to reside among the western Iroquois from 1668 until the 1680's, and this was the mission's most fruitful period.

New wars forced the suspension of the undertaking between 1687 and 1701. When it was resumed in 1702, the mission continued for less than a decade, then stopped for good.

"Cayuga," wrote one of the missionaries, "is the fairest country I have ever seen in America."[13] At the time the Cayuga mission was re-opened in 1668, the Jesuit assigned to it was Father Etienne de Carheil (1633?-1726), a Breton nobleman and one of the saintliest missionaries of New France. When he entered the Cayuga canton on November 6, 1668, he was undertaking his first missionary assignment. Still he was so well prepared that he amazed the Cayugas with his fluency in the Huron-Iroquois tongue. The Indians of Goyogouen built him a new chapel of St. Joseph on November 9th. The Cayuga capital and the other Cayuga villages were to be the scene of his labors from 1668 to 1671 and from 1673 to 1683. When illness forced him to return to Canada during the period 1671-1673, Father Pierre Raffeix (1633-1724) was his substitute.

Carheil's "parish" included three main villages of Cayugas. Besides Goyogouen proper (the Mission of St. Joseph), there were Tiohero (St. Étienne) four leagues to the north, and Onontaré (St. René) six leagues to the north. (A land league was about three miles.) Archaeologists think that St. Étienne was on the bank of the Seneca River near where Routes 5 and 20 cross the present René Ménard Bridge. They locate St. René some seven miles down the same stream, by Bluff Point, a couple of miles from the village of Montezuma.

At Goyogouen Father Carheil had a jewel of a companion in his French lay aide, René Richer. René not only performed the chores of the little mission household but also put to good use his skill at blending medicines and administering first aid. During the early part of their stay, both priest and layman were held in high esteem by the natives.

At the outset, at least, such crowds of Indians—Christian Hurons, pagan Hurons, captive Andastes and Iroquois—frequented the chapel that it had to be enlarged. The versatile René drew up a plan for a roomier building with a small chamber behind the altar. Except for its roof of bark the finished structure resembled a French house.[14] Crowds continued to come while Father Raffeix was in charge. He added a pleasant variant to the regular exercises—prayers and hymns translated into Iroquois and set to music for congregational singing. Each year the number of baptisms increased a little. In 1671, Chief Saonchiogwa himself, so long a supporter of the missions, took the step of entering the Church. By his own choice, however, he was received at Quebec.

At the time that Father de Carheil first set out for his Cayuga appointment in 1668, the new superior of the Iroquois mission had already undertaken his own assignment among the Senecas, where he was to remain for the next two years. This was Father Jacques Frémin (1628-1691) who came to Sonnontouan (as the Senecas called their country) and set up his center at Totiakton, the principal west Seneca village, on November 1, 1668. The chieftains welcomed him cordially; the Senecas built him a chapel which he dedicated to the Immaculate Conception of the Blessed Virgin Mary.[15] He had with him a lay aide named François Poisson. This Frenchman thus became the first recorded white lay resident of Monroe County.[16]

An epidemic broke out at Totiakton soon after Frémin's arrival. He was kept busy for some time, visiting cabin after cabin to instruct the afflicted and baptize the dying. By the end of a few months he had administered baptism to over 120 adults, ninety of whom had died.[17] He soon summoned an associate in the person of Father Julien Garnier (1643-1730).

The plague had ceased by the time Father Garnier reached Sonnontouan, but there was enough work to occupy two priests in such a populous nation. Garnier went to live in another village of the west Senecas, Gandachiragou. Here he had a chapel put up in 1669, dedicating it and the mission village to St. John. Indians from in and around Gandachiragou soon began to frequent the chapel of St. John for instructions. In his spare time Father Garnier compiled an Iroquois dictionary.[18]

Before he left the Senecas, Father Frémin commenced visits to the east Seneca villages. On November 3, 1669, he dedicated a chapel in honor of St. Michael in the Huron Christian village of Gandougarae.[19] For the two years 1670-1672 Garnier was the only priest among the Senecas. But from 1672 to 1680 he had the assistance of Father Raffeix, and from around 1673 to 1677 that of Father Jean Pierron. Father Pierron (1631-1700) took up residence in 1674 at Gannagaro, the chief east Seneca town, and built there the chapel of St. Jacques. Now there were four chapels among the Senecas.

Father Pierron, by the way, was something of an artist. While among the Mohawks he had invented a game of skill called "Point to Point," for which he had drawn symbols of the sacraments, commandments, virtues, vices, and so forth. The Indians along the Mohawk had taken to it readily and learned from it the chief elements of Christian practice. It is quite likely that Father Pierron taught his Senecas the same catechetical pastime.[20]

Some prominent Frenchmen visited Sonnontouan during the second mission period.

Most noted among these was the great explorer, Robert Cavelier de la Salle (1643-1687), who stopped by in August, 1669; December, 1678; and January, 1679. On the first occasion he was accompanied by two Sulpician Fathers, François Dollier de Casson and René Brehard de Galinée. During their stay of one week they took a side trip to the Bristol Valley to see one of the great natural wonders of the area—the "burning spring" which still sputters out its natural gas in a rustic glen.[21]

A colleague of LaSalle's, the Flemish Franciscan Louis Hennepin (1640?-1702) also made three recorded visits. In December, 1678, he dropped in on Fathers Garnier and Raffeix, who invited him to preach at the holy day Mass at Totiakton on January 1, 1679. Hennepin made a second stop the following June, while en route to explore the Mississippi; and a third in 1681 after his rescue from the Sioux, his face now bronzed by the sun and his wool habit patched with buffalo skins. His second stop is of most interest to us. The expedition paused for several days at Irondequoit Bay to take on provisions purchased from the Senecas. Hennepin was one of a band of four Franciscans on this "safari", two of whom were eventually to win martyrs' crowns: Gabriel de la Ribourde (1610-1680) and Zénobe Membré (1645-1689). While the provisioning was in progress, the friars set up "a small Cabin of Barks of Trees about half a league in the woods to perform Divine Services without interruption." This chapel, whether near the site of Our Lady of Mercy High School, or (more likely) off the east shore of the bay, was the first home of Christian worship in the Rochester metropolitan area.[22]

The routine followed by the Jesuits among the Senecas and Cayugas was much the same as that followed among all the Five Nations. It was essentially a stay-at-home apostolate, and there is no evidence that the missionaries visited the counties of the Southern Tier, although the Indians themselves often hunted there.[23] Their program consisted basically in catechizing the natives, at the chapel and at the cabins, in and out of season. What seriously complicated this program was the absence of most of the Iroquois for nine months of the year: the warriors on the war path, the hunters and their families at the hunting grounds. At such times only a few, principally the aged and infirm, remained in the towns.[24] In spite of this obstacle, the Jesuits at least achieved their objective of communicating to the savages the fundamental Christian truths, whether they accepted them or not. In 1672,

Father Dablon was able to write: ". . . there is not a family in all these countries which is not adequately instructed in the principal mysteries of our faith."[25]

Who, more specifically, were the objects of such great solicitude? First of all, there were the Christian Hurons. These were naturally the missioners' "joy and crown," and they loved them perhaps too partially. Most notable of the exiled Huron Christians were two leaders of St. Michel. One was Jacques Atondo, who spent most of his time in prayer, and ordinarily spoke only of God, whether to Christian or to pagan. The other was François Tehoronhiongo. St. Jean de Brébeuf had baptized François back in Huronia, and since his baptism he had never missed his daily prayers. Well instructed in his Faith and Bible history, this venerable and highly respected Indian had taught catechism before the Fathers arrived and continued to do so afterward.[26]

Many pagan Hurons entered the Church while living among the Iroquois. The Jesuits also converted captives who belonged to other nations, like the Eries, the Neutrals, and the Andastes. When humbled by adversity, these poor creatures were happy to give ear to Christian teaching, and often manifested a deeply Christian spirit.

The Iroquois themselves were another matter. A fair number of them, including some men of prominence, embraced the Faith. But a very large percentage of those whom the Fathers baptized were sickly or dying infants and adults.

Granted that the missionaries were unable to work among the Five Nations as long as they needed to, the fact remains that these Indians were not tractable and found spiritual concepts difficult if not boring. They possessed many natural virtues—more, perhaps, than the Fathers gave them credit for. Democratic, freedom-loving, loyal to benefactors, the Iroquois, when they were good, could be very good indeed. But when they were bad . . .! Carnal, arrogant, inconstant, sadistic, man-eating, even while sober they could pollute the atmosphere of the villages with a miasma of insecurity. And when they were drunk, they were devils incarnate. No wonder Father Frémin called the missionary's life among them "a continual death."[27]

After a few years of relative calm, French and Iroquois tension again began to mount in the 1670's. Victory over the Andastes made the Iroquois more insolent than ever, and the English spared no effort to stir up their anti-French sentiment. Now not only men but women and children became addicted to Albany brandy, with deplorable results. Despite the Jesuit efforts to maintain peace, the threat of a new war loomed large. At Goyogouen the proud and powerful chief Ourehaoué manhandled Father Carheil, pillaged his chapel and dwelling, and eventually, in the fall of 1683, compelled him to withdraw to Canada. By the fall of 1684 Father Garnier had been recalled from Sonnontouan, and no Jesuits remained in the whole State except the brothers Jean and Jacques de Lamberville, who tarried for a while at Onondaga, practically as hostages.[28] Father Jean, the last to leave, departed in 1687. The second Iroquois mission then came to an end.

In the turbulent years which followed, the French invasion of the Seneca homeland in 1687 was a leading event. The Senecas had persisted in ignoring the provisions of a peace treaty of 1684, and were constantly molesting the Indian allies of the French and interfering with trade. The French, layman and missionary alike, agreed that these Senecas would continue obstinate until they were made to eat humble pie. Therefore the new Governor of New France, Jacques René de Brisay, Marquis de Denonville (1638-1710) determined to lead a punitive expedition against them.

In theory, a punitive campaign against the western Iroquois was as sound a strategy in 1687 as it was in 1779 when General John Sullivan took a similar step. Practically speaking, Denonville's campaign was well planned. His own force comprised 1,800 French soldiers and seven hundred Christian Indians. By prearrangement, another force of four hundred Frenchmen and two hundred Indians, mostly pagan, came over from the West and met Denonville just at the moment of his arrival at the appointed rendezvous, Irondequoit Bay, on July 10, 1687. The "captains and the kings" were now all on land. There were the renowned French explorers: Italian-born Henri de Tonty (1650-1704); Baron Armand de Lahontan (1667-1715); and Daniel Duluth (+1709). There were notable Indian Christian leaders: Kryn "the Great Mohawk"; and Louis Garonhiagué ("Hot Ashes"), the Oneida chief who had assisted many Iroquois converts, including Kateri Tekakwitha, to escape from their pagan villages to the Christian Indian settlements in Canada. And there were several prominent chaplains: the Sulpician, Abbé François Vachon de Belmont (1645-1732); two veterans of the Iroquois Jesuit missions, Thierry Beschefer (1630-1711) and François Vaillant de Gueslis (1646-1718); and two Jesuits working among the western Ottawas, Jean Enjalran (1639-1718) and Jacques Gravier (1651-1708).[29]

In spite of its careful organization, the expedition was only moderately successful. Denonville had inaugurated the action by the treacherous arrest of Iroquois envoys, an unpromising beginning. True, the French won the only battle, which took place on July 13th at the site of

Victor, New York. But here the credit was due to the Christian Indians, who rallied the bewildered invaders when they were ambushed by a much smaller force 'of Senecas. Hot Ashes was numbered among the slain.[30] Instead of pursuing the Seneca assailants, Denonville spent the next week or so burning the villages, granaries, and standing crops of the east and west Seneca settlements. He was content, said Father Carheil rather tartly, "to make war on grain and bark, which offered no resistance."[31] The French army then returned to Irondequoit Bay, departing thence on July 24th.

Only in August, 1701, was a secure peace concluded between the Five Nations and the officials of New France. Thomas Dongan, Catholic governor of British New York, had previously hoped to send English Jesuits among the Iroquois. But he was now out of power, so the treaty allowed French missionaries to return.

Unfortunately, there were not enough Jesuit Fathers to fulfill the request for missionaries which each of the Iroquois nations presently made. In 1702 Father Jacques de Lamberville, a Jesuit lay brother, and a French blacksmith were sent down to Onondaga. Father Julien Garnier, though he was now "old and infirm," likewise took the road back to his beloved, if capricious, Senecas. He was accompanied by Father François Vaillant de Gueslis. Their stay was relatively brief, but upon the insistence of the tribal leaders, they subsequently returned—Garnier to remain at least through 1703, Vaillant until 1707. In 1707 Vaillant was replaced by Father Jacques d'Heu (1672-1742).[32]

After Denonville had destroyed their settlements, the Senecas rebuilt them on nearby sites. The west Senecas seem to have established their capital near Spring Brook on the Dann Farm, west of Honeoye Falls. The east Senecas appear to have moved their capital to Onaghee, on the McClure-Snyder farm in Hopewell township, three miles east of Canandaigua. The Hurons of St. Michel probably relocated on the present O'Brien-Kelaher farm, east of Boughton Hill and south of the Boughton Hill Road. While the missionaries of this third period most likely lived among the east Senecas, they took care of all the Seneca villages, and probably of the Cayugas, too, since there was no Jesuit resident in Goyogouen.

At first the course of the missionaries ran rather smoothly. In fact, the Iroquois ignored the advice of the British to dismiss the Jesuits. Towards the end of the decade, however, the Iroquois again became belligerent. The old provocations recommenced, so the missionaries were summoned back to Canada. This time the Senecas behaved better than some of the other nations, and Father d'Heu was at first unwilling to leave them. But he, too, finally changed his mind, and arrived in Montreal in 1709, accompanied by a French blacksmith and forty loyal Seneca guides.[33]

The year 1709 marked the practical end of the French Jesuit mission to the Five Nations. Before the question could arise of a fourth mission attempt, France signed the Treaty of Utrecht in 1713, which acknowledged the British as "protectors" of the New York Iroquois. True, the Senecas applied to the Governor of New France for French missionaries as late as 1721.[34] But this did not lead to any permanent reestablishment. It is quite certain, however, that Jesuits attached to the Iroquois mission village at Caughnawaga near Montreal came down to the Iroquois country on occasional secret visits.

In 1749, Father François Picquet (1708-1791) founded a large mission village on the banks of the St. Lawrence at the present Ogdensburg, New York.[35] At this mission, which he called La Présentation, the Sulpician priest welcomed a number of Senecas and Cayugas. His village functioned quite well during its decade-long existence. But it was forced to discontinue when the Peace of Paris of 1763, putting an end to the French and Indian War, positively excluded further Canadian missionary contacts with the Five Nations. (Or "Six Nations," as the Iroquois had become since the arrival of the Tuscarora Iroquois after 1712.)

On the face of it, the intermittent mission campaign which the Jesuits carried on among the Iroquois from 1656 to 1709 was no vast success. If by 1679 baptisms had reached 4,000, the majority of the baptized were still those on the verge of death, and the number of living Iroquois communicants remained relatively small. Some of the converts evidently remained in their New York homelands, for in the later Seneca cemeteries near Onaghee and along the Genesee River many "Jesuit rings" and religious medals have been unearthed. But the Seneca and Cayuga nations have long since departed from their ancient haunts, and the only tangible reminders of their missionary epoch, in addition to the Christian burials, are the native apple trees which the French Jesuits are supposed to have introduced.

Not that the Senecas or Cayugas or the other four nations have died out. At present there are at least 17,000 Iroquois living on reservations in the States of New York and Pennsylvania and the Provinces of Ontario and Quebec. This is fifty percent more than the Iroquois population at the height of the mission period! At least a quarter of them still profess a syncretist pagan religion. Yet even this cult, it is said, bears one dim testimony to the Jesuit catechetics: "Niio" or "Hawenniio," the modern Iroquois name for the supreme god, derives from the French word for God, "Dieu."[36] Probably one-half of today's Iroquois belong to one or another of the Protestant denominations.

But even today there are over 4,000 Catholic Indians from the old Iroquois country living in Canada and on the New York-Quebec border. Some of them are the descendants of the captive Hurons, most of whom eventually took the road to the Huron centers in the Province of Quebec. As early as 1677, for example, Francis Tehoronhiongo and his son and granddaughter moved to Montreal. There the granddaughter became a Sister of Notre Dame, took the name of Sister Mary Theresa Gannensagouas, and died at the age of twenty-eight, on November 25, 1695, with a reputation for great sanctity. Her devout grandfather had died five years earlier. Today the remains of both of them, buried in the cemetery of the Sisters of Notre Dame, are held in reverence.

The Catholic Indians of Caughnawaga (near Montreal) and at St. Regis are usually called Mohawks, and the Mohawks were perhaps originally in the majority among the Christian Iroquois immigrants. Actually, however, the Canadian mission villages welcomed converts from all five nations. Some of these must have been Cayugas who had fled to the short-lived Sulpician mission at Quinté, Ontario, in 1666; others, Cayugas and Senecas who passed over from La Présentation to the nearby St. Regis mission, founded at Hogansburg, New York, around 1755. We can surmise that some Christians of Sonnontouan and Goyogouen proper also followed the example of departing Huron Christians. And there must have been a number of individual conversions, like the extraordinary one of Chief Ourehaoué, the erstwhile persecutor of Father Carheil. This man was one of the Iroquois embassy treacherously seized by Denonville and packed off to France, where he was released by the King. Far from being embittered by the experience, he elected to stay in Canada, was baptized, and became a prominent Indian leader. When he died at Quebec in 1698 he was mourned as "a worthy Frenchman and a good Christian."

Thus, although the tribal lines have become blurred, the Catholic "Mohawks" of Canada are in large part descendants of the Senecas and Cayugas among whom the sixteenth-century Jesuits worked so diligently.[37]

What the Diocese of Rochester owes to these ancient missionaries is clearly not a native church of venerable age. It is rather the abiding spirit of a band of apostles who, assigned to one of the most difficult apostolates that history has known, gladly died a thousand dry martyrdoms to sanctify this soil.[38]

In the Mass for the feast day of St. Isaac Jogues and companions, the Church prays that "through their intercession the fine yield of Christians may ever and in all places increase." If in the former lands of the Senecas and Cayugas the fruits of our second sowing have been so plentiful, may it not be because the Garniers and the Carheils, having prepared the land for our later husbandmen, still continue to guide their hands?

CHAPTER TWO

SECOND SEEDTIME: 1783-1847

I T WAS THE American Revolution that opened western New York to settlers. And it was, of course, the presence of Catholics among the early settlers that brought the Niagara Country and the Genesee Country under the spiritual jurisdiction, first of the Diocese of Baltimore, and then of the Diocese of New York.

Before the Revolution, in 1768, the British agent Sir William Johnson had concluded a treaty with the Iroquois which reserved west-central and western New York for the Indians.[1] During the war, however, the pro-British Iroquois used western New York as a highway for anti-colonial raids. Considering the agreement violated by this action and therefore no longer binding, the American leaders, in August-October, 1779, sponsored a punitive expedition against the Iroquois under Major General John Sullivan and Brigadier General John Clinton. Their army engaged in only one real battle, at New Town, southeast of the present Elmira, on August 29th. The soldiers spent the remaining weeks of the campaign destroying crops and newly-abandoned Indian villages, moving up the Chemung River past the "painted post," up the east shore of Seneca Lake and both shores of Cayuga Lake, and cross-country to the Genesee River in the west and Owasco Lake in the east. Sullivan's forces therefore visited Tioga, Chemung, Steuben, Schuyler, Tompkins, Seneca, Cayuga, Ontario, and Livingston counties.

That this land of wooded hills, clear-running streams, placid lakes, and verdant valleys was both fair and fertile did not escape the ardent young soldiers. "These delightful wilds," Lieutenant Robert Parker called them in his journal; and he ventured to forecast their early settlement. "We may yet behold with a pleasing admiration those deserts that have so long been the habitation of beasts of prey and a safe asylum for our savage enemies, converted into fruitful fields, covered with the richest projects of agriculture, amply rewarding the industrious husbandman by a golden harvest; the spacious plains abounding with flocks and herds to supply his necessary wants."[2] Captivated by what they had seen during their invasion of the Iroquois country, many a veteran of the Sullivan-Clinton campaign later returned as a settler to the "delightful wilds" of western New York.

22

The present chapter treats the first half-century of settlement in western New York State. Such Catholics as found themselves among its pioneers were from 1789 to 1808 under the ecclesiastical jurisdiction of the Diocese of Baltimore, Maryland. Between 1808 and 1847 the same area belonged to the Diocese of New York. Here we shall consider, first, the Baltimore era; next, the trail-blazing work of Bishop Connolly, the first bishop active in New York; and finally, the work of his two successors, Bishops Dubois and Hughes.

1. ON THE FRINGE OF BALTIMORE.

On November 6, 1789, Pope Pius VI established at Baltimore the first Catholic diocese within the boundaries of the original United States. As its bishop he named Father John Carroll (1735-1815), who since 1784 had been general superior of the American Catholic clergy. Carroll was one of the greatest figures of American Catholic history. Member of a leading Maryland family; the brother of Daniel Carroll, a signer of the American Constitution; the kinsman of Charles Carroll of Carrollton, a signer of the Declaration of Independence; a Jesuit priest —until the Holy See suppressed that order—and blessed with an ample European education: John Carroll, first as bishop and then as archbishop of Baltimore brought to his task a rare combination of prestige, piety, leadership, and patriotism.

The original diocese of Baltimore was immense, occupying all the United States east of the Mississippi, except for Florida and the coastal parts of Louisiana, Mississippi, and Alabama. New York State was thus a part of Bishop Carroll's jurisdiction, although upstate New York was on its northern fringe. When Carroll was named to his see, the Niagara Country and the Genesee Country were occupied by very few white men. But the migrants began to arrive in greater numbers that very year 1789, and by 1810 the population of western New York had risen to 200,000, some of whom were Catholics.

Before we consider the Catholic element in this incoming population, we should briefly review the story of the pioneer settlement of the twelve-county district.

In the 1780's the district was divided into two segments by a "Preemption Line" which began at the Pennsylvania border, ran north along the present Steuben County-Chemung County border, and terminated at Lake Ontario. A third of the Rochester diocesan area lay to the east of the Preemption Line. Its northern counties were included in the "Military Tract," a region divided by the State of New York into townships adorned with such classical names as Scipio, Cato, and Aurelius, and allocated to Revolutionary veterans. South of the Military Tract there were several smaller tracts, acquired by land speculators from the State of Massachusetts or from private owners. To the west of the Pre-emption Line most of the land became known as the Phelps-Gorham Purchase from the two Massachusetts men, Oliver Phelps and Nathaniel Gorham, who bought it in 1788. Settlement began soon after Phelps and Gorham opened their lands, but in 1790 they forfeited the large remaining portion to Robert Morris, the well-known financier of the American Revolution. Morris also became owner, in 1791, of most of the lands west of the Genesee River and east of the Niagara. In that same year he sold the Phelps-Gorham Tract to the Pulteney Associates, a firm of British capitalists comprising Sir William Pulteney, John Hornby, and Patrick Colquhoun. In 1792-1793, he sold his westerly lands to a Dutch firm called the Holland Land Company, retaining for himself only the "Morris Reserve," a narrow strip immediately adjacent to the western boundary of the old Phelps-Gorham Purchase.

The original owners and speculators of these tracts are long since dead. But their names and the names of their friends still mark the land. Phelps, Gorham, Pulteney, Hornby, Bath, Henrietta, Troupsburg, Williamson, Mount Morris, Watkins—these and kindred titles remind us of the entrepreneurs of old who invited men to migrate into the promising paradise of western New York State.

Even before the speculators put their lands on the market, a few white men, squatters and traders, had entered the Finger Lakes area. Ebenezer ("Indian") Allen, when engaged by Phelps in 1788 to set up Rochester's first grist mill, had already been farming and trading for half a decade along the Genesee. By 1786, William Harris maintained an Indian trading store at "the painted post" in Steuben County; Horatio Jones operated another near the present Waterloo in Seneca County; and the Frenchman Dominick de Bartzch had still another near Geneva, on the border between Ontario and Yates County. Settlers had likewise begun to move into the Tioga County and Chemung County by 1785 or 1786.

But traders were essentially a transient element. Stable colonists arrived only after the land was formally opened. The Military Tract was rather slow to develop. Property titles there became confused, and for a time there was small assurance of legal tenure. The Pulteney lands, on the other hand, were exempt from this criticism. Furthermore, that Estate's canny Scots agent, Captain Charles Williamson, not only cleverly publicized his lands, but made them attractive by founding inns, mills and villages, and by inaugurating at Bath, a theatre, a fair, and horse racing. It is true that up to 1794 the Indians, still pro-British and rather hopeful that they and Britain might eventually oust the new settlers, discouraged abundant immigration by their churlish behavior. But in 1794, General "Mad Anthony" Wayne defeated the pro-British Indian confederates at the Battle of Fallen Timber, near the present Toledo, Ohio. After that, the Iroquois subsided.

The small stream of immigrants now widened into a steady river. Some of them came fresh from the British Isles. The majority, however, were younger folks from the older towns and countryside of eastern New York State and New England. For instance, on one day alone, February 28, 1799, five hundred sleighs of families bound for the Genesee country passed through Albany.[3] Others trekked up from Pennsylvania, New Jersey, and Maryland—British, German, or Irish in extraction. Those who had easy access to the Susquehanna River could paddle or pole their boats upstream into the Finger Lakes district; or, leaving that River's west branch at Williamsport, they could move northward to Painted Post and Bath by the road which Williamson in 1792 and 1793 had carved through the Pennsylvania wilderness. After 1800, the old Indian trails in New York State began to be replaced by turnpikes, which made migrant travel somewhat easier. To "turnpike" thereafter became practically a synonym for to migrate.

Most of the new arrivals took up farming. Their past experience had prepared them for the task of gradually clearing the wooded earth. Soon they had corn and wheat growing among the stumps, pigs grunting in their sties, and cattle grazing in the natural meadows. Where the soil was right, the pioneers also planted flax and hemp. Maples furnished them with syrup and sugar, they felled other trees for lumber, and burned the roots for potash. What they did not need for themselves, was readily marketable. Even in pre-canal days, the waterways of western New York, especially in the early spring, could carry substantial loads of grain, whiskey, and potash to distant marts; and the lumber of the Genesee Country was held in high regard along the St. Lawrence and Susquehanna River systems.

Not all the incomers established farms. A map of 1809 indicates the following villages then in existence: Geneva and Owego (1787); Canandaigua, Newtown (Elmira), Catherine's (Montour Falls), and Cayuga (all 1788); Seneca Falls, Ithaca, East Bloomfield, Hartford (Avon) (all 1789); Auburn and Bath (both 1793).[4] (Rochester itself was to come into existence only in 1812.) In these little communities log cabins eventually yielded to trim frame or brick houses in the Georgian or Classical Revival styles familiar "back home" in New England or Maryland. And when churches began to be built, they, too, were usually white clapboard buildings reminiscent of the meeting houses of the coastal States.

What was the religious complexion of the pioneers? The earliest denominational group was the colony called the New Jerusalem, established in 1788 near Dresden, Yates County, by Jemima Wilkinson, the religious matriarch who called herself the Universal Friend. This community was a passing phenomenon, however, Most of the incomers belonged to less singular Protestant faiths: some Quakers, some Unitarians and Universalists, some Methodists and Episcopalians, some Baptists, some Dutch Reformed, and a great many Presbyterians and Congregationalists.

The Presbyterians and Congregationalists were not only the most numerous but the best organized, thanks to the missionary efforts — eventually concerted — of the Presbyterian General Assembly and the Connecticut Missionary Society. Since both of these denominations were strong for revivals, religious camp meetings were a commonplace in the early history of western New York. Although they were prompt to organize into congregations, the settlers were too poor at the outset to build churches. It is said that the first Protestant church building in all western New York State was the Congregationalist church erected at East Bloomfield, in 1801.[5]

Dour-sounding old biblical names were borne by most of the pioneers, testifying to their Calvinistic background. Names like Abner Adams, Ephraim Rue, Jabez L. Bottom, Cotton Skinner, Shadrack Crane, Peleg Gorton, Zephaniah Hough. Were there any Catholics dwelling among the transplanted New England Yankees who brought with them the names, and, one may fairly assume, the stringent mores of Puritan New England? Yes, there were some Catholics. Few, no doubt, but some.

The earliest local Catholic on record was the trader, Dominick De Bartzch, who, as we have already noted, was trafficking among the Indians at the foot of Seneca Lake as early as 1786. He and his associate, one Joseph Poudre, were married to Iroquois women, and they exercised considerable influence over the local redskins. De Bartzch, a Montreal Frenchman, eventually left the district and moved farther west. Poudre remained longer, and in 1789 his right was acknowledged to 320 acres which the Iroquois had given him. We are rather sure that De Bartzch was a Catholic, for according to an old Yates County tradition, the first religious service in Yates County was conducted at De Bartzch's post at

Kashong, on the Yates County-Ontario County line, by a Catholic priest said to have been "from Oswego" (from Canada via Oswego?). This could have been as early as 1786.[6]

Monsieur De Boui, the crabbed recluse of the Wadsworth Flats on the Genesee River, may also have been a Catholic. An Alsatian, forced out of Santo Domingo by the French Revolution, De Boui had obtained permission of the Wadsworths, those grand pioneer squires of the Genesee Valley, to settle on their land. This was in 1793 or 1794. He and his mulatto slave Joseph, who was probably also a Catholic, stayed there for a few years, having little or no contact with their English-speaking neighbors. Then they decamped, bound, perhaps, for Asylum, the ephemeral colony founded by French emigrés—many if not most of them Catholic—on the upper Susquehanna in Bradford County, Pennsylvania.[7]

Major Charles Carroll of Bellevue was certainly a Catholic. Major Charles (1767-1823) was a Marylander, and by marriage a nephew of Daniel Carroll, signer of the Constitution, who, as we have already pointed out, was the brother of Bishop John Carroll. The Major and his brother Henry were educated at the Catholic English College at Liège, Belgium in the 1780's. He later became one of the early founders of Rochester.[8]

There was an interesting, if brief, colony of Irish immigrants undertaken in the early 1800's in the town of Tyrone, then in Steuben but now in Schuyler County. Thomas O'Connor, its founder, had fled Dublin after the abortive Irish revolution of 1798. Having come to New York, he purchased, in 1800, 4,000 acres in northeastern Steuben County. He and his wife and their infant son Charles moved there in 1804. His brother Dennis joined them and opened the first local store. Several other settlers soon arrived, among them the widowed Mrs. John Kernan with two sons and five daughters.

The Irish settlers did not remain long in Tyrone. Thomas O'Connor himself returned to New York around 1809, having decided he was a better journalist than trailblazer. His son Charles (who spelt the name O'Conor) achieved national fame. A noted lawyer, Charles O'Conor (1804-1884), was in 1872 nominated for the presidency of the United States by the Anti-Greeley Democrats. Despite his unwillingness to run, this first Catholic nominee for the American presidency polled 29,000 votes.

Apparently the only Tyrone Irishman who stayed on after his countrymen had left was William Kernan, the eldest son of the widow Kernan. He became the leading squire of the township and rose to brigadier general in the State militia—probably the only Catholic of his day to reach that rank in New York's amateur soldiery. We shall also meet him again on a later page. His son Francis, born in Wayne, was U.S. Senator from 1875 to 1881.[9]

Auburn, known as Hardenburgh's Corners until 1805, counted several Catholic Irishmen among its early citizens. The most prominent of them were Hugh Ward, who arrived in 1809, and John O'Connor, who likewise came before 1810.[10]

But the largest group of Catholic pioneers were the farmers who established themselves in the fertile lands of the Town of Greece, just west of the mouth of the Genesee River and northwest of the present city of Rochester. Parish tradition at Our Mother of Sorrows Church declares that the first of the pioneers was Felix McGuire (1770-1855), who moved into the Town of Northampton (out of which Greece Town was eventually carved) in 1808 or earlier. John McGuire, apparently his brother, arrived about the same time; and Cornelius Farnan (1776-1849) is also accounted one of the earliest of the colony. Later on, James A. Flynn, a ship's captain on the Great Lakes, joined them, married one of the McGuire girls, and started a second career as an agriculturalist. Relatives and friends of the McGuires, fellow landsmen and other Irish not so closely connected with the pioneers, migrated into the "Grecian" countryside in the subsequent years. It is no wonder that this farming neighborhood soon became known as "Paddy Hill."[11]

From the known we can argue to the unknown. The twelve counties doubtless attracted a number of other Catholics during the period 1789-1810. Identified or unidentified, however, they clearly constituted only a very small minority among the Protestant majority.

And what provision did Bishop Carroll of Baltimore make for western New York's scattered Catholics? None, directly. His diocese was so vast and his clergy were so few that he had to be content with setting up churches in the larger cities, commending to the care of the angels the faithful who were strewn across the remote hinterlands. When St. Peter's Church was opened in New York in 1786 it was the first post-Revolutionary Catholic house of worship in New York State, and its nominal parishioners were all the Catholics within the State boundaries.[12] The first upstate Catholic church, St. Mary's in Albany, began to function in 1798. This brought a parish church somewhat closer to the parishioners in the western part of the state.[13] Even so, the clergy of St. Mary's were never able to undertake missionary journeys to the western members of their congregation. And the organization of the Church in upper New York State progressed no farther than this while the State was under the jurisdiction of the bishop of Baltimore.

There were, however, two priests of the Baltimore Diocese who seem to have visited western New York during this period. Father James Pellentz (1727-1800) was pastor at Conewago, near Gettysburg in Pennsylvania. His parish included practically all the lands traversed by the Susquehanna River. In the course of a trip made north in 1787, Pellentz is said to have "reached the Wyoming Valley [near Wilkes Barre, Pennsylvania] and proceeded up the Susquehanna as far as Elmira."[14]

Another pioneer priest is known to have travelled east from Buffalo in 1805. Father Jean Dilhet (1753-1811) was a French Sulpician missionary. Summoned back to Baltimore from Detroit in the year 1805, he took a route which led him through New Amsterdam (now Buffalo), Niagara, Batavia, Canandaigua, and Geneva; and from Geneva south to Newtown (Elmira), where he secured transportation down the Chemung and Susquehanna to Baltimore. "There is no Catholic mission in these new settlements," he correctly testified at a later date. But he had discovered, he said, that "some Catholics may be found there."[15]

Did Father Pellentz celebrate Mass at Elmira or administer to the faithful there? It seems unlikely, for there is no evidence that Chemung or Tioga Counties had Catholic inhabitants as early as 1787. Did Father Dilhet, whose path lay across as many as six of the twelve counties, discover and give spiritual care to any Catholics living therein? This is more plausible, but no more capable of proof.

If other priests visited western New York in the same period, they, too, would have been transient rather than official figures. There can be little doubt that some of the first Catholic settlers suffered for want of the sacraments and religious instruction. Deprived of these aids for a long time, and under strong social pressures in a society overwhelmingly hostile to Catholicism, a number of them no doubt lost the Faith or saw their children lose it. This was, of course, one of the national tragedies of the struggling young American Church.

But if certain of the Catholic pioneers became lost to the Church, others clung to it with heroic courage, and made the long journey to their distant parish churches to receive their Easter Communion or have their children baptized. Faithful for the rest of the year to their catechism and their prayers, they hoped with an earnest hope that finally a priest might be sent to them.

In the second decade of the nineteenth century that hope began to be fulfilled.

2. The New York Diocese: Bishop Connolly.

On April 8, 1808, Pope Pius VII, by the briefs *Ex Debito* and *Pontificii Muneris,* divided the original Diocese of Baltimore into the Archdiocese of Baltimore and the dioceses of New York, Philadelphia, Boston, and Bardstown (later Louisville), Kentucky. The new Diocese of New York included New York State and the northern half of New Jersey.

The establishment of the Diocese of New York at this moment was particularly timely. Western New York was to reach a total population of 200,000 by 1810, and 500,000 by the end of another decade. Migration from New England still accounted for much of the increase. But European immigrants from Ireland, Germany and France, a large percentage of them Catholic, were also entering upstate New York, through New York or through Canada, in mounting numbers. While a bishop stationed in New York City would still have a major project on his hands, he would at least have a narrower territory upon which to concentrate than the first bishop of Baltimore had had.

Although founded in 1808, the Diocese of New York did not really begin to function until 1815. Richard Luke Concanen (1747-1810), an Irish Dominican priest resident in Rome, was named and consecrated first bishop of New York in 1808, but died in 1810 after waiting in vain for passage to America. Another Irish Dominican, likewise a Roman resident, was named to succeed him in 1814. The Right Reverend John Connolly, O.P. (1750?-1825) received episcopal consecration in Rome on November 6, 1814. But as the Napoleonic wars had delayed the departure of his predecessor, so the War of 1812 postponed Connolly's transatlantic crossing. He finally reached New York in November, 1815, on the packet "Sally." The trip took him over two months.

Once installed in St. Patrick's Cathedral (the *old* Cathedral on Mott Street, New York), Bishop Connolly began to realize the dismaying size of his new pastoral task. The majority of his Catholic diocesans still lived in New York City—between fifteen and twenty thousand, mostly Irish. There were two churches to care for them, St. Peter's, the original parish, and St. Patrick's Cathedral (dedicated in May, 1815, and heavily in debt). The only other fair concentration of Catholics was at Albany, where, as we have seen, there was one church. Three churches in the whole State, no more. The Bishop's informants could only hazard a guess as to the number of Catholics in northern and western New York State. And at the start of his episcopal career, this poor prelate had at times only three priests to aid him.

If Bishop Connolly proved to be more of a shepherd than an administrator, at least the Catholics of western New York could bless him for that trait. In 1817, he appointed Father Michael O'Gorman to be pastor of St. Mary's, Albany, with the understanding that O'Gorman would take regular mission journeys into the northern and western sections of the state.

The Bishop had chosen a good person for his assignment. Father O'Gorman (1792-1824) was a young Kilkenny man who had volunteered to serve Bishop Connolly, had come over to New York with him, and had been ordained to the priesthood by him.[16] He was a priest of genuine zeal. An old Catholic tradition at Auburn indicates that some months before receiving his appointment to Albany, O'Gorman had already visited Auburn and celebrated Mass for the four or five local Catholic families. Their leader, John O'Connor, a fairly prosperous citizen, had, it is said, requested that the Bishop send them a priest, promising to pay his stagecoach fare and other travelling expenses. On the occasion of that visit to Auburn in 1816, the missionary offered Mass in the home of O'Connor on Water Street. He also administered the sacrament of baptism.[17]

There is no proof that Father O'Gorman pushed farther west after this first visit to Auburn. But those who read the June 30, 1818, issue of Canandaigua's *Ontario Messenger* learned that the young pastor of Albany was to preach that very evening in the Canandaigua courthouse, and again in the late morning of July 5th at Williamsburg, Town of Groveland, in the present Livingston County. To what Catholics was he to preach? Well, the Catholic squire, Charles Carroll of Bellevue, lived in the Groveland neighborhood. Who the Catholics were in the vicinity of Canandaigua we cannot say. Perhaps O'Gorman was himself trying to find out.

"Rochesterville" on the lower Genesee had been founded only lately, in 1812. Nonetheless, it already had a population of about one thousand when it was incorporated as a village in 1817. It is quite likely that the missionary from Albany paid a visit to the Catholics in and around Rochesterville during the course of his trip to Canandaigua and Williamsburg.

In the case of Rochester, as in the case of many of our early settlements, there are conflicting accounts of the time and place of the first local Mass. The following story sounds the most plausible.

One summer, we are told—and the year was perhaps 1818—a Catholic woman from Maryland was a house guest of Rochester's principal founder, Colonel Nathaniel Rochester (1752-1831). Taken ill during her stay, the guest asked the Colonel to summon a priest. Colonel Rochester hastened to oblige, and sent a messenger as far as New York —the story says—to fetch the clergyman. A priest, unnamed in the record, came to Rochesterville and ministered to the ailing woman. Then he made known his presence to some of the local Catholic citizenry. One of the Catholics mounted his horse and rode far and wide to announce that a priest had come and would offer Mass in Colonel Rochester's home at Exchange and Spring Streets. The priest did offer the Mass, in the presence of a devout congregation. He furthermore tarried in Rochester a few days so as to be available to the Catholics of the vicinity.[18]

The time had not yet come to set up a parish in Rochester. But thanks to Father O'Gorman's efforts, the first parish in western New York was established at Utica in 1819. On January 25, 1819, nine laymen from the counties west of Albany met in Utica, with the approval of O'Gorman, and incorporated as the "Trustees of the First Catholic Church in the Western District of the State of New York." Three of the lay trustees represented the present Rochester diocesan area: Major Charles Carroll of the Genesee Valley, John McGuire of the Rochester environs, and John O'Connor of Auburn.[19] The fruit of their incorporation was St. John's Church, Utica. Bishop Connolly named Father John Farnan to see this project through. The church was dedicated by the Bishop on August 19, 1821, and Father Farnan continued as its pastor until 1823. Thereafter, at least for a short while, Rochester Catholics were parishioners of the new church at Utica.

A final word about Father Michael O'Gorman. The Bishop had recalled him to New York in 1819, to assist him at the Cathedral. Connolly held this eloquent, indefatigable, and worthy priest in such high regard that in 1824 he petitioned Rome to name him as coadjutor bishop, with right of succession. But Providence decided otherwise. Michael O'Gorman died on November 18, 1824, aged only thirty-two.[20] Members of the Diocese of Rochester should hold his name in benediction.

Father John Farnan (1799-1849) was himself only seven years a priest when named pastor of the Utica parish. He also had charge of the mission church lately dedicated at Carthage, Jefferson County, in northern New York; and of course he had custody of all of the western part of the State. To his enterprise we owe the establishment of what was the first church in *western* Western New York, and the first church in the present Diocese of Rochester: St. Patrick's Church, Rochester-ville.[21]

Father Farnan made his first missionary trip west in the summer of 1819. On July 11th, he celebrated Mass in the courthouse at Auburn. Six months later he was back in Auburn for another visit.[22]

It is quite likely that on each of these two occasions, Farnan pushed on to Rochester before returning to Utica. On July 12, 1820, he was in Rochester on a very special errand—to organize a parish and take steps toward the building of a church. At an official meeting of the vicinity Catholics there was formed the "Third Roman Catholic Church of the Western District." The meeting chose a board of managers: Felix McGuire, James Flynn, Patrick Buckley, and Patrick McCrisigan (Mc-Christian). A sixth person, Owen McGuire, was named secretary.[23] The post of treasurer was given to Felix McGuire. He was the real leader in the group. A zealous Catholic, reputed to have "brought the Faith into the Rochester area," he had already achieved enough local repute by 1810 to have won election as one of the township's "path masters."[24] All of the board members named on that July day were farmers from "Paddy Hill," with the exception of Buckley and McCrisigan, who lived in Rochester. Six years later Buckley, too, moved to the Irish farming community of Greece. No sooner had the committee been appointed, than they took up an initial collection for the building of a church.

Father Farnan held a similar meeting in Auburn later on in July, 1820, or early in August. Here the congregation chose, as managers of the "Fourth Catholic Church of Western New York," Hugh Ward, John O'Connor, James Hickson, Thomas Hickson, and David Lawler. On August 3rd, Farnan secured, for the nominal sum of five dollars, a lot for church and graveyard purposes located on the present Van Anden Street. Auburn Catholics now set about the building of Auburn's first Catholic chapel.[25]

There may have been a certain rivalry between the Rochesterians and Auburnians, both anxious to see their new churches finished and functioning. At first Auburn seemed to be leading the race. Possibly because the foundation walls were already built when it went to press, the New York *Catholic Laity's Directory* for 1822 stated that Albany, Utica, Carthage and *Auburn* were already provided with church buildings. Actually, the Auburnians never completed the construction. Perhaps for want of funds, perhaps because they lost heart when they learned that Bishop Connolly could not promise them a resident pastor or even regular care, they halted the project at mid-course. The property deed provided that if a church were not built on the lot within five years, it would automatically revert to the owners. The Auburn Catholics therefore had the double disappointment of losing both church and site.[26] Holy Family, Auburn's first church, was to be dedicated only in 1834.

The Rochester Catholics moved more deliberately but more successfully. On April 29, 1822, the congregation received the deed to a lot measuring 70 by 132 feet, located on the northeast corner of Frank Street (now Plymouth Avenue North) and Platt Street. They paid $200.00. Once again the lot was transferred for church and graveyard purposes, and once again reversion to the original owners was stipulated if the church was not up by the end of five years.[27]

But here there was no reversion. By the end of 1823, St. Patrick's Church was complete, except for the tower and certain other details. No pictures of this historic building are extant. Contemporary descriptions tell us that it was built of stone, measured a modest thirty-eight by forty-two feet, and was equipped "with large Gothick windows."[28]

Father Farnan, who had launched the movement to build St. Patrick's, was no longer its pastor when it was dedicated. In 1821 Bishop Connolly had assigned the western New York missions to Father Patrick O'Kelly (1792-1856). Like Michael O'Gorman and some other Irish priests engaged by New York's second bishop, Father O'Kelly was an alumnus of St. Kieran's College, Kilkenny. He was newly ordained when put in charge of the Catholics of Auburn, Rochester, and points westward to Buffalo. He had supervised the erection of St. Patrick's in Rochester; and although he was often absent on missionary trips, he seems to have resided in Rochester—in an inn or private home, since there was no rectory. O'Kelly is listed as pastor at Carthage, New York, in 1827. He must therefore have been transferred thence from Rochester at least by 1826.[29]

Bishop John Connolly died in February, 1825, at the age of about seventy-five years. It is not certain whether he ever made a personal visitation of the westernmost portion of his large diocese.[30] He had labored in New York State for ten years, but the fruits of his labors seemed pitifully small. By 1829, if not by 1825, there were close to 150,000 Catholics in New York State and 35,000 in New York City. To serve these there were still only three churches in the metropolis and five upstate. Outside New York City itself there were no Catholic schools or charitable institutions; and the painful lack of priests continued.

As his eyes closed upon his diocese, the second bishop of New York can only have had a salutary discontent with its condition. But this state of affairs was not of his making. He had done his best. And he had merited in particular the sincere gratitude of the Catholics of Rochester for having given them their first church and what was to be their first cathedral parish.

3. A TIDE STILL RISING: 1825-1847.

The third bishop of New York was the genial and apostolic Frenchman, John Dubois (1764-1842). Dubois was a member of the Society of St. Sulpice. A sometime refugee from the French Revolution, he had brought his zeal—and his French accent—with him. Prior to his appointment to New York on May 23, 1826, he had won note as the founder of Mount St. Mary's College in Maryland. Bishop Dubois' successor was one of America's most noted churchmen, John Joseph Hughes (1797-1864). Bishop Hughes was a native of the County Tyrone in Ireland, and was named coadjutor bishop to the aging Dubois (contrary to Dubois' own wish) on August 8, 1837. After 1839, when Bishop Dubois was incapacitated, Hughes was given full administrative authority; and upon John Dubois' death, December 20, 1842, he automatically became fourth bishop of New York. John Hughes was the last of the New York bishops to exercise episcopal jurisdiction over western New York State. In 1847, the whole territory occupied at present by the dioceses of Buffalo and Rochester was separated from the Diocese of New York and set up as the Diocese of Buffalo.

The year 1825—the very year in which Bishop Connolly died—saw the opening of the Erie Canal. Governor De Witt Clinton's "Big Ditch" was to play an important role in the later settlement and economic expansion of western New York. Not only did it furnish, of itself, quicker access to upstate and to the Midwest; it also inspired the digging of a network of auxiliary canals, particularly in the country west from Utica. By 1828, there was a Cayuga and Seneca Canal to join the waters of those two finger lakes with the Erie Canal. Three more canals completed this ramification to the south. The Crooked Lake Canal (1833) tied in Crooked [Keuka] Lake with Seneca Lake at Dresden, New York. The Chemung Canal and Feeder (1833) united the head of Seneca Lake with the Chemung River at Corning and Elmira. And the privately-operated Junction Canal, completed in 1858, connected the Chemung Canal with Pennsylvania's North Branch Canal. A more westerly spur of the system was the Genesee Valley Canal, which ran south from Rochester to Dansville and Olean. It was begun in 1836 and finished in 1857.

The canal era had scarcely begun when railroads put in their appearance. In the 1870's New York State's railways were to supersede all but the Erie Canal itself as common carriers; but at the outset they were quite unassuming. The Ithaca and Owego Railroad—second to win a State charter—opened in 1834. By 1842, however, there were enough of these small lines running across the northern tier of counties to enable a man to travel by train from Albany to Buffalo. The next step came in 1853, when these separate lines were joined to form the New York Central system. Meanwhile, the Erie Railroad, organized in 1835, had by 1853 forged its way west to Dunkirk, to become the longest single line in the nation. Although the Central and the Erie eventually took over north-and-south running links, the former remained essentially a Northern Tier railroad and the latter a Southern Tier railroad. This fact no doubt consolidated the tendency of Northern and Southern Tiers to develop relatively independent economies and cultures.

The part which the canals and railroads played in the growth of western New York was crucial. Place-names like Brockport, Spencerport, Bushnell's Basin, Fairport, Port Byron, Weedsport, and Breesport testify to the debt which these communities owe to the canal system. The Erie Canal could even make or mar a settlement. Rochester and Canandaigua, for example, were rivals in the early 1820's Then came the Canal, routed *away* from Canandaigua and *through* Rochester. As a consequence, the expansion of Canandaigua was inhibited, and by 1860 it had no more than 4,000 inhabitants. But Rochester, already an incorporated city since 1834, counted almost 50,000 citizens. The railways in turn benefited the towns along their rights of way. They augmented the prosperity of canal ports through which they passed, like Elmira, Corning, and Rochester; and they became prime factors in the economy of places like Hornell.

Catholicism in the twelve counties owes a great deal to these manmade rivers and iron highways. They not only gave Catholics as immigrants easier access; they also provided them with temporary or permanent jobs at construction and maintenance. As one Rochester Irishman proudly sang:

> The Cities and towns thro' this mighty Republic
> Are based on the sweat of the Irishman's face;

The Canals and the R.roads no man can deny it,
To Irish exertions you fairly can trace.

Ready jobs for manual laborers were a particular boon to the Irish newcomers, most of whom were unskilled. An incident at Elmira, although it occurred in 1848, is still a good case in point. That year opportunities were very good for common laborers on the Erie Railroad construction crews in the Elmira area. Learning of this, one Owen Mc-Greevey drove west to Elmira in his team and wagon; one Mark Cummings reached the same destination at about the same time; and the two were followed by hundreds of other Irishmen who came bringing their own shovels, ready to dig anything that had to be dug. Canal authorities had long since come to value the strength of the Irish laborer, and his dauntless stamina in the face of the most adverse circumstances. Had it not been for Irish grit, the Erie Canal might never have been carried across the vast swamps at Montezuma near Auburn.[31]

Similar scenes occurred on the "public works" in many a place in western New York throughout the mid-century era when immigration was at its height. Irish laborers were often attracted by one of the villages through which their work took them, and subsequently settled there with their families, which they usually brought over as soon as they had earned passage money for them. Some immigrants continued for many years in the employ of the canals or railways; others branched out into different employments; still others became tenant farmers, and eventually bought improved farms for themselves. The women-folk of the Irish families were meanwhile in great demand for domestic service, and their earnings contributed much to the support of the large families. At Brockport, Fairport, Victor, Nunda, Dansville, Scottsville, Mount Morris, Penn Yan, Hammondsport, Watkins, Ithaca, Waverly, Corning, Elmira, and a number of other upstate localities, a good proportion of the Catholic pioneers were men who had originally worked on the canals and railroads of the neighborhood.

While the Irish constituted the major part of the original Catholic immigration into western New York, the German element grew in size and importance. This was particularly true in Rochester and its environs.

John and Anna Maria Klem, natives of Klittersdorf, near Strassburg, Alsace, arrived in Rochester one day in 1816; and they and their family spent the night in the family wagon right in the middle of State Street. They were the second German-speaking family and the first Catholic family to establish a home at Rochester.[32] By 1835 the number of German Catholic Rochesterians had risen to 600. Some were Swiss, but most of them hailed from the western German districts: Alsace, Baden, Rhenish Bavaria, Württemberg, Luxembourg, and Hesse. Unlike the Irish arrivals, the Germans were usually skilled at some craft, or as bakers, butchers or brewers. Many, following their agricultural traditions, fanned out into the nearby townships, acquiring farms in Irondequoit or in the vicinity of Webster, Penfield, Walworth, Ontario, or Coldwater.

Germans also settled elsewhere in the twelve counties, although in smaller numbers. One group located briefly at East Bloomfield in 1830, then moved on to Rochester.[33] There was a larger and more stable concentration in the town of Dansville, then in Steuben County.[34] Between 1832 and 1838, a number of families from St. Wendel near Treves in Rhenish Prussia moved into the Dansville highlands. Their earliest center of population was on Sandy Hill, which rises to the south of Perkinsville. Later German immigrants bought land at Perkinsville proper, at Dansville village, Wayland, Liberty (now Cohocton), Naples, and Blood's (now Atlanta).

Germans likewise established themselves at other points in the Southern Tier: Hornell, Bath, Hammondsport, Corning, and especially Elmira. Along the Northern Tier there were small German colonies at Canandaigua and Lyons, and there was a large one at Auburn. Scattered German families could also be found in other parts of the present Rochester Diocese.

The French and the Netherlanders constituted the two smallest segments of the incoming Catholic population. On visiting Rochester in 1841 Bishop Hughes noted the "large and increasing numbers of Canadian and French Catholics."[35] Some French-speaking people took residence elsewhere in the district (like Vital Rèche of Dansville and Francis Wood [Houde] of Campbell), but the French colony in Rochester remained the largest. By the late 1850's there were also forty families of practicing Catholic Hollanders in or near Rochester.[36] Some of these may have arrived before 1847. But Belgians and Hollanders did not enter in large numbers until the later years of the century.

With so many more souls to visit in western New York, Bishops John Dubois and John Hughes must have thanked God for the canal boats and railways that eased and sped their travel. Each bishop came into the future Rochester Diocese at least four times.

Dubois' first visit was apparently in 1828.[37] In 1829 he once more passed through on the "grand visitation" of 3,000 miles, travelling the whole circuit alone because he could not afford to take a companion.[38] He was in Rochester again in the spring of 1832.[39] And in June, 1837,

as he drew near his golden jubilee of priesthood, he made his last official tour of the western part of the State, calling at both Rochester and
Auburn.[40]

While coadjutor to Bishop Dubois, John Hughes paid his first visit
to Rochester in August, 1839.[41] In the course of a more thorough survey
in summer, 1841, he paused at Auburn, Geneva, Rochester, and Greece.[42]
Local church problems brought him to Rochester once more in the late
fall of 1842.[43] In August, 1844, he again came to Rochester, to administer the sacrament of Confirmation.[44] Bishop Hughes does not seem to
have personally visited the twelve counties after 1844. But his coadjutor bishop, America's future first Cardinal, John McCloskey, made a
trip west in the summer of 1845, inspecting the parishes and administering Confirmation. He stopped at Dansville, Watkins Glen, and probably other places where there were Catholic congregations.[45]

Better acquainted with the facts and problems of western New
York and, as time passed, somewhat better supplied with priests and
funds, the third and fourth bishops of New York strove to satisfy as
soon as they could the upstate pleas for more churches.[46]

Within the twelve counties, between 1826 and 1847, twelve new
churches and chapels were begun. Some of these were put up by the
local Catholics themselves, in earnest of a future missionary pastor.
Others were erected on the more direct authorization of church authorities.

In Rochester proper, St. Patrick's congregation had become so populous by 1831 that it had to build itself a new church building, twice the
size of the original. Since the new structure was on the same site as its
predecessor, a schoolroom on Buffalo Street (Main Street West) was
used as an interim chapel.[47] Even the enlarged St. Patrick's soon proved
inadequate to the needs of the growing Catholic community. A second
parish, named St. Mary's, opened in 1834 in a former Wesleyan Methodist church building on South St. Paul Street (now South Avenue).
But the pastor, Father Patrick Foley (1799?-1839), could not make a
go of it, so St. Mary's closed in 1835. In 1841, however, the same building was once more purchased, and the parish reopened, now, as it proved, on a permanent basis.[48] St. Joseph's, Rochester's first German parish,
also bore the name of St. Mary's when founded in 1836. A second German parish, St. Peter's, was begun on Maple Street in 1842 to accommodate Germans living in the western part of town. And out in nearby
Greece, the Irish farmers of the neighborhood were worshipping in
their own country church by 1832. It stood beside Latta Road and bore

the name St. Ambrose. When St. Ambrose frame church was replaced by the brick church in 1860, the name of church and parish was changed to "Our Mother of Sorrows."

To the east of Rochester, churches were completed at Auburn and Geneva. Bishop Dubois' vicar general, the Very Reverend John Power, came up from New York to dedicate Holy Family Church in Auburn, on October 23, 1834, and St. Francis de Sales Church in Geneva, on October 26th.[49] A church was built at Seneca Falls in 1836. Its patron was St. Jerome, but a subsequent church building (the third) was given the name St. Patrick, which still denominates the parish.[50]

To the south of Rochester, in Livingston County, Charles Holker Carroll, the Episcopalian son of Major Charles Carroll, donated land at Brushville (now Tuscarora) for a chapel to serve the 300 Catholics laboring on the Genesee Valley Canal. The shanty chapel was opened in 1838 and closed in 1842, as no longer necessary. Many of the Brushville workmen are said to have settled at Mount Morris.[51]

In the Southern Tier proper, there were small churches at Sandy Hill, Dansville, and Greenwood, and an unfinished church at Salubria (Watkins Glen). The Germans of the Perkinsville district built their log church on the heights of Sandy Hill as early as 1839, although it waited five years for formal dedication to Our Lady of the Holy Rosary. The Catholic villagers of Dansville acquired a chapel of their own in 1845.[52] Meanwhile, Irish farmers had begun by 1834 to settle around Greenwood, in the hill country south of Hornell, Steuben County, rather close to the Pennsylvania border. In 1844, they began their small church —probably also of log construction—at a Greenwood rural intersection.[53] Over at Watkins, Attorney George Quin, Protestant son-in-law of General William Kernan of Tyrone, generously bought and donated to the Catholics a little hillside Presbyterian church. This was in 1845. The local Catholics did not finish outfitting the building until 1848.[54] (It seems that here as elsewhere the great poverty of the immigrants hampered them in realizing their desire for a church of their own. Canandaigua, too, had a little church begun in 1843 but dedicated only five years later.[55])

Two of the parishes we have enumerated deserve fuller notice: St. Ambrose on "Paddy Hill," and St. Joseph's in Rochester.

St. Ambrose was the first Catholic *country* parish in New York State. Felix McGuire, considered the area's pioneer Catholic, had been a legendary leader in the foundation of St. Patrick's Rochester. Subsequently he also led in the establishment of this rural church in his own township of Greece, on a site seven miles northwest of St. Patrick's

Church. Tradition says that they began to build the church in 1829. If this is true, it was another instance of slow completion, for the first Mass was celebrated in St. Ambrose only on February 5, 1832. The church lot was the gift of "Squire" Nicholas Read (1787-1864), a parishioner and prominent citizen of Greece Town since 1821. McGuire, who lived a bit to the south of Paddy Hill, donated the lumber. In 1834, not many months after the dedication of St. Ambrose, one Patrick Bulger "immortalized" the church in the columns of the New York *Truth Teller*. He commended the zeal of the congregation and described in romantic terms the little "church in the wood." The successor of St. Ambrose, Our Mother of Sorrows Church, standing in its picturesque old wooded graveyard, remained indeed a rural "church in the wood" until recent times, when it was finally engulfed by suburbia.[56]

St. Joseph's Church was an even more important foundation, for it was to play a key role in the German apostolate of the whole district.

Rochester's German Catholic families at first attended St. Patrick's. Here Bernard Klem, one of pioneer John Klem's sons, was an early trustee. When St. Mary's Church was opened on South Avenue in 1834, the Germans started to go to Mass there. After the closing of this church in 1835, the local Germans, disturbed by the crowded condition of St. Patrick's, and never quite reconciled to belonging to an English-language parish, were ready to consider establishing a congregation of their own. This was the recommendation of the Very Reverend John A. Raffeiner (1785-1861), Bishop Dubois' vicar for Germans, who visited the Germans of Rochester in 1834 or 1835. The Austrian Redemptorist, Father Joseph Prost (1805-1885), endorsed the same move, when a happy accident forced him to break off his journey at Rochester in 1835.

It was Father Prost's arguments that stimulated effective action. The 600 Germans of the locality may have come from many different locales in the old country, but they now not only concurred in desiring a parish but in begging Father Prost to be its pastor. Once he had agreed to do so, they set about securing a church. It was found that an unfinished African Methodist Episcopal church building on Ely Street in downtown Rochester was available. Therefore, on December 7, 1835, Bernard Klem, Ignatius Eichhorn, and John Wegman, as agents of the prospective congregation, purchased the building. Since the earlier St. Mary's Church, a stone's throw away, had now closed down, the name St. Mary's was adopted for the new church organization. This was confirmed on August 20, 1836, when the congregation elected six lay trustees and filed a certificate of incorporation for "St. Mary's Church in Rochester."[57]

Before Father Prost returned to Rochester, the new parishioners were served for a week by a young Austro-Hungarian priest who was just beginning a uniquely notable career. A native of Bohemia, John Nepomucene Neumann (1811-1860) had recently crossed the Atlantic to enter the service of the Diocese of New York. Bishop Dubois ordained him to the priesthood on June 25, 1836, and assigned him forthwith to the German farming community at Williamsville near Buffalo. He likewise told him to stop over at Rochester on a missionary visit. The next day, June 26th, Father Neumann celebrated his first Mass in New York and set out for his new post: "mit Sack und Pack," as he said. When his canal boat, the "Indiana," approached Rochester on July 4th, he was welcomed by the sound of cannons saluting Independence Day. He spent from the 4th to the 11th in Rochester. Here he performed the first pastoral functions of his priestly life. On July 7th at St. Patrick's Church, he baptized the infant Caroline Koch. On Sunday, the 10th, he delivered his first sermon at two Masses. He went on to Buffalo the next day. Father Neumann subsequently became a member, and later on the vicegerent of the American Redemptorists. From 1852 to 1860, he was bishop of Philadelphia. During his lifetime he was regarded as a living saint, and the Church eventually confirmed that belief. On December 11, 1921, Pope Benedict XV solemnly decreed that his virtues had been heroic; and on October 13, 1963, Pope Paul VI formally beatified him, raising him to the rank of "Blessed."[58]

Father Joseph Prost got back to Rochester on July 10, 1836, the last day of Father Neumann's sojourn. He was gratified to see the little church close to completion, and he soon established the routine of devotional life—German style—among his new parishioners. In late June, 1837, Bishop Dubois himself came up from New York for the opening. He dedicated Rochester's first German parish church—not as St. Mary's, but as St. Joseph's.[59] After ten years on Ely Street, the parishioners moved into the present St. Joseph's Church on Franklin Street. This, the oldest Catholic church building in Rochester, was designed by the firm of Jones and Nevin and built of stone mined in a special quarry on the nearby riverbank. The Very Reverend Peter Czackert, C.SS.R., dedicated it on the feast of St. Anne, July 26, 1846.

The transfer of St. Joseph's from Ely to Franklin Street engendered considerable friction, and the friction resulted in the foundation of a second German parish.

It was in 1838 that Father Prost, having purchased land on Franklin Street, announced to his Ely Street congregation that he purposed to build a new and larger church. The parishioners reacted strongly against his proposal, not a little because the Redemptorists rather than the congregation would be the owners of the new property. When the resultant bitterness reached a peak, Father Prost shook from his shoes the dust of Rochester, leaving the church without a residential pastor for several months. By the time he finally sent Father Simon Saenderl to succeed him, in 1839, the agitation of the people of St. Joseph's had largely subsided, and the majority, on second thought, favored moving to the new location.

Certain of the parishioners continued to hold out, however, because they were angry with the Redemptorists and because they wanted a German parish on the west side of the Genesee, where most of them lived. They therefore requested permission of Bishop Hughes to build a new church on the west side of town. The Bishop consented, on condition that Father Saenderl also approve. The Germans did not ask the latter's consent, probably because they believed he would not give it, but went right ahead with a new building at King and Maple Streets. Not knowing of Hughes' permission, Father Saenderl naturally reached the conclusion that the dissident Germans were guilty of a schismatic attitude. He refused to lay the cornerstone, and so did Father Bernard O'Reilly, pastor of St. Patrick's. The parishioners therefore performed the rite themselves. They sealed into the stone a rancorous document which declared: "Whereas we have been deceived by the Redemptorist Fathers, we are going to build in spite of them . . ."

The rancor had not abated by the time the church was up, so Bishop Hughes made a personal visit to Rochester to sit in judgment on the case. He decided in favor of St. Peter's congregation, and declared the new church to be a Catholic church on condition that the property be deeded to him in keeping with American Catholic church regulations. The trustees complied with this stipulation on December 13, 1842.[60] Bishop Hughes thereupon named as pastor a non-Redemptorist, the Austrian Franciscan missionary, Father Ivo Levitz (1790-1853). Father Ivo blessed the completed church on June 29, 1843.[61]

The building of new churches in those days did not always mean the immediate appointment of resident pastors. Priests were too few to permit that luxury. Instead, missionary rectors were usually named to central parishes and entrusted also with one or more outlying missions (that is, congregations with churches) or mission stations (that is, congregations without churches).

For example, Father Patrick O'Kelly, the first "resident" rector of St. Patrick's, Rochester, also had charge, as we have seen, of all other Catholic groups from Auburn west to Buffalo. In 1828 or 1829, Dubois established the parish of St. John the Baptist in Salina (now part of Syracuse). When in 1831 he named Father Francis O'Donoghue (1791-1845) to the "Salina Mission," he gave him jurisdiction over Carthage, Sackets Harbor, Oswego, and, in the present Rochester Diocese, Auburn and Geneva. After Father O'Donoghue had opened churches in Auburn and Geneva, he was reassigned to the "Geneva Mission," which by 1836 included Auburn, Seneca Falls, Ithaca, Watkins, and Elmira in the Southern Tier.

The Southern Tier counties were in general slower to receive consistent missionary care. It was easier at the start for Catholics along the Chemung River to obtain the occasional ministrations of priests of the Philadelphia Diocese who were working in northern Pennsylvania. Father Jeremiah Francis O'Flynn is said to have celebrated Mass at Elmira around 1830. This colorful Irish clergyman (1788-1831) had earlier been prefect apostolic of Australia; now he was circuit-riding pastor of an Irish colony at Silver Lake in the present Susquehanna County, Pennsylvania.[62] A decade later his zealous successor, Father John Vincent O'Reilly (1796-1873), found time to visit and offer Mass for canal laborers and other immigrants who had settled at Owego, Waverly, and Corning.[63] Only in 1843, when Father Andrew Doyle of the Diocese of New York was named rector of St. John's (now St. Patrick's) Church in Binghamton, did the Southern Tier receive its own travelling pastor. In the following year, jurisdiction over the congregation at Greenwood, westernmost of the Southern Tier's missionary stations, was entrusted to Father Thomas McEvoy (1823-1858), rector of St. Patrick's parish, Java (Wyoming County.)[64]

A still wider mission fell to the lot of the Redemptorist Fathers—the care of all the German-speaking Catholics of the district. As early as August 9, 1836, Father Joseph Prost, C.SS.R., visited the Germans in the township of Dansville.[65] In the years that followed, his colleagues and successors worked on a circuit which included not only towns near Rochester like Greece, Brockport, Penfield, Scottsville, and Webster, but remoter places like Auburn, Avon, Canandaigua, Clifton Springs, Clyde, Corning, Dansville village, Elmira, Geneva, Greenwood, Hammondsport, Hornell, Lyons, Mount Morris, Newark, Penn Yan, Perkinsville, Seneca Falls, and Waterloo. (After 1849 the Redemptorists of St. Mary's Church, Buffalo, assumed responsibility for those congregations, particularly in the Southern Tier, which were made up of both German-speaking and English-speaking Catholics.)[66]

By 1847, then, there were twelve churches, one still uncompleted, within the future Rochester Diocese. But that was not all. During the regimes of Bishops Dubois and Hughes four Catholic elementary schools were established and one charitable institution.

The German Rochesterians were the pioneers in parish education. St. Joseph's in Rochester opened its school in the basement of the Ely Street church in 1836. The first schoolmaster was Mr. Louis Kenning, who subsequently joined the Redemptorists as a lay brother—the first man to be admitted to that status in the United States. Pupils at St. Joseph's were taught "the English as well as the German."[67] The city's second German parish also had a school: St. Peter's School, opened in the same year in which the church was dedicated, 1843, was likewise conducted by a layman.[68] Redemptorist Father Benedict Bayer started school sessions for the German Catholics of Dansville village in 1842. When the Dansvillians acquired their own church in 1845 they opened a more formal school. The location was the old school building which the parishioners had used for several months as a temporary chapel. A Mr. Schario was the master.[69] Thus St. Mary's parish in Dansville had its own school even before it had a resident pastor.

The German parishes are therefore the indisputable founders of the present Rochester diocesan school system. Not until the days of Bishop McQuaid did the non-German congregations begin to overtake the German congregations in this respect. Still, St. Patrick's School in Rochester was one of the earliest in the area. It was first projected in 1832. The project did not materialize, however, until September, 1839, when the parish trustees hired as the first teacher the then sexton of the church, Mr. Michael Hughes (1799-1874). Schoolmaster Hughes' original classroom was in the church basement; but classes also seem to have been conducted in the second story of a store which stood on the southeast corner of State and Platt Streets.[70]

St. Patrick's Orphanage for girls was the one charitable institution founded in the twelve counties before 1847. Father Bernard O'Reilly, pastor of St. Patrick's, began to plan it as early as 1836. When it opened next door to St. Patrick's Church on July 5, 1842, there were twenty-four orphaned girls enrolled. A laywoman was house mother at the start, but it was the hope of the organizers that a community of Sisters might assume permanent charge. In 1844, the founding board (Father O'Reilly, Father Charles Ffrench, O.P., of St. Ambrose, Greece, and Messrs. George Wilkin and Patrick Barry), invited the Sisters of Charity of Emmitsburg, Maryland, to accept St. Patrick's Orphanage as a mission.[71] Emmitsburg consented, and on April 14, 1845, four black-capped members of Mother Seton's Sisters arrived in Rochester. To support themselves and their orphans, the Sisters opened a private or "select" school for girls in the following July.[72]

The coming of the Sisters of Charity to St. Patrick's Orphanage was a historic event in the annals of the parish and of social welfare in Rochester. But its historic importance was more than parochial and municipal. These four Sisters were the first Catholic nuns in all western New York.

While Bishops Dubois and Hughes had consolidated church organizations in the twelve counties, they had likewise built up the Church in the eight counties closer to Buffalo. By 1847 over half of the twenty-five missions in these eight counties had some sort of church building. Much remained to be done, but it was now time to divide the spiritual territory of the Diocese of New York and to constitute western New York as a new diocese with its own bishop.

On the recommendation of Bishop Hughes, and on the petition of the American Catholic hierarchy, Pope Pius IX severed upstate New York from the Diocese of New York and set up two new dioceses with seats at Albany and Buffalo. The Buffalo Diocese was established by the papal brief *"Universi Dominici Gregis"* of April 23, 1847. It included all of the counties west of the eastern boundary of Cayuga, Tompkins, and Tioga.[73]

The Pope appointed Buffalo's first bishop that same day. He was a priest of the Congregation of the Mission, or Vincentian Fathers, John Timon (1797-1867). Father Timon (rhymes with Simon) had become a well-known figure in his order and in the Church on the western frontier. Energetic superior of the American Vincentians, and sometime prefect apostolic of Texas, he was a true missionary after the pattern of St. Vincent de Paul. Although this son of Irish immigrants was a native of Conewago, Pennsylvania, he had been so intimately associated with the West that he was a little surprised to be named to an eastern episcopate. But he soon discovered that the twenty counties of western New York offered a challenge worthy of the most experienced missionary.

1   JOHN CARROLL
Archbishop of Baltimore
1789-1815

2   JOHN CONNOLLY, O.P.
Bishop of New York
1814-1825

3   JOHN DUBOIS
Bishop of New York
1826-1842

4   JOHN HUGHES
Archbishop of New York
1842-1864

5

JOHN TIMON, C.M.
Bishop of Buffalo
1847-1867

6 FATHER PATRICK O'KELLY

7 BISHOP BERNARD O'REILLY

8 ST. JOHN N. NEUMANN
C.SS.R.

9 FATHER JOHN V. O'REILLY

10 FATHER EDMUND
O'CONNOR

11 FATHER PETER CZACKERT, C.SS.R.

12 SISTER MARTHA DADDISMAN,
S.C. *(Brought Sisters of Charity to*
Rochester, 1845)

13 MOTHER AGNES SPENCER, S.S.J.
Pioneer New York State
Foundress, Sisters of St. Joseph

14 MOTHER CAROLINE FRIESS,
S.S.N.D. *(Brought to Rochester*
The School Sisters of Notre Dame)

15 MOTHER ALOYSIA HARDEY,
R.S.S.J.
Foundress, Academy of The Sacred Heart

16 MOTHER M. XAVIER WARDE,
R.S.M. *Foundress, Rochester Sisters of Mercy*

17 MOTHER HIERONYMO O'BRIEN,
S.S.J. *Foundress, St. Mary's Hospital*

18   THOMAS O'CONNOR   19   CHARLES O'CONOR

20 GEN. WILLIAM KERNAN   21 SENATOR FRANCIS KERNAN

22   JOHN O'CONNOR   23   MICHAEL HUGHES
          of Auburn

24   ANTOINE LANGIE   25   PATRICK BARRY

26   FRANK AND EVA RICHTER WEINMANN AND FAMILY (*circa* 1862)
(Frank Weinmann was a brewer in Rochester's "Dutchtown")

27　GEN. KERNAN'S "MASS HOUSE"
Wayne, New York

28　JOHN BRENNAN "MASS HOUSE"
Lima, New York

29　ST. PATRICK'S
ROCHESTER
(Second church, 1832)

30　HOLY FAMILY
CHURCH, AUBURN
1834-1861

31　ST. JOSEPH'S
CHURCH
(1846)

32　ST. PATRICK'S
CHURCH, OWEGO
1849-1889

33
ORIGINAL
CANANDAIGUA
CONVENT
*Sisters of
St. Joseph,
1854*

34
ST. MARY'S
HOSPITAL (1865)
*(First permanent
building, 1863-1959)*

35
MOTHERHOUSE,
SISTERS OF MERCY
*(Sold to St. Mary's
Church, 1916)*

36
HOLY ANGELS
ACADEMY, ELMIRA
1873-1906
*(Original building of
St. Joseph's
Hospital, 1908)*

CHAPTER THREE

BISHOP TIMON GATHERS HIS FLOCK

B EFORE ITS subdivision in 1847, the Diocese of New York had over 200,000 Catholics. About 40,000 of these were assigned to the new Diocese of Buffalo. By 1867, just before it lost its eastern counties to the new Diocese of Rochester, the Buffalo Diocese itself had reached a population of 200,000 souls. Throughout these two decades of rapid expansion, John Timon remained the faithful shepherd.

Some of the Catholic growth was, of course, the result of natural increase. With Catholics, small families were the exception, more often than not the outcome of infant mortality. Children were not only good company and good old-age insurance, but also, particularly in farming families, a real economic asset. Truck farmer Bernard Klem, the influential son of Rochester's first German Catholic citizen, married three times, and had, in all, twenty-two youngsters. Thomas Hendrick, Penn Yan shopkeeper, though not a farmer, could count almost as many offspring as Bernard Klem from his two marriages. Admittedly, these families were of record size; but families of ten or more were not unusual. Thus Edward Duffy, the Rochester Catholic merchant, had ten children.

Immigration nevertheless remained the principal factor in American Catholic increase. Political and economic conditions in Canada and Europe after 1845 prompted thousands of Catholics to escape to an America which offered peace, freedom, and greater opportunity to earn a living.

The Canadian French established their Rochester colony after the Canadian "troubles" of 1837. Others no doubt joined them after the further "troubles" of 1858.

About one-quarter of the two millions of Germans who entered the United States between 1841 and 1871 were Catholics. Potato shortages, a cholera epidemic, Protestant Prussian discrimination: these were the leading motives for German Catholic emigration in the 1840's. By 1855, Rochester had acquired a German community of 6,000, which ranked it second in size only to the Irish among the foreign-born segments of Rochester citizenry. A large number of the Germans who came to the "Flour City" were Catholics. Other Catholic Germans found homes elsewhere in the twelve counties. While German-speaking newcomers were poor upon arrival, they usually came trained in some skill or trade that enabled them to achieve before long a modest prosperity.

The Irish immigration during the same epoch was larger and more tragic. Between 1841 and 1871, 2,100,000 Irish, two-thirds of them Catholics, made their way to the United States. Long religious and cultural oppression, economic insecurity, and the harsh exactions of absentee British landlords, had in earlier years prompted some Irishmen to emigrate. Most of the Irish had stayed at home, however, persuaded that no matter how great were their griefs, the greatest grief would be to leave their beloved hearths.[1]

All that was changed by the terrible events of 1845 and after. A fungus blighted the all-important potato crops not only in 1845 but in 1846 and 1848. The British government, unprepared to meet so great an emergency, and unwilling to antagonize private enterprise, authorized sadly inadequate measures. Fortunately, sympathetic souls in other lands intervened with funds and foodstuffs to counter widespread famine. In 1847, the non-sectarian "Irish Relief Committee of the City of Rochester" contributed over $3,000.00 to the cause, and we may presume that the priests and immigrant faithful of western New York sent many personal gifts to their starving relatives and friends back home.[2] But starvation was only a part of the woes. Crop failure meant impoverishment; impoverishment meant a failure to pay rent; non-payment meant eviction by the landlords; eviction meant taking refuge in ruins, ditches, and burrows; filthy shelters of this sort fostered epidemics of typhus and relapsing fever; and fever and freezing weather further undermined the strength of those who tried to work. Overwhelmed by this vicious spiral of disaster, and ready to believe their native land had been laid under some awful curse, thousands upon thousands of Irish rushed in headlong flight to the ports, seeking sanctuary in Britain or in North America.

Nemesis did not abandon even those who crossed the Atlantic. Massed together in the unsanitary holds of rickety ships, a great number of the passengers fell victim to "ship fever"—typhus, once more, but under different conditions. Ship after ship which reached Canada was a traveling pesthouse, the stricken dying off like May flies. Over twenty thousand immigrants from Ireland's famine lay buried, sometimes in mass graves, near the port cities along the St. Lawrence River. Epidemics did not cause so much grief at United States ports, but poor health continued to vex the impoverished Irish arrivals. Bishop Timon reported in 1854 that one-third of the immigrants who reached Buffalo and were assigned to the poorhouse soon died as its inmates.[3]

Not all the incomers who reached western New York intended to halt there. Hundreds were in transit to the Midwest, travelling thither in another of the insulting devices of human greed, the crowded, dilapidated "emigrant train."[4] But thousands of European arrivals who moved along the Northern and Southern Tiers had already chosen as their destination Rochester, Auburn, Elmira, Hornell, Dansville, and other towns and townships of the twelve counties.

What was the image of these Catholic settlers, old and new? How did the first bishop of Buffalo make provision for them? And how, when the need arose, did he administer correction to them?

1. "THE SHEEP OF HIS PASTURE."

They were "little people," the early members of the Diocese of Buffalo. Although they came from backgrounds which differed from the backgrounds of those among whom they settled, they were, like them, ordinary human beings with their share of opinions, faults, and virtues.

A few of the Catholic immigrants were equipped by training or talents to achieve some measure of prominence and leadership. One thinks of the Rochester horticulturist Patrick Barry (1816-1890); of Patrick Kearney (1790?-1857), Rochester's second tailor and a founder of the city's merchant tailor industry; of carriage-maker James Cunningham (1815-1886); of the railroad builder and fuel merchant Antoine Langie (1814-1894); of pioneer journalist Henry O'Reilly (1806-1896).

Men like these were exceptions. The average incomer, German, Irish, Dutch or French, was cut out for a humbler role, and was content to live it. An epitaph in Canandaigua's Catholic cemetery pretty well summarizes his point of view:

> Patrick Breen is my name,
> Ireland is my nation,
> America is my resting place
> And heaven my expectation.

Immigrants were poorest, of course, in the earliest years of their American residence. Our economic depressions of 1837-1844 and 1857-1860 affected seriously those who qualified only as unskilled laborers. Because so many of them lived in substandard homes, they were easy victims of the epidemics of the day. In 1834, cholera made great inroads among the German farmers of Sandy Hill.[5] Cholera likewise struck Buffalo and the Southern Tier in 1849. The neighborhood of Watkins suffered most: at Millport there were approximately one hundred victims, of whom the majority were laborers.[6] The years 1848 and 1852 were cholera years at Rochester itself. Here again, Irish and German immigrants, living in small, unhealthful shacks, were among the principal victims. Thirty-two parishioners of St. Joseph's died of this plague in 1852.[7] Epidemics of the sort, nourished by poverty, in turn generated further poverty when they slew breadwinners or made orphans of children.

One clear indication of the genuinity of their poverty was the inability of the early Catholic settlers to build and properly adorn churches, although they dearly wished to have well-appointed churches of their own.

Consider the Catholics of Seneca Falls. Father Francis O'Donoghue gathered them in the home of Henry Graham, on Center Street, on October 4, 1835, and celebrated the first recorded Sunday Mass in the village. At least he *began* the Mass at the Grahams'. Before he had reached the end, the weak floor-beams collapsed under the weight of the crowd, the floor caved in, and celebrant and congregation were thrown into the cellar. Luckily, the priest managed to cling to the chalice. When he was able to climb out of the cellar window, he went directly to the house of James Hurley across the street, and there finished the Holy Sacrifice.

Despite the obviously straitened circumstances of the Seneca Falls Catholics, Father O'Donoghue urged them that very evening to undertake a church of their own. He led off the subscription with his own ten dollars. By the following May, parishioners had contributed out of their poverty a munificent $291.45. They had also bought a small building on Swaby Street, which was dedicated as St. Jerome's Church on May 24, 1836. St. Jerome's was little more than a shanty, unlathed and unplastered. Plastering, a stove, and other luxuries had to wait their turn to be budgeted. Plate collections never ran high: $16.88 at the grand opening, three cents at the initial prayer service. But the people were proud of their little church and never sent the collection plate back completely empty.[8] Even more populous churches had awkward moments, as when St. Patrick's and St. Joseph's in Rochester narrowly escaped foreclosure in the hard times of 1837.[9] And few of the early churches could afford copes or monstrances for Benediction.

A poor and sometimes mendicant segment of the upstate population, the Catholics were furthermore so slow to assimilate to the American culture that Protestant Yankees and Yorkers considered them incapable of assimilation. Yet it must be granted that the natives did not offer much assistance. Before immigrants began to arrive in large numbers, the Yankees from New England and the Yorkers from New York had long been at each other's throats. With the coming of the immigrants, especially the Irish immigrants, the two groups made peace with each other and formed a common front against these newcomers who threatened the Protestant American *status quo.* American natives were often friendlier to individual newcomers than to immigrant groups. But their hostility, condescending at its mildest, frankly discriminatory at its most fanatical, rankled in the hearts of the new arrivals. Some eventually capitulated, through indifference or in a bid for community acceptance, and abandoned the practice of their Catholic Faith. The majority remained content—or at least resigned—to seek company and consolation among their "own sort."

Yet Catholics, for all their common beliefs, were not monolithic, but retained national traits, and where they were numerous enough, formed more or less exclusive national groups. In the future Rochester Diocese there were three major national groupings, the French, the Germans, and the Irish. The French reached parochial proportions only in Rochester.[10] Elsewhere they blended imperceptibly into the local communities. Far larger was the German segment, for whose benefit German-language parishes were established in several places. English-speaking Catholics were mainly Irish. They, too, were strongly nationalistic, retaining an active interest in the politics and problems of the Emerald Isle. Priests of all three linguistic groups, far from discouraging old-country ties, tended to maintain them, even to the disadvantage of Americanization. German priests in particular believed that loss of the German tongue and Germanism were the preludes to loss of Catholic Faith.

Each national grouping of Catholics, therefore, clung to its own tongue and its own folkways. Among Rochester's French-speaking citizens there cannot have been a close social association, since those who spoke French came from three different countries: France, Switzerland, and especially Canada. German *Gemütlichkeit* no doubt ignored the diverse provincial origins of Rochester's Germans (with the possible exception of the Swiss). In the celebrations of church societies, the German Catholics could indulge in the vigorous pastimes and the *gute Speise und Lagerbier* which were traditional to German recreation. The

Irish, now melancholy, now gay (and sociable under either aspect) had their own traditions. Perhaps too much has been said of the funeral wake as an Irish practice. But it was indeed a very old custom, which even the deceased, in his own way, presumably enjoyed.

Even as Catholic members of the same diocese, the Irish and the German sections of the population moved in independent cultural circles, each group considering the other group "clannish." Intermarriage of Irish and German, at least where Germans were numerous, long remained a rarity. When both nationalities were in the same parish, friction was quite likely to develop, not over faith but over points of view. Thus, for example, the friction between the Irish minority and the German majority in Dansville prompted the breaking away of the former to found St. Patrick's parish.[11]

As new citizens in the world's most noted democracy, the immigrants naturally took an interest in politics. In an upstate traditionally Whig and Republican, the newcomers usually identified themselves with the Democratic party: the Irish, with its conservative, the Germans, sometimes with its more liberal wing. Only slowly did the foreign-born stand for political office, beginning on the ward level.

Parish societies played an important part in the social life of the early Catholics, particularly the Germans. Some of these organizations were of strictly spiritual character, others were mutual benefit associations. German pastors encouraged a multitude of parochial societies because, among other things, they provided a substitute for the sometimes radical and often indifferentist secular German societies in the locality. It was customary for each men's society, in both Irish and German parishes, to have its distinctive regalia: collars or sashes worn over the suit. When the societies thus adorned marched in processions or public parades, ah, it was a splendid sight!

Back home, the Germans had been used to many public religious processions. The Redemptorists made an effort gradually to inaugurate at St. Joseph's "all the old rites of the Church" practiced in Germany.[12] But public processions such as those of Corpus Christi were not feasible in this country, except in rural towns like Perkinsville. Occasionally, however, religious parades could be held even in Rochester. When a boy of St. Joseph's parish, Father Michael Mueller, celebrated his first solemn Mass on March 25, 1853, the school children, parishioners, and societies of St. Joseph's conducted him to the church in a gala march from his home through the adjacent streets of downtown Rochester. On the following September 18th, societies from St. Joseph's, St. Peter's and St. Patrick's, setting out from their own churches, marched to South Street to attend the laying of the cornerstone of the present St. Mary's Church.[13]

Irish parochial societies welcomed the opportunity to take part in Rochester's annual St. Patrick's Day parade. On this day even the local non-Catholics looked on the Irish with a more benign eye, especially if intemperance did not mar the occasion. In fact, the public authorities might sometimes grace the St. Patrick's rites with their presence. Thus on March 17, 1830, the first St. Patrick's Day after the British Emancipation Act of 1829 had given Ireland religious freedom, village president Elisha Johnson and other prominent Protestants of Rochesterville were honored guests at the banquet.[14] The fully developed order of the day in later years included a Mass and panegyric at one of the English-language churches, attended by delegations from each "Irish" parish. A parade followed, terminating, after 1857, at St. Mary's Hospital, where the marchers presented an entertainment for the sick. In the evening there was a banquet, with many toasts and much oratory. Elsewhere in the twelve counties similar celebrations took place, on a reduced scale. Each year the Irish-American national weeklies would devote column after column to reports of how the Irish commemorated the festival at Rochester, Seneca Falls, Brockport, Geneva, Greenwood, and in many other "little Irelands" across the nation.

The Irish pastor, like the other pastors of his day, exercised a stern but influential leadership in the spiritual and social life of his immigrant parishioners. Not all of the pioneer missionaries, it is true, lived up to the ideals of their calling. Father Farnham, organizer of St. Patrick's, Rochester, subsequently founded a schismatic church in Brooklyn, although he later repented his revolt.[15] Father John McCormick, sometime missionary to the Rochester Catholics, abandoned the priesthood.[16] Even in the days of Bishop Timon, when the clergy were more numerous and generally better qualified, the Bishop had trouble with some of his priests. None of the trials of our pioneer bishops were sadder than these.

But most of the priests remained firm, in spite of the hard and wearing life they had to lead; and several of them deserve special mention. Take, for example, Fathers Patrick O'Kelly, Francis O'Donoghue, and Thomas McEvoy, the "circuit riders" of the period between 1825 and 1847. All three were truly "apostolic pilgrims." After pioneering in New York State, the gaunt Father Kelly laid the foundations of the faith in Michigan and Wisconsin, and was buried at Dearborn, Michigan, in the cemetery named Mount Kelly in his memory.[17] Father

O'Donoghue had been the first resident priest in North Carolina before entering the service of the New York Diocese; and before his appointment to the Salina (New York) mission he had worked in New Jersey. He died at Lynchburg, Virginia, in 1845, having rounded out, in his eight last years on the Virginia mission, a "life spent doing good."[18] Father Thomas McEvoy was noted for his unremitting work and unsparing charity. Bishop Timon admired and praised his "apostolic merciful zeal."[19]

Especially important was the future second bishop of Hartford, Father Bernard O'Reilly (1803-1856), pastor of St. Patrick's, Rochester, from 1832 to 1834 and from 1835 to 1847. Born in Ireland but educated and ordained a priest in this country, Father O'Reilly merited wide admiration for his sound judgment and his quiet, thorough attention to duty. His predecessor at St. Patrick's, Father Michael McNamara, had been a pioneer in the Rochester temperance movement of 1828.[20] Father O'Reilly was also a staunch advocate of temperance among an Irish flock many of whom were victims of strong drink. By 1838 he had founded the Hibernian Temperance Society. In 1840 he established the Rochester Hibernian Total Abstinence Society. In this important social effort he had the good will and collaboration of Rochester's Protestant temperance crusaders. On September 4, 1851, that great Irish apostle of teetotalism, Father Theobald Mathew, O.M.Cap., (1790-1856), was greeted not only by Rochester Catholics but by the Mayor and prominent Protestants, when his train stopped briefly at the Rochester station. But as Bishop John Hughes had already proudly pointed out, Father O'Reilly's Hibernian Temperance Society, the first Catholic parish temperance union in America, was founded some time before Father Mathew began to administer the pledge in Ireland.[21]

It is difficult to single out the most representative of the Rochester Redemptorists, so outstanding were the contributions of this missionary community. Unique among them, however, was Father Simon Saenderl (1800-1878), who after a zealous pastorate at Rochester, entered the Trappists at Gethsemani, Kentucky, making his monastic profession in 1853.[22]

Father Thomas M. Brady's intellectual interests evidenced themselves during his pastorate at Seneca Falls. A keen mathematician, he was able to solve, in 1858, some prize problems proposed by the London magazine, the *Gentleman's Diary*. While in Seneca Falls, he established a parish school for children and a night school for working people, and he himself did much of the teaching. He transferred to the diocese of Detroit in 1860, spent the years 1862-1865 as Civil War chaplain of the 15th Michigan Infantry, and died soon afterward of broken health.[23]

Notable for quite different reasons were the pastoral efforts of Father Serge and Father Edmund O'Connor. Father Serge de Stchoulepnikoff was a Russian convert, whose knowledge of German, French and English made him available for almost any parochial assignment. At Dansville he ministered to both the Germans and the Irish, and waged a vigorous war against the local "dram-shops" and those who haunted them. Father Edmund O'Connor (1816-1873) was pastor at Canandaigua from 1848 to 1858. In 1856, when called upon to break the seal of the confessional, he steadfastly refused. A penitent of his who had stolen a watch gave it to Father O'Connor to return. Thereupon, Attorney Stephen V. Mallory cited the priest before Justice Alexander Howell, to force him to reveal the name of the robber. But almost on the eve of the day when O'Connor was to appear in court, the ambitious young lawyer died of typhoid fever. "Before he brought me to the bar of justice," Father O'Connor commented from the pulpit, "he is gone before the tribunal of God."[24]

Men of this caliber did yeoman work in providing for the spiritual and social needs of their transplanted faithful. Sometimes they arrived on the spot just in time to keep the immigrants from drifting away entirely from Catholic belief and practice. Thus, in 1836, when Father Prost, the Redemptorist, first visited the German Catholics who had settled in the Town of Dansville, he found them attending the Protestant German church, where they read their prayers out of Catholic prayerbooks. Since they were not completely comfortable with the compromise they had made, the missionary had little difficulty in persuading them to abandon it. The Protestant Germans, however, resented the departure of the Catholics from their congregation. Father Prost says they even planned to do him violence because of his interference. Fortunately, their plot misfired.[25]

That some isolated Catholics lost their Catholic identity is not surprising; that so many clung to their Faith heroically is indeed impressive.

Thrilling stories have come down to us of the efforts of the district's immigrants to obtain the sacraments. William Kernan of Tyrone took his infant son to New York in 1816 or 1817 to have him baptized. Tyrone was some three hundred miles overland from New York City.[26] Felix McGuire of Greece Town is said to have brought his two children to Albany for baptism a year or so later.[27] Corning's first Catholic couple, the Thomas Keatings, sought baptism for their son John in Buffalo, one hundred miles away, in the pre-railroad year of 1840.[28] And before they had their own church in Dansville, the Raubers did not hesitate to walk fifty miles to Rochester to make their Easter communions or have their children christened.[29]

The most notable sacramental pilgrimage was certainly that of Rochester's pioneer German Catholic matriarch, Mrs. John B. Klem. Anna Maria Klem, on October 31, 1818, gave birth to a daughter. Determined to have the baby baptized without delay, she informed her husband that she was going to take her to the nearest priest, and that she would return only when her mission was accomplished. Accompanied by her nine-year-old son, Mrs. Klem set out on foot for Albany, babe in arms. Unfortunately, the Albany priest was absent when she arrived. She therefore continued afoot to New York, kindly aided along her route (as she had been west of Albany) by sympathetic chance acquaintances. Family tradition says that the baby girl received baptism at New York, and that the valiant woman remained there until, aided in part by what her son could earn selling papers, she was able to return to Rochester in somewhat greater comfort.[30]

And those who had taken such pains to preserve their faith took equal pains to pass it on to others. They instructed their children in Catholic teachings. They instructed and refreshed each other on Christian doctrine: we hear of laborers on the canals and railroads who, as they worked, rehearsed each other on the answers of the penny catechism. They distributed Catholic reading: when Mathew Hogan came to "Paddy Hill" in 1821, he brought with him hundreds of religious books which he gave to others with a free hand. They taught Sunday school—often for many years, until their parishes could afford a parochial elementary school. Men were catechists as well as women. In fact we can cite Martin Hogan of Auburn as a good representative of all these lay apostles. Martin came to Auburn around 1843, and plied successfully his trade of dyer. But he found still greater happiness as a teacher in the Catholic Sunday school. Those who learned their religious rudiments from him always recalled his earnest admonition: "Keep bright the armor of your faith!"[31]

These were "the sheep of his pasture" over whom Bishop Timon was given charge: priests and laymen; men and women; Irish, German, French. They had in various degrees the frailties and faults of their own nationalities and of all the breed of Adam. But they were also capable of great virtue, and he who expended himself in their behalf might be sure of many consolations.

2. "In Journeyings Often."

Buffalo's first bishop-elect was consecrated in New York City by Bishop Hughes on October 17, 1847. He arrived in Buffalo on October 22nd, and on the following day, in St. Louis Church, he was formally installed in office.

Bishop Timon had visited Rochester even before his installation. He stopped on the 22nd, while en route to Buffalo, long enough to celebrate Mass at St. Patrick's Church and preach to a hastily mustered congregation. He returned on his first formal visit on November 27th. On this occasion he prolonged his stay until December 7th. His activities included the preaching of a retreat at St. Mary's Church, in the course of which he gave two meditations and four sermons each day, and heard confessions for six or seven hours. Nine hundred people received Holy Communion.[32] The conducting of retreats and missions throughout his diocese became thereafter a standard and a very fruitful practice of the Timon regime. This veteran missioner saw no reason for changing his old missionary practices.

At least for a while, the Bishop had to exercise considerable tact towards the Catholics of Rochester. The expectation had been that Rochester rather than Buffalo would be the see city of the new diocese of western New York. Bishop Hughes had favored Rochester, which was certainly more centrally located.[33] Civic rivalry was furthermore very strong at that date between the two "boom cities," both of which had a population of some forty thousand. Catholicism was also a little better organized at Rochester. Buffalo had three churches, no charitable institutions, and no nuns. Rochester had four churches, an orphanage, and the Sisters of Charity. But the Holy See had decided on Buffalo; and whenever Catholic Rochesterians complained to the new bishop about the rejection of Rochester, he reminded them that he himself had had no say in the matter.

The Catholics of Rochester must have soon recovered from this injury to their civic pride, although it is a fact that they contributed relatively little to the building fund of the Buffalo cathedral. Time eventually justified Rome's action, for Buffalo quickly outstripped Rochester in size. At all events, Rochester's aspiration to diocesan honors was not vetoed, merely deferred for twenty years. Bishop Timon meanwhile took care to prepare the Flour City for that inevitable dignity.[34]

Catholics of the twelve counties could never accuse John Timon of neglecting them. In the West he had engaged, like St. Paul, "in journeyings often." At Buffalo his radius was shorter but his diocesan circuits were no less frequent. Doubtless no bishop could have won total approbation from all his diversified followers. But it was surely no disadvantage that he was at the same time American-born, of Irish parentage, and well acquainted with both the French and the German languages. Though small in stature (not much over five feet tall), and not exactly young (fifty), the wiry Vincentian was a dynamo of apostolic energy, and seemed to thrive best and be happiest when the going was hardest.

Bishop Timon has left us an account of his earlier tour of the new diocese. It deserves to be summarized here because it shows both the methods and the effects of his urgent leadership.[35]

On January 18, 1848, he paid his first visit to Auburn, and gave the parishioners of Holy Family Church a short retreat. Since the Auburn church was now too small for the congregation, he preached in the city hall. He also had the warden of Auburn state prison conduct him to the cells of each of the four hundred prisoners. He found twenty-eight Catholics among them.[36]

His next stop, on January 24th, was at Seneca Falls. Here, too, he conducted spiritual exercises, preached, and heard confessions. Almost all the parishioners received Holy Communion, and he confirmed fifty-three. At Geneva, from the 26th to the 29th, he followed the same plan with equal success.

From Geneva he went by water to Jefferson (now Watkins), where he spent the 29th and 30th. As we have already seen, the Catholics of Salubria-Jefferson-Watkins had already been given a chapel, but had not completed it for actual use. Now the Bishop and his traveling companion, Father John Sheridan, finished the outfitting of the little church, and on the 30th Bishop Timon dedicated it as "St. Mary's of the Lake." On February 1st, he went to Hammondsport for the day, preaching there and confirming eighteen. En route he stopped at the home of General William Kernan at Tyrone, where he confirmed three more. He was back in Watkins for the night.

Since the following day was Candlemas, Bishop Timon conducted the candle rite at St. Mary's of the Lake. Then he was off to Ithaca. He preached in the town hall at Ithaca early that same evening, and spent the remaining hours hearing confessions and performing marriage ceremonies. On the 3rd he offered Mass in the town hall and confirmed twenty-four. That evening he and Father Sheridan went to Owego. Next day he began a retreat for the Owegans. He celebrated daily Mass in a little chapel which the devout tailor Daniel Connelly had constructed in his own home. But for public lectures and the like he used the courthouse. Here as elsewhere, many non-Catholics came to hear him: a judge, some lawyers, and even some ministers, all of whom seemed quite impressed by the logic of his addresses on Penance and other Catholic teachings.

On the morning of February 7th, the Bishop and his companion left by sleigh for Elmira. Soon travel along the wintry route became difficult. At one point, Timon was thrown out upon the ice, was stunned, and cut his hand. Not long afterward the sleigh itself broke down. The two clerics hired a horse-and-wagon to replace it, but now it was the horse that broke down. By this time the day was far advanced, so they decided to stop overnight at Factoryville (now Waverly). The delay proved providential, for it gave Bishop Timon an opportunity to instruct and hear the confessions of the Factoryville Catholics. On the morning of the 8th, he first offered Mass and preached in a private house, and then preached in the courthouse to a larger audience, mostly Protestants.

Their visit to Elmira was only overnight (January 8th-9th). The Bishop found that the candidates for Confirmation were not prepared, so he deferred that sacrament to a later date, and having preached in Elmira courthouse, went on to Corning. At Corning the Catholics, possessing no church of their own, had borrowed the Methodist church and were assembled there when he arrived. Timon lectured that evening on the Church and its sacraments. He celebrated Mass in the same building on the following morning, and, at the special instance of one of the Catholic Corningites, he directed his talk on the sacrament of Penance particularly to the Protestants in attendance, since they were known to have a distorted concept of the subject. The Bishop also directed the Catholics to begin planning for a church of their own; and he himself launched a building subscription which quickly mounted to $300.00, part of it contributed by generous non-Catholics.

As he was about to take carriage for Bath—there was as yet no railway connection—Bishop Timon was asked to call on a dying man who lived at a fair distance. Accompanied by a Presbyterian minister, who asked for the privilege, the Bishop set out afoot on his errand of mercy. He found the poor man on a rough straw bed in a wretched shanty. But there was rapt devotion in that little home as Timon, watched in silence by the family and the minister, administered the last rites. The clergyman was especially impressed. "God bless you," he said to the Bishop when it was all over, "that was very touching."

The audience which he addressed in the Bath courthouse that evening was largely Protestant. The Bishop spoke to them again on the following morning, after having said Mass in a private home. Then he went on to Greenwood, in bitterly cold weather. The fervor of the little congregation of Greenwood was a good antidote to the chill of their highlands. By the time he was ready to cross over into Allegany County, Timon had distributed Holy Communion to many, and had confirmed fifty-five.

Bishop Timon was back in Buffalo by February 17th. Before long he returned to Rochester to give two successive retreats in St. Patrick's Church: one to the English-speaking; the second, in French, to the French-speaking Catholics. There was now a fairly large number of the latter, so he urged them to found a parish of their own. On May 6, 1848, he made a trip to Canandaigua in order to dedicate St. Mary's Church. One week later he celebrated pontifical Mass at St. Joseph's in Rochester, confirmed 190, and preached twice in German. In the early evening he presided at pontifical vespers at St. Mary's Church in Rochester, and confirmed 167. And as if that were not enough, he concluded the evening with a lecture at St. Patrick's Church.

This was an arduous but a typical beginning. As long as he had strength, the first bishop of Buffalo did not slacken his apostolic pace. Given such rousing leadership, his Catholic people, poor though they were in worldly goods, responded enthusiastically to their Bishop's call for more and better churches, schools, and charitable institutions.

In the 1850's, several of the older parishes in the twelve counties found it necessary to enlarge their original churches or to build new ones. St. Mary's in Rochester moved into its present church in 1858. When Bishop Timon dedicated it he used not the ordinary blessing but a formal consecration. The consecratory rite, performed on October 24th of that year, made it the first consecrated church in the city and the present Diocese of Rochester.[37]

At Paddy Hill, a new brick church was begun in 1859 to replace the old St. Ambrose Church. The Bishop laid its cornerstone on June 19, 1859. His vicar general, Father Michael O'Brien, dedicated it to "Our Mother of Sorrows" on September 16, 1860. The French-born pastor and former African missionary, Father John M. Maurice (1812-1895) had undertaken and supervised the project. To adorn the sanctuary Maurice secured three large paintings from Rome through the agency of the Most Reverend Gaetano Bedini, secretary of the Sacred Congregation de Propaganda Fide. The dedicatory ceremony of the new church was made especially notable by the presence, as principal speaker, of that renowned and brilliant Irish scientist, editor, patriot and orator, the Reverend Doctor William Cahill (1796-1864). His address was on the Immaculate Conception of the Blessed Virgin.[38]

In Auburn, the Bishop himself dedicated the second (and present) Holy Family Church, on July 17, 1861. And on October 9, 1864, he laid the cornerstone of the third St. Patrick's Church in Rochester.[39] The latter church was a large Gothic edifice designed by Patrick C. Keely, the remarkable Brooklyn architect who drew plans, in all, for seven hundred American churches, including St. Joseph's (Old) Cathedral in Buffalo. St. Patrick's, finally dedicated in 1870, became the first cathedral of the Rochester Diocese. Probably Timon anticipated that it would.

Still greater signs of progress were the thirty-four new parishes opened by Bishop Timon in the twelve counties, and provided with resident pastors—permanently, for the most part. (He founded new mission churches and mission stations, too; but the parishes, as full-fledged foundations, were of more abiding importance.)

Six of the thirty-four were in Rochester proper. Immaculate Conception (1849) and St. Bridget (1854) were "Irish" parishes. St. Boniface (dedicated 1861), Holy Family (dedicated 1864), and Holy Redeemer (dedicated three months after Timon's death, in 1867) were German national parishes. The last of the six was French: Our Lady of Victory, which was simply referred to as "Ste. Marie" when it opened in 1848 in the Ely Street building which had originally housed St. Joseph's Church.

Elsewhere in Monroe County, the first bishop of Buffalo set up four other parishes. Assumption Church in Fairport was dedicated in 1856; the Church of the Nativity of the Blessed Virgin Mary, in Brockport, was dedicated in 1856 or 1857; the Church of St. Mary of the Assumption, in Scottsville, was dedicated in 1860; and Holy Trinity at Webster — basically a German parish — was dedicated in 1861.

The Bishop was also able to establish at least one parish, and often more than one, in each of the remaining eleven of his twelve eastern counties.

Thus, three new parishes came into being in Cayuga County. With the help of the Rochester Redemptorists in 1853, St. Alphonsus Church opened in Auburn. Most of its parishioners were German. St. Agnes (now St. Patrick's), Aurora, also opened in 1853. At Springport (now Union Springs), the first—and present—St. Michael's Church was dedicated around 1855: One pastor took care of both St. Agnes and St. Michael, the pastors living now in Aurora, now in Springport, according to their individual preference.

Father John Sheridan built Chemung County's first Catholic church in 1849. This was SS. Peter and Paul in Elmira. In less than a decade a new and larger building was necessary. Timon solemnly blessed it—the present SS. Peter and Paul Church—in 1857.[40]

Five new parishes were created in Livingston County. St. Agnes', Avon, dates from 1853; St. Patrick's, Dansville, from 1849; St. Mary's, Geneseo, from 1854; St. Rose's, Lima, from 1849. St. Patrick's, Mount Morris, was built in 1850, but was not given a resident pastor until 1855.

A resident pastor was assigned to Canandaigua in 1849. Bishop Timon founded three more parishes in Ontario County. St. Bridget's, East Bloomfield, was completed in 1852 and provided with a permanent pastor by 1857. The first church of the present St. Felix' parish in Clifton Springs bore the name St. Agnes. It was built in 1855 and received a rector in 1862. The original St. Francis Church at Phelps was built by its first regular pastor, and completed in 1856 or 1857.

There were two new parishes in Seneca County. The original St. Mary's Church was built at Waterloo in 1849, and opened on October 17th. Father William Carroll, who celebrated the first Mass and was pastor at Seneca Falls, seems to have resided at Waterloo, but it was a mission of Ovid for much of the decade after 1854. Father Terrence Keenan, assigned to St. Mary's, Waterloo, in 1863, appears to have been the first real resident priest. Holy Cross Church at Ovid was dedicated by Bishop Timon in May, 1851. Father William Gleason, who lived at Ovid from 1854 to 1856, apparently qualifies as the first truly resident pastor.

Steuben county gained five new parishes. Perkinsville became independent of the Sandy Hill parish when it built a church in 1850 and received a rector. St. Catherine's Church was erected at Addison in 1854 and assigned a pastor around 1867. St. Mary's in Bath (1850) was given a pastor in 1861, and St. Mary's in Corning became a full-fledged parish in 1854, five years after the Bishop had dedicated its first church. St. Ann's, Hornell, got its first church and pastor in 1849. (Troupsburg —with a chapel—was a mission of Greenwood, then of Rexville, 1866-1883.)

St. Patrick's, Owego, was the only parish in Tioga County. The first church building was opened in 1849, but the parish had already had a pastor since 1846. Immaculate Conception Church, Ithaca, was also the only parish in Tompkins County. The first pastor was appointed a couple of years before Timon dedicated the original church to St. Luke in 1851. It had a mission at McLean (St. Patrick's, 1851).

Two parishes were inaugurated in Wayne County: St. Michael's, Lyons (church 1849, pastor 1853); and St. Ann's, Palmyra (church

1849 or 1850, pastor 1850). A single parish was set up in Yates County. St. Michael's in Penn Yan had a church by 1850 and a resident rector by about the same time.

By 1867, therefore, eleven of the twelve eastern counties, in addition to mission chapels and stations, had one or more complete parishes with pastors in residence. The exception was St. Mary of the Lake at Watkins Glen, the only church in Schuyler County. Not until 1869 did it acquire a pastor of its own. That there were so many of the churches, even in rural communities, provided with settled clergymen is an indication of the success which Bishop Timon had in multiplying his diocesan priests. Indeed, when he had been in office for only twelve years, he had already succeeded in raising the number of priests in the Diocese from 13 to 102.[41]

Timon's first concern was with churches. He did not feel the time ripe to crusade for parish schools. But it is remarkable how many of the parishes of his day did found schools of some sort. All of the German parishes in the twelve counties, with the exception of the struggling St. Alphonsus' in Auburn, had parochial schools; as did Holy Ghost Church in Coldwater, just west of Rochester, (although it was still only a mission chapel) and St. Joseph's in Penfield, just east of Rochester. The "Irish" parishes in Rochester, with the exception of Immaculate Conception, likewise had schools of their own; and there were schools connected with the "Irish" churches in Canandaigua, Lima, Mount Morris, Seneca Falls, Waterloo, Corning, Bath, Dansville, Hornellsville, and perhaps elsewhere.

On November 13, 1859, Bishop Timon wrote a pastoral in which he authorized pastors to deny the Sacraments to parents who did not send their children to a Catholic school if one was at hand. This seems a little premature, since the original schools were staffed by laymen or laywomen of unequal talents, and the schools themselves sometimes proved ephemeral. The Bishop was, of course, trying to better these schools by inducing new religious teaching communities to enter the diocese. Two religious brotherhoods accepted his invitation. In 1857 a group of the La Salle Christian Brothers, headed by Brother Rodolphus (Henry McGee: 1829-1868) took charge of the newly built St. Patrick's Boys Academy in Rochester. These Brothers of the Christian Schools remained at St. Patrick's until 1872. From 1860 to 1862 they also taught at the grade school of St. Mary's parish.[42] The Marianist Brothers, a German group from Dayton, Ohio, staffed St. Joseph's School in Rochester from 1861 to 1899, and St. Peter's School in Rochester from 1868 to 1887.

The orders of nuns that heeded Timon's plea for teachers were more numerous and the foundations which they made in the twelve counties were usually permanent.

Briefest of all was the sojourn of the Brigidine Sisters, an ill-starred and somewhat uncanonical group only incidentally connected with the Irish religious of the same name. They taught at St. Mary's, Rochester, in 1855-1856.[43] Much longer, but also impermanent, was the Elmira career of the Sisters of St. Mary of Namur. Bishop Timon brought this Franco-Belgian order to Lockport in 1863. In 1866, a band came to SS. Peter and Paul's, Elmira, opened Our Lady of Angels Academy, a private girls' school, and taught in the parish school as well. Their mission was terminated in 1897.[44] Incidentally, the Sisters of Charity of Emmitsburg had been solicited to undertake this same Elmira mission in 1857. The designated sisters arrived that autumn and departed almost at once. Some disagreement, no doubt. This was the only assignment the Sisters of Charity ever accepted in the present diocese of Rochester outside Rochester itself.[45]

In 1855 the French Religious of the Sacred Heart of Jesus opened a private academy for girls on North St. Paul Street in Rochester. Eight years later they transferred this Academy of the Sacred Heart to its present location on Prince Street. The nuns had first founded the school at Buffalo in 1849, after Bishop Timon had concluded arrangements with the order's general superior, St. Madeleine Sophie Barat (1779-1865), and her American provincial, Mother Aloysia Hardey (1809-1886). But a wave of bigotry and an epidemic of cholera at Buffalo had so hampered the progress of the Academy there that it was transferred to Rochester, where it quickly prospered.[46]

It is to Bishop Timon, also, that the present Rochester Diocese owes the advent of the Sisters of St. Joseph, the School Sisters of Notre Dame, and the Sisters of Mercy.

In 1854, Timon requested the superior of the Sisters of St. Joseph of Carondelet, Missouri, to open a house at Canandaigua. That December, four sisters headed by Mother Agnes Spencer established a convent, a novitiate, a girls' academy, and a small orphanage, in a modest building on Saltonstall Street. Three years later, the Canandaigua convent sent forth another group of sisters to commence at Buffalo a school for deaf-mutes (now the famous St. Mary's School for the Deaf). And in 1864, in view of the orphaning of many children during the Civil War, the sisters at Canandaigua launched St. Mary's Boys' Home in Rochester.

The School Sisters of Notre Dame, a teaching community whose immediate background was German, arrived in Rochester in the fall of 1854 to assume direction of the girls' classes at St. Joseph's School. In 1855 they undertook a like assignment in St. Peter's parish, and during the next few years they were given missions in three other German parochial schools in the city: St. Boniface (1866), Holy Family (1867), and Holy Redeemer (1867). The School Sisters also staffed the parish school at Perkinsville from 1856 to 1869.[47]

As vicar of her community, Mother Caroline Friess (1824-1892) was principally responsible for the Rochester foundations of the School Sisters of Notre Dame. It was also a pioneer of the Religious Sisters of Mercy that brought her community into the United States, and established, among other foundations, the Sisters of Mercy of Rochester. Mother M. Xavier Warde (1810-1884), the loyal lieutenant of Mother M. Catherine McAuley, foundress of this Irish order, complied in 1857 with Bishop Timon's request to inaugurate a Convent of Mercy at Rochester. The convent adjoined St. Mary's Church on South Street. Here the original band opened a select school and a parish school, and engaged in their traditional works of charity. (They are also said to have taught at St. Bridget's, Rochester; but this may have been merely catechism classes.) From St. Mary's were established other Mercy convents at St. Bridget's, Buffalo (1858), and at St. Joseph's, Batavia (1862). All three of these convents were soon given independent status. In 1867, Mother M. Stanislaus McGarr, superior at Batavia, set up a Convent of Mercy at St. Mary's, Corning; and Mother M. Camillus Kelly of Rochester opened a convent at Holy Family Church, Auburn.[48]

During the latter half of the nineteenth century, the Catholic pastors in some upstate New York communities were able to reach an agreement with the local public boards of education to incorporate parochial schools into the public school system. The boards usually consented to pay a nominal rent for the parish school and the costs of its insurance and maintenance, as well as the salaries of the teachers. The pastor had to agree that the teachers would meet the teaching standards of the local board and be under its control and supervision, and that they would conduct no religious devotions or instructions during the official school hours. This plan is usually referred to as the Poughkeepsie (New York) or the Faribault (Minnesota) plan because the arrangement as worked out at those places received much publicity.

There were three parishes in the present diocese of Rochester where the public-parochial school arrangement was in effect. At St. Mary's, Corning, the parochial school was placed under the board of education in or before 1865, while lay teachers were still employed. Even after the Sisters of Mercy came to staff the school in 1867, the plan continued in operation until 1898. In Elmira, Father Peter Bede introduced the Poughkeepsie Plan at SS. Peter and Paul's School, one year after the arrival of the Sisters of St. Mary of Namur. It remained in effect from 1867 until 1876, when friction with the local board of education resulted in its abandonment. The Plan was apparently not introduced at Lima until 1874. Lay teachers staffed the school at the start, but when the Sisters of St. Joseph were given charge in January, 1875, the local board granted them the same status as public school teachers.[49]

In addition to encouraging elementary schools, whatever their mode of support, John Timon even attempted a boys' preparatory boarding school in Rochester. The "College of the Sacred Heart" ("Collegium Sanctissimi Cordis Jesu," as the stone inscription on its façade proclaimed it) opened on the corner of South St. Paul (now South Avenue) and Court Streets in 1848. A former journalist, Mr. Jesse A. Aughinbaugh, had made the building available to the Bishop, and had had himself constituted a corporation sole to administer the academy. Timon named as principal Father Julian Delaune, a Frenchman lately president of St. Mary's College in Kentucky. Father Delaune's faculty included a Kentucky layman named McAntee, and a certain Professor Wade, an alumnus of Trinity College in Dublin. The syllabus of this, the first Catholic secondary school for boys in the city of Rochester, included high school and college subjects. Since its primary aim was to attract vocations to the priesthood, the College was in a sense a preparatory seminary; but it also welcomed students who had no clerical aspirations. Seventy boys enrolled at the outset and participated in the festive opening procession. Father Richard Story, son of Richard and Elizabeth Story, early Irish pioneers of Rochester's "Dublin," was one of the early alumni. So were five laymen who later achieved local prominence: Walter B. Duffy, Robert Jennings, Charles and Frank Wilkin, and Edward McSweeney. Unfortunately, young Father Delaune soon took ill, returned to France in the spring of 1849, and died shortly afterward. Unable to obtain another principal of equal competence, the Bishop closed the College in 1851.[50]

A true spiritual son of the charitable St. Vincent de Paul, Buffalo's first Bishop, promoted Catholic charities. During his regime four orphanages were projected. A "Holy Family Orphanage" of Auburn was incorporated on July 21, 1853, but apparently did not materialize.[51] (Auburn's Catholic orphanage was a later and an independent enterprise.) The Sisters of St. Joseph, as we have seen, opened an orphanage at Canandaigua. It was incorporated on October 6, 1855, and operated on a modest scale until 1901.[52] St. Joseph's Orphanage in Rochester was incorporated on April 23, 1863, opened in 1867, and closed only in 1938. The School Sisters of Notre Dame were custodians of this asylum. It was adjacent to St. Joseph's Church and provided mainly, but not exclusively, for children of German families.[53] St. Mary's Asylum for Orphan Boys, another foundation of the Sisters of St. Joseph to which we have already alluded, was promoted by Father James Early, the pastor of St. Mary's Church, Rochester. Its doors opened on November 1, 1864, and its incorporation was recorded at Albany on January 17, 1865. In 1867, St. Mary's Asylum moved from its original locale on South Street to the corner opposite St. Mary's Hospital on Genesee and West Main Streets. In 1942 it amalgamated with St. Patrick's Girls' Orphanage and St. Joseph's Orphanage to form the present St. Joseph's Villa, incorporated on March 24, 1942.[54]

Unquestionably, the largest charitable institute which dates from Timon's days is St. Mary's Hospital in Rochester. The Bishop entrusted the setting up of this, the first real hospital in the city of Rochester, to the Sisters of Charity of Emmitsburg. The original founders were Sisters Felicia Fenwick, Martha Bridgman, and Magdalen Groell. Their superior was Sister Hieronymo O'Brien (1819-1898), who was to become a memorable figure in the history of Rochester welfare work. St. Mary's opened on September 15, 1857, in two remodeled stables which stood on its present property. Incorporation followed four days later.[55]

Bishop Timon, two years before his appointment to Buffalo, had inspired the foundation in St. Louis, Missouri, of the first American parochial conference of the St. Vincent de Paul Society.[56] Naturally he desired to see parish branches of this lay charitable organization established in the Diocese of Buffalo. Four churches in the twelve eastern counties heeded his recommendations. Father Thomas Brady initiated a conference at Seneca Falls. It was officially aggregated in 1858, but apparently did not function long. Conferences were begun in Rochester proper at St. Patrick's (1856), St. Mary's (1856), and Immaculate Conception (1857?).[57] Of these, only the St. Patrick's unit was destined to have a long career. But if the St. Vincent movement did not become very widespread in the twelve counties, several other parochial beneficent societies did flourish. There were a number of ladies' charitable organizations, and German and Irish parishes alike had their mutual benefit clubs. The Bishop himself could not afford to give alms to all these local works of charity, but he often gave "shilling lectures" for the benefit of the cause. In fact, the Rochester St. Vincent de Paul conferences, between 1857 and 1860, played impresario to a number of worthwhile money-making lectures. The speakers included such notables as Bishop Martin J. Spalding of Louisville, and James A. McMaster, controversial editor of the New York *Freeman's Journal.*[58]

Still another practical charity of John Timon was his advocacy of Catholic rural colonies within his diocese.

At that time a number of western bishops and priests favored the foundation of colonies of Catholic immigrants—a policy which was economically, socially, and spiritually commendable. In 1856, the Irish Immigrant Aid Convention met in Buffalo to consider measures for the national expansion of the immigrant colony plan. Unfortunately, Archbishop John Hughes of New York later interposed strong objections, and his opposition effectively thwarted the hopes of the Convention, which Timon, for his part, had encouraged.

Bishop Timon himself believed that immigrants should be invited to settle in unoccupied areas of the East before being counselled to "go west." Certain sections in the "near west" of western New York still offered many opportunities to immigrant farmers. For example, Father Peter Colgan, pastor at Dunkirk in the Buffalo Diocese, had some time before persuaded railroad laborers to buy cheap but good lands in French Creek township, Chautauqua County. The purchasers had been successful, had paid off their debts in a few years, and by 1859 were independent farmers.

Impressed by Colgan's success, Bishop Timon sent a letter to the Boston *Pilot* and the *New York Tablet,* two Irish Catholic journals widely read by immigrants, in which he recommended the Diocese of Buffalo to prospective immigrant agriculturalists. Throughout western New York, he pointed out, there were many improved farms abandoned by the original cultivators who had joined the current trek into the Far West. Thus, the western New York counties of Wyoming, Allegany, Cattaraugus and Chautauqua had much good farm land, available at reasonable prices. In the counties of Seneca, Cayuga, Tioga, Yates, Livingston, Chemung, and Monroe, some farm land, he said, was also available, although at a higher price. But there was still much good, inexpensive land in Steuben County, near Addison and Greenwood. The Greenwood district in particular, wrote Timon, was attracting many Catholic Irish farmers.

This letter appeared in both the *Pilot* and the *Tablet,* on May 7, 1859. The *Pilot* of June 30, 1860, carried still another of Bishop

Timon's open letters. Here he informed would-be settlers of good farming property in several townships of Chautauqua County.

The "advertisements" of the Bishop of Buffalo evidently generated considerable interest. Father Colgan subsequently reported that
he had received very many inquiries.[59] Quite likely a number of immigrants followed up these inquiries and moved into the Dunkirk area.
Some other settlers in the twelve counties may likewise have been attracted by the Bishop's suggestions. The Catholic population around
Greenwood-Rexville and around Addison certainly increased in the
1860's.

"In journeyings often," indeed! No part of John Timon's flock
lacked his present ministry and management. His was truly "the care
of all the churches."

3 TRUSTEEISM.

Trusteeism, always chronic, sometimes acute, was the most dangerous ailment which afflicted the American Church between 1785 and
the Civil War era. "Trusteeism" in American Catholic annals was the
tendency of parochial lay trustees and their partisans to assume excessive authority over church properties and even over church personnel.[60]

American civil law, geared to the American Protestant majority,
usually provided for only one type of parish incorporation, that which
confided parochial finances to a board of trustees or vestrymen elected
by the congregation. This was the substance of the New York State
Act of April 6, 1784, and of the 1813 revision of that Act. Here was
legislation which would have allowed even fallen-away Catholics to
vote for parish trustees; which gave parishioners and trustees wide control over church properties; which guaranteed the pastor no legal standing in his own parish corporation; and which, in case of a legal contest,
favored the lay incorporators over the Catholic hierarchy. Even so, as
Archbishop Hughes pointed out, the trustee corporation could have
operated successfully and saved the clergy many financial worries if
only the boards elected had been willing to interpret their powers in a
genuinely Catholic spirit. Unfortunately, in those parishes which did incorporate—and incorporation was not absolutely necessary—the trustees could seldom resist the fascinating temptation to usurp.

Many factors shaped this mischievous mentality. Sometimes a congregation built its own church before a bishop was able to assign a
pastor. When he did assign a pastor, the founding parishioners — influenced at times by recollections of European lay patronage, but more
often by the peasant's hard-fisted tenacity of property—were not easily

persuaded to deed over the realty to the bishop. Then there was the singular attraction which the democratic process exercised upon immigrants who came from more authoritarian countries. Although it may be hard for us to appreciate today, the newcomers delighted in voting and holding elective office, even in the very minor democracy of a church congregation. Malevolence was another important contributing factor. Where trusteeist friction arose in America, the ringleaders were almost always men undistinguished for their personal piety. But the principal factor, there can be little doubt, was the incorporation law itself: it gave to the trustees a Protestant form of organization and protected them in a Protestant interpretation of their prerogatives.

The first case of American trusteeism occurred in New York City in 1785. There were outbreaks in several other places in the east during the next four decades. In 1829, the American bishops, meeting in the first provincial council of Baltimore, issued three telling decrees against the abuse.[61] Decree number five urged that henceforth bishops refuse to dedicate any church unless, if at all possible, the church property had first been deeded to them in writing. This was intended to guarantee the control over church property which church law demands. Decree number six declared, against those trustees who had claimed the legal right to choose or depose their own pastors, that no Catholic lay trustees or parishioners had any such right. Decree number seven laid down canonical penalties applicable to any priests who in the future sided with rebellious trusteeists. It took a while for the bishops to make the decrees work in their own dioceses, but the enforcement gradually became effective. True, the anti-trusteeist campaign suffered a menacing setback in the 1850's, when trusteeists, backed by the anti-Catholic Know-Nothings, made a last stand. Their victory was ephemeral, however. By the end of the Civil War, the crusade against "trusteemania" had been substantially won.

There were several cases of trusteeism within the future Rochester Diocese. Here as elsewhere mere nationality assured no immunity to the disease. The trusteeist plague broke out among stubborn Germans as well as among stubborn Irishmen. It was Bishop Dubois who had the first brush with upstate trusteeism. Bishop Hughes, who succeeded him, practically eradicated it throughout the State. Bishop Timon fought and won the last bitter campaign.

The first outbreak in Rochester was at St. Patrick's. St. Patrick's Church became legally incorporated on April 20, 1829, six months before the convocation of the first provincial council of Baltimore. At the outset nine lay trustees were elected. They applied themselves to their task diligently, and remained for the nonce on good terms with their pastor, the intelligent and able Father Michael McNamara.

Nevertheless, there were early evidences that these trustees took themselves too seriously. On July 6, 1829, for example, they voted to publish an admonition "to persons who are in the habit of mocking and laughing during divine service of Sunday." Later on, on the plea of insufficient funds, they proposed to reduce the pastor's salary from six to four hundred dollars. Even the civil law did not give the trustees this right. In 1832, some of the board charged Father McNamara with too long absence on his collecting tour of the east for the benefit of the new church building. The trustees had earlier authorized this tour. Now their disaffected members accused him of taking some of the funds collected. Subsequently, Bishop Dubois removed the pastor from his pastorate. A few days later, on May 20, 1832, the Bishop named Father John F. McGerry to succeed Father McNamara.

But one party of the St. Patrick's trustees now absolutely refused to accept the new pastor. Dubois consequently interdicted the church, forbidding Catholic rites to be performed there. To provide for the loyal parishioners, Father McGerry established a temporary chapel in the rooms of the Catholic Association on Buffalo (now West Main) Street. Some time before, the trustees had commenced legal proceedings to compel the original owners of the St. Patrick's property to deed the property to the congregation itself. They won a favorable judgment in December, 1832, and the property was made over to the congregation by deed of January 16, 1833. This act further confirmed the trustees in their determination to maintain full control of the parochial assets.

Fortunately, an able new pastor had arrived on December 4, 1832. Father Bernard O'Reilly apparently had something to do with the removal of the interdict soon after his arrival, and with the abandonment of a concurrent project to establish a new parish. A diplomatic man, he eventually reconciled the dissenters, who seem, at any rate, to have been fundamentally men of good will.[62]

St. Joseph's Church in Rochester was the scene of the next outbreak. When Father Joseph Prost, C.SS.R., returned to the city in July, 1836, to assist in the establishment of this German parish, he was surprised to be told by his trustees just what his salary would be. Unaccustomed to the trustee system, Prost asked Father O'Reilly what such dictation implied. O'Reilly, probably with a shrug of the shoulders, assured him that trustee boards were common throughout the Diocese of New York.

Father Prost soon learned by experience what a nuisance the practice could be. At the next election of trustees at St. Joseph's, antagonistic members of the board saw to it that the new members elected were also men hostile to the pastor. When Prost became aware of what had happened, he denounced the maneuver and gave the congregation the choice of either overruling the election at once or seeing him depart. Sobered by this firm ultimatum, the parish voters rescinded the vote and kept the pastor. The victory was not quite so easy in 1838, however. At that time, Father Prost advocated building a new parish church on a lot to which he himself held title. Now it was the majority of the parishioners that opposed him, so the Redemptorist did leave Rochester, allowing his stubborn flock to remain some time without a pastor.[63]

As we have already seen, the Germans who in 1842 founded St. Peter's Church on Rochester's west side were largely anti-Redemptorist. While at St. Joseph's, this group had been party to such trusteeist impertinences as dictating the number of candles on the altar.[64] It is no surprise that they carried the mentality with them into the new parish. Eventually they drove their pastor to distraction with their meddling. By April, 1845, after only two years at St. Peter's, Father Levitz packed his bags and left for New York. True enough, the Vicar General for Germans, Father Raffeiner, succeeded in persuading the dejected Franciscan to return to his post; but after one more year he decamped for good.[65]

The trustees were also a cause of friction at Sandy Hill. Those at Geneva about whom Bishop Hughes complained seem to have been more inept than unruly.[66] Trusteeism may have affected other parishes, too, but we have evidence only of the cases discussed in the present chapter.

At all events, Bishop John Hughes launched a vigorous campaign against the plague in 1842. On August 29th, he convoked his first diocesan synod. One section of its decrees dealt with trusteeism, and aimed at strengthening the hand of the pastor in his parochial administration. The new regulations forbade trustees or lay parishioners to name, retain, or dismiss any parish employees without the consent of the pastor; to withhold salaries from the clergy when monies were available; and to rent church property or conclude church contracts without the approval of the parish priest. Pastors were henceforth to give the bishop an annual report of parochial finances, which implied that the trustees must open their accounts to their pastor on demand. Should the trustees or lay parishioners refuse to comply with the present decrees, the Bishop declared that he would take whatever disciplinary action the circumstances required. But he would certainly not permit a pastor to continue in residence in an incorporated parish which flouted the rules. Having adopted these anti-trusteeist decrees, the Bishop of New York published them in a pastoral letter of September 6, 1842.[67]

When they learned of the new synodal laws, the Catholics of New York State realized that their bishop meant business. Most of them accepted the legislation with proper docility. All but one parochial board of trustees acquiesced, and several would have transferred their church property titles to Bishop Hughes had he not declined the offer. The one board which absolutely refused to comply was that which governed the German parish of St. Louis in Buffalo. After in vain admonishing the members of this board to mend their ways, the Bishop allowed their pastor to depart.[68] Unfortunately, the remedy was not sufficient, and when Hughes handed over western New York to Bishop Timon in 1847, the St. Louis case was a dismal part of his legacy.

In the twelve counties, the trustees of St. Patrick's, Rochester, and the trustees at Sandy Hill spontaneously accepted the new rules. On November 6, 1842, the board at St. Patrick's voted to dissolve.[69] On May 22, 1843, the parishioners of Sandy Hill resolved to abandon the election of trustees and to entrust full administrative authority over their little church to the Bishop of New York and his successors.[70]

The other parishes of the present Diocese of Rochester seem to have been equally agreeable, with one notable exception—St. Peter's German Church in Rochester. Here the question did not concern the title to the church property, at least at the start. As we have already noted, the founders of St. Peter's had deeded their property to Bishop Hughes in late 1842, after he had authorized them to open the parish.[71] Hughes, in turn, transferred the legal title to Bishop Timon in 1848.

Some doubt arose thereafter about the validity of the original deed, so Timon asked for a new warranty deed to St. Peter's. In this connection, the Bishop of Buffalo, at the request of the parishioners of St. Peter's, made a written pledge that he and his successors would use St. Peter's "perpetually" for German Catholics, and that each year the regularly appointed pastor would name five parishioners as committeemen to assist with the temporal affairs of the congregation. Bishop Timon's pledge satisfied most of the congregation. All but five now voted to secure the warranty deed from the two parish couples in whose name the real estate had been originally recorded. The document was drawn up on September 17, 1849.

Before long, however, a radical minority in the Rochester parish began to agitate for the incorporation of the parish according to the troublesome trustee law.[72] Father Leonard Schneider, who served for a term as pastor of St. Peter's, seems to have inspired their stratagem. The movement grew, and in June 1851, its leaders requested the then pastor, Father Rudolph Follenius, to announce a meeting of the congregation for the purpose of electing the initial board of trustees as a prelude to incorporation. Father Follenius naturally refused. The ringleaders therefore convoked the meeting themselves. Assembling without the pastor on June 2nd, the parish electors chose a group of trustees, and on the following day filed a certificate of incorporation.

These proceedings were of dubious validity. The trustees, however, presuming themselves legally empowered, demanded that Bishop Timon and the pastor surrender the church property to them. Bishop and Pastor, confident that the majority of the parish was not party to the plot, rejected the demand. The trustees therefore initiated a lawsuit to force them to comply.

According to the civil law, the trustees were forbidden to exercise any control over the contested property as long as the suit was pending. Unfortunately, the "Blacks" (as they called themselves) could not restrain themselves from meddling in the affairs of the "Bishop's Party" during the six long years of litigation. In 1851, Bishop Timon appointed, as pastor of St. Peter's, Father Francis X. Krautbauer (1824-1885), a secular priest and the future second bishop of Green Bay. On his first Sunday in Rochester, Father Krautbauer was summarily ordered out of the church by one of the trustees, who told him "they did not want a *Jesuit*." Early in 1853, the impatient "Blacks" tried to seize the church, but were arrested and fined. Each year their partisans met in annual session to elect trustees. And each year the following of the "Blacks" obviously diminished. In 1855, only forty-five men participated in the election, though they claimed to represent the four hundred families of the parish. Furthermore, the chairman of the 1855 session was a man who had neglected for years to make his Easter Communion.

Eventually some of the "Blacks" went so far as to inaugurate an independent, and therefore schismatic, worship of their own in a neighborhood grocery. When they were told that this act of separation disqualified them from voting in the St. Peter's elections, they repudiated the notion. They considered themselves to be as good Catholics here as they had been in the old country. In the old country, they stated—incorrectly—"the priesthood ruled in things spiritual, not in things *temporal.*" If they had gone to law it was only in defense of the same principle. Leave it up to the American courts, they said. The courts would decide which was "mightier in rights of property—a council of priests or the Legislature of the State of New York." Language of this sort, voiced so often by embittered American trusteeists, was far more anti-Catholic than Catholic in sentiment.

Bishop Timon was meanwhile engaged in an even more strenuous battle with the trustees of St. Louis Church in Buffalo. These gentlemen likewise contended that the clergy should have no decisive say regarding parish temporal concerns. The Bishop finally interdicted St. Louis Church. When the trustees appealed from his action to Pope Pius IX, the Pope sent over a papal nuncio, Archbishop Gaetano Bedini, to hear their appeal and to attend to other business of the American Church. The Archbishop interviewed the trustees of St. Louis Church in October, 1853. Since they would not yield up their idea, so contrary to church law, that bishops have no real authority over church properties, the Nuncio regretfully informed them that they had no case against the Bishop of Buffalo.

Archbishop Bedini must have found Rochester a welcome refuge after his contentious hours in Buffalo. He arrived by an eastbound train at mid-morning on October 27th. First of all, he officiated at a benediction of the Blessed Sacrament at St. Patrick's Church. Then he was given a guided tour of the rest of the city's Catholic churches. St. Peter's was included in the tour, but nothing untoward marred his visit to that storm center. Late in the afternoon Bedini took part in another festive benediction ceremony at St. Joseph's Church. Here he preached in German. The Redemptorists played host overnight to the distinguished guest. He celebrated an early Mass on the 28th, and took the eight o'clock train to New York.[73]

The trustee parties at St. Louis', Buffalo, and St. Peter's, Rochester, still refused to give in. The O'Keefe Bill gave them a new opportunity to protest. In 1852, Archbishop Hughes sought to circumvent trusteeism by promoting a State law which would enable Catholic bishops to hold all church property in their dioceses as "corporations sole." In other words, the individual bishop would be recognized in civil law as a corporation legally empowered to hold all Catholic church property in his diocese. When they learned of this O'Keefe Bill, the trustees of both the Buffalo and Rochester churches protested loudly against it or any similar legislation. Laws of this sort, they claimed, were "contrary to our liberal and free institutions." The argument was deft, in that it appealed to both patriotic and anti-Catholic American sentiment. Much to the disappointment of the Archbishop of New York, the proposed bill was defeated in the Legislature.

The trusteeist overture to "native American" sentiment was an especially shrewd strategy because the era of anti-foreign and anti-Catholic Know-Nothingism was just dawning. In 1854, State Senator James O. Putnam, with the support of the trustees of St. Louis' and St. Peter's, presented the New York Legislature with a bill intended to *oblige* all Catholic parishes to incorporate according to the trustee law. By the provisions of the Putnam Bill, bishops would be *forbidden* to hold any church property in trust in their own names. If they should attempt to do so, the property would be subject to confiscation. After a spate of anti-Catholic oratory in the Legislature, this bill was passed and became a law on April 6, 1855. It was so patently unjust and discriminatory that everybody, even the cynical legislators who had supported it, knew it would eventually be repealed. Loyal Catholics simply ignored it, convinced that it was not enforceable.

Later on, the Rochester trusteeists boasted that they had played a real part in the enactment of the Putnam Bill. It was a dubious claim. As we have seen, they were reduced in numbers by 1855. True, the prolonged lawsuit against Bishop Timon was finally decided in their favor in 1857. But the Bishop appealed the judgment and it was reversed on March 7, 1859.

In the interim, the worthy parishioners of St. Peter's had tried to counter the trusteeists by voting into office another board made up of loyal Catholics. But the "Blacks" did not stop short of riotous disorder to maintain themselves in office. After the 1859 reversal, the congregation finally excluded the "Blacks" completely by electing a fresh slate of dependable trustees and reincorporating on March 10, 1859, as the "Trustees of Sts. Peter and Paul Church." Frustrated, the "Blacks" first countered by reincorporating themselves on May 19, 1859, as "the Christ Catholic St. Stephen's Congregation." But eventually they admitted defeat and abandoned their schismatic stand. Bishop Timon was finally able to jot down in his diary, under the date November 5, 1862: "Meet rebels of Old St. Peter's; pardon two, take off Ex [communication] . . . all present reconciled—only two absent hold out. *Deo Gratias*."

The year after Timon made this entry, the notorious Putnam Law was repealed. On March 25, 1863, a new state law was enacted which allowed a type of parish incorporation more harmonious with Catholic church law. According to the new law, parishes could be set up as "corporations aggregate," whose trustees would be the diocesan bishop, his vicar general, the local pastor, and two lay trustees. Since 1863, all the parishes in the present Rochester diocese have been incorporated or reincorporated under this law or its amended form. It has proved an effective antidote to trusteeism.

Meddlers would not cease to rise, of course. At St. Joseph's in Rochester, for example, one prominent and cantankerous layman carried on a private war against the pastor from 1855 to 1865. At the start, he had resigned from the choir. Then he had tried in vain to be readmitted. When the pastor refused, the layman adopted the annoying practice of sitting in the adjacent gallery and singing along with the choir. When he chose, as he sometimes did, to sing a Gregorian melody different from that which the choristers were singing, the effect was, to say the least, distracting.[74]

St. Mary's parish in Dansville also showed trusteeist tendencies in 1862:[75] In 1864, some parishioners of St. Boniface Church in Rochester caused vexation to their pastor.[76] Let it be said in all frankness that the clergy were not always blameless in these altercations, for pioneer pastors could be unduly authoritarian and intransigent. Saddest of all is the fact that, in the course of these troubles, some of the faithful became permanently alienated from the Church.[77]

It would make pleasanter reading if we completely ignored the ancient squabbles. But honesty demands that they be recalled. And did not Christ describe his kingdom-on-earth as a field in which cockle vies with wheat until the very harvest?

Besides, there is perhaps nothing which accentuates so well the great good will of the many as the malice of the few.

CHAPTER FOUR

NO-POPERY, SLAVERY, AND THE
AMERICAN WAY

DURING HIS two decades as bishop of Buffalo, John Timon became embroiled in three wars, each of a different type. The first was the war against trusteeism, which we have already described. The second was the war which Know-Nothingism declared upon immigrants and Catholics. The third was the American Civil War.

Historians have dubbed it "nativism," this recurrent tendency of native-born Americans to stem further immigration on the grounds that it is a threat to the "American way" of doing things. Anti-immigrationism, however un-neighborly, need not be anti-Catholic. There were American Catholics in Timon's own day who were concerned over the social and economic problems raised by uncontrolled immigration. But as a matter of fact, since so many of the pre-Civil War immigrants were Catholics, nativism did assume a deep tinge of anti-Catholicism.

In practice, nativist anti-Catholicism was directed more against Irish than against German and French immigrants. Since they spoke English and entered politics more readily, the Irish confronted Protestant Americans more frequently and more urgently. This very urgency only confirmed the anti-Irish attitude which the natives had already conceived. They resented the poverty of the Irishmen and their willing acceptance of substandard living conditions—conditions which were almost luxurious to the immigrants themselves, when compared to those which the Irish famine had imposed upon them. The Irishmen's lack of education, lack of skills, and social clannishness also met with prim disapproval; and the intemperance of some and the violence of others were considered both typical and incorrigible. Catholicism, the native Protestants concluded, was the cause of all this degradation.

For their part, the Irish, inclined to be hypersensitive, were too often ready to think themselves discriminated against for religious reasons alone, when as a matter of fact prejudicial acts against them might actually spring from social objections. But even the Protestants, in any given case, would probably have had difficulty in saying whether they disliked the Murphys or the McCarthys for social or religious reasons. All they knew was that Irishmen "just didn't fit in."

Close upon the heels of the Know-Nothing nativism of the 1850's came the Civil War, which had to turn for manpower to the "adopted" as well as the native American citizens. The loyal response of the immigrants to the battle trumpets did much to allay the earlier fear of born-Americans that immigrants could not be assimilated. Bishop Timon was to set a pattern of patriotism for his flock during the Civil War epoch. The nativist spirit was not dead, however, and Timon still had to combat discrimination in the postwar years of his regime.

1. THE NO-POPERY MEN.

That the Protestants of western New York should have had small respect for the Catholic Church is understandable. They had been reared in the conviction that Catholicism implied superstition and tyranny, and they read this conviction into the folkways and attitudes of Catholic immigrants. The United States they proudly considered to be a Protestant achievement, and they were persuaded that Catholics would never be truly American until they became Protestants. Still, tolerance even of the unpopular was an American principle. Therefore, so long as Catholics did not allow their exotic beliefs to offend against American social propriety, Protestants felt that they should be treated with fitting condescension.

While this gentlemen's agreement usually worked well enough even in the most hidebound era of native Americanism, there were so many points of possible friction between Catholics and Protestants that from time to time sparks were sure to fly. Especially after the British Emancipation Act of April 1829 had freed Irish and British Catholics from the shackles of official discrimination, American Protestants began to take a livelier interest in the Catholic Church as a growing American phenomenon. As we have seen, local Catholic celebrations of the Emancipation attracted the attention of non-Catholic Rochesterians. By order of Bishop Dubois, a *Te Deum* service of thanksgiving was held in St. Patrick's Church on June 21, 1829; and the Rochester Irish saluted the same event in the gala non-alcoholic observance of St. Patrick's Day, 1830.

There was nothing unseemly about either of these celebrations, yet they appear to have provoked the "No-Popery" sentiments of some Rochesterians. The *Rochester Observer* now launched a series of articles denouncing the alleged immorality of Roman Catholicism. The pastor of St. Patrick's, Father Michael McNamara, replied to the initial attack in a letter addressed to the *Rochester Daily Advertiser and Telegraph*. The *Observer* then opened its columns to an anonymous reply by one "Republicus," who seems to have been a local minister. McNamara rebutted the rebuttal in a letter addressed to the *Observer* itself. "Republicus" had asked whether any Catholic, as a Catholic, could be a loyal American. Father McNamara, deploring the innuendo, pointed to the record of Catholics in the American Revolution. He wrote intelligently and with verve, and should have won a fair hearing because of his own wide reputation for tolerance and good citizenship. But religious controversy of this sort was probably largely sterile.

Certainly the *Observer* itself remained unconvinced, and continued its petty and ill-informed attacks. So did "Republicus," who refused McNamara's challenge to doff his mask of anonymity. Now a Catholic layman, James Buchan, took up the cudgels, writing several letters against the *Observer* and "Republicus," and in favor of Father McNamara. Buchan's correspondence was less temperate than his pastor's, and it succeeded no more than his in thawing out the icy animosity of the Presbyterian-oriented daily journal.[1]

More ominous than verbal attacks against things Catholic were the occasional acts of physical violence. On March 7, 1830, somebody broke into St. Patrick's Church, Rochester, and engaged in a vandalism which seems to have sprung from malice. Early in 1835, a young Auburnian, after waiting until the congregation had assembled in Holy Family Church, set fire to the building. Fortunately, the fire was quickly discovered and quenched, and the culprit was arrested. He confessed the arson and said that others had prevailed upon him to make the attempt. Apparently the plotters had hoped to discourage the priest from making further visits.[2] We have already referred to the plot devised against Father Joseph Prost by certain non-Catholics of the Town of Dansville, after he had successfully persuaded the Dansville Catholics to stop attending Protestant services.

It was in Boston, New York, and Philadelphia that native Americans, witnessing with their own eyes the arrival of an endless flood of impoverished immigrants, felt most impelled to close the gates against further entry. In 1843, New York City nativists publicly proclaimed the foundation of the American Republican Party, a party dedicated to the restriction of immigration. Whatever merits their basic project may have had, it soon became charged with anti-Irishism and anti-Catholicism.

An immediate cause of this anti-Catholic slant was the movement recently led by Bishop Hughes of New York to obtain a portion of the public school funds for the elementary schools conducted by the Catholics in New York City. Governor William H. Seward had publicly intimated, in 1840, that he saw no objection to dividing public funds between public and parochial schools. On the basis of this statement,

Hughes petitioned the New York City Common Council for an allot-
ment of school monies. He maintained that the City's Public School
Society, which was independent of State educational control, operated
the City schools along militantly Protestant lines, thereby endangering
the faith of Catholics who attended. The Common Council turned
down the Bishop's petition, so Hughes sought redress from the State
legislature; and when the Democratic party refused to support him, he
reluctantly sponsored a ticket of his own in the 1841 elections. This
"Carroll Hall Ticket" polled only two thousand votes, but that was
enough to defeat the Democratic ticket. In 1842, therefore, the Democrats backed the Maclay Bill, which extended the control of the State
department of education over New York City and thus abolished the
authority of the City's Public School Society. The law furthermore
forbade sectarian teaching in any public school.

The Bishop had won his point, but he had also raised a tempest of
opposition among the nativists, who interpreted the whole episode as a
plot engineered by the Pope of Rome. The American Republican Party,
called after 1845 the Native American Party, made much of this charge,
as it bid for state and national political influence throughout the rest
of the decade.

The Native American Party was a transient phenomenon, and its
political program aroused little interest among Protestants in upstate
New York. Rochester nativists backed the Whig ticket, as usual, in
the election of November, 1845.[3] But if the party's platform did not
appeal to upstate Protestants, its anti-Catholic passion proved more con-
tagious. Forewarned by newspaper accounts of New York Catholic
"aggressions"; reminded by preachers of the wiles of Romanism; horri-
fied by such books as "ex-nun" Maria Monk's fictionalized "exposé" of
convent life; and roused by travelling nativist demagogues, many non-
Catholics of western New York felt impelled to take a more unfriend-
ly view of the tide of immigrants. Let it be said to the credit of these
Protestants that even in their hostile moments they seldom molested
Catholics. But there were all too many cases of rank discrimination,
especially against the Irish, and physical violence was not unheard of.

When Bishop Timon first visited Corning on January 9, 1848, he
spoke to his largely Protestant audience on the general notion of the
Church and its sacraments. Afterward, a poor Irish Corningite blessed
the Bishop for his clear exposition, but suggested that he might have
devoted more time to the subject of confession. "They do mock us so
much about it!"[4] In those days, there must have been a good deal of
this theological mockery. Nativist rowdies sometimes expressed a less

intellectual contempt. When the Rochester Irishmen, parading on St. Patrick's Day, 1842, came to the Buffalo Bridge on the present West Main Street, they were disconcerted to see an effigy of an Irishman dangling from a nearby flagpole. Some of the marchers, determined to take down the "Paddy," found it necessary to cut down the whole flagstaff. The *Rochester Republican* lamented the loss of the pole, but could scarcely blame the Irish for reacting as they did.[5]

On other occasions the show of bias was still more arrant. At the outset, Father Michael Gilbride (+1854) celebrated Mass for the Catholics of Ovid in the home of James Murphy at Benton's Corners. But the landlord soon told Murphy that if he continued to play host to the missionary, he would be evicted and the townspeople would no longer hire him. Something similar occurred at Geneseo a few years later. There a prominent nativist had the sheriff exclude the Catholics from further use of the courthouse for services. This happened when the benevolent General James Wadsworth was in Europe. When Wadsworth returned he was amazed to see the local Catholics kneeling on the porch of a small, crowded dwelling in which Mass was being celebrated. Learning what had happened, he straightway made a gift of a church lot to the Geneseo Catholics, adding a loan of $500.00, repayable at their convenience.[6]

Penn Yan showed even stronger antipathy to newly-arrived Catholics. Thomas Hendrick, the leader of the little flock of pioneer Catholic Penn Yanners, had to suffer for his leadership. Once two hoodlums tripped him with a rope as he came around the street corner, and gave him a trouncing. On another day he was beaten up badly in the American Hotel.[7] Had Hendrick been a tempestuous Irishman, one might suspect that he had invited the mayhem. On the contrary, Tom was an honest and peaceable citizen, the father of two future nuns, a priest, a bishop, a New York Supreme Court justice, and a United States consul.

In the late 1840's, the Mexican War and other more earnest issues stole the headlines, and nativism subsided a bit. A revolution in Rome also sent Pope Pius IX into exile in 1848, and those Americans who before this revolution had feared that the Pope was planning to invade the United States, began to breathe a little more easily. But after 1850, a new and stronger wave of intolerance arose. Know-Nothingism, as it is usually called, was to have a far greater impact on western New York than the Native Americanism of the 1840's.

The trouble was that the Catholic immigration kept coming, and in ever-swelling numbers. When St. Mary's Church was building in Canandaigua, a local Protestant said to one of the Catholic builders,

"Well, this beats the devil, to see a Catholic church in Canandaigua." "Faith, you're right, sir," replied the laborer. "It's the *only* Church that can do the same!"[8] The invasion of foreign Catholics into hitherto Protestant villages indeed seemed ominous to many of the local citizens. Was there not a real danger that these foreigners would take control and change everything? Had not Archbishop Hughes practically admitted such a conspiracy when he proclaimed in 1850 that his Church's mission was "to convert the world—including the inhabitants of the United States"?

Native Protestants, once more gripped by a nameless fear, organized for self-protection. Missionary societies like the American and Foreign Christian Union undertook the defense of international religious liberty and the conversion of the world's Catholics "to Christianity." Other movements embarked on a defense of obligatory bible-reading — the King James Version, of course — in the public schools. Still other activists, heeding the invitation of fractious Catholic trustees, favored state legislation which would oblige Catholic parishes to incorporate according to the "democratic" trustee system.

Controversialists, Protestant and Catholic, now entered the ring once again. A new spate of anti-Catholic literature gushed from the presses, ranging in character from the scholarly to the piously pornographic. Anti-Roman preachers and lecturers recommenced their round of the nation's pulpits and platforms. (One of the most effective of the newer agitators was the Italian ex-priest Alessandro Gavazzi, who went up and down the country denouncing Archbishop Bedini, the papal delegate sent from Rome to look into the appeals of Catholic trustee-ists.)

After the propagandists had laid their barrage, the political nativists moved in to recommend new legislation designed to restrict the admission and naturalization of immigrants, and to do whatever else could be done to preserve the Protestant *status quo*. It was an ideal time for such a maneuver. Both the Whig Party and the Democratic Party were divided into warring segments, and neither organization had an arresting political platform to offer. The nativists did not, however, move into politics openly, but through a society, the Order of the Star Spangled Banner. Founded in New York in 1849, this typical secret society was exclusively Protestant, and exacted from its members a militant effort to exclude Catholics from public office, and to exclude foreign and Catholic influence from American institutions. Since members, when questioned about the Order, professed they "knew nothing," the name "Know-Nothing" was quickly applied to the society itself and the movement which it fostered. In the spring of 1854, a member of the Order established a "junior branch," the "Order of Free and Accepted Americans," open to young men not old enough to qualify for the parent society. These youngsters, who soon adopted white felt hats as insignia, were eager to take part in the more riotous activities of Know-Nothingism.[9]

The Spangled Bannerites had pledged to follow the voting instructions of their superiors. As a result, this mysterious new political force, not yet widely known, made a dramatic bid for power in the New York State elections of spring, 1854. Members went to the polls armed with their own list of candidates, and sometimes by write-in votes of unnominated contestants elected whole tickets of unknowns. The Silver Grey Whigs (those opposed to Governor Seward) now hastened to ally themselves with this new political army, as did others whose allegiance to their own parties had been weakened. In the fall, the New York State Know-Nothings ran their own man for governor, Daniel Ullman. Ullman lost in his bid for the governorship, but he polled an imposing vote. Know-Nothing lodges now sprang up across the nation, and the leaders of the new party — officially named the American Party — adopted an "*anti*-anti-slavery" platform in 1855 in order to keep the good will of Southern members.

The party next aspired to win the presidency in the election of November, 1856. But by election day political Know-Nothingism had already entered into a decline almost as steep as its rise, and its candidate, ex-president Millard Fillmore, lost rather badly to James Buchanan, the candidate of the newly-formed Republican Party. Thereafter, the American Party grew weaker and weaker. Legislators whom it had put in office were furthermore unable to effect the anti-immigrant laws to which they were pledged. The only discriminatory act which the New York State legislature did carry through was the Putnam Bill, which as we have already seen obliged all Catholic churches to incorporate according to the odious trustee form of incorporation.

In the elections, however, western New York had gone staunchly nativist. Most of the elements of religious conflict which played a part in the formation of Know-Nothingism in New York City were also present upstate. In Rochester proper, the Monroe County Bible Society made concurrent efforts to place a bible in every home, although sixty-five percent of the families visited refused to accept the Society's bibles, apparently all in the Protestant version. The American Tract Society reorganized its Rochester group, and its agent called at many homes, one-ninth of which were households of Irish or German Catholics.

Rochester, too, had its branch of the American and Foreign Christian Union, but at Rochester the Union was less aggressive than elsewhere.[10]

Public controversies likewise recommenced. In May, 1851, the Reverend Henry W. Lee, rector of St. Luke's Church in Rochester, delivered two addresses on "The Papal Aggression." The following December, Bishop Timon preached on the same subject at St. Patrick's, apparently in reply. Henry Ward Beecher, the famous New England minister, could not refrain from attacking Catholicism in a lecture which he delivered that same month before the members of the Rochester Athenaeum. His diatribe drew a Catholic protest in the columns of the *Rochester Daily Advertiser*.[11] Elsewhere, too, Catholic citizens came to the defense of their Faith, devoutly if not always skillfully. Michael Murphy of St. Patrick's parish in Dansville was one of the contemporary lay champions.[12]

Dr. Lee's two lectures were subsequently published. In addition to this and other propaganda books there were many Know-Nothing newspapers, which specialized in anti-Catholic news and views, much of it "exchanges" from other Know-Nothing papers, or "boiler-plate" material. The Rochester *Daily American,* the Auburn *Daily American,* the Canandaigua *Repository,* the *Livingston County Republican,* the Seneca Falls *American Reveille,* and the Addison *Voice of the Nation* came under this heading; and there were also other papers which, while perhaps not so officially Know-Nothing, sang the same tune. Even some papers opposed to the American Party, like the *Corning Journal,* accepted advertisements for such literary gems as *The Escaped Nun; or, Disclosures of Convent Life and the Confessions of a Sister of Charity.*

The "Miss Carlson" who in 1855 lectured on the "secrets of nunneries" in Rochester's Minerva Hall was perhaps actually a former Sister. But most of the anti-Catholic speakers who now made the rounds were male: "ex-priests" and "ex-monks." Fortunately, Father Gavazzi did not come to Rochester to thunder against Archbishop Bedini, so the Archbishop's sojourn by the Genesee was more tranquil than it had been in some other places. Nor, it seems, did Pastor Charles Chiniquy, one of the most durable of the "ex-priests," visit Rochester, although he did speak in Geneseo in 1859. Giacinto Achilli, who lectured in Rochester in November, 1855, had already won some notoriety in England by reason of the suit of libel which he filed against the future Cardinal Newman. E. Leahey, who claimed to be an ex-Trappist monk, and a Reverend Doctor L. Giustiniani had delivered salacious anti-Catholic lectures in Rochester as early as 1848. Leahey swung through Rochester on another tour in 1852. On one of his circuits, the "ex-monk" gave a strong address at Auburn, arousing much excitement against Catholicism. Local tradition says that the Catholics felt obliged to stand guard over their little church, lest somebody try a second time to burn it to the ground.[13] Of all these worthies, Chiniquy and Achilli were indeed former priests of checkered careers. Giustiniani had apparently begun, but never completed, a Catholic seminary course; Leahey's position in the monastery seems to have been only that of a hired servant. While demagogues of their stripe probably did not attract the majority of upstate Protestants, it is regrettable that even a minority should have allowed themselves to be taken in by them.

Most picturesque and most dangerous of the lot was the "Angel Gabriel." John Sayers Orr was the real name of this British subject who went on a whirlwind tour of the eastern States in 1854. Wherever he went, he appeared in a long white robe and summoned his audience by blasts on a brass horn — whence his angelic nickname. He could have been written off as a laughable eccentric were it not that he had a real talent for inspiring the destruction of the homes and churches of Catholics.

The "Angel" may have visited Auburn as early as 1852.[14] But it was only when his reputation for mob-arson had reached its height that he "flew" into western New York, spoiling for discord. Orr came to Rochester from Buffalo on Friday, July 27, 1854, and remained in town until August 2nd. Maltby Strong, the Know-Nothing mayor of Rochester, gave him tacit backing, and on Saturday, July 28th, ordered out the Union Grays, a local company of militia, to put down any disorder that might break out that evening after his second lecture. This "emergency" move was quite unnecessary. The only "trouble" on the previous evening had been the mimicry of a waggish boy who had mounted a soap box on a downtown street and gathered an amused audience by tooting his own horn. Although Orr on that occasion made provocative remarks about the race and the faith of the Irish, the local Irishmen maintained admirable self-control. During the speaker's tirade of July 31st, somebody tossed a brickbat, which struck a policeman. The *Daily Union* suspected that a confederate of Orr's had thrown it. At any rate, Mayor Strong forbade him to deliver any more speeches in Rochester. After making one final attempt at the railroad station to cause a fracas, the Angel took flight from this unresponsive city.[15]

He did not flit far. That same evening he tried to raise hob in Canandaigua. But the local Catholics whom he wanted to needle had the commonsense to stay away from the public square where he was speaking.[16] Perhaps the Catholics were at that moment standing guard about St. Mary's Church. For there is a tradition that at one time or another during the Know-Nothing era the parishioners of St. Mary's felt obliged to take precautions against the burning of their church building.[17]

"Gabriel" seems to have made his next stop at Palmyra. Here he had better luck. He gave a typical harangue on August 4th, and left that same night. Perhaps he departed as quickly as he did because he sensed that he had really aroused some non-Catholic Palmyrans. It was always his policy to light the fuse and run. The explosion followed not long after he had left. A group of troublemakers marched on St. Ann's Catholic Church (the original building, which stood on Market Street, just behind the present church). They broke open the doors, tore down appointments of the sanctuary, threw some of the furnishings out of the window, and kindled a fire up among the front pews. Fortunately, the arsonists were rank amateurs, and the fire which they set sputtered out after having barely scorched one of the seats. But the sacrilege of the act burned deep into the hearts of Palmyra Catholics.[18]

Another act of vandalism was perpetrated at Holy Cross Church in Ovid, on April 4, 1855. Three teen-agers tore off the cross which crowned the church building and nailed an American flag to the remaining stump. A local committee, comprising Protestant as well as Catholic citizens, met next day and publicly denounced the deed. The *American Reveille,* Seneca Falls' nativist paper, in reporting the Ovid story on April 14th, insisted that juvenile delinquents, not the upright local members of the Know-Nothing party, were the guilty ones.

Friction between natives and immigrants also led to near-violence or actual violence elsewhere in the twelve counties.

In Owego, for example, freedom of conscience was supposedly the issue. A young Catholic girl who for a couple of years had been a domestic in a Protestant home finally began to absent herself from Sunday Mass. In April, 1855, the parish priest called on her and urged her, for the good of her soul, to change her job. One night soon after, a group of the girl's relatives gathered in front of the house, intent, it was thought, upon taking her away. Apparently nothing came of the gathering, but the *Southern Tier Times* warned its readers that "The Protestant spirit of Owego will not tolerate violence, nor permit a girl to be dragged to the confessional by force."[19]

We grant willingly that some of the Irish courted trouble. For instance, in February, 1850, a quarrel between laborers and a foreman of the Chemung Canal near Elmira almost turned into a pitched battle. When the sheriff and his aides intervened, the laborers banded together against them.[20] If these migrant workers of 1850 conceivably had a real grievance (as was often the case on the "public works"), those of 1853 certainly did not. After Mass on the holyday of the Assumption, August 15th, a number of the canal laborers decided to further "sanctify" the occasion by visiting the Elmira saloons. Sufficiently fortified by late afternoon, they overran the village, and the result was a regular Donnybrook Fair. The sheriff eventually clapped thirty-nine of the rioters in jail.[21]

Immigrants of this sort won little sympathy from native Americans for their nationality or their Faith. More understandable was the reaction of individual Irishmen to the taunts of the Know-Nothings and their auxiliaries, the "Wide-Awakes." On August 3, 1854, for example, two Irishmen walking near Rochester's Mount Hope Cemetery, accosted a passerby who wore a white "Know-Nothing" or "Wide-Awake" hat, that acknowledged badge of the aggressive nativist. One of the Irishmen planted himself in the path of the wearer and asked what business he had sporting that hat. In answer, the nativist surprised his questioner with a mighty punch in the eye that sent him heels-over-head into the gutter. Rochester's Know-Nothing paper, the *Daily American,* recorded this nativist triumph with great relish.[22]

For the most part, however, the average Catholic, following the counsel of his pastor and his own common sense, kept his peace in the face of sometimes strong provocation. Most deplorable of all, of course, was the unprovoked attack by native Americans on the life and property of poor but decent immigrants. One such attack was planned at East Bloomfield in the early 1850's, although fortunately it was thwarted.

At that time Irish laborers were working in Ontario County on the right of way of the "Peanut Line." Officially named the Canandaigua and Niagara Falls Railroad, the "Peanut Line" was a small railway subsequently absorbed by the New York Central system. While engaged on the project, a number of the workers, some with their families, were living in one-room shacks near East Bloomfield. Most of the Yankee inhabitants of East Bloomfield were fearful that these beggarly foreigners might take it into their heads to settle among them permanently. On two occasions the local anti-Irish feeling reached such a pitch that some of the Bloomfielders were dissuaded only with great difficulty from destroying the Irish shanties.

The agitators, twice frustrated, refused to be impeded the third time. One gusty winter's night, the Bloomfield nativists, inspired no doubt by some new "incidents," gathered together in high rage. This time the overwrought majority actually voted to march over immediately and set fire to the shacks of the migrants. A "burn-out," they thought, was the only effective way of warning the Paddies that their kind was not wanted in Bloomfield.

It was about 2:00 a.m. when the incendiaries set out on their grim errand. Although he himself had voted against the attack, Joe Steele, one of the Bloomfield Yankees, mounted his horse and rode along with them. When the mob reached its destination and was on the point of carrying out the plan, Steele suddenly turned his horse athwart their path and brandished a shotgun. If they should set fire to even one of the shanties, he warned them, the wind would quickly spread the flames to all, and they would incur the guilt of murdering sleeping men, women and children. This he intended to prevent, and he promised to shoot anybody who tried.[23]

Steele's strong stand quickly demoralized the rioters and sent them home thinking more sober thoughts. There was apparently no further talk of "burning out" the East Bloomfield migrants. Some of the Irish railroaders did settle in the neighborhood eventually, and others joined them later. Once the native Bloomfielders got to know them, they saw that Irishmen could become pretty substantial citizens after all.

Politically, the American Party won hundreds of votes in the twelve counties. In 1854, the Party's gubernatorial candidate, Ullman, carried Chemung, Livingston, Ontario, Schuyler, Seneca, and Steuben counties.[24] A year later, when the American Party succeeded in putting Joel T. Headley into office as New York Secretary of State, the counties of Livingston, Ontario, Seneca, Tompkins, and (again with a large vote) Steuben, contributed heartily to his victory.

In the presidential election of 1856, the Know-Nothing candidate Millard Fillmore won fewer votes in New York State than did some of the Know-Nothing nominees to state office. But the percentage of the American Party vote dropped off considerably that year, for the new Republican Party proved to have a wide appeal in western New York.

The Know-Nothings nevertheless continued in political existence, and there was some danger of their remaining a balance-of-power party if they could keep control of enough votes to swing future elections. As the elections of 1859 drew near, this threat seemed sufficiently strong to one prominent Irishman of the Town of Greece, to prompt him to suggest a new weapon against the American Party. Judge Nicholas Read, a prosperous Catholic farmer and leading citizen of Paddy Hill, proposed in the Rochester *Union and Advertiser* that his fellow "adopted citizens" form a common front and vote for an "anti-Know-

Nothing ticket," casting their ballots for those nominees of either the Democratic or the Republican parties whom the American Party had not endorsed.

A Catholic weekly published in New York City, the *New York Tablet,* seized upon Read's idea, and throughout October gave the recommendation considerable publicity across the State. Although the move came at the eleventh hour, the "adopted citizen" campaign nevertheless won several thousand votes in New York City and upstate. The nominees backed by the nativists did win the election, but by a slim majority. Judge Read's "Anti-Know-Nothing" ticket had at least contributed to the further weakening of Know-Nothingism in New York State.[25]

As a matter of fact, the political nativism of the 1850's was doomed from the start. Politicians had backed it merely as a handy political device. Anti-Catholicism was indeed an inborn American prejudice; but inborn too were the stronger sentiments of liberty and tolerance. The violent nativists were unrepresentative, and the Catholic immigrants knew that they could ultimately depend on the sense of fair play of the majority of Protestant Americans. Know-Nothing politicians themselves were often personally well-disposed to Catholics. In 1849, Protestant Millard Fillmore, at that time vice-president of the United States, had been the first parent to enroll his daughter in the Buffalo convent school of the Religious of the Sacred Heart.[26] And the leading Know-Nothings of Owego were said to have been the most generous Protestant contributors to the building of Owego's first Catholic chapel![27]

Although political nativism was predestined to short life, its campaigns against the Catholic Church did have the unfortunate effect of strengthening many Protestants in their antipathy to the Church and its members. What Bishop Timon had to fear was not so much violence as discrimination, particularly in welfare institutions.

In Rochester, for instance, the Protestant-founded "Home for the Friendless" had originally been liberal in its policies. But after 1854, its directors ruled that no Catholic priest might visit or minister to the unemployed young women who were under its protection. On at least one occasion this ruling had tragic results. The Monroe County Almshouse and the Work House likewise excluded Catholic instructions and services. On the other hand, Protestant proselytism was permitted in both of these institutions, in the Monroe County Jail, and even in the Auburn State Prison. The situation at the Western House of Refuge was even more grave. A State school of detention, and the forerunner of the present school at Industry, New York, the House of Refuge was then located in Rochester proper. Two-thirds of the three hundred boys held in custody by the House were professed Catholics; yet for "practical reasons," no Catholic priest was permitted to give them religious or moral instruction or to make Catholic worship available to them.

Timon urged the pastors of the Rochester district to maintain a united front against discrimination wherever it cropped up. In the matter of the Western House of Refuge, the Bishop, after working on the State government from 1861 to 1863, finally secured the appointment of two Catholics to its board of directors—one of them Patrick Barry of Rochester. But even the efforts of these men had not succeeded in tempering the rules of the House of Refuge by the time of Bishop Timon's death in 1867.[28]

2. THE WAR BETWEEN THE STATES.

However badly native Americans sometimes treated Catholic immigrants, the immigrants loved their adopted country and were ready to soldier for it.

As early as the War of 1812, some of the Catholic settlers in western New York rallied to repel the British attacks upon the United States. When the British commodore, Sir James Yeo, menaced the port of Charlotte in those exciting days of May 14-16, 1814, Felix McGuire of Greece is said to have been one of the rural "minute men" who gathered to protect the harbor. And family tradition says that another Grecian, James A. Flynn, commanded an American ship in the Great Lakes fleet, and was imprisoned for one day by the enemy.[29] Down in the Southern Tier, William Kernan, the Catholic pioneer of Tyrone, was a major in the militia regiment of General Frederick McClure of Bath. Some of the regiment took part in the American attack across the Niagara River in 1813, although Kernan himself does not seem to have served in the field.[30]

Many of the early settlers in western New York belonged to local companies of the State militia. Kernan, who eventually became a brigadier general in his militia regiment, probably had few if any Catholics in his command. But in districts where Catholics were more numerous, there were sometimes companies largely if not wholly Catholic in membership. This was probably true of the Irish Volunteers, founded in Rochester in 1827, and disbanded only in 1847. There were also Catholic members in other military organizations of Rochester, the Williams Light Infantry, for example. German Catholics like George Shale belonged to the German Grenadiers (1840); German Catholics like Louis

Ernst joined the German Union Guards (1848). But membership in these two German national units of Rochester was open to both non-Catholics and Catholics.

When the Mexican War broke out in 1847, the Government did not call up the militia regiments as such. Nevertheless, of the three hundred who enlisted in Rochester, a good many must have been former militiamen. Although volunteers were for the most part assigned to various regiments, the company of the 10th Volunteers formed at Rochester by Captain Caleb Wilder managed to retain its identity as the "Rochester Company." It was sent to Mexico and spent from July, 1847, to June, 1848, just south of the Rio Grande; but it never tasted actual battle.

Several Catholics from the Rochester neighborhood donned their nation's uniform on this occasion. Andrew Toal of Spencerport was a member of the Marine Corps. There were also Irishmen in the "Rochester Company." Wilder's first lieutenant in Mexico—and his former fellow-soldier in the Williams Light Infantry—was Edward McGarry, who was subsequently an Indian fighter, and a member of the California State legislature and State senate.[31] The known presence of Catholics in Wilder's unit may have persuaded Father Bernard O'Reilly, pastor of St. Patrick's Church in Rochester, to visit the company in its Mexican camp in July, 1847. The Rochester priest had a brother who had recently died in Matamoras, Mexico, after spending many prosperous years in Mexico as a merchant. Father O'Reilly was obliged to make the long trip from Rochester in order to take care of the deceased man's estate. Since the 10th Regiment was encamped near Matamoras, he took occasion of his visit to preach to its officers and soldiers on July 10th.[32]

Upstate Irishmen organized a number of new militia companies in the 1850's. The Shields Guards of Auburn came into being in 1853, the Emmett Guards of Corning in 1857. The Washington Life Guards, an independent Rochester company (1855-1858), seem to have been of the same category.[33] Were the "Irish Wideawakes," as well? Names which first appeared on the rosters of these military organizations frequently reappeared on the muster rolls of the Civil War.

The Civil War: the "irrepressible conflict." It was at Rochester, on October 25, 1858, that Governor William E. Seward first pronounced that prophetic phrase. During the three decades before the outbreak of the war, western New York had reechoed with the demands of "professional" abolitionists, and western New Yorkers had approved the abolitionists' ideals if not always their methods. Rochester's great Negro journalist, Frederick Douglass, had likewise been an active promoter of the "Underground Railroad," which was engaged in spiriting runaway slaves north into Canada. There is no evidence that Catholics in the twelve counties played any part either in abolitionism or the fugitive slave underground. As a matter of fact, in 1857, the *Rochester Democrat* twitted the "Romanists" for being "generally on the side of Slaveholders." Father Daniel Moore, the well-informed and patriotic pastor of St. Mary's Church, did not let the charge pass unchallenged. He wrote in reply that Catholics *were* opposed to slavery, slavery of all kinds. But they advocated ending Negro slavery by non-violent and legal means, although if it came to a question of national unity, they were ready to defend the Union even with their lives.[34]

This was indeed the stand taken by the Catholic hierarchy throughout the country. They expressed it in a national pastoral letter of May, 1858, at a time when the whole slavery issue had become so intensely political that an ecclesiastical commitment upon it would have been out of place. Bishop Timon's actions reflected the same wisdom. On October 30, 1860, he warned his clergy, gathered together in conference, against mingling in political matters.[35] Two days later he issued a circular letter to his diocese in which he urged the faithful, on the eve of the crucial presidential election, to vote honestly and according to their consciences. January 4, 1861, by order of the outgoing president, James Buchanan, was a day of nationwide "humiliation, fasting and prayer" for the continued peace of the whole country. Seconding the president's effort, Timon, in a pastoral of December 15, 1860, ordered that the collect for peace be recited at every Mass until March 19, 1861, and that Archbishop John Carroll's prayer for American civil officials be read each Sunday after the high Mass.

Unfortunately, the nation was not ready for the peace which it sought. On April 12, 1861, Confederate troops fired on Fort Sumter, North Carolina, and the Civil War began. It is not without interest that among the brave defenders of the invested fortress was a Rochester Catholic. Irish-born James Gibbons (1833?-1910) was a professional soldier in Captain Abner Doubleday's Company "E," 1st Artillery; and he played a brave part in the famous engagement.[36]

On April 15th, the new president, Abraham Lincoln, called for 75,000 volunteers. The fall of Sumter had caused a wave of patriotic horror to sweep across the North, and in city and town protestation and volunteering became the gestures of the hour. What was remarkable about the rallies in so many localities was the common front adopted by native Americans and "adopted citizens" against the enemies of national union.[37] When James Gibbons, granted a furlough to visit his wife and child, arrived in Rochester on April 22nd, he was given a grand surprise welcome at the station by the Light Guard and the Perkins Band. An immigrant, yet the lion of the day! At Palmyra, too, the wild warnings of "Angel Gabriel" had been forgotten. Villagers Catholic and non-Catholic foregathered to listen to stirring orations. One of the speakers, the immigrant James O'Dwyer, fervently declared: "I had a country once—I left it for a better . . . . It is the freest and the best on earth. And now, in this hour of our country's calamity, I offer all that I am, all that I have, to the last cent, for it has been given to me by this country, for the national defence."[38]

Catholic volunteers were numerous in the companies that formed in answer to Lincoln's first call. The federal government was unwilling to accept the militia organizations as such, but many of the militiamen sooner or later joined volunteer units, and not a few of these former citizen-soldiers helped to organize volunteer regiments.

The 13th New York State Infantry, formed in late April, 1861, was made up of soldiers from Rochester and vicinity. William F. Tulley was commissioned captain of Company "I," and Thomas Davis, of Company "H." Davis' company was subsequently transferred to the 26th Regiment. Both of these Rochester companies had a number of Irish Catholic members, and there was also a scattering of Irishmen in the other companies. Most of the local German Catholics who enlisted seem to have joined Captain Adolph Nolte's German company, Company "C."[39] Andrew Drost, Jacob Glass, Nicholas Martin, and Michael Schlaeger, who lie buried in Rochester's Holy Sepulchre Cemetery, belonged to Company "C" of the 13th. But there were also German Catholics in Company "I"—Jacob Ovenburg and E. Frankenberger, for example.

Owen Gavigan (1823?-1897), an officer in the Auburn Shields Guards, recruited Company "D" of the 19th Volunteer Infantry (which on December 11, 1861, was turned into the 3rd Regiment of Light Artillery). Many Catholics from the Auburn district enrolled in the 19th. The "Ontario Regiment" — the 33rd New York State Volunteers — also had an extensive Catholic personnel. Patrick McGraw of Seneca Falls headed Company "K." Company "C," the "Waterloo Wright Guards," and some of the other companies of the 33rd likewise had Catholic members. In the Southern Tier, there seem to have been some Catholics in the 23rd (Elmira and vicinity) and in the Ithaca Volunteers — Companies "A" and "I" of the 32nd Infantry.

Although one Catholic pastor in the twelve counties declined to urge volunteering from the pulpit, in general the Catholic priests of the area supported enlistment, sometimes with great enthusiasm. At Ithaca, Father Bernard McCool erected a new ninety-foot flagpole on his church property. Then when on May 9, 1861, Captain John Whitlock's Company "A" marched by the church to the railroad station, the Catholic parishioners ran up the Stars and Stripes on their new pole and fired a cannon in salute. The delighted soldiers replied with a cheer. At Phelps, in Ontario County, Father Francis Clark is said to have held special farewell services in St. Francis Church for the parish boys bound for the front; and Father James Early of Canandaigua was a featured speaker at local wartime rallies.[40]

The pastors at Seneca Falls and Auburn really outdid themselves in patriotic deeds. On April 28, 1861, Father Edward McGowan of Seneca Falls had a special church rite for his Catholic military men. McGraw's company of "Irish Volunteers" strode briskly from armory to church with flags floating and bands playing. The choir sang "The Red White, and Blue" (!) and the pastor delivered a stirring address. Father McGowan also spoke at the fair grounds on May 22nd, when the village bade its volunteers a formal farewell. The ladies of Seneca Falls gave the Company a flag, and McGowan presented Captain McGraw with a service sword, the gift of the villagers. In bestowing the sword, the priest told the Captain that he was confident he was putting it "in the keeping of a brave man." "I trust I am no coward," McGraw replied with soldierly brevity; "I'll do my duty."[41]

Even after their departure for the South, the pastor of Seneca Falls maintained his interest in the soldiers and their families. By the end of November, he had distributed some two thousand dollars to the families of the volunteers, and as Christmas approached he urged his parishioners to send their military men gift-packages of stockings and gloves.[42]

At Auburn, Father Michael Creedon, pastor of Holy Family Church, gave to Owen Gavigan's company of volunteers his fullest support. Creedon himself, it is said, had once been an officer in the British army.[43] He was also esteemed for his American patriotism by no less a judge than William E. Seward, his fellow Auburnian and Lincoln's Secretary of State.[44]

In the address which he gave to his parishioners on April 21, 1861, it was both the veteran and the patriot in Father Creedon that spoke out. There were, he said, only three types of citizens in his audience: those who loved their country and were willing to defend it; those whom age and responsibilities prevented from taking up arms; and those who were "traitors or craven cowards." He called upon the men of the first class to enlist.

The young men responded magnificently. Sixty arose, followed Owen Gavigan out of the little old church into the unfinished present church, and signed the roll. Forming then a double file, and headed by a flag, they marched off to the armory to enlist. By nightfall the company was complete.[45]

Like Father McGowan, Father Creedon followed the adventures of his parish Company with paternal interest. He visited the men at their Elmira rendezvous and later on at the front.[46] When the three-month term of enlistment was over, the Government commanded them to continue in the ranks. This possibility had unfortunately not been explained to the Auburn volunteers at the time of their enrollment, and most of them rebelled at the command. Creedon and Major General Nathaniel P. Banks finally succeeded in convincing most of the indignant soldiers to abide by the order.[47]

If the Catholic pastors of the twelve counties displayed such loyalty to the Union, it was with the knowledge that their bishop was of like mind. Early in May, 1861, Bishop Timon permitted some friends to float a flag from his residence. (Not from the cathedral, for he was unwilling to do anything which might discourage even a secessionist from entering the church.) A crowd gathered in front of the house when the flag was mounted, and the Bishop—surely not unprepared—came out and addressed them. Reiterating the stand he had taken in a sermon of April 21st, he declared: "Our country it is our duty not to question but to obey." ". . . The South began the war," he pointed out; "the North cannot back out without forfeiting its manhood, its honor, and its glorious future." "If," said he, "a war must be waged, let it be waged with vigor; thus alone can it be rendered less bloody, thus alone can it end speedily in peace."[48]

These were strong sentiments to come from one who had spent most of his adult life in slave States. They were also sincere sentiments. Throughout the war he was strongly anti-secessionist; he was a good friend of Secretary of State Seward; and when he was in Washington on July 13, 1861, Seward presented him to Abraham Lincoln.[49] Timon's outspoken pro-Union stand did much to allay the fears of upstate New Yorkers that when America's moment of decision should arrive, the "authoritarian" Catholic Church would reveal itself as pro-slavery.

Most of the pioneer regiments of western New York were mustered in at Elmira. The mobilization camps set up here could accommodate a large body of soldiers, although the armory at nearby Corning was used on at least one occasion to house a few overflow companies.[50] Mobilized at Elmira, the volunteers were sent by rail to the South, eager to fight but poorly trained and poorly equipped for battle. The 13th and the 27th N.Y.S. Volunteers, both from the Rochester area, arrived in Virginia early enough to participate in the first battle of Bull Run on July 21, 1861.

In the hopeless, tragic confusion of that engagement, the home regiments were not wanting in courage. The boys of the 13th made a good showing. Color Sergeant Daniel Sharpe of the Town of Greece bore the regimental flag through shot and shell. But there were also several casualties in the unit.[51]. Twelve were killed; and Charles Buckley, a resident of Rochester's "Dublin," was seriously wounded in the shoulder.[52]

Discharged for disability, Buckley returned to Rochester. When he got off the train on August 3rd—the city's first soldier to be wounded in action—he was given a splendid military welcome.[53] But the defeat at Bull Run had already sobered those at the front and those at home. This war, they saw, was no militia parade or military game. It was bitter and bloody and promised to be long.

Many Catholics from the twelve counties later enlisted in—or were drafted into—various branches of the armed forces, the Navy included. Not all on the Union side, by the way. Two local Catholics are known to have soldiered in the Confederate ranks.

In Peter Bacon's case, it was all a mistake. Peter, a Dansvillian, happened to be in the South when the war broke out. He was coerced into the Rebel ranks, and wore the Southern uniform for eighteen months. Then he somehow got north to St. Paul, Minnesota, and, to right matters, enlisted in the Union army.[54]

Edward McCrahon of Fishers Station, Ontario County, also joined the Southern forces, but under no compulsion. An agent of the Rochester nurserymen Ellwanger and Barry, he was traveling for them in Louisiana when hostilities broke out. The New Orleans Irish must have captivated Ed by their Confederate enthusiasm, for he soon signed up with Company "D." of Harry Hays' 7th Louisiana Infantry. The 7th fought battle after battle, from First Bull Run to Rappahannock Station, mostly under "Stonewall" Jackson. Ed was with the outfit until Rappahannock Station, where he was captured by Federal forces on November 7, 1863. It turned out that his younger brother, Alexander McCrahon, was in the same division that had taken Eddie captive. Previous to that, when Alec was a member of the New York State 108th, the brothers had opposed each other, without being aware of it, at Antietam and Gettysburg. So even at such an unexpected place as Fishers, New York, the Civil War had set brother against brother.[55]

Several of the upstate regiments which were organized in late 1861 and in the three years that followed had Catholic names on their muster roles. This was true, for example, of the 107th, mustered in on August 13, 1862. It was also true of another Southern Tier outfit, the 161st, formed on the following October 27th. Some of the officers and men of the 161st were former members of the Emmett Guard of Corning. Lieutenant Charles Kelly of Penn Yan helped recruit Company "M" of the 148th. But when that regiment was mobilized on September 14, 1862, his company was transferred, becoming Company "C" of the 44th.[56] The 108th (formed August 16-18, 1862) and the 136th (formed September 25-26, 1862) likewise had their Catholic soldiers. The units with the largest percentage of Catholic personnel seem to have been the 105th (March 15, 1862), the 140th (September 13, 1862), and the 188th (October 4-22, 1864).

The 105th began recruitment at Rochester in November, 1861. It was intended to be the "Irish Brigade," and Father Daniel Moore, pastor of St. Mary's Church, was scheduled to be its chaplain. But when only three companies had been filled, the military authorities suddenly ordered these three to consolidate with seven companies just organized at LeRoy in nearby Genesee County. Father Moore did not receive the chaplaincy, probably because the LeRoy companies already had a chaplain of their own. (But Rochester physician James W. Casey did go along as assistant surgeon.) The Rochester Irishmen were quite unhappy over the turn of events, and they had been at the Avon rendezvous only twenty minutes when they got into a free-for-all with the "LeRoy Methodists." Having thus purged their resentment, the "Irish Brigaders" made friends with their LeRoy adversaries, and both teams formed a common front against the enemy.[57]

Commanding officer of the 140th was Colonel Patrick Henry O'Rorke (1837-1863). O'Rorke was Rochester's most promising military figure. At his graduation from West Point in 1861, he had ranked first in the class. His lieutenant-colonel was Louis Ernst (1825-1892), a German-born Rochester toolmaker, who had held the rank of lieutenant-colonel in the old 54th New York State Militia. A large number of Irish Catholics and a fair number of German Catholics from in and around Rochester signed up with the 140th.[58]

Another Rochesterian organized and led the 188th. Colonel John McMahon (1834-1891), formerly a captain in the Rochester City

Cadets, had risen from private to captain in the 105th, and to major in the 94th, with which the 105th was subsequently consolidated. Many German Catholics from Wayland and Perkinsville enlisted in the McMahon regiment.

We may assume, according to the law of averages, that some of the immigrant soldiers from the twelve counties became deserters or were "bounty-jumpers." One gets the general impression, however, that the majority were faithful to duty. A number of them served with distinction. The vast majority fought in the ranks, rising no higher than sergeant. But there was a small percentage who entered the armed forces as officers or later won commissions. Louis Ernst, whose lieutenant colonelcy was apparently the highest rank attained by a local German Catholic, illustrates the first type. John McMahon, who illustrates the second type, rose from recruit to colonel, and, on his discharge, to a brigadier-general by brevet. A modest man, he never answered to any title higher than colonel; but he could not prevent his heirs from carving on his tombstone the highest rank achieved by any Catholic soldier from the Rochester district.[59] Distinction of another sort came to Dr. Richard Curran of Seneca Falls (who later moved to Rochester and became its mayor). As assistant surgeon of the 33rd N.Y. State Volunteers, he displayed great heroism at Antietam on September 17, 1862, taking care of the wounded under fire in that bloody field of battle. For this courageous devotion to duty he was later awarded the Congressional Medal of Honor.[60]

Catholic soldiers from the twelve counties fell victim in due proportions to the misfortunes of war. Some were imprisoned, some were wounded or disabled, some sacrificed their lives.

Those imprisoned in such Southern jails as Libby Prison and Andersonville Prison might accept their fate philosophically or reject it violently. Sexagenarian Michael Hughes, who three decades before had been the pioneer teacher at St. Patrick's School in Rochester, typified the philosophical prisoner. While locked up in Libby Prison, Richmond, he passed his time by writing poems which he pasted up on the prison wall. Family tradition says that General "Stonewall" Jackson, seeing the verses, invited Hughes to become his secretary. But however calm he was as a prisoner, the poet was no turncoat, and patriotically declined.[61] His exact opposite in temperament was Alexander Connolly, a spirited seventeen-year-old of the 108th regiment. Connolly was sentenced to the frightful concentration camp at Andersonville, Georgia; but the prison authorities had no reason to rejoice in his presence. After organizing breakouts from the camp and four times attempting to escape, this fantastically daring youngster made good his fifth attempt.[62]

Not all the upstate men detained at Andersonville were so fortunate. With the war's many wounded and incapacitated we must also list those who when finally released were living skeletons. It took long nursing in such hospitals as St. Mary's, Rochester, to bring back to health these shadows of men.

And among the dead there were also those who died in the Andersonville prison. One of them was Felix McGuire, Jr., the son of the patriarch of Paddy Hill.[63]

Many were killed in battle or died of wounds. The first wartime military funeral which took place in Elmira was that of Theodore Byrne, the teen-aged son of John Byrne the coppersmith, who was laid low at Gettysburg on July 2, 1863.[64] St. Agnes Church in Aurora lost a parishioner at the same place on the following day: Bartholomew Donahue was one of the ten Aurora parishioners who gave their lives in the war.[65] Martin Mahar and William McMahon of Corning, members of the 86th Volunteers, died in the Battle of the Wilderness and at Spotsylvania, respectively, on May 12, 1864.[66] And there were other victims from elsewhere in the twelve counties. Few if any Catholic parishes in western New York were wholly preserved from the grim calamities of the conflict.

Rochester Catholics offered up some of their best officers to the cause. Captain Thomas Davis of the 26th fell at Second Bull Run, on August 30, 1862.[67] Lieutenant Charles Buckley of the 105th (late hero of the 13th), died at Antietam on September 17th of the same year.[68] Captain Joseph E. Conway of the 1st Veteran Cavalry was mortally wounded at Martinsburg, West Virginia, on the 25th of July, 1864.[69] Mosby's Confederate guerrillas had already killed another Rochester cavalry officer at Kabletown, Virginia, on March 10, 1864: the dashing, beloved Captain Jerry Sullivan, who belonged to the same regiment as Conway.[70]

But greater than these and the rest of the local Catholic casualties was the loss of Colonel O'Rorke. Irish-born but American-bred (a Rochesterian since he was five years old), Pat had led his classes in the Rochester public schools before receiving the assignment to the United States Military Academy. Graduated at the very start of the war, he had merited rapid promotion. Although he was only twenty-five when named colonel of the 140th, he quickly built up the regiment into an effective fighting unit.

It was as commander of the 140th that he entered the Battle of Gettysburg. On July 2, 1863, he led his men in the occupation of Little Round Top—a rocky eminence which formed a crucial link in the line of Union defenses. But he and his troops had scarcely reached their goal and swarmed over the crest toward the enemy, when O'Rorke, sword in hand, was struck down at their head.

Rochester bestowed on this, its greatest Civil War hero, the fullest military honors. The Count of Paris, who had observed the battle, later wrote of the young colonel: "He had been destined, in the judgment of all his comrades, for the most elevated positions of the army."

God had chosen rather to leave to Rochester the memory of a gallant soldier and a true gentleman. And O'Rorke's family romance gave his history a storybook ending. He and his boyhood friend, Clara Bishop, had been married in St. Bridget's Church on July 9, 1862. After Patrick's death, a scant twelve months later, Mrs. O'Rorke became a member of the Religious of the Sacred Heart, and as a teaching nun spent the rest of her days in the cloister.[71]

While the military men were fighting and dying in the field, Bishop Timon was trying to solve the varied problems that the war gave rise to.

For one thing, the government did not provide enough chaplains for Catholic servicemen. More than once Timon pleaded with the Washington authorities, but to no avail. The draft of 1863 raised still another issue of concern to his flock. The draft law, as framed, worked to the disadvantage of the poor—which meant, most of all, the immigrants—in that it exempted from actual service any draftee who could afford to pay for a substitute. Many of the Irish workingmen of New York City were already feeling the strong competition of Negroes in the unskilled labor market. The draft capped the climax, and in July, 1863, New York's immigrant laborers exploded into devastating riot. It took the eloquence of the failing Archbishop Hughes to remind them of civil obedience, and the efforts of federal troops to reestablish order.[72] The Bishop of Buffalo was apprehensive that a similar flare-up might occur in western New York State when conscription was commenced among his own people. Therefore, on July 16th, he addressed a pastoral to his diocesans, urging them to accept the draft law peacefully and to lodge their trust in God.[73] There was no rioting. The people were resentful, but not disorderly.

Matters became a little complicated when four of Bishop Timon's diocesan priests were drafted. Three of these were stationed within the present Rochester Diocese: Fathers Dennis English of Penn Yan,

Patrick Lee of Clifton Springs, and Serge De Stchoulepnikoff of Dansville. The conscription law seems to have made no provision for the exemption of clergymen. Timon was evidently willing to make a test case of it, for he went to Albany to ask Governor Horatio Seymour about the priests. But the Governor advised the Bishop simply to pay for substitutes, and Father Creedon counselled him to forget about appealing to the federal government. It must have been the principle at stake rather than the expense involved that troubled Bishop Timon. The faithful of each priest's parish were quite ready to pay the exemption fee.[74]

The Bishop of Buffalo by no means forgot to urge upon his people the charities which war necessitated. In a pastoral of 1862, he ordered that in all diocesan schools and orphanages for girls a period be set aside each day for making and packing surgical dressings of lint for wounded soldiers.[75] In May, 1864, at the request of Pope Pius IX, he forwarded to the United States Sanitary Commission a papal check for five hundred dollars to be applied to the care of military casualties.[76]

The Elmira prison camp was another object of the Bishop's solicitude. In midsummer 1864, the government had turned one of the old marshalling camps at Elmira into a concentration camp. The camp was not adequate for the twelve thousand debilitated Confederate prisoners who were consigned to it during the next twelve months, and the death there of almost three thousand inmates won for it the title "Andersonville of the North." The Bishop paid the camp a personal visit in September, 1864, and straightway sent an order to New York for a hundred dollars worth of religious books to be given to the prisoners. Meanwhile, the pastor of SS. Peter and Paul Church in Elmira, Father Martin Kavanagh, succeeded in winning the grudging permission of the commandant to celebrate Mass once a week for the Catholic Southerners, provided that the Mass was not on Sunday. Father Kavanagh showed a courage worthy of his bishop in administering the last rites even to plague-ridden inmates of the prison camp.[77]

Timon scarcely needed to encourage the charity of the Sisters at Rochester's St. Mary's Hospital. Sister Hieronymo, the superior, was ready to do whatever she might for the suffering soldiery. As early as July, 1861, one of the Rochester Sisters of Charity was briefly detached and sent to Albany to nurse the stricken volunteers at that marshalling point. During 1862, St. Mary's welcomed a number of sick and wounded servicemen, committed to it, for the most part, by the local Overseer of the Poor. Then on March 10, 1863, the Hospital signed a contract with the federal government which gave it the rank of a "U.S.A. General Hospital." But it was not until June, 1864, that the government began to send it large consignments of wounded and ailing federal soldiers. From that time onward, St. Mary's shared with the newer Rochester City Hospital (the old Rochester General Hospital) the responsibility for hundreds of men whose homes were in western New York. By the close of the war St. Mary's alone reported that it had received 2,500 soldiers. This total probably did not include the servicemen cared for before the signing of the federal contract in 1863. The Sisters of Charity, true to their tradition, had performed their task well. But their success owed much to the constant aid given by Rochester citizens, Catholic and non-Catholic.[78]

Early in April, 1865, the Rochester *Union and Advertiser* lamented the death of "another brave soldier" from the city. Captain George French of the 107th Regiment was killed in action at Five Forks, Virginia, on April 1st. He was buried from St. Patrick's Church on April 9th.[79]

The very day of French's burial, General Robert E. Lee surrendered to General Ulysses S. Grant at Appomattox Court House, Virginia. The dreadful conflict was finally over. Several western New York regiments had participated in the last weary battles, and some were on hand for the capitulation. Captain James T. Reilly of the 188th wrote home a letter describing the surrender. Lee and Longstreet, he said, looked "careworn and sad." The Southern soldiers, on the other hand, seemed happy to have the war ended. The 188th gave them a square meal and a spot of whiskey.[80]

The nation had scarcely begun to rejoice when on Holy Saturday, April 15th, the tragic news of Lincoln's assassination the night before came burning along the telegraph wires.

Lincoln had never been universally popular. On the occasion of his death, Michael Hughes of Rochester, Catholic schoolmaster and army veteran, wrote a blistering poem *denouncing* the murdered president. Luckily this was never published.[81] Father Edward McGowan of St. Mary's Church, Rochester, spoke with a more Catholic voice. In his Easter sermon, the patriotic former pastor of Seneca Falls made allowance for widespread (and largely political) opposition to President Lincoln. But he entreated all to bury their prejudices in the face of "this national disgrace." Of the assassin he asked: "Can any punishment, then, be too severe for such a wretch?" But it was Bishop Timon who spoke for the whole diocese. He expressed public grief over the nation's loss and ordered public memorial services in all his churches. He also urged prayers for the recovery of Secretary of State William H. Seward, whom John Wilkes Booth's fellow-conspirator, Lewis Paine, had attempted to murder on the night that Lincoln was shot.[82]

Abraham Lincoln's funeral train passed through Rochester on April 27th, en route to Illinois. Although it stopped only briefly and at the inconvenient hour of 3:20 a.m., there was a dense crowd gathered at the Rochester station to pay a last tribute to the martyred president.[83]

It later transpired that upstate New York had had an incidental connection with the anti-Lincoln conspiracy, through John Harrison Surratt (1843-1916). Surratt was a Catholic Marylander who out of devotion to the Southern cause had served as a Confederate spy. After Lincoln's death, he and his mother, Mrs. Mary Surratt, were both charged with complicity in the assassination. Mrs. Surratt was tried, declared guilty (on the basis of insufficient evidence), and hanged. John fled to Europe, but was eventually seized and brought back to stand trial in 1867.

In the trial—which did not result in Surratt's conviction—it came out that he had not been in Washington the night of the murder, but in Elmira, engaged in an espionage assignment in connection with the prison camp. While in Elmira on April 15th, he maintained, he had heard of the assassination, and had set out at once for Canada. But because there were no trains available over the week end, he had lodged at Canandaigua's Webster House (later called the Pickering Hotel) until Monday morning, April 17th. He went to Mass on Easter Sunday at St. Mary's Church in Canandaigua. What would the parishioners of the old Saltonstall Street church have thought, that sad Easter morn, if they had known the identity of the gaunt young stranger who knelt among them?[84]

The end of the Civil War was the beginning of a new era. Soon the district servicemen who had survived, Irish, German, or other, returned to their homes to resume their civilian careers. Even "Stonewall Jackson" McCrahon, the Confederate from Fishers, was ready to renew his earlier association with the New York Central Railroad—provided he could still debate the old campaigns with his brother Alec and with any other Billy Yank who wanted to argue.

We have given much space to the Civil War, but for a very good reason. This was the last *great* American war fought principally by volunteer armies. During the decades before it broke out, nativists had persuaded American non-Catholics that Catholic immigrants could never be loyal Americans. How startled the old-stock Americans must then have been when they saw the "adopted citizens" rally with such conviction to the defense of the Union. "We were surprised," said Bishop McQuaid years later, "at the number of friends Catholics had in those days." It is true that Catholic patriotism during the war did not destroy the fortress of American nativism. But it did make the first irreparable breach in its walls.

3. JOHN TIMON IN RETROSPECT.

The pioneer bishop of Buffalo died in his see-city on April 16, 1867, two years after the close of the Civil War. He had headed his diocese just one week short of twenty years.

"Tireless" and "indefatigable" were the adjectives which came most promptly to the lips of John Timon's eulogists. To judge from his own diary, a record of incessant pastoral activity, Timon found in apostolic diligence a means of both doing his duty and performing salutary penance. When he chronicles the trials which often beset him, one can almost sense a joy at having been allowed these crosses. Take, for instance, the note about his journey to dedicate the new church at Trumansburg, Tompkins County, in April, 1857:

> . . . reach landing [on a Cayuga Lake boat which he had boarded at Seneca Falls] at 6-1/2 PM. No stage [-coach available]. Dreadful storm of snow, 2 feet 7 in. snow on ground. Start on foot, very hard, painful and dangerous, 2 miles up hill 600 ft. high. Reach Truemansburg [*sic*] at 8-1/2 PM . . . April 21. Bless new Church. Mass . . .

In addition to establishing and supervising parishes and schools, religious communities and charitable institutions, to giving sermons, lectures, retreats and missions, Buffalo's first Catholic bishop also issued many formal directives to guide his people in their spiritual and moral life. Many of these directives were published in the form of decrees at the synods which he held almost annually with his priests.

The synod of October, 1856, was especially memorable. It authorized the institution in each parish of the Society for the Propagation of the Faith, the Church's international mission-aid organization. It also inaugurated the Forty Hours' Devotion to the Blessed Sacrament. At least from August 8, 1857 onward, the *Buffalo Catholic Sentinel* published a list stating where in the Diocese the Forty Hours was being observed each week. Both the Propagation of the Faith and the Forty Hours' Devotion continued in existence in the twelve eastern counties when they became a part of the Diocese of Rochester.[85]

Strongly loyal to the Holy See, John Timon strengthened the bonds which linked the Pope with his distant American diocese. The Bishop went to Rome in 1854 to attend Pope Pius IX's formal definition of the dogma of Mary's immaculate conception. On leaving Rome after another visit in 1858, he bore a special oral communication from the Holy Father to Emperor Napoleon III.[86] He last visited the Eternal City in 1862, invited by the Pope to attend the canonization of twenty-six Japanese martyrs. At each departure from Buffalo, his people gave him a ceremonious *au revoir;* each return among them was publicly celebrated. After he arrived home, the papacy became for some time the main subject of his sermons and lectures, and wherever he went about the Diocese, he used the privilege given him by the Vicar of Christ to bestow the papal blessing. From time to time, Pope Pius IX also made jubilee indulgences available to the faithful. On these occasions Timon authorized the observances of the jubilee throughout his diocese.

In 1860, the King of Sardinia, Victor Emmanuel II, by means of diplomatic and military aggression, extended his jurisdiction over several small Italian states. One of these was the Kingdom of the Two Sicilies, a realm indirectly subject to the Holy See. Of the other states, three were provinces of the papal kingdom itself. Despoiled thus of its vassal state and of three constituent provinces, the Papal States was reduced to the single province of Rome—a district which the Italian monarchy also aspired to possess. Pius IX, unable to defend his small but ancient domain against the spoliation, turned to all the faithful for support and prayers.

On January 19, 1860, the bishops of the ecclesiastical province of New York issued a joint pastoral letter denouncing Italy's aggression.[87] In his own diocese, Bishop Timon instructed each parish to take up a special Easter collection for the Holy Father, and to write to His Holiness a letter of sympathy. The invitation was gladly heeded. The letter sent by St. Joseph's Church, Rochester, had 2,830 signatures appended, and the parish collection amounted to almost $500.00.[88] Auburn Catholics drew up their own communication, as did those of Corning, Elmira, and, presumably, the rest of the congregations in the Diocese.[89] All told, 25,691 names footed the Buffalo diocesan protest.[90] Pius IX answered Timon, on May 24, 1860, with a special letter of thanks. He was grateful, he said, for the offering, of which the first installment of $4,300.00 had arrived; and he was deeply consoled by the loyalty of the Buffalo diocesans.[91]

As bishop, John Timon did not simply administer his diocese, he *ruled* it. Himself a member and former superior of a religious order, he was perhaps too prone to expect from his priests and people unquestioning compliance. As one writer has said, "he was pastor of every parish."[92] Although Timon was most paternal with the clergy, he did not allow them much initiative. But since many of the early diocesan priests were not well trained, his policy of frequent transfers may have been well-advised.

He was especially strict in three matters: alcoholic drinks, indecorous funerals, and obedience to church regulations.

Timon himself was a firm teetotaler. He seems to have used whiskey only on doctor's orders, though he also tried it once as a *liniment*! Whiskey had been the downfall of many an Irish immigrant, and his Irish people needed to be reminded of this again and again. Thus, for instance, in his pastoral for St. Patrick's Day, 1857, he said: "We exhort all the pious and good to pray that no Irishman indulge in liquor next Tuesday [March 17th], that no Irishman make the holy faithful [day?] of Ireland's Apostle become a day of scandal and of sin, a festival for hell, and not for heaven."[93]

Drinking at wakes he also deplored. In fact, John Timon deplored the general decrease of reverence at the rites for the dead. Riding to funerals was becoming a symbol of status, and the popularity of a dead man was rated according to the number of carriages that followed his hearse. Families which could ill-afford it felt impelled to spend hard-earned money, not to aid the impoverished kin of the deceased, but to rent a barouche! The ride to the cemetery had thus become an ostentation. Besides, the riders often carried on most inappropriately. They behaved badly en route to the graveyard, and then raced their horses back to the stable.

The abuse was not limited to the Buffalo Diocese, but had become widespread, and called forth the protests and proclamations of more than one bishop. Timon dealt with the issue on several occasions. As early as his synod of 1854, he ordered that the number of hacks in the funeral procession be reduced. In the synod of 1858, he denounced unseemly gaiety during the funeral procession. In 1859, he ordered that there be no more than four carriages—five if the pall-bearers rode— at any burial. Although some bishops had limited funeral carriages to two, Bishop Timon's ruling was still quite stringent. But it was effective, and when in 1865 he asked his priests if they did not think it time to rescind the decree, they favored its retention. He also urged them on that occasion to prevent bands of music from playing at funeral corteges.[94]

Timon was accustomed to use many stiff canonical penalties in order to sanction church law and punish its infraction. Temporary suspension of the clergy from their religious functions was so frequently imposed as to cause some amusement. The Bishop employed a somewhat similar penalty against the laity at times, excluding them from Holy Communion, for, say, a year. Excommunication and the graver punishments were likewise resorted to when deemed necessary.

Bishop Timon's mode of enforcing the funeral rules is a case in point. In 1857, he decreed the major excommunication for those who by drunkenness and quarrels gave scandal at wakes and funerals. Priests who offended against the burial regulations were also warned that they would receive a punishment tailored to their guilt. Nor did the Bishop make easy exceptions to these laws. When, for instance, the heroic Colonel Patrick H. O'Rorke was given his grand military funeral from St. Bridget's Church in Rochester, many more carriages turned out than the Bishop's law permitted. This was, indeed, a civic as well as a religious event, and the pastor, Father William Payne, although he realized that the letter of the law was being transgressed, had gone ahead because he considered it to be a special case. Timon did *not* consider it a special case. Father Payne he suspended for a month; and to Father Joseph Jacobs, the Redemptorist who had preached at the grave, he gave a similar, if somewhat lighter, sentence.[95]

Something can be said for the opinion that John Timon was too uncompromising a disciplinarian. But he conscientiously strove to be just in dealing with a people who, for all their substantial faith, sometimes displayed an unruliness which only severity could correct. "He was firm," recalled the annalist of St. Joseph's in Rochester, "so that he could never be diverted from his decisions." "But," the Redemptorist added, "he was also full of charity."[96] Whenever it became plain to Timon that he had committed an injustice or an uncharity, he did not delay to make amends.

A man of versatility was John Timon of Buffalo. He was well read, an able literary stylist, a lucid but ever courteous publicist, a man whose social address made him acceptable—when duty brought him into their presence—to kings and presidents and civic leaders. Had he remained in the secular world, Timon could no doubt have attained prominence in almost any field of enterprise he chose. But his was a definitely religious destiny: earnestly to sanctify himself and the spiritual flock confided to him. By his unwearying effort he gave shape not only to the Diocese of Buffalo but to the Church in those counties which were to become a part of the Diocese of Rochester. And by his care and instruction—yes, and by his fatherly discipline—he helped to temper, in his uprooted immigrant children, precisely those crudities which most antagonized their new-found neighbors, the natives of the American republic.

CHAPTER FIVE

A DIOCESE FOR ROCHESTER

IN THE COURSE of a sermon which he delivered in St. Patrick's Church, Rochester, on September 9, 1866, Bishop Timon disclosed that the Holy See would soon establish a new diocese in western New York with Rochester as its see-city.[1]

In a sense, the announcement was premature, for the American hierarchy had not yet requested Rome for the diocese. That request was to be voiced by the Second Plenary Council of Baltimore, which convened from October 7th to October 21st, 1866. On October 8th, John Timon, now failing in health, asked the bishops of the New York Province to approve two petitions which he presented to them: first, that he be given a coadjutor bishop to assist him; second, that the eastern section of his diocese be cut off to form a Diocese of Rochester. The Provincial bishops were apparently unwilling to approve the first petition.[2] But they seconded the proposed new diocese and accepted the *terna* of priests recommended by Bishop Timon as candidates for its bishopric. Timon's nominees, listed as was customary in the order of preference, were: Very Reverend James M. Early, a Vicar General of the Buffalo Diocese and pastor of St. Patrick's Church, Rochester; Reverend Martin O'Connor, pastor of St. Bridget's Church in Buffalo; Reverend Joseph McKenna, pastor of St. Mary's Church in Canandaigua.

The Provincial bishops, adding their own advice on the matter, transmitted Timon's petition to the Fathers of the Baltimore Council, and the Fathers sent both papers to Rome. John Timon himself did not live to see the outcome. The Sacred Congregation de Propaganda Fide took up the question of the new diocese only in September, 1867, six months after his death. And it was on January 24, 1868, that Cardinal Alessandro Barnabò, prefect of the Sacred Congregation de Propaganda Fide, wrote to tell the Archbishop of Baltimore that the project had been approved.[3]

In the same letter to Archbishop Spalding, Barnabò announced the men chosen to succeed to Timon's divided jurisdiction. The Very Reverend Stephen Vincent Ryan, C.M., of St. Louis, was to be bishop of Buffalo; and the founding bishop of the Diocese of Rochester was to be the Very Reverend Bernard J. McQuaid, Vicar General of the Diocese of Newark, New Jersey. (Neither appointment was yet official: for both, the official date of appointment was March 3, 1868.)

Quite likely Timon had had Father Ryan in mind as his coadjutor bishop. Both men were Vincentians, and Ryan now held the same office of Visitor which Timon had held when named to Buffalo. But Father McQuaid, whom Bishop Timon had *not* recommended for Rochester, was quite clearly the choice of those bishops of the Province who came from the New York area.

If the Provincial bishops did not accept Bishop Timon's opinions on candidates for the see of Rochester, they did defer to his wishes in delineating the boundaries of the new diocese.[4]

Ten counties were included, it appears, in the original plan: Monroe, Livingston, Wayne, Ontario, Seneca, Cayuga, Yates, and Tompkins, plus Schuyler and Tioga. Since Tioga was bounded on the south by Pennsylvania, an obvious recommendation would have been to add to these ten counties Chemung and Steuben, the two other Southern Tier counties which lay to the west of Tioga and "underpinned" the rest of the designated counties. But Bishop Timon wanted to retain Chemung County for Buffalo; and, for that matter, Schuyler and Tioga Counties as well. It was finally decided to give Rochester the eight first-mentioned counties and to leave Tioga, Chemung, Schuyler and Steuben under the Buffalo jurisdiction. These were the dimensions indicated by Pope Pius IX when, by the apostolic letter *Summi Apostolatus* of March 3, 1868, he established the diocese of "Rochester-in-America."[5]

There were, of course, some arguments in favor of the retention of the Southern Tier by Buffalo. Even then, the Southern Tier belonged to a different economic and cultural area than the Northern Tier, and transportation was better from Buffalo to the southern counties than from Rochester to the southern counties. The Southern Tier might appropriately be constituted a diocese in its own right; but the question of where to locate the see or sees, difficult to answer today, was even more difficult to answer in 1868.

On the other hand, Tioga County was some 140 air miles from Buffalo, as compared to some 105 air miles from Rochester. There was also at least one place, Bernard McQuaid was to point out, where the bishop of Rochester had to cross a portion of the Diocese of Buffalo in order to get from one of his Rochester counties to another. And above all, the eight county solution divided the Catholic population inequitably. In 1868, before the subdivision, the Diocese of Buffalo had an estimated population of 220,000 Catholics. The Diocese of Rochester was given no more than 54,500 of these souls.[6] The city of Buffalo alone had almost that many Catholics!

From the start, Bishop McQuaid protested against the restricted boundaries which had been assigned to his diocese. Eventually his protests were to bear fruit. But this was after all an incidental matter. Having accepted the new assignment, he set about diligently to mould the eight counties entrusted to him into a new diocesan structure.

In this chapter we shall introduce Bernard McQuaid and describe his earliest efforts as the founder of the Rochester Diocese.

1. TWO NEW BISHOPS.

As first bishop of Rochester, McQuaid must be given primary attention during the next few chapters. But Bishop Ryan was to preside over the Catholics of the four Southern Tier counties until those counties were finally aggregated, almost three decades later, to the eight counties of the original diocese of Rochester. Let us therefore glance at the second bishop of Buffalo before we turn to his Rochester colleague.

Stephen Vincent Ryan was the son of an Irish immigrant couple, Martin and Catherine McCarthy Ryan. At the time of his birth, January 1, 1825, the family lived in Almonte, near Perth, Ontario, Canada; but in 1828 they moved to Pottsville, Pennsylvania. When he was fourteen, Stephen entered the Philadelphia diocesan seminary. In 1844, however, he joined the Vincentians, transferred to their seminary "The Barrens" at Perrysville, Missouri, and took his vows in 1846. He was ordained a priest on June 24, 1849.

Young Father Stephen was a wisp of a man with a shock of black hair and steel-rimmed eyeglasses. If his appearance was not prepossessing, his talents were, for he soon proved to be a capable writer, preacher and teacher, and a whole-souled missionary: ascetical, strict, diligent, but withal a good manager and a kindly person. A bare two years after ordination he was appointed president of his order's College of St. Vincent at Cape Girardeau, Missouri. So outstanding was his success, that when he was only thirty-eight he was advanced to the post of Visitor—that is, general superior—of the American branch of the Vincentians. And it was his success as Visitor that prompted the Pope in 1868 to select him to succeed Bishop Timon in Buffalo.

When informed of the papal appointment, Father Ryan, true to his natural modesty, made sincere representations to Archbishop McCloskey of his desire to decline the bishopric. The Archbishop of New York dutifully reported this to the Holy See. But on May 5, 1868,

Cardinal Barnabò wrote to Ryan, whom he addressed as "Bishop-elect of Buffalo", practically ordering him to accept. Commanded thus under obedience, Stephen Ryan, who as a religious had taken a special vow of obedience, accepted the promotion.

On November 8, 1868, Archbishop McCloskey, assisted by Bishop John Loughlin of Brooklyn and the Vincentian Bishop John J. Lynch of Toronto, consecrated the second bishop of Buffalo. The consecration took place in the Buffalo cathedral, (Old) St. Joseph's.

Father Patrick Cronin, the Buffalo journalist, and Bishop Ryan's close friend and biographer, has given us a good picture of Bishop Ryan by pointing out how he contrasted with Bishop Timon. While both men were ardent by nature, Timon could not always control his feelings, whereas Ryan could and did. Timon was a man of impulse, Ryan a man of deliberation. John Timon was an activist, brisk, outgoing; Stephen Ryan was more retiring, scholarly, and careful, despite the firmness of his convictions, to avoid public controversy. What Bishop Ryan may have lacked in nervous effort, he made up for in a calm and gentle dignity which won for him the admiration and reverence of his flock.[7]

When Stephen Vincent Ryan was consecrated, Bernard J. McQuaid knelt among the bishops in the Cathedral, already a seasoned episcopal veteran of five months.

Unlike his Buffalo confrère, and unlike many more of the American bishops of his time, Bernard McQuaid was a native of the United States and of New York City; and of both distinctions he was almost inordinately proud.[8] Although the first written record of his birth gives the date as December 15, 1825, Bishop McQuaid himself set it just two years earlier.[9] His parents were Bernard and Mary Maguire McQuaid, both natives of Ireland. A year or two after young Bernard's birth the family moved to Paulus Hook (now Jersey City), New Jersey, where the father secured employment in a glass factory.

At the time of the McQuaids' arrival in Jersey, there was no Catholic church at Paulus Hook to serve the need of the increasing number of Catholics. It was Bernard McQuaid, Senior, who led the movement to erect a church building. Meanwhile, Bishop John Dubois of New York, whose diocese then included northern New Jersey, promised the Catholics of Paulus Hook a monthly Mass. The first Mass in town was celebrated on November 29, 1829; and the site was the McQuaid residence (which later bore the address of 52 Sussex Street, Jersey City). Bishop McQuaid had a particular reason not to forget the event, for, being only three years old, he had been sent out of the house to make room for the adults, and had had to content himself with watching the mysterious ritual through the shutters.

If the McQuaids were a devout family, they were also a tragic family. Mary McQuaid had died in 1827, and the widower had married again about a year later. Then, in the spring of 1832, Bernard, Senior, himself died, the victim of an assault by a fellow worker. Young Bernard, now around eight, was thus completely orphaned. Nor did his stepmother give him proper parental care and affection. An unsympathetic woman, she treated him so badly that to his dying day Bishop McQuaid could not rid himself of the bitter memories of those desolate months.

Fortunately, there was one gentle friend of his parents who *did* care. On August 20, 1832, Mrs. Philip O'Brien, a warm-hearted New York Irishwoman, took the sad little boy to the Roman Catholic Orphan Asylum on Prince Street in Manhattan, and entrusted him to the kindly Sisters of Charity.

What Bernard McQuaid became he owed in large part to the motherly guidance which he received from the Prince Street Sisters, and most of all to Sister Elizabeth Boyle. This remarkable woman was one of the original trio sent by Blessed Elizabeth Seton in 1817 to establish a convent in New York City; and in 1846, when the New York Sisters of Charity were constituted an independent order, she was to be the first mother general. The Bishop never forgot her lessons in self-reliance, dogged perseverance, and happy poverty.

McQuaid furthermore attributed his vocation to the priesthood to Sister Elizabeth. In 1839, the same year in which he was discharged from the Asylum, he entered Chambly College, near Montreal, Canada. (Remote as it was from New York City, Chambly was still the closest preparatory seminary.) For his major priestly studies, he returned, probably in 1843, to the New York diocesan seminary, St. Joseph's, which was then located on the grounds of the present Fordham University. Vincentian Fathers staffed St. Joseph's upon his arrival; but in 1846 the Jesuit Fathers replaced them.[10]

In those days young McQuaid's physical strength did not measure up to his mental vigor. In his very first year at St. Joseph's, he was stricken with what appeared to be incipient tuberculosis—the white plague which destroyed so many pioneer Irish-Americans, including, perhaps, his own mother. Contrary to expectations, Bernard, after taking a year off, recovered. Fortunately, he was always welcome to spend his vacations at the Orphan Asylum, where the Sisters saw to it that he got rest and proper food. When he made his first trip to Rochester in 1846, it was also to visit the Sisters of Charity. In June, 1846, the Sister superior at Emmitsburg, Maryland, sent Sister Elizabeth Boyle to Rochester to head the little group of Sisters who the year before had established there St. Patrick's Girl's Orphanage. Sister Elizabeth remained only until late fall, but her stay was long enough to give the young seminarian an excuse for his first visit to western New York.

Thus McQuaid was still very much alive when it came time for ordination, so Bishop John Hughes ordained him a priest on January 16, 1848. His initial assignment was to St. Mary's Church, on Grand Street, Manhattan. But his mentor, the president of Fordham, Father James R. Bayley, felt that a country post would be better for a priest of such uncertain health; so he persuaded the Bishop to send Father McQuaid to Morris County, New Jersey. Therefore, on January 21, 1848, Father Bernard J. McQuaid was named assistant to Father Louis Dominic Senez, the French-born pastor of St. Vincent Church, Madison, New Jersey. By midsummer of the same year the assistant had been promoted to pastor of St. Vincent's.

Father Bayley's prescription worked. We hear no more of McQuaid's frail health, and there was only one side-effect left to recall it. His physician had persuaded him that hearty laughter was bad for a man with a "weak chest". So Bernard McQuaid, at the inevitable risk of being thought humorless, restricted his show of amusement forever after to a smile or a voiceless chuckle.[11]

It was during his New Jersey years that Bernard McQuaid forged his concepts of the needs and methods of the American mission. Since these same concepts were to govern his policies as bishop of Rochester, his Jersey apostolate must be described in some detail.

His first effort was to measure up to the proper norm of priestliness. Industriousness was doubtless already a part of his nature, and from the start he learned that having several irons constantly in the fire was a wholesome antidote to dull routine. It was also early in his priestly life that he resolved never to use strong drink. But the priestly virtue which he stressed perhaps most of all was apostolic charity. Bernard McQuaid had great financial talents, and before his ordination a New York banker had offered him a position in his own firm and a promise of inevitable wealth.[12] But McQuaid had already come to love and to supernaturalize the poverty in which he had been raised, and he saw in voluntary poverty a good symbol of the detachment and charity which should characterize the diocesan priest. He had not been a priest long before he made a vow that at no year's-end would he be possessed of more than twenty-five dollars he could call his own. He kept the vow until he became a bishop. Only then did he yield to the circumstances and take out his first bank book.[13] And as we shall see later he never departed from his conviction that avarice is one of the worst vices a priest can succumb to.

The Madison mission certainly proved a good training ground in missionary virtues. Its young pastor had to cover a territory which included all of Morris, Sussex and Warren Counties, and parts of Union and Essex. Morris and Sussex Counties now constitute two-thirds of the Diocese of Paterson; Warren is in the Diocese of Trenton; and Union and Essex are still a part of the Archdiocese of Newark. It is easy to see why in the early days when the only church in the area was at Madison, Father McQuaid had to spend much time on the road. With his own small money he bought two horses and carriages to transport him to the little clusters of Catholics scattered sparsely across a strongly anti-Catholic district. Frequently he spent the night in his carriage in order to be on hand in the morning to celebrate Mass on an improvised altar in some remote farmhouse.[14]

Challenge there was, and opposition, too. But it gave the young priest an occasion to develop further the ever-optimistic perseverance which Sister Elizabeth had taught him. "I had one natural gift in a high degree," he wrote a friend in later years, "and it was not a saintly one: the more opposition the stronger the determination to succeed in spite of the devil and every one else."[15]

One story is a case in point. When he was a bishop, McQuaid once recalled visiting the little home of a Catholic woodcutter in the course of one of his New Jersey missionary circuits. While he and the woodcutter's wife awaited the return of the head of the family, the priest baptized the baby. But their older boy strongly objected to being baptized, and ran and hid under the bed. Nothing daunted, McQuaid, with the mother's aid, dragged the lad out of his lair, and wrapping his left arm securely about him, poured on his head with his right hand the unwelcome waters of salvation. As was usually the case, Bernard McQuaid, by brooking no nonsense, achieved his purpose. He followed the later career of the boy and was pleased to learn, during the Civil War, that he had volunteered and proved an excellent soldier.[16]

It was also during his missionary years that Father McQuaid perfected the oratorical talents for which he was to become so noted as a prelate. He had taken a special course in elocution from one Professor Frobisher of New York, and had learned from him the art of precise and deliberate declamation.[17] (McQuaid's New York accent, with its broad "a", naturally made its own contribution to his sonorous delivery.) But Bernard McQuaid also had that faculty which an orator needs even more than rhetorical techniques: a clear, orderly mind, and firm convictions. And, added to this, he possessed a wide and deep literary background, acquired by extensive and perceptive reading.

His missionary flock was aware from the outset that their young pastor took his priesthood seriously. This "most undiplomatic of men," as journalist Katherine E. Conway later termed him, "courteous, but never courtly," immediately impressed those with whom he dealt as being "all business." As a result, they admired and respected him, and at the same time had a wholesome fear of rousing his apostolic wrath. He had made it quite clear, for instance, that he disapproved of dancing-parties and similar gatherings. One snowy winter's night a group of his young people got together, despite his admonitions, for one of the objectionable parties. In the midst of the merriment, the pastor himself suddenly appeared on the scene. In a moment the partymakers had all disappeared—some through the doors, others through the windows!

Church buildings throughout his counties headed the list of McQuaid's constructional agenda. First came Morristown, where the small Catholic flock, by pooling their nickels and dimes, erected Assumption Church, which Bishop Hughes of New York dedicated in March, 1849. Three years later Father McQuaid put up a mission church at Springfield, New Jersey; and in 1853 he was getting ready to erect another church, this time at Mendham, when he was transferred from the Madison mission to Newark.

Still more significant than his building of churches was McQuaid's opening of parochial schools.

He came to Madison deeply grateful for the Catholic elementary education which he had received at the orphanage, and strongly desirous of extending the same benefit to the thousands of Catholic youngsters who at that time had no such opportunity. The American parochial school movement had actually begun, but Bernard McQuaid was to be in the van of that movement. In September, 1849, he opened a school in the basement of St. Vincent's Church, Madison; and during the six months that he himself taught there he gained valuable pedagogical experience. This was the first permanent Catholic parochial school in the State of New Jersey. When he began to build the little Church of the Assumption in Morristown, he also took pains to provide it with a basement destined to house the State's second parochial school.

On November 15, 1849—midway between the foundation of these two New Jersey schools—Bishop John Hughes published a strong pastoral on the need of parish schools. The sight of so many of the children of immigrants who were growing up in a society and attending a public school system both of which were antagonistic to their Catholic faith, had impressed the Bishop with the necessity of strong, positive action. "I think," he declared, "the time has almost come when it will be necessary to build the schoolhouse first, and the church afterward." This was McQuaid's own view, and he was happy to have it confirmed as the official diocesan policy.

On July 23, 1853, Pope Pius IX established a new diocese, with its seat at Newark, to comprise the whole of the State of New Jersey, hitherto subject to the jurisdiction of the dioceses of New York and Philadelphia.[18] New Yorker McQuaid, "frozen" in his current appointment, thus became a Jerseyite. But the person who was appointed his new superior made the exile easier. It was Father James Roosevelt Bayley (1814-1877), Bishop Hughes's secretary and Bernard McQuaid's old friend and former mentor.[19]

One of Bishop Bayley's first acts was to appoint Father McQuaid, on October 18, 1853, to the rectorship of St. Patrick's Church, Newark, which had been designated the temporary cathedral of the new diocese. Preparations for welcoming the first bishop of Newark therefore fell to the lot of McQuaid. Spurning the counsel of those who feared it would incite anti-Catholic rioting, the rector planned to have thousands of the faithful gather at the railway station to greet Bayley and parade him to his pro-cathedral. When the Bishop arrived, on All Saints Day, crowds of Catholics were on hand to welcome him, and the whole ceremony went off like clockwork, with not a hint of anti-Catholic antagonism. McQuaid had had to sell his horse and carriage and borrow additional funds to pay for the clergy banquet. But it was worth that price to have everything go off properly. For Bernard McQuaid could never tolerate slipshod performances, especially in church ceremonials.

Bayley had made no mistake in choosing Father McQuaid as one of the key men of his administration. The two complemented each other effectively. Bishop Bayley was a good executive and had a fine zeal, especially for promoting Catholic education; but he tended to be conservative and timid, and was rather easily discouraged. McQuaid, on the other hand, rejoiced to carry out, with daring if need be, what the Bishop commanded; and he had enough happy aggressiveness for himself and his Bishop, too. There was apparently only one instance of their falling-out, as we shall see later. In general, Bishop Bayley valued his lieutenant precisely because of his decisiveness.

The first decade of the Diocese of Newark was a troubled one. Most of its Catholics were poor Irish immigrants, although German immigrants, no more affluent, made up a quarter of the diocesan population. The commercial crisis of 1853-1854 and the panic of 1857 created even more grievous problems for the poor Diocese and its impoverished faithful. Bayley decided to introduce the Conferences of St. Vincent de Paul to provide for the needy. In 1858, Father McQuaid set up one of these lay aid organizations in the cathedral parish. Four years earlier he had undertaken a still more positive work for the youth of Newark, the Catholic Institute. The Institute was an educational and recreational center for the Catholic Young Men's Association. McQuaid financed this project by creating a joint stock company, of which he was president. A successful enterprise, the Catholic Institute manifested the imaginative organizational talents of its creator.

As regards parochial schools, McQuaid and Bayley were in complete accord. The Bishop wanted a parish school in every parish. Father McQuaid was happy to comply whenever the occasion offered itself. He maintained a flourishing school at St. Patrick's, Newark; and when he founded the new parishes of St. Joseph's in Newark and Holy Cross in Harrison, he saw to it that they, too, were provided with combination church-school buildings.

If the initial reception of Bishop Bayley had not been marred by anti-Catholic demonstrations, the fear of such riots was a real one in the early 1850's. As a matter of fact, there was a serious riot in Newark on September 5, 1854. That day a procession of members of three bitterly anti-Catholic and anti-immigrant organizations, the American Protestant Association, the Orangemen, and the German Turners, was parading past St. Mary's German Catholic Church, when somebody (one of the marchers, it later transpired) threw a stone at their ranks. The nativists promptly attacked the watching crowd with pistols and daggers, killing one Irishman and mortally wounding another. Then they stormed into St. Mary's Church, destroying all they could lay hands on—except the Blessed Sacrament, which the pastor had had the prudence to remove at the start of the trouble.

There was great commotion until Father Patrick Moran, the vicar general, and Father McQuaid, arrived on the scene, and bit by bit calmed the agitated Catholics and dissuaded them from answering violence with violence. The Newark newspapers, and, at least at the beginning, the New York papers, gave slanted accounts of the affray, blaming the Catholics for starting it. When the mayor of Newark would give no redress, Bishop Bayley turned with better effect to the governor of New Jersey. The church authorities never did receive complete satisfaction. But Bayley did not hesitate to attribute to Father McQuaid's efforts the modicum of justice which was done to them.[20]

Bernard McQuaid was meanwhile attentive to his pastoral duties. He was always ready to preach or hear confessions. He saw to it that there were regular parish devotions, with good musical accompaniment. Here, too, he was a stickler for dignified rites. For instance, when the Pro-Cathedral celebrated, in December, 1855, the first anniversary of the definition of the dogma of the Immaculate Conception, he "adorned the church very beautifully with greens and thousands of lights."[21]

Father McQuaid's virtues included a very strong love of his native land. This manifested itself especially at the outbreak of the Civil War. It was on Friday, April 12, 1861, that Beauregard fired on Fort Sumter. On Sunday the 14th, McQuaid addressed his congregation on the need of preserving the Union. He was the first Newark clergyman to do so. Then on April 22nd, Newark citizens staged a massive demonstration of their patriotism. Bishop Bayley had the national flag run up on his Pro-Cathedral, and McQuaid gave an address to the crowd gathered before the courthouse. Greeted by a long applause, he admonished his listeners to rally without delay to the defense of the glorious Union against all her enemies. "Some of you," he went on, unwilling to pass up this rare opportunity, "Some of you, might, in the past, have supposed that because we Catholics stood aloof, we were not good Americans . . . But when danger threatened we had ever been found standing side by side with the defenders of the country . . ."[22]

The two Newark diocesan undertakings in which Bernard McQuaid played his chief role were the foundation of Seton Hall College and Seminary and the establishment of the Sisters of Charity of St. Elizabeth. These were, of course, authorized by Bishop Bayley; but it was McQuaid who played the leading part in both proposing and effectuating them.

The Seton Hall project began in 1854. This College-Seminary opened at Madison, New Jersey, in 1856, with an initial enrollment of twenty-five. Father McQuaid, who had gone about begging the funds to begin the College, served as president during the first year. Named president again in 1859, he continued to occupy the posts of president, director of the seminary, and professor of rhetoric until he was made a bishop. During his second term of office he moved the College-Seminary into two buildings on a sixty-acre tract in East Orange, in Essex County. In the following year, on March 8, 1861, the New Jersey Legislature incorporated Seton Hall as a college and even granted it the privileges of a university. The course in theology was added that same year. McQuaid saw to it that the syllabus of studies was strong and the faculty comprised the best men available under the circumstances. To increase student incentive, he persuaded benefactors to establish prizes and awards. He also tried to induce the more prosperous Catholics to endow professorships. Here his eloquence proved less effective; but the idea itself was sound, as he was able to prove in later years in connection with St. Bernard's Seminary in Rochester. All the experience which he gained during his years at Seton Hall was to serve him in good stead when he ruled a diocese of his own.[23]

The same can be said of the experience which he gained as superior of the Sisters of Charity of St. Elizabeth. When first appointed pastor of St. Patrick's, Newark, in 1853, Father McQuaid had induced his beloved Sisters of Charity of New York to send him two nuns to take charge of the orphanage connected with the Pro-cathedral. The New York community sent a few more Sisters to New Jersey during the next few years, but it was unable to provide Bishop Bayley with all the Sisters he needed for his schools.

The Bishop of Newark finally decided that he must establish his own diocesan order of nuns. He first asked the New York Sisters of Charity if they could not provide him with a few Sisters to form a nucleus of the projected community. When they replied that they could not oblige him even in this respect, he turned in another direction. In November, 1858, Father McQuaid conducted five young New Jersey women who aspired to membership in the new order to the motherhouse of the Sisters of Charity of Cincinnati, who had agreed to train them in the religious life. Eleven months later they returned to Newark. Here a modest motherhouse had been established, and two seasoned Charity nuns, released by the New York community for this purpose, were waiting to take over as mother general and mother assistant. They were Mother M. Xavier Mehegan and Sister M. Catherine Nevin. When Seton Hall College moved from Madison to East Orange in 1860, the Charity motherhouse was transferred to the former college building at Madison; and here at "Convent Station," the Sisters of Charity of St. Elizabeth still maintain their central headquarters. "The strongest conviction I had," McQuaid wrote much later of this undertaking, "was that there could never be success without a sisterhood for the diocese, and independent of all outside superiors." From the earliest days, he was the principal guide and spiritual counsellor of the new sisterhood; and in 1863 Bishop Bayley named him its superior general.

Bayley was also eager to induce religious priests to come into his diocese. He succeeded in persuading the Benedictine Fathers and the Passionist Fathers to found monasteries and assume charge of parishes in New Jersey. The Redemptorist Fathers declined a similar invitation.[24] Later on, as bishop of Rochester, McQuaid was firmly opposed to placing parishes in the hands of priests of religious orders. There is reason to believe that his opposition was based on his experience with the New Jersey parishes staffed by order men.

It was in 1863 that Father McQuaid and his Bishop had their first, and possibly their only real misunderstanding. That Lent, the Bishop decided to have the seminarians sing the Holy Week rites at the Pro-cathedral. Father McQuaid, as rector, was equally firm in his decision to have them conduct the ceremonies in the little seminary chapel. When Bayley insisted, McQuaid—spurred perhaps by other motives as well—gave the official books of the seminary into the keeping of his vice rector, departed for New York, and made arrangements with Father Arthur Donnelly, the pastor of St. Michael's Church in Manhattan, to become his assistant.

Quick action was necessary, so Father Patrick Moran, Vicar General of Newark, and Father Michael A. Madden of Madison, McQuaid's good friend, straightway set to work to talk sense into the stubborn refugee. McQuaid finally gave in, the seminarians went to the Pro-cathedral, and all was forgiven. It was probably the only time in his life that Bernard McQuaid, staunch enemy of caprice, ever played the prima donna.[25]

Far from penalizing McQuaid, Bishop Bayley, who was probably more amused than disturbed by the incident, continued to advance him to still greater responsibilities.

In 1864 he permitted Father McQuaid to make a tour of the Union Army camps in Northern Virginia. McQuaid had suspected that the disabled soldiers were not receiving adequate spiritual attention. His suspicions were verified when he reached Fredericksburg on May 20th and found that in the four corps hospitals in the area there was not a single priest to take care of the dying. He was unable to say Mass for them, since he had brought along no Mass-kit. But he did what he could for the casualties, and he wrote back to the Bishop requesting him to send down another priest to replace him. Diocesan duties called him back to Newark in the first week of June.

In 1866 Bishop Bayley named Father McQuaid vicar general of the Diocese. Now second-in-command, he accompanied the Bishop to the Second Plenary Council, held in Baltimore in October of that year. Here he was named a member of the Council's committee on metropolitans, bishops, priests, and seminarians.

Between March 20th and October 2nd of the following year, Bishop Bayley took a trip to Rome and the Holy Land, on the advice of his physician. Father McQuaid administered the Diocese during his absence, and kept the Bishop posted on the course of events at home. He took occasion of his superior's absence to discipline some troublesome priests. This was a task for which he was much better fitted by nature than the gentle Bayley.

The Bishop of Newark was very grateful to his Vicar General for the capable way in which he was discharging his administrative duties. Bayley was very much disturbed, therefore, when he learned, while still in Europe, that Father McQuaid was being considered for the bishopric of Rochester. On his return he wrote to Cardinal Barnabò to urge that the Newark Diocese would suffer unduly if it were to lose McQuaid at that time.[26]

Bernard McQuaid, upon receiving word of his appointment to Rochester, likewise demurred, and went to New York to explain to Archbishop McCloskey in person his motives for not accepting the assignment. After the Archbishop had listened patiently, he replied that he had put McQuaid's name on the list because he wanted him as his collaborator in the Province of New York. McQuaid could find no words to rebut this answer of his old and trusted friend.[27]

The Bishop-elect of Rochester would normally have received the official bulls of appointment not long after his acceptance had been confirmed. Actually, they arrived in New York only on July 10, 1868— six months after his selection. The reason for the delay was that they had been entrusted to a young Detroit priest, Father Ernest Van Dyke, who had just been graduated from the North American College and was returning to his home diocese. Unaware of the urgency of matter, he had made a grand tour of Europe before embarking for the United States. Father Van Dyke — subsequently Monsignor Van Dyke — was later to achieve distinction as a priest of the Diocese of Detroit. But in 1868 he had all the hierarchs of the New York Province guessing. As soon as these essential documents were in hand on July 10th, Archbishop McCloskey telegraphed the Bishop-elect that he would consecrate him two days later![28]

The rite of consecration took place at Old St. Patrick's Cathedral on Mott Street, New York. Archbishop John McCloskey, the consecrator, was assisted by Bishop Bayley and Bishop Louis De Goesbriand of Burlington, Vermont.

On the eve of Bishop McQuaid's departure for Rochester, his colleagues in Newark gave him a farewell banquet. On that occasion Father William McNulty testified to the high regard in which McQuaid had been held by the Newark diocesans. "The Bishop of Newark loses," he said, "a faithful and efficient auxiliary, the clergy an estimable associate, the people a tried and true friend, ever watchful over their well being." "We cannot recall a moment," he continued, addressing the guest of honor, "when your actions were not marked by the courtesy of a perfect Christian gentleman." His zeal, McNulty declared to the audience, had been inspiring, his motives disinterested, his life beyond reproach.[29]

One of McQuaid's friends had lately written to another that Bernard McQuaid's zeal "sometimes runs over and floods his neighbor's field." The priests who heard Father McNulty's eulogy were no doubt aware of that fact, too. But there is no reason to doubt that they accepted the eulogy as a correct expression of their sentiments.

Bishop McQuaid's major career now lay before him. It is quite clear, however, that he owed to the Newark Diocese the training for his episcopal career. What he formulated in Newark he fulfilled in Rochester.

2. THE FIRST STEPS.

On July 16, 1868 — a blistering day in a very torrid summer — Bernard J. McQuaid arrived in Rochester to assume his new duties. Delegates from each of the Rochester city parishes had met him in Syracuse and made the remainder of the railway trip with him. When the train pulled into the Rochester station, hundreds more of his future charges waited in anxious anticipation, not only to greet but to appraise their new superior.

The picture which McQuaid presented when he descended from the cars must have been favorable. He was now forty-five years old, a man of medium or somewhat less than medium height, with a large but shapely head and a fairly trim figure. His bearing was dignified, his features were firm and serious — though not unpleasantly so. How the Catholics of Rochester must have cheered their new prelate! And one can imagine that McQuaid, in response, lifted the high silk hat which throughout his episcopal life was to remain one of the badges of his status.

A carriage drawn by four greys was waiting, and when the Bishop was seated in it, the welcoming procession, led by Grand Marshal Louis Ernst, set out for St. Patrick's Church. Nearly a thousand participated in the march, including clergy, civil officials, delegations from parochial societies, and bands of music.

The third St. Patrick's Church, already designated the diocesan cathedral, was not yet complete. McQuaid was therefore installed more humbly in the "Shanty Church", a temporary frame building which served as a church while the cathedral was under construction. Greeted at the entrance by the parish officials, Bishop McQuaid vested in miter and cope and proceeded down the aisle to the strains of a "Reception March" that the organist, Professor Bauer, had composed for this event. Reaching the sanctuary, the new Bishop was installed on his episcopal throne — which happened to be a barber's chair — and received the obeisance of his clergy, some of whom were clad in white dusters![30] After the solemn hymn of thanksgiving, the *Te Deum,* Father James Early, the new vicar general, read an address of welcome. The Bishop, in reply, thanked priests and people for the splendor and cordiality of their greeting — a good indication, he said, that they appreciated "the reverence due the Bishop as the representative of the Church." He pledged to follow as closely as possible in the footsteps of his saintly predecessor, Bishop Timon.

Having concluded his remarks at St. Patrick's with a solemn pontifical blessing, McQuaid returned to his carriage, and the procession, reforming, conducted him to St. Joseph's, Rochester's pioneer German church. Although St. Joseph's was much larger than the St. Patrick's "Shanty Church", here, too, the crowd of spectators overflowed into the street. Addressing the congregation in St. Joseph's, the Bishop explained that he had spoken only briefly at his first stop in order to allow himself ample time to greet his German children gathered in their mother parish. The special purpose of this visit was to remind all that a bishop is shepherd of his entire flock, no matter what the nationality of its individual members.

On concluding his visit at St. Joseph's, McQuaid was finally driven over to the episcopal residence on Frank Street. Here he was officially greeted once again, this time in the name of the Catholic laity. The spokesman was Rochester's leading Catholic layman, Patrick Barry the horticulturist. The Bishop replied, now more informally, expressing his gratitude for the friendliness of his reception. Then he bade all a good night with a "God bless you" — a phrase which always remained his characteristic salutation and adieu.

The reception *had* been a happy one. Not that every detail had been perfect. The Bishop, who liked to have sacred functions performed the *right* way, must have taken a dim view of the priests' wearing dusters in the sanctuary of St. Patrick's. At St. Joseph's there had been a moment of musical disharmony. While Bishop McQuaid, kneeling before the altar, was singing the versicles, the musical band awaiting him outside in Franklin Street, struck up "The Wearing of the Green." Only when the chants of Bishop and choir were finished and the organist could let go full blast on the organ, did the congregation inside the church forget this Hibernian distraction.

But these were minor imperfections. In general, the new bishop was both impressed and impressive. The *Democrat* reported him to be of "a pleasing yet commanding appearance, and with a remarkably good voice and manner of delivery." His visit to St. Joseph's was a gesture of high and effective diplomacy. McQuaid had had pleasant and understanding associations with the German Catholics of New Jersey, and had arrived at a high estimate of the virtues of the German nationality. Two days after his installation, he wrote to Father Michael A. Corrigan of Seton Hall College, "My visit to the German Church of St. Joseph's has brought all the Germans to my side. I am sorry I cannot speak their language." Throughout his Rochester career, Bishop McQuaid remained on cordial good terms with his German diocesans. He laid the foundation for this friendship when he paid the shrewd but sincere visit to St. Joseph's Church on July 16, 1868.

For all the formality and excitement of the reception, there was one little human touch which proved that the new bishop was by no means lacking in sentiment. As he entered his new Rochester residence, the band serenaded him with "Home Sweet Home." Suddenly he became lonesome — an orphan again, far from the surroundings and friendships of these many years past. "At that moment," he wrote to Corrigan, "my thoughts were more with other friends than with the ten thousand that stood before me."

But Bernard McQuaid never allowed sentiment, much less sentimentality, to interfere with duty. The episcopal motto he had taken was *"Salus animarum lex suprema"*: "The supreme law is the saving of souls." The motto testified to his awareness of his new responsibility. He entered upon this responsibility as a man of both experience and courage. A teen-ager from Lima was in the audience when Bishop McQuaid was installed in office. Years later this Lima lad, now Archbishop James Edward Quigley of Chicago, used to recall McQuaid's words in his inaugural sermon: "I come here without fear, knowing what is to be done."[31] Ability and fearlessness were to be the hallmarks of his whole regime.

Let us look for a moment at the statistics of the area which the new bishop had to organize into a diocese.

The eight counties embraced 4,431 square miles. The total population (in 1870) amounted to about 377,000; but this population was far from evenly divided among the diocesan counties. Monroe County had 117,000 inhabitants. Cayuga County was a trailing second, with 59,000 inhabitants. The other six counties were even more distinctly rural, with still sparser populations: Wayne (47,000); Ontario (45,000); Livingston (38,300); Tompkins (33,000); Seneca (27,000); Yates (19,600). In the whole Diocese there were only two cities: Rochester (Monroe County) with about 60,000 inhabitants, and Auburn (Cayuga County), with about 17,000.

The Catholic flock in these eight counties was, as we have already stated, approximately 54,500; and from an economic point of view, the average member of this flock was poor. Catholics were most numerous in the city of Rochester. Here they numbered some 27,000 — a little less than half of the city's population. They were divided into ten parishes: four "Irish", five German, and one French. The "Irish" churches and their memberships were as follows: St. Patrick (5,000), St. Mary (4,000), Immaculate Conception (2,400), and St. Bridget (1,300); making a total of some 12,700 "Irish" parishioners. The German parishes were: St. Joseph (8,000), SS. Peter and Paul (2,500), Holy Redeemer (1,300), Holy Family (1,080), and St. Boniface (889); making a total of almost 14,000. The French church, Our Lady of Victory, had 370 members. Auburn had two churches: Holy Family (2,600) and St. Alphonsus (350, mostly Germans). Dansville, a village of about 3,000, was the only other community which had more than one Catholic church. St. Mary's (German) Church counted 600 communicants; St. Patrick's ("Irish") Church, 265. Geneva's St. Francis de Sales parish reported 2,107 parishioners (Geneva's total citizenry numbered 5,500). Seneca Falls had 2,000 Catholics (almost one-half of the local population). At Canandaigua the Catholic ratio was smaller: 1,650 to 7,000. Apart from these, there were no other parishes in the Diocese which had a membership over one thousand; and most of them fell far below this mark.

Let us see, specifically, what parishes and missions existed in the eight counties when they became the Rochester Diocese.

We have mentioned the ten churches in Rochester. All of these had permanent pastors except Holy Redeemer, which was still a mission of St. Joseph's. Elsewhere in Monroe County there were five other parishes with resident pastors. Assumption in Fairport and Holy Trinity in Webster had no out-missions; the other three had one or more. Nativity of the Blessed Virgin, Brockport, took care of St. John's, Spencerport; Our Mother of Sorrows, Town of Greece, took care of St. John's, Ridge Road, and Holy Cross, Charlotte; Assumption Church, Scottsville, took care of St. Patrick's, Mumford, and St. Fechan's, Chili.

Each of the four parishes in Livingston County had missions. St. Patrick's, Mount Morris (St. Mary's, Geneseo); St. Mary's, Dansville (St. Patrick's, Dansville); St. Agnes, Avon (St. Joseph, Rush, Monroe County); St. Rose, Lima, (St. Michael, Livonia Center, Livingston County, and St. Paul, Honeoye Falls, Monroe County). Holy Angels, Nunda (Livingston County) continued for some months as a mission of nearby Portageville in the Buffalo Diocese. Only in 1871 did Bishop McQuaid make it a regular mission of St. Patrick, Dansville. Ontario County had four parishes. Of these, St. Francis de Sales in Geneva and St. Mary in Canandaigua had no out-missions. But St. Agnes (now called St. Felix) in Clifton Springs had missions in Phelps (St. Francis); in Newark, Wayne County (St. Michael); and in Rushville, Yates County (St. Mary). The missions of St. Bridget Church in East Bloomfield were: St. Joseph, West Bloomfield; St. Mary, Honeoye Flats; and St. Patrick, Victor.

In Wayne County there were two parishes, each with an out-mission. St. John the Evangelist Church in Clyde also took care of St. Michael Church in Lyons. St. Ann, Palmyra, was responsible for St. Patrick, Mendon. Yates County had one full-fledged parish: St. Michael, Penn Yan. Seneca County had two: St. Patrick (Seneca Falls) and St. Mary (Waterloo). Holy Cross Church in Ovid was a mission of Waterloo. Tompkins County had only one parish, Immaculate Conception in Ithaca. But Immaculate Conception had two missions in the same county, St. James the Apostle in Trumansburg and St. Patrick in McLean.

Cayuga County could claim four parishes. Auburn, as we have seen, had Holy Family and St. Alphonsus. St. Alphonsus, under the tutelage of the Rochester Redemptorists, might be considered a mission of St. Joseph's Church in Rochester. St. Joseph in Weedsport was a parish, with two out-missions: St. John, Port Byron, and St. Michael, Montezuma. The pastor of St. Michael's Church, Union Springs, had three missions: St. Agnes, Aurora; St. Bernard, Scipio Center; and Our Lady of the Lake, Northville (now called King Ferry).

There were thus thirty-five parish churches and twenty-eight (or, with Nunda, twenty-nine) mission churches under the jurisdiction of the new Bishop of Rochester. The personnel of the Diocese comprised thirty-nine priests, three male religious orders, and five communities of nuns.

Many of the diocesan priests had only ordinary attainments, and a few were to prove rascals. But several were clerics of ability and even distinction.

Perhaps the most notable of all was the Belgian-born pastor of Our Lady of Victory Church in Rochester, Father Hippolyte De Regge (1830-1904). Bishop McQuaid named him his secretary and diocesan chancellor as early as February 5, 1869; and De Regge, who held the chancellery thereafter until his death, was to play a vital part in the formation of the diocesan clergy.[32] Father Francis Sinclair (1838-1907), the pastor of SS. Peter and Paul's Church in Rochester, brought permanent peace to that previously turbulent German parish. German-born (the foster-brother of Father Hermann Grueder, the first prefect apostolic of modern Denmark), and Roman-trained, Father Sinclair long remained McQuaid's intermediary with the Germans of the diocese.[33] Father John M. Maurice (1812-1895) was pastor of Our Mother of Sorrows parish, Paddy Hill, from 1856 to his death. This venerable and beloved man was a Frenchman who, before coming to America, had been a member of the first missionary band sent to Sierra Leone, Africa.[34] Father Peter Barker, D.D. (1831?-1871), was a graduate of the Urban College in Rome. He was pastor of St. Mary's, Rochester.[35] Another alumnus of the same Roman institution was the studious Father Myles Loughlin (1842-1879).[36] Father Patricio Byrnes (1835-75), was pastor of Immaculate Conception Church, Rochester. His Irish parents were living in Montevideo, Uruguay, at the time of his birth— hence the Spanish Christian name. (His brother William [1841-1915] became Brother Anthony of the Christian Brothers, and served as president of Manhattan College, New York, 1879-1886 and 1890-1894.)[37] Father Louis I. Miller, pastor of Assumption Church in Fairport, was of even more unusual antecedents. Formerly a Lutheran minister, Louis Miller once had a dream that he would enter the Catholic priesthood. When he announced this strange revelation to his Lutheran congregation, they took up a collection to help him achieve his goal![38]

The Redemptorists were the only religious order of priests in the new diocese, and so long as McQuaid was bishop they remained the only priestly order. The two other orders were teaching brothers, the

Brothers of the Christian Schools and the Brothers of Mary; and these were to continue their work in Rochester for some time. The five orders of women were: the Sisters of Charity (St. Mary's Hospital, St. Patrick's Girls' Orphanage, St. Patrick's Girls' School); the School Sisters of Notre Dame (St. Joseph's Orphanage and four schools); the Sisters of St. Joseph (orphanages in Rochester and Canandaigua, a girls' academy at Canandaigua); the Sisters of Mercy (an academy, free school and "industrial school" in Rochester, and a free school in Auburn); and the Religious of the Sacred Heart (an academy in Rochester).

Once installed in office, Bernard McQuaid set about organizing his diocese with whatever help these auxiliaries could give him. Of course, his earliest acts were more or less routine. On July 19th, three days after his arrival, he blessed the cornerstone of Our Lady of Victory Church. This, his first official function, was an intentional gesture of good will towards the French members of his flock. On August 15th, during his first visit to Auburn, he established his first new parish: St. Mary's.[39] Little by little he began to become acquainted with his spiritual domain and its people. And he even began to pay attention to such details as the improvement of the Cathedral choir and its musical selections.

Bishop McQuaid was summoned to Rome in the fall of 1869 to take part in the First Ecumenical Council of the Vatican. This Roman sojourn came scarcely a year after he had taken office, and it interrupted for nine months his acclimatization to the Diocese of Rochester. It is therefore all the more a tribute to his mettle that between July, 1868, and November, 1869, he had already made his mark as a religious publicist, established himself as a firm disciplinarian, and laid the foundations of his diocesan educational structure.

The Bishop of Rochester's first essay as a publicist was in a small newspaper controversy with the Right Reverend Arthur Cleveland Coxe of Buffalo, Episcopal Bishop of Western New York. Addressing his fellow Episcopalians in Rochester in August, 1869, this staunchly anti-Catholic prelate had denounced with a characteristic bitterness the alleged power politics of the Catholic Church, and had launched a special barb at the "corrosive management" of the Catholic teaching Sisters in New York State. Deeply stirred by this ungallant reference to the good Sisters, Bishop McQuaid replied from the pulpit on Sunday, August 29th. Since Bishop Coxe had left town, a local Episcopalian minister replied to the riposte with additional anti-Catholic charges. Bishop McQuaid retaliated with a letter to the editor of the *Union and Advertiser*. Neither on this occasion nor in a later controversy with the contentious Bishop Coxe, did the Bishop of Rochester succeed in correcting the opinions or the unseemly language of his adversary. But he did show Rochesterians that he was able to bring to a controversy logic of thought, clarity of expression, and genuine courtesy.

The first disciplinary problem which confronted Bishop McQuaid was a shattering experience, and a real test of his ability to rule. This was the case of Father O'Flaherty of Auburn, and we must discuss it at some length because of the great turmoil which it caused.[40]

During his pastorate at Holy Family Church (1845-1856), Father Thomas O'Flaherty had done good work in Auburn. Subsequently, however, Bishop Timon, for serious reasons, had suspended him from the exercise of his priestly powers. When he showed signs of repentance two years later, Timon had restored him to his pastorate, to the distress of many of the parishioners. These parishioners were right, as the sequel proved. Father O'Flaherty had not changed for the better. His loose behavior, his maladministration, and his abusive and calumnious language all pointed to one conclusion: the salt had lost its savor.

New measures were due against the unfortunate priest at the time McQuaid assumed office. On the very occasion of his consecration in New York, the Bishop-elect of Rochester had been handed a file on the case by Archbishop McCloskey, along with the personal counsel to "give O'Flaherty another chance."

Bishop McQuaid accepted the counsel, and for several months after his installation tried every device he could think of to reclaim the Auburn pastor and at the same time to mollify his opponents. The establishment of St. Mary's parish was one of these measures. But at the beginning of 1869, the Bishop was dissatisfied with the priest's parish financial report for 1868, and he asked for an itemized statement of the year's expenditures. Father O'Flaherty did not comply. McQuaid therefore consulted Father George Ruland, the superior of the Rochester Redemptorists, on possible courses of action. Father Ruland recommended that O'Flaherty be transferred to another post. Since Father O'Flaherty had publicly stated that he would never leave Auburn, Ruland reasoned that he would probably refuse the transfer, and thus render himself liable to suspension. The Bishop did not care especially for this roundabout approach, but it was at least one way to avoid a painful church court trial of the Auburn priest for grosser faults. So he accepted the advice, and wrote O'Flaherty that he was reassigned to St. Michael's Church, Penn Yan. O'Flaherty refused the reassignment, so on February 20, 1869, Bishop McQuaid informed him that he was suspended from his priestly functions.

What followed was a parable of waywardness. As justification for his disobedience, Father O'Flaherty claimed — without any basis — that since the Pope himself had confirmed him as pastor and rural dean, no bishop of Rochester could remove him. To Bishop McQuaid's public announcement he replied with vile innuendoes, and sought also to defame Father Martin Kavanaugh who had been named to succeed him at Holy Family. About one-fourth of the parishioners sided with O'Flaherty. The worst of the partisans were the dozen-or-so violent men who jeered McQuaid on his arrival in Auburn, and on two Sundays raised such a row in the church that the Bishop had to call off the services.

For the next month or so, O'Flaherty went to the parish schoolhouse each Sunday to say the rosary with his followers, whose numbers dwindled as time passed. Five hundred parishioners soon issued a statement of loyalty and obedience to the Bishop. The dissidents published a counter statement, claiming that they alone represented the parishioners. Here was an atmosphere in which a bad case of trusteeism might have broken out in the old days. As a matter of fact, Father O'Flaherty was quite likely thinking along these lines. The parish had reincorporated on September 23, 1868, according to the new and supposedly anti-trusteeist incorporation law of 1863.[41] McQuaid, Father Early, the Vicar General, and Father O'Flaherty thus became the clerical trustees. The two lay trustees were Michael Burke and Michael Chapman. O'Flaherty had named his partisan Chapman a trustee without consulting the Bishop or Father Early. He may also have exercised some influence over Burke, which would have given him a majority of votes on the board of trustees.

Whether or not the recalcitrant pastor was moving in this direction, the Bishop took prompt steps to block him. He met with Father Early and Father Kavanaugh on April 8, 1869, in the first official meeting of the new parish corporation. The Bishop reported that Michael Burke had resigned his office of trustee. The quorum voted to accept the resignation. McQuaid then stated that Chapman had been irregularly appointed, and was an adherent of the ex-pastor. The quorum therefore voted to reject him as invalidly named. The three clerics then proceeded to elect as lay trustees two men of undoubted loyalty, Owen Gavigan and Joseph Anderson. One of the bylaws adopted by the new corporation provided that parish business was to be conducted in conformity with the regulations of the Catholic Church and the Rochester Diocese.[42] Father O'Flaherty was thus deprived of the weapon of trusteeism.

But the dissident priest was far from surrendering. His followers now issued a public call to arms, urging the parishioners, in the name of *America,* to *resist* the attempt which was to be made on April 11th to force upon them "a Priest who is not recognized by us and whom we will never accept." Fearing possible violence on the 11th, the mayor of Auburn, Mr. J. M. Hurd, requested the two local companies of the National Guard to stand on reserve. A crowd did gather in front of the church that Sunday morning, but the presence of the police and the alerting of the guardsmen was enough to discourage any disorder that might have been contemplated.

Speaking from the steps of the church, the Mayor declared that he had ascertained that the present board of trustees was the legal possessor of the parochial property. He would therefore protect them in the exercise of their authority, and punish any persons who interfered with the morning's service.

There was no more commotion after that. But the O'Flaherty case itself was far from settled. For the next twenty-three years, the unfortunate priest sought reinstatement from Bishop McQuaid, now by calumnies, now by professions of repentance. The Bishop was always ready to remove the suspension if the priest would perform the customary penance, but this Father O'Flaherty constantly refused to do. Only in 1892 did the Bishop agree to the termination of the suspension, at the behest of the Apostolic Delegate, Archbishop Francesco Satolli. His sole condition was that he not be required to accept Father O'Flaherty back into the Diocese of Rochester.[43]

The O'Flaherty case caused Bishop McQuaid much pain, not only in itself, but in its wide repercussions. For Father O'Flaherty, a highly intelligent man, was shrewd enough to communicate to the local and the national press the manifestoes of his partisans, which of course represented the Bishop of Rochester as a despot who overruled the will of the parish majority. Partisan publicity of this sort did much to give the nation the picture of McQuaid as an arbitrary tyrant, and as late as 1894 his enemies would cite the O'Flaherty affair as primary evidence of the high-handedness of the Rochester prelate. Bernard McQuaid could, indeed, be excessively strict, as we shall see later on. One might flaw some of his actions with the Auburn priest. But fundamentally, the O'Flaherty case was a matter of routine and necessary discipline. The charge of despotism was therefore unjust.

Plying the rod is only a negative and incidental duty in the career of a teacher. As the official educator of his diocese, Bernard McQuaid was prompt to formulate a positive educational program. There were three items in the program. The first was to establish "Christian free schools" — true parochial schools — in every parish where that was possible. The second was to found a community of nuns trained to staff these schools under his own spiritual direction. The third was to develop a "home-grown" diocesan clergy, educated for their careers by members of the diocesan clergy.

Having reviewed the earlier career of Bernard J. McQuaid as a founder and defender of parochial schools, we shall not be surprised to find him arguing the same cause in the Diocese of Rochester. Apparently the first public intimation he gave Rochester of his plans was on July 19, 1868. At a dinner held in St. Joseph's hall after the laying of the cornerstone of the nearby French church, the Bishop stated that his first care would be to provide the children of his diocese with Catholic schools.[44] The place for this announcement was well chosen and probably chosen on purpose. Bishop McQuaid was quite aware that the local German parishes had done much more than the "Irish" parishes in the line of parish schools. There were five German parochial schools in Rochester, while only two of the local "Irish" parishes had schools, and these could not qualify as true parochial institutions. Before he left for Rome in 1869, the Bishop had already reached an understanding with Brother Patrick, the superior of St. Patrick's Academy, up to then basically a tuition school, to convert it into a true parish school.[45]

The foundation of a diocesan community of teaching Sisters was a little more involved.[46] Three of the congregations of nuns represented in the new diocese had headquarters outside New York State: the Religious of the Sacred Heart; the German-speaking School Sisters of Notre Dame; and the Sisters of Charity of Emmitsburg. McQuaid thought at first of securing a foundation from the Sisters of Charity of New Jersey, of which he had been superior. But it then occurred to him that the Sisters of Charity of Emmitsburg who conducted St. Mary's Hospital in Rochester, might consider this something of an affront. He did request the New Jersey mother general, Mother M. Xavier, to grant him one of her ablest nuns, Sister M. Joseph Plunkett, to assist him in his Rochester foundation. When Mother Xavier felt unable to do him this favor, the Bishop was disappointed, grumpy, and probably rather hurt.[47]

Choice was now narrowed down to two, the Sisters of Mercy and the Sisters of St. Joseph, both of which groups had small contingents in the Diocese. For some reason, he decided against concentrating his efforts on the Sisters of Mercy. Current personnel problems in the diocesan Mercy convents may have influenced his decision; but it seems also that they were under a special papal jurisdiction.

In the fall of 1868, therefore, Bishop McQuaid proposed to the Josephite Sisters stationed at Canandaigua and Rochester the choice of returning to the jurisdiction of the Buffalo Diocese, or remaining at their posts as charter members of a new diocesan community. Twelve nuns consented to remain: Sisters M. Stanislaus Leary, M. Xavier Delehanty, M. DePazzi Bagley, M. Claver Hennessey, M. Lucy Gorman, M. Patrick Walsh, M. Clare O'Shea, M. Michael Brown, M. James O'Connell, M. Ambrose McKeogan, M. Camillus Payne, and M. Paul Geary.

The Bishop therefore designated St. Mary's Orphanage in Rochester as motherhouse and novitiate of the new Rochester community, and named Sister M. Stanislaus to the post of mother general. Mother Stanislaus (née Margaret Leary, 1841-1900), a native of New York State, had been a resident of Corning in 1856 when she entered the sisterhood at Canandaigua. In 1857 she became one of the two first nuns to receive the Josephite veil in the State. The new community had its own first religious reception on January 1, 1869. One of those who took the veil on that occasion was Sister M. Josephine (Nellie) Leary, a sister of Mother Stanislaus; and a second sister, Bridget Leary, entered the order on December 31, 1869, as Sister M. Joseph. The three pious daughters of Michael and Ann O'Connor Leary were to play pioneer roles not only in the Rochester Sisters of St. Joseph, but also, after 1882, in the Sisters of St. Joseph of Concordia, Kansas, and the Sisters of St. Joseph of LaGrange, Illinois.[48]

To the intellectual and spiritual formation of the Sisters of St. Joseph Bishop McQuaid thenceforth devoted the closest personal attention. The sisterhood was to treasure the memory of his weekly conferences on spiritualized pedagogy, and it is quite likely that the Bishop began this practice at the very start. The diocesan Sisters of Mercy thus found themselves in a rather odd position. They were as true collaborators as the Sisters of St. Joseph, yet they seemed to be relegated to an inferior position. Now it would have been physically impossible for the Bishop to devote as much of his time to both orders as he was determined to give to the Josephite sisters. Still, one cannot escape the conclusion that he might have acted a little more graciously towards the tiny Mercy community, which, under the guidance of Mother M. Camillus Kelly (†1897), was trying to fulfill not only the educational but also the welfare commitments of its religious rule. On the other hand, Bishop McQuaid's reserved attitude did have the good effect of creating among his Sisters of Mercy a patient and persevering self-reliance which eventually received its reward.

The new Bishop, quick to formulate his parochial school and teaching personnel policies, was also quick to launch his program for native vocations. In those days when most American bishops were foreign-born, the common practice was to recruit secular clergy in Europe. Of the American-born first bishop of Rochester it has been said that he was "the first, and for a long time the only American bishop who came out openly in favor of fostering and building up a native clergy."[49]

One of the earliest steps he took in this direction was the appointment of a regular annual collection for the education of the clergy. In a letter written from Rome on June 30, 1870, McQuaid told Father Early that he hoped he might get home from the ecumenical council before the end of summer in order to take care of such important agenda as "the Seminary Collection . . . and the opening of the Latin School . . ."[50] The collection, as he introduced it, and as it remained until 1921, was not a basket-collection but a door-to-door solicitation undertaken in each parish by designated lay collectors. The Bishop promised to celebrate one Mass for living and one for deceased contributors. When the seminary collection was first taken up in 1870, $6,902.97 was realized. By the end of fifty years it brought in close to $40,000 annually.

On his return home from the Council, the Bishop lost no time in opening his "Latin School", which during most of its career bore the name of St. Andrew's Preparatory Seminary. We shall see more of St. Andrew's later. Here we merely point to the term "Latin School" as an indication of the rather unusual sort of preparatory seminary that his poverty obliged him to found. His reference to this school in the letter of June 30, 1870, implies that by then the plan to found it had already been given mature consideration.

Thus within barely a year after his enthronement, Bishop Bernard McQuaid had already identified himself as an articulate publicist, firm disciplinarian, and farseeing educator. He had also given evidence that he had a high concept of the authority which a bishop exercises in his diocese. Perhaps this concept was at times exaggerated; but so, one may conclude, was that of a good many of his contemporaries in the American hierarchy, particularly those in the Irish tradition.

Furthermore, it was this view of the episcopal office which Bernard McQuaid took with him to the First Vatican Council. And it was this view which he brought back, tempered in only one respect.

3. AT THE FIRST VATICAN COUNCIL.

Normally, a diocesan bishop concentrates upon the spiritual needs of that portion of the universal Church over which he has been placed. But he likewise shares with the pope and all other Catholic bishops a group authority and concern for the needs of the whole Church. Usually this group authority is exercised through communications issued by the pope. Thus, for example, in 1854, before Pope Pius IX reached the conclusion that he could proclaim the dogma of Mary's immaculate conception, he consulted with all Catholic residential bishops on their teaching and the belief of their faithful in this matter.

Sometimes, however, it is deemed wiser not to consult merely through correspondence, but in an ecumenical council, that is, a council in which all the bishops meet with the pope in person to discuss and vote upon matters of import to the whole Church. These councils occur once a century, on an average. Since the United States came into existence, there have been two: the First Council of the Vatican, which opened in 1869, and the Second Council of the Vatican, which opened in 1962.

Bishop McQuaid took part in the 1869-1870 Council. While this council was not in the strict sense a phase of the history of the Diocese of Rochester, it cannot be separated from that history. In the first place, the Rochester Diocese was represented there in the person of its bishop. In the second place, its bishop played a distinguished, if minor part, in the deliberations. And in the third place, the faithful of the eight counties were, of course, affected by the conciliar decisions.

Six hundred ninety-eight major prelates from across the world attended the First Ecumenical Council of the Vatican. The American delegation numbered forty-six: six archbishops, thirty-nine bishops, and one abbot-general. McQuaid was a "junior member" of the councillors, along with the eleven other Americans who had been named bishops in 1868.

Modesty alone suggested to the younger bishops at the council that they leave the leadership of the body in the hands of their older and more experienced colleagues. The Bishop of Rochester was, furthermore, more shepherd than scholar, and frankly inexpert in some of the more subtle issues which were brought before the council "Fathers." For all that, he took his task seriously, performed his homework diligently, and cast his votes conscientiously. On the council's burning issue, papal infallibility, he had the courage to take the unpopular side because he believed it correct; and the humility to accept the council's contrary decision because he believed the council spoke the truth.[51]

The Bishop of Rochester arrived in Rome on November 26, 1869, and remained there until July 18, 1870. Duty, not pleasure, motivated the sojourn. He found acclimatization difficult, and moved his place of residence three times — from the North American College to the Hotel Minerva to a private dwelling — until he found a satisfactory location. Furthermore, it was very trying to be away so long from the diocesan tasks that he had barely begun to become acquainted with. And he was lonesome for his new diocese. On December 16th, he confessed to Father Early: "If I had my own way . . . I would soon start for home." "It will do no harm," he wrote in January, "to say an odd prayer for my speedy return to my Diocese." As the proceedings dragged on through the summer heat, he became even more restive. The only consolation he derived from this necessary exile was that the separation "has caused me to think so much more of home and all my friends, priests and people in it."

Many passages in his letters to Vicar General Early betray the Bishop's tender feelings. On December 1st, he wrote Father Early that he had lately begun to celebrate each day's Mass for a different priest of the Diocese. He spoke sympathetically of the patience with which his Buffalo neighbor, Bishop Stephen V. Ryan, also in Rome, had borne what seemed at first to be a mortal illness. When Christmas came, he missed his good people of the Cathedral parish, whom he often remembered at Mass. He instructed Father Early to give a New Year's greeting and a special gift in his name to the diocesan charitable institutions: $30.00 to the boys' orphanage, $20.00 to the girls', $10.00 each to St. Joseph's and the Canandaigua asylums, and $20.00 to St. Mary's Hospital.

Major diocesan concerns were naturally communicated to him by Father Early. He was posted on such things as the O'Flaherty case, the latest attacks by Bishop Coxe, the development of educational plans. Distance and the slowness of the mails made it hard for him to deal effectively with some of the home problems.

Even when he was in the Council, however, Bernard McQuaid was thinking of his diocese, for he automatically judged its proposals in the light of the needs of his own diocesans.

Long as the conciliar sessions may have seemed to McQuaid, the council was of such unanticipated brevity that it was able to issue only two *constitutions* on doctrinal subjects. The first of these dealt with several contemporary errors against the fundamentals of Catholic Faith. The second treated the primacy of the popes and their personal infallibility as supreme teachers of faith and morals. The Bishop of Rochester was an attentive listener at the debates and voiced personal opinions during both discussions.

When the tentative draft or *schema* of the first constitution was distributed among the Fathers, they quickly agreed that it was too long and too academic to be practical. Sent back to committee for revision, it reappeared in a much more acceptable form. Of the revised draft, the Bishop wrote Early: "There are some obstruse [*sic*] metaphysical points which few can fathom and certainly will never trouble the brains of any but a German Philosopher for whose especial benefit they seem to have been made. The rest is quite simple Theology."

He wrote these words on April 24th, the day he had joined with the Fathers in a unanimous final vote of approval for the constitution. But at the earlier voting on April 12th, he had cast the ballot *placet juxta modum*, i.e. a conditioned *aye*. When a Father cast a conditioned aye, he was required to state in writing the reason for his objections. McQuaid did so. Like many others, he held that the expression "holy Roman Catholic Church" which the decree used was not traditional, for earlier councils had never used the adjective "Roman" in that position. He also agreed with a number of his colleagues that a conclusion added to the text of Chapter IV should be eliminated. The "canons" annexed to the chapter pleased him still less. In keeping with ancient conciliar practice, the council had added to the positive statement of doctrine a series of declarations of anathema against all who held the opposite. Motivated no doubt by irenic considerations, Bishop McQuaid boldly recommended the omission, not just of the word "anathema," but of the whole collection of canons.[52]

The conciliar commissions gave due consideration to all the amendments recommended by the bishops. Only one of those changes submitted by the Bishop of Rochester (and others) was eventually accepted: the initial words of Chapter I were changed from *"Sancta Romana Catholica Ecclesia"* to *"Sancta Catholica Apostolica Romana Ecclesia."* Still, McQuaid was satisfied and more than satisfied, for he marvelled at the infinite efforts that had gone into the preparation of the final draft. "It was wonderful," he wrote to Father Early on the evening of the 24th, "the care that was needed and the pains taken to make everything as it ought to be." And the splendor of that day's solemn session in St. Peter's, at which the bishops, in tribute to the Holy Ghost, had worn red copes, had thrilled him with its color and majesty.

If the discussion of the constitution on Faith was relatively calm, that on the papal primacy and infallibility was almost cyclonic.

Opposition to the concept of a personal papal infallibility, apart from the infallibility granted by divine guidance to the whole body of bishops, had a long history. When the Church, around the year 1400, had three claimants to the papacy, some had sought a solution for the riddle in what is called *conciliarism,* that is, the theory that it is the whole body of bishops rather than the pope which holds the real authority in the Church. In 1682 a group of French ecclesiastics had ventured to formulate this erroneous (and largely nationalistic) opinion in four articles. The fourth read: "In questions of faith the leading role is to be that of the Supreme Pontiff; and his decrees apply to all churches in general and each of them in particular. *But his judgment is not unchangeable, unless it receives the consent of the Church."* Here the conciliarism was tempered, but it still stood firm against the concept of a personal papal infallibility in that it required the consent of the bishops to guarantee the infallibility of any papal utterance.

The conciliarist (or "Gallican") view had lost much of its earlier popularity, but a number of the bishops at the council — German, Austro-Hungarian and Irish, as well as French — had been bred in this tradition. To this (uncertain) number must be added two other groups: those Fathers who opposed the definition because they thought papal infallibility was not so clearly revealed as to admit of dogmatic definition; and those who thought any such definition unwise in that it would create a further obstacle to the conversion of non-Catholics. Hence, even before the debates opened on the subject, there was already a strong bloc in the council opposed to definition either because they were Gallicans, or they doubted the doctrine's definability, or they believed its definition would be inopportune.

Bernard McQuaid was from the start opposed to the defining of papal infallibility. When he arrived in Rome, he was probably not fully aware of the extent of the struggle already in course between the European definitionists and anti-definitionists. But he and his American colleagues were quickly swept into the Roman maelstrom. What he now heard — much of it doubtless slanted gossip — only confirmed him in his conclusion that a definition of papal infallibility would imperil the Church. He wrote Father Early on December 1st that the Jesuits had mounted a strong campaign to promote the introduction and definition of papal infallibility. He was hopeful, however, that the majority of the council Fathers would vote against even bringing the subject up.

A month later, however, the "definitionists" gave a first show of strength. On January 1, 1870, a petition for the introduction of papal infallibility into the discussions was circulated among the bishops and won 380 signatures, ten of them American. Several counter-petitions were promptly filed, one of which was signed by McQuaid and twenty-six other prelates from the United States and England. The counter-petitioners pleaded: that the raising of the subject would disclose a great rift among the Fathers; that a definition would hamper future conversions to the Church; and that raising infallibility to dogmatic status would most likely engender such great disputes as to undermine the usefulness of the whole council.[53]

Opponents to definition lost this round. On March 6, 1870, the council was publicly informed that, the majority having favored the discussion of papal infallibility, the Holy Father approved of its entry in the agenda. One day later, a draft of the proposed constitution on the Church, containing a tentative definition of papal infallibility, was distributed to the bishops, and they were invited to submit written observations on it even before the debates began.

The draft was long, and if its chapters were to be treated in order, the chapter on papal infallibility would have had to wait a year or more to reach the floor. This would have pleased the anti-definitionists, who believed that delay favored their side. But the definitionists, among whom were many American bishops, outmaneuvered their opponents by seeing to it that the controversial chapter was given priority. Discussions thus began May 13, 1870, and ran on to mid-July. McQuaid was disconsolate at the loss of this round. "Somebody," he wrote to Father Early on May 1st, "will have a terrible account to render for having stirred up this question for many a soul will be lost no matter how it is disposed of, even if put to one side which is now impossible".

Why did Bishop McQuaid stand so firmly against the definition?

One reason, strong though perhaps secondary, was his belief that it would be inopportune. This caused him a long, acute anguish. "My head is fairly splitting with pain and anxiety . . .," he wrote to Father Early, "God help the Church is my constant prayer." As early as April 24th he confessed that the issue had been "such a disturbance to my mind since I came to Rome that once it is disposed of in one way or another I will never want to hear of its controversy again." He foresaw only the most dire effects: scandal to non-Catholics, schisms among Catholics — not in his diocese or in the United States, but surely in France, Germany, Austro Hungary, and the East.

What complicated his opposition to a definition was the fear that papal infallibility would be defined in such broad terms that some of the more controversial of the actions of popes-gone-by, like the deposition of monarchs, would be considered infallible.

Fortunately, extremists who favored too wide a concept of the papal prerogative were bound to yield, and the ultimate definition was bound to be couched in more restrictive terminology. The Bishop of Rochester nevertheless stuck by his guns throughout the battle. He did not address the gathering, but he submitted his reasons in a hand-written statement which was entered in the council's records.[54] Here he revealed that his stand against definition was based not only on prudence, but also on what he deemed theological reasons. Agreeing with most of the doctrinal historians of the minority, he stated his opinion that the matter of papal infallibility was not clearly enough a revealed doctrine to be capable of definition as a dogma of faith.

Since he had embraced the cause of anti-definition in full sincerity, the Bishop was shocked to receive, on May 24th, a letter from an American priest of another diocese, urging him to sacrifice his convictions and vote with the majority for the definition. "Just as though I could dare do such a criminal act!" he exclaimed in that evening's letter to Father Early. "Thank God so far every vote of mine has been according to my judgment and not according to the judgment of anyone else. When I could not fully understand a question I gave no vote at all, but kept my seat." Regarding infallibility, he said he had read authors on both sides of the question, but had seen no reason to alter his view. "I am open to a change of mind," he declared, "but it must be upon proofs and facts, and not on what someone else may happen to think or vote . . ."

Being still of this mind, he signed a protest on June 4th against the termination of the debates.[55] And however much the final definition hedged in the exercise of personal papal infallibility, he joined with seventy-six other American prelates in voting against the constitution. This preliminary vote on July 13, 1870, had demonstrated the relative smallness of the anti-definitionist party, for of the 601 Fathers present, 88 had voted *non placet,* 62 conditional approval, and 451 *placet.* The final public vote was taken in the presence of Pope Pius IX on July 18th. There were five hundred and thirty-three Fathers on hand, and all of these but two voted *placet.* The Holy Father then solemnly confirmed the constitution.

McQuaid, like many others of the minority, had preferred not to attend the last session so as not to have to cast a negative vote in the presence of the Pope. He had therefore asked permission on July 16th to leave for home. Departing on the evening of the 18th, he arrived in Rochester on August 24, 1870, purposely without fanfare, and very happy to be home.[56]

On Sunday, the 28th, he mounted the pulpit once more in his unfinished Cathedral, proclaimed his acceptance of the dogma of papal infallibility, and instructed his congregation on the matter with a precision born of his conciliar experience. "I have now no difficulty in accepting the dogma," he said, "although to the last I opposed it; because somehow or other it was in my head that the Bishops ought to be consulted". Some time later, however, Vatican authorities intimated that McQuaid should make a formal statement in writing. In 1875, therefore, he attached to his announcement of that year's papal jubilee indulgences, English translations of both constitutions which the council had issued. This act was entered in the official records of the First Vatican Council[57]. Fortunately, the vast disturbances that the anti-definitionists had anticipated failed to materialize.

There was nothing inconsistent in Bernard McQuaid's vote against the definition and his subsequent whole-hearted acceptance of it. In the sessions he had shown himself a good parliamentarian. He had reached his conclusions on the basis of study and of what he honestly conceived to be the best interests of the Church in America and throughout the world. He had realized even at the time the role which the "loyal opposition" had played during the council: ". . . It seems to me," he wrote to Father Early on May 24, 1870, "that God has used a small minority of 120 to 150 to hold the majority in check and compel them to act with care and deliberation". And his vote *contra* had been an added testimony to the freedom enjoyed by the Fathers. But what he had voted down as a mere theological opinion had been confirmed by the majority as a dogma. Peter had therefore spoken through Pius IX, the truth had been declared, and Bernard McQuaid as a loyal child of Holy Church had accepted it readily and without question.

The Diocese of Rochester has every reason to be proud of the truly pastoral part which its young first bishop, at the very outset of his episcopal career, played in the twentieth general council of the Catholic Church.

CHAPTER SIX

"LEX SUPREMA"

A S WE HAVE already noted, the first bishop of Rochester adorned his episcopal coat of arms with the motto: "The supreme law is the saving of souls" *("Salus animarum lex suprema").*[1] Few phrases could better summarize McQuaid's whole career as a bishop. And unless we judge his actions, as he himself did, in the light of their apostolic value, we can reach no proper estimate of the man.

We allot the next three chapters to the portion of the McQuaid era that ran from 1870 to 1909. A convenient dividing line in his administration is the year 1896, when he finally acquired, thirteen years before his death, the jurisdiction of the four contested counties of the Southern Tier.

Although the admission of the four counties was to add 10,000 more Catholics to the 80,000 which the Diocese included in 1897, and although by 1909 the Bishop could count 121,000 subjects, the Diocese of Rochester, even at the time of McQuaid's death, was still relatively small. It also remained relatively poor. If, therefore, Bernard McQuaid was unable to see all his dreams realized, it was because his Catholics were too few and too poor to provide him with the means. If, on the other hand, despite the major business depressions of the 1870's and 1890's, he accomplished as much as he did—far more than the bishops of some larger and richer dioceses—it was because of his canny stewardship.

However wanting his diocese may have been in size and prosperity, Bishop McQuaid never gave serious thought to moving on to a larger see. He declined the nomination to the see of Newark in 1872, and the coadjutor archbishopric of Cincinnati in 1879.[2] "Send a saint to Cincinnati," he answered in the latter case, "I am not the man."[3] In 1887, when there was some talk of the appointment of an American bishop as apostolic delegate to the United States, he waved off the suggestion that he was a possible choice.[4]

It is true that none of these appointments appealed to him. But neither did thoughts of self-aggrandizement influence him; nor, still less, thoughts of a higher income. What really pleased him in Rochester, it seems, was the opportunity to create and develop to maturity a new and model diocesan structure.

The Diocese of Rochester came into being early in the Industrial Revolution, and it grew up in an era of social turbulence. What effects this turbulence had upon its people we shall see later on. The present chapter deals with the early growth of the original eight-county diocese; the efforts of its first bishop to provide for its spiritual and educational needs; and the emergence of McQuaid as a national figure in the movement for Catholic parish schools.

1. "MASTER BUILDER OF A NEW HOUSE."

According to the United States census of 1890, seven out of the eight counties that composed the Diocese of Rochester had increased very little in population since 1870—if, indeed, they had increased at all. Cayuga had risen from 59,000 to 65,000. But Ontario's 48,000 represented a growth of only 3,000; Seneca's 28,000, a growth of 1,000; Wayne's 49,000, a growth of 2,000; and Yates's 21,000, a growth of 2,000. The total for Livingston County (37,000) and for Tompkins County (32,000) was 1,000 less than it had been two decades before. Monroe County, on the other hand, had continued its rapid expansion, rising from 117,000 in 1870 to 144,000 in 1880 and 189,000 in 1890.

It will be noted that the counties that grew most in population were those with cities. As late as 1890, the Diocese could still boast of only three cities. By 1892, Auburn had reached 27,000 (17,000 in 1870). Rochester, maintaining its repute as a "boom town", progressed from 62,000 in 1870 to 89,000 in 1880, 133,000 in 1890, 144,000 in 1892, and 150,000 (at least) in 1896. If Monroe and Cayuga counties owed most of their growth to the increased populations of Rochester and Auburn, the same was not true of Tompkins County. Here Ithaca, with a population of 10,000 by 1887, had acquired municipal status. The 10,000 had expanded to 13,000 by 1892. But the rural population had meanwhile fallen off, to the disadvantage of the total county population.

It is easy to conclude from these statistics that while the eight counties still remained basically rural, they had not escaped the current trend towards urbanization. Farming indeed continued strong, although it became more specialized: truck farming, grape and fruit growing, and in particular, dairy farming. But the cities and larger towns, turning more and more to industry, furnished increasing employment for rural youth as well as immigrants. Rochester's notable milling industry, nursery industry, and real estate business, were still active in the 1870's. After the depression of 1873-1875, however, they began to yield ground to the shoemaking and clothing trades. In the 1880's, the optical firm of Bausch and Lomb, the Eastman camera and film company, and the Gleason foundry, initiated wide programs of expansion. Auburn's largest fac-

tory was the D. M. Osborne Company, manufacturers of reapers. Drop
forgings, shoes, rugs, and pianos were also made in Auburn. The smaller manufacturing concerns of Ithaca produced many agricultural tools.

Some of the Catholic immigrants, especially the Germans, settled
in the countryside and lesser towns; but the cities and their environs
now attracted an increasing number. Irish immigration continued, but
was declining. The tide from Germany continued unabated, so that by
1890 almost one-half of the inhabitants of Rochester were German-
born. Of course, Catholics constituted only a part of this German colony.
Many were Protestants or Jews.

While Catholic immigrants of the "old immigration" (that which
originated in northern Europe) were now diminishing, Catholics of the
"new immigration" (from eastern Europe and the Mediterranean)
poured into America in torrents. The Poles were the first to arrive in
numbers. The Italians began somewhat later, but once they had begun
they more than made up for the delay.

There had been some Catholic Poles in Rochester during the years
1850-1870, and the Redemptorists of St. Joseph's Church had given
them some attention. New arrivals augmented the local Polish colony
after 1873. The pastor of St. Michael's German Church, Father Fridolin Pascalar (1841-1899), took care of the spiritual needs of the colony,
and eventually urged them to set up a parish of their own. Therefore,
on May 16, 1887, the Poles assembled at St. Michael's Church and
organized the Society of St. Casimir to carry out the project. Their dream
was realized on November 16, 1890, with the dedication of the original
St. Stanislaus church building. The new church had been built on the
corner of Hudson Avenue and Norton Street in what was then a suburban district, largely uninhabited. Attracted by the church, Rochester's
Polish people soon began to move into this neighborhood, which still
remains the center of local Polish concentration.[5]

Rochester's first known Italian citizen was the Genoese, Domenico
Sturla, whose name appears in the 1868 city directory. By 1875, there
were some thirty Italians in Monroe County, most of them in Rochester.
By 1890, there were 516, by 1893, 1000; and the number increased
rapidly thereafter. Canandaigua had a half-dozen Italian inhabitants
by 1877.[6] The first Italians arrived in Clyde around 1885; in Geneva
around 1890. In 1884 and after, the International Salt Company brought
a group of immigrants to Retsof to work in the salt mines. It is prob-
able that the majority of these exiles from sunny Italy worked initially
on the railroads, brought over by some Italian *padrone* who had arrived earlier, learned English, and set himself up as a labor agent. Many,

therefore, were migrants rather than settlers: indeed, a good many came to America intending to return home after they had "made a fortune".[7] Those who did settle down in Rochester were usually obliged by their poverty, as well as by their ignorance of English, to live first in slum "rookeries", on the west side of the Genesee River. Once they had married, they industriously plied their humble trades: manual labor, cobbling, barbering, popcorn-vending and organ-grinding. But the occasional violence of some of these uprooted and inarticulate Mediterraneans merely confirmed many of their American neighbors in an antipathy to the whole Italian group. And even Catholics, whose own parents had encountered unfriendliness on their arrival in the United States, often showed a like uncharity towards the poor newcomers.

Another immigrant group which began to colonize in the Rochester area after 1880 were the Flemings from Belgium. Five or six of these Belgians settled in and around Rochester in the early years of that decade. In 1879, Bishop McQuaid had appointed to the pastorate of Rochester's "French Church" Father Alphonse Notebaert (1847-1928). A Flemish Belgian himself, Father Notebaert quickly established contact with the Flemish parishioners, and when several other Flemings came over in 1882, he was able to secure employment for them. The news of his kindness got back to Belgium, and Notebaert became a willing committee-of-one to welcome new immigrants from both Belgium and Holland who came to join the earlier arrivals. He also discovered other families from the Low Countries who had settled elsewhere in Monroe and Wayne and Ontario Counties. They, too, became affiliated with Our Lady of Victory parish. By 1904, the parish had four hundred Belgian and Netherlandic members—almost as many as the parishioners of French stock. The Low Countrymen, many of whom were able farmers, soon made their mark as solid new citizens.[8]

Increase of population necessitated the enlargement of several old church buildings or their replacement by new. Once the cathedral of St. Patrick was finished, parishioners of Rochester's pioneer parish were of course well provided for. Although not yet completed, it was opened for use on March 17, 1869. The dedication took place on November 6, 1870, and it was a splendid affair. Fifteen bishops were on hand; Archbishop John McCloskey of New York officiated; and Father Isaac Hecker, founder of the Paulist Fathers, preached the sermon. "A remarkably good sermon," McQuaid noted in his diary.[9]

Elsewhere in Rochester, the parishes of Holy Family, Holy Redeemer, and St. Bridget erected new churches in the 1870's; and St. Boniface in the 1880's. Outside Monroe County new structures were built in the parishes of Avon, East Bloomfield, Geneseo, Lima, Mount Morris, Ovid, Waterloo, and elsewhere. In design, these new buildings usually followed the current Neo-Gothic style. One of the few local Neo-Gothic edifices that had any architectural distinction was St. Boniface Church, Rochester. Designed by William Schnickel of New York, this brick building continued in use from its dedication in 1887 to its destruction by fire in 1957. It had a richly carved wooden altar, installed in 1894. The sculptor was Anthony Halstrich (1858-1910) formerly of the Academy of Fine Arts in Munich, who had established the "Anthony Halstrich Christian Art Studio" in Rochester in 1893. His studio (and, after 1895, that of the Tyrolese sculptor Frank Pedevilla [1865-1927]), executed most of the altar-building and sculptural commissions awarded by contemporary pastors of the Diocese of Rochester.[10]

An exception to the ruling architectural style was Holy Redeemer Church in Rochester, dedicated in 1877. Here a Rochester architect, Christian Knebel, sought inspiration from the German Romanesque, and crowned the twin towers with the onion-shaped domes so popular in Bavaria and the Tyrol. They remain a touching reminder of the Fatherland.[11]

The foundation of new parishes was a constant need. Between the years 1868 and 1896, Bernard McQuaid promoted from mission rank or created twenty-six parishes, and established seventeen new missions.

Six of the new establishments were in Rochester—or, rather, on its outer fringe. St. Michael's German church was dedicated in 1874, and entrusted to German-born Father Fridolin Pascalar. His congregation grew with such speed that a second church, the present one, was erected, and dedicated on September 28, 1890. Adolphus Druiding of Chicago was the architect of the second St. Michael's—a Neo-Gothic edifice which is not only attractive as a period piece, but has a soaring quality and graceful silhouette that truly adorn the skyline of the fifth ward. The Bishop was delighted with it. "The best Church in my diocese," he said, "not excepting the Cathedral."[12]

St. Michael's was the eleventh Catholic church in the see city. There was no question in McQuaid's mind what to name the twelfth: he dedicated, on February 15, 1885, the Church of the Holy Apostles. In 1888, he formally blessed two more new parish churches: St. Francis Xavier (German) on October 28th: and Corpus Christi on December 4th. We have already noted the official inauguration of St. Stanislaus Polish church on November 16, 1890.[13] When the Bishop blessed Holy Rosary Church on January 1, 1890, it was as a mission church of the

Cathedral. As early as July, 1896, however, he raised it to parochial rank and assigned the pastorate to Father John G. Van Ness.

Five other mission churches in Monroe County were promoted in the same manner during the years we are considering: Holy Cross in Charlotte (1873); St. John the Evangelist in Greece (1876); St. John in Spencerport (1878); St. Vincent de Paul in Churchville (1873); and St. Paul of the Cross in Honeoye Falls (1875). Of these, the first three had been set up as missions by Bishop Timon, the last two by Bishop McQuaid himself.

Yates was the only one of the other seven counties that gained no new parishes during McQuaid's first three decades. In Seneca County, the Bishop reestablished Holy Cross, Ovid, as a parish (it had been one in 1854, but then was reduced to mission status). In Tompkins County the Trumansburg mission was made a parish in 1872, and St. Anthony parish was founded in Groton in 1874. In Livingston County, two missions were "promoted": St. Michael's in Livonia Center (1871) and St. Columbkill (Columba) in Caledonia (1889). Three missions in Wayne County were raised to the same grade: St. Michael's, Lyons (1876); St. Thomas the Apostle, Red Creek (1877); and St. Patrick's, Macedon (1883).[14]

Ontario County acquired four new parishes: St. Theresa in Stanley (1875); St. Januarius in Naples (1876); St. Patrick in Victor (1882); and St. Francis in Phelps (1885). Of these, the first two were completely new foundations; the last two, former missions.[15] In Cayuga County, only one of the four new parishes had never been a mission. This was St. Mary's in Auburn. The other three were former missions: St. Bernard's in Scipio Center (parish, 1872); St. Patrick's in Cato (1882); and St. Patrick's in Moravia (1888).

Bishop McQuaid likewise initiated a number of missions during the years 1868-1896. (The dates we give are those of the completion or dedication of the church.) There were three in Monroe County: St. Joseph, Penfield (1872); St. Louis, Pittsford (1874); and St. Leo in North Parma (now Hilton) (1884). There were five in Livingston County: St. William, in Conesus (1881); St. Simon, in Springwater (1881); All Saints, in Fowlerville (1884); St. Raphael, in Piffard (1887); and Holy Name, in Groveland (1894). St. Simon and All Saints have since been abandoned and their churches disposed of. The other three Livingston foundations continue as out-missions.[16]

The two new mission churches in Ontario County were St. Mary's, Honeoye Flats (now Honeoye), (church dedicated 1876); and St. Dominic, Shortsville (church completed 1885). Seneca County likewise acquired two: St. Francis Solanus, at Farmerville (now Interlaken), (1875); and Sacred Heart, at Romulus (1876). St. Joseph's, in the village of Cayuga (1870), was the only new mission begun in Cayuga County; and St. Andrew's, Dundee (1877), was the only new one in Yates County. Wayne County, on the other hand, gained three: St. Mary's of the Lake, Ontario (1870); St. Patrick, Savannah (1876); and St. Rose of Lima, Sodus Point (1886).[17]

Circumstances sometimes forced a change in the status of both parishes and missions. We have already noted that St. Januarius, Naples, soon reverted to the rank of a mission. Holy Ghost Church in Coldwater (Monroe County) had a resident pastor from 1867 to 1887, and then became a mission once more. St. Mary's in Rushville (Yates County) was a full-fledged parish from 1875 to 1878, but has been a mission ever since 1878. The church of St. Ann, Lummisville, Town of Huron (Wayne County) was incorporated in 1869; but the priests of Clyde, who had a mission station at Lummisville until 1874, ceased to go there after that date, before any church had been built.[18] The Church of Holy Angels, Nunda (Livingston County), has had many canonical ups-and-downs. As we have seen above, it remained for some time under the wing of the pastor of Portageville, in the Diocese of Buffalo. McQuaid was finally able to attach it to St. Patrick, Dansville. In 1874, he gave it a resident pastor. But the pastor quickly discovered that the Nunda congregation was not really large enough or prosperous enough to support a full-time pastor. The Bishop therefore assigned Holy Angels to St. Patrick's, Mount Morris. At the turn of the century it reverted once again, briefly, to the pastor of Portageville. Only in 1931 did it achieve a permanent parochial standing.

As the spiritual guide of his flock, Bernard McQuaid was more solid than showy. There were, of course, certain extraordinary rites that he was required to celebrate, and he celebrated them not only with good grace but with a flair. This was especially true when the Holy See was in any way involved in the observance. On November 11, 1870, when Pius IX had been forcibly deprived of his Roman territory, the Bishop of Rochester had addressed to him a statement of sympathy and solidarity from the people of the Diocese of Rochester.[19] Five years later, as we have seen, he loyally announced the indulgences of the papal jubilee; and in 1881 he proclaimed the new jubilee appointed by the Pope for that year.[20] One senses in McQuaid's reaction to the death of Pius IX a distinctly personal grief at the passing of the noble pontiff who had named him to the see of Rochester. On February 12, 1878, he celebrated and preached at a solemn Requiem for the deceased pope in the Cathedral. Six days later he celebrated another memorial Mass, as the climax of a procession of the faithful from St. Joseph's Church to St. Patrick's Cathedral. And he also preached at a memorial Mass offered at St. Mary's Church in Canandaigua, one of the many such Masses held for Pius IX throughout the Diocese.[21]

At the consecration of a bishop, the consecrating prelate asks of the candidate, "Will you teach the people?" The first bishop of Rochester never forgot the pledge he had made on that day to preach the Gospel. In addition to his addresses at confirmations and other rites, he often preached from the pulpit of his cathedral church. During Advent and Lent he made a practice of giving a series of sermons. In the more particular matter of instructing his clergy, he was diligent at presiding over the semi-annual clergy conferences, and at imparting special counsels to his priests when they gathered in the Cathedral rectory for their annual retreats.

We have already alluded to Bishop McQuaid's insistence that the sacred ceremonies be carried out with correctness and with edification. While he was not himself a trained musician, he had a good ear, a pleasant singing voice, and a discriminating taste for *churchly* church music. While in Europe in 1870 he kept his Cathedral choir in mind, and returned with the music of a number of appropriate Masses.[22] Soon after his arrival in Rochester he had dismissed the old choir at St. Patrick's and installed a new choir that was more ready to sing the chant and a type of figured music less reminiscent of opera house and concert hall.

Nor did he let the issue of good church music rest at that. In 1884, the Third Plenary Council of Baltimore ordered the reform of American Catholic liturgical music. Subsequent to these decrees, McQuaid established, in 1888, a diocesan music commission, and promised to issue a "White List" of acceptable Masses written by members of the Cecilian and other contemporary schools of church music. A year before this he had secured the services of a new and excellent artist as organist and choir director at St. Patrick's Cathedral. Professor Francis Eugene Bonn (1848-1935), a Bavarian-born and German-trained musician and composer, was to dedicate the rest of his life to the cause of ecclesiastical music in the Diocese of Rochester. As music director at the Cathedral, professor of chant at St. Andrew's Seminary (1888-1928) and St. Bernard's Seminary (1893-1903), this able, humble, and beloved layman did much to set the musical standard which his Bishop sought to achieve.[23]

Bernard McQuaid had a very good opportunity to state his own ideas on church music at three annual conventions of the American Cecilian Society: Rochester, 1877; Chicago, 1885; and Rochester, 1887. In his address to the 1877 convention, the Bishop deplored the abusive custom of omitting the singing of the proper of the Masses. He said he hoped that the revival of the chant would soon bear fruit, and he reminded his listeners that at sung vespers not only the clergy but the whole congregation should take part. Personally, he favored the chant. But he took no stand for or against other forms of ecclesiastical music. His only desire was that God be given the best music possible. (Later on, as he became better acquainted with the Cecilian school, a movement of German origin, he agreed that its approach was highly satisfactory.) [24]

The pioneer Bishop of Rochester was personally devout, with a consistent, manly devotion. While certain of his pious practices naturally remained private, there were two that he sought to commend to others because of their tested worth: the rosary of the Blessed Virgin; and prayer for the suffering souls in purgatory. A rosary well said, he often told his congregations, "becomes a study as well as a prayer."[25] He was in a position to know, for it was his custom to recite fifteen decades of the rosary daily between his Mass and meditation. His solicitude for the "poor souls" had a rather interesting origin. When he was a young priest at Madison, New Jersey, a fervent Negro woman had requested him several times a year to say Mass for those souls in purgatory who had nobody to pray for them. Soon he adopted the practice himself, and while bishop he offered every Mass that he was free to offer, for the dead—apart from the two Masses he celebrated weekly "for the intentions of the Mother of God." When he learned of the passing away of his friends, he tried to say Mass for the repose of their souls even before he wrote condolences to the survivors. He frankly attributed the success of his diocesan efforts in particular to the "poor souls." He declared that the souls in purgatory never failed him when he asked their aid in his projects.[26]

Another evidence of Bishop McQuaid's solicitude for the dead, and at the same time one of his noblest charities, was Holy Sepulchre Cemetery, which he founded at Rochester in 1871. Before that time, Rochester Catholics had been buried either in St. Patrick's Cemetery on Pinnacle Hill, or in the small parish graveyards of St. Joseph, SS. Peter and Paul, Holy Family, and St. Boniface. To provide a common burial ground sufficiently large for years to come, the Bishop purchased 109 acres on the Charlotte Boulevard (now Lake Avenue) to the north of city. He blessed one segment of this land on September 10, 1871. Subsequently most of the bodies were gradually transferred from the smaller cemeteries to this new burial ground.

Intent upon making Holy Sepulchre a place of dignity and devotion, the Bishop devised a good watering system for it and promoted a careful landscaping. (In Pierre Meisch, the superintendent, he found a competent landscape artist and able administrator.) On April 23, 1876, McQuaid laid the cornerstone of the Chapel of the Holy Souls. The building that rose on the spot—designed by A. J. Warner—was a handsome little structure of Early English Gothic pattern with an open hammer-beam ceiling. Less successful (but practical in that it also served as a water tower) was the tower, built, along with the twin gate houses, in the succeeding years. The building material was a mottled fossilized sandstone, dug from a quarry on the cemetery grounds.[27]

When the cemetery chapel itself was completed, the Bishop and his clergy gathered there on November 1, 1876, to sing a portion of the office of the dead in anticipation of the feast of the morrow, All Souls' Day. After the office, Bishop McQuaid and the priests inaugurated the Old-World practice of marching in procession through the cemetery to bless the graves. The Blessing of the Graves became an annual rite thereafter. However, the bad weather that usually occurred in early November subsequently prompted the Bishop to move the ceremony up to October 9th in 1881, and in 1894 up to the fourth Sunday of September, the date still observed up to 1966.[28]

The Blessing of the Graves captivated Rochester Catholics, and they turned out for it in large numbers. Five thousand were present October 9, 1881, according to the estimate. Transportation to this rural location was solved by the Charlotte branch of the New York Central Railroad, which, on that occasion, provided a special train of twenty-eight cars.[29] Around 1890 an electric railway was built from the city out to Charlotte, and this made it still easier to reach the Cemetery. The crowds sometimes reached fifteen or twenty thousand, according to newspaper accounts. By 1907, refreshment vendors had begun to appear on the scene *en masse,* giving a sort of carnival aspect to the gathering. The Bishop protested to the Town of Greece authorities, with the result that at the Blessing of 1908 the vigilant Greece policemen locked up ten popcorn outfits until the religious rites were over.[30]

Bernard McQuaid, despite his charity towards the dead, was also aware of the need of charity towards the living.

Many were his personal charities — "little transactions between friends," as he called them.[31] Naturally no records of these transactions were kept, except in the hearts of his beneficiaries. He was ever ready to permit and encourage parochial charities. Those at the Cathedral no doubt had his positive endorsement. There the Ladies' Aid Society, founded in 1875, sewed garments for the poor and visited and assisted people in distress.[32] The Cathedral conference of the St. Vincent de Paul Society was still functioning, as was that at St. Mary's Church. McQuaid likewise approved the foundation of two more conferences: St. Bridget, Rochester (1873), and St. Mary's, Auburn (1875).[33]

Urgent needs usually called forth special charitable efforts. The depression of 1893 was such an occasion. At St. Mary's Church, Rochester, Father James P. Stewart organized an aid society in the fall of 1893. Its purpose was to help all the needy within the parish boundaries, irrespective of their religious connections. The aid society members were also urged to admonish any neighborhood saloon keeper that was selling liquor to men whose wives and children were impoverished.[34] St. Michael's Church, around the same time, opened a soup kitchen.[35] Nor was the diocesan spirit of charity limited by the diocesan boundaries. In 1871, for example, the Bishop and his faithful sent both money and provisions to help four charitable institutions destroyed in the Chicago fire.[36] And in 1906, after learning of the earthquake and fire which crippled San Francisco, the people of the Rochester Diocese sent the Archbishop of San Francisco $10,420.00 for reconstruction and relief.[37]

These particularized philanthropies by no means interfered with the functioning of the charitable establishments within the Diocese.

While St. Mary's Hospital in Rochester was not strictly a diocesan institution, it was the only Catholic hospital in the Diocese, and as such received the Bishop's loyal support. Thus, when a large portion of the hospital building was damaged by fire on February 15, 1891, McQuaid gave strong backing to the campaign for reconstruction. St. Mary's, promptly rebuilt, re-opened on the following Thanksgiving Day.[38]

The number of orphans in the Rochester Diocese increased rather than diminished after the arrival of the first bishop. In 1872, therefore, McQuaid built a new St. Mary's Boys' Orphan Asylum on West Main Street just east of Genesee Street.[39] In 1893, he erected a new St. Patrick's Girls' Orphan Asylum, on Clifton Street, just south of the boys' orphanage. By 1896, there were 150 boys at St. Mary's Asylum and 100 girls at St. Patrick's. The asylums received their principal income from mammoth annual fairs plus the door money from public benefit lectures that the Bishop delivered. The German parishes of the city meanwhile supported St. Joseph's Orphanage, which in 1874 was also given a new home, adjacent to St. Joseph's Church. In 1896, the enrollment at St.

Joseph's Asylum was ninety-eight: sixty-six boys, thirty-two girls. Each of these three asylums, by the way, had its own school; and the Sisters who taught there were paid by the Rochester Board of Education.[40]

The orphanage at Canandaigua also continued in operation, but remained small. In 1896, there were twenty children under its care, housed in the present St. Mary's convent.[41] For the eastern part of the Diocese, Bishop McQuaid founded the Auburn Catholic Orphan Asylum. Incorporated on May 19, 1887, this asylum was meant to serve the needy children of the Auburn district. It therefore drew its support chiefly from the Catholics of Cayuga, Seneca and Tompkins Counties. Sisters of St. Joseph were in charge, and it was housed in a large frame building on North Street. In 1896, sixty boys and eighty girls were inmates.[42]

Orphans could be taken care of at the asylums only up to a certain age. Many, when they reached that age, were still too young to make their own way in the world. This posed a problem that called forth new solutions: industrial institutions for teen-age boys and girls.

On April 27, 1873, the Bishop opened a "Home of Industry" for boys. The boys—about fifteen to eighteen in number—lived in a frame building on Excelsior Farm, a sixty-five-acre property that is now the northwest section of Holy Sepulchre Cemetery. The Sisters of St. Joseph supervised and schooled the youths, who also devoted much time to cultivating a truck-garden, orchard and vineyard under the guidance of a couple of professional gardeners. At the time of the harvest, the boys helped to steam-can thousands of tins of vegetables. A portion of the grapes that they gathered were used to make altar wine for the churches of the Diocese. While Excelsior Farm had much, in theory, to recommend it, it had to be abandoned after 1879. An earlier effort to stabilize its operation by importing Belgian lay brothers had failed. Furthermore, the number of boys available had proved to be too small to justify the continuation of the project.[43]

Two Homes of Industry for girls were instituted in the same decade as Excelsior Farm, one by the Sisters of Mercy, one by the Sisters of St. Joseph.

When the Sisters of Mercy on South Street incorporated on May 21, 1857, it was as the "Rochester Benevolent, Scientific and Industrial School of the Sisters of Mercy." Within a decade, they were giving some industrial training to girls, and aiding them to obtain employment.[44] But the real industrial school dates from 1872. After that the Sisters received orphaned and poor teen-aged girls for a term of four years, during which they worked for their keep at plain and fancy sewing and thus learned the trade of seamstress. By 1884 there were some fifty pupils enrolled. The Sisters discontinued the undertaking only in 1900, when they found that it imposed too great a burden on their small numbers.[45]

The pastor of St. Mary's Church, Father James P. Stewart, was the great champion and benefactor of the Sisters of Mercy in those days. He supported the Industrial School, built the convent on South Street which served as their diocesan motherhouse, and bestowed upon them $12,-000.00 worth of property.[46] It was he, furthermore, who inspired the Mercy nuns to launch, in 1883, a "Crèche" or day-nursery—also referred to as a "kindergarten"—where working mothers might leave their small children for daytime care. Five cents a day covered the costs of food and supervision for each child. The plan proved feasible and popular, but the convent itself, where the day nursery started, could not accommodate more than a dozen children at a time. Therefore the Crèche moved, in the spring of 1892, into new quarters in the Sibley Building, where there was room for from thirty to fifty youngsters. Four years later it was still going strong.[47]

The Bishop authorized, but played no active role in, these undertakings of the Sisters of Mercy. He did give special backing, however, to the Home of Industry founded in 1872 by Sister Hieronymo O'Brien.[48] Sister Hieronymo, we will recall, was the foundress and for years the superior of St. Mary's Hospital in Rochester. On the expiration of her annual vows in 1871, she left the Sisters of Charity of Emmitsburg, and on the invitation of Bishop McQuaid, joined the Rochester Sisters of St. Joseph.[49] Assigned to St. Patrick's Orphanage (which the Bishop had entrusted to his own Sisters of St. Joseph in 1870), Sister Hieronymo instituted there, in the summer of 1872, a House of Industry. It was a department comparable to the industrial school of the Sisters of Mercy, in which adolescent girl orphans did needlework on commission. The plan quickly proved its worth. Consequently, the House of Industry, changing its name to the Home of Industry, acquired its own quarters in 1873, and eventually, in 1888, it constructed a fine building for itself on East Main, near Prince Street. By this time the girls of the Home were not only engaged in sewing, tailoring and embroidering for a large clientele, but manufactured shoes and slippers which were sold both at wholesale and retail. Its school department was financed by the local board of education after 1877. In 1896, there were 110 girls in residence. By that time, however, social circumstances were changing, and the Home of Industry was beginning to outgrow its usefulness. But while it functioned, this philanthropic project only confirmed the right of "Mother" Hieronymo (as she was affectionately, though unofficially, called) to rank with the leading humanitarians in Rochester history.

One more welfare institution of Bishop McQuaid's early episcopate remains to be recorded. Conscious of his success in establishing a youth organization in Newark, McQuaid attempted to do the same thing in Rochester. The Rochester Catholic Young Men's Association was incorporated on April 3, 1872. Its aim was to open an institute that would provide Rochester youths with an interparochial library, gymnasium, and recreation center. The Association launched a stock issue, and on October 29, 1873 opened its new $40,000.00 building at 120 West Main Street. Unfortunately, the C.Y.M.A., however well conceived, came into being at just the wrong time. The depression of 1873 was beginning when the Institute opened its doors, and its ultimate financial failure must be considered one of the casualties of those "hard times."[50]

So it was that Bernard McQuaid began to "build up a new house" in western New York—or rather a new kingdom of piety and benevolence. He built not only with diligence, but with verve, foresight, and imagination.

2. "The Schools Are My Greatest Glory".

Bernard McQuaid once declared: "I have plans, definite plans, which I shall carry through to the letter."[51] So it had been from the start. And of all these plans, a major portion were educational. Perhaps the Bishop did not succeed, for reasons beyond his control, in carrying out all his educational projects. But what he did accomplish exerted an influence far beyond his diocesan boundaries.

Educational institutions are commonly divided into primary, secondary, collegiate, and professional. McQuaid's greatest success was in primary education. Second only to his achievement in primary schooling was his foundation of St. Andrew's and St. Bernard's Seminaries. He accomplished less in secondary education, and never realized his dream to found a college.

Let us reverse the order and look first of all at McQuaid's secondary schools. The Bishop would have liked to set up at Rochester another Seton Hall, combining a boys' high school, a men's college, and a seminary. More than once he seemed to be about to carry out the project. As early as 1869, when the Methodist Seminary was planning to move from Lima to Syracuse, rumor had it (correctly?) that the Bishop of Rochester was considering the purchase of the Lima seminary buildings to house a college.[52] The rumor never came true. In 1875, he announced as one of his long-term diocesan projects the opening of "a seminary for clerics and a high school or college for secular boys." But the economic depression of that decade cut so deeply into his annual seminary collection that the plan of 1875 never got off the ground. Indeed, he was unable at that time to inaugurate even the "business college" which he thought might subsequently develop into a regular college.[53]

In 1878, Bishop McQuaid turned in another direction. He sought to persuade the Jesuit Fathers to open a boys' preparatory school in Rochester. Although this, too, failed of realization, it is of special interest for the light it casts upon McQuaid's attitude towards religious orders.

Having singled out a possible site—near Driving Park Avenue where Maplewood Park now stands—the Bishop contacted the Jesuits at Buffalo in the late summer of 1878.[54] McQuaid knew the Jesuits, of course, from Fordham, where they had for a time been his teachers. What he probably did not know at that time was that the Buffalo Jesuits, who had recently established Canisius in Buffalo, were considering moving that school elsewhere because of its small success. Of course, the Bishop's request had to pass along the Jesuit order's chain of command, so an answer was not quickly forthcoming. Only in March, 1879, did the Buffalo Fathers decide not to move to Rochester.[55]

McQuaid still cherished the hope that Jesuits might undertake a new foundation in his see city. But while he was in England in 1879, he was admonished by Cardinal Henry Edward Manning, Archbishop of Westminster, to take a cautious view of religious orders. The English bishops were then negotiating with Rome for rules which would regulate the relations between a bishop and the exempt religious orders functioning in his diocese. Bernard McQuaid did not give up his idea of having a Jesuit school; but he preferred (as he informed the Buffalo superior) to wait until the Holy See had issued a ruling on the religious orders question.[56] The ruling appeared in 1881, in the constitution *Romanos Pontifices,* and in 1885 its application was extended to the United States. After that, we hear no more of a Jesuit high school in McQuaid's Rochester. Quite likely the Bishop, intent by 1885 on founding a diocesan seminary, had neither the funds to build a preparatory school, nor the desire to have the Society of Jesus as a rival in attracting vocations to the priesthood.

Rochester finally got a Catholic high school in 1906. Cathedral High (later, Rochester Catholic High), run by the Diocese, was co-ed, but became a boys' school when re-established as Aquinas Institute (1922). Out of Aquinas sprang St. John Fisher College, the "new Seton Hall" that McQuaid himself never managed to found.

He was more fortunate regarding high schools for girls. To the existing academies (the Academy of the Sacred Heart, operated by the Religious of the Sacred Heart, and St. Mary's Academy, operated by the Sisters of Mercy) he added, in 1871, a third, operated by the Sisters of St. Joseph. Even while the last-named community resided in its original motherhouse at St. Patrick's Orphanage, it conducted a small "select school." In 1871, the Sisters moved their motherhouse, novitiate and academy to a roomier site near the Cathedral, on the corner of Jay and Frank (Plymouth Avenue, N.). Before they entered the new home, they had already secured incorporation for the "Nazareth Convent and Academy." Nazareth Academy was for many years a boarding as well as a day school, and like the other two academies, it had both grammar and high school departments.[57] Out of this Nazareth Academy yet another college eventually grew: Nazareth College of Rochester.

If Rochester's first bishop did not personally create the three diocesan colleges—St. John Fisher, Nazareth College, and Catherine McAuley College of the Sisters of Mercy, he did create two important seminaries for the secular clergy: St. Andrew's Preparatory Seminary (1870), and St. Bernard's Theological Seminary (1893).

We have already remarked that Bernard McQuaid was one of the first American bishops to give strong backing to the development of a native American clergy. It is significant that when he founded St. Andrew's, there were only seven other preparatory seminaries in the United States. For a while, the new Rochester minor seminary was called St. Patrick's, for it adjoined St. Patrick's Cathedral. But it was renamed St. Andrew's—officially after 1879, unofficially at least from 1874. The Bishop of Rochester-in-America thought it appropriate to place his seminary under the saint who had been the patron of the old see of Rochester in England.

St. Andrew's Preparatory Seminary opened in a remodeled stable. At the start it was a free school, and principally a Latin school, taught by a small part-time staff of unsalaried priests, aided, later on, by a couple of lay masters. President from 1870 until his death in 1904, was the diocesan chancellor, Father Hippolyte DeRegge. DeRegge, by his personal donations, enabled the Bishop to add a wing to the school in 1889, in order to accommodate the growing student body. By that time the Seminary course had been expanded to four years and given a broader scope. From the start, McQuaid hoped to build a dormitory to house students from out-of-town.[58] This dream neither he nor his immediate successor realized. Consequently, seminarians from outside of Rochester had to room with approved families. But St. Andrew's proved so effective as a day school that Bishop McQuaid became a valiant defender of minor seminaries conducted in this manner. He maintained that it was much better for teen-agers to live in a home than to board out during their formative years. After 1875, therefore, the Diocese of Rochester sent no more of its clerical aspirants to McQuaid's alma mater, St. Hyacinth's, at Chambly, or to St. Francis Seminary at Milwaukee.[59]

His theological students normally attended St. Joseph's Provincial Seminary at Troy, New York. However, when the Bishop was in Rome in 1879, officials of the Holy See asked him if he had a major seminary of his own. Now, a diocese as small and as poor as Rochester could easily have been excused from building or maintaining its own seminary. But the question fascinated the Bishop, challenged him, and eventually induced him, even though he had at the moment no funds to work with, to plan a Rochester diocesan theological seminary.

From that time on, he began to set aside "pin money." To the "pin money" he added a certain portion of the annual collection for seminary students. From 1882 on, he also sought to persuade more prosperous Catholics to endow the future institution with student burses and professorships.[60] (This was something new in the history of American Catholic seminaries. Only once before had it been tried: at Seton Hall by McQuaid himself. At Rochester the scheme subsequently met with better success.) As early as 1880 he promised to celebrate a monthly Mass for deceased benefactors. Nor had he forgotten the faculty to staff his seminary. In 1879, he sent Edward Joseph Hanna to the North American College in Rome to complete his priestly studies and prepare to teach theology. In the years that followed, the Bishop designated others of his most promising seminarians to prepare themselves for teaching careers.

In April, 1887, McQuaid purchased a good site for the new institution—a plot of more than twenty acres on the east side of Charlotte Boulevard (Lake Avenue), just south of Holy Sepulchre Cemetery. It was a bequest of five thousand dollars, left to him for the seminary by the deceased nurseryman Patrick Barry, that decided the Bishop to undertake the actual construction. The Barry will declared that the legacy should be paid to the head of the Diocese "when his seminary shall have been built." A building is "built", McQuaid's lawyer told him, when its walls are up and its roof on. So the Bishop decided to raise at least the shell of the building as soon as possible.

Construction commenced in 1891. A local architectural firm,

Warner and Brockett, drew up plans for a long main building, facing west; a chapel-refectory building, running off behind the main building at a right angle; and a separate convent building, also in the rear. The Rochester contractor, Hiram Edgerton, used stone from a neighborhood quarry near Hanford Landing Road. It was a mottled fossilized rock like that used in the cemetery buildings. Clergy and faithful, impressed by the urgency of the Bishop, came up with a generous contribution of $60,000.00. Now the building would not have to remain a mere shell.

By August, 1893, the work was done. On the 19th of the month, Bishop McQuaid dedicated the chapel to the Blessed Virgin, under the title of the Immaculate Conception. On the following day, the feast of St. Bernard, he blessed the whole institution.

On September 3, 1893, McQuaid's dream—which many had thought wildly impracticable—came completely true. Thirty-nine young seminarians, most of them transfers from the Troy seminary, the rest recent graduates of St. Andrew's Preparatory Seminary, took up residence as the pioneer students. A pioneer faculty of eight awaited them. Father James J. Hartley (1860-1943), was pro-rector, procurator, and professor of moral theology. (As procurator he had charge of the seminary farm that supplied the new school with meat, milk, fruit and vegetables.) His staff was: Father Edward J. Hanna, S.T.D. (1860-1944) Professor of dogmatic theology; Father Andrew J. Breen, S.T.D. (1863-1938), Professor of Hebrew and Sacred Scripture; Father Andrew B. Meehan, S.T.D. (1867-1932), Professor of Canon Law and Liturgy; Father Owen B. McGuire S.T.D. (1864-1950), Professor of Mental and Moral Philosophy; and Father Prosper Libert (1853-1931), a native of Belgium, Professor of Science and Librarian. Mr. Ludlow E. Lapham, M.A. (1860-1909), a convert to the Faith and himself a student for the priesthood, was Professor of English and German; and Professor F. Eugene Bonn was instructor in chant.

McQuaid entrusted the housekeeping to laywomen, supervised by a few sisters of St. Joseph.[61] This was an unusual step, and some more conservative Catholic clergymen criticized him for it. But the Bishop, as usual, had good reasons. In the first place, he said, only women can do domestic work properly. And in the second place, if the presence of women troubled the seminarians, they should ask themselves whether their vocation was to be diocesan priests or Trappist monks.

There is no question about it: St. Bernard's Seminary was the apple of his eye. So long as the Bishop lived, it was he, rather than Father Hartley, who was the actual rector. One of his policies was to welcome students from other dioceses. As early as 1894, the Seminary received one seminarian from the Syracuse Diocese and another from the New Orleans Archdiocese. Before long St. Bernard's, although conducted by the Diocese of Rochester, was in fact an interdiocesan seminary. As the founder fully appreciated, interdiocesan contacts gave seminarians a broader point of view.[62]

Still, it was the system of parochial schools that Rochester's first bishop called his "greatest glory."[63] "Christian free schools," as he loved to call them.

When this ardent and experienced champion of parochial schools arrived in Rochester to take up the reins of office, he discovered that his eight counties were almost completely lacking in Catholic grammar schools. The only true parish schools in Rochester were those of the five German parishes, which at that time educated some 2,300 pupils. They were staffed by the School Sisters of Notre Dame, although at St. Joseph's and SS. Peter and Paul these nuns taught only the girls, since the Brothers of Mary conducted the boys' classes.

St. Patrick's parish also had a school for girls, operated by the Sisters of Charity, and a school for boys, operated by the LaSalle Brothers of the Christian Schools. At St. Mary's parish, the teachers were Sisters of Mercy. But the schools taught by all three of these orders were not true parochial schools. Each of them had a tuition school, which was private, and a "poor school," for those whose parents could not afford tuition. Bishop Timon had disliked the undemocratic character of this double school, but because the orders depended for their support on the pay school, he had allowed the practice to continue. Bishop McQuaid also disliked it, and was determined to abolish the "poor school" plan, and to establish in every parish of the Diocese where it was possible, full-fledged parochial schools, supported by the congregations, for the free education of Catholic children.[64]

If the Catholic school situation in Rochester proper was unsatisfactory, it was still less satisfactory elsewhere in the new diocese. At Canandaigua, the Sisters of St. Joseph conducted a "free school," and the Sisters of Mercy at Holy Family Church in Auburn did the same. The Catholic parishes at Coldwater, Dansville, Webster, and perhaps also Ovid, had small schools taught by lay teachers. At Lima, the parish school, taught by a Catholic lay teacher, had been integrated with the local public school system, and had thus ceased to be a strictly parochial institution.

When he appraised this diocesan problem in 1868, the new bishop frankly stated that if St. Patrick's Church had not been under actual construction, he would have kept the "Shanty Cathedral" and devoted its building fund to parochial schools.[65] At any rate, he was not hampered by any existing parochial school system. He could therefore build up the sort of system he deemed best.

Careful planning went into the launching of his program for tuition-free parish schools. First came the publicity. On June 8, 1871, the feast of Corpus Christi, he staged a magnificent citywide procession of Catholic children of school age. Thousands of youngsters, white-clad girls and flag-waving boys, marched from each of the city parishes to the Cathedral, and from the Cathedral to Jones Square. Joined there by large delegations of their elders, they listened to addresses delivered in English, German and French. After the Bishop had given Benediction, the procession re-formed, marched back to Main Street, down Main Street to the Liberty Pole at Franklin, and then disbanded. It had been the Bishop's intention to show Rochester the size and the seemliness of Rochester's young Catholic population. To judge from the newspaper accounts, the message went home.

On September 3rd, the Bishop moved on to the next phase. He announced from the pulpit his intention to establish a diocesan-wide network of tuition-free parochial schools. The public schools, he said, simply did not give the complete education that Catholic parents want for their children. Even if the maintenance of a Catholic school system involved their paying, in effect, a double school tax, he felt that Catholic couples would not decline to shoulder this second financial burden.

His school plan? First he would reopen the Cathedral schools as one school, truly parochial in character. The Christian Brothers would continue to instruct the older boys. He intended to replace the Sisters of Charity with his own Sisters of St. Joseph as teachers of the younger boys and the girls. At the same time he was to open a new parochial school, likewise staffed by the Josephite Sisters, at the Immaculate Conception parish in Rochester. As soon as possible the other local English-speaking parishes were scheduled to inaugurate their own grammar schools, so that before long the Catholic parochial schools in the city of Rochester would be attended by five thousand youngsters—only one thousand less than were enrolled in the public schools. Nor would the Catholic schools be content, he said, with low standards. They would "give as good a secular education as can be obtained in the public schools, and a Christian education besides."

Once begun in the see city, the new program slowly spread out into the rest of Monroe County and the other seven counties of the Diocese. By 1896, all of the then fifteen parishes in the city of Rochester had their own schools with the exception of St. Stanislaus, where the schoolhouse was still under construction.[66] At the end of the same year there were also fifteen parochial schools outside Rochester: three in Auburn, two in Dansville, and one each in Avon, Brockport, Canandaigua, Coldwater, Geneva, Greece (Ridge), Ithaca, Lima (Catholic public school), Penn Yan, Seneca Falls, and Webster.

Two of the parochial schools functioning in 1896 were in the custody of the Sisters of Mercy (St. Mary's, Rochester, and Holy Family, Auburn). The five German Catholic schools in Rochester continued under the School Sisters of Notre Dame, although the Brothers of Mary (Marianists) had charge of the boys' classes at St. Joseph's until 1899.[67] All the rest (except Coldwater, with a lay teacher or teachers) were now staffed by the Rochester Sisters of St. Joseph. The community had grown so rapidly that by 1896 it had 198 professed nuns. After 1881 the Cathedral parish school had only Josephites on its faculty. The Christian Brothers had suddenly withdrawn in 1872 "before Bishop McQuaid could expel them," as they believed he intended to do. That this was his immediate intention seems unlikely, for he had to call 'n laymen to replace the Brothers, since there were not enough diocesan Sisters available. Daniel B. Murphy, James Rowan, and William E. Ryan succeeded each other as schoolmaster to the boys until 1881.[68]

Whatever may have been the Bishop's plan regarding the Christian Brothers, the rumor that he had intended to dismiss them spread, and doubtless helped to create the popular impression that Bernard McQuaid was hostile to male religious orders in general. This was not the case. He believed it a good thing to have a clerical order or two in a diocese, to provide confessors and counsellors for his priests and faithful. He himself often sought the advice and aid of the Redemptorists at St. Joseph's. He also had no objection to the presence of teaching orders within a diocese—as witness his own attempt to secure the aid of the Jesuits. What he did frown on was entrusting parishes to religious communities. Hence sprang his interest, already referred to above, in the papal constitution *Romanos Pontifices* which better determined the control that a bishop could exercise over male religious in his diocese.[69]

McQuaid wanted not only many schools, but *good* schools. If he concentrated on giving the Sisters of St. Joseph a special pedagogical formation, it was with the realization that he was settting a high educational standard that could not fail to have a salutary influence on the other religious communities who taught in his diocese.

The same motive of excellence prompted him as early as 1874 to have his parochial school children take the New York State Regents examinations. Fourteen pupils from various parochial and private Catholic schools went over to the Rochester Free Academy in June, 1874, to submit to the ordeal. Only one of the fourteen passed the tests. It was a poor beginning, but the Bishop did not give up. Gradually all the Josephite parish schools adopted the same annual practice, with increasingly good results; and the schools conducted by other religious communities eventually followed suit. After Nazareth Academy had received its state charter in 1891, the examinees in Rochester went there to try the State examinations. The Bishop was pleased to see that his pupils now held their own with those trained in public schools. The Regents tests thus provided both teachers and students with a strong incentive.

But incentive is not the only thing that teachers need. Without proper training a schoolmaster can accomplish little. Bishop McQuaid was well aware of this fact. He early saw to it that the Josephite Sisters received added instruction in pedagogy. In the late 1870's, he sent two of his nuns to a normal school at Bruges, Belgium. During the next decade other sisters were assigned to European study, some at Bruges, others at Kloster Bonladen in Württemberg, others at the Collegio Marcelline near Genoa.

In 1895, the New York State legislature enacted a law that established higher norms for the training of teachers who planned to teach in the public schools. Since a fair number of graduates from Nazareth Academy entered the teaching profession, it was important that the Academy, even though a private school, measure up to the new criteria. The Sisters therefore sought official approbation from the office of the State Superintendent of Public Instruction. They were required only to add a course in zoology and to extend the course in drawing. The rest of the Nazareth syllabus was already stronger than the new law required, so it met with immediate acceptance. On February 17, 1896, State Superintendent Charles R. Skinner notified the Academy staff of his formal approval.

In the same year, 1896, Father James P. Kiernan, rector of the Cathedral and general director of Nazareth Academy, organized a diocesan Institute for Religious Teachers, with the blessing of his Bishop. This was a new undertaking not only in the Rochester Diocese but in the American Catholic Church. It ran for two weeks, from July 20th to July 31st. The faculty comprised, in addition to Father Kiernan, one Jesuit priest, a laywoman who had graduated from a state normal school, two other laywomen who were teachers in normal schools, and a fourth laywoman attached to the State Department of Public Instruction. Two hundred and fifty Sisters representing five teaching communities were in attendance. They came not only from the Rochester Diocese, but from the dioceses of Chicago, Detroit, Boston, and Wheeling. On hand also were a hundred lay teachers, twenty-five priests and twenty-five visitors. The Institute was accounted very successful, and while it was not repeated in subsequent years, it led to the establishment of the present diocesan teachers' institutes, inaugurated in 1904. Finally, in 1898, the Sisters of St. Joseph opened their own Normal School.

As soon as a parish had an adequate tuition-free parochial school with competent teachers, Bishop McQuaid impressed upon the parents of the parish that they had a spiritual obligation to send their children to this school. In fact, he ordered that parents who failed to send their children to the parish school be denied absolution in confession until they complied. He could not impose the same penalty regarding high schools, for he was unable to provide Catholic high schools accessible to all Catholic children. But regarding the grammar schools, the Bishop considered denial of the sacraments the only appropriate penalty for mothers and fathers who demonstrated a stubborn neglect of their spiritual duty by deliberately entrusting their youngsters to public or other non-Catholic elementary schools.

This was a very strong stand. In 1874, his friend Archbishop Bayley pointed out to Bishop McQuaid that in the city of Rome, Italy, parents were allowed considerable freedom in their choice between Catholic and public schools. This gave the Bishop of Rochester some pause. However, on November 24, 1875, the Holy Office at the Vatican sent to the American bishops an instruction that strengthened McQuaid's hand. The instruction stressed the parental obligation to send Catholic children to Catholic schools, and declared that the refusal of sacramental absolution was justifiable when parents did not give their children adequate religious training, or, when there were good Catholic schools available, still sent them without reason or due precautions to a public school. The document did, indeed, imply that some Catholic schools might be considered inadequate if they were "little adapted to giving the young an education fit to their station in life." This and other nuances of the papal instruction seemed to make allowance for certain exceptions. But the Holy See left the determination, up to the local bishop. Bishop McQuaid continued, therefore, to follow his strict policy; and to justify it he appealed to the instruction of November 24, 1875.[70]

The Bishop's policy in enforcing attendance may at times have been too stringent, and one could perhaps discover other flaws in his program for parochial schools. But incidental faults do not nullify the general worth of an enterprise. Bernard McQuaid's campaign for parochial schools, begun in the face of widespread apathy and carried through in a truly progressive spirit, must be counted a real achievement.

3. THE EDUCATIONAL PHILOSOPHER.

Bernard J. McQuaid's reputation as an educator was based not only on the number and quality of the schools he founded but on his influence as an educational theorist, publicist, and controversialist. While he was not an educationalist in the academic sense, he was a born pedagogue whose intuitions were usually sound and practical, occasionally provocative, and seldom dull.

In 1897, for instance, McQuaid distilled four decades of thinking on seminary education into an article called "Our American Seminaries."[71] Part of the article describes the new St. Bernard's Seminary, and the glowing description of some of its modern "comforts" is rather amusing today. But a number of the practices which he had introduced and here defended represented a calculated break with older seminary customs. He paid relatively greater attention to the convenience of the students; he omitted regular reading at mealtime; he sent the seminarians on walks in smaller groups; he laid special emphasis on practice-preaching; he confided the domestic management of the seminary, as we have already noted, to female domestics. The motive behind these policies was that he was training secular priests, not monks; priests for the Americans, not for the Europeans or those in mission lands. For much the same reason, he defended the staffing of seminaries *for* diocesan priests *with* diocesan priests rather than with members of a religious community. But he insisted on top-level teaching, advocated the employment of priests who were non-members of the faculty as examiners, and anticipated the day when Rome would grant well-organized American seminaries the right to confer theological degrees.

In the section of the essay devoted to minor seminaries, the Bishop stated what he believed was the special merit of a day-school seminary like St. Andrew's. If a callow young aspirant continues to live at home, he said, a mother can "demand more of her son than any college would dare impose."

With the passage of time, many of Bishop McQuaid's seminary methods have become outmoded, even the more advanced. But his basic principle, that American seminarians should be trained in an American way for an American apostolate, has not lost its validity.

The conferences which the Bishop gave over the years to the Sisters of St. Joseph also had an important normative influence. He urged them to aim high as teachers, and to be discontent with anything short of the widest knowledge and the fullest effort. "A teaching community that rests satisfied with what they know will never make much advancement . . . Our Lord has a right to the best that we can give him . . ." Knowledge is not the only thing that counts, however. What really counts, he said, is the right use of knowledge; and every teacher should put "a certain amount of *individuality*" into her school work. The teacher in a Christian school should remember above all that she is called upon to be a teacher in the highest sense, an educator of the soul as well as the mind, and her very manner in class should reflect this role. She should not forget the physical welfare of her charges. She should never indulge in whipping: "It is lowering to your sex and I positively forbid it." In the last analysis, the careful preparation of her class work is the key to good discipline. Her aim should be always to "have God in your schoolroom," and always to see in each child "a soul redeemed by the Precious Blood of Jesus Christ." Hold to this purpose, then, he exhorted the nuns, and "whatever you teach, even if it be the ABC's or multiplication tables, let it be done so purely and so well for Him that the youngest children will recognize His presence."[72]

Advice of this sort amply demonstrated that the Bishop of Rochester was both a good shepherd and a practical pedagogue.

It was his lectures and articles on "Christian Free Schools" that brought Bishop McQuaid's educational philosophy to the attention of the largest audience. He began his career as an educational publicist with two lectures that bore that title, delivered in Rochester's Corinthian Hall on December 9, 1871 and March 15, 1872, and reported in full by the local *Union and Advertiser*. The thesis he advanced was that the native right to educate children belonged to parents. Parents therefore could in all justice demand for their children the sort of training that conscience required.

Now the public schools of those days, the Bishop continued, did not provide the complete education which Catholic conscience required. They failed to give to school work a proper and necessary religious reference, for in the public schoolhouse the orientation was either Protestant or, if religion was purposely avoided, "Godless." Consequently, Catholic mothers and fathers were justified in setting up their own "Christian schools." He denied that the State had a right to interfere with parental educational duties, or to monopolize education. The State did have a duty, however, to pay for the education of all its children in the necessary *secular* subjects, no matter what accredited school they might attend, public or private. In making his presentation, Bishop

McQuaid addressed his largely Protestant audience courteously but firmly and cogently, citing only Protestant writers to prove his points. In so doing he showed a remarkably wide acquaintance with current educational literature.

The first of the two lectures provoked a vigorous reaction, pro and con, from the pulpits and press of Rochester. This was, of course, just what the Bishop desired; and it confirmed him in his plan to plead his case insistently, in the hope that he might obtain for Catholic children the educational support due to them as citizens. He gave the same lecture at Albany, Buffalo, Clyde, Oswego and Syracuse. He also bought and circulated throughout the Diocese five thousand copies of the pamphlet *Who Shall Have the Child?* by the Paulist, Father Isaac Hecker.

The second lecture argued the same subject in still greater detail, quoting several additional non-Catholic educational authorities. The Bishop also delivered this talk from several platforms in and outside of the Diocese of Rochester. When the Rochester *Democrat and Chronicle,* disagreeing with the lecturer, asked for a fuller explanation, McQuaid was glad to oblige. It was no intention of his, he declared, to destroy the existing public school system. What he wanted to do was to expand that system. Should not Catholics who "fill the barn" be given at least a "handful of fodder?"[73]

Bishop McQuaid now reprinted the initial pair of lectures and distributed them. They also appeared in a German translation. Thereafter he took every opportunity, especially at conventions and the dedication of schools, to warn Catholics of the drift of the public schools away from religious implications, and to remind them that they had a duty as citizens to press for a solution by democratic agitation.

The only practical result of the Bishop's early efforts was a resolution, adopted by the Rochester Board of Education on June 7, 1875, to *prohibit* religious exercises in the local public schools. This was not at all what McQuaid desired. He believed that the teaching of some religion in public schools was better than the teaching of none, and he approved the use of Protestant devotions in those schools frequented exclusively by Protestants. But the action by the Board was an implicit admission that the Bishop had been correct in accusing the city schools of Protestant leanings. It only added to his arguments for parochial schools.[74]

On February 13, 1876, Bishop McQuaid delivered another lecture, "The Public School Question," at the Horticultural Hall in Boston, Massachusetts. Here his hosts were the members of the Free Religious Association, a freethinking group. At Boston, the Rochester prelate restated his now familiar case. Our public schools are inadequate for the Catholic conscience, for their religious slant is either Protestant or secularist, and therefore in both cases sectarian. Consequently Catholic parents have not only a right to maintain their own State-approved schools, but to obtain from the State, out of what they themselves have contributed in school taxes, sufficient public funds to pay for the basic training of their parochial school children. He recommended the expansion of the common school system, but suggested no definite plan, merely presenting his ideas as a matter for discussion.

McQuaid had already spoken rather favorably of one definite plan in a newspaper interview that appeared in the *Buffalo Courier* on November 24, 1875. In response to the reporter's query, he said there was one possible solution that at least deserved careful consideration. This was the so-called "Poughkeepsie Plan," according to which the local board of education rented the parish school building and paid its certified teachers—even if they were nuns—to teach the children the usual State syllabus of secular subjects. When this arrangement was adopted, it was agreed that during the official school hours there would be no religious instructions or exercises. Here was a form of common-school expansion that had been agreed upon in many localities across the country. Not only Elmira and Corning, both in the Buffalo Diocese, had such schools, but there was one in the Rochester Diocese, at Lima.[75]

Two important secular periodicals carried further articles by Bishop McQuaid in the 1880's. "Religion in Schools," appeared in the *North American Review* in April, 1881; "Religious Teaching in Schools," in *Forum*, December, 1889. Both essays discussed the by now customary subject. That in the *Forum* ventured to suggest two practical means of doing justice to Catholic parents. One way, he thought, might be to allow parents to apply the school taxes they themselves paid, to the education of their own children, provided that the children were educated according to State educational norms. Or, on the other hand, the State itself might pay instructional costs, in secular subjects only, for children who attended any school that met State requirements. These were the only approaches that seemed to him at all feasible. He was now inclined to reject the Poughkeepsie Plan. He admitted that it had functioned well in some places, but it labored under distinct disadvantages. Somehow it smacked of union of church and state. Religiously, too, it left much to be desired: "To some degree it weakens and deadens the Catholicity of our schoolrooms."

Certain arguments and positions that Bernard McQuaid set forth in these stimulating public statements were perhaps ill-considered then, or since that time have become irrelevant. Still, the school problem which he was bold enough to ventilate before so wide and varied an audience, is not much closer to a solution today than it was in 1871. What is most interesting is to observe how correctly the Bishop defended the parochial school and how clearly he discerned the strong trend towards monopolistic secularism in public education.

That such an articulate spokesman for Catholic education should also have played a part in the educational counsels of the American hierarchy is a foregone conclusion.

Sometimes it was a very lively part, as in the controversy over the Catholic University of America. The foundation of a great American Catholic center of higher education had often been discussed after the Second Plenary Council of Baltimore (1866), at which it had first been broached. In his seminary pastoral of 1882, McQuaid praised the general concept of a Catholic university and a higher school of theology, but said that it must yield place at present to the more important task of founding and enlarging diocesan and provincial seminaries. However, the Third Plenary Council of Baltimore, convening in 1884, was more optimistic about the proposed national university. In *Titulus V* of its decrees, the Council Fathers authorized the hierarchy to take steps to establish a higher school of theology (*seminarium principale*), which, it was implied, could form the nucleus of an eventual university. Bishop McQuaid was still not opposed to having an official American Catholic university. Indeed, when he theorized about the matter he was inclined to favor the establishment of *three* such institutions: in the East, Midwest, and Far West. But he still believed in 1884 that the time for such an undertaking was far off.[76] For the present, he was willing to go along with the decree for the setting up of the *seminarium principale,* to be supported, as he understood, not by the general faithful of the dioceses but by outstanding clergymen and wealthier Americans.

Almost from the start, however, the steps that the founding committee took displeased the Bishop of Rochester. They wanted to build at Washington, which McQuaid thought was a poor choice. They also wanted to set up at once not only the higher school of theology but other university departments. McQuaid completely disapproved of this, and predicted that if they had their way, the new institution would soon have to turn to the ordinary faithful for its support, contrary to the original plans.[77] For this reason, he joined with Archbishop Michael A. Corrigan of New York in opposing the university conception which Archbishop John Ireland of St. Paul and Bishop John J. Keane, rector of the projected university, were negotiating in Rome. Despite his opposition, the Catholic University was given papal approbation. The Bishop of Rochester was intentionally and obviously absent when the formal inauguration of the University took place in 1889.

McQuaid's prophecy was fulfilled in 1903, when the hierarchy felt obliged to authorize an annual collection in every American parish to help finance the Catholic University. As he had refused to allow solicitation in his diocese for the foundation of the University, so he now refused to take up the yearly collection in his parishes. To the end of his life he shunned the Washington institution and all its works and pomps.[78]

To a point, the Bishop of Rochester's motives in this issue were understandable. At the time the University project was launched, he was engaged on a number of diocesan projects, his major seminary in particular, that required the most careful economy of the funds available to him. To his way of thinking the scheme to open a complete university was premature, and he was unwilling to share the small and vitally necessary assets of his own small diocese with an educational undertaking that he considered abortive. A reasonable stand; but one wonders whether Bishop McQuaid would not have been wiser to come around, once the University had unexpectedly weathered its early storms. If the majority of the American hierarchy had now agreed to keep it going, he might better have yielded gracefully to the inevitable and given at least a token donation to the cause.[79]

There is reason to believe that Bernard McQuaid's attitude towards the Catholic University of America sprang in part from an insufficient understanding of the nature of a true university. But he did have a deep appreciation of the nature of seminaries and parish schools, and in these fields he was able to make a real contribution towards the educational legislation of the Third Plenary Council of Baltimore.

McQuaid excused himself from membership in the Council's committee on seminary education, but entered with interest into the discussion of its legislative proposals. Regarding minor seminaries, he advocated more intensive training in English studies than the submitted plan required. He took an active and influential part in formulating the syllabus for major seminaries. He opposed, with several other bishops, a decree that required each American seminary to have a summer "villa" or vacation-home. This was the custom in Europe, but McQuaid denied that the only way to preserve the vocation of seminarians was to keep them sequestered all year round. "We do not know," he pointed out, "what kind of priests we are going to have unless we have proved them while students by the test of experience."[80] (When he founded St. Bernard's Seminary nine years later, he gave it no "villa." This has enabled its students to engage in some appropriate summer work, to earn a bit of money, and to gain some valuable experience in the "outside world.")

The Council's action on parochial schools particularly engaged the interest of the Bishop of Rochester. In its final decrees, it confirmed the parish school as the normal agent of Catholic elementary education, laying it upon the consciences of Catholic parents to send their children to their parochial schools or to other "Christian schools," approved as such by the local bishop. Where there was no available parochial school or adequate "Christian school," the individual bishop could permit the sending of children to public schools, when their Christian training was otherwise guaranteed. McQuaid was satisfied with these regulations, for they confirmed his own views and policies.[81]

Less than a decade later, however, the so-called "School Controversy" arose, which Bishop McQuaid believed was subversive of the decrees of the Plenary Council. His stand brought him once more into conflict with Archbishop John Ireland of St. Paul. Archbishop Ireland and Bishop John Keane, usually backed by Cardinal James Gibbons of Baltimore, were leaders in what was called the "liberal wing" of the American Catholic hierarchy. McQuaid and Archbishop Michael A. Corrigan of New York, joined from time to time by the German-American bishops and several others, had won the name of "conservatives," applied in a reactionary sense. Both before and after the outbreak of the School Question, these parties engaged in open combat with each other over several issues of church policy. Played up in Catholic and the secular press, their conflicts became all the more notorious and disedifying.

In July, 1890, when the National Education Association met in annual convention at St. Paul, Minnesota, John Ireland, as Archbishop of St. Paul and a man of progressive educational ideas, was invited to address them. At that time there had been movements in more than one State to secure legislation outlawing parochial schools as incompatible with American democratic principles. The Archbishop decided to counter-attack by pleading with this group of public school educators for the State subsidy of parochial education. He framed his address, "State Schools and Parish Schools," in terms calculated to get through to his largely non-Catholic listeners.[82] Indulging his usual bent for the startling statement, Ireland not only praised the public schools, but expressed his regret that there was any need for parochial schools. Then he entreated the audience to help remove the need of parish schools by accepting Catholic elementary schools into the public school system. He suggested two methods by which this might be accomplished. One was the English system, in which the State granted tuition to any student, in any school, who passed the State examinations in the required subjects. The other was the "Poughkeepsie Plan" in which, as we have already stated, the local board of education "adopted" parochial schools into the common school system.

Archbishop Ireland's speech immediately caused a furore among American Catholics, especially those of a "conservative" trend, and the German-Americans in particular, chary as they were of a state control which might forbid the German language in their schools. But John Ireland went ahead in the summer of 1891 and approved the introduction of the Poughkeepsie arrangement in the parochial schools of Faribault and Stillwater, two parishes in his archdiocese. A pamphlet published in November, 1891, gave him moral support: *Education*: *To Whom Does It Belong?* The author was Father Thomas Bouquillon, S.T.D., professor of moral theology at the Catholic University. Dr. Bouquillon, who had written the essay at the request of Cardinal Gibbons, answered the question he posed in his title by asserting that the duty to educate children did not belong to the parents alone, but to the parents, the *State,* and the Church, working in harmony.

A history of the Rochester Diocese is not the place to recount in detail the ramifications of the controversy which now followed between the "liberal" and the "conservative" American Catholic parties. The upshot of it was that Archbishop Ireland had to go to Rome to defend the Faribault-Stillwater arrangement against the strong criticism that it conceded too much to the State and was subversive of the parochial school system which the late Plenary Council established as the norm. Even when the Holy See declared, on April 21, 1892, that the "Faribault Plan" could be "tolerated," the battle did not cease. Therefore, Pope Leo XIII sent over Archbishop Francesco Satolli to pour oil on the troubled waters. On November 17, 1892, the papal legate presented to the assembly of American archbishops fourteen propositions designed to clarify the issue.

Unfortunately, several of the propositions were more confusing than illuminating. They seemed to undermine still further the norms set up by the Council, and were widely interpreted as nullifying the Council's rule that parents send their children to parochial schools. The Pope therefore requested the American bishops to write him their individual opinions on the case. After that he put an end to the controversy on May 31, 1893, by declaring that the fourteen propositions were to be interpreted in the light of the legislation of the Third Council.[83]

Since the gist of Archbishop Ireland's 1890 address was substantially what Bishop McQuaid had long since defended, his stand against Ireland in the School Question may at first seem surprising. True, he took no public part in the war of words, beyond reissuing his collected educational articles in book form as a restatement of his views.[84] But the attitude of the "liberals" confirmed him in his growing distrust of Archbishop Ireland and Cardinal Gibbons. They were verging, he thought, into a sort of religious indifferentism. Furthermore, he agreed with a number of other bishops that Ireland and Bouquillon attributed too much educational authority to the State. Most of all, he feared that Archbishop Ireland was engaged in a one-man campaign to establish the "public-parochial school" rather than the parochial school as the norm, and was thus subverting the precept set down by the Third Plenary Council. He wrote of all this to the Pope, in response to Leo's invitation. With regard to Ireland's suggestions, he said he preferred the "English system" to the Poughkeepsie (or Faribault) plan, for the latter, in his own experience, had not been completely satisfactory. What he urged upon the Pope was that America would not be willing to do Catholics justice in educational matters for many years to come. The parochial school should therefore remain the rule.[85]

While Archbishop Ireland was far from opposing the spread of the Faribault arrangement, it now appears that McQuaid, not wholly through his own fault, misjudged the Archbishop's ultimate purpose. At any rate, it was not long before circumstances vindicated the parochial school as the most feasible policy even in Minnesota. For strong non-Catholic opposition led to the discontinuance of the "public-parochial" agreement at Stillwater in 1892 and at Faribault itself a year later.

The Bishop of Rochester and the Archbishop of St. Paul became involved in yet another school conflict in 1894. This time Bishop McQuaid waged a more active battle, and the Diocese of Rochester was more directly implicated. There were two issues: McQuaid's candidacy for the State Board of Regents: and an amendment to the State constitution denying public funds to denominational schools.

In 1894, the New York State Board of Regents, governors of the State educational system, had nineteen members, only one of whom was a Catholic. This Catholic member, Bishop Francis McNeirny of Albany, died on the second day of the year. Two Catholic priests presented themselves to the Legislature as candidates: Father Louis A. Lambert

(1835-1910), a priest of the Diocese of Rochester; and Father Sylvester Malone (1821-1899), a priest of the Diocese of Brooklyn.[86] Both were prominent, especially among non-Catholics, for their liberal views; neither one was really experienced in educational matters; and both had shown unrelenting public antagonism towards their own bishops. Rather than have an unrepresentative priest chosen for the position, the Bishop of Rochester reluctantly offered his own candidacy.

At this juncture, Archbishop Ireland intervened from far-off Minnesota. A strong Republican himself, and anxious to break off what he considered to be the dangerous alliance of the Church in New York State with Tammany Hall Democracy, he wrote to Republican politicians in Father Malone's favor. Lambert he urged to withdraw and to back Malone in the *Freeman's Journal* of which he (Lambert) was the editor. Father Lambert was happy to oblige, and it was with Archbishop Ireland's knowledge and enthusiastic approval that he assailed Bishop McQuaid in his columns as the Tyrant of Rochester.[87] The Rochester prelate lost out to his Brooklyn opponent in an election which the New York *Sun* did not hesitate to label an act of hostility to the Catholic Church.

Convinced that his intervention had been timely, Archbishop Ireland stepped into New York politics once more in November, 1894. He spent several weeks in and around New York City, never calling on Archbishop Corrigan, but appearing more than once on the campaign platforms of Republican politicians. During this period a new wave of anti-Catholic nativism was sweeping the country, intent, among other things, upon securing the enactment of State laws denying public funds to denominational schools. A secret society, the A.P.A. (American Protective Association) was in the process of assuming a major role in the drive, but it was by no means the sole participating nativist organization. Thus, it was the National League for the Protection of American Institutions that in 1894 proposed an amendment to the New York State constitution forbidding future grants of financial aid "directly or indirectly" to denominational schools.[88] The bishops of New York State rightly considered this so-called "Blaine Amendment" discriminatory. The State Democratic Party, asked to denounce creeping A.P.A.ism, had done so, though it did not denounce the Blaine Amendment specifically. The Republicans, also requested to denounce the current bigotry, had refused. If the latter won the fall elections, the revised Constitution was pretty sure of passage. But the Catholic bishops, feeling that a public stand against the amendments might seem too political, decided to give their opinion only privately upon being questioned, and to leave the matter to the consciences of Catholics of either party. It was at this critical point that the Archbishop of St. Paul strode onto the New York political stage.

There can be little doubt that Ireland's open support of the New York State Republicans contributed to their victory at the polls and to the passage of the proposed amendments. It is ironic that the Archbishop who had fought so hard for the Poughkeepsie Plan at Faribault and Stillwater should have assisted the enactment of a New York amendment that would soon be invoked to suppress the Plan wherever it still functioned in New York State. As a United States citizen, he had a right to favor any party he chose. He was wise in his general recommendation that Catholic clerics take the "large comprehensive view of national and ecclesiastical interests."[89] But his interposition in New York politics in 1894 was an error of judgment and taste. As Bishop McQuaid observed, "He has no sense of the propriety of things."

Did McQuaid's own explosive reaction to Ireland's "meddling" merit this same comment? The Bishop of Rochester had many complaints to make against his brother prelate, and the Archbishop's political interposition now capped the climax. Therefore, on November 25, 1894, Bishop McQuaid, spurning a last-minute caution from his vicar general, mounted the pulpit of his cathedral and delivered a carefully documented arraignment of the "meddlesome interference" of Archbishop Ireland in New York State politics.[90]

It was indeed an extraordinary action, and the public press made much of it. So, too, did Father Louis Lambert in his *Freeman's Journal,* utilizing information supplied by the Archbishop of St. Paul.[91] The newspaper predictions of his own deposition did not seem to disturb the Bishop of Rochester. Official reaction from his superiors caused him more concern. Archbishop Francesco Satolli, the Apostolic Delegate, wrote from Washington deploring McQuaid's address and forbidding him to discuss the matter further in the press.[92] In a somewhat calmer letter, the papal Secretary of State, Cardinal Mariano Rampolla, told the Bishop that Pope Leo XIII had been saddened by his course of action, and wished to remind him that the correction of bishops was the task of the pope rather than of fellow bishops.[93] The Prefect of the Sacred Congregation de Propaganda Fide, Cardinal Miecislas Ledóchowski, likewise wrote to Archbishop Corrigan of New York, instructing him to seek some amends from the Bishop of Rochester.[94]

McQuaid did not have to be pressed to reply to the Roman communications. To Cardinal Rampolla he stated his sorrow for having disturbed the Holy Father. In his letter to Cardinal Ledóchowski, February, 1895, the Bishop seized the opportunity to describe in detail his recent complaints against Archbishop Ireland. Then he went on to accuse Ireland of a long-term persecution of Archbishop Corrigan. He declared, furthermore, that Archbishop Ireland and Bishop Keane were exhibiting more and more a dangerous "spirit of false liberalism," which was causing confusion to the faithful and had to be countered.[95] More would be heard later on of this charge of "false liberalism", especially in the dispute over "Americanism."

Having received these replies, Rome took no further steps against the Bishop of Rochester. He certainly had had a strong case against the Archbishop of St. Paul. Secular newspapers were divided on the question of whether McQuaid had used the right method in taking John Ireland to task. That question could still be debated today, and even those who defended the negative would have to admit that Bishop McQuaid's action was both sincere and courageous.

At the same time, the public attack of one prelate upon another can only be regrettable. If the "supreme *law*" of action is "the saving of souls," charity still remains the supreme *virtue*.

37
BERNARD J. McQUAID
First Bishop of Rochester, 1868-1909
(Photo, 1904)

38
THE BISHOP
(*Around 1880*)

40   At the Trolley Stop.
State Street

39   McQUAID
Preaching at a Cornerstone Rite, 1892

41   COTTAGE, *the Bishop's Farm*
Hemlock Lake

42
STEPHEN V. RYAN, C.M.
Bishop of Buffalo
1868-1896

43
FATHER
JAMES M. EARLY, V.G.

44
MSGR.
HIPPOLYTE DeREGGE
CHANCELLOR

45
FATHER
JAMES F. O'HARE, V.G.

46
FATHER
JAMES P. KIERNAN, V.G.

47
MSGR.
JAMES T. McMANUS, V.G.

48
THOMAS A. HENDRICK
Bishop of Cebu, P.I.
1903-1909

49
EDWARD J. HANNA
Archbishop of
San Francisco
1915-1935

50
**ST. PATRICK'S
CATHEDRAL
ROCHESTER**
*(1870-1937)
Lady Chapel
at rear, on
the left*

51
**ST. PATRICK'S
CATHEDRAL,**
*Interior
(Photos, 1937)*

53
ST. MICHAEL'S
(German) **CHURCH**
ROCHESTER *(1890)*

52   LADY CHAPEL (1898)
St. Patrick's Cathedral
(Photo, 1937)

54
OUR LADY OF VICTORY,
ROCHESTER
(The "French Church," 1868)

55
ST. ANDREW'S SEMINARY
(The second building,
1904-1937)

56   ST. FRANCIS XAVIER *(German)* CHURCH
ROCHESTER, *1888-1915*
(A typical McQuaidian church and school building)

57   STUDENT GROUP, 1880's
HOLY FAMILY SCHOOL, AUBURN

58   BOYS' FIRST COMMUNION CLASS, 1894
ROCHESTER: ST. MICHAEL'S *(German)* CHURCH
FATHERS FRIDOLIN PASCALAR, *Pastor;*   HERBERT REGENBOGEN, *Assistant*

59
ST. MARY'S
BOYS' HOME
West Main St. ROCHESTER
1872-1942

60
ST. JOSEPH'S
(German) ORPHANAGE
Andrews Street, ROCHESTER
(1874-1938)

61
ST. PATRICK'S
GIRLS' ORPHANAGE
Clifton Street,
ROCHESTER
(1893-1942)

62
HOME OF INDUSTRY
East Main Street, Rochester
(1888-1906)

63
ST. ANN'S HOME *for The Aged*
Lake Ave. ROCHESTER 1906-1962
(Original Home in center. Photo 1965)

64   ST. BERNARD'S SEMINARY, ROCHESTER, 1893
(Photo, 1966)

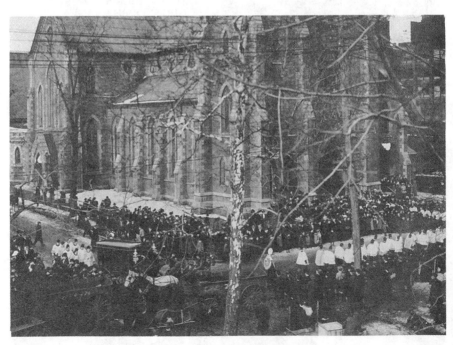

65   BISHOP McQUAID'S OBSEQUIES
(January, 1909)

THE MELTING POT

BY 1910 the United States had reached a young maturity. The national population had risen since 1896 from seventy to ninety million, and the State population from six to nine million. Rochester now had 218,000 inhabitants, with prospects of uninterrupted future growth. The census of the other diocesan counties showed light fluctuations, with a tendency to decline. This decline probably indicated the trend away from the land and into the cities and villages, where industry offered more attractive employment.

In the eight counties of the Diocese of Rochester, the number of inhabitants now totalled some 575,000. If we add to this the 177,000 who lived in the four Southern Tier counties acquired by the Diocese in 1896, we reach the total twelve-county population in 1910 of about 752,000, approximately one-sixth of them Catholic.

As in previous years, immigration had continued to be the primary factor in Catholic growth. Immigrants came in ever larger waves from the Mediterranean countries: some from the Near East (usually members of the Maronite, Melkite, Armenian and other Catholic Eastern Rites); some from Portugal (principally from Portugal's Madeira Islands); but the overwhelming majority from Italy. From the Russian and Austrian empires there was a continued influx of Poles, Lithuanians, and Greek-Rite Ukrainians and Rusins. At the same time, emigration from western Europe generally declined, although a fair percentage of Catholic Belgians and Hollanders took passage to America. All of these groups were represented among the new settlers of western New York, with the result that not only its cities but many of its villages became—to the frequent disrelish of their old residents—cosmopolitan communities.

As western New York moved towards the million mark in population, it lost all further claim to frontier status, and acquired all the gadgetry of modern progress. Two new steam railroads, the Lehigh Valley and the Delaware, Lackawanna and Western, now crossed the Rochester Diocese from southeast to northwest. Interurban electric railroads formed a network of passenger lines. But what promised to increase most was private transportation. Civil authorities were beginning to improve the roads, not out of compassion for carriage horses so much as to court the approval of the mounting number of bicyclists and automobilists. The 1890's saw bicycling rise to new prominence. (Bishop McQuaid learned from personal experience what a threat these swarming two-wheelers could offer to life and limb. In August, 1898, as McQuaid walked peaceably near St. Bernard's Seminary, a rattled bicyclist ran him down, fortunately without doing him serious injury.[1]) But automobiles were even then making a bid for still greater popularity. By 1907 there were 1,500 autos in Rochester alone. For the thousands who could not yet afford to recreate in motor cars, the phonograph and the new moving pictures provided cheaper, if more static, diversion.

Expanded means of travel and entertainment were the signs of a prospering economy. After the depression of 1893-1897, business moved ahead with renewed vigor. In Rochester, the Eastman Kodak Company gave promise of illimitable expansion. In smaller communities, too, manufactures took on added prominence. In Corning, for instance, there was a strong glass industry; Horseheads was noted for its brick works; and Seneca Falls, for its pumps and hydraulic machines. Labor and management still engaged in frequent disputes, but there had been a real advance in progressive labor legislation.

In the late 1890's the United States gave still another indication of the consciousness of its power by participation in the Spanish-American War. The war itself, which brought our nation willy-nilly into the ranks of the imperialist nations, ran its brief course between April and August, 1898. But the Philippine Insurrection that arose out of it was not put down until April, 1902. Catholics of the Diocese of Rochester were thus given as much chance as the rest of their countrymen to participate.

Thomas J. Cook, of Corning, a Catholic sailor in the regular navy, was at Cuba when it all began, assigned to the U.S.S. "Maine". On February 15, 1898, the ship was destroyed by an explosion which has never really been explained, but which American sentiment promptly blamed on Spain, at that time the ruler of Cuba. Tommy Cook was one of the luckier victims. Blown off the ship, but unscathed by the impact, he was rescued, still unscathed, from the waters of Havana harbor.[2] Not many Americans who "remembered the 'Maine' " and volunteered for service, reached the battlefields of the war before its brief hostilities ceased. Most of the Rochester diocesan men who died in the service were victims of disease (like Captain John A. Quigley of Auburn, James Clooney of Corning, George H. Mills and Thomas F. Quinn of Rochester); or of accidents (like Frank Kane of Rochester).[3] But there were doubtless other diocesan soldiers who lost their lives in combat over the subsequent four-year period. For example, in 1901 Martin O'Connor of Corning was mortally wounded in the Philippines.[4] Although there is no complete list of diocesan men who served during the conflict, the number of volunteers seems to have been relatively large, despite the absence of any specific encouragement on the part of the Catholic clergy. There is scarcely a Catholic cemetery in the Diocese that does not contain the grave of one or more veterans of the Spanish-American War epoch: Irish names, German names, Polish names.[5]

Not long after the American nation had thus asserted itself in international politics, the Catholic Church in the United States was officially recognized by Rome as having reached spiritual maturity. By the decree *Sapienti Consilio* of June 29, 1908, Pope St. Pius X transferred the American Church from the missionary jurisdiction of the Sacred Congregation de Propaganda Fide to the jurisdiction of the other Vatican departments that took care of churches in non-missionary areas of the world.

Bernard J. McQuaid reached his seventieth birthday in 1893. During the remaining fifteen years of his life he continued to make his valuable contribution towards the acclimatization of the Church and its polyglot membership to the American atmosphere. Because America has fused many immigrant races and nationalities into one nation, it has frequently been called "the melting pot". It is probably truer to say that in the United States there have been several melting pots. Catholics, for instance, have become entirely American, yet have not lost their religious distinctness.

What our early bishops had to do was to see to it that we became American yet remained Catholic, sacrificing our old non-American views but not our Catholic faith. This chapter studies some phases of the process in the Rochester Diocese: the care of expanding needs, spiritual and educational; the problems of nationalism and fraternalism; and other current issues which posed a threat to the Catholic Way.

1. EXPANDING NEEDS.

According to *Sadlier's Catholic Directory,* the Diocese of Rochester had a population of 80,000 in 1896. This flock was divided among sixty churches with resident pastors and thirty-three mission churches. Thirty-three of the parish churches (and one of the mission churches) had parochial schools, where 11,000 pupils were under instruction. The clergy numbered eighty-six: eighty-two diocesan priests and four religious priests (Redemptorists).

The *Official Catholic Directory* for 1909, the year of McQuaid's death, indicated a substantial growth since 1896. Now the Catholic population was 121,000; and there were ninety-three parishes; thirty-six missions; fifty-three parish schools (with 18,000 pupils); and 164 priests, six of them Redemptorists.

The Diocese had gained so sharp an increase mostly through the acquisition of four Southern Tier counties in late 1896. As we have already noted, when he first learned of the boundaries of his new diocese in 1868, Bishop McQuaid complained about the illogical exclusion of the adjacent Southern Tier counties. Because he and Bishop Ryan of Buffalo did not see eye-to-eye on many issues, no rectification was made during the Ryan administration.

Meanwhile, Stephen V. Ryan had taken good care of the Church in the four controversial Southern Tier counties. Immigrants of the Old and New Immigrations had settled here as they had settled in the Northern Tier. The second Bishop of Buffalo had established parishes for them in all the cities—one of them a Polish parish—and in some of the villages. He had promoted parochial schools, of which there were nine in the four counties by 1896: Cohocton, Corning, Elmira (three), Hornell, Owego, Perkinsville, and Wayland. Only St. Pius School, Cohocton, was taught by a lay teacher. The rest were staffed by nuns. Elmira could also boast of a flourishing school for girls. The Academy of Our Lady of Angels (1866) was managed by the Sisters of Mary of Namur. It served the girls and young women of the whole Elmira area, Protestant as well as Catholic; and there were about one hundred girls registered in its twelve grades.[6] St. Joseph's Orphan Asylum in Corning (1873) was the only Catholic charitable institution in the Southern Tier, and it was very small.[7]

Only six years before the transfer to Rochester, a Catholic hospital opened at Hornell—St. James Mercy Hospital. It owed its inspiration and its original funds to the Very Rev. James M. Early (1822-1890). We will recall that Father Early was Bishop McQuaid's first vicar general. Subsequently the two had fallen out, whereupon Father Early returned to the Buffalo Diocese, and ended his career as pastor of St. Ann's Church, Hornell. St. James Hospital was organized rather distinctively at the outset, no doubt in order to emphasize its role in the community. Father Early provided that the board of trustees should always comprise the diocesan bishop, the local pastor, the mayor of Hornell (*ex officio*), and six elected members. One of these elected members was to be the nun who was the current hospital superintendent. The other five electees were also to be members (resident or nonresident) of the Sisters of Mercy, the religious community to whose administration the hospital was entrusted.[8]

Bishop Stephen V. Ryan died on April 10, 1896. His death made it opportune to settle the old question of the Buffalo-Rochester boundary. As metropolitan of the New York ecclesiastical province, Archbishop Michael A. Corrigan of New York, at McQuaid's request, sought the opinion of his other suffragan bishops on the transfer of Steuben, Chemung, Schuyler and Tioga counties to the Diocese of Rochester. Bishop Thomas M. A. Burke of Albany had no objections, though he thought that it might be better to vote on it at a future provincial council, lest anybody be accused of taking advantage of the Buffalo vacancy to rush the change through.[9] Bishop Charles E. McDonnell of Brooklyn had an alternate suggestion. Fearing that a future bishop of Buffalo might still desire to retain Chemung County, McDonnell thought that a good compromise might be to set up a new see at Elmira, with jurisdiction over Steuben, Chemung, Schuyler, Tioga, Allegany and Tompkins counties.[10]

Bishop Burke's recommendation was apparently overruled, and Bishop McDonnell's compromise was rendered unnecessary. Pope Leo XIII, in the papal brief *Cum Ex Apostolico Munere* of December 10, 1896, decreed that the counties of Steuben, Chemung, Schuyler and Tioga in the Southern Tier be detached from the Diocese of Buffalo and added to the Diocese of Rochester.[11] By this act the jurisdiction of the see of Rochester was extended over twelve rather than eight counties, bounded on the north by Lake Ontario and on the south by the Pennsylvania border—a total of 7,455 square miles. The addition of 2,840 square miles did not, however, imply the acquisition of an extraordinary number of Catholics. There were probably no more than 15,000 Catholics in the Southern Tier Counties. These counties were largely rural, and therefore largely Protestant. The only cities were Elmira (30,000), Corning (10,000), and Hornell (10,000). Bath, Owego, and Waverly were sizable villages (4-5,000); but only Owego was strongly Catholic.

On January 21, 1897, Bishop McQuaid issued an official notification of the papal move to the clergy and faithful of the Southern Tier; and on that same day read the papal decree to his new clergy assembled in Corning.[12] There had been some fear that the division would cause complaint. Actually, the transfer was accomplished smoothly, criticism being voiced only by a couple of Buffalo diocesan priests. Archbishop Corrigan was happy to bear witness to this fact in a letter to Archbishop Sebastiano Martinelli, the apostolic delegate.[13] McQuaid himself made the transition easier by a nice diplomacy. The special reception which he gave to his new priests on February 3, 1897, at St. Bernard's Seminary, turned out to be a "very pleasant event."[14] Only two of the priests of the four counties elected to return to the Diocese of Buffalo. The others were continued in their former posts; and when they were subsequently transferred, it was normally to other assignments in the Southern Tier, where they would feel more at home.

Bishop Ryan's successor in the see of Buffalo deserved much of the credit for the smoothness of the shift. James Edward Quigley (1854-1916) was named third bishop of Buffalo on November 30, 1896. Although he was officially notified only after the realignment of the boundaries, he was on good terms with Bishop McQuaid, and cooperated fully with the move. His roots, after all, were in the Diocese of Rochester. When he was only five years old, his family had moved from Oshawa, Ontario, Canada, to Lima, Livingston County, New York. In 1870, the Quigleys moved once again, from Lima to Rochester, where his brother, Joseph M. Quigley (1858-1927), eventually became chief of police. By 1870, however, James E. Quigley had already been adopted as a seminarian by the Diocese of Buffalo.[15] The new bishop of Buffalo had furthermore received the backing of the Bishop of Rochester in his election to the episcopate.[16] Bishop Quigley maintained a neighborly good will towards his Rochester colleague until 1903, when he was promoted to the archbishopric of Chicago.

As it turned out, the admission of the nuns of the four counties was far more complicated than the admission of the priests.

In the first place, there were three communities of Sisters in the Southern Tier. The Buffalo (now called the Williamsville) Sisters of the Third Order of St. Francis taught in the German parish schools at Wayland and Perkinsville, four at each school. In Elmira, the Sisters of St. Mary of Namur conducted Our Lady of Angels Academy and the parochial schools of SS. Peter and Paul and St. Mary. There were twenty-one of these Sisters attached to the Academy, and perhaps a few more assigned to the two parish schools. Sisters of Mercy of the Batavia community staffed the schools of St. Ann, Hornell; St. Mary, Corning; St. Patrick, Elmira; and St. Patrick, Owego. To these teachers, who numbered about twenty, we must add the three nursing Sisters of Mercy then attached to St. James Mercy Hospital in Hornell.

As early as 1897, Bishop McQuaid replaced the Franciscan nuns of Wayland and Perkinsville with his own Josephite Sisters. He removed St. Mary's School, Elmira, from the jurisdiction of the Sisters of St. Mary of Namur, entrusting it also to the Sisters of St. Joseph. The Sisters of St. Mary continued to staff not only their own Academy but SS. Peter and Paul School, with which they had been associated for forty years. But in 1903, the Namur Sisters, feeling that they did not have the active support of the Bishop of Rochester, decided to withdraw from both of these Elmira schools. McQuaid thereupon replaced them at SS. Peter and Paul School with Sisters of St. Joseph. The Academy he closed down for good. In its former building St. Joseph's Hospital began its career on September 24, 1908. Sister Rose Alice Conway of the Rochester Sisters of St. Joseph was the Hospital's pioneer superintendent.[17]

Bishop McQuaid's desire to have Rochester-trained Josephite nuns in his schools was, of course, widely known. Furthermore, the Franciscan Sisters belonged to a Buffalo diocesan community, so their departure was not unexpected. It was a somewhat different case with the Sisters of St. Mary, who were members of an international religious order, comparable to the Religious of the Sacred Heart in Rochester. The chagrin which the Bishop's lack of sympathy caused the Sisters of St. Mary is therefore quite understandable.[18] What is even more regrettable is the fact that, educator though he was, the Bishop saw fit to suppress the only Catholic high school in the Southern Tier.

After the transfer, the Sisters of Mercy in the four counties passed from the surveillance of the bishop of Buffalo to that of the bishop of Rochester—a shift which gave rise to some nice problems of church law. On the counsel of Bishop Quigley, these Sisters decided in 1899 to sever their connection with the Batavia Mercy community, and to place themselves under Bishop McQuaid as an order in the Diocese of Rochester. But not as members of the existing Rochester Sisters of Mercy— no, as a separate community, centered at St. Ann's, Hornell, with Mother Angela Rogers as general superior.

A division of this sort was not so surprising then as it would be today. The rule of the Sisters of Mercy in those days apparently facilitated the establishment of small independent units. In the Diocese of Buffalo there had been two independent Mercy orders from 1867 to 1898; and from 1873 to 1881 there had been *six!*[19] Such an arrangement was impractical, however; so in 1901 Bishop McQuaid had the Hornellsville Sisters of Mercy vote on the question of union with the Rochester Sisters. The *ayes* won, and reunion was officially effected on July 26, 1901. Twelve of the Southern Tier nuns were allowed, on their own request, to return to the Buffalo Diocese. The twenty-four who remained in the Hornellsville community now joined the thirty-four members of the Rochester community, voting for the continuance in office of the current Rochester superior, Mother M. Teresa Gavigan.[20]

These twenty-four Sisters were a welcome addition to the small Rochester sisterhood of Mercy (which as late as 1909 numbered only ninety-eight). They were to give a long and faithful service to the community with which they affiliated in July, 1901. The last to survive was perhaps the most outstanding: Sister M. Liguori McHale, who died in 1963 at the age of ninety-three. As mother general of the Rochester Sisters of Mercy from 1907 to 1949, this remarkable administrator supervised the building of the present Rochester Mercy motherhouse, and of Our Lady of Mercy High School and its auditorium.[21]

Now is probably the best time to list the parishes and missions of the Southern Tier which the Diocese of Rochester acquired in 1896-1897.

First, the parishes. (The second date, or a single date, indicates when the parish was created a parish or promoted to that rank; a first date indicates when it became a mission with a chapel or church.) Parishes affected by the transfer were: *Addison:* St. Catherine (1854, 1867). *Bath:* St. Mary (1850, 1861). *Cohocton* [Liberty]: St. Pius (1861, 1880). *Corning:* St. Mary (1849, 1854). *Elmira:* SS. Peter and Paul (1848); St. John the Baptist (German) (1868, 1870); St. Patrick (1871); St. Mary (1872); St. Casimir (Polish) (1890). *Hammondsport:* St. Gabriel (1848, 1880). *Hornellsville* [Hornell]: St. Ann (1849). *Horseheads:* St. Mary (1866, 1879). *Owego:* St. Patrick (1846). *Perkinsville:* Annunciation (1850) (renamed Sacred Heart, 1884). *Rexville:* St. Mary (parish established at Greenwood, 1846, moved to Rexville, 1875). *Watkins* [Jefferson]: St. Mary of the Lake (1848, 1869). *Waverly* [Factoryville]: St. James (1853, 1891). *Wayland:* St. Joseph (1881).

We have already seen that in 1896 nine of these parishes had parish schools. Before that date four others had opened schools but had later discontinued them. For a short time there was a parochial school at St. Gabriel's, Hammondsport, taught by a lay person. Lay teachers also staffed St. Mary's School in Bath, which opened in 1862, and functioned for nine years. The Sisters of St. Mary of Namur conducted a school at St. John the Baptist, Elmira, from 1882 to 1890. And Rexville boasted a tuition school in the years 1889-1895, the faculty supplied by the Sisters of Mercy of the Buffalo (St. Bridget's) Mercy community.

Here are the Southern Tier mission churches involved in the change of diocesan boundaries. St. William, Cameron Mills (1886) was under St. Catherine, Addison. St. Joseph, Campbell (1872) was taken care of by St. Mary's, Bath. St. Joachim, Canisteo (1880) was under St. Ann, Hornell. St. Patrick, Corning (1886) was under St. Mary, Corning. St. Mary, Hendy Creek ("Dutch Hill") (1878), was a mission of St. John the Baptist, Elmira.[22] St. Patrick's, Owego, took care of St. John the

Evangelist, Newark Valley (1881); and St. Gabriel's, Hammondsport, had charge of St. Patrick's, Prattsburg (around 1868). The national Catholic directories from 1892 to 1934 list "St. Mary's", in Spencer, Tioga County, as a mission of St. Mary's, Horseheads (Chemung County). Although property for a church was purchased in 1891 at Van Etten in Chemung County (just west of Spencer), it appears that a church was not built at either Spencer or Van Etten.[23] Nevertheless, the 1896 Directory also listed Van Ettenville as a mission or mission station of Horseheads, with Millport as a third out-mission of the same parish. St. Mary's, Corning, likewise had a mission station at Big Flats, where a small chapel was opened around 1885.[24]

Bernard McQuaid had not long been in authority over the four counties before he set up therein two new parishes. In 1902, he raised St. Patrick's mission, Corning, to parochial status; and two years later he established, as a full-fledged parish, St. Cecilia's, Elmira. During the same period, 1896-1909, he created seventeen more parish units in the Diocese's eight original counties.

Five of these new Northern Tier parishes were on the outskirts of Rochester, and their foundation testifies to the city's unabated growth. Two were former missions of the Cathedral: Holy Rosary (mission, 1891; parish, 1896); and St. Augustine (mission, 1898; parish, 1906). The other three were parishes from the start: St. Monica (1898), Blessed Sacrament (1902), and Our Lady of Perpetual Help (1904).

The last of these was technically a territorial parish, but *de facto* it was German in population. Strictly national was Rochester's first Italian parish, St. Anthony (1906). St. Anthony Church, on Lyell Avenue at Plymouth, was outfitted to accommodate a congregation that had been formed in 1898 by Father J. Emil Gefell of the Cathedral staff, and had been holding its services since then in the Cathedral's new Lady Chapel. This same Father Gefell organized the Italians of the east side of town in 1904. They used the basement of Corpus Christi as a chapel until the opening of their own building, Mount Carmel Church, seven months after the death of Bishop McQuaid. The Bishop did not live to see the opening of still another national parish, St. George, in 1910. But he had authorized the organization of this Lithuanian congregation as early as 1906, and had permitted it to meet for Mass in the nearby hall of Holy Redeemer Church.

Holy Ghost Church in Coldwater, near Rochester, which had been a mission chapel since 1876, was finally given parochial rank in 1908. In 1905, the Bishop instructed Father Bernard J. Gefell to open St. Jerome Church in the railroad and manufacturing town of East Rochester. McQuaid dedicated its first and present church in 1907. Auburn was given three new parishes: St. Aloysius (1901); St. Hyacinth (Polish, 1907); and St. Francis of Assisi (Italian, 1908). Geneva's second Catholic church, St. Stephen's, started its career in 1904 in the old Dutch Reformed Church building. Three more missions advanced by the Bishop to parish rank were: St. Patrick's, Aurora, in 1901 (mission, 1855); St. Michael's, Newark, in 1903 (mission, 1863); St. Michael's, Montezuma, also in 1903 (mission, 1865).

McQuaid likewise founded four new missions: St. Thomas Aquinas in Moscow (now Leicester), a mission of St. Patrick, Mount Morris, in 1897; St. Catherine, Mendon, a mission of Victor, in 1902; St. Edward's, Auburn, a mission of St. Mary's, Auburn, in 1905; and St. Charles Borromeo, Elmira Heights, a mission of Horseheads, in 1905. To these we should add four lakeside chapels of ease: Star of the Sea (Grandview Beach, Lake Ontario, 1906); St. George (Summerville, Lake Ontario, 1907); St. Salome (Point Pleasant, Lake Ontario, 1908); and St. Margaret's (Conesus Lake, 1907).

Wherever it was possible, the Bishop insisted on the immediate establishment of a school in each new parish. The first parochial building was normally a modest two-story brick structure, one floor of which could be used for a church, the other for a school. When the congregation could finally afford a separate church building, the space formerly used for church purposes could be easily remodeled into schoolrooms.

Several of the parishes built themselves permanent churches during the latter years of the McQuaid regime. Corpus Christi and St. Stanislaus in Rochester, and St. Mary in Canandaigua were among the noblest of the structures erected. All three were the work of the Rochester architects Edwin S. Gordon and William V. Madden.

The church-building enterprise which engaged the Bishop's fondest interest was the enlargement and completion of St. Patrick's Cathedral. He launched the project in 1896, so as to have it finished in 1898, which marked the seventy-fifth anniversary of the building of the first St. Patrick's, and McQuaid's own fiftieth anniversary of priesthood and thirtieth of episcopate. The plans, drawn by Andrew J. Warner, provided for the construction of the hitherto unbuilt spire, the enlargement of the sanctuary and sacristies and the general overhauling of the interior, and the addition of a separate but connected "Lady Chapel" for lesser services. Sixty-thousand dollars was the estimated cost, half of which was requested of the Cathedral parishioners, the other half of the rest of the Catholics in the Diocese.[25]

The builders finished their work in time for the festivities of October 5, 1898. Early that morning, Archbishop Corrigan of New York performed the solemn rite of consecrating the main cathedral building.[26] At ten o'clock, the Apostolic Delegate to the United States, Archbishop Sebastiano Martinelli, celebrated the solemn commemorative Mass, and Bishop McQuaid preached the sermon. Present that day, in addition to two other archbishops (John Williams of Boston and Patrick J. Ryan of Philadelphia), were eighteen bishops, and five *monsignori*—the latter a rarity in those days. Sitting among the scores of priests in attendance was Father Michael O'Brien, of Lowell, Massachusetts, who as pastor of St. Patrick's, Rochester, had begun to build in 1864 what became St. Patrick's Cathedral. The organ and polyphonic music at the Mass was excellent. Seminarians from St. Bernard's and St. Andrew's Seminary sang the chant.[27]

Catholic schools were naturally given due attention in the jubilee sermon which the Bishop of Rochester delivered that morning. "It is Archbishop John Hughes' bold stand," he affirmed, "that has made the Catholic school system what it is today." McQuaid had no reason to regret that he had followed Hughes's lead. By 1909, fifty-three of his ninety-three parishes were to have their own schools. All the parishes in Rochester itself were so provided, even the little "French Church" and the new and struggling Italian church of St. Anthony. If many churches outside the see city lacked parochial schools, it was because of circumstances temporarily or permanently beyond the control of the church authorities. The magnitude of Bishop McQuaid's achievement had already become evident by 1890, when the Diocese of Rochester was outranked only by the Archdiocese of Philadelphia and the Diocese of Newark in the proportion of parishes blessed with their own schools.

The collapse of the "Poughkeepsie Plan" in New York State after 1894 had merely confirmed the Bishop in his opinion that parochial schools were and would long remain the only Catholic solution. As we have already seen, the "Blaine Amendment"— Article IX, Section 4, added to the State constitution in 1894—provided that public funds might not be paid even "indirectly," to schools under denominational influence. The article's effect was not automatic, however. Protests against "Poughkeepsie" schools had first to be lodged with the State Superintendent of Public Instruction from each public school district where the Plan was in operation.

Opponents of the Poughkeepsie Plan there certainly were, who for one reason or another were willing to voice the required legal appeal. The two schools in the Rochester Diocese where the system was still in effect did not escape this arraignment and its inevitable consequences.

On May 31, 1898, Charles R. Skinner, State Superintendent of Public Instruction, in response to the complaint of a group of non-Catholics of Corning, New York, ruled that two practices engaged in at Corning Public School No. 2 (St. Mary's School) constituted a sectarian influence and should therefore be discontinued. One practice was the use of the religious name "Sister" in addressing the teachers; the other was their wearing a religious habit during official school hours. Mr. Skinner naturally assumed that the Sisters of Mercy did not intend to abandon their titles or their habits while teaching classes, and he was, of course, correct. St. Mary's School was therefore removed from the local school system, its benefits and its burdens; and it reopened in September as a true parish school.[28]

In strongly Catholic Lima, the public-parochial school arrangement had been popular, and it was not until 1902 that opponents ventured to voice a protest against its continuance. Superintendent Skinner soon replied with the expected negative ruling. But the Lima Board of Education ignored the ruling, and it was only a further ruling, issued on November 4, 1903, that made the board members finally yield. That fall Brendan Hall, as the public-parochial school had been called, reopened as a strictly parochial school.

But the battle was not yet over. The literate and tenacious Father Simon FitzSimons, pastor of Lima's St. Rose Church, now brought suit against the village trustees for breach of contract and non-payment of salary to the nuns who had taught in the previously public school. The real intent of the suit was not so much to vindicate the contract and exact wages due, as to test the constitutionality of all the "religious garb" decisions issued by the State Superintendent. Father FitzSimons lost the first round when the New York State Supreme Court decided, on April 3, 1904, that the salary due the nuns before the announcement of the Skinner precept should be paid; but that the State Superintendent *did* have authority to issue such judgments. FitzSimons thereupon carried the case to the Supreme Court's Appellate Division. Here the outcome was even less favorable. The New York State Appellate Division, on November 25, 1905, stood by the verdict of the Supreme Court, but cancelled the salary award it had made. Undaunted, the Lima pastor brought the case before the State's highest tribunal, the Court of Appeals, charging that the nuns were being denied rights guaranteed by the Fourteenth Amendment of the American Constitution. Court of Appeals, on April 17, 1906, decided to restore the award of salary, but otherwise sustained the judgment of the Appellate Division. Father FitzSimons, by now short in funds (he had financed the battle himself), and sufficiently persuaded that his case was doomed, finally gave up.[29]

The Bishop of Rochester intervened in neither the Corning nor the Lima affairs. As we have already noted, the lukewarm interest which he had once had in the Poughkeepsie arrangement had long since chilled. Furthermore, it was not easy to fight a constitutional amendment, however much one disagreed with it. McQuaid must have taken a more active view of another suit brought in 1901 to enjoin the Rochester Board of Education from paying a salary to the Sisters who taught at St. Patrick's and St. Mary's orphanages. As we have already recorded, Article VIII, Section 14, of the 1894 State constitutional revision had allowed for this exception to the new general rule. James Sargent of Rochester, who initiated the suit against the Board of Education, was known to be anti-Catholic, and was said to be a leader in the A.P.A. The State Court of Appeals finally rejected his complaint on January 29, 1904.[30]

Meanwhile Bishop McQuaid never ceased to train his Sisters to acquire standards of competence that would make them the equals of public school teachers. After 1904, diocesan teachers' conferences were held annually. He collaborated closely with the second (and very able) superior general of the Rochester Sisters of St. Joseph, Mother M. Agnes Hines, who held office from 1882 to 1921. On December 27, 1898, he dedicated their new normal school and novitiate situated at Dewey Avenue and Augustine Street. Selected Sisters were still sent to Belgium, Germany and Italy for advanced study; and in 1899 four Rochester Josephites attended summer school at Cornell University. Outside contacts of this sort no doubt broadened the outlook as well as the learning of this community's educational specialists.[31]

The McQuaid scholastic program, so strong in elementary education, was still weak in its secondary aspect during the last decade of the Bishop's life. Outside the city of Rochester, St. Mary's in Corning and St. Rose's in Lima, had partial high school courses: the former, one year of high school (1904-1911); the latter, three years of high school (1900-1918). Nazareth Academy and the Academy of the Sacred Heart (both for girls) and Nazareth Hall (for boys) had high school departments; but these were private schools. From 1904 on, St. Joseph's parochial school in Rochester had a one-year commercial course for girls.

In 1902, a beginning was finally made towards a more truly diocesan high school. That year, Father Thomas F. Hickey, rector of St. Patrick's Cathedral, added a two-year commercial course to the eight grades of the Cathedral School. Pleased by Father Hickey's project, Bishop McQuaid expressed his hope that it would not stop there. It did not. In September, 1904, a freshman academic year was introduced, and in the next three years other superior grades, so that by 1907 there was a complete new institution called Cathedral High School. These upper grades had been housed at first in the old recreational section of the Cathedral School building. In 1906-1908 a new hall had to be built to take care of the recreational wants of the parish, for the High School needed all available room in the schoolhouse. Cathedral High was staffed by priests, Sisters of St. Joseph, and some laymen—the first of whom was Mr. Alphonse Sigl, a Catholic layman who was to win renown later on as a Rochester radio announcer and humanitarian. The High School graduated its first class in 1908, three in number: Gertrude M. Barry, Adelaide M. Carroll, and Cyril J. Curran. Unfortunately, Bishop McQuaid, then in his last illness, was unable to attend the commencement. Renamed Rochester Catholic High School in 1913, this last educational creation of the first Bishop of Rochester flowered, in 1922, into the present Aquinas Institute.[32]

To the very day of his death, Bernard McQuaid not only reigned but *ruled* in his diocese. Never the man to delegate much authority, he had the usual diocesan *curia* of officials, but their positions were more nominal than real. The diocesan consultors were not usually consulted. He named three rural deans in 1888, but as they died off he appointed nobody to succeed them.[33] During his lifetime only three of his priests were promoted to Roman honorary prelacies. He asked Pope Leo XIII to bestow, first the rank of papal chamberlain (1889), and then the rank of domestic prelate (1894) on the worthy Father Hippolyte De-Regge. He also requested the latter honor for Father James T. McManus, his vicar general, in 1889.[34] Father Joseph W. Hendrick of Ovid was another papal chamberlain, appointed on August 24, 1903. But the appointment was made at the behest of his brother, Bishop Thomas A. Hendrick, late of Rochester, on the day after the latter's consecration in Rome to the post of bishop of Cebu, Philippine Islands. Apparently this was done without the knowledge and approval of Bishop McQuaid, who therefore refused to allow Msgr. Hendrick to flaunt the purple of his prelacy in the Rochester Diocese.

Bernard McQuaid was not a trained canonist; furthermore, like a true pioneer, he found the rule of thumb a more practical episcopal norm. Yet he did not care to be thought arbitrary. On one occasion, at a dinner of the clergy which McQuaid attended, a distinguished guest, Archbishop James V. Cleary of Kingston, Ontario, ventured to speak humorously of the Bishop of Rochester. He said: "When he finds a law he doesn't like, and can't get around it, he goes *through* it". Those who knew Bishop McQuaid chuckled. McQuaid himself did *not* chuckle.[35]

Allowances are in order, however, before we judge the Bishop's monarchialism. In the first place, the complaints voiced against him in the early years of the 1900's were made of a man already advanced in age and naturally more imperious. In the second place, Rochester's first bishop shared his concept of diocesan rule with not a few of our early American hierarchs.

One thing which certainly strengthened him in his attitude was the series of lawsuits brought against him in the ecclesiastical courts by contentious priests.

The most regrettable of these, in one sense, was the suit preferred against the Rochester Cathedral by its former pastor, Father James Early, after he had withdrawn from the Diocese of Rochester and returned to that of Buffalo. McQuaid's firmness often brought out the stubbornness in others, and Early's own deathbed waiver of his claim proves that he had acted largely out of pique. But the contest caused considerable grief to the Bishop of Rochester.[36] Quite diverse from the case of the worthy Father Early was that of the unworthy Father Henry Egler. Bishop McQuaid removed him from his assignment because of his persistent misconduct. Egler appealed to the Archbishop of New York, and after New York's adverse judgment, to the Sacred Congregation de Propaganda Fide in Rome. Propaganda, in 1883, decided that the priest must make public reparation for his behavior, and ordered McQuaid thereupon to assign him to some chaplaincy. Here the chief trouble was that Father Louis A. Lambert of Waterloo, New York, at that time editor of the Philadelphia *Catholic Times,* rehearsed the case in his columns with a slant that made out Bishop McQuaid to be a despot. Deeply hurt, McQuaid complained to his friend Archbishop Corrigan, "I sometimes wonder how it is that I draw the fire of the enemy *so readily.* Shall I change tactics and let the Church go to the dogs?"[37]

Father Lambert's attack was the opening maneuver in a long and bitter war upon Bernard McQuaid. However disagreeable the episode may have been, it deserves our special attention here because it was a battle between Titans; a contest that caused repercussions not only throughout the Diocese of Rochester but throughout the nation.

Louis A. Lambert (1835-1910) was in all probability the Diocese's most distinguished literary figure. After his adoption into the Rochester

Diocese in 1869, he served as pastor of St. Mary's Church, Waterloo (1869-1888), and of Assumption Church, Scottsville (1890-1910). Meanwhile he engaged in journalism, for which he had a genuine gift. From his rectory desk he founded and for three years edited the *Catholic Times* of Waterloo (1877-1880); founded and for two years edited the *Catholic Times* of Philadelphia (1892-1894). And from 1895 until his death he was editor of the old and noted New York Catholic paper, the *Freeman's Journal and Catholic Register.* Father Lambert was a talented publicist, and his brilliant logic, native spunk, and urbane but caustic style made him an excellent controversialist. It was, in fact, out of his columns of religious controversy that he shaped his masterpiece, the *Notes on Ingersoll* (Buffalo, 1883), a famous and well-nigh irrefutable refutation of the "Great Agnostic," Robert Green Ingersoll (1833-1899). The *Notes* ran into many editions (although the author received no royalties); and Protestant ministers perhaps even more than Catholic priests thanked him for the weapons he gave them in this book and its sequel, *Tactics of Infidels* (Buffalo, 1887). For his anti-agnostic and other writings, for his strongly liberal views, and for his personal charities, he became a figure nationally revered by people of all faiths. In recognition of this fact, the University of Notre Dame in 1892 conferred on Father Lambert an honorary doctorate of laws.

It is too bad that this able journalist permitted a long contest with the Bishop of Rochester to mar his otherwise positive record. Unfortunately, Louis Lambert was a headstrong man, and perhaps a proud man, all too prone when antagonized to reply with invective. It was probably this trait, along with a tendency to neglect routine duties, that had brought him into conflict with some of his earlier superiors.[38]

Not long after he had admitted the former Illinois priest to the Diocese of Rochester, Bishop McQuaid became aware that Lambert was a poor administrator. It might have been better all around if a man like Father Lambert had been exempted from pastoral responsibilities so as to have more time for the literary career to which he was obviously called. But in those days a small American diocese could scarcely afford the luxury of an ordained but non-ministering litterateur.

The Bishop was at first pleased with the editor of the *Catholic Times* and his work; but as early as 1880, trouble began to brew. On one occasion, Father Lambert wrote so sharply of Bishop Edgar Wadhams of Ogdensburg that Bishop McQuaid compelled him to print a letter by McQuaid himself, defending that prelate.[39] Then there was the Egler case, to which we have already referred. In the course of his attack on the Bishop's policies, Lambert attacked the vicar general,

Father McManus, and the rector of the Cathedral, Father James F. O'Hare, in terms which McQuaid considered insulting. Father Lambert seemed, furthermore, to be collecting about himself a clique of anti-McQuaid diocesan priests. To head off this apparent trend and to caution the editor against further rashness, the Bishop restricted his priestly faculties to his own parish.[40]

Lambert appealed to the Holy See against the isolation to which his superior had thus subjected him; but Rome informed him, in August, 1884, that Bishop McQuaid had not exceeded his rights. Father Lambert did not mend his ways thereafter, so the penalty stood. Indeed, he was so far from repenting that he assailed unmercifully a pro-McQuaid letter that had appeared in the public press. The letter was anonymous, but practically everybody knew the author was the Bishop himself.

In 1888, Father Lambert appealed once more to the Holy See, counselled now by a popular American canon lawyer, the talented and artful New York priest, Father Richard Lalor Burtsell (1840-1912). But on July 31, 1888, Rome again rejected the appeal, informing Lambert at the same time that he was not actually a priest of the Rochester Diocese, because of certain flaws in the mode of his initial affiliation with Rochester. Bishop McQuaid had seized upon this technicality in good faith, thinking it might be the key to an easy solution of the whole problem. But as a matter of fact, Lambert *had* observed all the proper regulations in his transfer from the Diocese of Alton; and he was able to prove it to the Roman authorities in the course of a new appeal. This time the Bishop had to go to Rome in person to defend his side of the issue—a task which took him six months. Only on January 21, 1890, did McQuaid learn the Holy See's final decision. It was essentially a compromise. The controversial priest was required to submit an apology to his Bishop. The Bishop was not asked to restore Lambert to the Waterloo parish from which he had removed him, but to give him his choice of two other parishes of equivalent size. Father Lambert submitted a written statement of apology, which McQuaid accepted as sufficient without publication. When he was offered his pick of St. Patrick's parish, Victor, and Assumption parish, Scottsville, Father Lambert chose the latter.

Unhappily, the journalist was not content with a partial victory. So he renewed the war, first in the Philadelphia *Catholic Times,* then in the *Freeman's Journal.* As we have already seen, he plunged with vigor into the New York Regency campaign of 1894. Once more he dusted off the Egler case, presenting his readers with a biased version of it, prejudicial to the Bishop. Once more he called McQuaid names in print. Therefore Bishop McQuaid felt obliged to put the editor in coventry a second time. He refused to have any but the essential contacts with the priest until he made amends; and he implied to the other priests of the Diocese that they should follow the same course. In 1893, Archbishop Francesco Satolli, the new apostolic delegate, during his first visit to Rochester, tried in vain to persuade his episcopal host to give audience to the still impenitent Lambert.[41] Satolli apparently had no greater success two years later, when he sought to prevail upon Father Lambert to apologize for one notorious insult to his Bishop.[42]

Bernard McQuaid had adequate reasons for disciplining his literary priest, some public, some less public. It took no small courage on his part to administer an open correction to a man of Father Lambert's talent who had at his command the weapon of the press. Whether the Bishop chose his own weapons well in every case, he at least chose them thoughtfully, and he was sufficiently content with the ultimate canonical solution of the question. In the court of public opinion, however, McQuaid was the loser. Lambert, who for all his liberality of spirit never quite outgrew a strain of arrogance, focussed his journalistic big guns upon the Bishop. The latter was at a distinct disadvantage, for even if he had had the means of replying in kind, there were certain phases of the Egler and Lambert cases which charity forbade to be aired—as Lambert himself most likely realized.[43] The result was that Bishop McQuaid received a bad press as the "tyrant of Rochester", not only in some Catholic periodicals but in the secular newspapers, across this country and even in Europe. One quotation from *Truth,* a Buffalo journal, will illustrate in its worst form the caricature for which Lambert was in a large measure responsible. "Father Lambert, the brilliant pastor of St. Mary's, Waterloo, N.Y., has been dismissed by Bishop McQuade [sic] of Rochester . . . The cause was jealousy, pure and simple, on the part of the bishop." (September 16, 1888).

Rochester's first shepherd had, indeed, to engage in many battles, and since it is battles rather than routine achievements that make headlines, he came to be thought of by many as more bully than bishop. Such a notion is far off the mark. One of his close associates put it more fairly when he wrote: ". . . . Work was his constant occupation and the fights were rare episodes and these he took as a part of his work."[44] Most of his clerical problems were carry-overs from the regime of his predecessor. As he grew old in the episcopate, he could count on the cooperation of a better-trained and superior body of clergy, who, despite their occasional disagreements with him, were his loyal and admiring aides.

Bernard McQuaid did not, it is true, allow himself to become intimate with his priests or his faithful. But those who came into closer contact with him found him not only a just but a tender and thoughtful man. Only fragmentary records testify to his personal charities, but there were many of these. It was no proud despot that made a special inquiry about the missing Regents diploma of a tearful Nazareth Academy senior, who, just before commencement, had told him of her plight. "Well, my child, if your gown is ready, something must be done."[45] Bernard McQuaid was especially solicitous of the comfort and welfare of his seminarians and priests. He is said to have wept only twice in public, and on both occasions it was at the funeral of priests. One was that of young Father Andrew J. Brennan, the second priest whom he ordained to the priesthood, who died before he had completed his first year in the ministry. "The young priest lies still in death before us . . ." he began the eulogy. But that was as far as he could go.[46] The other was the funeral of his vicar general, Very Reverend James F. O'Hare (1846-1898), an able man whom he may have been considering for his auxiliary bishop.[47]

If, therefore, in meeting the expanding needs of his diocese, Bernard John McQuaid had at times to act sternly and to take boldly the calculated risks of disciplinary action, he by no means forgot the gentler phases of his task. What we have said, and will say later, on this point, will, we hope, correct the two-dimensional portrait that has all too long been considered the correct likeness of the pioneer Bishop of Rochester.

2. AMERICANIZATION AND FRATERNALISM.

The American-born son of Barney McQuaid of Paulus Hook yielded to none in the love of his native land. The man who as a priest in New Jersey had protested against Southern secession was no less the patriot after becoming bishop of Rochester.

On several occasions Bishop McQuaid gave public utterance to his deep sentiments of American loyalty. When we were observing the centenary of the Declaration of Independence in 1876, he addressed a pastoral to his flock. He thanked God for the self-government which our country had achieved through its Revolution. Since all Americans are fundamentally immigrants, he said, there is only one nationality here, the nationality of those "in whose souls burns a love of republican institutions". His sole fear was that our citizens would fail to live up to their responsibilities.[48] He struck a similar note in his pastoral of 1892 marking the fourth centenary of Columbus' discovery of America.[49] In 1880, he had devoted two sermons in the Cathedral to the virtue and burdens of patriotism.[50] In 1881 he gave a moving address at the civic memorial service in honor of the assassinated chief executive, President James A. Garfield. And on Memorial Day, 1892, when President Benjamin Harrison dedicated Rochester's Soldiers' Monument to the veterans of the Civil War, McQuaid sat by right among the "princes of the people".[51]

Willingness to serve the common weal also prompted Bishop McQuaid to accept a post on the Rochester Park Commission when it was founded in 1888. He remained a commissioner until his death; and despite the strong popular sentiment against the commission's plans to multiply city parks, he stood firmly for the extension of the park system.[52] Park commissioners were not, however, political figures. If they had been, McQuaid would have declined the appointment. He had made a pact with himself upon his appointment to the bishopric to sedulously avoid political partisanship as something out of keeping with his spiritual role. In fact, he carried his non-partisanship so far that while bishop he never voted in an election. Some criticized him for this, but he gave his critics a public answer. On two instances he explained from the pulpit that however great the duty was of every American citizen to take part in our elections, that duty was overridden in his case—to his way of thinking—by his duty as a bishop to keep clear of "entanglements with any political party."[53]

A man of such strong patriotic feeling was naturally desirous of promoting the Americanization of his multi-national flock. When Bernard McQuaid was entering upon his last illness, the Reverend George Chalmers Richmond, Rector of St. George's Episcopal Church in Rochester, praised him from the pulpit for his efforts on behalf of immigrants. "Passionately missionary, and zealously patriotic," the Rochester minister called the Catholic bishop; and he commended what he had done "to make good American citizens of these newcomers."[54]

Too often insufficient credit is given to American Catholicism for its great role in Americanization. In the case of Bishop McQuaid the credit was particularly deserved. One very interesting proof is to be found in the remarks which he made to various national groups in the Diocese when called upon to address them. He always allowed for the sympathy which the immigrants had for the land of their birth; but he likewise reminded them that since they were now Americans, their new allegiance must supersede the old.

"Your sons should grow up with the love of their native country," he told an Irish organization in 1894. He added, nevertheless: "While the best emotions of their souls will go out to the old land, yet it must always be second."[55] The same patriotic ideal inspired his remarks to the Poles of Rochester in 1890 at the dedication of St. Stanislaus Church. He rejoiced that there was a new parish in Rochester to represent a transplanted Poland. Still he would not have its members forget that all the national units in the Diocese constituted "one great, noble, Catholic family"; and he promised to send to St. Stanislaus, as soon as he could, school Sisters "who can speak both Polish and English so that thus your children will make rapid progress."[56] He had already made clear his attitude towards foreign languages in a sermon to the French Canadian Convention which met in Rochester in the summer of 1885. Keep your French language, he told his listeners. Nobody objects. But do not try to change the language of this country, English.[57]

No bishop of this frame of mind could have accepted "Cahenslyism." Cahenslyism was an ultra-nationalistic program named, rather unfairly, after Peter Paul Cahensly (1838-1923), a German Catholic layman and member of the German Imperial Reichstag, who devoted his life to the welfare of German immigrants to America. Cahenslyism, as advocated by a number of Catholic German-Americans with the backing of some German-American bishops, sought from the Holy See a guarantee of the preservation of Germanism in American church circles, and the selection of bishops in the United States according to the ratio of national percentages among American Catholics. While Bishop McQuaid deplored the shabby treatment which some American bishops gave to their German parishes, and while he made common cause with German-American bishops in their defence of the true parochial school, he could not in conscience accept a Cahenslyism aimed at retarding indefinitely the Americanization of all foreign-language immigrant elements. He begged to disagree with Archbishop John Ireland, who seemed to favor a quick and enforced Americanization. In McQuaid's view, the acclimatization of the immigrant should be neither impeded nor pressured, but allowed to work out naturally.[58]

Here was a moderate, rational and practical stand. The first bishop of Rochester did not succeed in avoiding all conflict with the sometimes highly sensitive national elements over whom he presided. But in the main he was able to retain the loyal and Catholic allegiance of his polyglot people—surely no small achievement.

His relations with the Germans of the Diocese remained substantially unimpaired throughout his regime. The Donner case of 1879-1880 only increased the respect in which they held him. Frederick Donner, editor of the Rochester Catholic weekly, the *Sonntagsblatt,* had launched scurrilous attacks on the pastors of three of the Rochester German parishes. The Bishop, having found the accusations unsubstantiated, forbade his German diocesans to read the *Sonntagsblatt*. Donner brought a civil suit against McQuaid, but the Circuit Court, in its final decision, ruled that the Bishop had been acting within his rights and in the fulfillment of his pastoral duties. At the conclusion of the trial, the parishioners of the three parishes in question (SS. Peter and Paul, Holy Family, and St. Michael) communicated to McQuaid their congratulations and gratitude.[59]

Because Bishop McQuaid allowed his national groups to work out their own destiny, the nationalistic frictions that caused such intense difficulty in some sections of the United States did not unduly trouble the Rochester Diocese. Journalist Katherine E. Conway spoke only the truth when she said of Rochester, "There is no Cahenslyism here."[60] As Bishop McQuaid himself admitted, with some amusement, he was widely looked upon as of "strong German proclivities." Only in the 1890's did he encounter difficulties with some of his German pastors. In this instance four of them stationed in Rochester reached the conclusion that a fifth of their number had merited dismissal from his pastorate because of public charges against his behavior. When the Bishop, who placed authority first, refused to remove the priest in question, the four pastors initiated proceedings in the ecclesiastical courts to force the dismissal. What had started out as a movement against a fellow German-American priest thus turned unintentionally into a movement against the Bishop. The campaign was not effective, but resulted in a certain coolness between McQuaid and the German pastors who had engineered it. But in this whole case, the disagreement was between the Bishop and some of his German pastors rather than between the Bishop and his German diocesans in general.[61]

Catholics of the Ruthenian rite entered the Rochester diocesan district in the last two decades of the nineteenth and the first two decades of the twentieth century. The largest concentrations were at Rochester and Auburn, and, in the Southern Tier, at Elmira Heights and Corning. The Corning Ruthenians were Rusins from the Podcarpathian section of pre-1919 Hungary. The others were Ukrainians from the old Austrian political province of Galicia. St. Nicholas, in Elmira Heights, was the first Greco-Slav parish established within the present Rochester diocese. This dates from 1894. SS. Peter and Paul Ukrainian Church in Auburn, was begun in 1901. Ukrainians began to arrive in Rochester in the early years of the present century, but their parochial development—like that in Corning and in Bath—belongs to the post-McQuaid epoch. Ruthenian immigrants posed a special problem in the years before 1907. Lacking churches of their own Greek rite, they were supposed to attend Mass and receive the sacraments in the Latin rite churches of the Rochester Diocese. In some parts of America, Latin rite Catholics, unable to understand the legitimacy of a Greek rite Catholicism, with its married clergy, were often less than cordial to the Ruthenians. Friction of this sort was apparently not extensive in the Rochester Diocese. We know from passing references that several of the Latin rite pastors in Rochester and Auburn gave their Greek rite neighbors a generous helping hand. In 1907, all Americans of the Ruthenian rite were given a bishop of their own, and thus they were no longer subject to the Latin rite bishops.

As for foreign-language groups of the Latin rite itself, Bishop McQuaid was often hard put to it to find qualified priests to assign to them. We have already indicated that Father Alphonse Notebaert, pastor of Our Lady of Victory, the Franco-Belgian Church, proved to be a real asset to immigrants from the Low Countries. In 1908 he was elected president of the newly-formed Association of Belgian and Holland Priests; and in the year that followed he toured western Pennsylvania and West Virginia in search of isolated groups of Belgians. He found several such groups and took steps to provide them with spiritual care. A staunch Belgian, Father Alphonse was decorated for his efforts by the King of the Belgians, and in 1921 was made an honorary canon of Bruges Cathedral.[62]

It was more difficult to secure priests for work among the Italians. In the 1880's, when Italian immigrants were only beginning to arrive, Father Edward J. Hanna, Rome-educated and a good Italianist, made the first efforts at gathering together the Italians of Rochester, for whom he began a Sunday School. But his principal contribution to the local Italian community was the social assistance which he gave the immigrants in the years that followed.[63]

More important, along parochial lines, was the work of Father J. Emil Gefell (1870-1959). Earlier in the present chapter we referred to his foundation of St. Anthony's parish and of the congregation that became Our Lady of Mount Carmel Parish.[64] Father Gefell was a Rochesterian of German parentage who had studied in Rome, Italy. Father Ernest Ziegan (1873-1916) was German-born, but had worked in Rome for some time before becoming affiliated with the Rochester Diocese. In 1905-1907 Ziegan organized the Elmira Italians into what became, in 1908, St. Anthony's congregation.[65] St. Anthony's Church was dedicated three years later. But of all the non-Italian priests who exerted himself in behalf of the immigrant, the man most deserving of credit was the pastor of St. John the Evangelist Church, in Clyde, Father John J. Gleeson (1857-1920). His knowledge of the Italian tongue was slight, but he more than compensated for this lack by his zeal for the spiritual and civic welfare of his many Italian parishioners. So diligently did he assist them in their accommodation to Amercian ways, that his parish became a sort of showcase of effective Americanization.

It seems that Bishop McQuaid was at first hopeful that he could entrust his Italian work completely to non-Italian priests, whom he believed to be better adapted to inculcate a systematic American Catholicism upon the casual Mediterranean immigrant. With precisely this aim in mind, he sent Father John R. Fitzsimmons to Italy in 1904 and Father Louis Edelman in 1905, to spend a year studying the Italian language.[66] In 1906, however, he changed his policy. Three years before this, he had invited a priest from Lucca, Italy, the Reverend Orestes Canali (1877-1948), to join the staff of St. Andrew's Seminary.[67] In 1906 he named Dr. Canali pastor of Our Lady of Mount Carmel Church. Pleased, it seems, by the work of Canali, the Bishop now induced two other highly educated Italian priests to join the St. Andrew's faculty. Father Crociano Cappelino (1878-1952), who held doctorates in philosophy, theology, and canon law, arrived in Rochester in 1906.[68] In 1907, Bishop McQuaid appointed him rector of St. Anthony Church. His successor at St. Andrew's was Father Albert R. Bandini, a Florentine (1878-1973). Father Bandini remained at St. Andrew's Seminary only two years, after which he left the Rochester Diocese for the West.

With the Italian population growing, Bishop McQuaid found it necessary to engage other Italian priests for pastoral work. Father John Robotti (1876-?) was first the pastor of St. Francis of Assisi Italian Church in Auburn (1907-1911), and then the pastor of Mount Carmel Church in Rochester (1911-1915). But like several other imported Italian clergymen, he subsequently moved out of the Diocese. In fact, the only Italian-born priest who was named pastor of an Italian parish by McQuaid and who spent the rest of his priestly life in the Rochester Diocese was Monsignor Adolfo Gabbani (1872-1949), appointed rector of St. Anthony's Church, Elmira, in 1908. (We exclude from this category four other Italian-born priests of the Diocese because they were in charge of regular parishes, not Italian national parishes: Fathers Arcangelo Paganini; Gilbert Nuonno; Eugene Pagani [1843-1928]; and Angelo Lugero [1834-1909].[69])

The problem of providing Italian-speaking priests continued to trouble the Diocese of Rochester long after its first bishop had passed from the scene. But one of the most potent factors in its solution was the gradual breaking down of the language-barrier through the schools. Bishop McQuaid and his teaching Sisters knew very well that the school child was the key to the Americanization of the immigrant family. One foreign observer, Abbé Félix Klein, took special note of this in 1904, when the Bishop took him on a tour of the parochial schools in Rochester. Later on, in a published account of his visit, Abbé Klein described the policy which the schools were following with Italian children. The children in the lower grades, he reported, "are kept in a room by themselves until they understand English; afterward—that is, in six or seven weeks—they are distributed among the general classes, where they soon (for usually they are extremely bright) learn to speak as well as the others. Here one sees, in almost mechanically perfect operation, one of the most effective agencies of assimilation."[70]

The troubles that Bernard McQuaid had with national minorities were secondary, with one exception. This was the tragic movement of a number of Rochester Poles which terminated in the foundation of a schismatic parish.

Conflict first broke out at St. Stanislaus'—as in many Polish-American parishes—in connection with a patriotic society. The Polish people of Rochester naturally retained a strong devotion to their native culture and to the cause of freedom for their native land. Now, in 1880 there was founded at Philadelphia a Polish-American organization, ostensibly dedicated to maintaining this double patriotic devotion. Its name was the Polish National Alliance, and although not professedly Catholic, it won quick popularity in American "Polonia". By 1900 there were three units of the P. N. A. in Rochester: Group 216 (founded 1893); Group 396 (1897); and Group 512 (1900). The three original Rochester units and the others established later on have in recent decades made a valuable contribution to the local Polish community. At the start, however, their status was more problematic; and for this reason they incurred the disfavor of the pastor of St. Stanislaus, Father Theophilus Szadzinski (1857-1909). They were, he pointed out, non-sectarian, and therefore suspect of religious indifferentism; and some of the members seemed to be tainted with socialism. He therefore concluded that membership in the P. N. A. represented a spiritual peril for Polish Catholics, who traditionally linked together Fatherland and Faith. Naturally, he could not permit the members to bring the insignia of the society into the church, for they were not an official church society. (This regulation on insignia was diocesan-wide, and applied to Catholics of all national origins.) Furthermore, in opposing the P.N.A., Father Theophilus knew he had the backing of Bishop McQuaid.

Unfortunately, the pastor's stand encountered strong opposition from a small but influential segment of the Polish parishioners.[71] What is more, a certain number of the lay people at St. Stanislaus' now began to agitate for greater lay control of the parochial finances. The parish was, of course, incorporated according to the 1863 law governing Catholic parochial incorporation. But some of the societies, in what seemed like a resurgence of the old-time trusteeist spirit, came to believe that they, rather than the official lay parish trustees, should have control over the church collections. Civil law, to say nothing of pastoral prudence, prevented both Bishop and Pastor from making such a concession. But antagonism to Father Szadzinski continued to mount, and in 1900 a "Committee for the Congregation", bringing moral as well as financial charges against their parish priest, urged Bishop McQuaid to remove him from his post.[72] The Bishop did not comply.

Thereafter the friction increased. In 1905, a group of parishioners once again petitioned McQuaid to remove their pastor and once again met with a refusal. This was the year in which the long battle began in earnest.

In the spring and summer of 1905, the Poles of Rochester were so fatally divided that there were frequent public rows and disorders on the parochial property and throughout the Polish neighborhood. The Bishop held his patience until August, but when complaints against the disturbances became city-wide, he saw that he must act. On August 21st, he addressed a letter to Father Theophilus to read to his people on Sunday, August 27th. The Bishop deplored the "barbarous conduct" which the dissidents had been guilty of during the past four months, and he declared that in his whole career he had never seen anything to equal it. Those who did not like the pastor were free to attend Mass at other parishes. At all events, the charges they had brought against him were exaggerated, erroneous, and slanderous. At the root of the opposition, he believed, was an ignorance of the laws of church and state. Those who did violence to priests and church property merited canonical penalties, and he promised he would mete out such penalties if need be. But interference with church funds, such as six of the Polish societies had attempted, was against civil law as well. So, too, was any disorderly conduct in public. In both instances, he warned, civil authorities could be depended upon to enforce law and order. It was the ringleaders that were to be blamed. The long-suffering Polish parishioners should therefore reject the guidance of these misguided men.[73]

If the Bishop's strong but carefully worded letter conciliated some of the parishioners, it accomplished nothing with the hard core of the adversaries. In July, 1905, they had appealed for help to Cardinal James Gibbons, Archbishop of Baltimore. Cardinal Gibbons, aware of his lack of jurisdiction over them, had refused to receive their delegation.[74] Then they turned to the Polish Conventual Franciscans of Buffalo. The Franciscans replied that they would be glad to help, but could do nothing, of course, without the permission of the Bishop of Rochester.[75]

In March, 1906, the complainants of St. Stanislaus congregation sent a special committee to lodge an appeal with Archbishop Diomede Falconio, the Apostolic Delegate. The Delegate gave them a hearing with all courtesy, as it was his duty to do. He sought to persuade them that Bishop McQuaid's policy was based on spiritual considerations, and that they should therefore abide by his wish. But he sensed that they were immovable in their antagonism to Father Theophilus. Falconio therefore suggested to McQuaid, in a subsequent letter, that a change of pastors seemed to be the wisest course.[76]

Bishop McQuaid, while defending Father Szadzinski in public, had not hesitated to call sharply to his private attention certain of the personal charges brought against him by the opposition.[77] Still he chose not to remove him from his post, despite the recommendation of the Apostolic Delegate. Quite likely he knew of nobody else who had the linguistic qualifications to replace him. Then, too, the majority of the parishioners seem to have been loyal to their pastor.

For the opposition, McQuaid's firm refusal was the last straw. Rumors were now current that the Bishop's attitude was really traceable to a bias against Polish nationalism, and that he wanted to change St. Stanislaus' from a national to a geographical parish. In view of McQuaid's known attitude towards Americanization, these rumors had all the earmarks of propaganda. At any rate, in 1907, while the stories were being spread, the dissident group turned to Bishop Francis Hodur with the request that he found for them in Rochester a parish of the Polish National Catholic Church. Francis Hodur (1866-1953) was a former Catholic priest who had accepted the invitation to become the founding bishop of this schismatic body. The Polish National Catholic Church, intensely nationalistic, gained much of its membership through divisions like the one in Rochester. The result was the foundation of St. Casimir Polish National Catholic Church on October 15, 1907. Bishop Hodur dedicated its church on Ernst Street, six blocks away from St. Stanislaus Church, on March 4, 1908.

After the split it became easier to judge the strength of the opposing faction. Some 150 families joined the St. Casimir parish. Some 400 families appear to have remained loyal to St. Stanislaus'. Of the latter, a certain number had favored the removal of the pastor, but were unwilling to carry their protest as far as schism. For months, now—indeed, even for years—an unauthorized guerilla campaign continued between the loyal and the seceding groups, men, women, and children of either side participating in scarcely Christian actions of mutual vexation. Thus it was a tense day, that July 5, 1908, when Bishop Thomas F. Hickey came, as delegate of the ailing Bishop McQuaid, to lay the cornerstone of the present St. Stanislaus Church. As he approached the scene, two policemen jumped on his hack to act as a bodyguard, saying they feared violence. In his address, Bishop Hickey praised Father Theophilus and his devoted people for the labor which they were expending on their parish. But he emphasized that there is only one Catholic Church, the Catholic Church founded by Christ and governed by the pope and bishops who have succeeded to the charge He gave to his apostles. "And let me remind you," said the Bishop in somber warning, "that anyone who joins or helps in building up any opposition church becomes thereby excommunicated and will be deprived of Christian burial."

A Polish-speaking priest translated Bishop Hickey's warning—apparently the first public admonition given by diocesan authorities since the dedication of the new schismatic church. A dramatic silence followed. The ban of excommunication was applicable to the friends, even the families, of many of those present. But when the address was finished, the parishioners applauded Bishop Hickey—a sign of their own faithful obedience.[78]

The second St. Stanislaus Church was dedicated on August 1, 1909, with great solemnity. Guest of honor was Bishop Paul P. Rhode, auxiliary bishop of Chicago, and the first Polish-American priest to be promoted to the American hierarchy. Bishop Hickey performed the ceremony of dedication, for Bishop McQuaid had died seven months before. Father Szadzinski himself, long declining in health and bent by trials, survived the dedicatory rite less than a month. He was only fifty-two at the time of his death. A fair number of the parishioners of St. Casimir eventually found their way back to the mother parish, which, thanks to increased immigration, became one of the city's largest Catholic congregations. Today St. Casimir's retains its independent status; but fortunately the old animosities between its parishioners and the Catholic Poles have long since died out. Whether Bishop McQuaid took exactly the right course in dealing with the dissidents of sixty years ago is a matter of opinion. The fact remains that this unfortunate tumult among the good Polish people of Rochester was the saddest chapter in the history of the Diocese.[79]

If Polish-American nationalist societies caused Bernard McQuaid many trying hours, Irish-American nationalist societies may well have caused him a more personal grief. When it came to Poland's fight for freedom, he could maintain an objective frame of mind. When it came to Ireland's—well, blood is thicker than water.

Daniel O'Connell by his brilliant peaceful tactics had led the Irish to victory in their campaign for religious emancipation. After O'Connell's death, in the subsequent campaign for home rule, Irish and Irish-American opinion had see-sawed between advocating peaceful and violent means. Advocates of violence were prone to form secret political societies, a type of fraternalism denounced by the Church.

One of these Irish secret political societies, the Fenian Brotherhood, had been condemned by Rome early in McQuaid's episcopal career. The Fenian Brotherhood, founded in the United States in 1859, was the American auxiliary of the Irish Revolutionary Brotherhood established in Dublin in 1858. Chapters of the Fenian organization were numerous at the end of the Civil War, no less in the Rochester area than elsewhere: it was expected that any Irishman worth his salt would belong.[80] Local Irish patriots, principally those who had seen service in the Civil War or the militia, took part, in May and June, 1866, in the fantastic armed Fenian invasion of Canada. Owen Gavigan of Auburn had recruited for this Fenian Army in Auburn; and Rochesterians Patrick H. Sullivan and Alexander Connolly had captained two of its companies. When the Fenians made another armed foray across the border at Trout River in May 26, 1870, Daniel Sharpe of Paddy Hill was quartermaster of the staff of General John M. Gleeson.[81]

On January 12, 1870, while Bishop McQuaid was attending the Vatican Council, the Holy Office, that papal bureau in charge of doctrinal matters, issued a decree condemning the Fenians as a secret political society of the sort forbidden by the Church. This confirmed the American bishops in their previous opinions of the Irish organization. But Bishop McQuaid, realizing that the American Fenian society had many worthy aims, expressed the belief that it could escape the papal ban by changing its name and severing connections with the secret and revolutionary elements in the Irish Revolutionary Brotherhood.[82] What the papal condemnation had not yet achieved, the ignominious failure of the second Fenian invasion of Canada largely accomplished, namely the general discrediting of Fenianism.

Another international Irish patriotic organization later arose to replace the Fenians—the Irish Land League. This was not a secret society. But both in Ireland and in America the bishops kept it under close surveillance lest it become infected with the Fenian spirit or resort to unjust means. The founder of the National Land League of Ireland (1879) was Michael Davitt (1846-1906). Its declared purpose was an open constitutional agitation for "three F's": Fair rents, Fixity of tenure, and Free sale. Suppressed by the British government in 1881, the National Land League reorganized in 1882 as the "Irish National League." The League, with its campaign against the abuses of landlordism, served as an effective instrument in the hands of the parliamentary leader and "uncrowned king of Ireland", James Stewart Parnell (1846-1891). Subsequently, the Holy See was to judge that certain of the League's methods—boycotting, withholding of rent, and the "Plan of Campaign" to compel rent-reduction—were morally inadmissible. In general, however, the League's program was both moderate and effective, and had the backing of the hierarchy both in Ireland and abroad.

It was the bad harvest of 1879 and its consequences that had prompted Parnell to act. On December 30, 1879, Bishop McQuaid launched a Rochester diocesan drive for Irish relief which netted $6,-300.00. In the Southern Tier, at that time still in the Buffalo Diocese, Catholic Irishmen contributed to the Buffalo diocesan relief fund.[83] Then on February 1, 1880, Michael Davitt organized at Rochester the first chapter of an American auxiliary to the National Land League, which bore the name of the "Irish National Land League Relief Association of the United States". From Rochester this auxiliary spread throughout the country. Soon not only the cities but even small country settlements where Irishmen lived had their Land League units.[84] In 1881, Miss Fannie Parnell (1854-1882), poetess and sister of the parliamentarian and a resident of the United States, launched a Ladies' Irish National Land League for Irish-American women. Many priests and a host of the most representative American Irishmen and Irishwomen joined one or another of these organizations—whose names changed, of course, after 1882 when the Irish National Land League, suppressed in Ireland, reappeared as the Irish National League.

Although he expressed reservations on some of the more violent remarks of Parnell, Bishop McQuaid found nothing to criticize in the early activities of the American Land League. In fact, he joined his voice with that of the League on March 4, 1881, when it protested against the recent British "Coercion Act." Later on, however, the National League in Ireland began to employ methods which the Irish hierarchy considered improper. Backing their stand, the Bishop of Rochester warned his own Irish Catholics not to compromise the cause by yielding to subversive elements or approving unjust tactics. This was a rather risky stand, for it prompted some of the Irish zealots to accuse Bishop McQuaid of being no true Irishman. McQuaid ignored their barbs, believing that those who threw them would eventually see the illogicality of their conclusion. Many did; some did not.

Bishop McQuaid was far less tolerant of Irish organizations which veiled their activities in ritual secrecy. There were a great number of societies founded in the last century that fell under suspicion as secret societies of the class condemned by Church law. In 1884, the Third Plenary Council of Baltimore set up the American archbishops as a standing committee to investigate suspect organizations and condemn them if they were found to be of the "forbidden" sort. If the committee could not agree in specific cases, it was to refer the case to Rome.

One of the Irish-American fraternal groups which McQuaid and the Archbishops carefully scrutinized was the Ancient Order of Hibernians (A.O.H.). Many of the American bishops suspected that the Order was affiliated with the "Molly Maguires", a secret organization that had allegedly promoted violence in Pennsylvania anthracite labor disputes of the 1870's. And was the A.O.H. not also connected with the suspect "Board of Erin" in Ireland? The Archbishops deferred action on the Order in 1886. Only in 1894 did McQuaid himself reach the conclusion that the Ancient Order was not connected, or at least was no longer connected, with more lawless Irish organizations. On June 25th of that year he addressed the Biennial State A.O.H. Convention, assembled in his own Cathedral. He frankly explained the motives for his earlier hesitation: the oath of secrecy they had at first required, and the danger of foreign political entanglements. These entanglements, he emphasized, were dangerous no matter what foreign country was involved: Ireland, Germany, Poland, Italy, or any other.[85]

The Bishop had stated his general attitude towards secret societies in a pastoral that he issued on October 4, 1878. He warned the faithful to avoid not only societies which the Church had condemned by name (the Masons, the Carbonari, and the Fenians) but all others that were secret or oath-bound, that practiced lodge rites of a religious character, or that were organized for reprehensible purposes.[86] This was, of course, the traditional Catholic stand—a stand rooted in opposition to the religious indifferentism of such associations, the suspicion of evil-doing that their secrecy prompted, the blasphemy of their extravagant oaths, and the immorality of their blind obedience. To these objections the first bishop of Rochester added his own personal detestation of what he called the "tomfoolery" of lodge ritual. In those golden days of fraternalism scarcely a fraternal society was founded, even a Catholic fraternal society, that did not feel constrained to adopt some sort of pseudo-Masonic ritual.

When it came down to condemning suspect societies, Bishop McQuaid was frankly on the strict side. He had no patience with those members of the Archbishops' Committee who took a more "liberal" stand: Cardinal Gibbons, Archbishop John Ireland, Archbishop Patrick Feehan of Chicago. In 1894, Rome overruled the conciliatory stand of these prelates towards the Odd Fellows, the Knights of Pythias, and the Sons of Temperance. McQuaid was pleased by the Roman ruling, for he had long since forbidden his own diocesans to join any of the three organizations. Societies which were not secret but were non-sectarian he likewise discouraged because of the religious indifferentism such organizations could conceivably foster. In 1872, for instance, he opposed the newly formed Rochester Irish Club because it welcomed non-Catholic as well as Catholic members.[87] And in 1897 he withheld his approval of the newly-established Knights of Columbus until the organization amended the Masonic rigmarole of its rite.

Not that McQuaid was anti-society. The formation of societies on a parochial, diocesan, or even wider basis, was a normal religious phenomenon, and so long as they had no spiritually objectionable characteristics, he was ready to give them his approbation.

One such association, which inspired a national movement, was the uniformed "German Catholic Union of St. Mauritius", founded at St. Joseph's parish, Rochester, in 1873, by Colonel Louis Ernst. The idea of a "parish militia" spread from Rochester across the country, among non-German as well as German parishes. Most of these uniformed parish units sent representatives to a convention held in Baltimore in 1879, where they amalgamated to form the national "Knights of St. John". In 1880, the associated units from Rochester itself joined this union, and were given the rank of "First Regiment". Since those days the uniformed Knights of St. John, always prompt to play their role as honor guards at church festivals, have added much to the decorum of American Catholic religious celebrations.[88]

Another type of society that met even more readily with the approval of Bishop McQuaid was the mutual benefit society. Since insurance benefits were one of the most attractive features of the forbidden fraternal societies, the Catholic insurance society, whether parochial or national, offered a rather good antidote to illicit fraternalism.

Many of these benefit organizations were small and short-lived.

We shall name a few that enjoyed greater stability. Both the Knights of St. John and the Knights of Columbus featured insurance benefits. The C.M.B.A. (Catholic Mutual Benefit Association) functioned over forty years. Founded in Buffalo around 1878, it received Bishop McQuaid's approbation after it had corrected its ritual, and thereafter rose into considerable prominence throughout western New York. The Polish National Alliance eventually outlived its early, more dubious reputation, and still remains a strong benevolent association among the Poles of the Rochester Diocese. The Catholic Benevolent Legion, founded in 1881, is also still in national operation, although its once large membership in the Diocese of Rochester has probably declined.

The favorite with the Bishop, however, was the Ladies' Catholic Benevolent Association, a national society founded in 1890. From 1896 until his death, Bishop McQuaid served as the L.C.B.A.'s Supreme Spiritual Adviser, and he discharged the tasks of that office conscientiously.[89]

But we have already said more than enough to illustrate the official diocesan views on Americanization and the popular societies during the administration of Bernard J. McQuaid.

3. OTHER CURRENT ISSUES.

The first Bishop of Rochester was obliged to take a stand on several other matters of public interest which involved the Church. Here we shall consider three such issues: freedom of worship in public penal and welfare institutions; campaigns for social justice; and so-called liberalism within the American Church.

The freedom of worship question, as we have already indicated, was in large part a carry-over from the Timon epoch. Bishop Timon had tried in vain to secure free worship for the Catholic youths committed to the Western House of Refuge. In 1869, Bishop McQuaid won the reluctant permission of that institution's managers to address the Catholic inmates on spiritual matters, subject to the dispositions of the House superintendent. Thereafter, the three Catholic members of the Board, backed by the Bishop, the pastors, and the parents of the inmates, kept up their efforts to achieve full liberty of contact. One of them, William Purcell, editor of Rochester's *Union and Advertiser,* finally brought in a minority report so conclusive that the majority capitulated; and on March 16, 1875, the Board voted, for the first time in its history, to engage two chaplains, one Protestant and one Catholic. Three years before, the managers of the Rochester Almshouse had decided to allow religious services upon Almshouse premises. They found, as the House of Refuge would also soon discover, that on-premises religious ministrations, far from having the divisive effect anticipated, made a positive contribution. Indeed, in 1888 the Visiting Committee of the House of Refuge requested McQuaid to designate three diocesan nuns to conduct a Catholic Sunday school. The Sisters continued this work as long as the Western House of Refuge was located in Rochester proper. When it was removed in 1906 to its present site at Industry, New York, the State erected chapels for the use of both the Catholic and the Protestant chaplains. (The institution is now called the New York State Agricultural and Industrial School.)

Not all the State's penal and charitable institutions were as prompt as the House of Refuge to provide for the spiritual needs of their charges. A "freedom of worship" bill was introduced in the State Assembly in 1881 with a view to enforcing a more liberal policy, but it failed to pass at that session and at subsequent sessions, largely because of the strongly anti-Catholic pressure of the United States Evangelical Union. When it finally did become a law in 1892, the precedent of the Western House of Refuge and the personal interposition of Bishop McQuaid were in a measure responsible for the victory.

The wind was now changing, slowly but surely. In 1894, the State announced its decision to establish the Craig Colony, a hospital for epileptics, at Sonyea, Livingston County, in the Diocese of Rochester. A Rochester Catholic, Mr. Daniel B. Murphy, was one of the charter members of the Board of Managers; and he saw to it from the outset that the religious side of the undertaking was not overlooked. In 1900, the Board agreed to support resident Protestant and Catholic chaplains. Taking this cue, Bishop McQuaid offered the Managers to build and pay for a Catholic chapel and rectory on the hospital grounds. His offer was accepted with pleasure, and in April, 1902, he dedicated the completed Chapel of the Divine Compassion. Towards the total cost of this chapel and rectory ($12,000.00) the Bishop himself had contributed $2,000.00; the Rochester Diocese, $6,000.00; and the other dioceses of the State, the remainder. During the same year McQuaid also raised $3,500.00, all within his own diocese, to build a rectory and weekday chapel for the Catholic chaplains assigned to the Soldiers' Home at Bath, Steuben County.

By 1902, there were likewise official Catholic chaplaincies at the State Hospital for the Insane at Willard, New York; at the Elmira State Reformatory; and at the State Prison in Auburn.[90] In the beginning, the priests assigned to the penal institutions were men attached to local parishes, to whom the State paid a salary for part-time work.

However, on January 1, 1907, Bishop McQuaid named, as the first full-time chaplain at the Reformatory, Father John A. Conway (1875-1954).[91]

Social justice engaged the Bishop's particular attention in the affair of the Knights of Labor and the affair of Henry George and his economic theories.

The Knights of Labor, founded in 1869, had by 1886 attracted a membership of some 700,000 American and Canadian workingmen, a large percentage of them Catholics. In its day it was the only national organization available to defend labor against the current exploitation. Unfortunately, although they had shed much of the Masonic secrecy which they originally practiced, the Knights still retained some secret ritual, and furthermore seemed to be flirting with socialism. On these grounds, the Canadian Catholic hierarchy, in 1884, forbade Catholics to be members of the Knights of Labor. Rome confirmed the Canadian ban.

Not until 1886 were the Catholic bishops of the United States informed of this Canadian condemnation. The Knights in Canada and in the United States were essentially one order, and in the normal course of events a Roman ruling on one branch would be extended to the other branch.

While a few American bishops looked askance at the Order and would have been pleased to have it declared out-of-bounds, it is evident that the majority of them thought the condemnation inadvisable on more than one score. Acting in the name of the Archbishops' Committee on forbidden societies, Cardinal Gibbons, with the assistance of Archbishop John Ireland and Bishop John Keane, then bishop of Richmond, submitted to Rome a brilliant memorandum urging that the authorities take a course that they seldom took regarding such societies — that of reversing their decision. The memorandum argued that the alleged secrecy was harmless, and the alleged association with socialists was unsubstantiated. Cardinal Gibbons believed that the Order was already declining, and therefore did not merit the special publicity which a ban would give to it. But most of all, he argued that if Rome were to condemn an organization which was fighting for the rights of the workingman, the Church would be branded as an enemy of social justice, and would lose face with the poor.

The Holy See actually did reverse its judgment, declaring on August 28, 1888, that membership in the Knights would be tolerated "provided there be amended those things in the statutes of the association that are stated less correctly or may be taken in a bad sense". It seems that the Bishop of Rochester held a generally neutral view of the Knights, although he scorned the "aid" they gave to the Rochester shoemakers and printers in their labor conflicts. From his point of view, the paramount norm for considering their acceptability was whether they constituted a spiritual peril to Catholic members. By 1891, when there was no evidence that the Knights had indeed "amended those things in the statutes" which the Holy See had stipulated, apparently as the grounds for reversing its decision, Bishop McQuaid was ready to make an issue of it. But by that time the Order had entered into its anticipated decline. Hence Archbishop Corrigan, although he himself disliked the organization, wisely pointed out to McQuaid that the reopening of the campaign would only have the effect of galvanizing it into a new life.[92]

In the Henry George affair, the conflict was fundamentally more doctrinal than disciplinary. Henry George (1839-1897) was an American Protestant economist dedicated to the quest of an antidote against poverty. Landlords, he decided, were the villains, and the chief agents of poverty. He recommended, therefore, that in place of all the other taxes which the people were obliged to pay, there be instituted a single land tax, payable by landowners alone, and equivalent in amount to the "unearned increment" of value accruing to their property. Since rent-paying, according to him, was the root of poverty, this single tax would eliminate poverty and restore the economic balance of the community. It was an ingenious theory, which is still arguable and still argued, although it has never been widely accepted.

The utter simplicity of George's solution won widespread approval among Irish-American Catholics, not only because they themselves were poor but because Georgism seemed to offer a handy theoretical basis to the contemporary war against landlordism in Ireland. Irish leader Michael Davitt had seen this relevance, and in his American campaign for the Land League he had frequently appealed to Henry George as an authority. Even more important in establishing the same connection was the prominent New York priest-publicist, the Reverend Dr. Edward McGlynn (1837-1900). McGlynn's advocacy of Georgist doctrine was bound to win a hearing in the New York metropolitan area, for the Irish of Gotham idolized this brilliant, eloquent, stormy Doctor, knight-errant of the impoverished and of Irish freedom.

Unfortunately, George and McGlynn (though not, in the last analysis, Davitt) felt that over and above the state's right of eminent domain in landed property, the denial of any right of private property in land was an essential postulate of the single-tax theory. Such a view apparently did not spring from Marxism, but it did savor of socialism and thus ran counter to the Church's traditional defense of the right of private ownership. As early as 1882, the Archbishop of New York, Cardinal John McCloskey, sought to persuade the unconventional Father McGlynn to reject this incorrect principle of Georgism. But the weight of the McGlynn problem devolved upon McCloskey's successor, Archbishop Michael A. Corrigan (1839-1902). In a pastoral letter of November 19, 1886, Archbishop Corrigan pointed out why the denial of private property in land was irreconcilable with Catholic teaching. When "the Doctor" stood his ground and participated actively in Henry George's unsuccessful campaign for the mayoralty of New York, Corrigan, with the backing of the Holy See, declared, on July 3, 1887, that Father McGlynn had incurred formal excommunication.

The strong-willed McGlynn let neither suspension nor excommunication deter him from touring the State that fall, stumping for the United Labor Party and attacking, if not the Church, at least the "ecclesiastical machine", which he said had interfered with his freedom of speech as an American citizen. Archbishop Corrigan, prone to rule by the book, sought from Rome a condemnation of Henry George's writings. But Cardinal Gibbons and Archbishop Ireland, who always opposed Church censures in matters where non-Catholics or non-religious factors were involved, interposed to thwart any such ban. As a result, the Vatican's Holy Office, in its decree of February 6, 1889, did reassert, against George, the Church's doctrine on "the right of private property, even as regards land," but in view of Gibbons' plea, the Holy Office forbade the publication of this decree. However, on May 11, 1891, Pope Leo XIII dealt with the same doctrine publicly in his encyclical *Rerum Novarum*. In the Pope's assertion that landownership is a natural right, Henry George saw the clear repudiation of his fundamental postulate. Consequently, he replied with an open letter to the Pope, expressing the hope that Leo would reconsider his stand, and would then, instead of defending private property in land, solemnly condemn it.

The Archbishop of New York felt the frustration of having in his hands a Holy Office condemnation which he was not free to use. But silence was probably the best policy in the long run, for the McGlynn affair had developed, at least in the New York metropolitan area, into something so complicated and emotional that it would take more than a subtle doctrinal condemnation to set things right. In the eyes of the liberal press and of many Catholics, the contest between the eloquent Doctor and his Archbishop was a struggle of social justice versus vested interests, of Irish freedom versus native Americanism, of political reform versus Tammany Hall. Archbishop Corrigan no doubt made certain errors of judgment in his attempt to solve what was probably under the circumstances unsolvable; but one can only marvel at the apparent disproportion of the bitterness visited upon him—a bitterness which has begun to be dissipated only in recent years. The McGlynn case came to a sudden termination on December 23, 1892, when Archbishop Francesco Satolli, acting as papal legate, absolved the controversial priest from his censures. Archbishop Corrigan, obliged by the terms of the absolution to give Dr. McGlynn a new pastoral appointment, assigned him to St. Mary's Church, Newburgh.

Satolli's action was based on a written declaration that McGlynn had made, at the Delegate's request, of his teachings on landownership. Four professors of the Catholic University, to whom the papal legate submitted the statement for examination, declared that it was in conformity with Catholic teachings. As a matter of fact, the McGlynn statement, though cautiously worded, reasserted George's basic denial of landownership; nor did the Doctor cease to maintain thereafter that Georgism was entirely Catholic on this point. That the Holy Office was of a different mind was evident from another document which it issued in 1893, expressing condemnation of "the doctrine of Henry George, which denies the right of private ownership and representing this ownership as contrary to the natural law . . ."[93] Small wonder, then, that not only in some American quarters, but in Rome itself, Archbishop Satolli's prompt absolution of Dr. McGlynn caused considerable surprise.[94] For the Delegate had rejected Corrigan's side of the controversy not only in the disciplinary aspect, in which he may have been at fault, but also in the theological aspect, in which he happened to be correct.

Western New York re-echoed, but less stridently, with the clangor of the Georgist war in New York City. When the Doctor, by now excommunicated, moved west on his lecture tour, a number of good Catholics gave him a hearing, on the assumption that attendance at a stimulating lecture on economics did not imply approval of the canonical status of the lecturer. For the most part, however, Catholics in the western counties played "hands off", and in this they usually had the backing of their priests.[95]

Bishop McQuaid took public action against Dr. McGlynn only on the occasion of his visit to Rochester on October 20, 1887. It is interesting to note the grounds on which the Bishop withstood McGlynn.

What he repudiated especially was the Georgist denial of the right of landownership.

Although he publicly commented on the McGlynn issue only when Dr. McGlynn came to Rochester to speak, McQuaid had been counselling Archbishop Corrigan on the case all along. He certainly advocated the strong rather than the gentle approach, and there may be some grounds for the opinion that Bishop McQuaid's advocacy of an "unconditional surrender" contributed to the prolongation of the struggle. What we must bear in mind, however, with respect to both McQuaid and Corrigan, is that they believed the crux of the question was not in his social theory nor in his political practice, but in his *theological* doctrine. "Stick to the declaration of McGlynn's letter," the Bishop of Rochester wrote to Archbishop Corrigan on October 9, 1887, "that there is no just ownership of land by individuals and confiscation without compensation is justifiable. Be cautious about what are called George's theories. They are one thing today and something else tomorrow." And three months later, on January 14, 1888, McQuaid reminded Corrigan, "The question of modes of taxation can be left to the people so long as they do not infringe on the right of individuals to hold real estate as owners."[96]

Most of our early American bishops were faced with disciplinary, not doctrinal problems in dealing with unruly priests. In the McGlynn episode, a doctrinal error was the basic issue at stake, if not the one most fully recognized. It is to the credit of both Archbishop Corrigan and Bishop McQuaid that they discerned this home-grown fallacy, and in the discharge of their role as teachers, strove to the best of their ability to warn their flocks against it.

Before we pass from the subject of social justice, we might ask what were the views of the founding bishop of Rochester on labor relations. Rochester had its share of labor troubles in the 1880's and 1890's. Did Bishop McQuaid on those occasions favor the manufacturers, who disliked the "dictation" of labor unions—and who included, in Rochester proper, such prominent Catholics as the Cunninghams, carriage makers, and the shoe manufacturers John Kelly and Patrick Cox? Or did he, despite the fatal inefficiency of the local Knights of Labor, stand rather on the side of the laboring classes to which most of his diocesans belonged?

The picture is not entirely clear, but it seems that the Bishop was disposed to allow capital and labor to work out their own salvation, reserving for himself only the right to interpose when doctrinal questions arose.[97] He welcomed Leo XIII's 1891 labor encyclical *Rerum*

Novarum. If he did not formulate, upon the basis of this encyclical, a positive social program, neither did most of his contemporaries in the American hierarchy, including Cardinal Gibbons and Archbishop Ireland. Only in 1919 would the Catholic hierarchy of this country promulgate their national platform for social justice based on the Leonine principles. Meanwhile, however, individual Catholic priests and laymen in the Rochester area were apparently not impeded in making their personal contributions to the theory and practice of social justice.[98] Nor is there evidence that the founding Bishop of Rochester took any step which brought about the alienation from Catholic loyalty of either the few capitalists or the many laborers who were members of his flock.

The last great battle which engaged the "liberal" and "conservative" American bishops of the post-Civil War decades was that over so-called theological "Americanism." Since Bishop McQuaid was a participant in this battle, it has, through him, some relevance to the Diocese of Rochester.

As we have already noted, McQuaid held views in common with the German-American bishops and other "conservative" prelates regarding several of the policies and practices of the "liberal" prelates —especially Archbishop John Ireland, Bishop John Keane, and Cardinal Gibbons, who usually joined Ireland and Keane when battle-lines were forming. More than once, Bishop McQuaid concluded that the "liberals" were too conciliatory to Protestant-minded America. In fact, he did not hesitate to state his belief to Rome that these prelates were manifesting a trend towards the theological liberalism — that is, religious indifferentism—which the popes of the nineteenth century had strongly condemned. In the mid-1890's, the "progressive" prelates lost, for the nonce, their favor with the Holy See. Leo XIII requested Msgr. Denis J. O'Connell to resign from the rectorship of the American College in Rome, evidently because he had been too active a partisan of the "liberal" group of American prelates. One year later, in 1896, the Pope made the same demand of Bishop Keane, the founding rector of the Catholic University of America. McQuaid's opinions, communicated to Rome, had no doubt been a factor in both dismissals; and the Bishop of Rochester felt that this action of the Holy See was wise and timely.[99]

The "Americanist" controversy was of French origin, and concerned the applicability of American progressive ideas to French Catholicism. Here, too, Archbishop Ireland was the darling of the French Catholic "progressives." His flamboyant dedication to the American theory of "manifest destiny" struck many American Catholics as excessive; but those Frenchmen who favored republicanism over monarchy hailed it precisely because it was flamboyant and dynamic.

Now, in 1897, one of John Ireland's staunchest Gallic admirers, the Abbé Félix Klein, published a somewhat inexact translation of the *Life of Father Hecker* written by Father Walter Elliott. Father Hecker, with whom Bishop McQuaid had been on good terms, was the convert-founder of the American religious community known as the Paulists. Conceiving his Congregation of St. Paul as called to the special vocation of carrying the Catholic faith to American Protestants, Father Hecker had formulated some new theories about the best methods for winning the mind and soul of the Yankee. Father Elliott, devoted disciple of Hecker that he was, had been at pains to incorporate much of Hecker's theory into his biography. Archbishop Ireland, in the Introduction which he wrote for the *Life,* confessed his own debt to Father Hecker's inspiration, and with typical Irelandic vigor praised the sterling Americanism of Hecker's apostolic approach. In their context, the thoughts expressed by Hecker and Ireland in the Elliott book merited no substantial criticism; out of context they could rather easily lend themselves to misinterpretation. When the book came out, in 1891, it bore the *imprimatur* of Archbishop Corrigan.

Klein, in presenting *Le Père Hecker* to his French audience, added to the original biography and to Ireland's original introduction an equally enthusiastic preface of his own, in which he laid stress on just those points of the book that were the most disputable. Hence *Père Hecker* quickly ignited a blazing controversy that spread from France into Italy and Spain. While the Europeans who were pro-Hecker and anti-Hecker represented various shades of theological and political thought, the campaign against Heckerism in France was basically the campaign of French monarchists and ultraconservatives against French democrats and progressives. Abbé Charles Maignen was the opposition's most vocal prophet of doom. According to him, all the evidence proved one conclusion: this "Americanism" which French progressives wanted to introduce into France was a collection of theological novelties, semi-Protestant attitudes, Masonic and Jewish chicaneries, and schismatic trends. In 1898, when Maignen received an *imprimatur* for his book, *Le Père Hecker: est-il un saint?* from Father Lepidi, the Pope's own official theologian, the Holy See itself became enmeshed in the dispute.

America itself was drawn into the Americanist discussion belatedly and almost incidentally. Arthur Preuss of St. Louis, editor of the ultra-conservative German-American *Fortnightly Review,* sponsored the circulation of a translation of Maignen's *Father Hecker: Is He a Saint?* Maignen, said Preuss, had presented therein a *true* picture of the situation in the United States. This was a controversial view, and it soon sparked a new controversy. Opposing lines now re-formed among the American bishops; but most of the prelates saw no strong resemblance between Maignen's portrait of "Americanism" and the sort of Americanism they knew. Cardinal Gibbons interposed once more to avert a Roman condemnation. Although he spoke up too late, his plea apparently did influence Leo XIII's manner of phrasing the warning he was about to give. The papal letter *Testem Benevolentiae,* dated January 22, 1899, carefully pointed out that the errors lately labelled as "Americanism" had nothing to do with Americanism in the cultural or political sense. Rather, they were a cluster of conclusions which flowed from one false principle: namely, that in view of the modern trend to liberty, greater freedom should be allowed in the theological interpretation of even defined doctrines. Among these blameworthy conclusions were: that "active" virtues were now more important than "passive" virtues; that religious communities without vows were now preferable to the old orders which require vows; and that new apostolic methods should supersede the traditional methods.

Once the Pope had spoken, the sincere French "Americanists" hastened to accept his judgment, and Abbé Klein withdrew his book from circulation. The American hierarchy also hastened to express its acceptance, declaring that the condemned errors were by no means the teaching of the Church in the United States. Nevertheless the German-American bishops of the Milwaukee Province did indicate in their joint reply to the Pope that they believed the erroneous doctrines were actually taught in this country. Archbishop Corrigan, too, in the letter which he composed in the name of McQuaid and the suffragan bishops of the New York Province, intimated, although less strongly, that these false doctrines had already begun to crop up in the United States.[100] However the two letters may have phrased it, they were making a serious accusation against the doctrinal vigilance of the American episcopate. Consequently, at the next formal meeting of the American Archbishops, both Archbishop Ireland and Archbishop Patrick W. Riordan of San Francisco demanded that a thorough investigation be made into the charge that theological "Americanism" was actually defended anywhere in the United States. However, Archbishop Corrigan countered the move as imprudent, and it was tabled. Obviously, the "Conservatives" did not want to make an issue of the point, so it was on this note that the American phase of the "Americanist" controversy ended.[101]

That catechists are sometimes tempted, in addressing this religiously pluralist nation, to make compromises in doctrinal teaching, is undeniable. Pope Leo's *Testem Benevolentiae* was, and still is, a salutary warning to religious teachers never to set out along new paths of instruction without taking as their guide the compass of tradition. Some of the accusations brought by Maignen against American Catholicism were indeed reflections, however distorted, of tendencies which actually existed among us. The American "liberal" leaders were dynamic, and did not spurn new approaches. Today we can consider them pioneers in what we now term the "ecumenical spirit." But one can fairly ask whether, in their day, either Catholics or Protestants were ready for ecumenical dialogue. The exceptions which Bishop McQuaid took to some of the practices of the "liberal" bishops must not be judged in the light of the conditions of today but of the conditions of the late nineteenth century.

Although the Americanist discussion seems to have understandably roused little interest or comprehension among the Catholics of the Rochester Diocese, there is no doubt that they were aware of many of the controversial issues which had divided the United States hierarchy. The subjects of discussion were not, it must be remembered, Catholic doctrines, but methods of accommodating Catholic practice to the non-Catholic American milieu. Clashing opinions, however sincerely held, might well have been voiced less bitterly, had not the Catholic and the secular press offered themselves enthusiastically to the contesting parties as media of expression. Catholics of the Diocese of Rochester and of other dioceses were thus furnished with all too much information on disagreements that might better have been settled privately. And when bishop began to argue with bishop in the newspapers, the chance for a real meeting of minds became even more remote.

Only the experience of World War I would convince the members of the American hierarchy that they needed very much a forum in which they could discuss quietly and without untimely and confusing publicity, those problems of policy that faced them all. Had the National Catholic Welfare Conference and the annual bishops' meetings been functioning as early as 1880, there can be little doubt that the many thorny questions of the following decades could have been solved more easily, more gracefully, and more charitably.

CHAPTER EIGHT

REQUIESCAT

DURING THE last decade of Bishop McQuaid's episcopate—1899 to 1909—Rochester's pioneer Catholic bishop completed the basic organization of his diocese. By the time he reached the fortieth anniversary of his episcopate, the diocesan population had risen from the initial 54,000 to 120,000. While the population in 1908 was not great enough to rank the Rochester Diocese with the major American dioceses, it was sufficient to place Rochester among growing sees of middling size. The number of diocesan clergy had also increased remarkably. In 1868, there had been 39 priests; by 1909 there were 158—a large proportion of them "home-grown" and "home-trained", thanks to McQuaid's campaign for a native clergy. And there were still more clerical candidates on the way up: in 1909 St. Andrew's Seminary had 74 aspirants; St. Bernard's, in a total student body of 187, had 54 seminarians enrolled for the Diocese of Rochester. Parochial schools, 14 at the outset, now numbered 53, and took care of 18,280 pupils. The most populous of the religious orders of women serving in the Diocese were local Mercy and Josephite communities. In 1868, there had been about 10 Sisters of Mercy; now there were 98. In 1868, there had been 12 Sisters of St. Joseph; now there were 417.

Bernard McQuaid reached the golden anniversary of his priesthood on January 16, 1898. His seventy-fifth birthday was only eleven months off. The last ten years of his episcopate were therefore "borrowed time". This is not to say that McQuaid, even as an octogenarian, lost control of his abilities or of his diocese. As a matter of fact, some of his finest accomplishments date from these latter years. Nor were they years free from problems, trials, and challenges such as he had encountered before and was still able to stand up to.

In general, however, the old prelate's last decade was serene. To the gratification of being allowed a long autumn in which to perfect his work was added the special consolation of reconciliation with some of his former adversaries. When he finally reached the end of his long life, he died, as he had lived, a bishop of the grand manner, lamented by a reverent body of clergy, faithful, and fellow citizens, and hailed as one of the most influential builders of American Catholicism.

1. THE BUSY AUTUMNTIDE.

As he neared the age of seventy-five, Bishop McQuaid began to think of asking the Holy See for an auxiliary bishop. Not to *share* his authority, of course. McQuaid, as we have seen, was a strict interpreter of the *monarchial* episcopate. But to take over some of his episcopal duties.

There were several able priests in the Diocese who might have been considered episcopal timber. The Chancellor, Monsignor Hippolyte De Regge, was now too old for the honor; but had he been younger he would have deserved consideration. Two Redemptorists who served as rectors of St. Joseph's Church were high in the estimation of the Bishop of Rochester: Father Mathias Kuborn and Father William Kessel. But Father Kuborn died in 1895; and it is highly unlikely at all events, that a secular bishop—especially the Bishop of Rochester—would have selected as his auxiliary a member of a religious order. Outside the city of Rochester there were several conceivable candidates. Among them was the pastor of St. Patrick's Church, Elmira, Father James J. Bloomer (1841-1931). Father Bloomer was a strong-willed man, who had stood his ground against Dr. Edward McGlynn in 1887, and, in 1894, against the "seditious" attitude of an Elmira organization, the Father Mathew Catholic Total Abstinence and Benevolent Society. He was highly esteemed by the Southern Tier Catholics.[1] At Auburn, there was the able Father William Mulheron (1844-1913), who had built up St. Mary's parish plant and founded the Auburn Catholic Orphan Asylum. At Geneva was the gentlemanly Dean William A. McDonald of St. Frances de Sales Church (1855-1917), who was actively interested in Catholic schools. Still more of a scholar was Father Simon FitzSimons of St. Rose Church, Lima (1848-1928). It was he, we will recall, who fought the Lima School Case practically single-handed. He had a flair for controversy and was a writer of both articles and books. But he was perhaps *too* bookish, and too mercurial.

There is no real indication that Bishop McQuaid considered any of the seven above-named priests as possibilities. Nor that he considered a younger man, Father Augustine M. O'Neill (1859-1921), who was very promising, but of uncertain health. There is, however, a strong likelihood that McQuaid had practically decided on his vicar general, Father James F. O'Hare (1846-1898). So high did the pastor of Immaculate Conception Church stand in the eyes of his Bishop, that McQuaid obtained for him, in 1889, an honorary Roman doctorate of divinity. The unexpected death of Dr. O'Hare grieved McQuaid deeply; and the loss of a potential auxiliary bishop may have been an additional factor in that grief.[2]

Next in order of preference, it would seem, was Father James Kiernan of St. Mary's Church (1855-1900). Father Kiernan also had much to recommend him. As rector of the Cathedral from 1886 to 1898, he had shown himself devout and unassuming, yet zealous and progressive. Although not essentially a man of learning, he had contributed his genuine administrative energy to the development of the diocesan school system and, in particular, of Nazareth Academy. Interested in adult education, he sponsored the Rochester Literary Coterie, a club of young men bent on self-education. He was likewise vice-president of the Catholic Summer School of Cliff Haven, New York.[3] But Kiernan, too, was snatched away in the springtime of his promise. He died on May 13, 1900, profoundly lamented by McQuaid and all others who had known this excellent and wise priest.

There were now three priests left who seemed to qualify, more or less, as episcopal candidates: Thomas Hendrick, pastor of St. Bridget's Church, Rochester; Edward J. Hanna, professor of theology at St. Bernard's Seminary; and Thomas F. Hickey, rector of the Cathedral and vicar general.

Father Hendrick (1849-1909) was the son of Thomas Hendrick, whom we have already met as the leading Catholic pioneer of Penn Yan. A versatile man, Thomas, Junior, had shown himself a "live wire" in his pastoral assignments both in the country and in Rochester. His interests ranged much farther afield than the strictly parochial duties. Public welfare and Republican politics engaged him deeply; and he was such an expert on the breeding of horses that he regularly wrote a column, under the pen name "Aurelius", for a horse-breeders' journal. From 1901 to 1903 he was a member of the New York State Board of Regents.

Nevertheless, it is not likely that Bishop McQuaid considered Father Hendrick, then or later, as a possible auxiliary bishop. Hendrick was notoriously absent-minded, for one thing; and McQuaid may well have thought him too immersed in politics. At all events, Hendrick became a bishop of a see of his own in 1903, before the Bishop of Rochester had reached any decision on a Rochester auxiliary. For in the spring of 1903, President Theodore Roosevelt, desirous of having the Spanish-born bishops in the Philippine Islands replaced by Americans, informed Cardinal Gibbons that he would appreciate it if his friend Father Hendrick were named archbishop of Manila.[4] Asked by the Cardinal what he thought of Hendrick for the post, Bishop McQuaid encouraged the appointment.[5] Actually Leo XIII named Hendrick bishop of Cebu, P.I., rather than archbishop of Manila, confirming the nomination on June 26, 1903.[6] Bishop Hendrick, a simple, direct man, always interested in human betterment, fought a gallant defense of the rights of his Philippine diocese. He died an untimely death on November 30, 1909, on the eve, it seems, of his transfer to a see in the United States.[7]

It is certain that Bishop McQuaid considered the Reverend Doctor Edward Hanna as a possible auxiliary bishop of Rochester. Hanna (1860-1944) was a native Rochesterian whom McQuaid had sent to the North American College in Rome in 1879 to prepare himself for a professorial position in the proposed St. Bernard's Seminary. After a brilliant scholastic career, Hanna had returned to Rochester in 1887, to spend six years as assistant at the Cathedral and member of the faculty of St. Andrew's Seminary. Upon the opening of St. Bernard's Seminary in 1893, he assumed the chair of dogmatic theology. An excellent teacher, he continued also to assist the Bishop with much of his secretarial work, to engage in various priestly ministrations, to aid Italian immigrants, and to participate in many social welfare activities. For some time, Hanna was deemed the obvious choice for the post of bishop-assistant. But in 1903 and 1904, Bishop McQuaid grew wary of Hanna's known differences of opinion on several matters of policy. He finally reached the conclusion that the Professor, should he happen to succeed him as bishop, (always a likelihood, if never an inevitability, in the case of auxiliary bishops), might not maintain the traditions, especially the educational traditions, which he, as founder of the Diocese, had labored to establish. He seems to have feared also that Hanna's many Catholic and Protestant friendships in Rochester might hinder rather than help him should he subsequently become second bishop of Rochester. As the sequel was to prove, McQuaid was convinced that Hanna was of episcopal stature—but he should rule some see other than Rochester.[8]

Father Thomas F. Hickey was therefore the man of election. He could certainly be counted on to carry out the McQuaid policy.

On February 29, 1904, the Bishop wrote to Rome requesting that the Holy Father grant him an auxiliary bishop in the person of Father Hickey, whom he warmly commended. Replying to this request, the Roman officials informed McQuaid that the current practice of the Vatican was not to grant mere auxiliary bishops, but coadjutor bishops, with the right to succeed to the bishopric when the bishop whom they assisted resigned or died.[9] This complicated matters, for now the diocesan clergy (the consultors and the "irremovable" rectors) would be obliged to compose a ticket of three nominees, to be sent to Rome along with a similar list drawn up by the bishops of the New York Province. McQuaid presided at the balloting of his clergy-electors on

October 18, 1904. He clearly intimated that he did not want Dr. Hanna's name to appear on the list, but otherwise he left them to choose their own ticket. Eight names received votes. Those who fared the least well were Fathers James J. Bloomer (Elmira), Simon FitzSimons (Lima), Francis Naughten (Hornell), and Michael J. Nolan (St. Andrew's Seminary). The three who led, and whose names were submitted, were all Rochesterians. Listed in their preferential order, they were: Father Thomas E. Hickey, the vicar general; Father Augustine M. O'Neill, pastor of Immaculate Conception parish; and Father James J. Hartley, Pro-rector of St. Bernard's Seminary.[10] The New York provincial bishops also placed Father Hickey first on their trio of names, November 10, 1904. The names of the candidates were then sent to Rome. Hickey was appointed to the titular see of Berenice on January 18, 1905, and assigned to Bishop McQuaid as coadjutor with right of succession.[11]

On May 24, 1905, the Coadjutor Bishop-elect was consecrated in St. Patrick's Cathedral, Rochester—the first consecration rite performed in St. Patrick's parish or within the Diocese of Rochester since that of Bishop Bernard O'Reilly in 1850. The consecrating prelate was Archbishop John M. Farley, of New York; the assistant consecrators were Bishop McQuaid and Bishop Patrick A. Ludden of Syracuse. To add to the solemnity, Archbishop Diomede Falconio, the apostolic delegate was on hand.[12] After receiving consecration, the new Bishop, whom McQuaid continued in his office of vicar general, took up residence on Lakeview Park, on call for whatever service the eighty-two-year-old Bishop of Rochester might ask of him.

We shall see a great deal more of Bishop Hickey in future chapters. Now we must return to our account of the activities of Bernard McQuaid after the diamond anniversary of his birth.

McQuaid continued to be interested in charitable institutions. He supported two drives which St. Mary's Hospital was obliged to make in the 1890's: that which followed the fire of February 15, 1891, and that launched in 1899, to pay off the hospital debt.[13] It was also with his blessing that the Sisters of St. Joseph opened St. Joseph's Hospital, Elmira, in 1908. But Bernard McQuaid's most notable charitable effort of his last years was the foundation of St. Ann's Home for the Aged, in Rochester.

Even as early as 1876, Mother Hieronymo's Home of Industry had begun to welcome a certain number of elderly women as permanent guests. After Mother Hieronymo's death in 1898, those in charge of the Home of Industry concluded it had outlived its original purpose. They therefore decided to use the building exclusively as a home for aged Catholic women.[14] Some refurnishing was done with this in mind, but the arrangements remained rather unsatisfactory.

Now, in late 1903 and early 1904, Bernard McQuaid suddenly realized that he himself was getting old. A long bout with pneumonia had necessitated a prolonged period of convalescence in Savannah, Georgia. As he lay abed, prostrated by this sickness and unable, for once, to help himself, the Bishop began to think of the sad lot of the aged who had nobody to take care of them. He therefore decided that he would "build a home for the aged that would be worthy of my declining days."[15]

On his recovery, the Bishop began to lay plans. "St. Ann's Home for the Aged" would be built on Lake Avenue near St. Bernard's Seminary. The initial unit, in addition to a chapel, would have accommodations for 150 women and 30 men. (Neither he nor his successor quite got around to constructing another unit which he had originally intended to add: "a small house for old married couples".) How was it to be financed? By grand fairs, such as had financed the local orphanages for many a year, McQuaid once more interceded with the Poor Souls in Purgatory to assist the drive. The Poor Souls did not ignore his plea, for the fairs netted $55,000.00. Economically built for a little less than twice that sum, and entrusted to the Sisters of St. Joseph, St. Ann's Home was formally dedicated on January 6, 1906. That fall the same Order reopened the original Home of Industry as St. Agnes Institute, a school of art and music, the forerunner of St. Agnes High School.[16]

But education still remained the primary enthusiasm of the aging prelate. As time passed, more parishes that had had no schools acquired them, and several old parishes enlarged their earlier schoolhouses or built new ones. The opening of St. Agnes Institute advanced the diocesan secondary school program another step. And there were useful developments in the direction of adult education: the parish reading circles and the Catholic Summer School on Lake Champlain.

The Reading Circle Movement was national in scope. Inspired and supported particularly by the Paulist Fathers of New York, it was launched in earnest in 1888. Rochester early responded to the call. On March 10, 1889, the Rochester Catholic Reading Circle was founded in the Cathedral parish. The founder was Miss Emily Gaffney (1856-1903), daughter of the well-to-do Rochester clothing merchant, Owen Gaffney, and an apostolic woman who later established and for a long time edited the monthly *Cathedral Calendar*.[17] Subsequently, other circles were inaugurated in Rochester: the Nazareth Academy Reading

Circle; the Cardinal Newman Reading Circle (St. Bridget's); the Columbian Literary Circle (Immaculate Conception Church); and the Catholic Literary Circle. Several other units sprang up outside the see city, for instance at Dansville (St. Patrick's), Clyde, Mount Morris, and Canandaigua.[18] The purpose of these ladies' organizations (men could be only honorary members) was programmed reading, lectures, discussion, and social activities. The circles therefore had a certain amount of intellectual "tone" to them, and this is probably why they did not spread into every parish. Where they did arise, it was usually where the pastor was a man of more than usual culture. Since they concentrated on English literature, they were not likely to be popular in the German or other foreign language parishes of the Diocese.

However restricted the Reading Circle movement may have been, it led to something broader and better: the foundation, in 1892, of the Catholic Summer School Movement. The Catholic Summer School opened in 1893 at Cliff Haven, on Lake Champlain, New York, and continued to function until after World War II. Essentially, it was a Catholic Chautauqua, patterned on that larger and more durable Protestant movement for popular culture which has long maintained its headquarters on Lake Chautauqua, in western New York State. Unlike the Catholic Reading Circles, the Catholic Summer School welcomed male as well as female memberships. Rochester's Emily Gaffney was one of its founders. Father James Kiernan of Rochester was also fervently involved. In 1897, he accepted the post of moderator of the newly formed Alumnae Auxiliary Association, a group organized to raise funds for the Summer School. He was also chosen president, that same year, of a new stock corporation formed to finance and build a "Rochester Cottage" for Rochesterians who attended the Cliff Haven sessions. The Cottage was put up in 1898 and saw many years of service.[19]

While the Reading Circles and the Summer School at Cliff Haven were not of his own inspiration, Bishop McQuaid gave them his support. He attended the meeting of the central board of the local reading circles at least once.[20] And he was scheduled to preach at Cliff Haven during the summer sessions of August, 1897.[21]

What may have impressed the Bishop especially in these enterprises was the backing given to them by Miss Katherine Eleanor Conway. Miss Conway was a native of Rochester, who, thanks to McQuaid's constant interest and encouragement, became a rather prominent literary figure. This is perhaps the most convenient point at which to tell her story.

Katherine E. Conway, the daughter of James and Sarah Agatha Conway of the Cathedral parish, was born on September 6, 1852. Her father was a bridge and railroad contractor of some means. Katherine attended the Academy of the Sacred Heart in Rochester, the Manhattanville Academy of the Sacred Heart in New York City, and the Miss Nardins' Academy in Buffalo. Along the line, she discovered that she had a knack for writing. On her return to Rochester, in addition to teaching at the Academy of the Sacred Heart, she became the editor of a little monthly journal launched to publicize the needs of St. Mary's Hospital and the Catholic orphans. In her hands, this *West End Journal* became something of a diocesan paper and literary journal as well. From 1872 to 1878 (when it gave way to a true diocesan paper, the *Catholic Times*), Katie Conway *was* the *West End Journal:* editor, contributor, reporter, bookkeeper, and circulator of its 2,000 monthly copies.[22]

When the *Journal* suspended publication, Miss Conway was for five years a member of the staff of the *Catholic Union,* Buffalo diocesan newspaper (1878-1883). In 1883 she submitted a poem called "Remember" to the *Pilot,* well-known Boston Catholic organ, edited in those days by the prominent Irish-American writer, John Boyle O'Reilly (1844-1890). On the strength of this poem, O'Reilly offered Katie a position on his staff. Encouraged by Bishop McQuaid, as she had been in her previous literary ventures, Miss Conway accepted, moved to Boston, and remained with the *Pilot* until 1908. From 1905 to 1908 she held the post of managing editor. Thus she became closely associated with the interesting Catholic literary group that centered in Boston in the late nineteenth and early twentieth centuries: John Boyle O'Reilly, Dr. Robert Dwyer Joyce, George Parsons Lathrop, James Jeffrey Roche, Susan Emery, Mary Elizabeth Blake, Louise Imogen Guiney, etc. Interested also in social and educational welfare, Katherine served on the Massachusetts Prison Commission and on the board of trustees of the Boston Public Library. Her last editorial position was on *The Republic,* a Boston periodical published between 1908 and 1926. But her range of activity expanded as time passed. In addition to her work with the Reading Circles and the Catholic Summer School, she was from 1911 to 1915 adjunct professor of literature at St. Mary's College, Notre Dame, Indiana. Two of her Indiana pupils later achieved note in the literary field: Sister M. Eleanore (Brosnahan), C.S.C., and Sister M. Madeleva (Wolff), C.S.C. Katie also authored sixteen books: two novels (*The Way of the World and Other Ways,* Boston, 1900; and

Lalor's Maples, Boston, 1901); two collections of poems; and twelve volumes of essays.

The honors that Katherine Conway received bore witness to the esteem in which she was held. In 1907, the University of Notre Dame awarded her its annual Laetare Medal; and in 1912, Pope St. Pius X bestowed on her the decoration "Pro Ecclesia et Pontifice". She was, in fact, an excellent editor. Said O'Reilly, "She is poet and logician: she has the heart of a woman and the brain of a man". Today her poetry and other writings seem dated, characterized by an old-fashioned idealism. But that was just the point: her idealism was not put on, she lived by it. Her fortitude during the last long illness (she died at Roxbury, Mass., on January 2, 1927) was only one more proof of her solid Christianity. She did not belie the hopes which Bishop McQuaid had in her. As long as he lived she kept up with him a loyal and daughterly correspondence, and the recollections which she published of him after his death revealed much of the gentler side of the first bishop of Rochester.[23]

But to get back to the Bishop's own educational efforts. Bernard McQuaid did not forget his seminaries during his last years. In fact, his solicitude for them pretty well proved that of all his institutions, these were the closest to his heart.

St. Andrew's Seminary had been enlarged in 1880. (Monsignor De Regge, who continued to be its rector until 1904, personally contributed $1,500.00 of the cost of $2,000.00 which the 1880 wing entailed.) Another small wing had to be added in 1889. Still the school grew, so that by 1903 it had sent forth over one hundred alumni and was already too small for its enrollment of sixty-five boys. In 1903, the decision was reached to build a completely new schoolhouse adjacent to the Cathedral: a fireproof building 33' by 104', with five classrooms, a study hall and a gymnasium, all designed to accommodate one hundred day-students. Proposed as a monument to the ailing Monsignor De Regge, the new seminary building attracted a generous response. The Bishop himself gave $1,000.00; and the alumni of St. Andrew's agreed to underwrite the remainder of the estimated cost of $10,000.00.

On September 9, 1904, the Apostolic Delegate, the Most Reverend Diomede Falconio, dedicated the new structure. It was only regrettable that Monsignor De Regge was unable to see that day. He had died in Antwerp, Belgium, on June 13, 1904.

With the opening of September sessions, St. Andrew's added another year to its curriculum. Now it had, in addition to the four years of high school, a first year of college.[24]

Since 1893, St. Bernard's Seminary had been, to all intents and purposes, the Bishop's home, although he still maintained his suite of rooms at the Cathedral rectory. He furthermore continued to be the real rector of St. Bernard's. In addition to the frequent conferences which he gave to the students, he took charge of the classes in reading and preaching. In the fall he gave the annual student retreat; and by his attendance at spiritual exercises he set a splendid example to the young seminarians. While he did not "fraternize" with them, Bishop McQuaid did make a point of attending the students' matched baseball games, for he found that he could sometimes learn more about the character of the individual student on the ball field than in the classroom.

Since the student body at St. Bernard's had begun as early as 1894 to include men from outside the Rochester Diocese, physical expansion of the Seminary plant was soon necessary. A new wing, the "Hall of Philosophy and Science" was constructed south of the main building at the turn of the century and dedicated on October 3, 1900. By that time there were over one hundred students registered, and the student body continued to increase. Therefore, in 1905 McQuaid laid plans for a five-story "Hall of Theology" to be constructed north of the main building. Concomitant with this, the chapel-refectory building was to be extended. Under the Bishop's diligent personal supervision, the two structures were completed, as economically as ever—stone from his own quarry in the town of Greece; bricks made on the premises. The new building was ready for use when classes were resumed in the fall of 1908. That year 188 students matriculated, representing 36 dioceses.

It was not mere ambition that prompted Bishop McQuaid to enlarge his seminary; it was his apostolic desire to supply priests, well-trained priests, wherever they might be needed. That he was still a missionary at heart became evident when the Philippine Islands, acquired by the United States as a result of the Spanish-American War, suddenly became the missionary responsibility of the American Catholic hierarchy. Were it not for his advanced age, he then declared, he would willingly volunteer for this new mission in the Far East. But if he could not actually undertake such missions, he could at least contribute to the cause. Hence he made available over a dozen free places at St. Bernard's Seminary for seminarians from our southern States, from Puerto Rico, and from the Philippines.[25]

Quality in education still took precedence in his eyes, and this was especially evident in McQuaid's efforts to improve the scholastic standards at St. Bernard's. While he was in Rome in late 1900, he requested that the Holy See give to his seminary the privilege of granting academic degrees in philosophy and theology. Pope Leo XIII consented, and in the papal brief *Romani Pontifices,* expedited March 21, 1900, bestowed the right *in perpetuum* to confer the requested degrees. The Sacred Congregation de Propaganda Fide followed up the papal document with a special implementary decree on April 23, 1901. When the Bishop of Rochester published this decree, he issued a general circular to the American hierarchy in which he stated that it was his intention to exact the maximum rather than the minimum requirements for earning the new degrees. He was as good as his word, and he called in theological experts from outside the Diocese to serve as degrees examiners.[26]

So far, so good. Pleased with the effectiveness of the degrees program in philosophy and theology, the Bishop, in February, 1908, took another step. He solicited from the Holy See the additional privilege of conferring degrees in canon law. Father Andrew B. Meehan, professor of canon law at St. Bernard's, had just returned from Rome with a doctorate in that subject; he would be an able mentor for those who might study for canonical degrees at the Rochester seminary. This time, however, the Sacred Congregation de Propaganda Fide turned down McQuaid's petition, principally because it was unwilling, as the explanation stated, to "place a seminary on the same level as a university".[27]

Was Bernard McQuaid trying to develop St. Bernard's Seminary into a rival of the Catholic University at Washington which he had so strongly opposed? It seems that he was. At least he was attempting to set up the sort of *seminarium principale* or ecclesiastical *"universitas"* which he still maintained the Third Council of Baltimore had envisaged, rather than the full-fledged university that had been founded at Washington.[28] To his Rochester associates he spoke more than once of eventually seeing the houses of religious orders rise in the broad meadows across from the Seminary, to accommodate the student priests who would enroll for advanced degrees at St. Bernard's. Perhaps he was speaking seriously; perhaps tongue-in-cheek. But at other times he had dreamed the seemingly impossible and his dreams had come true. Rome's disappointing refusal to approve a canon law faculty had dissipated this particular revery. But by the time the answer reached Rochester, the ailing Bishop was no longer in a position to really care.

Bernard McQuaid gave still another proof in these latter years that he had lost little of his educational daring. This was his unfulfilled Cornell University plan.

What prompted McQuaid's Cornell plan was the increasing number of Catholic young people who were entering Protestant or secular colleges and universities. A similar problem had arisen earlier in England, and Cardinal Manning had taken a firm stand against the attendance of Catholics at Oxford and Cambridge. Bishop McQuaid followed the Manning line in his own diocese. In 1890, he denied permission to Bishop John Keane of the Catholic University of America to lecture at Cornell University, in the Diocese of Rochester, on the basis that his appearance would seem to confer a semi-official approval on Catholic matriculation there.[29] As time passed, however, McQuaid saw a little more clearly that it was idle to oppose the matriculation of Catholic young men at non-Catholic universities and colleges, especially those institutions that had specialized departments and professional schools with which Catholic universities could not compete. But he did not yield in the matter of Catholic young women. By the turn of the century, more Catholic girls were beginning to be interested in carrying their education beyond high school. Bishop McQuaid had the strong impression that this trend was a passing fad. He therefore made it known in the fall of 1903 that Catholic women of the Diocese of Rochester who frequented non-Catholic colleges and universities would be denied sacramental absolution within his diocese so long as they remained at those schools.

A rumor that the Catholic girls who attended Cornell University had made a joint protest against this ruling soon came to the attention of the well known New York secular periodical, *The Outlook*. The editor of *Outlook* asked Bishop McQuaid for a clarification, and the Bishop willingly complied with a statement, dated November 24, 1903. The reasons for his decision, he said, were: 1) that the teaching of philosophy, psychology, and history in such institutions was perilous to the faith of students; 2) that obligatory attendance at chapel services ran counter to Catholic principles; and 3) that coeducation was fraught with moral dangers. Now, he reasoned, a woman who willingly remained in so perilous an environment showed that she lacked the repentance necessary for absolution. Catholic young women, he concluded, should therefore attend Catholic colleges for women, of which there were several in the United States. *Outlook,* commenting on the Bishop's letter, judged it unusually strict.[30]

At least in the last of these points, McQuaid gave an erroneous impression. Catholic colleges for men were fairly numerous; Catholic colleges for women, though increasing, were very few. There was no Catholic women's college in New York State before the opening, in 1904, of the College of New Rochelle—over two hundred miles away from Rochester. Of the five others established in the Middle Atlantic

States by 1903, the College of St. Elizabeth at Convent, New Jersey (1899), and Trinity College in Washington (1897) seem to have been the best qualified; but both were still in the formative state. A Catholic girl from the Diocese of Rochester had therefore to travel quite far from home if she decided to attend a Catholic college.

Not that Bishop McQuaid failed to look into this matter. It was rather natural that St. Elizabeth's should occur to him as a place to recommend to the young women to whom he had interdicted all but Catholic colleges. This college was conducted by the New Jersey Sisters of Charity whose community McQuaid practically founded. In the spring of 1903, he asked the Sisters in charge about the standards of St. Elizabeth's, and whether its degrees were recognized by the New York State Board of Regents.[31] Satisfied by the answers he received, he began to direct Catholic girls to the New Jersey college at Convent Station.

Meanwhile McQuaid held the line in his denial of absolution. In fact he extended the denial, in 1904, to parents resident in his diocese who allowed their daughters to frequent any non-Catholic colleges. Three illustrations will show how this practice worked out.

At Cornell University, the situation was rather anomalous, since the Bishop had for some time been permitting his own nuns to enroll there, at least in the summer sessions. Catholic girls from outside the Rochester Diocese were not, of course, affected by the ban of 1903, nor were their parents touched by the extension of the ban in the following year. But Catholic girls from the Diocese of Rochester *were* penalized. There were only a few of these; and if they were aware of their canonical right to go to confession outside the Diocese, they apparently did not make use of it. At the same time, it seems that there was no denial of absolution to the Catholic diocesan girls who attended Elmira College for women, which was a strongly Protestant institution.[32]

One of the leading figures in the L.C.B.A., of which Bishop McQuaid was Supreme Spiritual Adviser, was Mrs. John A. (Cora) McParlin. The McParlins wanted their daughter Leah to go to college, but John McParlin, a railroad dispatcher, could not afford to send her out of the State to a Catholic institution. The University of Rochester was only a step away from their home, so Leah registered there as a day student in 1902. When the Bishop's veto became known the following summer, Leah and, subsequently, her mother were penalized by it. Oddly enough, the father, John McParlin, seems to have escaped involvement. The Bishop also warned Mrs. McParlin that if she sought national office in the L.C.B.A., he would be obliged to oppose her candidacy. The situation became quite painful, but Mrs. McParlin was fortified by the opinion of her pastor, Father Dennis J. Curran, that the Bishop had in this instance exceeded his authority.[33]

More personally painful for Bishop McQuaid was the case of the Daniel B. Murphys. Daniel Murphy, one of the Bishop's early protégés, had risen into a position of wealth and prominence in Rochester, and had distinguished himself as a Catholic lay leader in civic undertakings. In 1903, he and his wife decided to send their daughter Harriett to Smith College, in Northampton, Massachusetts. The Bishop opposed this move, but the Murphys thought that Trinity College, suggested as a Catholic alternative, did not measure up to the Northampton institution. Much as their rejection of his alternative grieved him, McQuaid firmly informed the parents that they would be denied sacramental absolution if they persisted in their decision. Harriett, apparently because her college was outside the Rochester Diocese, was given no specific information that she herself was subject to the exclusion. The parents, advised, it seems, by Father Edward J. Hanna, went thereafter into the Buffalo Diocese whenever they wished to receive the sacraments. The penalty was automatically rescinded after Harriett's graduation in 1907.[34]

If this disciplinary policy of the Bishop—admittedly dictated by earnest pastoral motives—was in some cases agonizing, inconsistent, and at times of questionable fairness, it did work out advantageously in other instances. For example, when Miss Margaret E. Flynn of Palmyra asked Bishop McQuaid in 1903 whether she might be permitted to take advantage of a partial scholarship granted by Syracuse University, McQuaid naturally said no. Where, then, could she go? asked the weeping girl of the aged prelate. The Bishop suggested St. Elizabeth's. She followed his advice a little ruefully; but she ultimately fell in love with the New Jersey college, applied its lessons well in a long career of public school teaching, and ever after sang hymns of gratitude to the Bishop for having guided thither her reluctant steps. At St. Elizabeth's she was also joined by several other girls from the Rochester Diocese who had been diverted by the Bishop's ruling from non-Catholic institutions and set on the road to Convent Station.[35]

But censures and St. Elizabeth's College did not really solve the problem of Catholics at non-Catholic colleges, and Bishop McQuaid knew it. Other Catholic leaders, equally aware that a positive solution was needed, were beginning to point out possible new directions. One thoughtful essay on the subject appeared in the February, 1906, issue of the *American Ecclesiastical Review*. In this article, which seems to have moved the Bishop of Rochester to take action, Father Francis B. Cassilly, S.J., suggested two conceivable remedies: either the appointment of permanent Catholic chaplains at secular colleges, to be provided, perhaps, with special chapels for the use of the students; or the establishment of Catholic colleges affiliated with a secular university.[36]

When the archbishops of the United States met in April, 1906, they read a communication from Bishop McQuaid that reminded them of the urgency of the secular college problem. Provision had to be made for these Catholic collegians, he said; and he, for one, favored the setting up of Catholic colleges connected with the secular universities, but staffed by Catholic professors who would be supported, if possible, by State university funds.[37]

McQuaid did not expect the archbishops to take direct action on his memo; he simply wished to present the issue and to indicate the course of action that he himself intended to take. On April 16th, he published the scheme he had in mind. A census of the student body at Cornell University had indicated that there were in attendance some 250 Catholic students (about 210 men and 40 women) from various dioceses. Bishop McQuaid had therefore decided to erect a building close to the Cornell campus, equipped with a chapel and lecture hall, and staffed by one or two priests especially trained to give lectures in fields closely related to Catholic faith and morals. This method, he believed, would make up for what was lacking in the college courses that the Catholic students frequented. It was a method, furthermore, which had a recent precedent in the arrangement worked out between St. Michael's Catholic College, Toronto, Canada, and the University of Toronto. The St. Michael's students were given academic credits by the University of Toronto; and McQuaid hoped that Cornell University might agree to the same procedure.

The Bishop received support for his proposal from the president of Cornell University, Jacob Gould Schurman, and from his predecessor in office, Andrew D. White. But the scheme subsequently met with frank opposition on the part of many elements of the University faculty. Although repulsed on the academic front, the Bishop still intended to carry out the ecclesiastical phases of his plan. In September, 1907, he made it known that he proposed in the near future to set up a chapel for the Cornell students, and then gradually to carry out the other points of the program.

Actually, McQuaid did not even get to build the chapel. In 1907 and 1908 he was obliged to concentrate his attention and his financial efforts on the erection of the north wing of St. Bernard's Seminary; and by the beginning of 1909 he was in his last illness, and his new projects came to a halt.

If Bishop McQuaid did not live to carry out his Cornell Plan, the plan itself was not forgotten. In 1914, five years after the Bishop's death, a Cornell Newman Club was organized. In 1946, this student group acquired its own "Newman Oratory" off-campus. The permanent Catholic chaplains, provided with many opportunities to contact his Catholic university students, are able today to achieve at least some of the counselling and instructional work which Bishop McQuaid envisioned. Of course, the Newman Oratory is far from being a college integrated academically with the University. Had McQuaid been successful in achieving this portion of his program—necessarily in a manner somewhat altered from his original conception—Catholic collegiate education in this country might have developed along totally different lines.[38]

2. INTO CALMER WATERS.

One day around 1905 Bishop McQuaid had a casual meeting with George Eastman, Rochester's enterprising photographic inventor and manufacturer. Eastman, already prosperous enough to afford a couple of the then newfangled automobiles, invited the Bishop to take a ride in one of his horseless carriages. "Maybe," he added, "I can get you one for yourself." McQuaid replied, firmly, but with a twinkle in his eye, "Only when an automobile can take me to my farm on Hemlock and bring me back the same day will I be persuaded. And then I'll buy my own!"[39]

This anecdote casts an interesting sidelight on the position which Bishop McQuaid enjoyed in his adopted community. He was held in high regard by Rochesterians Catholic and non-Catholic, as a man of principle, talent, and drive. With prominent non-Catholic citizens he was on cordial good terms, yet he never solicited their company, keeping to his own way. In the case of prominent Catholics of the locality, he occasionally accepted their dinner invitations; but in these instances, the privilege was the host's rather than the guest's. More than once he turned for aid or expert advice to leading Catholic figures on the Rochester scene, like the manufacturers James Cunningham (1815-1886), Patrick Cox (1842-1896), John Kelly (1837 ?-1898); to horticulturists Patrick Barry (1816-1890) and his son William C. Barry (1847-1916); to journalists Joseph O'Connor (1841-1908) and William Purcell (1830-1905); to merchants Owen Gaffney (1824-1893), Charles J. Burke (1832-1892), Charles FitzSimons (1829-1888), Alex-

ander B. Hone (1831-1909), Walter B. Duffy (1840-1911), and Daniel
B. Murphy (1848-1922). But these men knew well that his confidence
in them depended on their faithful adherence to Catholic ideals and
practice. They realized that they could expect from him no greater reward than thanks and deserved praise. For example, when the admirable Patrick Barry died, the Bishop himself, breaking with his customary policy against funeral eulogies, preached at the funeral. Barry, he
said, had merited this public commendation because he had constantly
set so good an example, bringing his faith and its principles into every
activity of his life.[40]

The Bishop naturally felt freer to socialize with the clergy. Not
with his own diocesans so much, but with clerics from outside his own
jurisdiction. He had stayed at home pretty much during the earlier years
of his episcopacy in order to attend to pressing business. Later, as he
became the butt of widespread criticism in the "liberal"—"conservative" frays, he remained away from national ecclesiastical gatherings
because unfair publicity had wounded him. After 1893, however, he
sallied forth more often, now courting extensive contacts with the bishops of other States, in order to acquaint them with the new seminary
which he had opened—and to which they *might* be interested in sending their theological students. This was informal advertising, but it
proved effective.[41]

Even when he had been more a "stay-at-home", McQuaid had
played the gracious and enthusiastic host to many a prominent churchman. If they came to Rochester proper, he could always find room for
them, despite the fact that he had no real "episcopal palace" of his
own. In the summer he entertained them at his farm overlooking Hemlock Lake. He had purchased this farm of more than five hundred acres
early in his Rochester career. A staff of farmers carried on the truck-
farming and stock-raising which eventually provided the Seminary with
fruit, vegetables, mutton and milk. Furthermore, the farm had eighty
acres of vineyard, which by 1905 were annually producing 20,000 gal-
lons of wines of various types for altar and table use.[42] Viticulturist
McQuaid was especially proud of the diploma he had been awarded
for his wines, which he called "O-Neh-Da" after the Indian name of
Hemlock Lake. Not all Americans, and certainly not all visitors from
France, shared the Bishop's admiration of his rather tart beverage. But
from the rubrical point of view, the Hemlock wines had the required
purity, hence priests from many States ordered their altar wine from
the Bishop of Rochester.

The "star boarder" at McQuaid's busy farm was the Bishop's dear friend and colleague, Archbishop John Williams of Boston (1822-1907). On the face of it, their close friendship was rather surprising, for the Bishop of Rochester was loquacious and the Archbishop of Boston was the most taciturn of men. Beyond the difference of speech, however, the two had much in common. McQuaid deeply admired Williams; and it was his hope, unfortunately unfulfilled, that he might survive Boston's first Archbishop long enough to write his biography. When the Bishop first invited John Williams to vacation among the New York Finger Lakes, Williams was especially moved to accept by the assurance that the Hemlock farm was remote from railroad and telegraph. For two days after his arrival, however, he ventured no comment on the farm, despite the anxiety of his host to learn whether he was pleased. Finally, on the third evening, as the two prelates sat on the porch of the simple cottage and gazed down the meadows and wooded slope to the darkling blue waters of Hemlock Lake, the Archbishop of Boston unlocked his jaws and spoke. "Well", he said, "this is what I call solid comfort". And he returned to that "solid comfort" summer after summer, until 1907.[43]

The guests whom the Bishop of Rochester entertained in Rochester or at the farm were a distinguished group. They included, besides a host of bishops, Cardinals James Gibbons of Baltimore and Michael Logue of Armagh; Apostolic Delegates Francesco Satolli, Sebastiano Martinelli, and Diomede Falconio; Archbishop Patrick W. Riordan of San Francisco (many times); the future Cardinals Raffaelle Merry Del Val and Aidan Gasquet, O.S.B., the Paulists Fathers Isaac Hecker and Walter Elliott; Father Daniel E. Hudson, C.S.C., editor of *Ave Maria;* Msgr. Denis J. O'Connell, Rector of the North American College in Rome; Abbé Félix Klein, of the Catholic Institute of Paris; and Professor James Farnham Edwards of the University of Notre Dame. (On one occasion McQuaid even welcomed hospitably a visiting "cleric" who passed himself off as a missionary bishop. But when McQuaid learned that the visitor's Mass at the Academy of the Sacred Heart had been notable for its odd rubrics, he sent word to St. Bernard's that it would be "more fitting" for His Lordship to offer the next Mass in the Cathedral rather than at the Seminary. Whereupon, "His Lordship", saying that he must then change his clothes, returned to the Seminary's guest room, climbed out the window bag and baggage, and strode across the meadows into Dewey Avenue and oblivion. It was eventually learned that the pseudo-prelate was a former Benedictine lay brother from Canada who had later served a bishop, and on severing his connections had appropriated that bishop's garb.[44])

Several of these guests who arrived in Rochester with preconceived notions of their host's character left with quite altered views.

Professor Edwards, for instance, though tarrying in Rochester in 1900, was at first loth to accept the suggestion of a Rochester priest that he call on Bishop McQuaid before he left the city. "I had an idea," he later confided to his diary, "that the Bp. was a stern forbidding character. When he came into the parlor I was surprised to find a small man instead of the large one I had pictured to myself, a cordial man beaming over with kindness and good nature." McQuaid gave the Professor the usual grand tour of the diocesan institutions. As a result, Edwards was completely converted. "Bishop McQuaid is a wonderful man, a man of ideas and a man of detail."[45]

An even more significant "conversion" was that of Abbé Félix Klein (1862-1953). Pure accident—if there is such a thing—landed him in Rochester during his visit to the United States in 1903. By another pure accident, he met Father James J. Hartley, Pro-rector of St. Bernard's Seminary, who insisted that he not leave the city without calling on its Bishop. This French professor who had so praised the "liberal" American bishops during the "Americanist" controversy, agreed only reluctantly. But Bishop McQuaid soon put Klein at his ease with the warmest of welcomes, trotted him about town on a tour of the Catholic sights, and sent him off next day with a hearty *au revoir*. In 1907, Klein did return, at the Bishop's special invitation, to speak to the seminarians at St. Bernard's Seminary. By now Professor Klein was ready to compare "this venerable, original man, in certain respects to Cardinal Lavigerie, to Bishop John Lancaster Spalding, to the strongest figures that I have chanced to meet during the course of my life."[46]

But the happiest "conversion" was that of Archbishop Ireland. One of the Archbishop's two nun-sisters—presumably it was Mother Seraphine Ireland, S.S.J.—seems to have inspired the reconciliation. When she came to Rochester to inspect the Catholic schools, Bishop McQuaid showed her great courtesy. On her return to Minnesota, she is said to have admonished her brother not to let the old Rochester prelate die without extending to him the olive branch. (The Archbishop was McQuaid's junior by fifteen years.) After Archbishop Corrigan passed away in 1902, a thaw did set in in the Ireland-McQuaid relations. In June of the following year, Ireland wrote the Bishop of Rochester to ask him if he would be able to make his O-Neh-Da altar wines available to the priests of the St. Paul Archdiocese. It was a gracious and effective move for the reopening of diplomatic negotiations. In the following year, the L.C.B.A. decided to have its annual summer convention at St. Paul. McQuaid, planning to attend the convention, dutifully wrote to the Archbishop for permission to address the Association on the occasion of his visit Archbishop Ireland sent back a hospitable and jolly reply; and during the Bishop's sojourn in the convention city he no doubt treated him with all proper kindness.[47]

In reciprocation, McQuaid now invited the Archbishop to come to Rochester and view its churchly achievements. Ireland accepted, and in the company of Bishop James McGolrick of Duluth, he spent December 2-4, 1905 in Rochester as Bishop McQuaid's guest.

It was, by all accounts, a happy visit. The crowning event was a dinner at St. Bernard's Seminary. That day Archbishop Ireland was the life of the party. After the dinner, he gave a speech. When engineers were digging the Suez Canal, he recalled, there was some fear that when the two segments of the canal finally came together, the Mediterranean and Red Seas which they connected might turn out to be of different level, and the meeting of the waters might be tumultuous. But the final breakthrough proved that the fear had been groundless: waters merged gently with waters, showing that neither sea was higher than the other. "I have discovered on this visit," Ireland concluded, drawing the moral, "that St. Paul and Rochester are on the same level."[48]

And the Archbishop was quite right. The two leaders had a great deal in common—more perhaps than they themselves realized.

Visitors to whom Bishop McQuaid gave his customary "grand tour" were impressed not only by what they saw, but even more by the zest of their guide. It was his constant policy to stress the positive side of what had been accomplished; and he was displeased with Father Hartley, the Pro-rector of St. Bernard's Seminary, because he was prone to apologize to guests for what the Seminary *lacked.*

McQuaid had something worth "selling", and he was a good salesman. But his salesmanship naturally amused those who knew him, and became the subject of many a gentle joke. One story had it that he died and went to heaven, where he straightway got into conversation with St. Peter. The Saint was describing the splendors of heaven. The Bishop listened respectfully, if a bit impatiently. Finally, when St. Peter stopped for breath, McQuaid said, "But Your Holiness should see St. Bernard's Seminary!"

And then there was the story of the Rochester nun who sang the wrong response at devotions. The celebrant chanted: "Let us pray for our bishop, Bernard . . ." Sister replied with vigor ". . . who made heaven and earth." Still, Bernard McQuaid was never mesmerized by his own sales talk. When he told the students of the American College in Rome what wonders his diocese had accomplished, he added, "Pray for the boastful Bishop of Rochester!"

It is regrettable that in those last conciliatory years of the aged prelate's life he had to bear a trial that pained him acutely because it reflected on the reputation of his beloved major seminary. This was the accusation of theological unorthodoxy brought against the Seminary's professor of dogmatic theology, the Reverend Doctor Hanna.

Bernard McQuaid was pleased to have his professors write for learned publications. Several of them contributed to the *Catholic Encyclopedia,* then in the course of publication. Among Edward J. Hanna's contributions was an article on "Absolution", which appeared in Volume I, issued in 1907. About the same time, Father Hanna also wrote a review article titled "Some Recent Books on Catholic Theology", for the *American Journal of Theology,* edited by the Protestant Divinity Faculty of the University of Chicago (January, 1906 number). And the *New York Review,* a new learned journal published by the faculty of St. Joseph's, the New York Catholic archdiocesan seminary, carried his three-part essay, "The Human Knowledge of Christ", in 1905-1906. In all three articles—"Absolution," the review, and the three-part study—there were occasional aspects that vaguely suggested certain avant-garde attitudes current among advanced European Catholic theologians. One Roman theologian raised questions about the *New York Review* articles when they first came out.[49] Nobody in the United States seems to have registered any public protest.

In April, 1907, Archbishop Patrick W. Riordan of San Francisco, in search of a progressive, able priest to be his coadjutor and successor, asked Bishop McQuaid if he thought Doctor Hanna would fill the bill. As we have already seen, the Bishop of Rochester objected only to Hanna's possible designation to the see of Rochester. He therefore strongly recommended him for the coadjutor bishopric of San Francisco. Other prelates whom Riordan consulted concurred with McQuaid, so in August, 1907, the Archbishop submitted the two required lists of three nominees to the Apostolic Delegate in Washington to be forwarded to Rome. Hanna's name stood in the first and favored place on both the *terna* of the San Francisco priests and that of the bishops of the ecclesiastical Province of San Francisco.

In the meantime, however, Pope St. Pius X had suddenly issued a document which was to have an important bearing on the case of the coadjutorship of San Francisco. This was the decree *Lamentabili* of July 3-4, 1907, which condemned, under the name of theological "modernism", a trend that the Pope pointed out was completely subversive of the body of Catholic doctrine. This "heresy of heresies" was a complicated and highly subjectivist view of the Catholic faith, evolutionist in its approach and agnostic in its conclusions. But its principal and most shocking opinion was that dogmas of faith can change in value with the passage of time, so that what is true today may be false or outmoded tomorrow. It is easy to see why the Pope should have denounced such a medley of errors and why he proceeded to take drastic measures to eradicate them. Unfortunately, the heresy was so subtle that in the course of its suppression some Catholic scholars who were quite orthodox fell under a heavy suspicion of heterodoxy.

Archbishop Riordan's list of nominees would normally have been acted on in October, especially since the list was accompanied by high recommendations of Hanna written by some outstanding American prelates. But October passed, and no communication reached the Archbishop from the Holy See. Only in early November did Riordan learn the reason for the delay. Somebody had sent to Rome copies of Hanna's *New York Review* article, and had seriously questioned its orthodoxy and the orthodoxy of the author. The Archbishop forthwith departed for Rome, to battle for his favored nominee. Before long the story of the accusation got into the secular press; and early in January, 1908, the newspapers reported the further news that the person who had delated Dr. Hanna was an unnamed fellow professor at St. Bernard's Seminary. Bishop McQuaid, scarcely believing such a report could be true, requested that each member of the faculty declare under oath that he himself had not been the delator. Only one refused to sign the declaration, thus identifying himself as the man in question. It was the professor of Sacred Scripture, the Reverend Doctor Andrew E. Breen (1863-1938). The Bishop thereupon requested Dr. Breen to resign his professorship.

Early in December, 1907, a second party, who has never been identified, called the attention of the Sacred Congregation of Propaganda Fide to Dr. Hanna's article on "Absolution" in the *Catholic Encyclopedia*. Commentaries on the theological correctness of both this article and the essay in the *New York Review* were submitted to the Vatican authorities, on request, by Father Alexius Lépicier, O.S.M., the same Roman professor who had earlier criticized Hanna's *New York Review* essay in his public lectures. Although Riordan's private informants assured him that the Cardinals in charge of the case were not convinced, but only cautious about Hanna's alleged unorthodoxy, the

Archbishop's expectation of a favorable decision was balked on January 13, 1908, when these same Cardinals voted to defer action.

Archbishop Riordan, Bishop McQuaid, and other friends of Hanna in America and abroad now renewed their efforts to convince the Sacred Congregation of the Rochester professor's orthodoxy. Hanna himself twice declared to the Holy See his acceptance of the decree *Lamentabili;* and when requested to restate his position on the human knowledge of Christ and on absolution, he did so in two new articles published in the *New York Review.* The Vatican authorities found these new statements unexceptionable. Riordan began to be more hopeful that the Sacred Congregation, in a fall meeting, would finally agree to give him the coadjutor of his choice.

Meanwhile, however, the third Hanna article ("Some Recent Books on Catholic Theology") had come to the attention of the Vatican officials. There is reason to believe that it was again Dr. Breen who submitted this review article which had appeared in the *American Journal of Theology.* Father Lépicier, requested once more to submit an opinion on its contents, handed in, on March 21, 1908, a report in which he cited seven points that he considered questionable. The review article may well have decided the whole issue, for in their meeting on September 7, 1908, the Cardinals, after a three-hour discussion, voted against the acceptance of Dr. Hanna. However, lest this decision be interpreted as a reflection upon either Hanna or the other candidates, the Cardinals simply rejected the whole list on a technicality, and requested that Archbishop Riordan submit three other names.

Bishop McQuaid assuredly liked publicity for the Seminary, but not *this* sort of publicity. At the outset of the episode, he was understandably concerned about how it would reflect on the reputation of his professor and his seminary. The only factor of Hanna's rejection that consoled him at all was the fact that the Vatican authorities had acted on the basis of negative rather than positive doubts. Furthermore, the theological climate in Rome at that moment had certainly influenced this final decision. Since the Holy See had just launched a total war against Modernism, it would have been something less than judicious to promptly approve as bishop a man whose name had become, at least for the nonce, theologically controversial.

In the United States, Dr. Breen seems to have been the only person who seriously believed that Hanna was prone to formal Modernism. Hanna's *Review* article had perhaps been incautious in summarizing various false opinions without refuting them. He had also used a few of the phrases that an incipient Modernism had made "stylish". But he had written all these essays several months before the heresy was officially exposed and denounced. Bishop McQuaid, in particular, remained convinced of Hanna's substantial orthodoxy, and convinced that in due time he would still become a bishop, and something more than a bishop. He even ventured to prophesy this to Mother Xavier Mehegan, his old colleague in the foundation of the New Jersey Sisters of Charity, when she came to see him in November, 1908, during his last illness. "My boy will go to San Francisco, Mother, and he will later be made an archbishop, so all is well. The gilded edge of every cross is resignation to the divine will." Furthermore, before his death the Bishop set aside one of his episcopal rings, instructing Bishop Hickey to give it to Dr. Hanna if and when he was promoted to the hierarchy.[50]

The prophecy came true in 1912-1915, as we shall see later on.

The founding bishop of Rochester enjoyed robust health during most of his episcopal years. Only one serious illness marred the early decades of his episcopate: a bout with typhus during his Roman sojourn in 1879, which had brought him to the threshold of death.[51] In 1903-1904, as we have seen, he contracted pneumonia, and had to go to Savannah, Georgia, to recuperate. The next winter, though in good health, he returned to Savannah as a precautionary measure.[52]

But Bernard McQuaid, apart from the organic ailments that come with old age, was still so hearty in 1907 that some madcap Italian immigrants threatened him with murder unless he gave them $5,000.00. In his address at that year's blessing of the graves, he revealed to the listeners this recent threat to his life; and he went on to assure them that even if he had that much money — which was not the case — he would rather be picked up in the street with a stiletto in his back "than pay one dollar that would reflect on the might and power of the law to protect me." But the Bishop made it clear that he was not lecturing just one national group: *all* immigrants to America, not the Italians alone, he said, must be taught to respect the law of the land.[53]

Despite his relatively good physical condition, the Bishop admitted to his closer friends that he felt a certain weariness of life. On October 22, 1907, he wrote to Sister M. Pauline Kelligar of New Jersey: "I am beginning to feel like an old gnarled oak, left solitary and alone in what was once a forest of trees, old and young."[54] What particularly depressed him that fall was the death of Archbishop Williams on August 30th. McQuaid had been invited to preach Williams' eulogy, but had declined. "I would have broken down at the first opening of my mouth," he explained to Father Daniel Hudson.[55] Even the farm at Hemlock lost its charm for him after that because of its association with the deceased Archbishop. As he confided to Katherine Conway, "I think I can never face the old house again . . ."[56]

They would soon be tolling Bernard McQuaid's own knell. In May, 1908, he experienced the beginnings of what was to be his ultimate illness. It was not an urgent ailment, still he was unable to shake it off.

What he feared most was the illness might interfere with the plans for the observance of his fortieth anniversary of episcopal consecration, on July 12, 1908, and—more important—the gala dedication of the new Hall of Theology at St. Bernard's on the feast of its patron, August 20, 1908. As it turned out, he was indeed too incapacitated to participate in the Mass of thanksgiving offered in the Cathedral on his anniversary. But the dedication he had no intention of missing. For this reason he had himself removed betimes from his suite in the Cathedral rectory to his suite at St. Bernard's.

If he was unable to participate actively in the rite of dedication, he at least had the satisfaction of watching it. As the Apostolic Delegate, Archbishop Diomede Falconio, accompanied by a large crowd of bishops, prelates, priests and educators, moved in procession to the new wing, McQuaid, in his invalid's chair, observed them gravely from the adjacent building. He did not attend the dinner which followed in the newly enlarged refectory; but at its conclusion, he was wheeled in so that he might make a short address to the assembled priests and guests. After alluding briefly to the significance of the occasion, he sounded a somber warning against the "commercialism", that is, the tendency to greed and financial speculation, which he had lately detected in some of the older clergy and against which he cautioned the younger. As he reached the climax, he spoke with all his strength, pounding the floor with his cane. Then he concluded more quietly, "What a glorious career is before you, young man of St. Bernard's. I would say more but my strength is failing." And with that he collapsed against the back of his chair in a dead faint.

It was a dramatic moment. All present looked on, breathless. Archbishop Quigley urged the administration of the last rites; but the Bishop's physician, Dr. Leo F. Simpson, who was at the side of his patient, assured Quigley that it was not necessary. Bishop McQuaid soon came to, but the edge of the gaiety had been dulled, and the visitors filed silently out.[57]

The main subject of McQuaid's address might at first seem strange and out of keeping with so happy an occasion. But it was really quite in character, the last utterance of a man who had always advocated a voluntary practical poverty for the Catholic secular priesthood. Bernard McQuaid, devoted to clerical poverty while a simple priest, had not given up his ideal upon becoming a bishop. Even as bishop of Rochester he did not possess a horse or carriage of his own; his comely silk top hat was always a bit worn; and his neat Prince Albert coat was always a bit shiny. When he died, his personal estate amounted to some $2,000.00—just enough to pay his funeral expenses and recompense his three executors.[58]

In his 1908 pastoral on the Seminary, dated August 24th, McQuaid announced that he had begun to erect an infirmary building and to provide more space for the seminary library. He was not to see the completion of these projects. Now he entered upon a slow decline that increased in pace only after November 18, 1908, on which date he was driven back to the Cathedral rectory in a hackney coach. Even so, the last months had their recompenses. There was time to bid formal farewell to Bishop Hickey and to his priests, especially the Cathedral staff and the professors at the two seminaries, and to speak to them parting words of encouragement. He was given reminders of peace achieved, like the telegram which Archbishop Ireland sent to Bishop Hickey on August 21, 1908: "Present to the old hero my most sincere sympathy. I pray the weakness be but temporary." And final efforts were made to mend other bridges. Bishop McQuaid requested that the list of his honorary pallbearers include Daniel B. Murphy, now no longer banned from the sacraments since his daughter had graduated from Smith College. Indeed, it seems that even Father Louis A. Lambert, prevailed upon by Father William Kessel, C.S.S.R., the rector of St. Joseph's Church, paid a conciliatory visit to his failing superior.[59]

Bernard McQuaid died a very edifying death on January 18, 1909. After funeral obsequies in St. Patrick's Cathedral on January 22nd, he was laid to rest in the original bishops' crypt of the chapel at Holy Sepulchre Cemetery.[60]

3. The Legacy of Bernard J. McQuaid.

While Bishop McQuaid was still alive, somebody commented that he was the only bishop in the United States who would still be ruling his diocese a quarter-century after his death.[61]

Like all really witty statements, this prophecy contained an element of truth. There was scarcely a phase of diocesan activity or a type of diocesan institution that McQuaid, in his foresight, had not provided. His successors therefore fell heirs to a sound establishment. For some time that establishment would require only maintenance; and even when the later bishops of Rochester decided that new institutions were necessary, they would as often as not erect them on foundations already laid by the pioneer bishop. This thoroughness with which Mc-Quaid constructed his diocese is the main reason why we have given so much space to the history of the man and his episcopate.

"It is difficult to gather his character as a man," said the Rochester *Union and Advertiser* of the dead prelate, "so closely did he invest himself with his dignity as bishop."[62] This was certainly the case with regard to his public image. However, those relatively few diocesans, and those others on the outside, with whom he could converse more freely, discerned in the uncompromising dignitary a man of strong faith and staunch piety, of genuine tenderness of heart wherever tenderness would not be taken for weakness, and of sterling natural patriotism. Of his patriotism we have already spoken. Also of his tenderness; and the children in the orphanages bore added witness to this trait. His faith was childlike in its simplicity and strength. The seminarians at St. Bernard's were especially able to testify to his piety—that undemonstrative but solid piety that he evidenced to them and sought to communicate to them. And beyond these, in a category of its own, was his courtliness of bearing, something not innate but acquired, and a tribute both to his own sense of the appropriate and to the training that his early mentors had given to the frail young orphan from Paulus Hook.

Bernard McQuaid's effectiveness as a bishop sprang primarily from his gift of leadership. His was the positive type of mind that reaches conclusions with quick and imaginative logic, acts upon them promptly, and thus generates in others confidence and willing cooperation. "The Bishop of Rochester had no opinions," wrote Bishop Francis C. Kelley. "What he had were convictions, and his convictions were dogmas only a little below those of the Faith." Or as Father Augustine O'Neill observed, "He never asked, 'Is it popular?'; but 'Is it right?'" There was a certain jauntiness in the self-confidence that this trait engendered. It prepared McQuaid not only to storm the fortresses of the seemingly impossible, but, on the other hand, to call off these same sieges with cheerful resignation, in the few cases in which they had patently failed. His convictions also made him a firm but courteous controversialist. Conviction was likewise a basic constituent of his skill as a preacher and lecturer; for he was an able speaker, much in demand, and his eulogies of Bishops Richard Gilmour and Edgar Wadhams were considered classics.[63] Having received a vocation as a spokesman, McQuaid was always ready to speak, in script or *viva voce*. His sermons, lectures, conferences, articles, and abundant correspondence thus communicated his conclusions and his ideals to a wide audience across the country and even beyond its borders.

The positive man must be ready to make mistakes—and enemies. Once a woman said to Bishop McQuaid, in praise of his vicar general, "Father Kiernan has no enemies." The Bishop replied, "If he has no enemies, then he's not doing his job." But he took incidental blunders with equal nonchalance. "It is a long while," he wrote to a friend in 1908, "since I made a rule for myself not to worry unless I had done something wrong and of which I was justly ashamed."[64]

Whether in some instances he aroused avoidable enmities, and what in particular were his mistakes will remain controverted questions. It seems to us that he might have yielded more graciously to the accomplished fact of the Catholic University of America; that his penalties imposed on parents who refused to send their children to Catholic schools were sometimes too stringently applied; and that his penalties for attending non-Catholic colleges were in some cases inequitable. Where Bernard McQuaid was perhaps oftenest at fault was in his at times too rigid regard for the letter of the law. In general, however, his logical mind led him to decisions that were sound, prudent, and defensible.

What was especially remarkable was that those whom Bishop McQuaid penalized on debatably sufficient grounds seem not to have questioned his motives. For he was a transparently honest man. One knew where he stood, and one respected his stand as reasoned and sincere, even when one strongly dissented from it.

Writers are naturally fascinated by the personality of strong men, and delight in analyzing and summarizing the characteristics that make them unique. One of the most acute analyses of Bernard McQuaid appeared in an editorial by his friend, Father Daniel E. Hudson, C.S.C., in the *Ave Maria*.

He was more like St. Jerome than St. Augustine; and yet with all his apparent inflexibility, he was easily influenced by persons in whom he reposed full confidence. Had he not been a man of resolute character, doubtless his admirers would have been far more numerous and his opponents less aggressive. He was too honest, and held the world's opinion in too light esteem, either to conceal his foibles or to care what might be said of him. The valuation that he set upon himself and upon all that he did or attempted was estimated in the light of eternity. Such men are often misjudged, their very virtues sometimes appearing as defects. The satisfaction of right intention or honest endeavor is so much to great souls that unpopularity and opposition count for nothing.[65]

That Bernard McQuaid did indeed view his decisions in the light of eternity was evident from his frequent insistence on this point. "God has a right to the best and we are bound to give it to him." So he summarized it in one instance. And when he did give his best and succeeded, he knew whom to thank. "God has been very good to us . . . He will always help those who strive to do the best for his cause."[66]

His chief claim to fame, as we have already emphasized, lay in his achievements as an educator. With foresight and, in view of the relative poverty of his diocese, with remarkable success, he created an excellent elementary school system out of which institutions of secondary and higher instruction could easily grow. To staff these schools he trained a large number of Sisters in pedagogy and Christian educational philosophy. He organized two seminaries that were models of their kind. And in the wider field, he agitated for the nationwide spread of parochial schools; for a Catholic educational program second to none in quality; for American seminaries adapted to the characteristic needs of the American Church. Bishop John Lancaster Spalding, the leading educational philosopher among Bishop McQuaid's colleagues, did not hesitate to say that McQuaid had done more than anybody else in America for the cause of Catholic education.[67] Nor did his efforts benefit Catholics alone. Since they were directed to the Americanization of a large immigrant population, they benefited the community and the very nation. Quite likely Pope St. Pius X had this broader effect in mind when he sent a personal letter to congratulate McQuaid on his fortieth episcopal anniversary. "The education of the young," wrote the Pope, "and especially of those intended for the priesthood . . . is a thing so great that there is nothing of more importance to the church and nothing of more importance to the state."[68]

If in certain respects, particularly in the controversies over policy in which he and his fellow bishops were engaged, McQuaid sometimes showed less vision and less elasticity, the mistakes he made were well within the allowable margin of error. The Diocese of Rochester could meanwhile rejoice in having had Bernard McQuaid as its founding bishop. He was neither totally "conservative" nor totally "liberal". Like all sensible men, he was something of both. His progressivism was most notable in the field of education. In certain other questions he opposed change. But even when he took his strongest "anti-liberal" stance, he made a valuable contribution to the Church in the United States, by questioning and tempering trends that might otherwise have become exorbitant. His was the "loyal opposition" which the democratic spirit encourages.

The word "great" should be used with caution. But it does not seem excessive to say that for his zeal, his uncompromising devotion to duty as he conceived it, his "leonine courage," his magnificence of dream and deed, Bernard John McQuaid deserves to be ranked among the great bishops of the American Church.

CHAPTER NINE

BISHOP HICKEY
AND THE WAR YEARS

T HE SECOND Bishop of Rochester, Thomas Francis Hickey, took over the reins of his office just a few months before 1910. His first ten years in office thus coincided with the period in which immigration, the primary source of American Catholic increase, reached its final peak. During these same years, in a sort of reverse action, vast numbers of American men set sail from the United States to the European battlefields of World War I. National needs, whether in peace or in war, now imposed upon Americans, even more urgently than before, the obligation to concentrate on better organization, in order that they might serve more efficiently the manifold needs of mankind.

What was true of the nation in this regard was no less true of the Diocese of Rochester.

Catholic immigration continued to follow the same trends that had begun in the 1890's. The numbers who arrived from Ireland and Germany were much reduced. The Irish in the Diocese had become rather well acclimatized to American culture. The Germans remained particularistic a good while longer, their language serving as a special bond to the past. The existence of German national parishes naturally fostered a certain separatism, whether the parishes were rural, like those in Dansville, Perkinsville, and Wayland; or urban, like Holy Family, Rochester (which presided over "Dutchtown"); St. Boniface (at the center of "Swillburg"); and St. Michael's (in the heart of the old farming neighborhood called "Butterhole"). But even in these staunchly German parishes, the demands of a more Americanized second generation brought about a gradual reduction of German sermons and services. The process began towards the beginning of the Hickey regime and was already completed by 1925.

A modest immigration from Belgium and Holland still continued. Between 1891 and 1911, over 800 Belgian Flemings had settled in Rochester proper, and no less than 4,000 in the whole diocesan district.[1] By 1914, the colony of Hollanders in Rochester had reached 1,500. The Catholic Hollanders, like the Belgians, tended to affiliate with Our Lady of Victory, the Franco-Belgian church.

But the majority of the "new Americans" still represented the "later immigration," stemming from Eastern Europe and the Mediterranean.

A fair number of Poles arrived to augment the Polish population of the Rochester Diocese. Outside of Rochester, Polish centers arose in East Rochester, Auburn and Elmira, and later on in rural sections of Steuben and Tioga counties. The rural colonies were mostly peopled by Americanized Poles who had moved in from other parts of the country. Thus, there was a good deal of Polish migration north from the Pennsylvania coal-mining counties into the Rochester Diocese, as the Pennsylvania mining industry gradually declined.

Catholics of the Greek Ruthenian Rite continued to emigrate to the United States from the Russian and the Austro-Hungarian empires up to the outbreak of World War I. Groups of these settled at various times in Rochester, Auburn, Elmira Heights, Corning, and Bath. By 1910, the Ukrainian Ruthenians in Rochester itself had reached a total of 600. On July 4th of that year they opened their first little church, St. Josaphat's, on the Remington Street site now occupied by St. Nicholas Syrian Catholic Church. Bishop Hickey was guest of honor on that occasion—a symbol of the cordiality that generally existed between the city's Latin-rite and Greek-rite Catholic clergy. Hickey was not present as the bishop of the Ukrainians, however. The American Ruthenians had received a bishop of their own rite in 1907; and it was he, Bishop Soter Stephen Ortynsky (1866-1916), who actually officiated at the Remington Street dedication.[2] By the 1930's, the population of St. Josaphat parish was to rise to 5,000.

Syrians, Portuguese, and Italians represented the Mediterranean peoples who now found homes within the Diocese. The Syrians belonged, more often than not, to eastern rites of the Catholic Church, especially the Melkite and Maronite rites. They settled in various parts of the twelve counties. The majority found their way to Rochester, but the Rochester Syrians were still not numerous enough to think of building a church to serve their own rites until the mid-1920's. In the interim, they affiliated with the Latin rite parishes of their neighborhoods.

The Portuguese arrivals came mostly from the Madeira Islands. While some of them settled in Corning in the latter half of the last century, the largest Portuguese colony was in Rochester proper. By the outbreak of World War I, the Rochester Portuguese numbered from sixty to eighty families. Too few to ask for a national parish of their own, they attended St. Augustine's Church, within whose parish boundaries they had for the most part established themselves.

But the Italians still continued to constitute the largest percentage of the newcomers. Many of them, it is true, came to America with no intention of remaining permanently. Furthermore, hundreds of Italian men were recalled in 1914 at the outbreak of the War to serve in the Italian army. Nonetheless, the proportion of Italians who stayed on was so great that there was scarcely a city or town in the whole Diocese in which Italians did not soon outnumber the other foreign-born inhabitants and compose an impressive bloc of the local population.

As a result of immigration, migration, and natural growth, the population of the twelve counties mounted from 750,000 in 1910 to 815,000 in 1920. Monroe County, acquiring 70,000 new residents, once again enjoyed the greatest expansion of any of the diocesan counties. The growth of Rochester proper was, of course, the prime explanation: from 218,000 in 1910 to 295,000 in 1920. Except for Wayne County, whose inhabitants rose by 8,000 and Chemung County, which gained 11,000, the rest of the twelve counties experienced neither growth nor decline. Elmira now outnumbered Auburn by 9,000, and was entitled by its population of 45,000 to the rank of the second city in the Rochester Diocese.

Not all the Catholics who had moved into the diocesan district remained in the Catholic Church. A certain number of Italians—many of whom left the mother country poorly instructed—accepted not only the philanthropy but the doctrines of Protestant missionaries, as the existence of several small Protestant Italian parishes still bears witness. Far larger, no doubt, was the number of immigrant Catholics who simply became indifferent about their Catholic religious duties, sometimes because there were not enough priests who spoke their language, sometimes because they fell victim to the American mood of a practical secularism. At all events, the official estimates of diocesan population —121,000 in 1909 to 172,000 in 1920—are almost certainly too low.

It was the good fortune of the second bishop of Rochester to inherit a diocese already well established in its structures and its ideals. Nevertheless, his flock was so rapidly increasing, and its needs in war and peace were so rapidly mounting, that Bishop Hickey was to have little time for leisure.

1. Thomas Francis Hickey.

Thus far, we have referred to Bishop Hickey only incidentally. Now that he has become the head of the Rochester Diocese, it is time to speak more fully of his background and personality.

Thomas Francis Hickey was the first native Rochesterian to be elevated to the episcopacy of the Catholic Church. He was born in the small and humble family homestead at 494 Clinton Avenue, South, on

February 4, 1861, the second child of Jeremiah and Margaret Griffin Hickey. Margaret Griffin was a native of County Limerick, Ireland. Jeremiah hailed from nearby County Tipperary. But both had come to America as children—he when about twelve, she when a very small child. Hence one could almost consider them "second-generation" Irish-Americans.

It was a difficult delivery that brought Margaret Hickey's first son into the world. Apparently the child's death was feared, for he was given emergency baptism. But Margaret, a woman of deep faith, consigned her son into God's good hands that day; and God fully accepted the gift.

In 1866, the Hickeys sent Thomas to the Cathedral School. Laywomen instructed him in the lower grades; the Christian Brothers in the upper grades. He was no doubt disappointed when the Brothers withdrew from the school in 1872. At all events, his own parish, St. Mary's, opened its own parish school in 1873. So it was at St. Mary's that he finished the last year of his elementary course.

When a boy, young Tom Hickey often used to play at "saying Mass," with a playmate named "Lew" as his "server." Many a Catholic boy has played the game of priest but ended up as a butcher, baker or candlestick maker. In Tom's case, the game proved prophetic. He had enrolled as an altar boy while in parochial school, and now that he had completed the eighth grade, he decided to study for the priesthood. In 1874, he entered the then quite new St. Andrew's diocesan preparatory seminary. When he graduated with honors in 1879, Bishop McQuaid sent him to St. Joseph's Provincial Seminary, at Troy, New York. Here he was a schoolmate of the saintly Thomas Francis Cusack, (1862-1918), future bishop of Albany, and of Joseph Henry Conroy, (1858-1939), subsequently bishop of Ogdensburg. Thomas Hickey and Joseph Conroy remained especially close friends in later life. At Troy Hickey showed himself as diligent a student as he had been before. In due time, therefore, he was advanced through the minor orders of the clerical state and on December 23, 1882, received his first major order, the subdiaconate.

Thus far all had gone well; but some months before Thomas Hickey was due to receive the sacrament of the priesthood, his father suffered a financial reverse which posed the question whether Tom would ever realize that dream.

Jeremiah Hickey was a competent custom tailor, and also carried a line of ready-to-wear clothing. Unfortunately, he was less gifted in finances than in handicraft. He was the sort of haberdasher, we are told, who would remain firm about the price of a suit, but when he had won the haggle, would throw in a pair of free suspenders. What he had done for his family thus far, he had done at no small sacrifice. Tom himself, while studying at St. Andrew's, often had to spend long hours after school delivering packages from his father's shop. But now, around 1883, Jerry Hickey's little business definitely failed, and the shop was padlocked. When word of this reached Thomas at Troy, he came home. He told his parents that if need be he was quite ready to give up his studies for the priesthood, and go to work to provide for the family.

Hard pressed as they were, the family could not bear the thought of Tom's not going on to the priesthood. Particularly insistent that he return to Troy was his young brother, Jeremiah, Junior. Jeremiah G. Hickey (1866-1960) was later to become co-founder of the clothing manufacturing firm of Hickey-Freeman. In 1883, he was only seventeen; but, having been obliged to discontinue grammar school in order to earn his own keep, he had already begun to feel at home in the business world. He told his brother that he was quite confident that a solution would be found for the family financial problems. So Tom went back to the seminary.

On March 25, 1884, the day of the priesthood finally dawned. Bishop McQuaid ordained Thomas F. Hickey in the Rochester Cathedral. It was a triumphant occasion for the whole Hickey family: but not least of all for young Jeremiah, who to his dying day would rejoice that he had been able by his own labors to provide the Church with a worthy priest.[3]

On April 4th, less than two weeks after Father Hickey had celebrated his first solemn Mass, the Bishop assigned him to the position of assistant pastor of St. Francis de Sales Church in Geneva. It was not the easiest possible appointment. Living conditions at the rectory were poor, and the pastor, Dean James T. McManus, while a devoted priest, was apparently difficult. One year after his appointment to St. Francis, Father Hickey wrote a discreet letter to Bishop McQuaid suggesting that, all things being equal, he *might* do a more effective job in some other parish.[4] The Bishop, it seems, did not even reply. Hickey, making the best of the matter, plunged all the more ardently into his parochial duties. He eventually got to know his people well, and was very active among them. In later years he loved to return to this parish which he had at first found so frustrating. He could still call the old parishioners by their first names; and it was clear that they held his own name in benediction.[5]

In those days, there was no long internship as an assistant before a diocesan priest was named a pastor. Father Hickey was given his first pastorate, St. Patrick's Church in Moravia, on August 26, 1888, barely four years after ordination. With this Cayuga County rural parish went two rural missions in adjacent Tompkins County: St. Anthony in Groton, and St. Patrick's in McLean. The care of the three churches involved a Sunday journey of twenty miles, by buggy in fair weather and cutter in snowy. At Christmas, the pastor, reversing the usual order, celebrated midnight Mass at McLean, early morning Mass at Groton, and late morning Mass at Moravia.

When he learned of his appointment to Moravia, Hickey informed his schoolmate, Father Joseph Conroy of Ogdensburg, that Bishop McQuaid had sent him to the parish farthest removed from the see-city. "Congratulations!" replied the jovial north country priest. But McQuaid had not by any means forgotten the pastor of Moravia. On March 20, 1895, he reassigned him, now to a post in Rochester. Hickey was to reside at the Cathedral Rectory and serve as chaplain of the New York State Industrial School.

The young priest had enjoyed parochial life; now he threw himself with zest into this new and challenging apostolate. As a State employee he was obliged to travel a good deal to investigate parolees. If his extensive train-riding at times became tedious, at least it gave him an opportunity to prepare his sermons. He had already begun to win a reputation as a preacher. Gradually more and more Catholics who lived in the vicinity of the Industrial School—which was then located on the grounds of Rochester's Exposition Park—began to attend the Sunday Masses he celebrated in the hall of the School, largely to hear him preach. Hickey also delivered sermons reguarly at the Cathedral, and when his turn came up, both the body of the church and its galleries were often filled. While his sermons were never strongly imaginative, they were solid, well-composed, well-delivered, and not unduly long.[6]

Father Hickey was now subjected to the close scrutiny of his bishop, and Bishop McQuaid was well impressed by what he saw. On January 31, 1898, when he promoted Father James P. Kiernan from the rectorship of the Cathedral to the pastorate of St. Mary's Church, he named Thomas Hickey to succeed him.

The thirty-six-year-old new rector applied himself with customary earnestness to his new job. Under him, the parish monthly, the *Cathedral Calendar,* became more varied and valuable. His own reputation as a preacher also grew ever wider.

Of all his duties, however, the care of the Cathedral School seems to have been closest to Father Hickey's heart. He was interested in its work not merely for religious but for educational reasons. Little Kathryn Kirk, of the seventh grade, testified as much in a little note that she contributed to the *Calendar* of April, 1905.

> Last week Very Rev. Father Hickey gave us a delightful treat by reading Hawthorne's description of the Concord River. He pictured the scene so vividly that we were much impressed, and imagined we were there, viewing the river. Compositions were written on this subject, and many of them were very good.

To serve as a bond of union among the alumni of the Cathedral School, Hickey established on December 11, 1898, the Cathedral School Association.[7] Each year thereafter until the late 1920's or early 1930's, the alumni gathered together at a festive banquet. At least in the earlier years of its existence, the Association engaged noted Catholics to speak at these annual meetings.

But the principal contribution that Father Hickey made while rector to Catholic education was the foundation of Cathedral High School. An outgrowth of the Cathedral School, the High School was launched with a two-year business course in 1902. In 1905 a regular four-year academic course was added, under the New York State Regents. By fall 1906 students from other than the Cathedral parish were being welcomed on a tuitional basis. Thus was Bishop McQuaid's dream of a Catholic secondary school finally realized.[8]

In 1900, the diocesan vicar general, Father Kiernan, died suddenly. Nobody was particularly surprised when the Bishop named Thomas Francis Hickey to succeed him. Father Hickey discharged his new duties so satisfactorily that Bishop McQuaid continued him permanently in that position.

When the pioneer bishop of Rochester decided in 1905 to ask the Holy See to create Father Hickey a bishop and appoint him auxiliary bishop of the Diocese, he certainly had had ample time to size up the man of his choice. The young Vicar General was without doubt a worthy, modest, and devout priest, studious in his habits, and seemly in bearing. He was an able speaker and a dutiful and apostolic cleric; a rather good businessman; and an educator devoted to the tradition of parochial schools that McQuaid had established. While he apparently had no wide reputation outside his native diocese, Hickey was at least notable enough to have been awarded the honorary degree of Doctor of Laws by the University of Notre Dame in June, 1903.[9]

There was, admittedly, one flaw in the temperament of Thomas Hickey which we must mention here because of its bearing on his later career. It was his tendency to scrupulosity of conscience. Although this infirmity became acute only after he assumed the government of the Diocese, it had long since been discernible to his priest-associates. Did Bishop McQuaid himself discern it? Quite possibly he did not, or at least he underestimated it, positive man that he was. Or perhaps he apprehended it only as a lack of aggressiveness—a trait that might not have displeased him, since he desired a successor who would be sure to follow established policies.

Nobody could have shown more loyalty to the aged Bishop of Rochester than his young coadjutor. Especially during McQuaid's last sickness, Bishop Hickey was attentive to his slightest wish. His solicitude sprang in part from a strong filial reverence, in part from a genuine love and admiration of the leonine pioneer.

If Bishop McQuaid went to his rest in the conviction that Bishop Hickey would abide by his policies to the last jot and title, he was mistaken. McQuaid had refused either to purchase or to accept an automobile. Hickey raised no fuss at all when in 1909 his parishioners presented him with a Selden touring car. [10] McQuaid had opposed the Knights of Columbus. While Hickey restricted clerical membership, he gave the Knights his general approbation. McQuaid had not bothered to fill vacant deanships; Hickey, in 1914, named three new deans: Father James J. Bloomer (Elmira); Father Francis J. Naughten (Steuben and Livingston); and Father John T. Hickey (Auburn).

Bishop Hickey furthermore appointed Father Andrew E. Breen to the pastorate of St. Patrick's, Mount Morris, soon after McQuaid's death, although Breen had been *persona non grata* to McQuaid since the Hanna affair. Three years later the cloud that had hung over Dr. Hanna's head since 1907 was dissipated by his appointment as Auxiliary Bishop of San Francisco. It was Bishop Hickey who officially announced this welcome move; and when the papal delegate, Archbishop John Bonzano, consecrated Edward J. Hanna on December 4, 1912, Hickey was the preacher.[11] Thomas Hickey had also preached in 1910 at the funeral of another old antagonist of McQuaid's, Father Louis Lambert; and he had not hesitated then to praise Lambert, as "a simple man, simple in all his greatness."[12] Nor did he subscribe to all of his predecessor's views on institutions of higher learning. He did not renew McQuaid's impracticable ban on attendance at non-Catholic colleges. And he finally added Rochester to the roster of the American dioceses which took up an annual collection for the Catholic University of America.

In the last analysis, however, these divergences of policy were few in number. In the main, Thomas Francis Hickey, convinced that Mc-Quaid had given him a mandate to carry on, adhered very closely to the course mapped out by the founder. Even when he blazed new trails, they were ramifications of the old established highways.[13]

On acceding to the bishopric of Rochester, Bishop Hickey confirmed in the position of chancellor the beloved, priestly Father Michael J. Nolan (1870-1931), whom McQuaid had appointed chancellor and rector of St. Andrew's Seminary in 1904 after the death of Msgr. De-Regge. At the same time the new bishop chose as vicar general the pastor of Corpus Christi Church, Father Dennis J. Curran (1857-1922). Father Curran, a good administrator and a manly but unobtrusive priest, was to prove a dutiful lieutenant. Hickey also filled some minor offices: a secretary (Father Edward B. Simpson); parish priest consultors; and members of some new diocesan standing committees.

With the aid of this staff, Bishop Hickey now set about the active administration of his diocese. Between 1909 and 1919, he established three new territorial parishes on the perimeter of Rochester proper: Sacred Heart, in the northwest (1910); St. Andrew's, in the north (1913); and St. John the Evangelist, in the east (1914).

Outside the see city, Hickey, in the same decade, founded only one completely new territorial parish: St. Vincent de Paul, in Corning, where he dedicated the combination church and school in March, 1914. But he raised nine other mission churches to full parochial status. They were: St. Louis, Pittsford, Monroe County, 1911 (mission, 1866?); St. John the Evangelist, Newark Valley, Tioga County, 1914 (mission, 1881); Our Lady of the Lake, King Ferry, Cayuga County, 1913 (mission, 1870); St. Mary of the Lake, Ontario, Wayne County, 1915 (mission, 1870); St. Joseph, Livonia Station, Livingston County, 1915 (mission, 1912); St. Thomas Aquinas, Leicester[Moscow], Livingston County, 1916 (mission, 1897); Good Shepherd, Henrietta, Monroe County, 1916 (mission, 1911) and St. Januarius, Naples, Ontario County, 1911 (mission, 1879).

The special interest which Bishop Hickey took in rural churches was perhaps a reflection of his own experience as a country pastor. In addition to advancing to parish status these nine rural missions (two of which he had himself established as missions), he founded, in his first decade, six new missions. In Cayuga County, there were St. Ann at Owasco and St. Hilary at Genoa, both set up in 1911. In Steuben, there was St. Matthias at Atlanta (1914). In Tompkins County, there was the chapel built at Ludlowville to take care of the Catholics of that vicinity, who were largely Slavonian (1913). In Wayne County, there was St. Gregory at Marion, where the Catholics were principally Flemish and Hollanders (1914). And in 1919, the Bishop set up Our Lady of Lebanon Chapel, on the west shore of Canandaigua Lake, for the benefit of summer vacationers.

During his first decade, the Bishop was also preoccupied with the needs of the other foreign-language groups that had settled in the Diocese; and when they were numerous, he sought to provide them with churches or at least chapels of their own. In 1910 he dedicated, in Rochester, the first and only Lithuanian church within the Diocese. It is now called St. George, but its original name was St. John Kanty.

Most of the new foreign language parishes were, of course, Italian. In 1909, the Bishop laid the cornerstone of the combination church and school of Our Lady of Mount Carmel, Rochester: a parish organized by McQuaid, as we have seen, to accommodate Italians on Rochester's East Side. In 1912, Bishop Hickey himself organized an Italian parish on the west side of the city. Its parishioners first made use of the old SS. Peter and Paul church building at King and Maple Streets, lately vacated by its congregation on the completion of the present SS. Peter and Paul's on West Main Street. By 1913, however, Hickey was able to dedicate their new church-school combination on Troup Street, under the patronage of the Sicilian martyr, St. Lucy.

But the majority of the incoming Italians continued to settle on the east side of the Genesee River. An increasing number took residence along Niagara Street, in a neighborhood once staunchly German and a part of the German parish of St. Francis Xavier. To take care of this new Italian salient, the Bishop in 1914 purchased the former Niagara Street Baptist Church, a frame building at the corner of Niagara and Dake Streets, and blessed it as an Italian mission church under the name of Our Lady of Sorrows. (During the whole period of its history, from 1914 to 1938, Our Lady of Sorrows was an Italian mission chapel rather than a full-fledged parish, although after 1930 its full-time administrator, Father Patrick Moffatt, lived no longer at Mount Carmel, but in a rectory behind the church on Dake Street.[14])

Another body of Italians now moved into the northeastern part of Rochester, along Norton Street and "The Lots" of Irondequoit just to the north of it. This was a poor and at times disorderly neighborhood, but it certainly deserved spiritual attention. It was priests from the Cathedral parish who established and serviced a new Italian mission on Norton Street near North Goodman Street. Here the Diocese, in 1917, built a basement church, with the manual aid of the Italian men. The chapel was originally named "St. Agnes", and because it was almost wholly below ground, it was often referred to as the "catacomb church." Only in 1923 was a very inexpensive superstructure erected. By the time the Bishop blessed this on April 18, 1923, the official title had already long since been changed from "St. Agnes" to "Annunciation," apparently because of the part the Italian "Annunciation Society" had played in its early career.

During his first decade, Thomas Hickey also made provision for Italian congregations elsewhere in the Diocese. The Italians of Elmira, after four problematic years, finally finished St. Anthony Church and School in 1911, and the Bishop dedicated it on May 27th.[15] In 1914, he blessed the Italian mission church of the Assumption, in Mount Morris.[16] Although officially a mission, this church was given a full-time priest from the start. Another Italian chapel, Santa Maria de Mercede, was constructed in 1914 at Cuylerville, also in Livingston County. A group of Italians had been brought in by the Sterling Salt Company to operate its Cuylerville mine. It seems that the Company not only donated a church-lot for their use, but built the little frame church itself.[17] Santa Maria de Mercede ceased to be used as a mission church around 1933, for when the mine at Cuylerville closed it was no longer needed. The abandoned building was destroyed by fire some seven years later.

Meanwhile, another mining firm, the International Salt Company, had been prospering at Retsof, some five miles north of Cuylerville. Here, too, a large number of Italians were employed; and this Company likewise provided the employees with a church, St. Lucy's, which was opened in December, 1911. Technically, St. Lucy's was more a territorial congregation than an Italian congregation; and by a rather odd arrangement, the Company refused to transfer the property to the Diocese, allowing its use only on a rental basis. But International Salt always intended to convey the property eventually to the Rochester Diocese, and finally voted to do so in early 1957. The deed was handed over on March 23, 1959.[18] St. Lucy's has always been a mission church, entrusted to St. Mary's Church, Geneseo, until 1931, and to St. Thomas Aquinas, Leicester, since that time.

The financing of the diocesan Italian parishes and missions presented many problems. Still another problem was to staff them with Italian priests. It was difficult to secure their services in Italy, and when they came it was difficult to sustain their interest in their impoverished and multi-dialectal flocks. There were, however, three Italian-born priests who entered the Diocese early and devoted the rest of their lives to its missions. The Reverend Doctor Mario Catalano (1881-1926) was pastor of St. Lucy's, Rochester from 1912 to 1926. Father Peter Moia (1885-1935), was pastor of St. Francis of Assisi, Auburn, from 1911 to 1935. Father Adolfo Gabbani (1872-1949), served in the pastorates of St. Anthony, Elmira, St. Francis of Assisi, Rochester, and St. Francis of Assisi, Auburn.

If Bishop Hickey held fast to the basic norms set by his predecessor, this adherence was most obvious in his educational efforts. In the first pastoral letter which he wrote on the diocesan seminaries, on August 20, 1909, Hickey revealed that Bishop McQuaid had urged him, on his deathbed, to carry on without halt the educational program which he had initiated. He therefore pledged to his people that he would keep faith with the founding bishop's wish, and devote his most earnest efforts to the "sacred cause" of religious education.

As a result, whenever the existence of the "Christian free schools" was challenged, or there was a threat of undoing them by taxation, Thomas F. Hickey spoke out in defence of their economic and social value to the community.[19] And whenever a parish was able to support a school, the Bishop gave it one, usually located, as in McQuaid's day, on the second floor of a combination church-and-school structure. Thus the second bishop of Rochester opened ten new parochial schools in the first decade of his regime. Five were in Rochester: Sacred Heart (1911), St. Lucy (1913), Our Lady of Mount Carmel (1910), St. Andrew (1915), and St. John the Evangelist (1916). The first two were assigned to the Sisters of St. Joseph; the last three to the Sisters of Mercy. Outside of the see city the schools were at St. Francis of Assisi, Auburn (1910-1916); St. Vincent's, Corning (1913); St. John's, Clyde (1914); St. Patrick's, Mount Morris (1911); and St. Anthony, Elmira (1911). Of these, the first three were entrusted to the Sisters of Mercy, the last two to the Sisters of St Joseph.[20]

Assigning additional schools to the Sisters of Mercy was quite a departure from the practice of Bishop McQuaid. Bishop Hickey naturally admired the Sisters of St. Joseph, and always maintained close contact with them. On the other hand, he could scarcely forget the Mercy nuns who had taught in his home parish, St. Mary's. He was therefore readier to accept them than was his predecessor as trusted auxiliaries in the expanding educational work of the Rochester Diocese. Even now, the Rochester Mercy community was small and struggling. In 1916, their original convent and motherhouse on South Street was seriously damaged by fire, so they disposed of the property. Having no other building to take over as an administrative center, they moved out into their frame summer house on St. John Park in lakeside Charlotte, and this drafty dwelling had to serve as motherhouse until 1930. Nevertheless, the advent of Bishop Hickey marked a real turning point in their expansion as a community.[21]

Nuns from all three of the orders that taught in the diocesan parish schools attended the annual diocesan school conference held each summer. Able educators were brought in from outside to share their information and pedagogical experience with the sisters. The Bishop naturally backed this practice: he himself had inaugurated it in 1904.[22]

Secondary Catholic education moved ahead a few paces during the first Hickey decade. Several parish schools experimented with a ninth grade. This was the case in at least three schools conducted by the Sisters of Mercy. St. Patrick's School, Elmira, seems to have had a ninth grade; St. Mary's, Corning, maintained one from 1904 to 1911; and St. Mary's, Rochester, after some experimentation, abandoned its ninth grade only in 1912. The Sisters of St. Joseph followed a similar practice in at least two instances: at the Cathedral School; and, prior to 1913, at Immaculate Conception School, Rochester.

In addition to those schools which tried a non-academic ninth grade, there were four others which added an extra year with the hope of developing a full academic course. St. Rose in Lima led the way. Here, from 1900 to 1918, the Sisters of St. Joseph conducted a small but accredited three-year high school course. Unfortunately, circumstances forced the Sisters to reduce, rather than expand, the length of the schooling: to two years in 1918, and to one year in 1920. But the academic department itself was maintained until 1946. At St. Mary's in Rochester, the Sisters of Mercy registered a freshman academic class in 1913, but had to give it up in 1916. Their colleagues at St. Ann's School, Hornell, were a little more successful. They started an academic year in 1912 and later added a second year. Classes were held in the Federation Building, a parish and civic center constructed in 1912 by the pastor, Father Francis Naughten. The academic course, subsequently reduced to one year, continued to function in the Federation Building until the building was sold in 1947. After the sale, the academic class moved into the parish school building, but was discontinued three years later.

Equally modest in its beginnings, but far more prosperous in its development, was St. Francis De Sales High School in Geneva. With the encouragement of Father William A. McDonald, pastor of St. Francis De Sales Church and dean of the Geneva deanery, the Sisters of St. Joseph, in September, 1912, opened two advanced courses in their parish school building: one commercial, one academic. A priest was the principal (Father John Muckle). Two nuns constituted the initial teaching staff; and seventy-two boys and girls made up the student body. Each year for three years thereafter, another academic year was added, so that at the end of four years the pioneer Class of 1916 was graduated. By 1928, the staff comprised two priests and eleven sisters, and there were 225 students on the roster. Thirty years later, the school, still flourishing but at another street address, changed its name to De Sales High School, the better to declare its inter-parochial status.[23]

While the Bishop was doubtless delighted to see his old Geneva parish assuming educational leadership, he had no time to play an active role in the development of De Sales High. For in the see city itself, there was an even greater need of Catholic secondary school facilities. Having talked the matter over with the Rochester pastors in 1913, he had practically decided by November of that year to build two new secondary schools in Rochester, one for boys and one for girls.[24]

As it turned out, however, the project for a boys' school was shelved, in favor of the girls' school—a new Nazareth Academy to replace the original school near the Cathedral. Once built, a girls' academy could absorb the girls enrolled at Cathedral High School, which had thus far been coeducational. As a result, Cathedral High could be continued as an all-boys' school. This was wise, for Cathedral High had won a good reputation. It had already been granted a Regents charter in 1909. In 1913 it was granted an improved Regents charter, which hailed it by its new name—more appropriate because its students had long since come from many parishes—"The Rochester Catholic High School."[25]

The new Nazareth Academy was formally opened in the fall of 1916. This is the tawny brick building that remains the original part of the Academy complex on Lake Avenue at Lakeview Park. Architect Joseph H. Oberlies designed it to accommodate 1,500 students. The forty-five year-old Academy soon became a major diocesan educational institution, thanks chiefly to Sister M. Marcella Reagan (1858-1940), who was in charge through the transition. She had been named principal in 1882; she was to continue her notable career at Nazareth Academy until her death in 1940. When she died, Mr. Frank P. Graves, the New York State Commissioner of Education, did not hesitate to declare: "I have never come into contact with a greater educator than Sister M. Marcella."[26] The Bishop was certainly blessed in having the assistance of such a pedagogue in his expansion of secondary education.

Another phase of education to which Bishop Hickey gave special attention was catechetics. In the encyclical letter *Acerbo Nimis* of 1905, Pope St. Pius X had ordered that a unit of the Confraternity of Christian Doctrine be established in each Catholic parish. How quickly and how extensively this formal program was adopted in the Rochester Diocese it is now impossible to determine. But there was certainly an active unit at the Cathedral by 1913. Here a group of parish young women applied themselves to the study of Catholic teachings, and then passed on their knowledge to the Catholic children, mostly from immigrant families, who attended the public schools.

Still more ambitious was the catechetical work of the Catholic Charities Guild of Rochester, which, as we shall see, the Bishop brought into being in 1912. Its Catechetical Department employed the services of a large number of volunteers, divided into the Fishers and the Catechists, in proper C.C.D. style. The Fishers had the task of rounding up the Catholic children enrolled in public schools throughout the city. The Catechists did the actual work of instruction in the Sunday school classes. All worked under the close surveillance of Bishop Hickey, who met his catechists at the Chancery each Friday and gave them lectures on catechetical approaches. By 1918 there were eight catechetical centers in Rochester and more than 250 Rochester Catholic women were engaged in this important work.[27]

A further ramification of the religious educational work was the vacation school. In 1916, the Bishop launched a summer school program, six weeks in length, for the benefit of the children of Italian immigrants. It was conducted in two places: Cathedral Hall, for the west side of Rochester; Mt. Carmel School, for the east side.[28] A third center was established at St. Lucy's School in the following year. Programming at the vacation schools included not only catechism, but reading and writing, singing, sewing, cooking, and some manual training.[29]

Rochester's second bishop also gave firm support to the unique apostolate of the deaf that the Redemptorist Fathers had undertaken at St. Joseph's Church in 1908. In that year, Father William Kessel, C.SS.R., had organized the Ephpheta Society for the Catholic deaf-mutes of the Rochester district. He and Father Aloysius Englehardt, C.SS.R., gathered them together once a month for religious instruction in the basement of St. Joseph's School.[30] Most noted among their resident successors was Father Charles Burger, C.SS.R., whom Bishop

Hickey named head of the diocesan apostolate to the deaf in 1926, and who, in 1931, opened St. Francis de Sales Chapel for the Deaf in a room in St. Joseph's School.

In view of his active interest in all these forms and instruments of religious instruction, Thomas F. Hickey can never be charged with neglecting his task to teach the Faith. He was no less solicitous in encouraging devotional practices among his people.

The movement for the more frequent reception of Holy Communion, had, for example, received a powerful impetus under Pope St. Pius X. In the legislation of the Third Synod of Rochester, held June 9, 1914, the Bishop of Rochester embodied into diocesan law the papal decrees on frequent Communion of 1905 and 1906, and the decree of 1910 which declared that children might be admitted to Communion when they had reached the age of reason.[31] Of course, the papal legislation had already been in effect from its promulgation; but it was during the Hickey epoch that the practice of frequent Communion, both by children and adults, began its gradual but magnificent rise.[32]

Another movement sponsored by Rochester's second bishop was the Holy Name Society. In October, 1910, Bishop Hickey promoted a parade of the city-wide membership of this men's organization. Ten thousand marchers turned out, to make it perhaps the largest male demonstration of the sort in Rochester history.[33] One good turnout deserved another, so the procession was repeated in 1911, 1912 and 1913. In 1914, however, the practice was discontinued, in favor of the corporate reception of Holy Communion in the separate parishes.[34] The Holy Name Society, designed to combat profanity and encourage the frequentation of the sacraments, had meanwhile been activated throughout the Diocese; indeed, the 1912 procession in Rochester had included delegations from several parishes outside the city. Hickey had apparently desired to show, by means of the processions, the triumphant solidarity of Catholics in the face of an often hostile world. There is reason to believe that he discontinued them not solely because they had sufficiently served that purpose, but because they had themselves evoked new signs of hostility in a current prewar wave of anti-Catholicism.

A second international spiritual movement which Bishop Hickey encouraged was the Apostleship of Prayer, promoted by the League of the Sacred Heart. The Bishop announced his intention, in the spring of 1916, to establish branches of the League in every parish in the diocese.[35] The intention was carried out.

The Holy Name Society and the Apostleship of Prayer were established on clerical initiative. The Laymen's Retreat League of Rochester owed its origin to lay enterprise.

In 1915, two Rochesterians, Mr. James C. Connolly, a postal employee, and Mr. James P. B. Duffy, an attorney, fell under the sway of Father Terence Shealy, S.J., a priest of Fordham University who was actively furthering the lay retreat movement. Having agreed that the Rochester Diocese would profit by affiliating with the movement, the two laymen requested Bishop Hickey to permit the holding of lay retreats in Rochester. The Bishop consented, and arranged to have annual retreats given at St. Bernard's Seminary during the summer vacation season. Thirty-five laymen made the first retreat, in August, 1915. Before separating, these pioneers organized a diocesan Laymen's Retreat League, electing Connolly to the presidency and Duffy to the secretaryship. The League has continued in existence up to the present, an organization whose sole purpose is to encourage lay retreats and finance their costs by voluntary donations.

At the outset, the pastors of the Diocese considered the Retreat League a novelty, and took little interest in it. Only in 1928 did the League undertake a program of publicity. Despite that fact, the retreat practice did grow gradually in popularity, for a man who had made one retreat would often return to the next one bringing new retreatants to whom he had communicated his enthusiasm. Thus by 1928, the last year of Bishop Hickey's episcopate, the number of those attending the annual retreat had risen to 145. Usually the retreat masters were Jesuit Fathers, although this was not always the case. The men on retreat cooperated generously with the priests in charge, and edified all by their devotion. There can be little doubt that the foundation of the lay retreat movement in the Rochester Diocese was one of the milestones in its spiritual history.[36]

It was thus, in efforts administrative, educational, and devotional, that Thomas Francis Hickey began his career as spiritual father of the old and the young, the religious and the lay, of his diocese.

2. Social Questions and Answers.

The second decade of this century was a period of active political and social reformism throughout the United States. A number of Rochesterians were extensively engaged in the quest for social solutions. Rochester Catholics played no prominent part in these intercredal endeavors. But this is not to say that they had no interest in the problems involved, which were all too often the very problems that confronted many of the poorer Catholics. Especially in the face of increasing socialist trends, more Catholics now became interested in the Church's doctrines on social justice. And the Diocese meanwhile saw the need of better systematizing its works of charity.

A few Catholic diocesan spokesmen kept on the alert against seemingly socialistic trends in government actions, whether national, state or local. One of the most articulate of these Rochester spokesmen, who communicated his ideas through addresses, letters to the daily press, and editorials in his own parish magazine, was Father Augustine M. O'Neill of Immaculate Conception Church. In 1919, for instance, he bespoke a common Catholic apprehension in the face of the possible establishment of a federal Department of Education, on the grounds that it would be an invasion of the authority of the States.[37] A decade before, he had opposed the projected program of free textbooks in Rochester's public schools for the reason that it was not only "pork-barrel" legislation but might provide an opening wedge for state socialism.[38] Speakers at Rochester's experimental "social centers" also evoked critical remarks from Father O'Neill. These were city-sponsored clubs for cultural betterment held on public school property. But when certain of the invited speakers began to show partiality to socialism and animosity towards Catholicism, O'Neill and other Rochesterians, Catholic and non-Catholic alike, protested against the use of public school auditoriums for programs that were socially or religiously subversive.[39]

Father O'Neill's arguments were sometimes a bit strained, but he usually had a good point, defended it well, and on some public issues won a considerable following among Rochesterians of other faiths. Not all Catholic opposition to socialism was so well informed. The *Catholic Journal,* for instance, seemed too ready to see socialism where it was not. Nevertheless, there was real apprehension that some of the local Poles and Germans, in particular, might be hypnotized by immigrant fellow-countrymen who arrived in America afire with a collectivist ideology.

Far more important than the search for socialist bogeymen was the active diffusion of Catholic social principles. In forward-looking parishes, there was an increasing number of lectures delivered and articles published along these lines. In 1909, for instance, the Lenten sermons in St. Bridget's Church, Rochester, were devoted to social problems. In March, 1913, the Holy Name Society of Holy Family parish, Rochester, was treated to a lecture on socialism by the well-known convert from Judaism and former socialist, David Goldstein. In March,

1917, Father Joseph Baierl of St. Bernard's Seminary, addressed the Holy Name Society of St. Andrew's Church on "The Social Question."[40] Father O'Neill wrote and published several essays along the same line in the *Immaculate Conception Church Magazine* which he edited. His biggest editorial scoop was two apparently exclusive articles, written by the leading American Catholic authority on papal teaching, Father John A. Ryan, of the Catholic University of America.[41] Another alert diocesan pastor, Father William L. Harrington, reprinted in full in the October, 1916 issue of *The Parish Record* of Immaculate Conception Church, Ithaca, the excellent Labor Day address recently given in San Francisco by the former Rochesterian and labor champion, Archbishop Edward J. Hanna.[42]

But it was the Germans of the Rochester Diocese who made the most systematic effort to deepen their knowledge of Catholic social principles.

The main force behind this effort was the Catholic Central Verein, a national German Catholic federation which was represented in Rochester by a diocesan federation of the societies in all the German parishes. In 1908 the Central Verein, whose center was in St. Louis, Missouri, had set up a Central Bureau for the Promotion of Social Education; and in 1909 it began to publish *Central Blatt and Social Justice*, a bilingual journal, to diffuse social information and agitate for labor legislation. The affiliated parishes in the Diocese of Rochester welcomed the program and sought to put it into effect locally.[43] Their Rochester officers saw to it that the lay-edited Rochester *Catholic Journal* was regularly supplied with articles on social justice syndicated by the St. Louis office of the Central Verein. In the late spring of 1914, the statewide membership of the Verein, called the New York State Federation of German Catholic Societies, held its three-day convention in Rochester. Bishop Hickey addressed one of the sessions. Another speaker was the director of the Boston School of Political Economy, Mrs. Martha Moore Avery (1851-1929). Since her conversion from Marxism to Catholicism in 1904, this dedicated woman had campaigned vigorously for Christian social justice.[44]

Another contemporary national movement for social justice was the American Federation of Catholic Societies. The A.F.C.S. had been founded in 1901, with the backing of the American hierarchy, to coordinate the work of all American lay Catholic organizations. In 1910, it established a Social Service Commission to work on a program of education and labor-law advocacy comparable to that of the Central Verein. That its program was similar to that of the Verein is not surprising: both programs had been outlined by the same man, the national pioneer and gadfly of American Catholic social organization, Father Peter E. Dietz (1878-1947).[45]

Although inspired initially by a German Catholic organization—the Knights of St. John—and spurred on by a German-American, Father Dietz, the A.F.C.S. was intended to embrace Catholic American societies of all native backgrounds. That was evident in the participants of its national convention held in New York in August, 1916. The Rochester diocesan delegation included not only Father Mathias Hargather, pastor of St. Michael's German Church, but also Father Curran, the Vicar General; Father Nolan, the Chancellor; Father Augustine M. O'Neill, of Immaculate Conception; Father Simon FitzSimons of St. Mary's Church; and Father James J. Bloomer, dean of the Elmira deanery. Bishop Hickey gave one of the addresses. He urged Catholic unity, solidarity, and progress—not in the direction of forming a Catholic politial party, but of applying Catholic principles to everyday life. In announcing the convention, the *New York World* called the Bishop of Rochester "one of the most powerful pulpit orators in the American hierarchy."[46]

If the Rochester clerical delegation to the A.F.C.S. meeting was mostly Irish, the lay delegation from Rochester to the 61st annual convention of the Central Verein, held in New York at the same time, was mostly German. Mostly, we say; for there were actually two delegates who were of Irish background: Patrick Gaffney and Philip H. Donnelly. Philip Donnelly (1877-1945) deserves special comment. A self-made man, a lawyer, and subsequently a Monroe County judge, Donnelly was an indefatigable exponent of the teachings of the popes on social justice. For this reason he felt particularly at home among the members of the Central Verein, of the Windthorst Study Circle at Holy Redeemer Church, and the Catholic Social Lecture Circle of St. Joseph's Church. To a questioner who asked why he, of Irish background, should belong to these German groups (rather an eyebrow-raising practice in those days), he answered: *"They* listen to me!" When Judge Donnelly died, Bishop James E. Kearney, the fifth head of the Rochester Diocese, referred to this zealous man as "an unconsecrated priest."[47]

Father Peter E. Dietz not only sought to organize Catholics, but to bring Catholic principles into the American labor movement. With this end in view, he founded, in 1910, an organization made up of Catholic labor unionists and labor leaders. It was called the Militia of Christ. Among the original officers were a vice president of the A.F.L. (American Federation of Labor), John Mitchell, and a Rochester labor administrator, John Sibley Whalen (1868-1913). Whalen had been secretary of state of New York State (1907-1909), and in 1912 was to be appointed First Deputy State Commissioner of Labor. He was a close associate of John Mitchell. John S. Whalen was a member of Rochester's Cathedral parish.[48]

In pursuit of his aim, Father Dietz made a practice of attending the A.F.L. national conventions. Thus in November, 1912, he came to Rochester, where the labor organization was holding its convention, and gave a forceful address at one of the meetings. On November 21, 1912, with the aid of some of his Militia of Christ associates, he composed and sent from Rochester a letter to Cardinal Gibbons of Baltimore, in which he urged that the American Catholic hierarchy publish an official program of social justice based on the teachings of Pope Leo XIII. No action was taken by the hierarchy at that time; but in 1919 the American bishops, with the backing of Gibbons, did publish an official social program that more than fulfilled the dreams of Father Dietz. It is of some interest, therefore, that Dietz's original proposal was dated from Rochester.[49]

On at least one occasion, Father Dietz asked another clergyman to represent him at an A.F.L. convention. When Dietz found it impossible to attend the 1915 convention, to be held in San Francisco, he asked his friend, Archbishop Edward J. Hanna, to represent him.

Father Dietz had chosen his representative well. Dr. Hanna, who in 1907 (as we have seen) had been challenged without warrant for his theological correctness, had also gained wide note in Rochester for his interest in labor problems. Trained in Italy, and ably conversant with classical Italian and even with some Italian dialects, Hanna had devoted a good deal of his time to the spiritual needs of Rochester Italian immigrants. From spiritual ministrations he had turned naturally to an interest in their social problems. Having thus won their confidence, he was in a position to assist them when they became involved in labor difficulties. In June 1910, laborers in the building trades, most of them Italians, went on strike against their employers. Tempers rose quickly and violence seemed imminent. One day when the strikers were parading in the streets, Father Hanna halted them and warned them that they would forfeit their chance for success if they resorted to force. Fortunately, his advice was heeded.[50] When Mayor Hiram Edgerton undertook to make peace between the workers and the contractors that August, Hanna played an important role in the negotiations which finally put an end to the contest.[51]

Two years later, the same seminary professor was again called upon to serve the public welfare, this time in the matter of adequate working conditions. In 1911, State Senator Robert F. Wagner (1877-1953), who later became famous as a social legislator in the United States Senate, launched a statewide investigation of laboring conditions. His investigator found that there were substandard conditions in all but two of the thirty-three garment factories in Rochester. The *New York World* followed this up with an investigation of its own, which resulted in an even more sensational and stinging indictment of the Rochester clothing manufacturers. Badly wounded by the double-barrelled attack, the Rochester Clothiers' Exchange requested that the local Chamber of Commerce commission an impartial committee to undertake still another investigation of the Rochester factories. Dr. Hanna was named to chair the eight-man committee. For four months this group made a careful study of all the industries in question. In November, 1912, the Chamber published their report, *An Investigation of the Conditions Existing in the Clothing Factories of Rochester, N.Y.* While the committeemen were happy to state that working conditions ranged from good to excellent in 86% of the factories visited, they frankly declared that in the remainder the facilities in heating, lighting, and sanitation fell short of the standard.[52]

By the time that World War I arrived, the socialist movement in the United States had lost its drive. The Catholic Diocese of Rochester had, it is true, mounted no formal campaign against it. But the diocesan clergy and laity had at least done enough, positively as well as negatively, to warn Catholics against the fallacies of Marxist teachings.

If Bishop Hickey blazed no new trails in the quest for social justice, he did pioneer in the organization of diocesan charities.

We are not concerned here with parish aid societies as such. As for the Conferences of St. Vincent De Paul, there were only three in the Diocese: the Cathedral conference, which after many years of good work closed its books in 1918; and new conferences established in Canandaigua and Elmira around 1910.[53] Out of the Elmira conference developed the "St. Vincent de Paul Society", incorporated in 1910, as an essentially lay citywide organization of Catholics interested in volunteer charitable work. Funds for this work were principally raised, during the next dozen years, by an annual gala Charity Ball, which brought in an average income of $2,000.00.[54]

During the same decade there were social centers operating in some of the parishes of the Diocese. For example, the Young Men's Club of the Cathedral parish opened a reading room in Cathedral Hall in 1916. In Hornell, as we have already noted, Father Francis Naughten built the Federation Building in 1912. This not only housed the parish high school, but had an auditorium and meeting rooms for the use of all the parishioners.[55] Rather different from both of these was the Big Brothers Club, launched in 1914 by the Catholic industrialist J. Adam Kreag to provide wholesome recreation for Italian youths in the neighborhood of the Rochester Public Market.[56]

More essentially diocesan efforts were the cemeteries and welfare institutions. Bishop Hickey added a forty-three-acre annex to Holy Sepulchre Cemetery, Rochester, in 1915. He likewise acquired, in 1909, a twenty-one-acre addition to the property of St. Ann's Home for the Aged; and three years later he opened a new (north) wing of the Home itself, constructed at a cost of $36,000.00.[57]

St. Joseph's Hospital, Elmira, acquired an annex in 1914.[58] A half-decade afterward, on September 9, 1919, the Bishop dedicated the fourth diocesan hospital—Mercy Hospital in Auburn. This hospital had been incorporated on July 11, 1917. Father William Payne, pastor of St. Mary's Church, Auburn, was the leading figure in its organization. The original home of the hospital was the Thornton farmhouse near the site of the present Mercy Hospital building. Originally, there were accommodations for only twenty-six patients. To staff it, the Bishop turned to a Syracuse community of nuns, the Third Franciscan Order of Sisters, Order of Minor Conventuals; and the superior of the order sent, as pioneers, Sisters M. Veronica Powers, M. Mildred Weber, M. Agnes Moyer, and M. Stephen Kane. This was the first new religious community of women to be assigned a mission within the Diocese since the days of Bishop McQuaid. Like the other three hospitals in the Rochester Diocese, Mercy Hospital had its own school of nursing.[59]

While Auburn gained a Catholic hospital in Hickey's first decade, it lost its Catholic orphanage. An Auburn Orphan Asylum Building Association had been formed in 1908 to bolster, if possible, the declining funds of the institution. Since nothing had come of its effort by March 9, 1909, Bishop Hickey issued orders to send the orphans to St. Mary's and St. Patrick's orphanages in Rochester.[60] By November 2nd, St. Patrick's had welcomed seventeen little girls from the Auburn home; and by March 13, 1910, St. Mary's had added forty-nine Auburn boys to its roster.[61] When the old orphanage on Auburn's North Street was sold in 1917, the price realized, $8,600.00, was handed over to the Rochester orphanages: three-fifths to St. Mary's, two-fifths to St. Patrick's.[62]

Two of the more stable institutions founded in the city of Rochester during Bishop Hickey's first decade were the St. Elizabeth Guild House and the Charles Settlement House.

The following account has come down of the origin of the Guild House. One rainy night, apparently in November, 1913, a young woman from out-of-town rang the bell at Blessed Sacrament Rectory; and when the pastor, Father Thomas F. Connors, answered the door, she asked if he could recommend an inexpensive Catholic women's club where she might find lodging. There was no such place, so he had to direct her to a private home. Father Connors had been chatting, when the bell rang, with a caller, Mr. J. Adam Kreag (1858-1927). As we have already implied in our reference to the Big Brothers Club, Mr. Kreag was interested in social welfare. He was a man of means, the treasurer of the Shinola Company, Rochester manufacturers of shoe blacking; and he devoted much of his wealth to worthwhile causes. When he heard from Father Connors of the young woman's plight, he said, "It's a shame that we haven't a girls' boarding house for cases like this." He quickly offered a large sum—at least $10,000.00—to that end. Bishop Hickey approved the project, and in 1915, the Diocese purchased and remodeled the former Pinnacle Club at No. 1 Field Street. It reopened on October 21st as the St. Elizabeth Guild House, a residence for girl students and working girls. It was enlarged in 1925 so as to accommodate forty-two—seventeen more than its original capacity. When the Pinnacle Road property was condemned to make way for the Inner Loop Expressway, the Guild House changed its address in 1959 to 1475 East Avenue, the former Walter Todd home. But the House had clearly outlived its usefulness by 1965, so it was discontinued in that year, after a half-century of service.[63]

The Charles House, the first Catholic settlement house in Rochester, opened its doors on November 30, 1917. In this instance, the prime movers were a group of Catholic young women who wanted to do settlement work among the Italian immigrants under Catholic auspices. With the permission of Bishop Hickey, the group organized and chose as their president, Miss Harriet Barry. Harriet Barry had, in fact, been the first to suggest the undertaking. She had had experience in social work at Washington, D.C., where she was associated with Miss Mary Virginia Merrick, founder of the Christ Child Society. Granddaughter of Patrick Barry, Rochester's leading pioneer Catholic philanthropist, and daughter of his son Charles, who had also been a representative Catholic layman, she decided, when given the privilege of naming the new center, to call it the Charles House in memory of her father. The Charles House was originally located at 52 Magne (now Broad) Street. Italians were fewer on the West Side than they were on the East Side. But the East Side already had one center, the

Lewis Street Settlement House. Furthermore, a Protestant mission had lately been established on the West Side, and it was desired to counter the attempt to proselytize the Italians of the neighborhood.

In general, the Charles House followed the typical settlement program: classes and supervised recreation for the boys and girls; meetings for the mothers; recreation for the working girls; hygiene classes; and a certain amount of clinical work. To these routine functions catechism classes were added. As assistants, Miss Barry had: Mrs. Daniel B. Murphy, General Adviser; Mrs. Frank X. Kelly, Vice President; Miss Margaret Fee, Treasurer; Miss Monica McLean, Registrar; and Miss Helen Beattie, Chairman of the Sewing Circle. Self-supporting from the start—the only non-volunteer was the matron-in-residence—the Charles House soon proved to be an effective social medium.[64]

If the social institutions of Rochester doubled and trebled in the years before World War I, this development, praiseworthy in itself, certainly posed another problem—the problem of an inefficiency which comes from overlapping. As early as 1908, in the wake of the panic year of 1907, Rochester social leaders came to the conclusion that it would be better all around if the various social agencies and institutions in the city could unite, at least to the extent of setting up a central coordinating bureau.

In the fall of 1908, two civic leaders decided to agitate for some sort of amalgamation of charitable efforts. They were the Reverend Dr. Henry H. Stebbins of Central Presbyterian Church; and Mr. Henry R. Noyes, Jr., an industrialist. The following January, those agencies that had responded to their appeal met to organize, under the sponsorship of the Rochester Chamber of Commerce. In order that the projected union might be truly representative, the formative committees were made up of Catholics, Protestants, and Jews, clerics and laymen. The Catholic delegates were: Father Edward J. Hanna, Mr. James P. B. Duffy, and Mr. Daniel B. Murphy. What came out of the consultation was the United Charities of Rochester, incorporated on May 17, 1910 to coordinate the work of all local charitable agencies without destroying the identity of any one of them.

When this movement for federation began, Bishop Hickey showed considerable enthusiasm for it, and it was at his invitation that Messrs. Duffy and Murphy cooperated with the founding group. Later, however, his fervor cooled, most likely because he feared that full participation would somehow involve a loss of autonomy on the part of the Catholic charities. The Bishop's subsequent withdrawal from United Charities was a source of great disappointment to its promoters, who had earnestly hoped their body would be truly citywide. Individual

Catholics did remain active in U.C., among them Messrs. Murphy and Duffy, Father Hanna, Mrs. Daniel B. Murphy, and the educator Joseph P. O'Hern. But by 1919 other non-Catholic groups had withdrawn from the organization, so United Charities reincorporated as the Social Welfare League of Rochester. Having again changed its name in 1930 and 1946, the League continues today as Family Service of Rochester.[65]

However much he disapproved of the amalgamation of all city social agencies, Thomas Hickey became increasingly aware of the need of coordinating the efforts of his own diocesan charitable institutions. As early as January, 1911, he inaugurated a diocesan Catholic charities collection designed to finance the care of the orphans, the aged, the dependent and the delinquent of the Diocese, and to support the catechetical program and other "missionary work." According to the *Catholic Journal* of January 26, 1912, the collection that first year amounted to $6,800.00. The appeal was repeated during the next few years, but at no time did it net more than $8,000.00. Clearly, this would never suffice to meet growing needs, or even to replace the old bazaars, donation parties, and the like, from which the various institutions had drawn their support in McQuaid's day. So Bishop Hickey quickly saw that he would have to seek new sources of revenue.

In 1912, the Bishop took an important step towards the integration of diocesan charitable institutions into one governing body. Calling together a group of active Rochester Catholic laywomen, he presented to them his thoughts on the problem. The meeting thereupon decided to establish the Catholic Charity Guild. Bishop Hickey was elected president; Fathers John Francis O'Hern and Jacob Staub, vice presidents; Miss Mary Jennings, general secretary; and Miss Elizabeth McSweeney, general treasurer. The original members were the Misses Elizabeth Clark, Anna Casey, Mary Jennings, Alice Kirk, Elizabeth Madden, Kathleen D'Olier, Elizabeth McSweeney, Cecilia Lennon, Ella Geraghty, Catherine Connolly, Margaret Dempsey, Helen M. O'Reilly, and Mesdames Daniel B. Murphy, Beekman C. Little, and Martin J. Calihan. At the end of its first year of existence membership in the Guild had risen to 200.

Guild members were now able to undertake an ordered program of volunteer charities financed by dues, voluntary gifts, benefit socials, and lesser sources. They did admirable work, especially among the city's immigrants for whom the current "poor laws" did not provide. Some of the ladies, as we have already indicated, taught catechism at Sunday schools and in summer vacation schools conducted in the city's immigrant neighborhoods. Others, having secured in 1914 a center on Niagara Street, engaged in a sort of settlement work: sewing classes for girls, supervised recreation and picnics for both girls and boys. The Department of Hospitals and Literature visited the sick in the city's hospitals; the Layette Department prepared clothing for infants; and the Child Helpers' Department distributed layettes and Christmas presents among the poor. A Department of Child Visitors made home inquiries about Sunday School attendance, and sometimes about family needs. Still more forward-looking were the Social Inquiry Guild, devoted entirely to the relief of indigent families; the Physical Relief Department (home nursing by nuns and nurses from St. Mary's Hospital); and the Police Court Department (aid to delinquent girls). It was also the Catholic Charity Guild that helped to bring the St. Elizabeth Guild House into being.[66]

From 1914 on, the Guild added a new and important branch of activities, the Relief Department. What precipitated this move was a threatened run on a Rochester bank. In October, 1914, the East Side Savings Bank at Clinton and East Main was reported to be on the verge of financial collapse. When anxious depositors began to gather outside its doors demanding the return of their deposits, an S.O.S. was sent to Father Jacob Staub, vice president of the Guild and diocesan troubleshooter in welfare matters. Father Staub hurried over and appealed to the excited creditors in firm language. He urged them not to seek the return of their funds, declaring that he himself had no intention whatever of withdrawing the account of the Catholic Charity Guild. There would be no failure, he assured them; the Bank would fulfill its obligations. Mollified by the eloquence of this well-known, dynamic pastor, the crowd gradually dispersed. There was no run on the Savings Bank, and it remained solvent.

Meanwhile, the experience had taught Father Staub a salutary lesson. He had not realized how widely Rochesterians had been afflicted by a recent business recession until he read the fact in those frightened eyes. The realization prompted him to advocate the establishment of a relief department by the Guild. This Relief Department began to function on November 5, 1914, staffed by Staub himself (part-time), assisted by Miss Elizabeth McSweeney ("Miss Mac") as a full-time volunteer, and an interpreter. In 1915, the new Department secured a warehouse in which to store the clothing, furniture and bedding brought in by the Guild's Garment Service Department. At this warehouse, jobless people who were able to work were given employment mending the clothing and furniture for distribution. Until the outbreak in America of World War I, when employment opportunities increased, the Relief Department warehouse hummed with activity.

Once the Guild acquired a central office, the case work among the poor also increased.[67]

The more the Guild's activities expanded, the more need there was for additional funds. On April 11, 1915, Thomas F. Hickey tried a new device. He gathered a number of leading Catholic laymen together and announced the foundation of a Catholic Men's Charity League. His audience thereupon elected a ticket of officers: Peter A. Vay, president; Frank J. Hone, vice president; Frank Yawman, secretary-treasurer. By 1918 membership in the C.M.C.L. had risen to 1,236. Through this new organization, the Bishop derived an annual amount of some $7,000.00—the principal source of the Guild's income for the next couple of years.[68]

Rochester was not the only New York State diocese that was searching in those days for a better type of charities organization. All six of the State's bishops were faced with the same problem. In 1916, with the strong backing of Bishop Hickey, Cardinal John M. Farley, Archbishop of New York, engaged the service of Attorney Charles J. Tobin of Albany to keep the bishops of the New York Province informed on pending State legislation relative to charities and other matters of Catholic interest. Then on January 25, 1917, the bishops of New York State met in New York to discuss still closer collaboration. Cardinal Farley, as chairman, proposed the foundation of a State Council of Catholic Charities. In the interim, the bishops named Bishop Hickey and Bishop Thomas F. Cusack of Albany as a committee entrusted with two duties. The first duty was the preparation of a statewide plan for the placing-out of Catholic dependent children through diocesan agencies. The second was to work for the protection of Catholic interests in the State other than charities.[69]

Around this same date, and quite likely before it, the Bishop of Rochester had asked his Catholic Men's Charity League to study how best to coordinate all the Rochester Catholic charitable projects into one unit. There was not much precedent to work from, but the League eventually came up with a promising scheme. Backed by the bishops of the New York Province, Bishop Hickey now had the Rochester attorney, Thomas P. McCarrick, draw up a bill for the Legislature which would permit Rochester or any New York State diocese to form a diocesan charities aid association. Introduced before the State Legislature by Assemblyman John Malone of Albany on April 2, 1917, an "Act to Incorporate Catholic Charities Aid Associations" subsequently passed both houses and was signed into a law on April 24th by Governor Charles S. Whitman. This legal achievement, which more than fulfilled the mission assigned him by his fellow bishops, remained one of the chief accomplishments of Bishop Hickey's regime.[70]

On June 28, 1917, the charities of the Rochester Diocese—at least several of them—were incorporated as the Rochester Catholic Charities Aid Association (the simpler name, Rochester Catholic Charities, was adopted only on January 22, 1924, as the result of reorganization). Incorporators under the law were the Bishop himself, four Rochester pastors, and eighteen prominent Catholic laymen. Some friction arose in the selection of the ruling board. Most of the laymen wanted to have the R.C.C.A.A. under lay control, and Father William E. Cowen, one of the active organizers, favored their view. But the Bishop put his foot down, and firmly. The memory of lay trusteeism was still too fresh for him to want to flirt with it in the new organization, so he insisted that the trustees chosen be men not opposed to close ecclesiastical control. The officers elected to the Association were: John J. Keenan, president; William T. Farrell, secretary; William C. Barry, treasurer; William T. Nolan, general secretary. Father Staub was continued as director of the Relief Department. The Association then engaged a professional case worker, Miss Kathleen D'Olier, who, like Mr. Nolan, now began a long and valuable professional career in the charitable ministrations of the Diocese of Rochester.[71]

Then came the big question of financing this growing enterprise. Hitherto, several of the agencies now confederated into the R.C.C.A.A. had fended for themselves, or been supported parsimoniously out of an assortment of purses. Father Staub's Relief Department was able to turn, when in urgent need, to the Rochester branch of the Catholic Women's Union—a ladies' auxiliary of the Central Verein, national in scope, founded, largely through the instrumentality of Staub himself, for charitable work.[72] But now a relatively vast sum was needed to meet the budget of the whole organization. The officers of R.C.C.A.A. decided that the only possible course was to launch a drive for $50,000.00.

Today a campaign for that amount would not cause surprise even in a small country parish. In 1917, as the Bishop himself admitted, it was "a bold thing." Nothing of the sort had ever been attempted in the Rochester Diocese. But the solicitors, organized into fifteen teams, campaigned like troopers from November 5th to November 12th. A few outstanding gifts from individuals helped: George Eastman, J. Adam Kreag, and Philip J. Yawman each contributed $5,000.00. Just before midnight on the last day, Father William E. Cowen announced triumphantly to the two hundred campaign workers that the drive had brought in pledges of $74,333.64. This was almost 150% of the amount sought, and all but $4,000.00 of it was eventually collected. The Diocese of Rochester was never timid thereafter about launching drives. In fact, Bishop Hickey decided to conduct a campaign for funds yearly; and he would have done so had he not succeeded, in 1919, in affiliating the R.C.C.A.A. with the Rochester Community Chest.[73] When, at length, the New York State Council of Catholic Charities (known after 1933 as the N. Y. State Catholic Welfare Committee and after 1966 as the New York State Catholic Committee) was formally established on January 30, 1918, the Bishop of Rochester naturally played a prominent part in its activities.[74]

Bishop Hickey would have been the first to admit that his success with Catholic Charities had stemmed from the assistance of many loyal helpers. The assistance, for example, of generous laymen like J. Adam Kreag, "godfather of the Rochester Catholic Charities", and Philip H. Yawman (1839-1921), president of Yawman and Erbe, and "grandfather" of Catholic Charities. The assistance of generous priests, like Father William E. Cowen (1878-1961), of St. Bernard's Seminary; Father Augustine M. O'Neill, pastor of Immaculate Conception Church; and Father Jacob Staub, pastor of Holy Redeemer Church.

Father O'Neill, while not a trained sociologist, was a sound theoretician of philanthropy. In 1918, he was elected president of the New York State Conference of Charities and Correction.[75]

Father Jacob Staub, on the other hand, epitomized the practical philanthropist. Jacob Staub (1865-1933) had established, in 1905, Concordia Hall, a model parish recreational center adjacent to his parish church, Most Holy Redeemer. Thereafter, Staub's name figured in most of the progressive welfare movements of the city. Only in 1919 did he retire from the active management of the social welfare department of the R.C.C.A.A. which he had founded and developed. He had meanwhile become so well known for his connection with the Relief Center that when, on April 26, 1917, the Windthorst Study Circle of the parish gathered to honor him, their printed program paid him the following homespun tribute:

> Everybody works poor Father
> At the Charity Guild.
> You should see them gather,
> Telling their tales of woe.
> Some want shoes and stockings,

Others look for coal,
Everybody looks for Father
From morn till night.

His store is most surprising
Down on Andrews Street,
One can buy a hairpin
Or shoes for any feet.
You can get a dresser
Or an automobile,
Carpets, rugs or washtubs
And get them cheap.

A slight, intense, but cheerful man was Jacob Staub, impatient of timidity and red tape, and not afraid to soil his hands. It was not surprising that he was later associated with Professor Meyer Jacobstein in the attempt to settle the building trades and shoe strikes that plagued Rochester after World War I; for he had always championed the underdog and the man who cried out for social justice. Father Jacob Staub can be called, without exaggeration, the Saint Vincent de Paul of the Rochester Diocese.[76]

3. The First World War.

Much of the organizational work of Rochester's Catholic charities took place under the shadow of World War I. Long before that European storm broke upon America, the second Bishop of Rochester had had a brush with it in the Europe in which it originated.

Thomas F. Hickey's first episcopal trip to Europe took place in 1907, when he went as Bishop McQuaid's vicar general to report to the pope on the condition of the Diocese. Other destinations on this extensive journey had been Palestine, Lourdes, and his ancestral city, Tipperary.[77] When he went to Rome a second time to report, in 1914, it was as the head of the Diocese of Rochester.

The Bishop prepared carefully for this official trip. In order to obtain the data for his formal report on the state of his diocese, he spent late 1913 and early 1914 conducting a visitation of all diocesan parishes.[78] Then, on June 9, 1914, he presided over his clergy, assembled in the Cathedral, in the Third Synod of the Rochester Diocese—the first during his own regime, and the first since McQuaid's Second Synod in 1887. Part of its sacramental legislation, as we have already noted, dealt with the changes made by St. Pius X in the age for first Communion, and with the matter of frequent Communion. Following the Synod, Bishop Hickey named several new deans and diocesan officials.

Thus equipped with data and legislation, the Bishop sailed for Europe on July 1, 1914, aboard the S.S. "Ivernia." He was one of a group of some sixty Catholic pilgrims, clerical and lay, from several dioceses. A number of Rochester priests accompanied him, among them Father J. Francis O'Hern, Rector of St. Patrick's Cathedral; Reverend Doctor John Francis Goggin, a professor at St. Bernard's Seminary; and Father George V. Burns, pastor of Sacred Heart parish. Italy was the first country on the itinerary. After that, most of the pilgrims were scheduled to move north to Vienna, Berlin, Paris, and London, and to sail for home on August 26th from Queenstown, Ireland.

The schedule was observed, point by point, during the first lap of the journey. Bishop Hickey had his audience with Pope St. Pius X on July 23rd; and subsequently the Holy Father received the whole group of American pilgrims. Part of his business at the Vatican was to request the rank of domestic prelate for Father Dennis J. Curran, his vicar general, and for Father James J. Hartley, the rector of St. Bernard's Seminary. The request was readily granted. Then the travelers began to move north on the rest of their trip.

But the journey was soon forced to detour, and ended up in an anti-climax. On June 28th, a fanatical Serbian had assassinated Archduke Franz Ferdinand, the heir to the Austrian throne. One month later Austria-Hungary declared war on Serbia; and this was only the beginning of the tumult. Germany declared war on Russia on August 1st, and on France on August 3rd. On August 4th, German armies invaded Belgium, and Britain declared war on Germany. Europe suddenly lost its attraction for tourists. The voyagers from Rochester had apparently cancelled their visit to Vienna and Berlin soon after the assassination, and had struck out for France. But they reached the Franco-Italian frontier the very day that Belgium was invaded.

Our travellers now passed through a period of inconvenience and anxiety. Railroad schedules were of course in great disarray, and they had difficulty getting transportation out of both Basel, Switzerland, and Belfort, France, since their route west lay across the lower fringe of embattled Alsace, and at station stops along the way they saw French casualties just brought down from the field of battle. At Paris and at London they experienced similar delays in securing ocean passage because of the disruption of transatlantic shipping. On August 20th, they were saddened to learn of the death of the saintly Holy Father—a death no doubt hastened by the shock of this widespread conflict.

As if these complications were not enough, Father O'Hern fell ill in Paris; and since he had not recovered by the time the others were due to leave, he was obliged to stay on, and arrived home only late in October.

The Catholics of Rochester had meanwhile been concerned about the welfare of the Bishop and his companions. It was therefore with double joy that a large crowd of them greeted Hickey at the Rochester depot on September 11th, and paraded him in triumph to the Cathedral. He had finally docked at Boston on the S.S. "Laconia", along with a record shipload of 5,370 fugitives from war. however, the Bishop did not dwell on the terrible struggle that night in the Cathedral, but simply said, with deep feeling, "War is terrible. *We* comprehend what it means." He urged all to accept loyally the policy of strict neutrality proclaimed by President Woodrow Wilson. Of the late Pope, this holy man with whom he had conversed a scant six weeks before, Hickey spoke very tenderly. But a new pope had already been chosen to succeed him, so Catholics, he reminded them, should now look to the new Holy Father for guidance: "Pope Pius X is dead; Benedict XV reigns; the papacy still lives!"[79]

When St. Pius died in August, Father Curran, the vicar general, in the absence of the Bishop, had ordered that memorial Masses be celebrated for him in all the parishes. On returning from Europe, Bishop Hickey issued a pastoral letter on the deceased Pope and cabled congratulations to his successor. Pope Benedict replied, blessing all the faithful of the Rochester Diocese. Hickey also ordered the holding of a *Te Deum* service in honor of the new pontiff on October 4th. But with a mind on the war, he further prescribed two devotions on behalf of world peace: a special prayer to be recited by priests during each Mass; and exposition of the Blessed Sacrament on each Friday of that October.[80]

It was not always easy to observe Thomas F. Hickey's injunction to maintain a "strict neutrality", for most of his diocesans retained strong attachments to the European lands of their birth or ancestral origin. Of course, the German invasion of "little Belgium" evoked a powerful wave of sympathy from most Americans. Rochester's Belgians were naturally racked with grief, and they received strong assurances of sympathy from their non-Belgian fellow citizens. The first twenty-seven recruits to leave Rochester for the European front were parishioners of Our Lady of Victory Church. A Belgian Rochesterian also became the city's first military chaplain in Europe. Father Prosper P. Libert, a priest who taught at St. Bernard's Seminary, was vacationing in his native land at the outbreak of hostilities. When war was declared, he asked and received permission to remain in Belgium as a chaplain to the Belgian forces. That same autumn, the pastor of Our Lady of Victory, Belgian-born Father Alphonse Notebaert, organized a citywide drive for Belgian relief.[81]

American papers—including even the Rochester *Catholic Journal* —continued for some months to give fuller publicity to German wartime operations than to those of the Allies. Presumably this was because German propaganda was at that stage better organized. German-Americans on the whole were inclined to blame England for the existing state of affairs. But if Rochester's German Catholics were pro-German in this sense, they were unwilling to be considered un-American. It was Catholic German-Americans of Rochester who now led the way in setting up new flagpoles at Catholic institutions. When the flagpoles were dedicated, strong sentiments of American patriotism were voiced —as, for instance, at the dedication of the flagstaff of Holy Family School on October 11, 1916. A still more pointed gesture was the blessing of a new flagstaff at St. Bernard's Seminary on the same day. It had been erected with donations from the young priests of the city who were of German antecedents.[82]

There was, of course, something a little self-conscious about these flag-floating gestures. But under the circumstances, self-consciousness was easily understandable. Especially after Germany began its U-boat warfare and, on May 7, 1915, sank the liner "Lusitania"—with three Rochesterians on board—German-Americans as well as German nationals became the object of increasingly irrational suspicion across the nation. As German-born Father Dietrich Laurenzis of Holy Family parish later wrote: "A 'devilish' hatred against the Germans whom they called 'the Hun' was created by ignorant people all over the U.S. And they call themselves a Christian nation!" To cite a rather comic example, there was the case of the pastor's parrot at Our Lady of Perpetual Help Church. Father John P. Schellhorn, himself a native of Rochester's "Dutchtown", had trained his parrot—surely with no subversive intent—to cry *"Hoch der Kaiser!"* ("Hurrah for the Kaiser!"). One day Frances, his housekeeper, set the cage out on the back porch to give the bird a breath of fresh air. Polly, prompted by some minor devil, soon began to shriek: *"Hoch der Kaiser!"* in an all-too-human voice. Frances rushed out, snatched the cage, brought it into the house, and slammed the door. What would have been a capital joke before 1914 might now have caused an ugly incident.

Some more recent immigrants from the belligerent countries returned home voluntarily, or were called back, to serve in their nation's forces. We have already mentioned the Belgian group. Hosts of Italians —1,700 from Monroe County alone—sailed away to fight for Italy after Italy declared war on Austria on May 24, 1915. Plans were laid that same year for an international Polish Legion. Eventually, 248 Rochester Poles enlisted in this group. The majority of the servicemen from St. Hyacinth's Polish parish in Auburn were members of the same outfit. The Polish Legion did not move across the Atlantic until December, 1917 (three Poles from Rochester were in the first contingent: Lieut. Ladislaus Czaban; Lieut. Thaddaeus Gedgowd; and Sgt. John Pospula). Many of the Legion's soldiers served in Poland after the War, under General Joseph Haller, during the months when order was being reestablished in the new Republic of Poland.[83]

Woodrow Wilson's attempt to maintain national neutrality had merited the gratitude of the American people, and the pro-Wilson slogan "He kept us out of war" was no doubt effective in winning him re-election in 1916. But circumstances finally demanded that even Wilson abandon his neutralist stand. On April 7, 1917, he made the dramatic announcement that a state of war existed between our country and Germany.

Just a few days before the President's announcement, when the declaration of war was presently expected, Bishop Hickey had publicly declared to Mayor Hiram W. Edgerton the attitude of his Catholic flock. "No true American," said the Bishop, "is eager for war; but should it come, no true American will fail in his duty to his Country. It is then with feelings of deepest pride that I make known to you, the chief executive of our City, the attitude of the Bishop, priests and people of the diocese of Rochester in the matter of loyalty and obedience of [*sic*] our country and its President. Representing fourteen nations of the world, the Catholics of our diocese under the guidance and direction of Bishop and priests hold allegiance to but one flag and one leader—the Stars and Stripes and the President of the United States. This is no mere sentiment but a patriotism and loyalty arising from the dictates of conscience according to which we recognize and obey the lawfully constituted authority of our Country."[84]

What he had declared before that ominous April 7th, the Bishop later reaffirmed on more than one occasion. On April 15th, at a public ceremony sponsored by the Knights of Columbus at the corner of Main Street and East Avenue, he blessed a flag that was about to be unfurled. In the address which followed, Hickey promised to the banner, as the symbol of our nation, the fealty of his flock. "I pledge to you in peace and war, love, loyalty and devotion for myself, my two hundred priests, and for one hundred and seventy thousand souls who claim my spiritual parental care . . . May God bless the Republic of the United States!"[85] Then on the Fourth of July, the Bishop took part in a great Independence Day rally held at Exposition Park. He gave the benediction at the end of the demonstration.[86] Nor did the Bishop of Rochester announce his vows of loyalty to Rochesterians alone. He joined his voice with that of the other American Catholic bishops, in the official letter sent by the hierarchy to President Wilson in April, 1917.

Our atomic age is more cynical, and generally more questioning in its attitude toward armed defense and civil authority. It is harder for us today to comprehend the patriotic feeling, naive perhaps but splendidly idealistic, that gripped the Americans of 1917. Swept on by this wave of devotion to the cause, Catholic and non-Catholic alike took part in the gigantic effort to turn our non-military nation, at least for the time being, into a military power, so that the world might be made "safe for democracy."

One large item on the agenda was the four "Liberty Loans"— drives to sell government bonds for financing wartime expenditures. Bishop Hickey naturally backed these campaigns to the full, and made a very special appeal regarding the Third Liberty Loan.[87] One of the features of the drives was the appearance, at bond rallies, of boards of able local speakers, called, by the publicist George Creel who created them, the "Four-Minute Men." Catholic priests were usually included in these speaking committees throughout the Diocese along with prominent Catholic laymen.[88] But parishes also bought bonds. For instance, Rochester's Immaculate Conception Church, had soon invested $5,000.00 of its parochial funds in war bonds. This parish not only pioneered parochial bond-buying in the Rochester Diocese; it is said to have been the first church in the country to do so. Subsequently this same parish took out additional bonds, to the grand total of $46,-000.00[89] Meanwhile, in Immaculate Conception School, as in the other parochial schools of the Diocese, the children were urged to purchase war savings stamps and thrift stamps.

Now that the Army Nursing Corps had begun to flourish, and the American Red Cross had expanded across the country, there was no need to employ Catholic nuns as nurses. But Red Cross, as the "Greatest Mother in the World" offered an even better opportunity than had existed in previous wars for American laywomen to assist in relief work. The women of every community could participate in sewing, knitting and bandage-making under Red Cross auspices, whether at home, in the Red Cross centers, or in parish halls. Committees of women also arranged to greet the troop trains as they halted in railway stations large and small, with gifts of tobacco, candy and notions. At Mount Carmel in Rochester, a group of young women was organized not only to distribute gifts of this sort, but to pray regularly for "our doughboys."

Supplying the needs of warfare naturally implied some self-denial at home. Coal was chronically insufficient, hence national fuel conservation had to be inaugurated in 1917-1918. Food was short, too, so on January 26, 1918, the federal Food Administrator, Herbert C. Hoover, launched a food-conservation campaign. By then housewives had already begun to use "substitute" foods. Hoover asked for a voluntary observance of wheatless Mondays and Wednesdays, meatless Tuesdays, pork-less Thursdays and Saturdays; and for the use of the "Victory loaves"—bread made from grains other than wheat. On July 1, 1918, sugar was rationed: no person was permitted more than two pounds per month. No wonder the verb "to Hooverize" caught on as a synonym for "to conserve food." Of course, the food shortage was somewhat offset by the produce of the "war gardens" that many citizens took to cultivating. And along with the campaign on food-saving, health authorities declared public war on the housefly as a source of contagion. "Flyless Week" was observed in the spring of 1918, during which movie theaters showed educational "anti-fly" slides between reels, and Boy Scouts dutifully distributed fly swatters to use against this other airborne enemy.

To a certain extent, the impulsive patriotism backfired. From swatting at flies, Americans all too frequently turned to swatting at everything and everybody considered Germanic. At times American chauvinism led to absurd extremes. Thus the title of the comic strip, "The Katzenjammer Kids" was timidly amended to the more *Yankee* "Shenanigan Kids." Sauerkraut was rebaptized "Liberty Cabbage". There was even an attempt to alter the name "German measles" to "Liberty measles"! Dr. Joseph Roby, Rochester's acting health officer, treated this latter effort with the amused scorn that it deserved; but even his witty reply was properly anti-Germanic. " 'Liberty', he said, "is altogether too good a word to attach to any disease, and the disease is nowhere near bad enough to be called German."[90] More serious still was the rejection out of hand of the German language. The *Catholic Journal* joined Rochester's *Post Express* in commending the Metropolitan Opera of New York for abandoning its German operas.[91] St. Mary's German Catholic parochial school in Dansville now dropped the use of German, and other German parish schools probably followed suit around the same time. So did Rochester Catholic High School and, it seems, all public schools.

It may have been necessary to keep enemy aliens under governmental surveillance during the war months. But even American citizens of German background had to tread lightly lest they rouse suspicions of disloyalty among self-appointed vigilantes. And citizens of impeccably non-German ancestry might also be looked at with jaundiced eye if they were considered too friendly with the German-minded. A good illustration is the case of Father Francis Naughten, pastor of St. Ann's Church, Hornell. As a loyal alumnus of the German Jesuits of Canisius College in Buffalo, he was judged by some to be of dubious patriotism. This impression was as widespread as it was silly, but it prompted Father Naughten to excuse himself from participating with the local "Four Minute Men,"—a role which he decided it was wiser to delegate to his assistant, Father Charles F. Shay. If the misplaced diligence of unofficial detectives did not cause much grave injustice, it was owing largely to the common sense of Mr. John D. Lynn, U. S. Marshall for the seventeen-county district of western New York.[92]

One of the most important effects that the war had on the home front was to bring Catholics into close cooperation with their Protestant and Jewish fellow citizens. Cooperation was particularly strong in the recreational work for the benefit of those in the armed forces. The Knights of Columbus took charge of this nationwide phase of Catholic action, but the general Catholic supervisory agency was the National Catholic War Council, organized August 11-12, 1917 (and reorganized in the following December) to coordinate, under a committee of American bishops, all Catholic efforts bearing on war-created problems.[93]

Early in 1918, the Knights of Columbus had a national drive for the $10 million necessary to sustain their program here and abroad. In Rochester proper, the campaign topped its quota of $100,000.00 by $18,000.00. Bishop Hickey, in Washington on official business on the final day of the drive, telegraphed to the Rochester campaigners a message of commendation from Newton D. Baker, U. S. Secretary of War.[94] With a fund such as this, the national Knights of Columbus was enabled to set up and operate its own recreation "huts". One of these was the K. of C. "hut" opened at Dansville, New York, on December 20, 1918, in connection with the temporary federal hospital established there.[95]

More interesting than the "huts" run by K. of C. personnel—at least from a social point of view—were the recreational projects at

Kodak Park and Mechanics Institute in Rochester, which were experiments in interdenominational collaboration. The Eastman Kodak Company sponsored an Aerial Photography School from February, 1918 to January, 1919, training, in all, some 2,700 servicemen. The recreation "hut" opened for them was apparently unique, in that it was operated not by the K. of C. alone nor by the Y.M.C.A. alone, as was usually the case, but jointly by both. Three secretaries represented the Y.M.C.A.: John A. Wells, Gilbert C. Cox, and Edward R. Foreman; three others, the Knights: Angelo J. Newman, Cyril J. Statt, and Elroy Miller. Father Frank W. Mason, assistant pastor of nearby Sacred Heart Church, was appointed chaplain to the Catholic soldiers. In May, 1918, Bishop Hickey himself gave a four-day mission for the soldiers of the School in Sacred Heart Church. The cooperative arrangement at the "hut" seems to have been amicable and efficient. Angelo Newman, one of the Catholic secretaries, died of pneumonia in October, 1918—a death attributable in large part to his devotion to the duties of his assignment.[96]

The project at Mechanics Institute was smaller. Between May 1, 1918, and January 3, 1919, 761 servicemen were enrolled as students. The K. of C., Y.M.C.A., and Jewish Welfare Board joined hands to provide recreational facilities for them. Father Augustine M. O'Neill, pastor of the nearby Immaculate Conception Church, kept a watchful eye on the Catholic soldier-students. Whenever these men received Holy Communion at the church on Sundays, the parish ladies served them breakfast; and when their barracks finally closed down and they were about to leave town, Miss Katie Hurley and her co-workers treated them to a bountiful farewell supper.[97]

But the major cooperative effort in Rochester was the War Chest of Rochester and Monroe County. After the Red Cross Drive of 1917, the K. of C., the Y.M.C.A., and Jewish Welfare Board had all had their own campaigns for funds. So had the Rochester Catholic Charities. The response had been generous in all cases; but civic leaders saw that this policy, if continued, could become distasteful and inefficient. George Eastman and other leading citizens began to advocate a joint fund for wartime needs. New York, Syracuse, and Columbus, Ohio, had tried such a drive, and with considerable success. As the plan began to crystallize, Bishop Hickey was asked whether Rochester Catholic Charities would go along. The Bishop consulted with his trustees on March 13, 1918, and on March 18th submitted the answer. Catholic Charities *would* go along, and accept a just proportion of the proposed fund—provided that their agency might retain its autonomy. Not only because the projected organization of the War Chest depended on Catholic participation, but also because Mr. Eastman could see no reason to oppose the Bishop's stipulation, the organizing committee accepted the proviso.

Thirty-six organizations in Rochester and Monroe County now joined the War Chest, which in May, 1918, sought incorporation as the "Rochester Patriotic and Community Fund, Inc." The Bishop and twelve Catholic laymen were listed among the incorporators, and Bishop Hickey served as a member of the executive committee. In a mammoth drive held May 20-27, 1918, $3,750,000.00 was the goal, and $4,838,093.00 was pledged. Generous sums were allotted from this fund to Catholic institutions: K. of C., $150,000.00; Catholic Charities Aid Association, $24,267.00; St. Mary's Hospital, St. Ann's Home, St. Elizabeth Guild, and the three local Catholic orphanages, portions of $109,870.00. From all angles, the War Chest proved to be a satisfactory undertaking. The Bishop of Rochester deserves to be remembered not only for his active participation in the Chest but for his part in forming its policy of respecting the autonomy of member institutions. The organization of the Rochester War Chest was widely imitated thereafter in other localities.[98]

But we must not linger unduly long on the home front. While many members of the Diocese of Rochester were supporting the armed forces at home, many more were battling in the trenches to "make the world safe."

As in the case of the nation's earlier wars, many young men had hastened to volunteer in the armed forces upon the declaration of war. The days of '61 and '98 seemed to have returned as the first enlistees were paraded to the trains in their various communities and sent off proudly with a sermon and a sigh. At Dansville, for instance, the citizens gave an ardent patriotic farewell to sixteen accepted men and forty-three recruits. The village fathers of Dansville gathered on the speakers' rostrum; and Father Leo G. Hofschneider, as one of the day's orators, gave the enlistees "words of tender counsel and his fervent blessing." No doubt several of those whom he addressed were members of his parish, St. Mary's, or of St. Patrick's parish. When the parade formed, the twenty-eight local members of the G.A.R. appropriately led the way, bearing a battle-scarred banner of 1861.[99]

Of course, there were not wanting protests on the part of some American mothers, who naturally disliked the thought of their sons' marching off to possible death. The popular pacifist tune re-echoed their maternal grief: "I didn't raise my boy to be a soldier; I brought him up to be my pride and joy." But what had been an acceptable sentiment in the days before we entered the war was no longer suitable afterward. Thus, when some grieving Rochester mothers sought to persuade Father Thomas F. Connors, the pastor of Blessed Sacrament parish, to deter their sons from enlisting, the usually benign Father Connors sternly announced from the pulpit that he would do no such thing. During the period of national neutrality, he reminded his people, he had never in his sermons advocated any warlike measure. But now the nation was at war, and the case was altered. "Patriotism and love of country," he said, "is one thing that the Catholic Church has always taught." He would therefore never discourage enlistment. "We want no cowards—no slackers in this parish . . . When the call comes we want every Catholic young man who can aid his country to respond. Their faith should strengthen and help them. It will take away the fear of death."[100]

Apart from the diocesan men who were professional soldiers, sailors and marines, those who first got into the fray were the federalized units of the National Guard. The 3rd New York Infantry of the Guard had played an uneventful part in General John J. Pershing's Mexican Border Campaign of the summer of 1916. After we entered the European war, the federalized guardsmen were given intensive training, and set foot in France on June 1, 1918, as part of the 108th Infantry, in Major General John F. O'Ryan's 27th Division. There were a good many of Ryan's men, and a good many Catholics who came from the Rochester, Geneva, Auburn, and Elmira areas; and they kept busy from July to November, 1918, hammering away at the Hindenburg Line in the French provinces of Artois and Picardy.[101]

But World War I was not fundamentally a volunteers' war, it was a draftees' war. The national drawing of draft numbers took place on July 20, 1917; and by October the earliest group of the drafted was already engaged in its six-month period of military training. Conscription *imposes* military service. But the conscription law of 1917 was far fairer than that of the Civil War era; and for the most part those drafted accepted their national obligation loyally and discharged it even heroically.

What was particularly interesting was the reaction of the draftees of the later immigrant stock. The Italians especially, who had so often been labeled by American natives as immutably alien, showed as much zeal as those of old Yankee stock for the American cause. Take the case of John Dombrocci of Gates. Mr. Stephen J. Warren, a member of the draft board of Monroe County's District #2, told a reporter in August,

1917, that Dombrocci had appeared before the board and proved to them that he had ample reasons to warrant exemption. But once he had proved his case, he asked that his claim be waived and that he be drafted at once. The board was very impressed. But Dombrocci was just one such case. "You'll find Italians right up to the front," Warren concluded. "We haven't found a slacker among them yet, and we've dealt with a lot of them."[102]

No systematic records were kept of Rochester diocesan service personnel. But the parishes did have their "service flags", and the known totals of their stars present a cross section of diocesan participation.

The Cathedral service flag had acquired 133 stars by April, 1918, and no doubt gained many more afterward. Immaculate Conception Church in Rochester could boast of 361; SS. Peter and Paul, of 130. No doubt Mount Carmel Italian parish also had a large number of soldier-members, but that tally has unfortunately not come down to us. St. Mary's, in Canandaigua (Ontario County), counted 129; St. Mary's, in Dansville (Livingston County), 31. St. Thomas, in Red Creek (Wayne County) had five stars; St. Patrick's, in Aurora (Cayuga County), 18. The flag at Sacred Heart (German) Church, Perkinsville, bore ten stars; that at the mission parish of St. Joseph, Campbell, two stars. (Both parishes are in Steuben County.) St. Cecilia's, Elmira, (Chemung County) listed 100 servicemen; St. James, Waverly (Tioga County), listed 79. And so forth. Furthermore, these soldiers, sailors, marines, merchant marines, Army nurses, and Red Cross employees, represented the same cosmopolitan origins as American Catholicism itself. There were a few old-stock Americans like Major Winthrop Chanler of Geneseo; there were very many of Irish, German, French, Belgian and Holland Dutch stock of the earlier immigrations; and there was a large number from the later immigrant groups: Lithuanians, Poles, and especially Italians.

As there is no record of the whole diocesan service personnel, so there is no complete record of those diocesans who gave their lives for the cause. Because Monroe County kept careful lists, it is possible to state that of the 609 deaths among County servicemen, at least 236 were Catholics, some 43 of them of Italian extraction.[103] One or more Catholic war victims hailed from the following places outside Monroe County: Auburn, Avon, Cato, Corning, Dansville, Elmira, Geneva, Honeoye Falls, Horseheads, Ithaca, Leicester, Lima, Penn Yan, Rexville, Seneca Falls, Stanley, Waterloo, Waverly and Weedsport.

A few of these casualties deserve special mention. John Arthur Sturla, of the 57th Artillery, was mortally wounded on November 8,

1918. He was the only American-born Italian among the Italian war victims from the city of Rochester. His grandfather, Domenico Sturla had been the first Italian to settle in Rochester (1868).[104] Henry A. Milliner, on the other hand, represented the oldest American breed. His great-great-grandfather had been a drummer-boy in the Revolution. Corporal Louis C. Whitman, killed at Belleau Wood, personified the German-Americans among the soldiery. Through his grandmother, the Baroness Emma von Saucken, he was a first cousin once-removed of Field Marshal Paul von Hindenburg, the principal German military leader. Clarence F. Tracy sustained the fighting Irish tradition. He enlisted in November, 1917, giving his age as eighteen. Actually, he was only fifteen; and when he died in the second Battle of the Marne he was only sixteen—the youngest of all the Rochester casualties. Equally touching was the death of Louis Koscielny of St. Stanislaus Parish. He was an immigrant who had joined the Polish Legion in Canada in October, 1917. He was killed in action in France on July 14, 1918. When they were preparing him for burial, his comrades discovered, over his heart and stained with blood, a tiny American flag.

Several diocesan servicemen won special awards for gallantry. The French Croix de Guerre was bestowed posthumously on Frank J. Cullen and Henry A. Milliner. America's Distinguished Service Cross went, also after his death, to Michael Vigliotti (*alias* Vigilterre), an Italian casualty from St. Lucy's Parish, Rochester. At least two living diocesan men received this same decoration. One was Sergeant H. Grover O'Connor of the 78th Division, a native of Hornell and resident of Wayland; the other was Private William Cornelius Coughlin, of the 312th Infantry, who was from Aurora.[105] Major Joseph R. Culkin, M.D., was decorated with the Distinguished Service Medal, on account of his exceptional service at Camp Upton, New Jersey, during the influenza epidemic of 1918.

At the outset of the war, the aforementioned Father Connors, urging his young parishioners to "do their bit" in the service, had promised that Catholic chaplains would be on hand to guide them. Other diocesan pastors were able to make the same pledge, for government regulations in World War I made better provisions for chaplains than ever before. National Catholic authorities assigned to the Rochester Diocese the task of providing a quota of eight chaplains. Actually, ten priests of the diocese eventually received commissions. They were: Fathers Charles J. Bruton (1890-1956); William M. Cassidy (1888-1929); John B. Crowley (1882-1956); Walter J. Donoghue (1889-1962);

John J. Ganey (1885-1946); George T. Jones (1875-1924); George F. Kettell (1887-1945); Arthur A. LeMay (1888-1955); Frank W. Mason (1887-1964); John M. Sellinger (1891-1945).

Chaplains Cassidy, Crowley, and Donoghue were given military appointments within the United States, although Father Donoghue did serve abroad after the war with the Army of Occupation. The other six priests crossed the Atlantic with the American Expeditionary Forces. Three of them, Fathers LeMay, Sellinger and Ganey saw action in the offensives of St. Mihiel and the Meuse-Argonne. Father LeMay, attached to the 64th Infantry, 7th Division, was badly gassed. He won the Purple Heart and Silver Star medals. Father Sellinger (7th Field Artillery, 1st Division), was twice awarded the Silver Star medal. Father Ganey (38th Infantry, 3rd Division) received no military decoration, but those who witnessed his battlefield career agreed that he, too, should have been formally commended for heroism.

While Rochester chaplains were attending to American boys in France, a prominent French army chaplain came to America and to Rochester to communicate the heartfelt thanks of the French people. Abbé Patrice Flynn (1874-   ), the son of an Irish father and a French mother, was a citizen of France who was to become, in 1932, bishop of the French diocese of Nevers. He had spent months in the thick of the war as foot soldier and chaplain, and now his government had entrusted him with this American goodwill tour. During his three-day stay in Rochester (April 15-17, 1918), Abbé Flynn addressed the Chamber of Commerce and thousands of factory workers. Catholic delegations were well represented wherever he held forth, for he was not only highly respected, but spoke eloquent English. At the final civic mass meeting held in his honor, Bishop Hickey, at the request of Mayor Edgerton, voiced the thanks of the city for the inspiring message that Chaplain Flynn had brought to all.[106]

That fall a sadder bond united those in the service and those on the home front: the grave epidemic of Spanish Influenza. This plague had already stricken many of our soldiers abroad. Now, in the late weeks of autumn it swept over America itself like a poisonous wave.

The Rochester Diocese lay in the direct path of the wave. In Rochester itself, by the end of October, 1918, there were 10,000 registered cases of influenza; and by the year's end, 1,100 people had died of the disease or its complications. In some instances whole families were wiped out. Eventually, the grave diggers at Holy Sepulchre Cemetery had to use machines to accomplish their task, so numerous were the burials.

Outside Monroe County, the epidemic also struck hard—at times terribly hard. For instance, the priests at St. Patrick's Church, Seneca Falls, buried twenty-six victims in twenty-four days. Two hundred people died in Elmira and Chemung County.[107] At Corning, seventy-two citizens perished, out of the 3,500 stricken.[108] Auburn lost 133 of its inhabitants to influenza and thirty-five to pneumonia, between October and January. Geneva, somewhat more fortunate, recorded 1,128 cases, thirty-nine deaths. In all these last four communities we may be sure that some of the victims were Catholics. The Fourth Horseman plays no favorites. Not since the cholera days of the mid-1800's had the twelve counties suffered such widespread contagion; not since the cholera days had the care of the afflicted called forth such widespread and, indeed, such heroic devotion. The Rochester Catholic Charities Aid Association was obliged to open, in the E. Frank Brewster residence at 141 Fitzhugh Street, a temporary nursery for children whom the epidemic had deprived of parents. (This was subsequently continued as the Anna M. Wilkin Nursery, on Fulton Avenue.[109]) Two zealous diocesan priests fell prey to the disease: Father Mortimer Nolan, the principal of Rochester Catholic High School; and Father Otto Geiger, of Holy Family Church. At St. Mary's Hospital, the hospital facilities and the strength of Sisters and staff were severely overtaxed. Kindly laywomen, Red Cross nurses, and the Sisters of Rochester's other religious orders also rallied to the need. The School Sisters of Notre Dame were kept busy with the many ailing nuns of their own convents. The Sisters of Mercy, true to their title, delegated several of their number to the public care of the sick. Some from St. Mary's Convent worked among the sick Negroes on Troup Street. Some from Mt. Carmel Convent nursed in the temporary hospital on Davis Street. At Owego, where certain social workers fought shy of visiting the diseased, the Sisters from St. Patrick's Convent bravely undertook their care, winning the praise of their fellow citizens.[110]

The epidemic bore down hardest in Livingston County. A large percentage of the victims were Italians from Mount Morris and Retsof. At the former place, the pastor, muscular Doctor Andrew Breen, dug the mass graves with his own hands. The Rochester Sisters of Mercy sent Sister M. Hilary Carroll to do nursing at the Sonyea Colony for Epileptics. Sisters of St. Joseph from Rochester volunteered to serve in Mount Morris proper. First they nursed in the homes; later on in a theater that had been turned into a temporary hospital. Two of these

Josephite sisters were victims of their own charity. Sister Francis Xavier Byrnes died that fall; Sister St. Mark Quinn, the following March.[111]

Who can describe the explosive joy of Americans on the morning of November 11, 1918, when the definite news of the armistice was bruited across the land? In Rochester proper, the ban placed on school sessions and church services because of the "flu" epidemic—a ban so strange and so trying—had been lifted only the day before. Now even the influenza victims in each community were cheered by the din of bells, sirens, and whistles that rent the air with a greeting to peace. But beneath all the hectic joy there ran a current of grateful prayer. Let one example serve for all. On Armistice Day a slight woman in black handed an envelope to Father J. Francis O'Hern, rector of St. Patrick's Cathedral.[112] On opening it he found the sum of $5.53 and the following note:

To Whom it may Concern:

I have promised to beg the kind people for what little change they can spare as a donation to St. Patrick's Cathedral. As I have promised to do this as soon as peace comes to the world, I trust you will help me in this matter.

Respectfully,
Miss Barsilla Hannah,
Syrian.

Bishop Hickey set aside Thanksgiving Day for the official expression of his diocese's gratitude to God. He celebrated a solemn pontifical Mass in the Cathedral, which had been decorated with festive joy. The Bishop spoke briefly and very feelingly, on the significance of the occasion. But it was Father John Cavanaugh, the forceful president of the University of Notre Dame, who delivered the formal thanksgiving sermon.[113]

The "doughboys", discharged and sent home as soon as possible, were greeted by their fellow citizens with happy adulation. As time passed, the remains of many soldiers who had died in Europe were brought back for reinterment in American soil. Memorial Day, 1919, thus took on a special significance. On that day, for instance, the service flag at Immaculate Conception Church in Rochester, was "demobilized" in a symbolic rite. The Misses Mary and Julia Fennessy were chosen to sing "America"—they had lost two brothers to the cause. And the man who slowly lowered the flag was Private Daniel Hyland. He had surely merited that privilege, with his record number of eighty-nine shrapnel wounds![114]

The great European War caused worldwide suffering. But it proved once more that American Catholics, even the foreign-born, were devoted to their country. It accelerated the Americanization of several immigrant groups. And it taught Rochester Catholics another important lesson in cooperation with those of other faiths in projects of concern to the whole community.

66   **THOMAS F. HICKEY**
Second Bishop of Rochester
1909-1928

67 **FIRST DIOCESAN LAY RETREAT** (1915)
*Organizers: James C. Connolly (front row, third seated
figure from left). James P. B. Duffy (rear row, arrow).*

68 **BISHOP HICKEY** breaks soil for **AQUINAS INSTITUTE** (1924)
*Clergy, left to right: J. Emil Gefell, Arthur A. Hughes (partially
obscured), Walter A. Foery, J. F. O'Hern, Joseph S. Cameron, John
B. Sullivan, John M. Boppel (with valise), John Muckle, Andrew
B. Meehan, John G. Behr, C.SS.R., Sebastian Englert (in fur cap).*

69
MSGR.
DENNIS J. CURRAN,
V.G.

70
MSGR.
MICHAEL J. NOLAN
CHANCELLOR

71
MSGR.
ANDREW B. MEEHAN

72
FATHER
AUGUSTINE M.
O'NEILL

73
FATHER
JACOB F. STAUB

74
SISTER
TERESA MARIE
O'CONNOR, S.S.J.

75
LAWRENCE O.
MURRAY

76
EDWARD J. DUNN

77   **RELIGIOUS PROCESSION** (1917)
        Annunciation Italian Chapel

78   **RECREATION "HUT"** *jointly operated by the Y.M.C.A. and K. of C.*
        for soldiers attending Kodak Aerial Photography School (World War I)

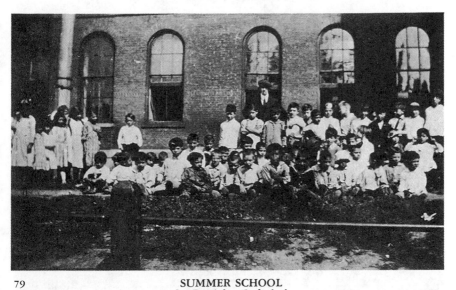

79   SUMMER SCHOOL
St. Patrick's Cathedral
(1919)

80   BISHOP HICKEY, *Roman visit (1924)*
with Fathers J. F. O'HERN and THOMAS F. CONNORS
(seated), J. F. GOGGIN and WALTER A. FOERY (standing)

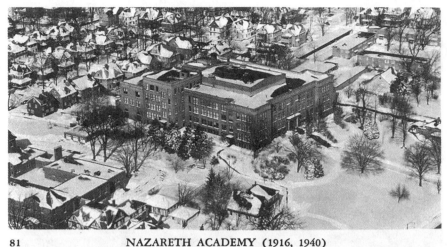

81   NAZARETH ACADEMY (1916, 1940)
(Photo 1960)

82   AQUINAS INSTITUTE (1925)
(Photo 1961)

83   MERCY HIGH SCHOOL (1928, 1941)
and SISTERS of MERCY MOTHERHOUSE (1931)

84 SS. PETER & PAUL CHURCH
(1912)

85   ST. JOHN'S CHURCH
SPENCERPORT
(1915)

86   ST. FRANCIS XAVIER CHURCH
(1915)

87   **SACRED HEART CATHEDRAL**
Parish Church (1927), Pro-Cathedral (1937)
Cathedral (1952), Consecrated 1961

CHAPTER TEN

BISHOP HICKEY: THE LAST DECADE

ARMISTICE Day 1918 may have marked the end of World War I, but it was one thing to conclude worldwide hostilities and another to reestablish worldwide tranquility. Even though President Woodrow Wilson was one of the architects of the Treaty of Versailles of 1919, the United States Senate, by refusing to accept that treaty, deferred until 1921 the signing of peace with the German Republic.

The domestic scene was also disturbed up to 1922 by strikes and a recession. In this troubled atmosphere, doctrinaire Marxism, come into new prominence through the Russian Revolution of 1917, raised its voice. As a result, a hysterical "Red scare" swept across the country, culminating in the highly controversial case of Sacco and Vanzetti. In industry, capitalists used the anti-Bolshevik panic to justify their new campaign against unionization. The revived Knights of the Ku Klux Klan likewise pointed to the wiles of foreign-born agitators as an argument in favor of the new nativism which the Klan was seeking to foment.

Actually, the Federal Government itself was now becoming "nativist" in a sense. Large-scale immigration had resumed after the Armistice, so that in 1920-1921 as many as 800,000 immigrants arrived in this country. But Congress, with the law of May 19, 1921, began a series of enactments which drastically reduced the number admitted into the United States each year. After that date the "Golden Door" that had welcomed so many prospective Americans—and so many Catholics—would never again open quite so wide.

Except in the case of America's farmers, prosperity began to reassert itself in 1922. During the next six years, the national economy zoomed to new heights. Mass-production methods in industry, particularly in the automotive industry, were largely responsible for this great economic upsurge.

Today the 'twenties seem to be remembered best for their discreditable events and trends: the Teapot Dome scandal; the Scopes "Monkey Trial"; the Florida land-boom; the feverish stock speculation; the Ku Klux Klan; the tinseled and polygamous Hollywood stars; the extremes of female "emancipation." These were indeed phenomena of the time, but they meant far less to the average American than the really notable occurrences of the decade. For the 1920's were also marked by many great deeds and events. A large body of progressive legislation was enacted, as, for instance, the program of social welfare effected in New York State by Robert F. Wagner and Alfred E. Smith. Then there was that national Catholic triumph, the great International Eucharistic Congress held in Chicago in June, 1926. And one should never forget two epochal airplane flights whose heroism thrilled the whole world: the flight of Richard E. Byrd and Floyd Bennett over the North Pole in 1926; and the great transatlantic solo flight of Charles A. Lindbergh in 1927.

This is not to say that the decade was free of instability. On the contrary, there was a great deal of giddiness, fostered by sudden wealth and stimulated by "bootleg" liquor. The Church faced many problems engendered by a hectic worldliness on the one hand and, on the other, by the side-effects of the prohibition era.

Prohibition had long been practiced in many localities and its enactment into federal law had long been favored in certain circles. Through the years, the saloon, without a doubt, had ruined many men and impoverished many families. During World War I, the concept of legal prohibition gradually gained ground. In New York State an increasing number of communities voted to go "bone-dry" by virtue of the "local option" allowed to them. For example, in April, 1918, five lesser cities in the Rochester Diocese, Canandaigua, Hornell, Corning, Auburn and Ithaca, voted for local prohibition.[1] Meanwhile, a new amendment to the federal Constitution, the Eighteenth Amendment, was in the process of being ratified by the States. It won quick backing and went into effect on January 16, 1920. By that date the National Prohibition Act (the "Volstead Act") had already been passed to reduce to a minimum the manufacture and sale of alcohol. It defined an alcoholic beverage as one which contained more than one-half of one percent of alcohol.

Enforcement of the Eighteenth Amendment was to prove a difficult, costly, and thankless task. The smuggling and the illicit manufacture of liquor were too tempting to the lawless elements of society, and "bootlegging" often led, at least in the major centers of population, to gangsterism, gang warfare, and bloodshed. Thus what had begun as a "noble experiment" in compulsory social betterment brought on widespread blackmail, violence and murder.

It was in this worldly decade—or at least the first eight years of it—that the essentially unworldly Thomas F. Hickey passed through the last years of his episcopate. He took a dim and somewhat old-fashioned view of the tumult of those days. Still he continued faithfully about his duties, quite aware that however pleasure-mad many Americans had become, that spirit had not yet deeply affected the fundamentally strong faith and goodness of his own flock.

1. EXPANDING FACILITIES.

Population increased somewhat in the twelve counties after the end of the European War. The federal census of 1920 reported 816,000 inhabitants there in 1920; 924,000 in 1930. Diocesan figures—as usual unscientific—gave 172,000 Catholics for 1920 and 208,000 for 1928, the year in which Bishop Hickey retired. Once more, the increase was largest in Rochester and Monroe County. Apart from a modest growth experienced in Tompkins County, the Catholic population in the other counties remained stable.

A rather large number of Italians and Poles immigrated into the Diocese between 1919 and 1921. Protestant agencies engaged in some proselytism among the Italians. Hickey did not deem it necessary, however, to erect any new Italian parishes. But for the Poles he did set up one new parish and one new mission. The parish was that of St. Theresa of the Child Jesus, Rochester, cut off from the southern part of St. Stanislaus parish. Its building, a combination church and school, was dedicated in December, 1928. The Bishop entrusted St. Theresa's to the Polish Conventual Franciscans. The new Polish chapel was St. Stanislaus, opened at Bradford in Steuben County—a rural district into which a number of Polish agricultural families had been moving of late. The first resident rector at Bradford was Father Ignatius Klejna. When he was assigned to the post in 1926, he was given St. Joseph's "Irish" Church, Campbell, as his mission. The Bishop moved Father Klejna elsewhere after a year, and having no other Polish diocesan priest with whom to replace him, he appealed for help to the Polish Conventual Franciscans of Buffalo. These Franciscans continued to administer the Bradford chapel for the next nine years.

The only other "national" church established in the 1920's was St. Nicholas Church, Rochester—a little building dedicated in 1927 for the use of Syrian Catholics, principally of the Melkite (Greek) Rite. The parishioners have apparently never numbered more than 150, but their devotion to their own eastern rite has always made them desire a church of their own. Since there was no Melkite bishop in this country before 1966, they remained subject to the jurisdiction of the bishops of Rochester.[2]

Seven new territorial parishes came into being in the Rochester suburbs between 1919 and 1928. Two of these were in Irondequoit

Township: St. Thomas the Apostle (established 1922, combination church dedicated 1923); and St. Ambrose (established 1921, permanent church-and-school dedicated 1923). In Brighton Township, Our Lady of Lourdes parish dates from 1928. St. Theodore (1924) was wholly in the Town of Gates; Our Lady of Good Counsel (1928) was partially so. In the northern part of Greece, the Bishop founded St. Charles Borromeo parish (1925). He dedicated its temporary church the following year.[3] Up along the Ontario lakefront just west of Irondequoit Bay, the Bishop in 1925 promoted to parochial rank St. Salome's Church, which had been a chapel-of-ease for Sea Breeze, Point Pleasant, and the adjacent farming area since 1908.[4]

Two more parishes round out the number of those set up by Hickey in his latter episcopal years. St. Dominic, Shortsville, (Ontario County), had been a mission since 1885. It was made a full-fledged parish in 1922. On the other hand, the Church of the Epiphany, founded at Sodus (Wayne County) in the same year was a full-fledged parish from the start. The allocation of a parish to Sodus seems to have been motivated to some extent by a criticism voiced against Bishop McQuaid. Wayne County Catholics had long complained that while McQuaid had set up sufficient churches east of Rochester along the route of the New York Central, he had neglected the towns farther to the north along the present Route 104. The church at Sodus was authorized in 1922, but its church was ready for dedication only in 1924. Catholics in this neighborhood were still relatively few, and the early pastors considered the town of Sodus itself to be cold and unsympathetic towards the Church.

While the McQuaidian policy of a combination church-school building was still followed, whenever possible, some of the churches built in the 1920's were simple frame structures inexpensively designed to serve for no more than a couple of decades. But a few of them still remain "on active duty" today.

Not many of the permanent church buildings constructed in the late Hickey regime were of notable architectural merit. Sacred Heart Church deserves particular mention because it became the second cathedral church of the See of Rochester. Charles H. Prindeville, a Chicagoan, was the architect. Bishop Hickey dedicated it in 1927. Smaller but more distinguished was the Church of the Nativity of the Blessed Virgin Mary in Brockport, the work of a Pittsburgh architect, William F. Hutchins. The Bishop dedicated it in the same year as the future cathedral.

The best church designs by Rochester architects came from the firm of Edwin S. Gordon and William V. Madden. They produced the churches of SS. Peter and Paul and Blessed Sacrament Church in Rochester, and St. Stephen's Church in Geneva. Blessed Sacrament and St. Stephen's have unquestionably the finest sanctuary wood sculptures in the whole Diocese. William F. Ross and Company of Cambridge, Massachusetts, were responsible for the designs, and the carving was done by John Kirchmayer, one of the ablest American woodcarvers of the early twentieth century.

But the worthiest group of church structures erected under Bishop Hickey are without doubt those created by the Pittsburgh architectural firm of John T. Comes and John E. Kauzor, who were represented in the Rochester Diocese by supervising architect Charles W. Eldridge of Rochester. Mr. Comes designed the following churches, all still in use: St. Monica, Rochester; St. Francis Xavier, Rochester; Holy Rosary, Rochester; St. John, Spencerport; and St. Mary, Dansville. All were dedicated in 1915, with the exception of Holy Rosary, whose turn came in the following year. While Comes used now Romanesque, now Gothic, now Spanish Renaissance styles in drawing the plans for these structures, he gave to the traditional styles an inventive freshness. His last work in the Diocese was the shrine of the Sacred Heart in St. Stephen's, Geneva, which he designed and John Kirchmayer executed in 1921.

While we are treating ecclesiastical property, we can also mention two other property transactions that the Diocese concluded under Bishop Hickey. One was the purchase, in 1917, of the Ritter residence at 947 East Avenue, to serve as a residence for the bishops of Rochester. An imposing building, at that time only eight years old, the bishop's new house was financed by quotas assigned to each parish in the Diocese. The second property exchange was a sale—the sale of Bishop McQuaid's farm and winery at Hemlock Lake. Bishop Hickey had found the continued operation of the farm, and particularly of the winery, an increasing burden. The many legal controls imposed by national prohibition complicated the manufacture of sacramental wine. Furthermore, the vintners had not yet succeeded in correcting the sourness of the "O-Neh-Da" wines. At all events, Bishop Hickey on May 11, 1925, sold the 527-acre property, the winery, and its stock of wine, to the Society of the Divine Word, a well-known order of missionary priests. Actually, the Society had already assumed control of the farm on July 1, 1924. The price was low—$40,000.00—and the Diocese of Rochester—or rather, St. Bernard's Seminary, to which McQuaid had bequeathed the farm—agreed to generous terms. But eight years later the new owners, not quite happy with their acquisition, considered selling it to the Oblates of St. Francis de Sales. Fortunately, the resale did not go through, for a year later, in December, 1933, the Eighteenth Amendment was repealed. In 1934 the Divine Word Fathers reorganized the winery to produce O-Neh-Da wines on a commercial basis, having now found a way to correct the acidity of the Hemlock grapes.[5]

The arrival of the Society of the Divine Word at Hemlock brought another religious order of men into the Diocese. As is evident, Bishop Hickey was more willing than his predecessor to welcome new religious communities. As early as 1913, he had accepted a member of the Congregation of the Sacred Hearts as assistant pastor of Our Lady of Victory Franco-Belgian Church. This priest, Father Camiel Van der Meulen (1868-1955) subsequently became pastor there after the death of Father Alphonse Notebaert in 1927; and the parish has since that time been in the hands of the Fathers of the Sacred Hearts. We have already noted that the Bishop later called on the Polish Franciscan Conventuals to assist him in the Polish apostolate. In 1926, one year before he commissioned them to found St. Theresa Church in Rochester, he had entrusted to their pastoral care St. Hyacinth Church, Auburn, up to then administered by diocesan clergy. Conventual friars were also given the care of the Bradford mission, as we have already noted. In 1928, Hickey welcomed into the Diocese members of a teaching order, the Congregation of St. Basil. At the Bishop's request, the superior in Toronto assigned six Basilian fathers to the staff of Aquinas Institute, where they joined the current faculty, a composite of diocesan priests, sisters, and laymen.

Bishop McQuaid surely would have been less hesitant about welcoming *teaching* orders like the Basilians, or seminaries of religious, such as the Divine Word Fathers eventually established at Conesus. But consigning diocesan *parishes* to religious orders was quite another thing, and McQuaid had always been against it. If Bishop Hickey changed this diocesan policy, it was largely because he had no alternative.

Three new communities of nuns entered the Diocese under Hickey after World War I. Sisters of the Third Franciscan Order of Minor Conventuals assumed the direction of Mercy Hospital, Auburn, in 1919, as we have already pointed out. In 1926, the Missionary Servants of the Most Blessed Trinity opened a "cenacle" or convent in Holy Family parish, Rochester. (The Trinitarian sisters, established at Holy Trinity, Alabama, in 1909, engage in home visitation, catechetics and recreational work in underprivileged neighborhoods.) In 1928, the school at St. Theresa's Polish church, Rochester, was consigned to the Polish-speaking Franciscan Sisters of Saint Joseph, whose motherhouse is at Hamburg, New York.

Bishop Hickey of course continued to open new parochial schools whenever circumstances permitted. Seven of these came into being during his last decade in office: one at St. John's, Spencerport, Monroe County; the rest in suburban Rochester. Of the recently established suburban parishes, only two—Our Lady of Good Counsel and Our Lady of Lourdes—were unable to undertake parish schools, at least for the nonce. Of the seven new schools, three were committed to the Sisters of St. Joseph (St. Ambrose, St. Theodore, and St. John, Spencerport); and three (St. Salome, St. Charles, and St. Thomas the Apostle) to the Sisters of Mercy. Two Sisters of Mercy were also appointed to the faculty of Aquinas Institute in 1921, at the request of the Bishop.

Another evidence of Bishop Hickey's friendliness towards the Mercy community was the firm backing he gave to Reverend Mother M. Irene Considine in her plans for a girls' high school and new motherhouse. Planning began in 1923. The Bishop broke soil for the projected high school on the Blossom Road property, Town of Brighton, in November, 1927. Our Lady of Mercy High School, swung open its doors to eighty freshmen on September 8, 1928.[6]

The Bishop's interest in the Sisters of St. Joseph nevertheless occupied a primary place. He had a justifiably high regard for the talents and wisdom of Reverend Mother Sylvester Tindell, who directed the community from 1921 to 1939. The project of a new motherhouse, which was completed on East Avenue near Pittsford in summer 1928, engaged his active attention.[7] Doubtless he was even happier when the Sisters opened Nazareth College of Rochester on September 24, 1924. For this foundation represented the complete flowering of the educational apostolate which Bishop McQuaid had entrusted to his Josephite sisterhood. The College began unpretentiously in the former Rouse residence at 981 Lake Avenue—the "Glass House" (so called from its glassed-in veranda)—adjacent to Nazareth Academy. Sister Teresa Marie O'Connor was dean, and the initial faculty comprised three nuns and two priests. There were twenty-six girls in the pioneer class. Fifteen of them were graduated in June, 1928, at the first and last commencement held in the "Glass House." Hickey was still at the helm of the Diocese when this graduation took place. It was also with his permission that the College moved, that same summer, into the former motherhouse on Augustine Street, lately vacated when the new motherhouse was opened at Pittsford. Nazareth College had meanwhile been incorporated by a state law signed in April, 1925, by Governor Alfred E. Smith.[8]

More directly under the control of the Bishop than either Mercy High or Nazareth College were St. Bernard's Seminary and Rochester Catholic High School. It was on his own initiative that Hickey undertook to re-finance the seminary and to give the high school a new home, Aquinas Institute. Both of these accomplishments must therefore be inscribed high in the list of his personal achievements.

Knowing well the special solicitude which Bishop McQuaid had had for his two seminaries, Thomas F. Hickey kept their needs clearly in view. He continued the custom McQuaid had inaugurated of taking up an annual diocesan-wide collection for seminary education. Here the only change he made was to replace, in 1922, the traditional door-to-door solicitation with an envelope collection.[9] Towards the end of his episcopal career he expressed his hope that the minor seminary might be provided with a more adequate home.[10]

Even though he was prevented from building new quarters for St. Andrew's Seminary, in 1919 he made a very positive contribution to the stability of St. Bernard's by authorizing a drive to cancel the large debt which that institution had carried since the death of McQuaid.

Hickey first explained the need in a circular addressed to his priests on January 16, 1919. His predecessor had had to borrow heavily to finance the seminary buildings dedicated in 1908; and in 1918 the debt still amounted to $225,000.00, of which $177,153.00 was in notes and mortgages. The war and many other concerns had thus far prevented Bishop Hickey from doing much about this debt, beyond accepting (with pleasure) the sum of $55,000.00 pledged by the priests to the Seminary in July, 1918, on the occasion of the golden jubilee of the Diocese. Now the Bishop launched a drive for $100,000.00 during "Jubilee Testimonial Week", January 26-February 10, 1919. Well organized, this debt-cancellation campaign brought in pledges for $194,-000.00—$17,000.00 above the amount of the debts in notes and mortgages.[11] The ready response was a triumph for the Bishop, and proved once more how devoted were the people of the Rochester Diocese to the cause of their seminaries.

We have already indicated that Rochester Catholic High School, which Hickey himself had founded in 1905 as Cathedral High School, had ceased to be coeducational when Nazareth Academy occupied its Lake Avenue building in 1916. The departure of the girls made room temporarily for more boy students, but the erection of a new building for the High School could not be postponed indefinitely. As early as 1920, Bishop Hickey told the alumni of Catholic High that he wanted very much to establish a Catholic college in Rochester, but that a boys' high school came first on the agenda, and "in the not distant future."[12] Two years later, the Bishop engineered the passage of a State law which recognized the educational establishment called "The Aquinas Institute of Rochester," and granted to it the right not only to give academic instruction but also "to conduct a college or university of higher learning . . . to confer literary, scientific, technical and professional degrees and in testimony thereof award certificates and diplomas . . ." The bill passed on March 16, 1922, and was signed into a law by Governor Nathan L. Miller.[13]

Rochester Catholic High School was thus incorporated under a new name. From November 9-19, 1923, the Bishop held throughout Monroe County a drive for the biggest single sum ever sought by the diocese thus far: $650,000.00. Once again, the response was excellent —$919,152.42 was pledged.[14]

Land for the new Aquinas Institute was purchased from the Sisters of St. Joseph. It was a parcel of their large motherhouse property on Augustine Street—the section facing on Dewey Avenue. Here the Bishop ceremoniously turned over the first soil on the feast of St. Thomas Aquinas, March 7, 1924.[15] J. Foster Warner was the architect of the new plant, which eventually cost $720,000.00 unfurnished. Aquinas Institute opened as a school on September 8, 1925, with an initial student body of 850 boys. Formal dedication took place on September 29th. The officiant was Cardinal Patrick Hayes, Archbishop of New York. Positions of honor in the large crowd of spectators were occupied by the Bishop of Rochester and six other bishops. Not since the consecration of the Cathedral in 1898 had a diocesan dedication been resplendent with so much prelatial purple.[16]

If Bishop Hickey deserves special credit for having founded the Cathedral High School and carried it through to this notable conclusion, he also deserves special credit for his part in another important venture in religious education—the released-time arrangement in the public schools of Rochester and New York State.

In January, 1920, the Rochester Board of Education passed a resolution permitting public school children to be released, if their parents so requested, for one period a week, during which they would attend religious instructions given by official representatives of their own religious denominations.[17] Rochester was the first city in the State to take this step. It went into effect on February 6th, and kinks in the program were ironed out as it progressed. Gradually many other upstate communities adopted the "Rochester Plan." To the regret of the Catholics of Auburn, the Auburn Board of Education refused to follow suit in 1923. But by 1933 released-time had been accepted by six other communities within the Diocese: Geneva (1924); Waterloo (1925); Ithaca (1928); Penn Yan (1929); Newark (1932); and Mount Morris. On April 9, 1940, Governor Herbert H. Lehman signed into a law the Coudert-McLaughlin Bill which gave to released-time official status throughout the State. The Rochester Board of Education could well congratulate itself on the part it had played in this interesting and, from a legal point of view, rather delicate development.[18]

The "Rochester Plan" could not have succeeded, of course, without the close cooperation of Rochester's religious denominations. The Catholic authorities had responded, according to Herbert S. Weet, Superintendent of the public schools, "eagerly and in a very wholesome spirit."[19] When first called into consultation on the matter, Bishop Hickey had made a detailed study of the proposal. Then, as soon as the original resolution was adopted, he had initiated a census of the Catholic children attending the local public schools. Within ten days after the beginning of the program, he had over 600 children from Public School No. 18 under released-time instruction. He himself attended the first catechetics class. By the end of 1920, there were 4,200 students coming to the new religious instruction classes. Instructions were given by forty-two priests and five lay persons. When the Trinitarian Sisters came into the Diocese in 1926, they were added to the staff. The Bishop's contribution to the "Rochester Plan" was therefore a substantial one. In fact, Bishop Walter A. Foery of Syracuse, when he delivered the funeral eulogy of Thomas F. Hickey in 1940, did not hesitate to call Hickey's part in the promotion of the Plan the "greatest achievement" of his whole administration.[20]

What had facilitated the Bishop's prompt cooperation was the catechetical program which he had already developed for those children who did not attend parochial schools. Since 1913 the Cathedral had had a strong chapter of the Confraternity of Christian Doctrine, whose staff was made up principally of women who were teachers in the public schools. Catechetics was also one of the programs of the Catholic Charities Guild established in 1912. Even before the official released-time resolution was passed by the Rochester Board of Education, one of the catechists at the Italian parish of Our Lady of Mount Carmel, a former teacher at School No. 18, had persuaded the principal of that school to let the Catholic children off early once a week so that they might be taken to the church for instruction. The Diocese subsequently engaged several experienced catechists for this "Italian Work," on a regular basis, paying them a modest annual salary. Of this group the Misses Catherine C. Connelly, Lily Best, Bertha Martens and Elvira Paolone held the longest service records.

While the priests, sisters, and laity made a contribution of increasing importance, we must not ignore the catechetical work in Rochester proper by students of St. Bernards' Seminary. Since the time of Bishop McQuaid, some of the seminarians had been actively engaged in teaching catechism, first on Sundays, and later on free days as well. When released-time began to expand, the St. Bernard's men were ready and eager to take part in a program of religious instruction which afforded them a practical opportunity to apply the catechetical methods they were learning at the Seminary.

Catechism was also on the agenda of the "summer schools," first inaugurated, as we have already seen, in 1916. But another motive behind the continuance of vacation programs was the need to protect the faith of the Italian children against proselytism through the Protestant vacation programs established in the immigrant neighborhoods. In 1924, the Catholic Women's Club of Rochester assumed the sponsorship of a Catholic summer school, the vacation school conducted by Father George A. Weinmann at Annunciation Mission on Norton Street. The Club paid a salary to the directress; the rest of the staff was volunteer.

Released-time has never been a perfect solution of the problem of how to give to public-school children the doctrinal and moral instruction that public education itself is prevented from providing. If Catholics have been able to derive ampler benefits from the arrangement than some other denominations, it is no doubt due in large part to the long-standing Catholic catechetical tradition.[21]

Some might gently disagree with Bishop Foery's opinion that Hickey's role in developing released-time was his "greatest achievement." They might prefer to apply that label to his role in the foundation of the Rochester Community Chest. And a good case could also be made for this opinion.

Once he had begun the annual drives for the support of the diocesan charities, the Bishop had intended to make them an annual practice. But his experience with the Rochester War Chest had been a pleasant one, and it had persuaded him that the citywide collaboration of charitable agencies was a good thing, provided that the member organizations were not required to give up their autonomy. Now, on January 17, 1919, Hickey was officially informed that a permanent community chest was under consideration. Would the Catholic agencies go along? The Bishop replied with another question: Would the proposed Chest allow Catholic Charities to retain its autonomy? George Eastman, who had seen no objection when the same question was raised relative to the War Chest, saw no objection in this instance. So the Rochester Community Chest was inaugurated with the collaboration of the Catholic diocesan charities organization. Hickey was named to the board of directors and held that office until resignation from the helm of the Diocese in 1928. The Catholic Charities case work department, St. Patrick's and St. Mary's Orphanages, St. Ann's Home, the Wilkin Nursery and the Charles House were soon voted into charter membership in the Chest. This made it unnecessary to renew the annual drives for Catholic funds. All in all, it was a happy development. Not only were Catholic institutions of benevolence provided with adequate financial aid; Catholics also acquired through the arrangement a better sense of "belonging" to the local community. The creative part which Thomas F. Hickey had played in the development of the Rochester Community Chest was by no means forgotten. Oscar W. Kuolt, the initial chairman of the Community Chest, used to point out that George Eastman's intellectual contribution to the Chest had been the idea of "participation"; while Bishop Hickey's had been "autonomy."[22]

Father Jacob Staub resigned the office of director of the Catholic Charity Guild in 1919. The Bishop appointed a full-time director to succeed him. He was a former Army chaplain, Father John B. Crowley (1882-1960); and he assumed his duties in the Catholic Charities office at 25 Exchange Street on August 1st. Mr. William T. Nolan retained the general secretaryship.

The diocesan charities reincorporated on January 22, 1924 as Rochester Catholic Charities. Rochester Catholic Charities now took over the work of the old Catholic Charity Guild, and expanded the program to include adoptions, parole work, immigrant service, work with unwed mothers, and child welfare. It is true that Catholic Charities discontinued the Anna M. Wilkin Nursery in 1925. But the closing of this small foundling home that had been set up during the influenza epidemic was motivated by practical considerations rather than by any failure in management. One of the constant perils in foundling homes is the spread of infectious disease. When six of the infants died in an epidemic it was decided to avoid the possible recurrence of this tragedy by closing the nursery and solving the foundling problem in safer ways. In other forms of social work, the facilities of R.C.C. were expanded. From 1923 to 1926 the Charles House provided clinical services for the neighborhood. In 1924 the Charities board voted to take over the Big Brothers Club which J. Adam Kreag and the Knights of Columbus had conducted for the Italians at Union Street and Central Park. Renamed the Genesee Institute, the Big Brothers Club was reopened as a settlement house under the management of a special committee of which Father Walter A. Foery was priest-in-charge.[23]

Rochester's Council of the Knights of Columbus was an old and relatively active council, but prior to World War I it did not have a real home of its own. In 1919, the Knights took an option on a valuable downtown property at the corner of Chestnut and Lawn Streets, with a view to building an appropriate headquarters. Their drive for funds in 1922 brought in pledges for $576,665.91—an unexpectedly large total. In an optimistic mood, the Knights—or rather the corporation set up for this specific purpose by the Knights— decided to add several stories to the four-story building originally planned. The finished building, they thought, could serve as a self-supporting social and recreational headquarters for general Catholic use. Unfortunately, the funds eventually ran out, and in 1927 only the forlorn and silent skeleton of the structure bore witness to the original dream. Another campaign for funds that year enabled the directors to recommence construction, and the Columbus Civic Center was finally completed in March, 1928.[24]

Another organization interested in social welfare was the Catholic Women's Club of Rochester. Formed in 1919 and incorporated in 1923, this Club enjoyed the special approval of Bishop Hickey, whom it had early invited to be its spiritual director. The Club's program embraced a wide variety of charitable and social welfare projects, including participation in the local interdenominational Big Sister movement. To the diocesan catechetical efforts it made a substantial contribution, and it subsequently pioneered Catholic Girl Scouting on the local scene. The Club also conducted a Catholic girls' camp for over twenty-five years. Around 1919, Mrs. Mary F. Nier, matron of the St. Elizabeth Guild House in Rochester, had inaugurated a small camp for Catholic women at Menteith's Point, Canandaigua Lake. It was called Camp Madonna. In 1923, the Women's Club purchased the camp and continued to operate it along the same lines. By 1928, however, the Club began to make provision for little girl campers; and from 1930 on Camp Madonna was conducted solely as a girls' camp. It was never a large undertaking and no more than forty youngsters could be accommodated at each encampment. But in the period from 1930 to the date of its discontinuance (February 1, 1957) Camp Madonna made a worthwhile contribution to youth work in the Diocese.[25]

A camp for boys had meanwhile been established in 1926 at Mc-Pherson's Point on Conesus Lake. It was started in a rented cottage by two enterprising students at St. Bernard's Seminary, Gerald C. Lambert and Eugene B. Hudson. One of those who admired and approved of their efforts was Mr. Max Russer, the prominent Catholic head of a Rochester meat-packing firm. In 1927, to encourage the two camp directors, he purchased and loaned to them for camp use a large lakeside property somewhat to the north of McPherson's Point. Camp Stella Maris has occupied this excellent location ever since. Russer intended to deed the property to the Diocese of Rochester, but his untimely death prevented the fulfillment of that intention. In 1930, however, the Diocese acquired the locale and adopted the camp as one of its official institutions.[26]

Catholic Scouting received the nod of the Bishop of Rochester after the close of the First World War. Boy Scouting had been introduced into the United States as early as 1910. St. Mary's Church in Canandaigua had a troop as early as 1917. The Catholic hierarchy was at first hesitant about this nonsectarian educational movement. But the National Catholic War Council subsequently gave it formal approval, and Pope Benedict XV blessed the efforts to promote Catholic Scouting. In 1919, Bishop Hickey named Father J. Ernest Brophy, the young assistant pastor of Immaculate Conception Church, to the post of director of the Catholic Extension of the Rochester Council of Boy Scouts. When Father Brophy died prematurely in 1920, Father Francis J. Lane, his successor at Immaculate Conception, was designated to continue the work. By March of the following year, Immaculate Conception parish boasted three troops—#68, #69 and #70. And these three units comprised 120 scouts—the largest number of scouts reported by any school or institution in Rochester.[27]

One last beneficent work in which Thomas F. Hickey took a special interest was Holy Sepulchre Cemetery, Rochester. Here he opened a new North Division and erected an office and several new buildings. In 1923 he also established a new policy which required that all future purchasers of graves and lots contribute to the Cemetery's fund for perpetual care.

Meanwhile, three old parochial cemeteries, no longer used for interments, were in danger of being neglected. Mayor Clarence D. Van-Zandt suggested to the Bishop of Rochester that it might be better to transfer the bodies to Holy Sepulchre where they would be better provided for. Hickey agreed, and on April 26, 1925, announced to the Rochester parishes the reasons behind his decision. The burial grounds involved were St. Patrick's Cemetery, on Field Street (the old "Pinnacle" graveyard); St. Boniface Cemetery, on Clinton Avenue, South; and Holy Family Cemetery, on Maple Street. Reinterment was a long process, requiring a full decade to complete. Four thousand bodies had to be removed from the Pinnacle graveyard alone. Thus all—or practically all—the remains of Rochester's Catholics were finally laid at rest in a common ground.[28]

2. CHURCHMAN AND CITIZEN.

During his later, as well as during his earlier years in the episcopal office, Bishop Hickey projected the image of an earnest churchman and a patriotic citizen.

There was never a question about his earnestness as a shepherd. He was essentially a teaching bishop, and especially in the midst of postwar worldliness he spoke out again and again on behalf of eternal principles and eternal aims.

Sermons were the medium he used most frequently for reiterating Christian ideals. An able and popular preacher, doctrinal in his emphasis, and cogent, if not particularly inventive, in his presentation, Thomas Hickey was often invited to preach outside the Diocese on special occasions. At the dedication of a church, for instance; or at the installation of new bishops; or at great funerals, like those of the saintly Bishop Thomas F. Cusack of Albany, or of Cardinal John M. Farley, Archbishop of New York.[29] His wide reputation as an orator stemmed particularly from the annual course of Advent and Lenten sermons which he faithfully delivered from the pulpit of his own cathedral.

Not many of his diocesans were in a position to hear their Bishop preach often. But through his pastoral letters he could reach all. Two basic points which he constantly returned to in these circulars were the need of personal self-denial and the need of strong family life.

Sometimes he alluded to self-denial by focusing his attention on particular abuses, like the revels of New Year's Eve.[30] Sometimes he mentioned it in passing, as when he recommended that those who spent much on pleasure devote a portion of their recreational funds to the support of the seminaries.[31] But the annual Lenten circular was naturally the place to deal specifically with sacrifices. In Hickey's day the rules of fast and abstinence were still strict. It was only in 1918, for example, that the church rules permitted both fish and meat to be taken at the same meal.[32] Breakfast for fasters was stringently limited to "a small piece of bread with a cup of coffee, chocolate, or the like." True, the American "workingman's" privilege permitted laborers and their families to take meat once a day outside of Friday; but "workingman" was interpreted restrictively, so as to exclude from the benefit members of the "liberal professions." Dispensations from either fast or abstinence were given so rarely that Catholics were rather shocked when they were declared. Now, there may have been some American bishops even in those days who placed a more benign interpretation on certain of these regulations. If there were such bishops—and it is not likely—Thomas F. Hickey was surely not of their number. He admitted that self-denial implies pain and that nature shrinks from pain. But he reminded his faithful that the pain of self-abnegation was inescapable to him who would make the necessary choice between the standard of the world and the standard of Christ.[33] These were not comfortable words, but they were true. And there is no reason to believe that until more recent times the exacting Lenten rules were not substantially observed in this country.

Bishop Hickey was likewise most solicitous to preserve strong Catholic family life in a generation that was turning more and more to divorce, contraception, and free love. He hoped and prayed for an increase of vocations to the priesthood and sisterhood.[34] But he realized that most of the faithful would have to fight for heaven on the battlefield of the world. It was with this thought in mind, for example, that he issued his circular on weddings, October 11, 1926. Here he prescribed that six hours of instruction on Catholic doctrine, particularly matrimonial doctrine, be given to non-Catholics who were entering a marriage with Catholic parties. To curtail abuses that had arisen, he instructed pastors that when couples asked to be married on Saturday, their request be granted only if the couple indicated that they would not prolong festivities into Sunday, and thus dissuade members of the wedding party from fulfilling their Sunday Mass obligation. The Bishop also deplored the practice of submitting the bride and groom to an "ordeal of levity" at the church door; and of attaching "objects of any kind" (pans, cans, and old shoes, for instance) to the vehicle in which the newlyweds left the church. In general, he reminded young people that they should choose their partners-for-life seriously and with the greatest care.[35]

Concerned about trends toward greater worldliness on the part of his flock, Bishop Hickey devoted another Lenten pastoral to a strong penitential exhortation. Families should take Lent very seriously, he said, and should omit theater-going, dances, and bridge parties. And "let the young lady who has begun the habit of cigarette smoking stop it, and permanently."[36] Several years before this, in a circular issued in the summer of 1922, he had warned parents to supervise very carefully the summer reading and the summertime companionships of their children. In 1924 he spoke out strongly against a rumored attempt to alter the State law on movie censorship.[37]

The Bishop's strongest statement on Christian family life came in a long pastoral read from the pulpits on January 8, 1928. Here he resumed those points he had so often made before: that each member of a family should frequent the sacraments; that mutual love and obedience should prevail within the bosom of the family; that in recreation, patronage should be withheld from entertainers who "give the people what appeals to them"; that the Holy Family should serve as a model to every Catholic household. Almost with anguish, the Bishop solemnly asserted, "In the name of God, we call upon our people to heed this word of warning and to take the stand of right against the existing dangers to the youth of our day."[38]

Thomas F. Hickey continued to speak on current evils in positive and general terms. Specific controversies he left for those priests who had a gift, or at least a flair, for polemics, like Augustine M. O'Neill, Simon FitzSimons, and the professor of church history at St. Bernard's Seminary, Father Frederick J. Zwierlein, D.Sc.M.H. (Louvain).[39] What we have quoted above will suffice to prove that Hickey was a man of personal conservatism and a strict moralist. What gave his teaching particular force was that he himself was strongly ascetical and unworldly. If he insisted relentlessly that all Christians must bear their crosses, he set a magnificent example by loyally bearing his own.

Bishop Hickey's churchmanship, though it was exercised principally within his diocese, naturally involved him in wider responsibilities towards the Catholic Church in New York State, in the nation, and even across the world.

We have already alluded to the part the Bishop played in the formation of the New York State Catholic Welfare Committee, a consultative association of the State bishops which kept close watch on State laws that had a bearing on religious and charitable matters. On September 29, 1919, over a year after the formation of the State committee, the bishops of the whole United States formed an even broader consultative body called the National Catholic Welfare Council (or, after 1922, the National Catholic Welfare *Conference*). The Welfare Council was largely an outgrowth of the bishops' National Catholic

War Council, in whose ably coordinated wartime work Bishop Hickey had actively participated. The Welfare Council filled a need long felt among the Catholic bishops of the country, for prior to that they had had no permanent forum or clearinghouse for mutual socio-religious problems. It was all the more disconcerting, therefore, when on February 25, 1922, the Holy See, as the result of complaints made by certain of the American bishops, announced the suppression of the N.C.W.C. Fortunately, the majority of the hierarchy protested this action, Bishop Hickey among them, and the Council was spared, to become a model to the hierarchies of other nations.[40] A former Rochesterian, Archbishop Edward J. Hanna of San Francisco, was elected and reelected to the post of chairman of the N.C.W.C. from 1920 until his retirement from the See of San Francisco in 1935. Bishop Hickey himself was never chosen by the hierarchy to hold office on the relatively small executive staff of the Conference.

Thomas F. Hickey showed the normal solicitude for the mission needs of the universal Church. In a circular letter of April 22, 1926, he announced the establishment of a diocesan office of the great international mission-aid organization, the Pontifical Society for the Propagation of the Faith. To the post of diocesan director, he named Father Leo C. Mooney (1894-1964). In another circular dated January 17, 1927, the Bishop stated that he was introducing into the Diocese a second mission-aid society, the Catholic Near East Welfare Association. From the fall of 1928 on, "Mission Sunday" was observed each year throughout the Rochester Diocese.

Hickey's filial devotion to the Bishops of Rome was unwavering. When Cardinal Giacomo della Chiesa was elected pope in 1914, and took the name Benedict XV, the Bishop of Rochester cabled congratulations.[41] During the war, Hickey, on the diocesan level, heartily seconded the conciliatory efforts of this peacemaking pope. On the occasion of Benedict's untimely death in 1922, Bishop Hickey not only celebrated an official diocesan Requiem in his memory, he also wrote a special pastoral circular on the deceased pontiff.[42]

Thomas Hickey never met Benedict XV personally. But he did meet his indomitable successor, Pope Pius XI, on the occasion of his *ad limina* visit to Rome in 1924.

As in 1914, Hickey prepared for this official decennial visit by holding a diocesan synod. The Fourth Synod of Rochester, which took place on May 15, 1924, was content, for the most part, to repeat the legislation of the Third Synod. Certain alterations were necessary, however, in view of the publication in 1918 of a Code of Canon Law applicable to the whole Latin Church. Among the newer specific rules laid down by the Fourth Synod, two dealt with the clergy. Decree #9 forbade priests to attend moving pictures or theatrical performances in any public theater, whether inside or outside the Diocese. Decree #10 forbade assistant pastors to own automobiles, or even to drive automobiles owned by others except in the course of strictly parochial business.[43]

Having completed his quinquennial report—which stated, among other things, that his diocese had a population of 194,578—the Bishop of Rochester sailed for Rome via Germany on Independence Day, 1924. Four leading priests of the Diocese accompanied him: Fathers John Francis O'Hern, Thomas F. Connors, John F. Goggin, and Walter A. Foery.[44] The Bishop had the customary private audience with Pius XI on July 30th. He was thrilled, as he afterward put it, to sit "side by side" with this scholarly, discerning, and—as events would prove—heroic successor of St. Peter. One pleasant and unusual feature of the audience was Hickey's presentation to the Holy Father of a white Corona typewriter. It had been made especially for the Pope by the Corona factory at Groton, New York, where Bishop Hickey had once been the pastor.[45] On the completion of his Roman business, the Bishop traveled north through Florence, Milan, Switzerland, Belgium, Ireland, and England before finally embarking for home.

The homeward trip from Europe was not nearly so eventful as it had been in 1914, although it did have one misadventure. As the Bishop and his party sped up the Hudson Valley towards Rochester, the train narrowly escaped derailment by a landslide. Even though their arrival was delayed three hours, they still found a delegation of Rochester priests and laymen awaiting them at Syracuse; and the 2,000 patient Catholics who greeted the Bishop at the Rochester depot were all the happier to welcome him when they learned of the hazard which had caused the delay. Late though the hour was, the devoted throng paraded Hickey to the Cathedral. After a brief address to the crowd assembled there, the Bishop bestowed the papal blessing. Then he was given another pleasant surprise—a seven-passenger Lincoln sedan, the gift of the priests of the Diocese. He went home in the new car.[46]

A few days later, the Bishop solemnly blessed the purple vesture of three of his priests whom Pius XI, at his request, had named domestic prelates. The three *monsignori* were John Francis O'Hern, the Vicar General; Michael J. Nolan, the Chancellor of the Diocese; and Andrew B. Meehan, the rector of St. Bernard's Seminary. Six years before this, Monsignor Meehan, a devoted churchman and knowledgeable canon lawyer, had declined the appointment to the bishopric of Trenton. It was easier for him to accept this honorary papal prelacy which placed no strain upon his uncertain health.[47]

The 1920's were beset by several problems that veered into the religious: labor relations, prohibition and its consequences, and a resurgent anti-Catholicism. While Bishop Hickey did not often speak out in these matters, he did at times give backing, or at least encouragement, to others who took action; and at times he brought his influence quietly to bear in the search for solutions.

In the early years of the decade an increasing friction between Capital and Labor led to a rash of strikes. Catholics often played a part in these conflicts, for many of them were in the ranks of the aggrieved. But Catholic leaders also participated in the quest for a solution to the underlying problems.

Labor relations were strained in several places throughout the Rochester Diocese. In Retsof, for example, the workers went on strike in 1920 against the management of the International Salt Company. For their guidance, the acting pastor, Father J. Edward Bayer, laid down the ethical rules for strikers prescribed by Pope Leo XIII. "The men" said Father Bayer "are in justice to receive a wage enabling them and their families to live in frugal comfort. Their demands must not be extreme. They must not use violence or force. They ought to settle their difficulty by arbitration."[48]

In Rochester itself, still largely anti-unionist, Labor took occasion of the turmoil to make an all-out drive for unionism. But at the Bausch and Lomb Company, the union organizers were categorized as "reds," and the firm strove to offset the benefits pledged by the unions with matching benefits of their own concession. A like policy was followed by the Eastman Kodak Company.

The greatest trouble, however, was in the shoe, clothing and building trades.

In 1920, the large Rochester shoemaking industry became the center of an inter-union battle. Capital, represented by the Boot and Shoe Manufacturers Association, moved against unionism in general by declaring an open shop. A lockout followed, in 1922-1923, throwing 3,500 workers out of employment. The dispute was never fully settled, and afterwards the city's large shoe industry went into a permanent decline.[49]

Fear of a similar fate had earlier prompted the Clothiers' Exchange to adopt a more realistic policy. In January, 1919, through the instrumentality of Professor Meyer Jacobstein, Messrs. Simon Weil and

Jeremiah Hickey, the chief representatives of the clothing manufacturers, signed an arbitrational agreement with Sidney Hillman, president of the Amalgamated Clothing Workers. After that date the only local tailoring firm that had labor problems was Michaels Stern and Company, which was not a member of the Exchange.

Building contractors made an effort in April, 1919, to thwart union demands for a raise in wages by declaring an open-shop rule. The unions stood firm, and a strike took place during the next two months. An armistice followed, but hostilities recommenced in 1920. Anti-unionist forces in the city now rallied in favor of the contractors. To oppose them, a pro-workers organization was formed, led by Judge Arthur E. Sutherland, two Protestant ministers, William R. Taylor and Paul Moore Strayer, and the pioneering priest of Rochester Catholic Charities, Father Jacob Staub.

Much more dangerous than this ideological war was the violence that erupted on the job between strikers and strikebreakers. Strayer, Staub, and the State and Federal mediators could not prevent serious disorder at the picket line. Mayor Hiram H. Edgerton finally appointed a special "Mayor's Committee" to exhort the embattled parties to submit the case to arbitration. The Committee comprised Judge Adolf J. Rodenbeck, the Reverend W. S. Stone of First Presbyterian Church, and Father Augustine M. O'Neill of Immaculate Conception Church. Fortunately, the Mayor's Committee succeeded in its assignment.

If Bishop Hickey did not become personally involved in these contests for social justice, it was because he knew the Catholic experts involved were performing their task competently. His brother Jeremiah, co-founder of the Hickey-Freeman Company, clothing manufacturers, was one of Rochester's pioneers in achieving amicable labor relations. Attorney Philip H. Donnelly, as counsel for the various locals of the United Shoe Workers of America and the milk drivers' local, had ample opportunity to put Catholic social principles into actual practice.[50] Father J. Edward Bayer (1889-1929), a gifted priest whose career was to be tragically brief, was, as we have indicated in connection with the Retsof strike, well informed on Catholic social doctrine. Fathers O'Neill and Staub we have already described as influential figures in welfare circles. None was so ready to praise Jacob Staub's social sensitivity as Professor Jacobstein, that Jewish scholar of the University of Rochester who contributed so much to management-labor peace in Rochester. When Father Staub died Jacobstein eulogized his sympathy for the needy and his firm adherence to principles.[51]

Before taking leave of the subject of economics we should mention "Father Naughten's Mine"—the copper-mining venture undertaken by the Royal Development Company and actively promoted by the pastor of St. Ann's Church, Hornell, Father Francis J. Naughten.

Only one other case has come to our attention in which a priest of the Diocese of Rochester became an entrepreneur. In 1892 the pastor of St. Mary's Church, Dansville, Father Frederick R. Rauber, played a part, it seems, in the establishment of a Catholic Health Institute in Dansville. This was a "Kneipp Water Cure" sanatorium. Not only the visiting patients but, it would appear, many of the villagers became "addicted" to Father Kneipp's prescription. Old-timers at Dansville can still remember seeing native Dansvillians soberly following Kneipp's prescription to walk barefoot in the dewy morning grass.[52]

If Father Rauber was indeed a promoter in this Dansville enterprise, his business involvement in it must have been minimal. Father Naughten, on the other hand, launched a large-scale operation. His brother, James Naughten, was a mining engineer who lived at Butte, Montana. Father Naughten was not himself a "gambling man." But the thought grew on him that a good copper mine, financed by private stock sales, might earn a welcome income for many Catholic institutions of the Buffalo-Rochester area and for many individual Catholics of slight or moderate means.

When a promising vein of ore had been secured in the Cascade Mountains (at Phelps Ridge, Chelan County, State of Washington), the Royal Development Company, on the basis of its charter of February 5, 1917, began the semi-public sale of stock. Scores of Catholics in western New York excitedly subscribed to shares of the stock, to "royalty certificates," or to "participating contracts;" and the rectory at St. Ann's became a minor New York Stock Exchange. The money collected for stock—over $1.6 million—was carefully invested in government bonds deposited in New York. The Company could use only the income from these bonds, according to its own specific regulations. Thus the original amounts invested in stock remained intact, capable of being returned to the investors should the enterprise be called off. This was not true, of course, of the two types of royalty certificates and the participating contracts. Their income value was based upon actual production, hence they were strictly speculative in character.

Mining operations got under way soon enough, but lost momentum in the late 1920's. The market crash of 1929 certainly did not help the cause, nor did Father Naughten's death in 1930. It eventually transpired that the ore in the mine, while genuine, was of lower grade than had been anticipated. It could still have been mined by other methods, but the cost of those methods would have been much higher than the operating income, and the rules of the company forbade invading the capital sum invested in stock. Therefore in 1940, after much delay and bickering, the stockholders voted to dissolve the Royal Development Company and to return the invested capital to the stock investors. Litigation followed, for possessors of royalty certificates and participating contracts also wanted to be reimbursed. The contest was carried to New York State Supreme Court, in the case of *Maier-Corcoran v. Royal Development Company et al.* But the Court decided, on September 22, 1942, that only holders of the stock itself were entitled to recompense. The corporation was therefore dissolved on April 3, 1948, and in 1949 the depositors were paid off, receiving something more than eighty-five cents on each dollar. Thus ended Father Naughten's noble experiment. If the "little people" who had invested in Royal stock in the hope of reaping a fortune failed to do so, at least they did not suffer much loss through their investment.

What was the view of the Bishop of Rochester regarding the Royal Development undertaking? Quite likely he knew very little about it at the start, so unpublicized were its negotiations. When he became more fully informed, there was not much he could do but tolerate it. Only after the death of Father Naughten did the Diocese of Rochester become directly involved in this Southern Tier enterprise, for Naughten had left a portion of his own large block of stock to Rochester diocesan charities. To this extent, at least, the benevolent, if ill-advised, dream of the Hornell priest—that the Royal Development might benefit diocesan institutions— was realized.[53]

Another "noble experiment" of the Hickey years caused the Bishop graver concern. As we have already noted, national prohibition had been voted into constitutional law with a view to destroying the saloon, so long a bane to countless American families. Many Catholic families, and especially many Irish Catholic families, had suffered greatly because of the abuse of alcoholic drink. There had always been some pastors in the Diocese of Rochester who waged a personal war upon the "Demon Rum."[54] For the most part, however, Catholics of the Rochester Diocese agreed with their fellows throughout the country that it is one thing to embrace temperance or teetotalism voluntarily, and quite another to have it imposed by civil law. Catholics, particularly those raised in a beer-drinking or wine-drinking tradition like the Germans and Italians, were inclined to look upon prohibition either as a Calvinistic invention or a Federal invasion of local or even personal rights, and, in any case, something fundamentally unenforceable. Whatever their reason for objecting to the Eighteenth Amendment, American Catholics were probably no more punctilious than their neighbors in taking occasional advantage of the illegal traffic in alcoholic liquor. But the national bootlegging industry, which by 1926 involved $3.6 billions a year in income, and millions in law enforcement, was in itself a powerful argument against the wisdom of trying to legislate national sobriety.

When the abstemious Bishop Hickey deplored the worldliness of the 1920's, we may be sure that he had in mind the new excesses in social drinking that the prohibition era favored. The Volstead Law also caused him much worry in a particular sphere, that of sacramental wine. Not only was he interested in providing his priests with sufficient sacramental wine in a desiccated nation; he himself, as proprietor of Bishop McQuaid's O-Neh-Da vineyard on Hemlock Lake, was the operator, however reluctantly, of a wine-producing industry. As early as September, 1919, when the War Prohibition Act was still in force, he made inquiries about sacramental wine at the Federal office of Internal Revenue, and reported to Cardinal James Gibbons of Baltimore that he had received the necessary assurances.[55] Under the Volstead Act, the Treasury Department, on October 29, 1919, made special provisions for sacramental wine and the bonding of its producers; however, the regulations were not only intricate but inadequate, and eventually had to be amended.[56] Nor was that all. New York State had its own laws to enforce prohibition, and the Bishop of Rochester was at pains during the next six years to see that Catholic interests were borne in mind when legislation on alcohol came up for consideration in Albany.[57] For instance, a change was made in the State Liquor Tax Law in 1920. Bishop Hickey was largely responsible for the introduction of this measure before the State legislature and played a role in guiding it through.[58]

Anti-Catholicism had diminished considerably by the 1920's; but it still made its presence felt from time to time, now openly, now indirectly. There were two waves of nativist agitation during the Hickey decades: the first, a more anonymous movement of pre-World War I days, led by the publishers of the widely circulated anti-Catholic paper, the *Menace;* the second, the Knights of the Ku Klux Klan, which began in 1915 and reached the peak of its power a decade later.[59]

The *Menace* first appeared in 1911, hurling the old accusation that Catholics were trying to gain political control of the United States. Before a year was up, its Rochester subscribers—ever mounting in numbers—were being fed a regular diet of systematic bigotry. Readers made some attempt to pass on issues of the paper to Catholics, to teach them the "real story" about Roman wiles. Each week, for a while, indignant parishioners at Immaculate Conception Church, Rochester, brought in copies to show their pastor; and when the priests at Sacred Heart Church opened the rectory door, they more than once found an issue of the *Menace* defying them from the stoop.[60]

The *Menace* mentality was doubtless more appealing in the countryside than in the cities of the Diocese. For instance, a "Menace Campaign Committee" circulated a strongly anti-Catholic political letter in Ontario County during the campaign weeks of 1914.[61] Still, Rochester Catholics were not immune to petty attacks by the *Menace*-minded or by associates of another diehard group, the Guardians of Liberty. Sometimes these attacks were directed against the Bishop himself.

A favorite ploy of the *Menace* group was to circulate an oath allegedly taken by Fourth Degree members of the Knights of Columbus. This forgery, which pretended to pledge the Knights to work for the annihilation of "heretics," was actually an adaptation of another well-known forgery first circulated in the seventeenth century.[62] It may have been making the rounds in Rochester during the fall of 1914, for Bishop Hickey in his Columbus Day address to the local council of the K. of C. in that year, denounced the "insidious attack made against Catholics in this country."[63] At any rate, nativist Robert L. Long, sojourning in Rochester in March, 1915, published an editorial in the *American Citizen,* a Boston paper of which he was editor, denouncing the Bishop of Rochester and the St. Elizabeth Guild House which he had just announced his intention to found. The Guild House, Long declared in true *Menace* style, was being organized by men who were for the most part politicians, office holders and liquor dealers. He warned Rochesterians to beware lest the Catholics try to secure support for the Guild from public sources.[64] Robert L. Long was a notorious demagogue, and Bishop Hickey did not dignify his editorial with a reply. But his onslaught on the Guild House and the increasingly anti-Catholic mood of the moment seem to have prompted the Bishop to discontinue the public Holy Name processions in Rochester.[65]

The Bishop had already been caught in the cross fire of a somewhat comparable incident the year before. On February 24, 1913, the Union Ministerial Association of Rochester publicly charged the Diocese of Rochester with officially opposing the appointment of a Reverend Dr. Arthur O. Sykes to the post of assistant director of the State Industrial School at Industry. On February 25th, Hickey wrote an open letter to the president of the Association, the Reverend Dr. James Bishop Thomas, denying the charge. The Catholic protest against Sykes, he said, had been taken "without my knowledge and never received my official sanction." Investigation, furthermore, had proved that the group working against Sykes was small and unrepresentative of Rochester Catholicism, not to say of Catholicism in the Diocese. The Bishop said that he himself endorsed, "as every true American must," non-discrimination in public appointments. Nevertheless, he had always believed, and here restated his belief, that "it is inadvisable to appoint to an administrative office in a state institution a clergyman of any denomination." He announced that he was sending a copy of this open letter to the Governor of the State. What Hickey feared, apparently, was the possibility of a recurrence of religious discrimination in public institutions, against which Bishops Timon and McQuaid had been obliged to fight so strenuously. It seems that Dr. Sykes did not finally receive the administrative appointment at the Industrial School. But he long served as its Protestant chaplain.[66]

Not all the virtue was on the Catholic side, however. Some Catholics were still prone to see bigotry where it did not actually exist. For example, the editors of the Rochester *Catholic Journal* used the word "bigot" too often to be convincing. On one occasion in 1916 the paper applied the term with patent injustice. The *Journal* and the Buffalo *Catholic Union and Times* both declared that a Mr. George M. Neal of Bergen, New York, was a notorious distributor of anti-Catholic literature. The accusation proved to be completely erroneous, so both papers had to retract their charge.[67] Nor did Catholics always turn the other cheek. Around the period of World War I, a Protestant evangelist, the Reverend J. J. Kennedy, pitched his tent on the mall at Glendale Park—a Rochester street—and began a summertime revival. This was in Holy Rosary parish, then a staunchly Irish neighborhood. The rumor soon circulated that Kennedy had been attacking the Catholic Church. The next night a gang of pugnacious "Irishmen" gathered outside the revival tent, sang *"Tipperary"* to drown out the preacher, stoned the tent, and finally cut its ropes so that the canvas fell limp around the large congregation. Nobody inside was hurt, apparently, but all were understandably resentful. Some of the "victims" went so far as to stage a march on Holy Rosary parish, where they pelted the convent with tomatoes and cabbages. The police were called in, but no arrests were made on either side, and the flare-up quickly subsided.[68]

While actual religious conflicts were rare, the fact remains that Catholics as a group were still rated rather low in the estimation of their local Protestant brethren. Certain of the newspapers manifested this unfairness, too, in their editorial attitudes. The Rochester *Democrat and Chronicle* is a special case in point. What paper nowadays would accept an advertisement like the following?

> Wanted—Man to work and drive team; no booze fighter or cigarette smoker or Roman Catholic need apply: State wages with board. H-23, this office.

Yet it appeared in the *Democrat.*[69] And the *Democrat* always seemed ready to print attacks on Catholicism, but reluctant to allow Catholic spokesmen equal time for a rebuttal. At least this was the case until around 1920. Then one day Father John Francis O'Hern, the Vicar General, arranged for a meeting between the editor, Mr. Allen Ross, and the Diocese's principal "champion," Father Frederick J. Zwierlein, Professor of Church History at St. Bernard's Seminary (1881-1960). Father Zwierlein had often submitted corrective letters to the *Democrat* only to be informed: "Sorry, no space." In their interview, he succeeded in convincing Editor Ross that the Catholic side of controversial matters had up to then not been given a fair hearing. At the end of the conversation, Ross agreed that his paper would thereafter accept Catholic replies written by Zwierlein, either as letters or as news articles, provided that they were submitted through the diocesan chancery. And the editor kept his promise.[70]

World War I brought Catholic and non-Catholic closer together as citizens. Denominational divisions were for the time being forgotten, or at least submerged. Only after peace had been renewed could Americans once more afford the luxury of nativism. The Ku Klux Klan recommenced its northward expansion, and by 1922 has established a broad beachhead in New York State itself. Here the Klan did not indulge in the violence it was accused of practicing in the South, but it retained all the Southern Klan's opposition to Catholics, Jews, Negroes, and "foreigners." Fortunately—and this was an encouraging sign of increasing maturity on the part of Americans—city dwellers for the most part not only deplored but denounced the Klan. This was certainly true in Rochester proper.[71] KuKluxism still proved attractive, however, in some rural communities. On July 8, 1923, villagers of Nunda witnessed the first "fiery cross" in Livingston County. The burning of huge wooden crosses was, of course, the trademark of the K.K.K.; and the twelve counties saw many a flaming cross during the months that followed—some "official," others, no doubt, the work of pranksters or independent cranks. There were Klan activities at Henrietta (Monroe County) and Hemlock (Livingston County) in the fall of 1923, with the usual fireworks.[72] In 1925, when Father Daniel O'Rourke arrived to take over the pastorate of the Church of the Epiphany in Sodus, he was greeted by a fiery cross burning across the street from the rectory. There were Klan rallies at Penn Yan in 1926, and at Geneva and Corning in 1927.[73] In all or most of these instances, we should point out, the communities themselves merely tolerated the demonstrations. Those Klansmen who were the leading demonstrators were usually outsiders: the local members were generally chary about exposing their prejudices to their fellow townsmen.

The largest Ku Klux convention in Western New York was the "Konvocation" of the Seventh Province, held September 25-26, 1926, at East Rochester, a village in which the Klan was probably stronger than anywhere else within the diocesan boundaries. Nineteen thousand Klansmen and their wives came flocking from ten neighboring counties into the suburban meadows where their tent-city had been pitched. The violence feared by public authorities failed to materialize, largely because bad weather obliged those "konvoked" to restrict their demonstrations and demagoguery to the camping area. Three crosses were burned at the climax of the affair, one of them fifty feet in height.[74]

The Klan enjoyed a relatively short life in western New York. As a matter of fact, by the time it reached its crest of influence upstate, it was already out of style in the States where it had attained its original strength. One factor that stemmed its growth in New York State was the law of 1923 which required the Klan and comparable societies to file notarized membership lists with the public authorities.[75]

Klan activities were too innocuous in western New York to call for public comment from Bishop Hickey. But he did speak out on a national issue on which the Klan had taken the anti-Catholic side. This was the Compulsory School Law enacted in 1922 in the State of Oregon (*Oregon Laws,* sec. 5259), which insisted that all children in that State be educated at public schools. If allowed to take effect at the scheduled date, 1926, this law would have destroyed all private schools in Oregon, as well as all parochial schools, Catholic or Lutheran. What is more, anti-Catholic groups in the other States were awaiting the opportunity to press for similar legislation in their own legislatures. The matter was therefore one of national significance; and the National Catholic Welfare Conference, as representative of the American Catholic hierarchy, was glad to lend its assistance to Archbishop Alexander Christie of Oregon City in his joint effort with other aggrieved Oregon parties to have the United States Supreme Court declare this Compulsory School Law unconstitutional. The Diocese of Rochester, along with the other dioceses of the New York Province, made a sizable contribution to the "Oregon School Defense Fund."[76] Fortunately, the Supreme Court did declare the law unconstitutional in a memorable decision delivered on June 1, 1925, several months before this rankly discriminatory measure was scheduled to take effect.[77]

Since the N.C.W.C. had assumed charge of the campaign against the Oregon law, the Bishop of Rochester was not called upon to take a more active part in it. But in the midst of this national campaign for educational justice, Hickey was obliged to answer a Rochester voice raised in praise of the Oregon legislation. It was the voice of the Reverend Orlo J. Price, a local minister, who expressed this view in the November 22, 1922 issue of the *Bulletin of the Rochester Federation of Churches.* Parochial schools, Mr. Price flatly declared, were inadequate. Their teachers did not meet full requirements, and the training which they gave in citizenship was substandard. Parochial school instruction, he concluded, was not of the quality "that free American citizens are entitled to."

Now a reasoned critique of parochial schools was then and always would remain in order, so long as it was objective and based on facts. Mr. Price's critique showed not only a lack of information but a definite animus. His conclusions were therefore as offensive as they were unjust.

Thomas Hickey, as a great schoolman himself and the successor of a still greater educator, Bernard McQuaid, could not leave Price's challenge unanswered. Hickey's reply was one of his best efforts in controversial writing, dignified and persuasive. Actually, the antagonist had played into his hands, for it was easy to disprove his general charges, at least so far as the Diocese of Rochester was concerned, by a reference to actual facts. But the Bishop pressed on. The real difference between public and parochial schools, he pointed out in phrases worthy of a McQuaid, was that the parochial schools teach a positive religion, "the basis of the best citizenship and of the highest standard of morality." Rather than deprive their children of this spiritualized education, Catholic parents were willing to pay for the support of both the public and the parochial schools. The Rochester public school system, he pointed out, profited by this policy, for it saved local taxpayers some $1.25 millions each year.[7b]

Bishop Hickey spoke on this occasion as the good citizen that he truly was, interested in whatever could benefit community and nation. And it was just such a stance, increasingly evident on the part of patriotic American Catholics, that had gradually convinced thinking Protestants that anti-Catholic nativists were talking nonsense. The remarkable fact about Alfred E. Smith's presidential campaign in 1928 was not that he lost (and religion was only one factor in his defeat), but that he had even been chosen to run by a leading political party. His nomination proved that the Know-Nothing spirit was well on its way to extinction.

What sensible Americans have always respected in fellow Americans is achievement and civic interest. If a citizen is capable and civic-minded, his religious beliefs will usually not prevent him from being recognized by other Americans of divergent views. Two priests of the Diocese of Rochester can serve as modest exhibits in proof of this statement. Canandaiguans of every religious belief long cherished the memory of Father James T. Dougherty, who distinguished himself in patriotic and social leadership. And Father Daniel O'Rourke, who, as we have seen, had been greeted by a fiery cross on arriving in Sodus, subsequently established most cordial relations with the village merchants and even became a fast friend of the man who had lighted the flaming cross!

What was true of a considerable number of the priests was true of the increasing number of Catholic lay persons who assumed positions of prominence in the community.

Let us mention three such men as representatives of Rochester proper. Attorney James P. B. Duffy (1878-   ) was active in welfare projects and on the Board of Education. In 1930, when he was completing a quarter-century on the Board, School Superintendent Herbert S. Weet did not hesitate to declare: "No person in public life has ever been more devoted or sincere."[79] Prominent figures among Rochester Catholics of German ancestry were Peter A. Vay, vice president of the Lincoln National Bank (1860-1931), and Andrew Wollensak (1862-1936), founder of the Wollensak Optical Company.[80] They, too, were held in high civic esteem.

Elsewhere in the Diocese the sons and grandsons of immigrants were likewise moving into positions of some importance. At Dansville, for example, nurseryman Edward H. Maloney (1875-1929) was named postmaster. John Connelly of Elmira was active in civic affairs and was the pioneer president of the Elmira Chamber of Commerce (1860-1929).[81] One of the most universally respected citizens of Ithaca was the merchant James Lynch, a self-made man (1867-1916). A worthy husband and father, he was most diligent at attending not only the regular Masses but the devotional services at Immaculate Conception Church. President Woodrow Wilson, on July 23, 1914, named him postmaster of Ithaca. When the confirmation was somewhat delayed, somebody asked Lynch if he thought the appointment was being held up because of his race or religion. "I don't know," the merchant confessed. "But I couldn't change the one and I wouldn't change the other."[82]

Thomas Carmody (1859-1922) was from Penn Yan. He was elected Attorney General of the State of New York in 1910 and again in 1912.[83] Even a talented foreign-born citizen could achieve some status. Michael Grace of Weedsport (1856-1941) was a native of Ireland. He became a leading architect and builder in northern Cayuga County, was twice elected president of Weedsport, twice elected to the State Assembly, and served from 1918 to 1933 as deputy clerk of the New York Senate.[84] But it was a man from a farm on Addison Hill, Steuben County, who held the highest appointive office in governmental service. Lawrence O. Murray (1864-1926) served as United States Comptroller of Currency from 1908 to 1913.[85]

In many ways, the most influential Catholic layman in the Diocese was a *laywoman!* Mrs. Margaret Terry Chanler (1862-1952) came not of recent immigrant stock but of old British-American lineage. Half-sister to the renowned novelist F. Marion Crawford, and, as her published memoirs subsequently proved, an able author in her own right, Mrs. Chanler belonged to a wealthy and cosmopolitan New York family. Surprisingly enough, she was also an ardent and knowledgeable Catholic. She and her husband first became acquainted with the Genesee Valley in 1903 when they came to Geneseo for the fox-hunting season. Taking a liking to the Valley, they purchased Sweet Briar Farm as a permanent residence for themselves and their seven children. Now Geneseo had never been especially warm towards the Catholic Church, whose local members were then the largely Irish families that earned their bread in the service of the great landowners. Mrs. Chanler changed all that. Whenever she was in residence, she threw herself into the activities of the little Catholic parish. When the altar boys failed to turn up, she would stride up into the sanctuary, take the bells back to her pew, and respond to the Latin prayers of the Mass. She sponsored many benefits for the parish in Emerald Hall (the parochial auditorium), and gave benefit garden parties on her own estate. Even the most offish squires could scarcely withstand this persistent matron when she approached them to buy tickets. Furthermore, in 1913, she built a little public chapel, St. Felicity's, on her own farm, and got permission from the Holy See to reserve there the Blessed Sacrament and have Mass celebrated in it a couple of weekdays each week while the family was in residence. As the result of her positive Catholic emphasis, Catholicism, previously ignored in Geneseo, became not only acceptable, but rather stylish.[86]

Although Thomas Hickey himself was a representative second-generation Irish-American, he shared with most of his tribe a fond interest in the welfare of Ireland. Rochester's old St. Patrick's Day parades were, of course, a thing of the past—the *Catholic Journal* had complained as early as March 26, 1909, of the abandonment of the annual procession. But the feast was still staunchly observed by Irish societies, and the Bishop naturally saw to it that St. Patrick's Cathedral had its annual patronal Mass with the traditional panegyric.

Few men of warm Irish blood could fail to follow with interest Ireland's continuing struggle for her still unrealized political independence. That warm blood seethed to the boiling point during the "Troubles" of the early 1920's. The Easter Rebellion of 1916 had tragically failed to achieve its immediate aim. But at long range it was quite successful. Practically all those Irishmen who were elected to office in 1918 won on the platform of the independence movement, Sinn Fein ("Ourselves Alone"). Refusing to take their parliamentary seats in London, they set up in Dublin an "Irish Parliament," the Dail Eireann, and in the first days of January, 1919, they declared Ireland a republic, with Eamon de Valera (1882-1975) as its president. The British government was naturally not disposed to accept this bold declaration of independence, but the campaign of suppression which Britain now launched, though increasingly violent, proved increasingly ineffective. The importation of harsh British veterans—the "Black and Tans" —to put down the "republicans" generated still more bitterness. But it was the Irish who eventually won. In 1922 Ireland—or at least southern Ireland—was officially acknowledged as possessing dominion status: the Irish Free State. This was a step—though not the last—towards final emancipation.

Ireland's century-long struggle, renewed in fact and in symbol during the "Troubles" could only stir up the bile of Americans of Irish ancestry. In those days, outspoken priests like Father James Bloomer of Elmira did not hesitate to denounce England in public as the "beacon light of hell." However strongly Bishop Hickey may have felt on the issue, he could not well speak out so emotionally, nor could he take an active part in the political activities of the Irish-American societies. But when it seemed possible in 1919 that the Allied powers might be able to grant to Ireland and other smaller nations the right of self-determination at the forthcoming peace conference of Versailles, the Bishop gave public expression to his hope. He took part in a mass meeting for Irish freedom held in Rochester on March 4, 1919. He also sent to President Wilson the following telegram:

> Independent of any organization, general and particular, and speaking as an American citizen, representing in our birthplace or ancestry twelve nationalities, moved by regard for a country loved by us all, I ask in my name and in the name of the clergy and laity of this diocese your interest and influence in securing self-determination for Ireland.[87]

The Bishop of Rochester was sorry that the Versailles Conference subsequently did nothing about the matter of Ireland's freedom. Still he did not lose hope. Preaching in his cathedral on the feast of St. Patrick, 1920, he voiced the strong desire that the mounting violence in Ireland would give place to peace and independence. But he also prayed that in Ireland's struggle "no means will ever be used which would be contrary to the laws of God and which would fail to receive the respect and confidence of the great civilized nations of the world."[88]

In the Irish movements of yore there had been a close contact between Irish political leaders and the Irishmen of Rochester. The bond was even firmer in this instance, for Eamon de Valera's mother had been a resident of Rochester since 1895, and he came to see her more than once in the course of his many political trips to this country.

Mrs. Catherine Coll de Valera (1858-1932) was a highly intelligent colleen from rural Bruree in County Limerick. She came to New York City from Ireland in 1879, and in 1881 married a Spanish sculptor and musician, Juan Vivion de Valera. She bore him a son, Eamon, the future statesman, on October 14, 1882. Unfortunately, Juan Vivion died when the boy was only two years old. Obliged now to earn her own living, Mrs. de Valera decided to send her fatherless child over to Bruree "temporarily" to be raised by his Irish kinsfolk. The "temporary" arrangement became permanent, and Eamon, though half-Spanish by blood and American by birth, grew up a thorough Irishman. Educated in mathematics in the Royal University, the tall, gaunt professor must have seemed a very unpolitical figure when he joined the independence movement in 1916. But he came to rank with the very greatest Irish leaders of all time.

Not for thirty-four years after he was sent to Bruree did Eamon see his mother again. She had remarried in 1887. Her second husband was Charles E. Wheelwright, a native of England. It was he who in 1895 brought her to Rochester, where he secured employment as a groom with a prominent Rochester family. The Wheelwrights had two children: Annie, who died in childhood; and Thomas (1890-1946) who became a Redemptorist priest. The mother and her firstborn had thus moved along divergent paths. She returned to her homeland only once; but she was always happy to welcome her "Eddy" to the little house at 18 Brighton Street.[89] Whenever the local Irishmen had a big rally or festival, Kate Wheelwright was ready to grace the occasion as a special guest of honor.[90] Kate died on June 12, 1932, and was buried in Holy Sepulchre Cemetery. Her son Eamon had been elected five months before as President of the Executive Council of the Irish Free State. Naturally he could not attend the funeral, but he sent as his representative the Irish Minister to the United States. A fortnight later "Dev" had the consolation of hearing a detailed account of his mother's last days. Monsignor Charles F. Shay, rector of the Rochester Cathedral, was head of the Rochester delegation to the International Eucharistic Congress held in Dublin on June 24-26. In a private interview with the Irish president, Monsignor Shay told him the whole story. When Kate's will was admitted to probate, it was learned that she had left one-half of her modest estate to each of her two sons, the President and the priest.[91]

Bishop Hickey's sympathy for needy nations was not restricted to the Emerald Isle. He demonstrated his interest in the foreign missions, as we have already noted, by establishing a diocesan office of the Society for the Propagation of the Faith. In 1916 he took up a diocesan collection for the relief of the needy in Poland, Ireland, Germany, Belgium, Austria and Italy—a charity which transcended the political alignment of the nations involved.[92] In 1920 he joined in the nationwide protest against the mass oppression of Jews in the Ukraine.[93] In 1922 he authorized a collection for the relief of Russians and other Europeans in distress.[94] By a circular of December 27, 1923, he announced another diocesan collection for the relief of the impoverished Germans. Persecution of the Church in Mexico at mid-decade engaged his particular compassion. Under the direction of Pope Pius XI, he enjoined upon his flock by a circular of July 18, 1926, special prayers to be recited for Mexico on August 1st, the feast of St. Peter in Chains. Some weeks before this, on May 24, 1926, he had written a personal letter on the same subject to the Department of State in Washington, protesting the anti-Catholic actions of the Mexican government.[95]

Thomas F. Hickey does not seem to have entertained as many bishops, foreign or domestic, as Bishop McQuaid did. Of course, he often had as guest his old schoolmate, Joseph H. Conroy (1858-1939), the third Bishop of Ogdensburg. Bishop Conroy was always able to make Hickey forget his worries for a while and laugh. Bishop Hickey also welcomed back to Rochester, in 1910, Cardinal Michael Logue of Ireland. In the same year the Italian Cardinal, Vincenzo Vannutelli, paid a visit to Rochester's bishop while en route as papal legate to the International Eucharistic Congress of Montreal. And it also became Bishop Hickey's duty in 1926 to greet the seven Cardinals who passed through the see city on their way to the International Eucharistic Congress being held in Chicago. One year later a future Cardinal stopped in Rochester: Archbishop Francesco Marchetti-Selvaggiani, president of the supreme council of the Society for the Propagation of the Faith.[96] These and others the second Bishop of Rochester received as graciously, though perhaps not as energetically, as his predecessor.

Bishop Hickey took an even greater interest in three other prelates who came to him in the name of their suffering flocks.

The best known of these churchmen was Cardinal Désiré Mercier (1851-1926). He was the brilliant and heroic archbishop of Malines, Belgium, who during the first World War had perhaps more than any other Belgian come to symbolize his nation. Mercier came to America in 1919 professedly to thank the citizens of the United States for the support they had given to Belgium during the struggle. Actually, his visit was a triumph, for city vied with city to do him honor. His twelve-hour stay in Rochester on October 13th was marked by a whirlwind program of religious and civic events. The activities culminated in a grand mass meeting. George Eastman, the president of Kodak, Justice Arthur E. Sutherland, and Bishop Hickey all gave addresses, and the president of the University of Rochester, Dr. Rush Rhees, presented His Eminence with the City's gift—a check for $25,000.00.[97]

Two prominent bishops from conquered and impoverished Germany also came to Rochester in quest of funds during the decade after World War I. One was Christian Schreiber (1872-1933), then bishop of Meissen, and later bishop of Berlin. He lectured in this country in 1927-1928, and during that time stopped in Rochester, perhaps more than once. On February 25, 1928, with the permission of the Bishop of Rochester, he administered the sacrament of Confirmation at Holy Family German Church in the see city.[98]

The other German prelate was the Archbishop of Munich-Freising, Cardinal Michael von Faulhaber (1869-1952), who a decade later was to take such a brave stand against Adolf Hitler. His local visit occurred on May 25, 1923. The Bishop of Rochester cordially received the Cardinal, who made no formal appearance or appeal during his stay but seems to have solicited private donations. Faulhaber did not depart from Rochester without an adventure. Msgr. John F. O'Hern, the Vicar General of the Rochester Diocese, his assistant, Father Emmett Magee, and some other diocesan priests formed a farewell committee to see the German prelate off at the railroad station. While he waited on the platform for the arrival of the train, His Eminence set down the little black bag in which he was carrying the funds he had collected for his needy archdiocese. The train came, and the Cardinal boarded it; but as it pulled out of the station with increasing momentum, he appeared at the rear door gesticulating frantically at the black bag—still on the platform. Monsignor O'Hern quickly telegraphed to the Cardinal that the money would be delivered to him at the railway station in Lyons, New York. Then he sent Father Magee to Lyons on the next train. When Father Magee reached the Lyons station, Faulhaber rushed up with thanks, took the precious bag, handed Magee an autographed photograph, and clambered aboard his departing train.[99]

All these illustrations are more than enough to prove that Thomas Francis Hickey was thoroughly ecclesiastical and thoroughly patriotic. To two great institutions he gave unwavering loyalty: his Church and his native land.

3. The Archbishop of Viminacium.

On May 24, 1925, Bishop Hickey observed the twentieth anniversary of his consecration as a bishop. On that occasion he received two notable tributes. One was from his flock: a "spiritual bouquet" of Masses and prayers pledged to him by the devoted Catholics of his diocese. The other was from Pope Pius XI, who on May 4, 1925, bestowed on him the honorary title of Assistant at the Papal Throne.[100]

Three years later, to the surprise of the Catholics of the Diocese of Rochester, Monsignor O'Hern, the Vicar General, announced that the second Bishop of Rochester had resigned his post for reasons of health. The announcement was made on October 31, 1928, five days after the Pope, in accepting the resignation, had declared it to be effective. On October 30th, Pius XI promoted Bishop Hickey to the titular episcopal see of Viminacium, with the honorary rank of Archbishop. Thus ended the Rochester episcopate of a prelate who had headed the Diocese for nineteen years and eight months.[101]

In a superficial sense, the plea of "poor health" as grounds for resignation was conventional. In a deeper sense it was entirely true. We have already mentioned that Thomas Hickey was constitutionally prone to scrupulosity. After he took over the government of the Diocese in

1909, this tendency grew gradually more acute. In the final stage, the Bishop became so indecisive in the face of crucial sacramental and administrative tasks that his effectiveness as an executive was gravely impaired. Early in 1928, the apostolic delegate, Archbishop Pietro Fumasoni Biondi, took cognizance of this difficult problem. Without informing Bishop Hickey of his intentions, he came to Rochester and undertook a private investigation. The upshot of the inquiry was that Rome —no doubt with genuine regret—requested Hickey to submit his resignation.

At first, Bishop Hickey was startled and shocked by the unexpected request. He had evidently never considered taking this course. He would probably never have done so spontaneously; for even if he had reached the conclusion that duty required him to step down, his very indecisiveness would most likely have hindered him from taking action. As it was, a few hours of prayerful thought—plus, no doubt, the counsel of those on whose wisdom he relied—convinced him that the voice of Peter was the voice of God.

After the news was announced, Cardinal Hayes of New York, who was not only the metropolitan of the Bishop of Rochester but his close friend, wrote Hickey a kindly and reassuring letter. "No one, my dear Bishop," said His Eminence, "has had, during the years I have been privileged to know you, greater appreciation and warmer admiration of your singleness of purpose in the successful upbuilding of the Kingdom of Christ." Touched by this sincere tribute, Archbishop Hickey thanked Cardinal Hayes for his sympathetic message. Then he went on in his reply to reveal his final frame of mind. "As you can understand, the severing of ties that were very close can easily be followed by feelings of sadness, but with God's help the consoling thought will be that before the great interests of Religion the individual in the case will not be considered."[102]

There was true pathos in this whole episode: that a man should be asked to retire from office not because he had been irresponsible but because he had been too painstaking. And if that is a paradox, we may add to it a second paradox. At no time, perhaps, in his career as bishop of Rochester, did Thomas F. Hickey come closer to true greatness than when, out of deep humility and concern for the welfare of his diocese, he requested to be removed from its stewardship.

The clergy of the Rochester Diocese, who always held the Archbishop of Viminacium in high personal esteem, continued to be most considerate of him after his retirement. Among other gestures, they arranged a pleasant banquet for him at the motherhouse of the Sisters of

St. Joseph on January 9, 1929, the twentieth anniversary of his succession to Bishop McQuaid. His dearest friends in the hierarchy were invited to the celebration: Bishops Thomas J. Walsh of Newark, Thomas C. O'Reilly of Scranton, and Joseph H. Conroy of Ogdensburg. At the climax of the dinner, Monsignor O'Hern, Apostolic Administrator of the Diocese, presented Hickey with a check for $10,000.00 in the name of the diocesan clergy. A year later they also arranged a commemoration of the Archbishop's silver jubilee of consecration.[103]

But Archbishop Hickey, who was only sixty-seven, had no intention of enrolling in the inactive list, nor did others hesitate to seek his service. During the earliest years of his retirement, when he was living at St. Stephen's Church, Geneva, Hickey taught religion in DeSales High School. After he returned to Rochester and took up residence in the motherhouse of the Sisters of St. Joseph, he taught classes at one time or another at Nazareth College, Nazareth Academy, Our Lady of Mercy High School, and Aquinas Institute. He also gave instructions and conferences at the motherhouse itself and at the motherhouse of the Sisters of Mercy; and he taught homiletics and gave spiritual talks at St. Bernard's Seminary.

The Archbishop's oratorical skill had not waned, and although the style of his rhetoric, like the style of his classes and conferences, was a little old-style, he could still be counted on as a good preacher for important occasions. Thus on August 3, 1936, he delivered the funeral eulogy of Monsignor Nelson F. Baker of Lackawanna, the saintly philanthropist and vicar general of the Buffalo Diocese, who at one time had served within the Rochester Diocese.[104] A year later, on August 8, 1937, he preached in St. Patrick's Cathedral when Father Walter A. Foery, his former director of charities, was consecrated fifth bishop of Syracuse.[105] But the most moving of his grand discourses was his sermon at the consecration of the man who succeeded him as bishop of Rochester. Speaking on March 19, 1929, at the Mass of consecration of Bishop John Francis O'Hern, Archbishop Hickey took opportunity "to render to the clergy and laity whose love and co-operation and loyalty has been known to me for years, an expression of my deep gratitude, and to tell them that to my dying hour it will always be held by me in cherished memory." "May the church of Rochester," he concluded, "give glory to God and blessings to the world."[106]

It was thus that the gentle, diffident old prelate spent the last twelve years of his life in limited but active pastoral work. We have already described the many services, some of them truly distinguished, which he had rendered the Diocese and the Church during his term of office. Even after his retirement he lived up to his concept of the role of a bishop—a servant of the flock—to the best of his waning ability.

Now we have only to round out our account of Thomas Hickey's official accomplishments with a few personal details.

He was, in the first place, a deeply spiritual man. When he exhorted others to devotion, he spoke as one who stood firm in his own devotional life. By disposition he was austere, and singularly unworldly. He was more of a "priest's priest" than a "layman's priest"; and unless other anxieties happened to be disturbing him, he could relax best in the company of the clergy. Nevertheless, even among priests he was "always the bishop." He never lost sight of the dignity of his office or of his conscientious duty to give good example.

Bishop Hickey knew his flock well, and took a personal interest in the pastoral problems of his priests. One instance will suffice as an illustration. In 1925, the Bishop decided to raise the St. Salome mission, at Sea Breeze, to the status of a parish. He knew that the first pastor would be faced with no easy task. Not only was the parish territory still largely agricultural, but it included a resort neighborhood on the lakefront which set small store by the laws of God or men. It was with tears in his eyes that the Bishop asked Father Edward J. Eschrich if he would consent to accept the assignment. Father Eschrich consented on the condition that if he felt after a trial that he was not succeeding he would be immediately relieved of the pastorate. Hickey agreed to the condition. As a matter of fact, the new pastor, by quick, firm action, soon had matters well in hand, and began to develop successfully a parish district which has since been divided into three flourishing parishes. But even after his resignation the Archbishop continued to pay regular visits to St. Salome's rectory, and he seldom failed to remind the pastor that if he desired a transfer, it could still be arranged.[107]

Finally, Thomas Francis Hickey was a generous and charitable man towards individuals in need. He had especially demonstrated this self-sacrificing kindliness during the last months of Bishop McQuaid, by undertaking to perform even menial tasks in order to add a little to the dying Bishop's comfort. We can only guess at the extent of his personal charities. At his death on December 10, 1940, he left an estate of less than $2,000.00, all of which he bequeathed to the current bishop of Rochester.[108] Nor did he hesitate to beg from others alms for the needy which he himself could not supply. Once, for instance, he learned of a family that faced disgrace if the father could not immediately secure a substantial sum. He turned for help to his Jewish friend, Mr.

338 / *The Diocese of Rochester*

Simon N. Stein of the Stein-Block Company. The clothing manufacturer replied: "I don't want to know the name; here is the money."

On another occasion, in the midst of the business recession of 1921, Mr. Carleton Brown, general manager of Corona Typewriter Company of Groton, confessed to the Bishop that his firm, which employed 800, was on the verge of failure; but he said it could be tided over if only he was able to secure a pending order from a New York organization of which Cardinal Patrick Hayes was a director.[109] Bishop Hickey forthwith wrote to the Cardinal suggesting that he use his good offices to direct the business to Corona. That Company's solvency meant much to the little village which had once been part of Hickey's Moravian pastorate.[110]

The second Bishop of Rochester was a truly good man and a most devoted bishop. He had chosen *"Fides et Constantia"* ("Faith and Constancy") as his episcopal motto, and he did his utmost to live up to its implications.

For that effort, Thomas Francis Hickey deserves to be held in reverent memory by the Diocese of Rochester.

CHAPTER ELEVEN

JOHN FRANCIS O'HERN

THE FOUNDING bishop of Rochester had governed his diocese forty years; his immediate successor, something less than twenty years. John Francis O'Hern, third Bishop of Rochester, though only fifty-four at the time of his appointment, was to live only a few weeks beyond his fourth anniversary in office.

World conditions in the period 1929-1933 were anything but tranquil, even though there was no international war raging. In Russia, Mexico, Spain, the revolutionary climate stifled religion, and American Catholics in particular gave sympathetic ear to the cries of the persecuted. But the major grief of these years was an economic one—the Great Depression, which began in America but inevitably affected the economy of many another nation.

While American business in 1929 was undermined financially, its instability was not obvious, and the sudden collapse of the New York stock market on October 29, 1929, took most Americans by surprise. Depressions had occurred before, but the nation had usually been able to shrug them off before very long. National leaders, on down from Herbert C. Hoover, the newly inaugurated president, were at first confident that the slump would be brief. But as months lengthened into years without bringing deliverance, Americans realized that they were in the midst of such "hard times" as the nation had never before suffered. Each year the national income declined. Each year unemployment rose: from four million in 1930 to fifteen million in the blackest year, 1932. Drought in some rural areas of the nation further added to the plight of both farmer and consumer.

Local and State charities did their best to provide relief, but as the number of needy increased beyond measure, Americans turned more and more to the federal government to solve the crisis. "Hunger Marchers" swarmed up to the White House clamoring for jobs. Eleven thousand jobless veterans converged on Washington to demand that Congress pay them the balance of the federal soldiers' bonuses. President Hoover, under constant pressure to "do something", eventually did take several constructive steps.

It was a foregone conclusion that in the presidential campaign the main issue would be the Depression. Actually, the Democratic candidate Franklin Delano Roosevelt was in many ways better equipped to deal with the problem than the man whom he defeated. As governor of New York he had recently sponsored a number of valuable anti-depression measures. He was more ready than his predecessor to take daring and economically unorthodox steps. Furthermore, he had a notable sense of public relations, which quickly won from most of the nation, and especially—as he termed the unemployed American—from the "forgotten man," an enthusiastic response to the "New Deal," his dramatic war on economic pessimism. "The only thing we have to fear," he declared at his inauguration, "is fear itself." And from that day, March 4, 1933, throughout the next hundred days he took many measures, by proclamation and by law, to provide relief for those in need and to give the federal government a surer control over the finances of the nation. Culminating all these governmental measures was the National Industrial Recovery Act of June 16, 1933.

Bishop O'Hern had been in office for only seven months when the market crashed. He died in the midst of Franklin Roosevelt's "One Hundred Days." His administration was therefore contemporary with the worst years of the Great Depression. It was also colored by it, hobbled by it. What the third Bishop of Rochester accomplished and what he failed to accomplish, at least in material achievements, must be judged in the light of these circumstances.

1. The New Shepherd.

Like the prelate he succeeded, J. Francis O'Hern was a priest of the Diocese of Rochester. He was not, however, a native of the Diocese.

John Francis O'Hern was the son of Patrick and Ellen Casey O'Hern. He was born on June 8, 1874 at Olean, New York, in the Diocese of Buffalo. Patrick O'Hern, who had a farm outside Allegany, was a man of modest means. The couple had fourteen children, eleven of whom reached maturity.

It was a happy family that Patrick and Ellen raised—affectionate and almost proverbial for their exuberant optimism and rollicking humor. It was also a devout family. Ellen was a native of Ireland, and so, apparently, was Patrick; and they infused their deep Irish piety into their children. They were among the pioneer Catholics around Allegany, and as such gave notable assistance to the Franciscans who founded St. Bonaventure College and Seminary in 1856. This is the sort of family that most frequently produces religious vocations; and the O'Hern family, through no parental pressure save that of prayer and good example, gave four priests to the Church. The oldest of these was Dennis (1865-1911). He became a priest of the Diocese of Erie, and subsequently president of Little Rock College, Arkansas. Next in order was Frank, the bishop. Lewis O'Hern (1876-1930) entered the Paulist Fathers, and subsequently became rector of the Apostolic Mission House connected with the Catholic University of America; and executive secretary of the Catholic Army-Navy Bureau, under Cardinal Hayes, Ordinary of Catholics in the American armed forces. In these roles he acquired considerable influence. Thomas (1880-1961) was the only one of the four to serve in the diocese of his birth. At the time of his death he was a prominent pastor in Buffalo and a protonotary apostolic. Edward P. O'Hern (1872-1945) wore another sort of uniform— that of the United States Army, which he entered from West Point, and in which he reached the rank of colonel. (But his son, Edward Philip Jr., joined the Paulists.) The Patrick O'Herns furthermore had three cousins who were priests. One of them was attached to the Rochester Diocese: Father John E. Casey (1865-1929), who at the time of his death shortly after the consecration of Bishop O'Hern was pastor of St. John's Church in Clyde.[1]

Surely, a most Catholic family!

Frank was baptized in the College church of St. Bonaventure's; attended, it seems, a parochial school; and then went on to Olean High School, where he showed himself a very bright student.[2] After attending this public high school, he decided to enter the seminary. Why he chose to enter the service of the Diocese of Rochester is now unknown, although it is said that Father Edward J. Hanna, professor at St. Bernard's Seminary from 1893 on, had some responsibility for the arrangement.[3] At all events, the young man from Olean first went to St. Andrew's Seminary, and then, in 1895, to St. Bernard's.

In 1897, Bishop McQuaid decided to send three of the outstanding Rochester "philosophy" students at St. Bernard's to complete their priestly training in Rome. They were Edmund J. Wirth and J. Francis Goggin (both of whom were destined to become professors at St. Bernard's) and Frank O'Hern. Frank was happy to be a student at Rome's North American College, where he officially registered on October 18th. He enjoyed the cultural advantages of a Roman residence, and became acquainted with, and fond of, the Italian language and the Italian people. At the theological university where the American students then studied—the Athenaeum of the Urban College de Propaganda Fide—he made a distinguished course and on one occasion bore off an academic medal. He was awarded his bachelor's degree in Sacred Theology (June 15, 1898) and his licentiate (June 18, 1900). He would normally have won his doctorate at the end of the spring semester of

1901 and then gone on to higher studies in Scripture, as Bishop Mc-Quaid evidently desired. Unfortunately, he suffered an impairment of health at the beginning of that year. His superiors thought it would be better for him to return home directly without waiting out the remainder of the last semester. He was therefore ordained a priest in advance of his class, on February 17, 1901, by Cardinal Pietro Respighi, vicar general of Pope Leo XIII. Departing shortly thereafter, he was back in America in March.[4]

Young Father O'Hern's illness soon disappeared after a few weeks at home. Consequently, Bishop McQuaid appointed him, in May, to the position of assistant pastor of St. Mary's, Rochester. Four months later the Bishop transferred him to St. Mary's Church, Auburn; but in July, 1902, he brought him back to Rochester and assigned him to the staff of St. Patrick's Cathedral.[5]

Never again was O'Hern to hold a post outside the see city. He performed his tasks so well at St. Patrick's that when Bishop Hickey, on succeeding Bishop McQuaid in 1909 as head of the Diocese, relinquished his office of Cathedral rector, he named Father O'Hern to the rectorship. O'Hern made a notable rector, and a very popular one, among Catholics and non-Catholics alike. For he was genuinely devout, friendly, energetic in the discharge of his pastoral duties, and very charitable.

Father O'Hern made a genuine effort to foster public piety among his parishioners. One example is his attempt to introduce congregational singing. Shortly after his appointment as rector, he decided to persuade his congregation to sing the Mass. Pope Pius X had strongly urged this in his memorable decree of 1903 on church music. Within months after launching the project, the new rector had trained the Cathedral School children to sing the Latin Creed and responses of the high Mass. He engaged Father John M. Petter, director of music at St. Bernard's Seminary, to coach the congregation in its own part. It is doubtful that much was attempted along these lines elsewhere in the Diocese. It is a tribute to Father O'Hern's desire to do the right thing that he should have kept urging parochial singing for at least the next two or three years. An Irish congregation was perhaps the hardest group to begin with, for the Irish had no singing tradition. German parishioners would have been easier to win over. Had John Francis O'Hern been living in our own days of the renewed liturgy, his parish would certainly be one of the most advanced in congregational singing and participation.[6]

By 1923 O'Hern was one of the best known priests in the Diocese.

The *Catholic Journal* called him "an ardent worker in the affairs of his parish and in charitable activity not of a public nature." In addition to the rectorship of St. Patrick's he was a diocesan synodal examiner and an associate director of the diocesan Children's Welfare Bureau. He had also been, since 1914, chaplain of the Monroe County Penitentiary. From this latter task, which he enjoyed, he developed an abiding interest in the apostolate of penal institutions. We have already noted that he accompanied Bishop Hickey to Rome on the *ad limina* journey of 1914. This was only one more indication that the Bishop held him in esteem. Therefore, when Msgr. Dennis J. Curran died, few were surprised to learn on January 9, 1923, that Hickey had named O'Hern successor to Curran's double office—vicar general of the Diocese and pastor of Corpus Christi Church. On August 13th of the following year, Pope Pius XI conferred on the new vicar general the rank of domestic prelate.

Monsignor O'Hern, as second in diocesan command, naturally moved into greater prominence in the affairs of the Diocese and the organizations associated with it. He played a larger role, too, in various civic movements. For example, he was a director of the Society for the Prevention of Cruelty to Children from March 3, 1920 until the date of his voluntary resignation, January 10, 1933.[7]

When Bishop Hickey resigned the bishopric in 1928, the Holy See named Monsignor O'Hern to serve as apostolic administrator of the Rochester Diocese until a new bishop was chosen.[8] The rules governing the selection of bishops for sees in the United States had changed in 1916. It was now no longer the task of the administrator to assemble the major priests of the Diocese in order to have them select three candidates. According to the new regulations, the bishops in each province compiled every two years a list of possible candidates from each suffragan diocese. Since this list was confidential, there is no way of knowing at present the names on the list submitted to the Holy See in 1928. Normally the names of the various vicars general would appear among the nominees, and the name of Father O'Hern would thus have stood at the head of the Rochester group of possible bishops. Father Lewis O'Hern, the Paulist brother of the pastor of Corpus Christi, was closely associated with Cardinal Hayes and with the Apostolic Delegate, Archbishop Fumasoni Biondi; and some have thought that this association may have had a bearing on Rome's eventual decision. Nevertheless, if a Rochester priest was to be selected, John F. O'Hern doubtless had more to recommend him at that time than any of his confrères.

On January 4, 1929, the Holy Father's decision was announced.

John Francis O'Hern was named bishop of Rochester. His consecration took place at St. Patrick's Cathedral, Rochester, on the feast of St. Joseph, March 19, 1929. Cardinal Patrick Hayes of New York was the consecrator. Co-consecrators were two of the new bishop's best friends: Rochester-born Edward J. Hanna, Archbishop of San Francisco, who had played an influential part in O'Hern's earlier career; and Thomas Charles O'Reilly, bishop of Scranton, one of O'Hern's Roman school-mates. Twenty other bishops, the O'Hern brothers, Admiral William S. Benson, leading civic officials and a large body of priests and lay people witnessed the rite. Archbishop Hickey delivered the sermon, one of his finest. The Rochester radio station, WHAM, broadcast the whole ceremony to the Diocese, from 9:00 A.M. to 2:30 P.M. This was not only the most pretentious program thus far attempted by a Rochester radio station; it seems to have been the first broadcast on record of the solemnities of a Catholic consecration.[9]

The new bishop's earliest official act was to name the vice-chan-cellor, Father William M. Hart, to the position of vicar general. (Father Hart was designated a domestic prelate on August 8, 1929, by Pius XI.) On the following day Bishop O'Hern appointed a new as-sistant chancellor in the person of Father Charles R. Reynolds. Once installed in office, the Bishop lost no time in undertaking a schedule of pastoral activities heavier than either of his two busy predecessors would have dreamed of.

There was to be no great growth in diocesan population during the next four years. Growth in the nation itself was now more the re-sult of natural increase than of immigration, for the old flood of immi-grants had dwindled to a small, carefully controlled stream. In the twelve counties of the Rochester Diocese the general population rose from 880,000 in 1925 to 900,000 in 1930. As before, Rochester and Monroe County experienced the greatest expansion; in the other coun-ties the number of inhabitants remained relatively stable. According to the *Official Catholic Directory*, there were 208,000 Catholics in the Rochester Diocese in 1928, and 214,000 in 1933. Whatever the validity of these figures, they at least point to the conclusion that diocesan in-crease would henceforth be less dramatic than during the immigration era.

Two natural factors limited the new bishop in his efforts to set up new parishes. One was the brevity of his episcopal career, the other the current shortage of funds. He created only two completely new parishes in metropolitan Rochester. The founding of St. Margaret Mary, in Iron-dequoit, he entrusted to the former Army chaplain, Father Charles J.

Bruton; and he dedicated its first church, a frame building, on September 15, 1929. The second church was St. Anne's, Brighton, which the Bishop formally blessed on February 9, 1930. Father George J. Schmitt organized this parish and built its wooden church, and was officially designated its pastor in 1931 when its parish lines were finally established.

Bishop O'Hern also set up five new mission churches in and around the see city. St. Helen's, in Gates, was blessed on February 29, 1930, and placed in the care of St. Augustine parish. It was designed to serve all the Catholics within its boundary irrespective of nationality. The other four were mission chapels for Italians: Our Lady of Sorrows, on Niagara Street (1930); St. Francis of Assisi Church, on Whitney Street (1929); St. Philip Neri Church, on Clifford Avenue (1929); and the Church of the Most Precious Blood, off Lexington Avenue on the western fringe of the city (1930). Father Anthony Pece, an Italian-born member of the Precious Blood Fathers, was assigned to this last church as rector.

The Bishop instituted two parishes outside Monroe County. In 1930 he detached Holy Angels Church in Nunda, Livingston County, from St. Patrick's, Mount Morris (whose mission it had been), and gave it parochial rank, with a mission of its own—Holy Name Church in Groveland. He named Father Raymond Lynd the first pastor. In 1931 he divided the large old parish of St. Ann's, in Hornell (Steuben County), apportioning the southern part of St. Ann's territory to a brand-new parish, St. Ignatius, with Father Ignatius X. Cameron as pastor. St. Joachim's in Canisteo was given parochial status in 1932, but reverted to mission status in 1934. Another Steuben County mission, St. William's in Cameron Mills, came to an end in 1930, after a career of forty years. Automobile travel to Addison, of which St. William's was an out-mission, was doubtless one of the factors that persuaded the Bishop to close down the rough little structure and sell it for $200.00. Around the same time St. Edward's Mission Church in Auburn was razed to make way for the permanent building of Mercy Hospital.

During the 1920's a fair number of Polish people moved into the Diocese to engage in farming. We have already mentioned those who came to Bradford, Steuben County, for whose benefit Bishop Hickey founded St. Stanislaus Church shortly before his retirement. Other Polish families settled in Prattsburg, in northern Steuben County. These were taken care of by St. Patrick's Church, Prattsburg—a mission of St. Gabriel's, Hammondsport. Towards the end of the 1920's a larger group of Polish-Americans from the district of Scranton, Pennsylvania, were induced by a speculator to take up farming around Catatonk, near Owego in Tioga County. O'Hern interested himself directly in their situation, and in 1931 blessed for their use a new little church named after St. Francis, which he attached as a mission to St. John the Evangelist Church, Newark Valley, Tioga County.

In founding this Polish mission church, the Bishop had relied once more on the loyal assistance of the Polish Conventual Franciscans. Father Callistus Szpara organized the little congregation at Catatonk. As we have already noted, the Polish Franciscans took over the administration of St. Stanislaus, Bradford, in 1927. Here Father Method Szymanski, aided by a donation of $25,000.00 from the Catholic Church Extension Society of Chicago, erected the present St. Stanislaus Church in 1930. Bishop O'Hern dedicated it in November of that year.

Circumstances did not permit the construction of ambitious church buildings in the depression years. Simplicity and serviceability were the standards. Thus St. Ignatius, Hornell, opened in a double store. Even today, St. Francis of Assisi, in Rochester, still occupies its original home —the former Ideal Theater, a neighborhood movie house. Most of the new church buildings in and around Rochester were neat and unpretentious frame structures, built, and in some cases designed, by the Rochester carpenter, Seraphin Schwartz.[10]

Only three new parochial schools date from the days of Rochester's third bishop, and all three were in Rochester. The school of St. George parish, the city's only Lithuanian congregation, started off in 1929 with four grades. Parish laywomen staffed it the first year, but in 1930 they were succeeded by the Lithuanian Sisters of St. Francis of the Providence of God, an order whose motherhouse is in Pittsburgh. Another community of Sisters new to the Diocese opened parish schools in 1930 at both Our Lady of Good Counsel and St. Margaret Mary. They were the Sisters of St. Francis of Allegany, New York. (A third group of Franciscan sisters, the Polish Franciscan nuns, had replaced the Sisters of St. Joseph at St. Hyacinth's, Auburn, in 1921.)

If the Bishop opened only three new parochial schools, it was not at all because he was unenthusiastic about Catholic schooling. On the contrary, he agreed completely with the ideals of his two predecessors. As late in the Depression as July, 1931, he reiterated (somewhat unrealistically) their watchword: "Every Catholic child in a Catholic school."[11] He had already taken a more practical step in 1929. That June he appointed Father John M. Duffy as the first full-time director of diocesan schools.[12] Father Duffy, a graduate of Oswego State Normal School, had taught in the public school system before entering the seminary. He now became responsible for working out the first real diocesan educational program.

Bishop O'Hern's major scholastic contributions were on the secondary rather than the primary level. He enlarged the staff at Aquinas Institute, Rochester, by bringing in some Basilian Fathers in 1928 and some Franciscan Friars Minor in 1930. On Memorial Day, 1930, he dedicated the new building of DeSales High School in Geneva.[13]

In the fall of 1930, the Bishop opened two new high schools outside Monroe County, one in Auburn, the other in Elmira. Like DeSales High School in Geneva, both of these new schools were perforce coeducational. Both began under humble auspices; even so, it took some courage to launch them in the depression years.

The Auburn institution was called Holy Family High School. In 1930, O'Hern, observing that there were vacant classrooms in Holy Family parochial school, suggested that the pastor, Father John Conway, might use them to inaugurate a high school department. Father Conway agreed, and in September, 1930, he initiated the freshman year of Holy Family High with thirty-two registrants. Two teachers constituted the original faculty: Sister M. Martha Lavey, R.S.M., and Father Donald M. Cleary. A year later two more were added: Sister M. Julia Ryan, R.S.M., and Father Leo Hastings. After the school had received State approval in 1932, Father William Davie was named principal. The first commencement took place in 1934.[14] Twenty-one years later, Holy Family High School yielded to the present Mount Carmel High School conducted by the Carmelite Friars.

Elmira Catholic High School arose out of similar circumstances. SS. Peter and Paul School also had some extra classrooms. On July 18, 1930, Father Duffy, as diocesan superintendent of schools, and Father John J. Lee, pastor of SS. Peter and Paul's, made the joint announcement that a Catholic High School was to be commenced the following September at SS. Peter and Paul School. Twenty-five boys and girls signed up for the pioneer class, some choosing the academic course, some the commercial course. The Sisters of St. Joseph, who staffed the elementary school, were invited to provide teachers for the secondary grades; and Father Francis J. Reilly, assistant at SS. Peter and Paul's, was designated principal. Two years later, the Bishop blessed the ampler quarters into which Elmira Catholic High School had moved, on the third floor of St. Patrick's parochial school.

In 1933, the Sisters of St. Joseph found it impossible to provide sufficient teachers for the expanding high school program. The Rochester Sisters of Mercy agreed to replace them, and Sister M. Isidore Doyle took charge. State Regents' approval was granted in 1934, and in June, 1934, diplomas were awarded to the nineteen members of the first graduating class.[15] In 1955, Elmira Catholic High School acquired a fine new home on the south side of Elmira, and with it a new name, Notre Dame High School. The Sisters of Mercy remain in charge.

For those Catholic children unable to atend Catholic schools, the diocesan program of catechetics was, of course, continued. However, in most parts of the Diocese the program of religious instruction was adapted to local conditions. Ambitious vacation school projects of the type provided in Rochester were usually impossible; and released-time had been accepted by only a few communities outside of Monroe County. Thus, the Auburn Board of Education still declined to accept the "Rochester Plan." In the course of a public address which he delivered in Auburn in the fall of 1930, Bishop O'Hern did not hesitate to protest this stand. Its effect, he declared, was to deprive children of every denomination of a God-given right.[16]

John F. O'Hern was also solicitous for the well-being of St. Andrew's and St. Bernard's Seminaries. In the days of the Depression he urged his people to heed the annual seminary appeal. The most important action that he took regarding St. Bernard's was the replacement of the Sisters of St. Joseph (who for forty years had managed the domestic department) with sixteen members of the Canadian Sisters of St. Joan of Arc. These French-speaking nuns, installed at St. Bernard's on September 8, 1932, were specialists in the domestic management of church institutions. Bishop Hickey had begun negotiations to secure their services five years before.[17]

O'Hern himself took the initiative in making an important addition to St. Andrew's Seminary. The Minor Seminary had hitherto been strictly a day-school. But as the number of non-Rochesterian students increased, it became less feasible to quarter them in private homes. Therefore, in the very month of his consecration the Bishop leased a large dwelling at 46 Greig Street, about a mile south of the Seminary. By the time he dedicated its chapel, on September 26, 1929, it had twenty students in residence. A year later the number of out-of-town seminarians had increased to fifty-one, and it was necessary to lease another residence near "St. Andrew's House of Studies" for additional sleeping quarters.[18]

One reason for the increase of seminarians in 1930 was the "drive" for vocations that O'Hern conducted that year through the parishes. The initial response was most gratifying. Seventy-seven entered the freshman year at St. Andrew's in September, 1930 (compared to forty-nine in 1929), and ninety-five entered the following year. Unfortunately, the number dwindled drastically along the line, so that only two of the entrants of 1930 finally reached the priesthood.[19] The Bishop's drive for vocations to the sisterhood was more successful. In May, 1930 and May, 1931, he enjoined a novena for increased religious vocations on all parishes of the Diocese. In 1930, thirty-nine candidates entered the Sisters of St. Joseph (as compared with thirteen in 1929); and in 1931 there was a class of forty-five candidates. Thirty-three of the 1930 class persevered and took final vows; thirty-six of the 1931 class. The class of candidates which entered the Sisters of Mercy in 1931 had nineteen—very large for those times; and fifteen of these subsequently made their profession.[20]

Bishop O'Hern's campaign for priestly vocations had been dictated by a real need. Thomas F. Hickey, finding himself short-handed, had invited neighboring bishops to loan him priests for temporary service. O'Hern was obliged to continue the practice. Thus several priests of the Albany Diocese came to serve for a while in the Diocese of Rochester. Nor was Bishop O'Hern hesitant about inviting the help of religious orders. The Basilian Fathers, who under Hickey had sent several men to teach at Aquinas, increased the number assigned to that faculty. To these O'Hern added Franciscan friars—ten in all, over the years. We have already alluded to the Polish Conventual Franciscans and the Precious Blood Fathers. St. Francis de Sales Church, Geneva, likewise had an Italian Dominican Father for assistant in 1930-1931. And toward the end of O'Hern's career Vincentian priests were added on a temporary basis to the faculty of St. Bernard's Seminary.

Mention has also been made of the advent of two new teaching orders of nuns, the Lithuanian Franciscans and the Franciscan Sisters of Allegany. In 1930, the Bishop entrusted the specialized task of educating girls with problems to still another religious community, the Sisters of Charity of the Refuge. On his invitation, the Buffalo convent of this cloistered order sent to Rochester Mother Mary of St. Agnes Zimmerman and six other Sisters. The official foundation of the new convent took place on July 6, 1930; but Holy Angels Home, built on a twelve and one-half acre plot on Winton Road, was not finished for another seven months. Bishop O'Hern dedicated it on February 8, 1931.[21]

A second cloistered order of nuns, contemplatives rather than educators, was likewise welcomed into the Diocese in 1930. These were the Discalced Carmelites.

O'Hern, deeply aware of the power of prayer for the benefit of any diocese, had in 1929 invited the Carmelite nuns of Philadelphia to found a monastery in Rochester. To his great pleasure, the nuns consented. He therefore secured a locale for their convent, the large house at 151 Saratoga Avenue which had been the residence of Clarence A. Barbour. This had to be outfitted and fenced about, in accord with the Carmelite rule, before the nuns could come to Rochester. When all was ready, the Carmelites set out from Philadelphia for their new home. There were six in the pioneer group: three choir nuns, two lay sisters, and an "out-sister" to live outside the cloister area and act as a middleman between the cloister and the "world." The Bishop formally inaugurated the Monastery of Our Lady and St. Joseph on the feast of Corpus Christi, June 19, 1930. On hand as the special guest of the Bishop was the papal internuncio to Haiti, Archbishop George J. Caruana. The Archbishop spoke prophetically when he declared in his address, "This convent will become the storehouse of all spirituality in the Diocese."

That was certainly the hope of the foundress and superior of the new monastery, Mother Beatrix of the Holy Spirit (1845-1939). She was eighty-four when she came to Rochester, but had a sprightly vigor and a wide experience that enabled her to govern with a sure hand. Possibly not since Mother M. Xavier Warde established St. Mary's Convent of Mercy in Rochester some seventy years before, had a nun of the eminence of Mother Beatrix set up a new foundation in Rochester.

Born Camilla Josephine Magers, of a prosperous Catholic family of Baltimore, Sister Beatrix had made her studies at St. Joseph's Academy, Emmitsburg, Maryland, during the Civil War years, and had entered the Carmelite monastery of Baltimore on June 24, 1868. Her religious profession took place on July 27th of the following year. The Baltimore monastery is the oldest house of Carmelite nuns in this country. It was founded in 1790 at Port Tobacco, Maryland, and moved to Baltimore forty years later. Sister Beatrix, as a nun of the third generation, had an opportunity to be trained in the religious life by nuns of the second generation who had been associated with the pioneer American Carmelites. She thus became an authority on the customs of Carmelite life, and an important link between the earliest American foundation and the many that have sprung from it in the present century. Consequently, she had served in many posts of authority before coming to Rochester. She was prioress at Baltimore, Wheeling, West Virginia, and Philadelphia. She herself founded the Boston Carmel (1890) and supervised the founding of the Philadelphia Carmel (1902). Sisters trained by her norms established several more monasteries across the nation. She gave valuable counsel to the Foreign Mission Sisters of St. Dominic (Maryknoll) when they inaugurated a cloistered convent at their Hudson Valley motherhouse. She played an important role in popularizing in this country devotion to St. Therese of Lisieux and in promoting her canonization. Mother Beatrix gave the Rochester Carmel nine years of leadership and good example. She died on January 29, 1939 at 1530 East Avenue—a new Rochester "Carmel" into which she and her nuns had moved in June, 1934. At the time of her passing, this ninety-three-year-old religious was said to be the oldest Carmelite nun in the world. Rochester and the Diocese could never know how much it owed to her hidden, prayerful presence.[22]

John Francis O'Hern was a firm exponent and defender of Catholic faith and morals; and firmness sometimes must lead a bishop into public controversy. As we shall see later, O'Hern was by nature irenic rather than controversial. It seems that he became embroiled in only one public altercation, and that was a brief one over birth control.

In the 1920's and 1930's, Margaret Sanger was campaigning against the civil laws which forbade the dissemination of contraceptive devices and instruction in their use. She came to Rochester as early as February, 1922, and presented her case for eugenics with a variety of arguments, some thoughtful, others less so. On that occasion, Father Frederick J. Zwierlein answered her in a sermon at Sacred Heart Church.[23]

Ten years later, Mrs. Sanger returned under the sponsorship of a local group for a more public appearance, on January 20, 1932. She had in the meantime been convicted and imprisoned for breaking the New York State anti-contraception laws. Bishop O'Hern arranged for Mrs. Eugene Dwyer, wife of the diocesan attorney, to attend the meeting and make a report. Mrs. Dwyer and her daughter, Mrs. Mary Katherine Keenan, did so. That evening, Mrs. Dwyer issued a public statement stating that while the speaker had used general terms in the lecture proper, she had later on given to a group of questioners specific contraceptive pointers that seemed to go counter to section 1142 of the State Penal Law. Mrs. Sanger and her sponsor promptly denied the charge. Attorney Dwyer reiterated the accusation. The press considered the attorney's intervention as an official action of the Rochester Diocese.

It *was* an official action, at least indirectly. But the diocesan officials can scarcely have intended to do any more than give the birth control movement a salutary legal warning. The controversy, as a controversy, ended on that note. The Bishop himself uttered the last public word on the subject a week later. Mrs. Sanger, in her address, had stated that Italy, currently intent on increasing its population, was re-quiring that every married woman who did not have a new child every two years report to the health bureau and explain why. "Italy, it seems," concluded Mrs. Sanger, "would breed humans like animals." She pre-dicted that Italy's bursting population would undoubtedly overflow into France. This was one of her typical arguments, and it was expressed in bad taste. Cesare Sconfietti, the consular agent for Italy residing in Rochester, telegraphed to the *Democrat and Chronicle:* "Her state-ments regarding Italy are entirely contrary to facts and her uncalled for comments could only be imputed to extreme need of notoriety." Then on January 27th, Bishop O'Hern addressed a large audience of Italo-Americans at the Columbus Civic Center. He took this occasion to deplore Mrs. Sanger's remarks on the Italian people. Our good Italian people, he said, had no need to apologize for their domestic traditions to Americans, "much less to an ex-convict."[24]

Unhappy and rather infelicitous in controversy, Bishop O'Hern, who was cheerful and sociable by nature, felt completely at home at public festivities, whether devotional or social. One celebration that occurred during his term of office splendidly combined both of these aspects: the grand centennial of Our Mother of Sorrows Church in the Town of Greece.

As we have already mentioned, this, the first Catholic rural parish in the State, was built between 1829 and 1832, and for the first three decades of its existence bore the name St. Ambrose. Father Daniel B. O'Rourke, named pastor of the church in the 1920's, was a great stu-dent of its romantic history. He resolved to commemorate the centenary with no small ceremony. The Bishop fell in readily with his plans. June 8, 1930, was chosen as the date of the main observance. That morning, when O'Hern offered the solemn pontifical Mass in the crowd-ed little building, Governor and Mrs. Franklin Delano Roosevelt oc-cupied the front pews as guests of honor. After the Mass was over, the Governor and other guests, standing on a platform erected outside the church, addressed the large crowd that had gathered for this notable event. Here O'Hern was in his element, and thoroughly enjoyed him-self. Nor had the future President any reason to regret that he had accepted the invitation.

Father O'Rourke might well have complimented himself on the success of the affair. Later on, Roosevelt, with a knowing touch, did something else that warmed the heart of the pastor. The usher had been carefully instructed *not* to pass the basket to the Governor and his wife at the offertory of the Mass, and he had carefully obeyed. But Roosevelt had apparently *wanted* to give an offering. So he had it delivered to the pastor *post factum*.[25]

2. "SERVIRE REGNARE EST."

When he was named a bishop, John Francis O'Hern chose as his heraldic motto a phrase from the votive Mass for peace *"servire regnare est"*—"to serve (God) is to reign." And he took that motto literally. "My motto shall be service," he declared on the occasion of his consecration. "The episcopate places a man to rule in the Church of God, but to rule only in a way that will mean constant and devoted sacrifice of self in the service of the people of God." This statement, made in 1929, sounds curiously like a passage from the Constitution on the Church proclaimed thirty-five years later by the Second Vatican Council. For O'Hern it summarized a pact which he made with God at his episcopal consecration, and which, according to his lights, he strove as bishop to fulfill.[26]

We have already described the outlook of Rochester's third bishop as irenic, conciliatory. It is probably no exaggeration to say that he dedicated his whole regime to bringing people together, high and low, rich and poor, Catholic and non-Catholic, in justice and Christian love.

As head of the Diocese, he had first of all to deploy his clergy well and maintain with them a fitting relationship. He early added to his clerical administration three new commissions, one on building projects, one on church music (see his special pastoral and instruction of February 6, 1930), and one on organ building. He also set up (did this trouble the shade of Bishop McQuaid?) a diocesan chapter of the Friends of the Catholic University of America. He went out of his way to establish a social rapport with his priests. He invited them in to dinner in groups, and at public functions he was loth to halt the speeches until all of the clergy in attendance had been called on for "a few words." In assigning his priests he made a sincere effort to take seniority and merits into consideration; and when he gave an order he phrased it as a request rather than a command. He took a genuine interest in their problems, and sympathized with them in their griefs. His endeavors were not, of course, completely successful. The decisions he made did not please all, and many found it tedious to sit through his interminable programs of after-dinner speakers. But even those clergy who faulted the acts and practices of their diocesan leader never doubted his good will towards themselves.

The third prelate of Irish ancestry to govern the Diocese of Rochester, Bishop O'Hern was as loyal to Ireland as his predecessors had been. He was nevertheless persuaded that Bishop Hickey had not—at least of late—paid sufficient attention to diocesans of other national strains. Consequently, a year after the death in 1931 of the beloved diocesan chancellor, Msgr. Michael J. Nolan, O'Hern named to succeed him the gentle, patient pastor of St. Boniface German Church, Monsignor John M. Boppel (1869-1947). He likewise relied much on the services of the talented pastor of Holy Redeemer German Church, Msgr. F. William Stauder (1882-1955), and the unselfish pastor of St. Michael's German Church, Father Ferdinand P. Scheid (1873-1934), and thus engaged the particular loyalty of these two capable men.

The Bishop also manifested a special interest in the Poles of the diocese. It was on his own initiative that in 1931 he provided the Polish farmers of Catatonk, Tioga County, with their own church. The Poles of the Diocese, and especially the parishioners of St. Stanislaus and St. Theresa churches in Rochester, were naturally proud of their countryman, the great Ignaz Jan Paderewski—pianist, composer and patriot. When he came to Rochester for a concert on February 5, 1932, a committee of local Polish men and prominent citizens waited on the virtuoso to present him a gift "From the Poles of Rochester to the Master of the Piano." The Bishop of Rochester was one of that committee.[27]

If there was any national group which Bishop O'Hern favored more than the others, it was the Italians. Two factors in particular led him to focus attention on his Italian diocesans. In the first place, he retained fond memories of his own student years in Italy, and had a fair acquaintance with the language of Dante. In the second place, he realized that Italians and the descendants of Italians would before long compose a large proportion of the Catholics of the Diocese. When he learned that in 1928 one-tenth of the Catholics born in the city of Rochester were born into the families of parishioners of Mount Carmel Church, he could only agree with Father Foery, the pastor of that parish: "We see who our future citizens will be." This thought motivated the Bishop in his establishment of the several Italian "mission chapels" that we have already alluded to. This was a better policy, he thought, than setting up full-fledged "national" parishes. Chapels could be more easily promoted, in due time, to the rank of full-fledged territorial parishes. This would facilitate Americanization. It was also in the interests of such Americanization that the Bishop had Father Foery enlarge his parochial school.

Bishop O'Hern extended the hand of welcome in 1931 to a group of over forty military directors of physical education direct from Italy. They had been sent over to take a course in Dansville at the Bernarr Macfadden school of physical culture. When he learned of their sojourn in his diocese, O'Hern quickly saw the pastoral and ceremonial possibilities of the situation. He therefore planned to give them a weekend of his time. On April 11th, he went down to Dansville and announced he would be available for confessions in Italian. The next day, Sunday, he celebrated a pontifical Mass for them in Dansville's St. Mary's Church. It was a grand affair. Cesare Sconfietti, the Italian consular agent at Rochester, was on hand; Father Philip Robotti, O.P., preached; and the Bishop himself greeted the visitors most cordially. That these visitors had been sent by a Fascist government did not disturb the Bishop of Rochester, nor should it have. These were gymnasium directors, not ideologists or policy makers; and to O'Hern they were simply nice young Italians far away from home, most likely lonesome, appreciative of a little splurge, and perhaps in need of a little spiritual pull . . . or push.[28]

The Italians of the Diocese itself were quite aware of the Bishop's fondness for them, and they were always ready to return generosity for generosity. They paid him their most notable tribute at a banquet given in his honor at the Columbus Civic Center on January 27, 1932. Scores of representative Italians turned out for the affair, which was climaxed by the presentation of a lifesized painting of Bishop O'Hern, executed by one Signor D'Ambrosio, an Italo-American portraitist from New York. It was the intention of the donors that O'Hern hang the picture in the Columbus Civic Center, and he accepted it on this understanding. In expressing his gratitude, the Bishop praised Italy and the artistic genius of its people.[29]

Almost a year before this presentation by local Italians, John F. O'Hern had been honored by King Victor Emmanuel III of Italy with the decoration of knight commander of the Order of the Crown of Italy. The local Italian consular agent, Mr. Sconfietti, announced the award on February 17, 1931, which was the thirtieth anniversary of O'Hern's ordination to the priesthood. Only one other Rochesterian had thus far been accorded this distinction—George Eastman, in acknowledgment of his contributions to relief after World War I, and to art.[30] The Bishop of Rochester was no less deserving of official Italian recognition. Not only had he done much for Americans of Italian descent; apparently he had already played some part in the establishment of the Eastman Clinic in Rome. When the Clinic was ready for dedication in

1933, O'Hern was scheduled to go to Rome to dedicate it. Ill health and, subsequently, his death prevented the realization of that plan.[31]

Bishop O'Hern thought that Bishop Hickey had tended to slight not only his non-Irish diocesans but also the clergy and faithful who lived outside Monroe County. Whether the latter opinion was correct or not—and if it was, surely Bishop Hickey's neglect was not intentional—it did lead O'Hern to forge more intimate bonds of friendship between the headquarters of the Diocese and its remoter members. At the outset, the new bishop—himself a native of a Southern Tier county—launched a campaign to "bring the Southern Tier back into the Diocese." Thereafter he made a point of visiting Elmira practically once a month. In the fall of 1930 he conducted the blessing of the graves not only in Rochester but at Geneva and Auburn. He likewise showed a nice diplomacy when he went to confirm or speak in the more rural communities. His secretary, Father Charles Reynolds, had standing orders to provide him well in advance with a basic history of the parish he was preparing to visit. These historical memoranda served a double purpose: they acquainted the Bishop with parochial histories, and they gave him topical material for his address. Naturally the parishioners were pleased and edified to listen to a bishop who knew sometimes even more than they did about their local Catholic annals. And his conquest was complete when he was able to exclaim, "Why, goodness gracious, Sister Mary So and So comes from here!"

John Francis O'Hern was much more a "layman's bishop" than either of the two prelates who preceded him. Naturally, therefore, he took a special interest in the lay apostolate.

Of the several Catholic organizations founded under O'Hern the Nocturnal Adoration Society was the most purely spiritual in nature, and yet one of the most popular.

The Nocturnal Adoration Movement is an old one, begun in France in 1815 and brought to these shores in 1882. It is under the tutelage of the Blessed Sacrament Fathers. The movement was introduced into the Rochester Diocese in 1929, as a by-product of the flourishing Rochester Laymen's Retreat League. Two Retreat League members, William G. Wynn and James P. B. Duffy, proposed to Father Charles F. Shay, rector of St. Patrick's Cathedral, that a branch of the Nocturnal Adoration Society be established in the Cathedral parish. Father Shay agreed, on condition that the Bishop would consent. Bishop O'Hern gave his approbation readily and named Shay the moderator of the Society.

On the opening date, October 28, 1929, two hundred men from

many parishes in the city assembled in the Cathedral's Lady Chapel to register as members. By 1932 there were 600 names on the membership roll. Delighted with this development, Bishop O'Hern circularized his pastors throughout the Diocese in February, 1932, urging them to set up Nocturnal Adoration branches in their own districts.[32] During the next few months enrollment began at Auburn, Geneva, Hornell, Seneca Falls, Elmira and Ithaca; and in later years additional chapters have been set up elsewhere in the Diocese.[33] (Mr. Harry P. Somerville, a member of the Rochester Nocturnal Adoration Society, even became responsible for introducing the movement in the Nation's Capital after his transfer to the managership of the famous Willard Hotel.) By 1955 there were 4,000 laymen of the Rochester Diocese registered as members of the Society, over half of them in the Rochester metropolitan area.[34] By 1965, there were eighteen centers across the Diocese. What is most amazing about this growth is that the N.A.S. is strictly spiritual in purpose and quite demanding in rule. Each member must spend one full hour a month in night adoration before the Blessed Sacrament. While the "bands" operate in staggered hourly shifts, so that no member is perpetually assigned to the "wee small hours," the program still remains a sacrificial one. Quite likely it was the very challenge involved that made this virile devotion so popular. The introduction of the Nocturnal Adoration movement into the Rochester Diocese was certainly one of the most solid accomplishments of the O'Hern regime.

Most of the lay organizations that the Bishop encouraged had social as well as spiritual aims. In the 1920's and 1930's Pope Pius XI was strongly advocating "Catholic Action," which he defined as the participation of the laity in the efforts of the hierarchy to restore the reign of Christ over men. Activist as he was by nature, Bishop O'Hern was happy to encourage the lay societies which already existed and to create new federations along the lines recommended by the Holy Father.

Of the interparochial organizations already existing in the Rochester Diocese, the most prominent were the German Catholic federations of men and women; the Holy Name Society; and the Sodality of Our Lady. The German Catholic Men's Federation and Catholic Women's Federation had long been active in the lay apostolate; with them it was merely a case of stepping up their efforts.[35] After Father F. William Stauder had been designated diocesan director of the Holy Name Society in 1931, that organization sprang into new life. A feature of the program of the diocesan Holy Name Union was the candlelight rally. The first rally was held in Rochester's Red Wing Stadium on June 12, 1932. Fourteen thousand Holy Name men from all parts of the twelve counties were on hand, and six thousand spectators. When they lighted the tapers, studding the grandstand with a myriad of twinkling flames, it was a breathtaking sight.[36] The Sodality offered even greater opportunity for apostolic projects. In November, 1932, O'Hern named Father Robert J. Fox of Rochester to the post of diocesan sodality moderator. An organizational meeting held in the Columbus Civic Center on November 11th, attracted close to one thousand young women representing forty parishes. Assisting at this first convention was the national organizer of the Sodalities of Our Lady, Father Daniel J. Lord, S.J. The Bishop himself attended and addressed the Sodalists.[37]

A few months before these larger organizations were reactivated, a smaller and more specialized Catholic Action group had been inaugurated. A number of Rochester Catholic physicians, on April 26, 1929, formed a St. Luke's Guild. They elected the Bishop their honorary president.[38]

Catholic Action, as a definite apostolate, was variously organized in different countries. In the United States, Catholic Action implied affiliation with the National Catholic Welfare Council, the coordinating agency of the American hierarchy. John F. O'Hern held two offices in the N.C.W.C. He was elected by his fellow bishops to the Administrative Board in 1930, 1931 and 1932.[39] He was also appointed to a special committee to study the Catholic press, and to another to study the organization of the N.C.W.C. itself with a view to reshaping it more effectively.[40] Since he was thus a policy-making member of the national body, he no doubt felt a still more urgent responsibility to federate his diocesan men's societies with the Conference's National Council of Catholic Men, and his diocesan women's societies with the National Council of Catholic Women.

The diocesan council of the National Council of Catholic Men was organized with a flourish in November, 1931. The Rochester Diocese had played host, from October 11th to October 15th, to the National convention of the N.C.C.M. The convention had welcomed a host of delegates from across the nation—prelates, distinguished laymen (among them Rear Admiral William S. Benson), and experts on social justice. The current financial depression had much to do with the choice of subjects discussed: social needs, trade unionism, unemployment relief. Speakers included Frederick P. Kenkel, prominent lay leader of the Central Verein; and Fathers John A. Ryan, Raymond A. McGowan, and Francis J. Haas, acknowledged authorities on social ethics. The highlight of the convocation was Father Ryan's proposal of an antidote to the contemporary unemployment—a five billion dollar federal program of public works. This was a good eighteen months before Franklin Delano Roosevelt, having taken the oath as president, embarked on just such a program.[41] It was with fresh memories of this convention that laymen from each of the diocesan deancries met with Bishop O'Hern on November 8, 1931, to form the Rochester Council of Catholic Men. The newly formed diocesan Council held its first convention at Geneva on May 15, 1932.[42] In its early months of existence the Rochester group functioned actively. Attorney Frederick J. Mix, one of the diocesan officials, was also a delegate to the national organization, and as such participated in the setting up of the Catholic Hour, a nationwide radio broadcast that still continues to operate in television. However, Archbishop Mooney, who succeeded Bishop O'Hern as head of the Diocese of Rochester, took more interest in the National Council of Catholic Women than in the National Council of Catholic Men. As a consequence, the local N.C.C.M. chapter never lived up to the hopes that O'Hern had reposed in it.[43]

The Diocesan Council of Catholic Women was formed on April 23, 1931, also under the watchful eye of John Francis O'Hern. Several hundred women, representing 150 Catholic organizations throughout the Diocese, took part in the original meeting. The delegates chose presidents for each deanery unit, and conferred the diocesan presidency on the able and dedicated Rochester Catholic social leader, Miss Cecilia M. Yawman (1865-1950). After a couple of preliminary meetings, this Diocesan Council held its first convention, on October 21-22, 1931.[44] Since its establishment, the Council has remained active. Diocesan meetings and workshops have kept the membership informed on late developments, especially along social welfare lines. In its earlier years, the local Council participated in scholarship program of the National Council's School of Social Service in Washington. In more recent times, it has sponsored the Marian Award of the diocesan Girl Scouts, the Pre-Cana Conferences, and the annual drive for used clothing.

Generous man that he was, Bishop O'Hern was always ready not only to praise the deeds of his clergy and laity—with superlatives—but to bestow upon leaders among them tokens of reward.

As regards honors for the clergy, Bishops McQuaid and Hickey had both solicited them occasionally from the Holy See. Bishop McQuaid, as we have seen, requested the title of monsignor for a couple of his priests; in a few other cases he petitioned Rome for honorary doctorates of divinity. Bishop Hickey went somewhat farther, asking domestic prelacies for his principal officials. But neither he nor most of his American confreres made many such requests in those days. In 1928 monsignori were still so relatively few in the United States (700) that the *Official Catholic Yearbook* of that year listed all the American monsignors together in a special nine-page section. However, the number of these honors was certainly mounting even then.

John F. O'Hern did not adhere to the example of McQuaid and Hickey, but went along with the newer trend. Between 1929 and 1932 he petitioned for the domestic prelacy for thirteen of his priests. The group included not only his vicar general and chancellor and the Seminary rector, but the diocesan consultors and some of the rural deans. In this way the Bishop was able to make a gesture of recognition both to his German diocesans (two of the monsignori were Germans: Father Boppel, the Chancellor, and Father John P. Schellhorn, a consultor) and to the Southern Tier (three of the monsignori were deans there; a fourth was dean at Geneva). For Msgr. James J. Hartley, a domestic prelate since 1914, Bishop O'Hern secured the added honor of protonotary apostolic on November 26, 1932. Monsignor Hartley was the first priest in the Rochester Diocese to be granted this. higher distinction.[45]

In soliciting papal and quasi-papal awards for prominent lay diocesans, O'Hern took a step which his two predecessors had not taken.

One of the papal awards was the medal *"Pro Ecclesia et Pontifice"* ("For Church and Pope"). Pope Pius XI first granted it, at the Bishop's request, to the beloved musician, Professor F. Eugene Bonn. O'Hern pinned the medal on the octogenarian organist at a special ceremony held in the Cathedral in November, 1930.[46] In March, 1932, the same decoration was accorded to five leading Catholic laywomen. They were: Mrs. Teresa Ganster, national president of the Ladies' Auxiliary, Knights of St. John; Mrs. Cora McParlin, Supreme Trustee of the nationwide Ladies' Catholic Benevolent Association; Miss Alice P. Kirk, president of the Rochester Catholic Women's Club; Miss Cecilia M. Yawman, president of the Rochester Diocesan Council of Catholic Women; and (from outside the see city) Miss Elizabeth A. Harmon, District Deputy of the Auburn district, Catholic Daughters of America. The papal medals were conferred on the five recipients with all due public ceremony.[47] (It will be recalled that Mrs. McParlin was one of those to whom Bishop McQuaid had refused the sacraments because she sent her daughter to other than a Catholic college!)

March 19, 1931—the second anniversary of the O'Hern consecration—was a red letter day for honorifics. It was on that day that he himself received the decoration from the King of Italy, as we have related above. During the course of the day's observance the Bishop conferred the garb of their rank on four new domestic prelates: Monsignori John Boppel, John Brophy, George V. Burns, and Joseph Cameron. Finally he set a precedent by conferring the insignia of the papal knighthood of St Gregory upon five diocesan laymen, carefully chosen as representatives of the Irish, German, Polish and Italian segments of the faithful of the Diocese. The recipients were: Eugene Dwyer, official attorney of the Diocese; Attorney James P. B. Duffy, president of the Duffy-Powers department store and a lay leader; Joseph H. Weis, furniture merchant and an official in the Knights of St. John; Walter Wojtczak, owner of a large Polish bakery; and Harry C. D'Annunzio, chief designer at Fashion Park, one of Rochester's principal clothing factories.[48]

On Sunday, May 24, 1931, the Bishop presided in the Cathedral at the investiture of three Rochester laymen in a still rarer knighthood, that of the Sovereign Order of Malta. This military religious order, established in the twelfth century to further the efforts of the Crusades, still continues as a hospitaller order engaged in international philanthropy. On O'Hern's petition, the Grand Master in Rome conferred knightly rank upon James P. B. Duffy, already a recipient of the papal Order of St. Gregory the Great; Jeremiah Hickey, clothing manufacturer and brother of Archbishop Hickey; and Dr. Joseph P. O'Hern (1868-1939), deputy superintendent of the Rochester public schools, and the Bishop's cousin. Officiating at the installation in the name of the Grand Master was the Master of the American Chapter of the Knights, Mr. James J. Phelan of New York.[49]

Finally, on April 24, 1932, Bishop O'Hern delivered to another group the insignia of still a third equestrian order, that of the Holy Sepulchre. This is a distinction, also of crusade origin, which is granted by the Latin Patriarch of Jerusalem. On the occasion of the conferral, the Bishop himself was awarded the rank of Knight Commander with Medal; and the cross of Knight Commander was conferred on Msgr. John Francis Goggin, rector of St. Bernard's Seminary. The other ten admitted to the Order were diocesan laymen, chosen, once more, with a view to representing the various national origins and localities in the Rochester Diocese. Six were from Rochester proper: Augustine J. Cunningham, Thomas W. Finucane, Frank H. Biel, Frederick J. Weider, Peter Tettelbach, and William E. Maloney. Of the other four, two were Elmirans (J. John Hassett and Michael A. Del Papa); one was a Corningite (Frederick F. Pfeiffer); and one was an Auburnian (Frank J. Lesch). Most of these men were businessmen or executives.[50]

If this last investiture took place more quietly in the Bishop's private chapel, it was not because O'Hern had planned it thus, but because he was at that date recuperating from an illness. The third Bishop of Rochester placed great stock in splendid ecclesiastical functions not just because "everyone loves a parade," but because he believed that imposing affairs had a distinct publicity value.

One close observer has put it, "Bishop O'Hern had a superb sense of public relations." "Why not make the Church better known?" he would argue: "Bigotry is the product of ignorance." He had long been aware of the worth of press publicity. While rector of the Cathedral he edited the monthly *Cathedral Calendar,* a miscellaneous parish magazine. He was also prompt to communicate Catholic news items to the daily press. As bishop, he maintained most cordial relations with the Fourth Estate. He did not have to seek out reporters; they came to him. He was always picturesque and newsworthy, and the journalists knew that he would give them correct information on any matter of Catholic interest. News photographers found him a cooperative subject. There was a standing joke among them that John Francis O'Hern would stop in the middle of anything to accommodate them.[51]

It was, of course, Bishop O'Hern who in 1929 adopted the *Catholic Journal* as a diocesan paper—the first official Rochester diocesan paper since the *Catholic Times* of the 1880's.

There had been three other English Catholic newspapers in the Diocese since the demise of the *Times.* One was the *Catholic Citizen,* a tabloid put out by the Kennedy Brothers, Rochester printers, in the early years of this century. From 1922 to 1933 or 1934, the *Echo,* a Buffalo Catholic paper, issued a Rochester edition, under the editorship of Thomas H. O'Connor. In its latter years the Rochester edition was called the *Rochester Echo.* But the oldest local Catholic paper was the *Catholic Journal,* established in 1889 by two printers, Edward J. Ryan and Thomas H. Donovan, and a cub reporter, Willard Marakle. Bishop McQuaid gave their project his blessing, but assumed no responsibility for it. The *Journal* could be more properly called an advertising sheet directed to a (limited) Catholic audience, than a newspaper systematically dedicated to reporting Catholic news. In 1929, a group of Catholic laymen purchased this paper from the owners, and on March 15th of that year, with its name changed to *Catholic Courier and Journal,* it reappeared as an official diocesan publication. For the nonce, the paper remained the property of the new purchasers; but on April 7, 1932, the Diocese assumed fiscal responsibility for it. However, the *Catholic Courier and Journal* was not fully reorganized until after the death of Bishop O'Hern.[52]

John F. O'Hern was also aware of the potentialities of motion pictures as a medium of publicity and religious education. In 1931, he collaborated with Eastman Teaching Films, a subsidiary of the Kodak Company, in the production of a sixteen-millimeter, two-reel silent film, "The Sacrifice of the Mass." It was a complete enactment of the rite of the Mass—the first, it was said, to be produced in the United States. Father William E. Brien was the "celebrant"; seminarian William Gioseffi was the "server"; and Father Wilfred T. Craugh of St. Bernard's Seminary edited the film and prepared the explanatory booklet that was distributed with it. After its release, "The Sacrifice of the Mass" was widely used. Had it not been for the Great Depression, the Bishop would doubtless have carried out his further plan of producing documentary films on the other sacraments.[53] But he still placed a high value on the moving picture camera as a means of recording history. With his encouragement, his secretary, Father Charles R. Reynolds, took as many as ten thousand feet of sixteen-millimeter motion pictures of parochial and diocesan events. Much of this footage, preserved today, constitutes a unique record of church activities in the late 1920's and early 1930's.[54]

Bishop O'Hern was equally enthusiastic about the potentialities of religious radio broadcasts. Rochester's pioneer radio station, WHAM, pleased with the reception given to its broadcast of the O'Hern consecration in March, 1929, decided to present five religious broadcasts that same fall, featuring discussions between a Catholic priest and a Protestant minister. The Bishop fell in with the plan and designated Father Leo C. Mooney to represent the Catholics. The minister was the Reverend Dr. Justin Wroe Nixon, pastor of Rochester's Brick Presbyterian Church, a clergyman distinguished for what would today be called the "ecumenical spirit." Then on February 2, 1930, with the generous cooperation of the same station, a strictly Catholic program was initiated. Father Charles F. Shay, the rector of the Cathedral, was in charge of the presentation (which was soon extended to a full hour); and it comprised choral music, an address, and a question-box period. This pioneer program yielded, on October 23, 1932, to a "Catholic Radio Hour," directed by Father Leo C. Mooney for the next decade and more.[55] Auburn Catholics followed suit, and on April 2, 1933, the radio station at Auburn, WMBO, launched a Catholic program.[56] Meanwhile nationwide Catholic programs were multiplying. The N.C.C.M., on March 9, 1930, started the national broadcast of a popular and durable series of lectures by a rising young professor at the Catholic University of America named the Reverend Doctor Fulton J. Sheen.[57] The

Bishop of Rochester himself addressed a national audience over station WHEC on November 22, 1931. The program was on Catholic church music, and the day—well chosen—was the feast of the patron saint of church music, St. Cecilia.[58]

Looked at from our present point of time, the early radio efforts of the Diocese of Rochester would seem amateurish. Even in their own day, they were pretty homespun. It is arguable that the Rochester Diocese—and the same can be said of most American Catholic dioceses—has never sufficiently utilized radio or television as a channel of religious communication. If local Catholic broadcasting during the O'Hern regime lacked expertise and wide impact, the Bishop himself must nevertheless be given credit for making this further attempt to inform non-Catholics about Catholic rites and beliefs.

A bishop, as an instructor in Christian virtue, must not neglect to inculcate the virtue of patriotism by word and example. John Francis O'Hern was too transparently idealistic to forego this duty. Though his episcopate ran its course during a war-free decade, he was always devoted to the needs of his nation, as his support of the government's anti-depression efforts amply proved. His personal devotion to America was perhaps best expressed in the moving address he gave at the "presentation of flags" to the parochial school children of Rochester on May 3, 1933, just a few days before his death. "Patriotism," he said, "is love of country and loyalty to its highest and best needs: a love tender and strong—tender as the affection of a son for a mother, strong as the pillars of death." He pointed out that true patriotism must avoid two extremes: a "superior nationalism" on the one hand, and, on the other, a pacifism which opposes preparedness. Praise was due to the parochial schools, he declared, for teaching their children true patriotism. Americans, he said, should glory in their national heritage. If St. Paul claimed *"Civis Romanus sum*—I am a Roman citizen," the American can make a still nobler claim: *"Civis Americanus sum*—I am an American citizen."[59]

In the last analysis, patriotism is not so much love of a whole nation as love of the *patria,* the district, of one's birth. John O'Hern was truly fond of the Genesee Country. He was born near the headwaters of the upper Genesee River and spent most of his priestly life near its lower reaches. It must have pleased him when, in early 1932, the Society of the Genesee, at its annual banquet in New York, chose him its official chaplain.[60]

The Bishop, finally, was alive to the interests of his adoptive city, the seat of his episcopate: to its health and welfare, its culture, its prosperity, its history.

He gave strong backing to the Community Chest and the Red Cross. In July, 1929, he sent a circular to Catholic parents of Rochester and vicinity urging them to cooperate in the Statewide drive for diphtheria immunization.[61] In the following year, disturbed by the report of overcrowded conditions at the Rochester State Hospital for the Insane, he urged his diocesans to vote "yes" to a State bond issue for the improvement of all New York State mental hospitals.[62] One of his first public acts as bishop was to commend the Civic Music Association of Rochester.[63] The local Chamber of Commerce received his warm support, and he attended its meetings regularly. Civic observances appealed to him scarcely less than church celebrations. Thus he was happy to take part on September 9, 1931, in the national commemoration of the foundation of the American Red Cross, held in Stony Brook Park near Dansville. As bishop of the Diocese that contained the two communities—Rochester and Dansville—in which the foundress of American Red Cross, Clara Barton, had begun her great work, he shared the microphone with Governor Franklin D. Roosevelt, who attended the celebration, and President Herbert C. Hoover, who broadcast from Washington.[64]

But the Bishop's spirit of public peace and reconciliation was never more strongly exhibited than in his public dealings with citizens of other faiths.

The first and second bishops of Rochester, as we have seen, had known and respected many Protestants and Jews of the area, and had not been slow to indicate their personal esteem. For the most part, however, they had concentrated on purely Catholic concerns. John Francis O'Hern was much more outgoing and outspoken. Thus in 1929 he paid public tribute to the late Charles Brent, the able Episcopal Bishop of Western New York.[65] In November, 1930, when two thousand Rochester Jews assembled in a mass meeting to protest the British curtailment of immigration into Palestine, he sent them a letter of sympathy.[66] Then on Christmas, 1931, in a broadcast originating from the Cathedral, the Bishop extended Christmas greetings not only to the Catholic faithful but to Protestants and Jews of the area, "with a prayer that the Christ Child may bless them and theirs in all their hearts' desires at this Holy Season."[67] He was also friendly with the Rochester

Masons; and when one of their members, Esten E. Fletcher, was chosen by the American Shriners as their Imperial Potentate, he publicly congratulated him on his new office.[68]

By time-honored custom, Catholic clergymen have usually taken part with non-Catholic clergymen in civic celebrations. Bishop O'Hern was ready to carry social collaboration even farther. On February 1, 1932, he was guest of honor at a luncheon meeting of the Ministerial Association of Rochester, held at the Central Presbyterian Church. Before screening for them the newly completed film, "The Sacrifice of the Mass," he addressed his clerical hosts in a most conciliatory vein.[69]

He encouraged the Newman Movement at non-Catholic colleges and universities in much the same mood. He appointed priests to serve as chaplains to the Catholics attending both the men's and women's campuses of the University of Rochester; and to Catholic girls enrolled at Elmira College. These were part-time assignments. At Cornell Bishop O'Hern installed a full-time chaplain—a highly intelligent and university-trained priest borrowed from the Diocese of Albany, Father James T. Cronin, Ph.D. (1897-1952). What prompted this move was the fact that Cornell was very progressive in making provision for religious emphasis among its students. The Cornell University Religious Work (C.U.R.W.) had originated in 1919. It was initially a corporation comprising students and chaplains, organized to coordinate Protestant religious activities on the campus. But in 1929, C.U.R.W. expanded its compass by inviting Catholics and Jewish students to join its board. Father Cronin became principally responsible for developing the Catholic phase of C.U.R.W. participation. In October, 1930, Bishop O'Hern went to Ithaca and celebrated Mass for the Catholic students at Cornell in Barnes Hall. The whole ministerial staff of C.U.R.W. attended the rite.[70]

In our own day, when Catholics, under the leadership of Pope John XXIII and the Second Vatican Council, have bidden welcome to the Ecumenical Movement, the interfaith gestures of John Francis O'Hern would seem far from radical. In his day, however, they were received with mixed emotions. Most of the diocesan priests, though encouraged by their Bishop to imitate him in interdenominational action, preferred to beg off. Non-Catholic clergymen—apart, at least, from such admirable bridge-builders as David Lincoln Ferris, Episcopal Bishop of Rochester, and Dr. Justin Wroe Nixon, pastor of Brick Presbyterian Church—were apparently no more comfortable about these novel contacts. The attitude of the Catholic priests was, in a sense, understandable. On more than one interfaith occasion, some non-Catholic spokesman had voiced the sentiment that "one church is as good as another," a view in which Catholics could not honestly concur. Nor was the non-Catholic distrust of Catholicism yet in decline. The Bishop himself might be invited to offer Mass in a Cornell hall; but afterward the Secretary of C.U.R.W. was called upon to justify the invitation.

In other words, the old religious antagonisms were still too strong in the 1930's to allow for a truly ecumenical view—to admit firm differences in faith, but to encourage mutual discussions in the hope of finally resolving divisions in God's good time. Bishop O'Hern himself was far from possessing a well-defined ecumenical philosophy, and sometimes in these affairs he spoke out of turn. What was admirable about his interfaith efforts was his intuitive apostolic zeal coupled with his genuine friendliness. Before undertaking to appoint a full-time chaplain to cooperate with the Cornell University Religious Work, he had first consulted with certain Roman authorities. He received a sound reply: "Take care of your people wherever they are." It was to make the Catholic faith better known that he embarked upon his interfaith effort. Today we can at least credit him with striking out in the same general direction that Pope John XXIII, another bishop of apostolic charity, was to take three decades later, when divided mankind was readier to follow.

It is just possible that John O'Hern, by reason of his Roman education, had in some respects a more cosmopolitan view than his predecessors in the bishopric. At any rate, he showed a deep interest in the Church across the world. We have already noted his concern for the foreign missions. So far as fund-raising went, that concern was productive. In 1929 the Rochester branch of the Society for the Propagation of the Faith turned over to the international agency almost $154,000.00. This sum was second only to the returns from the Archdiocese of New York—$183,000.00.[71]

But O'Hern's interest in the Church Catholic was broader than even its missionary enterprises. For example, as a former Roman student he took a particular joy in the signing of the Lateran Pacts of February 11, 1929. These pacts terminated a half-century of painful friction between the Italian Government and the Holy See: an achievement which certainly merited the solemn *Te Deum* service the Bishop held in the Cathedral to signalize it.[72] On the other hand, he was deeply disturbed by the persecution current in Russia in 1930. He was the initiator of a mass meeting held in Rochester on April 8th of that year to protest the actively anti-religious stance of the Soviet Union. Five thousand Catholics, Protestants and Jews, clerical and lay, turned out for the demonstration. The guest speaker, Father Edmund A. Walsh, S.J., was a recognized authority on Russia, and presented a picture of Soviet anti-Catholicism and anti-Semitism based on the latest documentation.[73]

Bishop O'Hern took part in another mass meeting in Convention Hall on March 29, 1933. On this occasion Rochester's citizenry convened to protest against recent steps taken by Nazi Germany against religious bodies, particularly the Jews.[74] His attendance at this convocation, held a scant two months before his death, only emphasized more strongly his unswerving desire to give of himself to others, to become "all things to all men."

3. "THE LOVE OF CHRIST IMPELS US."

The Great Depression cast a pall over most of the 1930's, but the shadow was deepest during the years of Bishop O'Hern's regime. Widespread want hampered the administrative efforts of the Diocese of Rochester and at the same time taxed its beneficence.

Not that the hard times struck all the twelve counties with maximum fury, or any one of them with equal impact. In Rochester proper, the banks stood firm. However, by November, 1930, the number of unemployed Rochesterians had risen to 19,000. Many of them were Italians, who were still discriminated against in certain of the local industries. As in other large cities, jobless men sold apples on Main Street; and when the fear of further losses began to grip even those who were solvent, the civic efforts to relieve unemployment became ever more ineffectual. On the other hand, Corning's glass industry held its own quite well, so that that city suffered relatively little. Elmira was less fortunate, but could have been worse off. It was sometimes the smaller communities that were hit the hardest, particularly if their major industry declined. Phelps and Victor were in this category. And at the railroad center of Shortsville-Manchester the economy received a bad jolt when fifty percent of the one hundred local railroad workers were laid off.[75] Lessened personal income naturally meant lessened parish contributions. Bingo games now became a popular (and necessary) diversion in many Catholic parishes. Nevertheless, more than one pastor suffered an impairment of health in his effort to pay off heavy parochial debts contracted in more abundant days.

What was lacking for recovery was not the will to work but the opportunity. Unemployment was therefore the root problem; but it was easier to diagnose the case than to cure it. Rochester itself made a rather prompt move to grapple with the issue. On March 15, 1930, representatives of local industry, labor, business, and social welfare agencies, met and formed a Civic Committee on Unemployment, whose purpose was to provide jobs on civic projects at standard wages. If the Committee's program bore fruit only very slowly, it was not for want of citywide backing. As a matter of fact, the pioneering enterprise of the Rochester Committee more than once evoked the praise of Governor Franklin D. Roosevelt. Rochester Catholic Charities was a charter member of the Civic Committee on Unemployment, and the Bishop of Rochester gave the undertaking his warm support.[76]

But the blaze was too big for one fire company to handle. Eventually the State and the federal government had to lend a hand. In New York State, Governor Roosevelt set up TERA (Temporary Emergency Relief Agency) to assist the local communities in their work. The Diocese of Rochester went along with this trend, and in November, 1932, Father Walter A. Foery, as director of Rochester Catholic Charities, urged all Catholics to vote "yes" to a proposed State bond issue of $30 million for unemployment relief.[77] A year later, Franklin D. Roosevelt, having moved from the Capitol in Albany to the Capitol in Washington, launched a Federal Emergency Relief Administration (FERA), similar to the TERA he had established in New York State. On April 5, 1933, he created an Emergency Conservation Work to give reforestation jobs and similar tasks to jobless young men.

Roosevelt's inaugural address on March 4, 1933 had inspired the nation with a new hopefulness. That same month, the Rochester diocesan Holy Name Union and the Catholic Men's Federation both issued resolutions in support of quick federal action against the Depression.[78] Bishop O'Hern, speaking on March 19, 1933 at a reception given in honor of his fourth anniversary of consecration, praised Rochester for the fine optimism it had displayed in welcoming the new President's call to action. The Bishop himself had already ordered that prayers be said each Sunday throughout the Diocese for the welfare of the nation. In his anniversary address he echoed the stirring watchword of President Roosevelt's inaugural speech "The only thing we have to fear is fear itself." O'Hern urged one and all: "Let fear be banished forever from our heart . . ."[79]

However important it was to alleviate unemployment, there still remained a need for much almsgiving on the part of government and social agencies. Nor did the Bishop of Rochester and his flock ignore their duties of Christian charity.

By fall 1931, the Great Depression had already made itself felt throughout the world. On October 2, 1931, Pope Pius XI issued an appeal to all Catholic bishops to counter its effects to the best of their ability. Bishop O'Hern forthwith ordered that there be a triduum of prayer from October 23rd to October 25th for economic recovery. He urged the pastors to cooperate with local welfare agencies, and instructed them, if they had as yet no parish aid society, to establish one.[80]

Actually the Bishop had been working on this problem of almsgiving for many months. He had made a generous personal contribution to the Rochester Community Chest; and he had performed many acts of personal charity, especially by paying the coal bills of families which were without funds. Pastors throughout the Diocese engaged in similar acts, on their own or with the cooperation of their flocks. At Sacred Heart Church in Rochester, Father George V. Burns and the parish ladies raised and administered special relief funds. At St. Salome Church in Sea Breeze, Father Edward Eschrich distributed not only staples furnished by the Government, but also chickens and rabbits raised at the rectory, and even pigeons. At St. Mary's, Canandaigua, the St. Vincent De Paul Society, a ladies' aid organization, was encouraged in its solicitation of charity donations by the pastor, Father Michael C. Wall. St. Hyacinth's parish in Auburn in 1932 raised $1,-335.99 for the relief of the unemployed. Father Albert Geiger, assistant pastor of Holy Redeemer Church, Rochester, made a contribution of a different sort. In 1923, he and a parishioner, Mr. Joseph Stoecklein, a carpenter, had established the Aljo Club, a recreational organization open to youths and young men of all faiths. In May, 1932, the Club acquired an athletic field on Hudson Avenue; and this, too, was placed at the disposal of youths. In a day when personal funds for entertainment were low, the Aljo facilities—as widely used as those of the Y.M.C.A.—served as valuable antidote to delinquency. Its methods furthermore inspired the Rochester Inter-Religious Court Committee to follow suit in programming its own interdenominational recreation work.[81]

Rochester Catholic Charities was meanwhile striving valiantly to keep abreast of the requirements of the needy. In 1930, Miss Kathleen D'Olier, who for some time had been acting director of the organization, recommended to the Bishop that he again place a priest at the head of operations. O'Hern first requested Father John O'Grady, secretary of the National Council of Catholic Charities, to make a study of the Rochester Catholic Charities. On the basis of his report, the Bishop appointed a new director, Father Walter A. Foery (1890-   ). Father Foery was pastor of Mount Carmel Church, and was also a member of

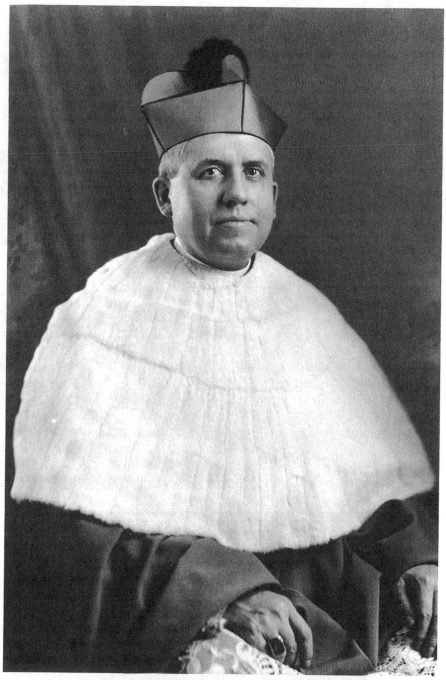

88   JOHN FRANCIS O'HERN
Third Bishop of Rochester
(1929-1933)

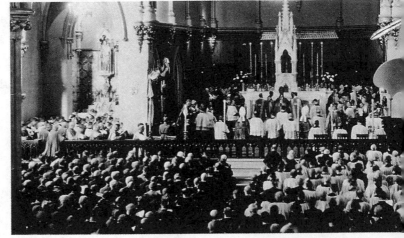

89   CONSECRATION OF BISHOP O'HERN
(March 19, 1929)

90
BISHOP O'HERN
lays the
cornerstone of
ST. CASIMIR'S
SCHOOL, ELMIRA
June 29, 1929

91
BISHOP O'HER
breaks ground
for Nurses' Hor
ST. JOSEPH'S
HOSPITAL,
ELMIRA
May 1930

EDWARD MOONEY
Fourth Bishop of Rochester
(1933-1937)

93
Installation of
ARCHBISHOP
MOONEY,
1933
(with Msgri. J. F. Goggin,
George V. Burns,
Charles F. Shay)

94
The Archbishop
at an
academic rite

95

The Archbishop dedicates
ST. GEORGE LITHUANIAN CHURCH
August 11, 1935

WALTER A. FOERY
Priest of the Diocese of Rochester 1916-1937
Fifth Bishop of Syracuse, 1937

97
MSGR.
WILLIAM M.
HART, P.A.
Vicar General,
1929-1962

98
MSGR.
JOHN F. BOPPEL
Chancellor
1932-1936

99 FATHER JOHN H. O'LOANE, C.S.B.

100 KATHLEEN D'OLIER

101 MOTHER BEATRIX of the Holy Spirit Magers, O.C.D.

102 MOTHER MARY OF ST. AGNES ZIMMERMAN

103 JUDGE PHILIP H. DONNELLY

104 JEREMIAH G. HICKEY K.S.G., K.M.

105   MERCY HOSPITAL,
AUBURN, 1931
(Photo 1967)

106   ST. STANISLAUS POLISH
CHURCH, BRADFORD, 1930

107   COLUMBUS CIVIC CENTER,
1928 *(Diocesan building, 1931)*

108 ST. PHILIP NERI CHURCH
*(A "temporary" church, 1929;
destroyed by fire, 1967)*

109 CARMELITE MONASTERY,
*1530 East Avenue (Second Rochester
home of Carmelite Nuns, 1934-1956)*

the Relief Committee and the director of the Genesee Institute. During the next seven years, until he became bishop of Syracuse, Father Foery was to guide Catholic Charities with a sure and knowledgeable hand.

From 1931 to 1943, Rochester Catholic Charities benefited by public relief funds in the discharge of its increasing case work. In 1932 alone it spent $51,872.00 for administration. This sum almost equalled the entire amount it received from the Community Chest in 1925[82]. The diocesan settlement houses were also called upon to counter trends towards juvenile delinquency. In the fall of 1930, the Genesee Institute became the Genesee Settlement House, open to both boys and girls up to twenty-five years of age. The board entrusted the House to Miss Anne Gray, an experienced social worker. She coordinated the program of the Genesee Settlement House with that of its branch, the Merrimac Center, which had been opened in April, 1926, at 270 Merrimac Street. From 1930 the Genesee, the Merrimac, and the Charles settlement centers were under the jurisdiction of the diocesan charities director.[83] Early in 1930, the Bishop announced that the local Knights of Columbus were to sponsor a "St. Francis Charitable Society" whose purpose was to train lay volunteers for work with Rochester Catholic Charities.[84]

The major event which occurred under O'Hern in the development of the diocesan charities was the foundation of Elmira Catholic Charities. This organization opened on January 31, 1930, in a small office in the Elmira Federation Building. Miss Mary E. FitzGerald took over as executive director on that date. On March 13, 1930, she was joined by Mrs. Clara Rensel, who became secretary, receptionist, and intake worker. The new organization replaced the St. Vincent de Paul Society, whose work we have already recorded. This was the first year of the Chemung County Community Chest, and the Elmira community welcomed the addition of the new Catholic agency which came into existence during the most trying period of the Great Depression. On July 17, 1930, a permanent organic structure was accomplished. Incorporated as a "benevolent order," Elmira Catholic Charities had as its initial officers Bishop O'Hern, president; Fathers James J. Bloomer and John J. Lee, Elmira pastors, as vice presidents; Attorney Cornelius O'Dea, chairman of the board; Mrs. Edward J. Dunn, vice chairman; William Flannery, treasurer; Martin T. Purtell, secretary. The directors numbered twenty-one. This organizational form had been based on the recommendations of Father John O'Grady of the National Conference of Catholic Charities. While the Elmira agency was thus an independent entity, it became an affiliate of Rochester Catholic Charities, and moved one step further towards becoming a truly diocesan unit. Early in 1930, Attorney O'Dea was able to report the good work which Miss FitzGerald and Mrs. Rensel had done during the first busy twelve-month. Between January, 1930 and January, 1931 the new Elmira Catholic center had taken care of 1,063 needy individuals.[85]

Another liability of the business depression was the ambitious Columbus Civic Center. The Center, undertaken under the auspices of the Knights of Columbus, had finally opened after much delay in March, 1928—just nineteen months before the beginning of the financial slump. In April, 1930, the Center was incorporated by a special State law as a welfare institution dedicated to improving the physical, social, intellectual and moral welfare of young men and women.[86] But even at the moment that the law took effect, the directors were without sufficient funds to make the upcoming payment on the second mortgage. Bishop O'Hern issued a circular that month announcing a quiet campaign for enough cash to keep the wolf away from the door of 50 Chestnut Street.[87] His effort ultimately failed; so in the spring of 1931, the Bishop decided to have the Rochester Diocese take over the Center and its debt of $485,000.00. This was a big undertaking, but O'Hern reached his decision only after having first sought the advice of his diocesan consultors and of Cardinal Hayes, the Archbishop of New York, and the permission of the Holy See.[88] In August, 1931, the transfer was effected from the original trustees to a new board comprising the Bishop and his Vicar General, twenty-four other Rochester priests, and nine laymen.[89] Thereafter the Diocese began gradually to move its various offices into the Center—the Society for the Propagation of the Faith, the diocesan schools office; the Chancery (after the sale of the Cathedral property in 1937); and, around the same time, the Charities office. Here, too, the Niagara University School of Business, Rochester Division, was housed after 1935. Plans were evolved as early as 1931 to use the gymnasium and swimming pool for an expanded Scouting program; and in that same year the Columbus Club was founded to make these recreational facilities available to a wider public.[90]

Not unconnected with the social needs of the 1930's was the moral guidance of those committed to penal institutions within the twelve counties. If John Francis O'Hern was actively concerned in this apostolate, it was no new interest. For fourteen years prior to his election to the episcopate, he had been chaplain of the Monroe County Jail, and during that period he had made an extensive study of criminal psychology. So attached had he grown to this work that he did not give up the chaplaincy even after his consecration.[91] At the Monroe County Penitentiary, the chaplain (who also held the chaplaincies of the State Hospital for the Insane, the County Hospital, the Almshouse, and Iola Tuberculosis Sanitarium) was the jolly and dedicated Father Eugene Golding (1895-1955). The Bishop continued him in his Penitentiary assignment. In July, 1931, he appointed to the post of first full-time Catholic chaplain of Auburn State Prison, Father William F. Bergan, up to then a professor at St. Andrew's Seminary. Bishop O'Hern possibly had something to do with the establishment of this chaplaincy by the State government. At any rate he made the appointment shortly after the full State salary became available.[92]. It is certain that O'Hern later intervened personally to persuade the State to raise the salaries of chaplains at State-supported penal and welfare institutions.[93]

One factor that had focussed Statewide attention on penal institutions and had no doubt been in some way responsible for the establishment of a full-time chaplaincy at Auburn Prison was the rioting that occurred in that prison in 1929. Since the two prison outbreaks involved Catholic priests and laity of Auburn, they deserve to be mentioned here.

The first of the two riots — a rarity in the history of this century-old penitentiary—occurred on a broiling Sunday, July 28, 1929. The prisoners attempted a massive break for freedom. Four men actually succeeded. The rest were restrained by the prison custodians, but only after a bitter battle in which two were killed, several were wounded, and the industrial wing was set on fire. While guards, State troopers and militiamen were engaged thereafter in collecting guns from the 1,750 angry convicts, two local priests entered the prison yard, and moving among the rioters, begged them, in God's name, to yield and return to their cells. The priests were Father Frederick G. Straub, the pastor of St. Alphonsus Church, and his assistant, Father John Bohmwetch. From 3:00 P.M. to 10:00 P.M., the two argued, pleaded, and cajoled; and eventually their words had an effect. Meanwhile, six other priests from the vicinity had arrived to give such assistance as they could, along with one priest from Rochester—Father Bergan, the future chaplain.[94]

Father Straub, rough-cut, blunt, and lovable, seems to have had a way with turbulent inmates of the prison. A few months later, on August 9, 1930, he succeeded where others had failed in bringing down a frenzied prisoner who had scaled the wall and was hanging from the roof.[95]

The second riot of 1929 took place on December 11th. Not all the firearms had been recovered from the rioters in the July row: the convicts had managed to conceal some of them for future use. Now, in December, they decided that the time was ripe. Four desperate criminals, the ringleaders of the new uprising, seized the warden and seven other officers, and using them as hostages, demanded their own liberation as the ransom. On this occasion, it was another Auburn priest who played an important role—Father Donald M. Cleary, assistant at Holy Family Church. At the risk of his life, Father Cleary talked with the ringleaders through the barred door, and when they gave him an ultimatum, he carried it back to the prison officials, whose reply he conveyed, in turn, to the rioters. The officials eventually gained the upper hand through a stratagem for which the convicts wrongly blamed the priest who had served as middleman. Once the final battle was over and peace had been reestablished, Father Straub and the other Auburn priests came in to assist the wounded and dying.[96]

But let us go back to the Depression proper and the Bishop's part in fighting it. His best-known effort to combat unemployment was his sponsorship of a widespread building campaign among the diocesan institutions. The idea of creating work-opportunities was, of course, not original with O'Hern; in fact, he made his appeal as a part of the joint action of the various Rochester agencies. Nevertheless, he does deserve credit for his attempt to engage the Diocese in a concerted program of building and repairs.

As early as March 16, 1930, Bishop O'Hern saw to it that an appeal was read from all the pulpits of the Diocese for cooperation in the anti-unemployment drive. The return of spring, he pointed out, suggested the repairing and improving of property. If Catholic priests, fraternal orders, and laymen would only seize this chance to renew or remodel buildings in their care, they would create new jobs and thus make a positive contribution towards local economic recovery. The Diocese, for its part, was not shirking its duty. Building projects slated for 1930 in the twelve counties of the diocese involved an expenditure of $2 million. New churches, new schools, new parish buildings were on the agenda, as well as a $100,000.00 infirmary wing at St. Ann's Home for the Aged. Largest of all the diocesan projects was a nurses' residence and medical building at St. Joseph's Hospital, Elmira. These two Elmira structures were to be financed principally from a legacy of a million dollars left by the Elmira industrialist, Edward J. Dunn (1868-1927).[97]

Rochester authorities commended the Bishop of Rochester for thus marshalling his diocese into the army against unemployment; and the news service of the National Catholic Welfare Conference gave considerable publicity to what it termed the nation's first diocesan anti-unemployment campaign.[98] But the Bishop did not rest on his laurels after issuing the pastoral of March, 1930. For example, whenever he addressed the Knights of Columbus, whether in or outside of Rochester proper, he urged its members to do their part in creating and procuring jobs for those out of work.[99]

During 1931, almost $2 million more were spent on additional diocesan construction.[100] Auburn's new Mercy Hospital, which cost $400,000.00, was the most important single undertaking. Rochester items included the new Motherhouse of the Sisters of Mercy ($234,-000.00); Holy Family School ($200,000.00); St. Stanislaus School ($180,000.00); and Holy Cross School in Charlotte ($200,000.00). In 1932, the Bishop was kept busy dedicating or rededicating diocesan structures. One of the lesser projects was a gateway on the Dewey Avenue side of Holy Sepulchre Cemetery in Rochester. This ornamental entrance was formally blessed as a special symbol of what the Cemetery, a diocesan corporation, was doing to provide greater employment. A few months before that, many local industrialists had begun to cut wages. The Cemetery corporation, throwing its weight in the other direction, had raised its wages by ten per cent. And on the very day the gate was dedicated, the Cemetery managers launched a "Share Your Work" plan so that each of its seventy-five employees might have enough work-hours each week to earn a decent living.[101]

Now it is quite true that some diocesan organizations undertook building projects more because the Bishop pressed them than from their own choice. At Charlotte, Father Alexander McCabe would doubtless not have built his twelve-room school addition and auditorium had Bishop O'Hern not insisted. Nor would Father Stanislaus Szupa have added the large wing to the parochial school of St. Stanislaus. In fact, there was considerable complaint among the diocesan pastors when their superior saddled their parishes with such fat debts in such lean days. One could fairly argue from his insistence that the Bishop was too impulsive a businessman to be a good one. Nevertheless, the passage of time was to prove him wiser than his contemporary critics were willing to admit. When the pastors finally paid off their large debts in the 1940's and 1950's, they had to acknowledge that they had saved a pretty penny by building during the depression years.

On May 7, 1933, John F. O'Hern dedicated All Saints Church at Ludlowville, Cayuga County. This dedication was not only the last he was to perform in connection with the manifold building projects of the Depression: it was the last such ceremony of his life. On Monday, May 22nd—seventeen days before his fifty-ninth birthday—he died of a heart attack at his episcopal residence.

The sudden death of the Bishop shocked his associates, but did not really surprise them. Heart trouble was apparently a family ailment, and the Bishop had already suffered two attacks since 1929. The first occurred a couple of days after his consecration, and was quite likely brought on by the strict fast he had observed before the rite and the feverish activity of those first days. The second seizure had taken place in December, 1932. This time a rest of three months was necessary before he could be about again. Even then, experts at Walter Reed Hospital in Washington warned him that his heart had been irreparably damaged, and that he must beware of over-exertion. He heeded this warning at least to a point: when administering Confirmation, for example, he sat in the Sanctuary and let the candidates approach him. But nobody really expected a man of such nervous energy to comply fully with the doctors' orders. And he himself often indicated to close associates that he preferred to die "in the harness." As a result, he eventually overtaxed his strength.[102]

On May 23rd, the consultors of the Diocese met and voted to name the Vicar General, Msgr. William M. Hart, as Vicar Capitular, to serve as diocesan administrator until the Holy See designated a new bishop for Rochester. It was under Monsignor Hart's direction that the great funeral took place. The city itself was in mourning, for Mayor Percival Oviatt ordered that all city buildings float their flags at half-staff and that at 10:00 A.M. a moment of city-wide silence be observed. Hundreds packed St. Patrick's Cathedral for the funeral Mass on May 26th. Cardinal Patrick Hayes of New York presided at the throne, and Bishop William Turner of Buffalo, offered the Mass. The preacher was Bishop Emmett J. Walsh of Charleston. Archbishop Hickey was one of the five bishops who performed the absolutions at the end of the Mass. The remains of the third Bishop of Rochester were then solemnly conveyed to Holy Sepulchre and laid away in the bishops' vault.[103]

On the day of O'Hern's death and for many days afterward a flood of messages of condolence poured in.[104] They came from cardinals, archbishops, bishops, religious superiors, and lay leaders. Some were political figures: former Governor Alfred E. Smith; President Franklin D. Roosevelt, Secretary of Labor Frances Perkins; Postmaster General James A. Farley. Municipal and civic authorities also expressed their grief. So, too, did industrialists (among them Thomas J. Watson of I.B.M.); and labor organizations (like Local #86 of the International Brotherhood of Electrical Workers). Non-Catholic spokesmen were especially warm in their personal tributes. "I loved him as a brother," declared Episcopal Bishop David Lincoln Ferris. "I have never known a more tolerant soul," said Presbyterian pastor Justin Wroe Nixon. The deceased bishop, asserted Rabbi Solomon Sadowsky, had done much towards "creating an atmosphere of good will for all mankind."

But the "little people"—the ordinary Rochesterians who passed four abreast to view his remains—were doubtless the ones who missed him most. For this handsome white-haired priest, with his gay smile, his free-handed cordiality, and his word of greeting for everybody, had long since engaged their affection. Many of them he had singled out for special attention. He had given them an alms, perhaps; or perhaps he had stepped out of the procession in church to bless their babe-in-arms; or perhaps he had visited them on their golden jubilees or on their nine-tieth birthdays. Among his devotees were his old parishioners, whom he never forgot; the friends whose *friends'* funerals he had attended; the cleaning woman with whom he had chatted in the New York Central Station; the Italian immigrant whom he had counseled; the parolee whom he met in the County Jail. One and all, they knew that he was their own bishop in a very special way.

John Francis O'Hern was a man of impulse, and was therefore in-judicious at times in word or deed. But even when a good man's heart outstrips his judgment, his very love will not permit him to go very far astray.

It is easier for us to see today the providential role which Bishop O'Hern played in the history of the Rochester Diocese. He had suc-ceeded two men who were admirable but austere, and who concentrated their attention on their own flock. The time had come for another sort of diocesan leader—one who would reach out towards non-Cath-olics, and symbolize to them as well as to his own people the endearing human element in the Church of Christ, its attractiveness, its solicitude for all mankind.

This was a new departure, rather dismaying to those of his priests who were accustomed to walk their Catholic way with eyes straight ahead. Nor did he actually succeed in convincing non-Catholics in gen-eral that the Church Catholic was as winsome as he himself was. The important thing is not that he succeeded, but that, like Pope John XXIII in our own time, he *tried*. "He was," said Bishop Walsh in the eulogy, "the representative of Jesus Christ Who reduced all to the law of charity . . ."

CHAPTER TWELVE

THE FUTURE CARDINAL MOONEY

O NE WEEK when it had been raining constantly in Rochester for several days, the weather man of one of the local papers, weary of announcing to the sodden citizens "Today: Rain", simply stated: "Today: More of the same."

The economic weather in the United States likewise remained tediously poor throughout and beyond the brief Rochester episcopate of Bishop O'Hern's successor. The efforts of President Franklin D. Roosevelt to promote national recovery bore their fruit, but only slowly and uncertainly before the end of the decade.

What was most worthwhile about the Rooseveltian program was the "New Deal" legislation—not only its measures for immediate relief but the more important laws that promoted social justice and aimed at stabilizing the economy against future depressions.

A leading item in his early program was the National Industrial Recovery Act of June 16, 1933. The NRA set forth a business production code and favored collective bargaining. Those firms that accepted the code—and to decline to do so was unpopular—were allowed to flaunt the "Blue Eagle" label in the windows of their factories or shops. The motto on the label was "We do our part." Although this Recovery Act was declared unconstitutional by the federal Supreme Court two years later, by then it had already served the purpose of rallying goodwill across the nation.

Two relief agencies which "F.D.R." established were of special importance. One was the WPA (Works Progress Administration), which provided jobs to various unemployed, among them writers, artists, musicians, and historians. A special assignment given to the last-named group was to index the archives of the parishes and institutions of religious denominations, including the Diocese of Rochester. The National Youth Administration, set up in June, 1935, expanded the work of the Civilian Conservation Corps, which had been launched as early as March, 1933, to undertake reforestation and other public works. There were a number of these conservation camps in the twelve counties of the Rochester Diocese.

More permanent in their import were: the formation of the National Labor Board in 1933 (later called the National Labor Relations Board); the Social Security Act of 1935; and the creation of the Federal Housing Administration in 1935. These were measures of great value to Catholics of the Diocese of Rochester as well as to all Americans.

Of course, the "New Deal" enjoyed an uneven success. Its measures were often widely criticized, and it did not come up with an answer for every problem. Hence there were a number of contemporary public figures who proposed to wide audiences their own personal solutions of the dilemmas of the Depression.

One of these publicists who gained some followers in the Rochester area was Dr. Francis E. Townsend of Los Angeles. From 1934 on he gave nationwide publicity to his "Old Age Revolving Pension Plan." Still more popular was the Detroit radio priest, Father Charles Coughlin. In 1934 he organized the National Union for Social Justice. He had earlier won a wide audience for his explanations of the doctrine of the papal social encyclicals. Now he began to advance upon less sure ground with a concrete program for economic recovery.

Among the others who were proposing nostrums in those days were the Communists. The years 1935-1939 were the heyday of American Communism. The Stalinists, posing as 100% Americans, hoodwinked many an American liberal and political innocent into signing up with one of the countless "popular front" organizations that espoused some cause consonant with the Communist party line. Since so many liberals were active in the "New Deal", the Communists wooed them mightily. Even Eleanor Roosevelt, the compassionate and ebullient wife of the President, lent annual support for some years to one of these "fronts", the American Student Union. In the Rochester diocesan district, the principal Communist threat lay in the Party's attempt to gain control of the Committee for Industrial Organization, which arose in 1935 under the leadership of John L. Lewis as a dissident group in the American Federation of Labor. Labor itself was on the offensive, especially after 1934, when "sit-down" strikes became a popular technique. Communist manipulation was suspected in some of these strikes.

The international scene was also increasingly disturbed as the 1930's progressed. It is true that the United States proclaimed its neutrality in both the Italo-Ethiopian War of 1935-1936, and the Spanish Civil War of 1936-1939. But both of these contests were symptoms of a more widespread and threatening malady. Hence Americans viewed with apprehension the welding of the Rome-Berlin Axis by Adolf Hitler and Benito Mussolini on October 25, 1936, and the signing of the German-Japanese Anti-Comintern Pact one month later.

The years 1933-1936 were thus, at home, years of continued economic depression and therefore of continued poverty and social agitation. Abroad, they were years of rising totalitarianism. It was during this brief and inauspicious period that the fourth bishop of Rochester administered his diocese.

1. AN ARCHBISHOP FOR BISHOP.

Late in August, 1933, a distinguished but rather reserved American prelate arrived without fanfare at Seattle, where he intended to embark for Tokyo. He was the Most Reverend Edward Mooney, Titular Archbishop of Irenopolis-in-Isauria; and he was returning to the post which he had occupied since 1931: that of apostolic delegate to Japan. His age was fifty-one, rather young for an archbishop. But as a matter of fact, he had been consecrated to that rank in 1926, when he was only forty-three, on the occasion of his appointment to the highest Vatican diplomatic office entrusted thus far to an American priest—apostolic delegate to India.

The Archbishop had taken his vacation in America that summer, visiting family and friends in Ohio. He did not expect to return to his native land for some time once he was back in Japan. But on August 28, 1933, Pope Pius XI named Mooney bishop of Rochester to succeed Bishop O'Hern. The Holy See sent immediate instructions to the departing voyager to cancel his trip to Tokyo. With typical diplomatic finesse — and thoughtfulness — the Bishop-designate at once sent the following telegram to Cardinal Patrick Hayes, metropolitan of the church province of New York to which the Rochester Diocese belongs.

> Intimation appointment to Rochester interrupted voyage at Seattle. Ever ready obedience to Holy See rendered particularly easy and delightful by fact that it affords opportunity to work under esteemed direction of Your Eminence.[1]

The See of Rochester, widowed of its bishop since May, and not a little anxious to discover who would succeed him, was surprised but gratified by the news. As Vicar Capitular, Monsignor William M. Hart sent the official word of welcome to his new superior. The Rochester newspapers described the wide experience of the new bishop—teacher, spiritual counsellor, educator, diplomat, and, for a brief while, parish priest. During the next few weeks, while Mooney, back in Ohio once more, was making the necessary preparations, the *Catholic Courier* set forth even fuller information about his person and his achievements.[2]

Who was this man who was about to become the fourth Bishop of Rochester? He was, without question, one of the ablest leaders—and also one of the most self effacing whom the Catholic Church in America has known.

The first bishop of the Diocese had been a New Yorker, by way of New Jersey. The second and third had been priests of the Rochester Diocese before their elevation. Archbishop Mooney was an Ohioan who, until he was promoted to the episcopate, was a priest of the Diocese of Cleveland. Although associated most of his life with Ohio and the Diocese of Cleveland, Mooney was a native of Maryland. He was born in Mount Savage, on May 9, 1882, the child of Thomas Mooney and Sarah Heneghan Mooney. It was Father Patrick F. O'Connor, the pastor of St. Patrick's, the only church in the little village, who on May 14th baptized him Edward Alexander Mooney.[3]

Mount Savage may not have been populous, but it was almost solidly Catholic. Situated in the hill-country at a point where western Maryland, Pennsylvania, and West Virginia almost meet, it early attracted many Irish immigrants who sought work in its foundries or the nearby mines. Today this hamlet with its narrow streets, tortuous roads and quaint old-fashioned parish church, is reduced in population. But prior to 1926 its staunch Catholic citizens had given nineteen of their boys and twenty of their girls to the service of the Church.

Thomas Mooney was a native of the County Galway. His wife Sarah was American-born but the child of immigrants. The couple had seven children: Mary Angela (Byrne), Frank, John, Margaret, Joseph, Charles B., and the baby, Edward. Mr. Mooney worked in a foundry. His hillside home, razed only in recent years, was of the mining-village type, with a siding of unpainted vertical planks. This structural simplicity suggests strongly that Thomas Mooney was far from prosperous.

What bears out the impression is the fact that in 1886 or 1887 Tom Mooney sought employment elsewhere. He took his family to Youngstown, Ohio—some 130 air-miles distant from Mount Savage. Here he got a job with the American Tube Company. Youngstown was a steel-working city, and the factories engaged many Irish laborers. The Mooneys settled in a neighborhood where the Irish were numerous. Their street was called Poland Avenue; but the neighborhood was popularly referred to as "Kilkenny."

Mr. Mooney was apparently able to bring home better wages from the Youngstown Tube Company than from the Mount Savage foundry.

Unfortunately, he died in 1893, leaving the responsibility of raising the family in the hands of his wife Sarah. It was a struggle for her, even though the older boys were now able to earn a living and give her some assistance. But she was a valiant woman, and she kept faith with the trust which Tom Mooney had bequeathed to her.

All this background of Irish parochialism, mining, and metal-working, seems a strange setting for an archbishop, a papal diplomat to the Far East, and a prince of the Church. But unless we are aware of Cardinal Mooney's origins, we cannot appreciate several important facets of his character, particularly his simple tastes, his sympathy with those in trouble, and his deep interest in labor relations and other social problems.

In Youngstown, the Mooneys belonged to St. Columba's parish (which in 1943 was to become the cathedral parish of the newly erected diocese of Youngstown). Young Edward attended St. Columba's School—all nine grades of it—and it was here he first made his mark. The Ursuline nuns who conducted the school quickly discovered that Eddie was an arrestingly bright student. In only one subject was he poor —music—for he was tone-deaf. All the rest, whether language, mathematics, or religion, he learned and retained easily.

Some bright boys are nuisances. Edward Mooney was both bright and winning. He had a fine, well-balanced personality: a bit shy and unassertive, but good-humored, modest, and naturally kind. Although he preferred to be a spectator, he had both initiative and leadership; and when two of his classmates got into a scrap, it was usually Eddie who patched things up. One of his teachers, Sister Vincent—to whom he attributed in large part his vocation to the priesthood—was so enchanted by the lad and his talents that she took pains to be assigned to the grade in which he was, so as to enjoy the privilege of teaching him another year. The pastor, Father Edward Mears, also kept a watchful and approving eye on the youngest Mooney; and when Ed showed an interest in studying for the priesthood, he guided him with manly hands.

Not that Mooney was anything but regular. He made fast friends with his contemporaries and never let those friendships die. Nor did he consider that his love of books excused him from other duties. When he was thirteen, he offered to get a summer job in order to contribute something to his mother's support. It was the mother who decided the matter: "The books are for you, Eddie!"

That same year, Eddie had debated one of his schoolmates on the subject of the gold standard. Father Mears was so amazed at the maturity of the boy's reasoning, that he took pains to find out whether he had borrowed his arguments from some other source. It turned out that the argumentation was all original. That same sagacity appeared once more in the valedictory that he gave at his graduation from St. Columba's School. He spoke of one's vocation in life.

> And if in that vocation we are faithful even to the least of its obligations, though from a human standpoint our career may not have been a brilliant one, yet in the all-seeing eye of God we have achieved a victory brighter than the subjugation of a nation, more enduring than the wisdom of the Philosophers . . . His is the grandest life who has lived it nobly, made the most he could of it, and endeavored to be true to his God, to himself, and to humanity. In all our undertakings let us be positive—negative in nothing.

The future Cardinal exemplified these principles in his own adult career.[4]

Edward Mooney entered St. Charles College, Ellicott City, Maryland, that same fall, 1897. What had happened in parochial school happened once more in this preparatory seminary. He was the star student of the Class of 1903, carried off all the prizes, and was rated by the faculty as one of the three top students in the history of the school.[5] But once again, he did not allow his triumphs to distort his sense of values. Classmates who were slower scholars than himself knew that they could turn to him with their questions about studies and receive satisfying explanations, given generously and without a trace of patronage.

It was the same story when Mooney began his philosophy studies at St. Mary's Seminary in Baltimore. In his two years there he won the top prizes in Philosophy and Sacred Scripture, and was granted his A.B. and his A.M. *maxima cum laude.*[6]

The Bishop of Cleveland, Ignatius F. Horstmann, singled out Edward Mooney as a deserving young man and a promising future teacher; and on the completion of his philosophy years, he sent him to Rome to complete his priestly training. He officially enrolled in the American seminary-residence, the North American College, on October 22, 1905. With the rest of the men who lived in the College, he attended classes at the Athenaeum (University) of the Urban College of Propaganda Fide. Even in this international, polyglot student body, the Youngstown boy still stood out. He won "full points" in fundamental theology, dogmatic theology and moral theology; and in the first year he made off with the gold medal in fundamental theology. At the end of his course, in 1909, he passed the examination for the doctorate of sacred theology. (He had meanwhile also acquired a doctorate in philosophy from the Roman Academy of St. Thomas.[7]) On Saturday, April 10, 1909, he was ordained to the priesthood by Cardinal Pietro Respighi.

When he returned to Cleveland in 1909, Doctor Mooney was given a post for which he had been preparing and was well equipped: professor of dogmatic theology in the Cleveland diocesan seminary, St. Mary's (Our Lady of the Lake). He discharged this task well during the next seven years. "He was an outstanding professor," says one of his former theological students. "He left an indelible mark on his students. They admired him for his brilliance and his sincerity."[8]

In 1916, "Doc" Mooney was transferred to another, completely different corner of the educational field. Bishop John P. Farrelly decided to start a non-resident Latin school in Cleveland, hoping by means of it to attract more vocations to the priesthood. Because he had this vocational purpose in mind, he decided to ask the Seminary to sacrifice Father Mooney so that he might serve as founder and principal of the new boys' high school.

The Cathedral Latin School opened in temporary quarters in 1916, and moved into its permanent building in June, 1918. As president, Doctor Mooney showed that he could adapt readily to the mentality of adolescent students. He also gained valuable administrative experience in his new task. And his fertile imagination inspired him to work out a novel plan for teaching Latin and other languages which was so effective that it was subsequently adopted by the Cleveland public schools. As a result, Mooney engendered in the boys of Cathedral Latin not only a spirit of industry, but an admiration of, and a gentle affection toward himself. For he was strict with them, but just, straightforward, and stimulating.[9]

When Joseph Schrembs became bishop of Cleveland in 1921, he decided that because of the diocesan shortage of priests he would turn over the complete management of Cathedral Latin School to the Marianist Brothers, who had already been represented on the teaching staff. The founding president was therefore deprived of his job. In June, 1922, Bishop Schrembs appointed Father Mooney pastor of St. Patrick's Church in Youngstown.

At St. Patrick's Mooney faced a totally new sort of task. But at least he was back in his home town, and there was a new church building to be undertaken and much else to keep him busy.[10]

Although he began to make long-range plans for St. Patrick's, Father Mooney's planning was soon interrupted. Scarcely had he celebrated his first Christmas as a pastor, when he was called to Rome on a new assignment—spiritual director of his Alma Mater, the North American College. He assumed the new duties on January 31, 1923.

The choice of Mooney for this task was a good one. He knew Rome, he knew seminarians, he knew theology, he knew what challenges the American priest should be prepared to meet. If the American College students first found him rather on the quiet side, they quickly learned to appreciate the keenness of mind he displayed in his conferences, and the very balanced judgment he manifested in his private counselling. One project which received his enthusiastic support was the foundation of an American College branch of the Catholic Students' Mission Crusade. The branch was called the Blessed Isaac Jogues Mission Unit, and its aim was to pray for the foreign missions and provide missionaries with funds. The support which Mooney gave this mission unit revealed his special interest in the missionary field.[11]

As the months passed in Rome, Doctor Mooney was gradually invited to undertake other tasks outside the College walls. He was asked to teach pastoral theology at the Collegio dei Sacerdoti per la Emigrazione Italiana—an institution which prepared Italian priests to work among Italian immigrants in the United States and elsewhere. He was also chosen as an advisor on the commission for the compilation of an international catechism, headed by Cardinal Pietro Gasparri. Furthermore, he was named a consultor on the Sacred Congregation of the Council. On June 3, 1925, Pius XI bestowed on Father Mooney the honor of domestic prelate.[12]

In 1925 Monsignor Mooney was called upon to play a part in a property negotiation between the North American College and the Sacred Congregation de Propaganda Fide. The College and the Congregation had agreed to the joint purchase of a large parcel of land on Rome's Janiculan Hill, but a fine diplomacy was necessary for the working out of the precise dividing line of the property. Mooney showed himself adept at this task—genial but firm. His expertise particularly caught the attention of Archbishop Francesco Marchetti-Selvaggiani, who was himself the Secretary of the Propaganda Fide Congregation.

Now just at that moment in history, Cardinal William Van Rossum, C.SS.R., Prefect of Propaganda Fide, happened to be in search of a diplomatic churchman to settle once and for all the problem of the "Double Jurisdiction" in India. The Government of Portugal had for ages claimed the right to nominate bishops, pastors, etc., in the sees in

India, on the grounds that Portugal, as the pioneer Latin Christian state to colonize India, had been granted rights of patronage. The Sacred Congregation de Propaganda Fide, finding that this old grant hampered modern missionary work, had insisted that such nominations be under its own control. The dispute was partially settled in the nineteenth century; but there was still much friction. For instance, some parishes belonging to old Portuguese dioceses were still in the middle of dioceses set up by Propaganda Fide. It was a delicate issue, involving long traditions and nationalistic sensitivities. The papal diplomat sent to deal with it could not be Indian or Portuguese or even Italian, for in all these cases he would be suspected of prejudice. Archbishop Marchetti now confided to Cardinal Van Rossum that Monsignor Mooney seemed to be one who could turn the trick. The Cardinal agreed.

When Van Rossum called Mooney in on January 7, 1926, and told him that the Pope had named him a titular archbishop and papal delegate to India, the Monsignor was completely surprised. The only comment he could make was that the Holy Father, in his opinion, had had a lot of courage to choose *him*. But as Mooney wrote to his sister a few days later: there was a job to be done; his selection was "the Lord's doing and not my own"; so he would be as happy to serve God in India as anywhere else.[13]

Monsignor Mooney was consecrated to the episcopacy by Cardinal Van Rossum on January 31st. Then he set out for India via Youngstown, where he said good-bye to his mother. As both silently surmised on that occasion, it was their last meeting.

The Titular Archbishop of Irenopolis did not disappoint the Pope or the officials of Propaganda Fide. As the result of his patient efforts, Portugal signed an agreement with the Holy See on the jurisdictional problem on May 3, 1928, and a supplementary agreement on April 11, 1929.[14] Archbishop Mooney had another gratifying experience shortly afterward. He participated in the first stages of the process by which two bishops and many of the faithful of the separated Indian Jacobite Church became reunited with the Holy See. The reunion was achieved in 1930, when Rome recognized the group as the Malankara Church. For the rest, Mooney worked hard at his task, covering in his journeys out of Bangalore, his headquarters, every diocese and vicariate in India. No previous delegate had undertaken this arduous visitation personally; he found it well worth the pains. As the result of his accurate reports, the Holy See set up eleven new dioceses and transferred the direction of three others to bishops of the Indian clergy. Meanwhile, Mooney became fast friends with those he met, and won the admiration of such leaders as Lord Halifax, the British viceroy.[15]

On February 25, 1931, the Holy See (much to the regret of the Indian hierarchy) transferred the Archbishop to the post of apostolic delegate to Japan. During his two years in Japan, he is said to have paved the way for permitting Japanese Catholics to perform certain public rites in pagan temples. Careful study showed that these rites, which all citizens were expected to carry out, were purely civic in character. Therefore, on May 26, 1936, the Roman authorities officially declared them permissible to Catholics.[16] Mooney also made a visitation of Korea, at that time under Japanese control; and on September 21, 1931, he celebrated at Seoul a solemn pontifical Mass to commemorate the centennial of Korea's first diocese. While there he likewise supervised a thirteen-day synod of the five bishops of Korea—a milestone in the history of Korean Catholicism.[17]

After the Japanese invaded Manchuria in 1931, tension gradually arose between the United States and Japan. This fact was probably the principal reason why Rome took the American apostolic delegate away from Tokyo, and gave him another assignment. While the appointment to Rochester probably surprised Mooney, it had no doubt been understood all along that he would eventually be named to some episcopal see in the United States. And the Holy See doubtless intended by now that it should be a notable see, as a reward for notable diplomatic labors.

This has been a long résumé, but we have thought it essential to an understanding of the remarkable talents of the man who was now Bishop-designate of Rochester. It was nevertheless typical of the Archbishop's simplicity of taste that he should have written to the secretary of Cardinal Hayes from Youngstown, apropos of the forthcoming installation: "I am hoping that he [the Cardinal] does not take to a high hat on such occasions." The secretary of the metropolitan of highly traditional New York sent back a comfortless reply: "The Cardinal will wear a high hat."[18]

Archbishop Mooney could hope even less to escape the populous and warm welcome he received in Rochester's Central Station on October 11, 1933. Hundreds of Catholics greeted him as he entered the waiting room in the company of his own personal friends and a delegation of Rochester diocesan officials who had met him in Buffalo and made the last lap of the trip as a guard of honor.

Cardinal Hayes performed the simple rite of installation next day in St. Patrick's Cathedral. Archbishop Mooney (the Holy See allowed him to retain the title of archbishop as a personal distinction) delivered a very fine sermon. It was discerning and strong, though carefully and diplomatically phrased, and it breathed a noble devotion to the Apostolic See. Tokyo and Rochester, he said, might seem far removed from each other. "But Tokyo and Rochester are not far apart in the eye of Peter, whose horizon is worldwide. What is Catholic in Asia is bound to what is Catholic in America, not only by the cords of Adam but by the yoke of Christ." He praised his predecessors on the See of Rochester, and assured his listeners that he was truly concerned about the responsibilities he was now assuming. He reminded himself that the Church needs bishops who are "strong but not headstrong." That he might fulfill this trust, he asked the prayers of all.

Archbishop Hickey was the main speaker at the luncheon which followed the installation. The new Bishop's own remarks centered on his heraldic motto *"Domino servientes"* ("Serving the Lord").[19] Mooney also spoke at the civic reception given in his honor that evening. Here his theme was Catholic Action: its great value, but also its necessary subordination to Church authority. In these three initial addresses, therefore, the Archbishop-Bishop clearly set forth his understanding of the relationship of bishop and flock: a flock active in good works, but under the direction of pope and bishop; a bishop who is loyal to the Holy See, and strong yet wise in directing his people.

At the outset, Archbishop Mooney retained the services of the waggish, capable and loyal Monsignor Hart as vicar general, and the gentle and patient Monsignor John F. Boppel as chancellor. Father Lawrence Casey soon became the sole vice-chancellor and served as the Archbishop's secretary. But a senior vice-chancellor was added three years later. He was Father William F. Bergan (1889-1947). Father Bergan had had experience in business, in professional-style baseball, in seminary teaching (St. Andrew's Seminary for fourteen years) and in penology (chaplain at Auburn State Prison, 1931-1935). When the aging Monsignor Boppel retired from the chancellorship in 1936, Father Bergan was named to succeed him. These three priests, Fathers Hart, Bergan, and Casey, were to be the principal aides of the Archbishop during his Rochester career. They complemented each other so well that Mooney once declared: "Father Hart always says 'Yes, yes'; Father Bergan always says 'No, no'; and Father Casey takes the middle road." Their assistance was very valuable to him, for the job of administering a diocese was to him something new. If he later proved an efficient steward in the See of Detroit, it was largely because of the schooling he received during the Rochester years.

2. THE CARE OF SOULS.

Between 1933 and 1937 the population of the Diocese of Rochester increased from 214,000 to 223,000. While these figures offered by the *Official Catholic Directory* are more symbolic than mathematical, the fact remains that during the Mooney episcopate the diocesan population remained more or less stable. Even if economics had permitted it, therefore, there would have been no urgent reason for founding a host of new parishes.

Archbishop Mooney did establish three new parishes, by promoting three mission churches to full parochial status. Two of these were Italian mission churches created on the West Side of Rochester by Bishop O'Hern: Most Precious Blood (a mission since March 2, 1930), made a parish in July, 1934; and St. Francis of Assisi (a mission since August 15, 1929), made a parish in 1935. The third was St. Charles Borromeo, Elmira Heights, Chemung County. Launched as a mission church in 1897, it was raised to parochial rank and given a resident pastor on January 23, 1935.

The Archbishop also opened one new mission: St. John Fisher, at East Bay, in Wayne County. The East Bay mission was begun in 1933 as a mission station of St. Thomas Church, Red Creek, at the request of vacationers who summered in this Ontario lakeside neighborhood. At first, Mass was celebrated in a school building by Father Lawrence Casey; but on June 30, 1935, the new little frame church was opened. St. John Fisher, Bishop of Rochester, England, was chosen as its patron. St. John and St. Thomas More, martyrs under Henry VIII, had been canonized on May 19, 1935. The East Bay chapel thus became the first institution in the Diocese of Rochester-in-America to be dedicated to the martyred bishop of Old Rochester. It was possibly also the first church in the whole United States to be given his name.

Archbishop Mooney did at least have the pleasure of *blessing* a few new buildings in his diocese, including two new parish church structures.

The first of these two churches was St. George's Lithuanian Church, in Rochester. Mooney laid its cornerstone on November 11, 1934, and dedicated the completed building on August 11, 1935.[20] The second was St. Ignatius Church, Hornell, which he blessed on September 19, 1935.

There was one small but gracious building project for which the Archbishop himself was more directly responsible. It was a new crypt for the deceased bishops of Rochester which he ordered to be constructed in the base of the tower of Holy Souls Chapel in Holy Sepulchre Cemetery. This was designed to replace the original crypt, located in the basement of the Chapel. It was not completed and dedicated until 1938, after Mooney's departure. In connection with its dedication, the remains of Bishops McQuaid and O'Hern were transferred to two of the several burial compartments that line the walls of the room.[21]

Archbishop Mooney showed great interest in studying the plans of the few construction projects undertaken during his Rochester tenure. That interest in building, frustrated in Rochester, was to enjoy free rein in Detroit, where Edward Mooney developed into a noted builder.

As the diocesan population remained stable, the Diocese had more than enough priests to go around. As a matter of fact, the graduating classes at St. Bernard's Seminary were growing larger. There had been only five new priests ordained from St. Bernard's in 1929, seven in 1930, eight in 1931, eleven in 1932; but from 1933 to 1943 the number never descended below ten, and in 1940 there were twenty who presented themselves for ordination. Priests borrowed from other dioceses could now be sent home. There were only a couple of instances in which borrowing continued. It was still necessary to bring in one Italian-speaking priest and two Polish-speaking priests to assist in national or multi-national parishes.[22] And it was also necessary to engage three new secular priests as temporary members of the theological faculty of St. Bernard's Seminary.[23] For the rest, the Diocese of Rochester now began to ordain supernumerary graduates of St. Bernard's Seminary on the understanding that they might be loaned to another diocese after their ordination.

On the other hand, the years of 1933-1937 witnessed the advent to the Diocese of members of three priestly religious orders. Completely new to the Rochester Diocese were the Vincentian Fathers. Three of these served from 1933 to 1935 on the staff of St. Bernard's Seminary. Another group of Vincentians, also from Niagara University, established a Rochester Division of the Niagara University School of Business Administration. It opened in the Columbus Civic Center on February 6, 1934, and served its purpose well during the decade of its existence.[24] The Society of the Divine Word was not a newcomer, for as we have already seen, that religious community had purchased Bishop McQuaid's old farm and vineyard from Bishop Hickey. But in October,

1935, the Divine Word Fathers announced their intention of starting a preparatory school for aspirants to their own Order. St. Michael's Divine Word Seminary opened in 1936 with a student body of twenty-five "belated vocations." Several more priests had been added to the staff by then to serve as a faculty; and from that year on, these true missionaries have given willing and valuable week-end assistance to the pastors of parishes south of Rochester. The increase of residents on their property also made it possible to cultivate the farm more extensively and to revive the wine-making.[25]

Nor were the Basilian Fathers newcomers. They had furnished some priests to serve on the staff of Aquinas Institute. But on September 1, 1936, Archbishop Mooney concluded an agreement with the Congregation of St. Basil to take over the complete management of Aquinas Institute in the following year.[26]

Early in his Rochester career, Archbishop Mooney showed his interest in getting to know his priests and their views. He started at St. Bernard's Seminary. On various occasions he gave conferences to its students, particularly to those who were about to enter major orders. His experience as a spiritual counselor and as a churchman made his talks very practical. But he doubtless considered his personal interviews with the candidates even more important. Provided with the records of each student, he received them one by one in a very informal audience. By conversation and deft questioning he strove to draw them out. Since he was a good judge of men, he was able to learn much about his prospective priests from this informative dialogue.

Another group of clerics to which Edward Mooney paid special attention was the ill and disabled priests. Whenever he learned of their disability, he made a point of paying them a visit. But for that matter, he went out of his way to establish contact with all his priests. He memorized their names—which naturally gratified them. He gave them to understand that he was available to them, and when they called he straightway put them at their ease. He assured them—and they knew that he meant it—that he wanted them to be frank with him. As a result of the Archbishop's efforts in this direction, it could truly be said, by the end of four years if not sooner, that he and his priests knew and understood each other.

For the better regulation of the Diocese, the Archbishop held the Fifth Synod of Rochester in St. Patrick's Cathedral on December 12, 1934. This was the first diocesan synod convened since 1924. It made no great change in diocesan rules, but it expressed them much more briefly, and brought them up to date.[27] On January 3, 1936, Archbishop Mooney communicated to his priests three extra-synodal decrees which altered certain of the decrees of the synod itself.[28]

The 1934 Synod, in decree No. 90, spoke of forthcoming parochial quotas for the support of disabled priests of the Diocese. Mooney quickly implemented the decree, establishing the Clergy Relief Society, one of the more notable achievements of his Rochester regime. On July 11, 1935, a committee named to study the matter presented its findings to the assembled clergy. The report was accepted, and the Rochester diocesan Clergy Relief Society came into official existence on August 1st, with the Archbishop as its head, Msgr. Walter J. Lee of Geneva as vice-president, Msgr. Joseph Cameron of Rochester as secretary, and Father F. William Stauder of Rochester as treasurer. The new organization succeeded the "Infirm Priests' Board" established by Bishop Hickey in the Synod of 1914; and it was better gauged to achieve its purpose than the Board, which had sought to support incapacitated priests by a quota of $15.00 assessed annually to each parish. A report issued in 1959 showed that since 1935 the Clergy Relief Society had collected $617,852.80, and distributed from that sum $450,303.62.[29] The disabled and needy diocesan priests who were beneficiaries of this "insurance" had Archbishop Mooney to thank for making it available to them through Clergy Relief.

The Rochester clergy felt especially honored when, on May 26, 1937, Pope Pius XI named Father Walter A. Foery, the pastor of Holy Rosary Church, to be fifth Bishop of Syracuse. Clergy and laity alike appreciated what the *Catholic Courier* termed the Bishop-elect's "quiet and decisive manner" and "brilliant yet unostentatious achievements." Archbishop Mooney, who concurred with these sentiments, must have had a hand in promoting the appointment.

Father Foery had indeed deserved well of the Diocese of Rochester. As we have already seen, he proved an able manager of the diocesan charities organization, of the Columbus Civic Center and of the Columbus Youth Association. As an administrator, he had made many firm friendships in the Rochester business community. And it was his reputation as a director of charities that led to his designation, in the summer of 1936, as the sole delegate of the National Catholic Welfare Conference to the Third International Conference on Welfare Work, held in London, England. But in addition to this special work, he had had extensive parochial experience. As assistant at Mount Carmel Italian parish from 1916 to 1922, this non-Italian priest had quickly been dubbed "Padre Fiori"; and even though he could not converse in the native language of his parishioners, they were pleased to have him as their pastor from 1922 to 1932. In 1932, he had been transferred to the territorial parish of Holy Rosary. Father Foery was therefore a man of wide pastoral experience and proven competency.[30]

Walter Andrew Foery was born in Rochester on July 6, 1890. His father, William, was of German descent; his mother bore the Irish name of Agnes O'Brien. Walter Foery attended the parochial school of his parish, St. Bridget, where he finished his elementary course in 1905. Then he went on to St. Andrew's and St. Bernard's Seminaries, in both of which he made a notable record. In those days, St. Bernard's Seminary still enjoyed the privilege granted in 1901 by Pope Leo XIII of conferring academic degrees in philosophy and theology. Foery won the degree of Doctor of Philosophy in 1914, and that of Licentiate of Sacred Theology in 1916.[31] Bishop Hickey ordained him to the priesthood in St. Patrick's Cathedral on June 10, 1916.

It was on August 18, 1937, in the same Cathedral and before the same altar, that Archbishop Mooney consecrated the Bishop-elect of Syracuse. Assistant consecrators were two other members of St. Bernard's "famous Class of 1916" which eventually gave five members to the episcopate. The senior co-consecrator was Most Reverend Emmet M. Walsh (1892-1968), Bishop of Charleston at that time (1927-1949), and subsequently Coadjutor and then Bishop of Youngstown (1952-1968). The junior co-consecrator was Most Reverend Francis P. Keough (1890-1961), then Bishop of Providence (1935-1947) and subsequently Archbishop of Baltimore (1947-1961). Archbishop Hickey, now seventy-six, delivered the sermon to an audience which included two other archbishops, sixteen bishops, the Episcopal Bishop of Rochester, the mayors of Rochester and Syracuse, and a delegation of local businessmen of various faiths. The consecration of Bishop Foery was the last of the four consecrations of bishops performed in St. Patrick's Cathedral. Just a few days later the historic old building was sold, and not long after the completion of the sale it was razed.

On August 31st there were over a thousand people on hand—including many of his old friends and former parishioners—to say farewell to Bishop Foery as he boarded the train for his new diocese. He was installed on the following day in the Cathedral of the Immaculate Conception, Syracuse.[32]

If Archbishop Mooney was prevented by circumstances, during his brief Rochester years, from establishing new parochial schools, he nevertheless took two positive steps of educational significance. One step was to welcome into the Diocese on September 1, 1936, a new order of catechist sisters—the first group of the sort since the arrival of the Trinitarian Sisters. These were the Religious Teachers Filippini, a community of Italian origin, who opened their convent in the parish of St. Mary of the Lake, Watkins Glen.[33] The other step—one of wider import—was his insistence that the nuns of the diocesan teaching orders continue their studies so as to qualify for academic degrees. The Archbishop won wide praise for framing this latter policy.[34]

A good deal more was accomplished in secondary education during the years 1933-1937. We have already referred to the opening of the Divine Word Missionary Seminary in 1936. While this was not a diocesan institution, it was nevertheless within the Diocese. As an old "seminary man", the Archbishop naturally took a special interest in his own diocesan seminaries. He approved of the building of a new heating plant at St. Bernard's and the construction of a new residence for the students of St. Andrew's. The frame residence, St. William's House, opened in 1936 and still in use, was at 1150 Buffalo Road, on the front of the property where St. Andrew's Seminary was built after World War II.[35]

Aquinas Institute had meanwhile become increasingly difficult to finance. Bishop Hickey had desired to charge no tuition, and with this intention in mind, he had levied annual quotas on the Rochester parishes. But the depression had cut into the quotas and interfered with the liquidation of the large debt. To balance the decline of the parish payments, Archbishop Mooney now launched two drives for $90,000.00 —one in 1934, the other in 1935. The first drive brought in $88,000.00; the second, only $74,000.00.[36] Obviously, another approach was necessary; so the Archbishop decided to turn the school over to the Basilian Fathers.[37] He asked that the city pastors pledge to pay one-quarter of their quotas every year until 1960. The pastors were content with the arrangement. However, the diocesan priests on the Aquinas faculty were less happy. Devoted to the school, and unwilling to see it pass out of the hands of the diocesan clergy if that could be avoided, they informed Archbishop Mooney that they would be willing to serve without recompense for a stated period if this would stay the transfer. The Archbishop appreciated their generous gesture, but stood by his decision as the only feasible arrangement.

We have already stated that the Diocese and the Basilian Fathers of Toronto reached their agreement on September 1, 1936. The Basilians consented to take over the property and its liabilities. The Diocese promised to pay an annual sum to provide for whole or partial scholarships for five hundred students; it promised likewise that during the next fifteen years it would open no new boys' high school in Rochester, and that even after that time it would establish no such school in the vicinity of Aquinas.

In fulfillment of this contract, the Basilian Fathers took charge of the high school at the resumption of classes in September, 1937. Since they did not have enough priests and scholastics of their own community to fill the ranks of the faculty, they continued for some years to engage the services of a few diocesan priests and a number of Sisters of St. Joseph and Sisters of Mercy. But Father Joseph E. Grady, who had served ably as principal since 1928, was transferred to the vice-rectorship of St. Bernard's Seminary, and made a domestic prelate on June 23, 1937. Father John H. O'Loane, a Basilian, succeeded him in the principalship.

One other interesting stipulation of the Basilian contract was that their Congregation should be given the priority in the future establishment of any Catholic men's college in Rochester or within a radius of forty miles. It was as a result of this phase of the agreement— prompted, perhaps, by the charter of incorporation of Aquinas Institute, which envisioned the Institute's development into a college—that the Basilian Fathers opened St. John Fisher College in 1951.[38]

We have noted above the inauguration of the Rochester Division of the Niagara University School of Business Administration in February, 1934. Nazareth College for Women was meanwhile growing apace, and its humble frame quarters on Augustine Street were becoming yearly more inadequate. The Sisters of St. Joseph had already decided to build a permanent campus adjacent to their new motherhouse on East Avenue. The Archbishop, however, disagreed with this proposal. He believed that it was not wise to have the college so close to the motherhouse. The Sisters therefore purchased another property on the edge of Pittsford, about a half-mile away, and in 1937 launched a drive for funds. Mooney warmly commended their plans and their cause to prospective benefactors.[39]

It was during the Mooney regime that New York State finally adopted a law granting free bus transportation to children who attended parochial schools. While the Archbishop did not act personally in promoting the law, the New York State Catholic Welfare Committee gave effective backing to the legislation, and Archbishop Mooney was, of course, one of the Committee, represented in Albany by the Rochester diocesan superintendent of schools, Father John M. Duffy, and his associate, Father Charles J. Mahoney. It was furthermore a

Rochester legislator, State Senator George B. Kelly, who played perhaps the most important role in getting the law through the State Legislature.

The campaign to obtain free school transportation and other "auxiliary services" for parochial school children has been a long and arduous one in New York State. Laws conceding such "services" eventually came up against the so-called "Blaine Amendment" (Article IX, 4) which as we have seen above was written into the 1894 State Constitution under anti-Catholic pressure. This forbade not only direct public financial aid to denominational schools, but "indirect" aid. Consequently, almost any form of public assistance to parish schools or to their students—even police or fire protection—could easily be accused of unconstitutionality under so wide a formula.

State Senator George B. Kelly crashed into this legal barrier in 1935 with his Kelly-Corbett Bill, designed to provide free bus transportation. The Bill passed, in both Senate and Assembly, but Governor Herbert Lehman vetoed it. Nothing daunted, the Senator revamped the proposed law, which passed as the Kelly-McCreery Bill on May 5, 1936. This time the Governor accepted it, signing it into a law on May 13th; and it took effect on September 1st.[40] When the bus law got through, Mr. Charles J. Tobin, counsel of the N.Y.S.C.W.C., told Archbishop Mooney and the other bishops of the State that the legislation was "epoch-making". But he warned them that local school authorities might still hesitate to apply the law.[41]

The prophecy was soon fulfilled. In Rochester itself, the Board of Education decided that the law referred only to rural districts, not to cities.[42] This decision was based on a judgment made by Charles A. Brind, Jr., director and principal attorney of the Law Division of the State Department of Education.[43] Senator Kelly protested that he had intended to furnish bus transportation to all school children.[44] Nevertheless, the Rochester Board, after having declared in March, 1937, that it planned to grant comparable transportation to public and parochial students, in the following month whittled down the number of eligible children from 200 to 37. The Rochester diocesan authorities protested.[45]

The main argument which had been advanced by promoters of the bus law was that free transportation was a service not to the schools that the children attended but to the children themselves. Now, however, a series of test cases were brought against the school transportation law, alleging that it really provided "indirect" aid to the parish schools, and as such fell afoul of the "Blaine Amendment." In 1938, the New York State Court of Appeals decided that the Kelly-McCreery

Act was indeed an infringement of this constitutional provision.[46]

After the 1938 decision, the only course open to Catholics and other interested parties was to work for a new State constitutional amendment that would permit free bus transportation. This was accomplished in the constitutional convention of 1938, and the enabling clause was voted into the State Constitution on November 5, 1938, as an amendment to the Blaine provision, now re-numbered Article XI, 4. On May 16, 1939, the Legislature altered the Education Law so as to authorize free bus transportation to all children who needed it, "for the promotion of the best interests of such children."[47] But by the time this long-overdue adjustment was made, Archbishop Mooney had been promoted to Detroit.

Edward Mooney by no means neglected the devotional life of his flock. He did not, it is true, preach as frequently as his predecessors had. A certain hesitancy of utterance may have deterred him from mounting the pulpit. (Some identified this as a stammer, although it seems rather to have stemmed from the word-watching which diplomacy had forced upon him.) A more likely reason was that he was a perfectionist in literary composition. Nevertheless, when he did speak, on more solemn occasions, he could be depended upon to deliver a strong and able discourse, carefully organized and composed, and aimed more directly at the mind than at the heart. One could cite, for instance, his sermons on world peace delivered in the Cathedral at the Christmas midnight Mass in 1935 and 1936.[48] He gave another admirable address at the Seventh National Eucharistic Congress (Cleveland, September, 1935) to a large gathering that included about one thousand Rochester delegates.[49] The baccalaureate sermon that he delivered at the University of Notre Dame in June, 1936, was also very well conceived.[50]

No devotional practice engaged his enthusiastic support so readily as one which involved the Holy See and the Vicar of Christ; for he was not only outstandingly loyal to the papacy but also to Pope Pius XI, with whom he was on close friendly terms. Thus, the Diocesan Synod of 1934, in Decree #15, directed that on the Sunday within the octave of the feast of SS. Peter and Paul (June 29th), when the annual collection was taken up for the pope, there should be a special sermon on the Holy See, with a view to strengthening the attachment of clergy and laity to the successor of Peter. This was an innovation in the Diocese. The Archbishop was also happy to proclaim to his faithful their eligibility for the jubilee indulgences of the special Holy Year of 1933-1934.[51] And it must have been with tender personal feelings that

Mooney presided over a diocesan observance, on May 30, 1937, of the eightieth birthday of the indomitable Pope Pius XI.[52]

One phase of Catholic devotional life which was developing in the 1930's was the Liturgical Movement. The first widespread evidence of this new emphasis was the increased use of the small missal. Adults were urged to own a missal and to follow it during the Mass. In the parochial schools the same practice became a part of the program. Thus, for example, the *Catholic Courier* of January 7, 1937 reported that children in the sixth, seventh and eighth grade of Corpus Christi School, Rochester, were now regularly reading the missal at Sunday Mass.

The Diocese of Rochester was anything but a pioneer in the full-blown liturgical drive, prior to World War II. However, it did continue to sponsor the cultivation of good liturgical music. Father John M. Petter (1875-1938), professor of music at St. Bernard's Seminary, had marched along the trail blazed by Professor Eugene Bonn. He was active in the councils of the Society of St. Gregory of America, and served as its president from 1927 to 1938.[53] Another local priest-musician, Father George V. Predmore (1886-1961), received favorable notices in the Catholic press for his *Sacred Music and the Catholic Church* (Boston, 1936).[54]

Particularly constructive were the Summer Schools of Liturgical Music held in Rochester in 1934, 1935, and 1936. The project arose out out of a series of concerts of liturgical music presented in Rochester in January, 1934, by the Pius X School of Liturgical Music of Manhattanville College, New York. Sponsored by the Rochester Diocesan Schools Office, these concerts won high praise from local music critics and from Dr. Howard Hanson, the Director of the Eastman School of Music.[55] The warmth of praise suggested the feasibility of conducting a summer school of church music under the direction of Mother Georgia Stevens, R.S.C.J., of the Pius X School.

Though no musician himself, Archbishop Mooney had shown great interest in the original concerts. He was consequently happy to announce the plans for the summer school. When the time drew near for beginning of the two-week August sessions, he urged the diocesan priests to attend along with their organists and choir directors. The undertaking proved successful, so it was repeated in the two following years, again with the personal support of the Archbishop.[56]

If John Francis O'Hern had been ever-ready to give a newspaper interview or to pose for a press photographer, Edward Mooney went to the other extreme in his avoidance of either type of publicity. He disliked being photographed even for his diocesan paper. Nevertheless, he strongly encouraged the efforts of the Rochester *Catholic Courier* to increase its circulation.[57]. The *Courier* had, indeed, slowly improved since the Diocese assumed management. In addition to articles on churchwide and diocesan subjects, it printed several features of its own. One regular contributor was the Reverend Dr. Owen B. McGuire, a retired professor of St. Bernard's Seminary, whose column "Believe It . . . Not" appeared weekly after October 20, 1934. Dr. McGuire wrote discerningly on a wide range of subjects, and displayed a cosmopolitan knowledge and a real, if minor, talent as a publicist. Another columnist was a young instructor in English at St. Andrew's Seminary, Father Benedict A. Ehmann. Father Ehmann had been principally responsible for opening the Catholic Evidence Library in the lobby of the Columbus Civic Center in 1933. His *Courier* column, the "Library Signpost," was devoted largely to reviewing and commenting on books available in the Evidence Library; but its format was broad enough to permit essays on any current subject. At the same time, Father Ehmann, a capable musician, was beginning to move through the gateway of church music into the national liturgical movement, which was starting to expand. A third columnist was Mr. William A. Lang, a young journalist, who wrote the athletic column, "Along the Sports Horizon." "Bill" Lang eventually moved from journalism into business, and became president of the Rochester Transit Corporation.

On May 20-22, 1937, the Rochester diocesan paper played host to the national convention of the Catholic Press Association. The Archbishop greeted the officers, delegates, and distinguished guest speakers. It was on this occasion that the C.P.A. for the first time staged an annual Catholic Press Exhibit in connection with its meeting.[58]

The editor of the *Courier,* Father Leo C. Mooney, continued to be the key Catholic figure in local Catholic radio work. Other priests were guest speakers from time to time on his Rochester Catholic Hour, broadcast on Sunday noon over WHAM. Archbishop Mooney himself gave the talk at the opening of the fifth year of this radio series. On that occasion, the Archbishop declared, with his typical forthrightness, gentle but frank, that the purpose of the Catholic Hour was to educate not only Catholics but non-Catholics in the Catholic faith.[59] It must be admitted, however, that this and the other diocesan Catholic radio programs still suffered from an amateurism that diminished their appeal in the eyes of a public accustomed to the finesse of professional radio broadcasts.

As we have already pointed out, Edward Mooney's interest in the foreign missions was an enduring one. This interest had no doubt stood him in good stead during his India assignment. It had likewise whetted his desire to see the faith spread in Japan; and it had led him to promote the introduction of the Maryknoll missions into that country before his transfer to Rochester. This missionary spirit by no means left him as he became "domesticated" in his first American see. Thus, in Spring, 1934, he gave the seminarians of St. Bernard's a lecture on the foreign missions that revealed his wealth of information on the subject.[60] When Bishop James A. Walsh, founder of Maryknoll, died in April, 1936, it was Mooney who celebrated his funeral Mass in the New York Cathedral.[61] To further advance the cause of the foreign missions in the Rochester Diocese, he named Father John S. Randall assistant director of the Society for the Propagation of the Faith in July, 1936, and he authorized the development of the Missionary Cooperation Plan.[62] He made much of the annual Mission Sunday in October. For example, on October 20, 1936, he presided in the Rochester Cathedral at the solemn Mission Sunday Mass. A Rochester-born Maryknoller, Father Charles Hilbert, celebrated the Mass; and the preacher was the newly-consecrated Vicar Apostolic of Kaying, China, who seventeen years later was to meet a martyr's death at the hands of Chinese Communists—Bishop Francis X. Ford, M.M. (1892-1952).[63] A year later, the Archbishop himself preached a very feeling Mission Sunday sermon on his own experiences in the mission lands of Asia.[64]

It was doubtless the same missionary urge that prompted Edward Mooney to start missionary work among the Negroes of Rochester. His part in this effort is little known, but deserves to be recorded, particularly because it sprang from his own initiative.

The story began on June 9, 1935, when the Archbishop administered Confirmation at the poor little Italian mission chapel of the Annunciation on the northern outskirt of the city. Along with the Italo-American children, he also confirmed that day an adult who automatically arrested his attention. It was Mr. Jethro Urius Pinckney, a fifty-year-old Negro. After the ceremony, Mooney invited the priest in charge, Father George A. Weinmann, to have lunch with him at his residence. When they met at the Bishop's House, the Archbishop asked for further information about Mr. Pinckney. Father Weinmann said that he had become acquainted with Jethro when the Negro had volunteered to assist him in laying the cement floor of the church basement. As the two worked on the building project it gradually came out that "Pink", while living in Buffalo, had already taken some instructions with a view to becoming a Catholic. Weinmann offered to complete the training and to receive him into the Faith. Pinckney agreed and eventually entered the Church on June 3, 1933.

The Archbishop then disclosed his mind to Father Weinmann. He wanted to begin work among the Negroes, and he wanted Weinmann to make the approach in whatever way he thought best.

Father Weinmann decided that the best way to start would be to gather a few Negro men together for social meetings under Church auspices. So he paid "Pink's" carfare to go around Rochester and invite whatever friends he thought would be interested. A rather good number responded, pleased with the opportunity of getting together in Annunciation Hall without any cost to themselves beyond a voluntary offering. In June, 1935, this group organized as the St. Peter Claver Society. The original officers were Albert Broco, Sr., President; Wilfrid Quamina, Vice President; O. J. Green, Secretary; and Reverend George A. Weinmann, Treasurer and Chaplain. The Chaplain then made available for distribution to all interested parties a descriptive notice of the Society the text of which Archbishop Mooney had approved:

> The purpose of this Society is to unite Colored People especially under Catholic auspices. It has the approval of the Rt. Rev. Archbishop Edward A. Mooney. Membership is open to all Catholic Colored People and to all others who are interested in getting exact information about the Doctrines and Practices of the Catholic Church.

On March 1, 1936, the young Society sponsored an important Meeting on Racial Cooperation at the Columbus Civic Center. Father Weinmann was in charge of arrangements, assisted by Father John C. O'Donnell, a teacher at Aquinas Institute and moderator of its student Mission Unit. The Chancery, in a circular letter, instructed the local pastors to announce the affair in their parishes and to direct each parish society to send a delegation. As a result, a capacity crowd attended.

The quality of the speakers guaranteed a worthwhile evening. They were two representatives of the Catholic Interracial Council of New York City: Father John LaFarge, S.J., a pioneer in Catholic interracialism; and Mr. Elmo Anderson, a prominent New York Catholic Negro.

Time was to prove Father LaFarge's 1936 address prophetic. He warned his Rochester hearers that the North would eventually have to face a serious racial problem by reason of the accelerated migration of

Negroes from the South. He therefore urged all his listeners to be prepared to assist the Negro in hurdling his great initial barrier—lack of education. Meanwhile they should strive to remove, by their own tolerance, charity, and good example, any other obstacles that might hamper the Negro in his effort to better his condition. LaFarge, who had long done missionary work among the American Negroes, was fully aware of the delicacy of racial confrontation. Black was black and white was white, and it took more than ordinary good will to overlook that accidental but socially troublesome truth. But he admonished his white audience: "If you don't like the Negroes, at least don't harm them." Then, in a truly memorable figure of speech, he reminded them: "Men are like the white and black keys on a piano. Their color may be different, but that does not prevent them from playing in harmony."

Three local Negro ministers were present and took part in the open forum that followed. Their participation added a new and fitting interracial note to the gathering, and emphasized its importance as a civic convocation.

By the time this meeting took place, the membership of the St. Peter Claver Society had risen to fifty. Soon the members expressed a desire to have quarters of their own closer to the Negro centers of the city. After careful investigation, Father Weinmann secured a residence at 13 Rome Street, near the main Post Office. The price asked for was originally $5,000.00. The Society acquired it for $1,300.00, with the substantial personal assistance of Attorney James E. Cuff, who had chaired the interracial meeting and was also grand knight of the local Knights of Columbus Council. Now the "Claverites" could expand their activities.

The center on Rome Street was made available not only to the members but to any other Negro group that wished to use it. For about a year it served as the address of the Catholic Worker movement, of which more below. Summer vacation school was likewise conducted here by the School Sisters of Notre Dame.

During the Sundays of the school year, the Sisters of St. Joseph taught catechism on Rome Street to integrated groups of children. The leading figure in this undertaking was Sister Rose Miriam Smyth of Nazareth College. She was imbued with a strong missionary spirit, and had a special interest in the Negro. As a matter of fact, it was she who, through her nephew, Father John C. O'Donnell, had urged the St. Peter Claver Society to hold the interracial meeting of March 1, 1936. Sister Rose Miriam's work with Negroes had an interesting sequel. In July, 1939, she was elected superior general of the Rochester Sisters of St.

Joseph. As we shall see later on, in 1940 the new Mother General sent a group of her nuns to conduct a Negro school for the Edmundite Fathers in Selma, Alabama.[65]

By May, 1937, Father Weinmann, as the result of his contacts with local Negroes, largely through the Society, had received thirteen Negroes into the Church. But the St. Peter Claver Society was more widely valuable as a gesture of Catholic friendliness towards the local Negro population. Through its efforts, too, the first Negro students were admitted to Aquinas Institute and Nazareth Academy.

In 1944, as we shall see, the Diocese decided to take a different approach to the Negro apostolate. The Peter Claverites therefore disposed of the Rome Street property and gave the sale-price, $2,400.00, to the Diocese towards the new Negro work. Their organization thus ceased to exist six years after its foundation. Its contribution had been modest, but it had been positive; and this is to the particular credit of not only the priests, sisters and layfolk who collaborated, but to Archbishop Mooney who initiated the program.[66]

Edward Mooney, as we have already indicated, preferred the unobtrusive life. As a result, he was slow to make friends with the Catholic laity of Rochester. With only two laymen did he build up a fast friendship: Dr. Leo F. Simpson, the physician, and Mr. B. Emmett Finucane, the banker.[67] Nor did he make any real effort to extend his personal acquaintance among the non-Catholics of the diocesan area. This was a curious trait, to which the term "detachment" might apply more exactly than "aloofness." For the Archbishop, once engaged in interview, was very sociable and sympathetic, and a good conversationalist. The only regrettable thing was that as a result of his attitude of reserve, Archbishop Mooney's Rochester diocesans had small opportunity to discern in him the talents which later brought him into national and worldwide prominence.

But the limitation which Mooney placed upon his personal contacts was of his own choosing, so he did not lament its effect. Nor did it interfere with his active leadership of the laity, particularly through Catholic Action, on a diocesan, national, and international basis. An able executive can do much through delegation, through correspondence, and—one of Mooney's favorite methods—over the telephone.

In the Diocese itself, the Depression had not yet lifted its deadening hand, so Rochester's fourth bishop had to concern himself with the works of charity and of social justice. In institutionalized charity he played a prominent role. He was elected a director of the Rochester Community Chest on October 13, 1933.[68] *Ex officio* he headed Catholic

Charities; and when Father Walter A. Foery, the Charities director, was made bishop of Syracuse, Archbishop Mooney, then administrator of the Rochester Diocese, appointed Father Gerald C. Lambert to succeed him, with Father Hubert A. Bisky as director of the Family Division and Father Joseph E. Vogt as director of the Social Action Division.[69]

Another sort of scourge struck the Southern Tier of the Diocese on July 4, 1935, when the Chemung River system went on a rampage. The flood caused much anguish and destruction in Yates and Tompkins Counties, and even more in Steuben County. Four parishes of the Diocese suffered property loss. St. James Church in Trumansburg became an avenue for the rushing waters. At Watkins, one parishioner lost a child, and 200 were driven from their homes by the deluge. At Hammondsport, St. Gabriel's Church was badly damaged, and Father Patrick W. A. Kelly, the pastor, and his two sisters had to be rescued from the second story of the shaken and waterlogged rectory. At Hornell, St. Ann's Church was inundated. The new St. Ignatius Church, soon to be dedicated, was not harmed by the flood itself; but its undelivered pews were seriously injured in the local woodworking factory.

Shocked by the news of the disaster, Archbishop Mooney made a tour of the stricken area, visited the damaged churches, and left a generous donation. The mayor of Rochester also set up a Mayor's Flood Relief Committee, chaired by Mr. B. Emmett Finucane, which collected funds by sponsoring benefit movies at three Rochester theaters. The Rochester Knights of Columbus and the Catholic Women's Club backed this campaign, which added $7,500.00 to the relief fund. Elsewhere in the Diocese, especially in the afflicted centers themselves, Catholic clergy and laity lent a hand to the work of rescue and rehabilitation.[70]

As for the national economic depression, the Diocese of Rochester continued its support of federal and State efforts. On September 26, 1933, before the arrival of Archbishop Mooney, Rochester staged a mammoth procession to champion the National Recovery Administration (NRA). The Sunday before the parade, the priests of Rochester preached on the merits of the federal recovery measures and urged the faithful to accept them. Catholic Rochesterians played a prominent part in the parade, which involved 65,000 citizens.[71] Elsewhere in the Diocese, the Catholic clergy took the same stance. One of the most knowledgeable defenders of the NRA was Father Michael B. Groden, pastor of St. Mary's, Horseheads.[72] A year later, when the State submitted to a vote a proposition to set aside further funds to combat unemployment, Father Foery, as director of diocesan charities, again urged all to vote "Yes."[73]

One phase of federal and State relief work that imposed new pastoral obligations on Archbishop Mooney was the Civilian Conservation Corps. The federal government set up this project as an emergency measure in 1933, and continued it as an independent undertaking from 1937 to 1943. The young men joined the program for one six-months' term, and could reenlist for a second. They were housed in barracks in rural or State park areas, each center accommodating on an average of 200-300 men. In 1935, at the peak point, there were sixty-seven Civilian Conservation camps in New York State. After that year, the number was gradually reduced. Catholic Corpsmen were apparently able in some localities to attend Mass at nearby parishes. In most cases, priests of the vicinity visited them more or less frequently, to offer Mass, hear confessions, and be available for consultations. Diocesan priests from Aquinas Institute were assigned to the Corpsmen in the two eastern camps in Letchworth Park. The Howland's Island Camp was taken care of from Auburn; the Fillmore Glen camp, from Moravia; the Watkins Glen Park camp from Bradford; the Stony Brook camp from Dansville; the Fair Haven camp from Cato; and the Hamlin Beach camp, presumably from Brockport. A priest from Corning visited the camp at Monterey, and one from Hornell, the camp at Arkport. In all, there were over a dozen camps within the twelve counties.[74]

Three interesting works of benevolence had their beginnings in the Mooney regime, and with his permission, even though they were not under the direct jurisdiction of the diocesan charities. The St. Gerard Maternity Guild was established by the National Catholic Women's Union, the ladies' branch of the German-Catholic Central Verein. The Central Verein itself introduced parish credit unions into Rochester. And the third new charitable enterprise was the Catholic Worker group, inspired by the New York movement of the same name.

As its name suggests, the St. Gerard Maternity Guild had as its purpose the supplying of funds, maternity clothes, layettes, etc., to needy expectant mothers. The Rochester chapter was founded on June 18, 1935, with the willing approval of Archbishop Mooney and under the direction of Father Joseph J. Schagemann. The original officers were: Mrs. Mary Klos (President); Mrs. Margaret Spiegel (First Vice President); Mrs. Benedict Ehmann (Secretary); Mrs. Lawrence Weider (Treasurer). The spiritual director was Father Joseph H. Gefell, pastor of Holy Family Church. While the Guild has never been large, and is called on for aid very infrequently today, it was nevertheless able to make a positive contribution to needy mothers in the late years of the Depression.[75]

Rochester's first parish credit union dates from 1937. Parish credit unions, popular abroad and in Canada, offer a good opportunity to people of small means to borrow money without exposing themselves to the usury of professional loan companies. The parish credit union is operated *by* parish members *for* parish members. They join by taking out at least one share of stock in the union, at a few dollars a share, and are thereby entitled to borrow short-term loans at about one percent monthly interest "for productive or provident purposes." As early as 1925 the American Central Verein had embarked on a campaign to "sell" this scheme to its parish units across the country.

Rochester Verein members had been toying with the idea of a local credit union since 1934. Finally, at the end of 1936, Attorney Joseph H. Gervais and Mr. John J. Ammering, both local Verein members, recommended the plan effectually to their Rochester confreres. With the active backing of the pastor, Father Joseph H. Gefell, the Verein associates of Holy Family Parish in Rochester organized the city's first parish credit union. Founded on January 7, 1937, it received its State charter on April 4, 1937. The Holy Family credit union has been most successful. By 1956 its assets were close to $350,000.00; and between 1937 and 1962 it made loans to the sum total of $3 million. It was of benefit to its members during the depressed years, but even more during the 1950's, when home loans were very much needed.

After Archbishop Mooney's departure from Rochester, four other German-oriented parishes of Rochester established credit unions, also under Central Verein auspices. These four were never so large as that of Holy Family, and the last of the four suspended operations in 1965.[76] By that time banks and company credit unions were offering too great competition. But the local Central Verein had no reason to regret its efforts. The credit unions had done a valuable service in a time of genuine need.

The Catholic Worker movement was inspired by the movement of the same name begun in the New York City slums in 1933 by Dorothy Day, a former Communist, and Peter Maurin, a French-born social philosopher. The founders aimed at opposing the spread of Communism by preaching a doctrine of social justice based on the papal labor encyclicals, and illustrating that doctrine by an ardent "personalist" charity towards the city poor, whom it welcomed to its slum-centered "Houses of Hospitality." The movement did not hesitate to use certain tactics that the Communists themselves used, but in order to achieve counter-Communist aims. Among these methods was the publication of the *Catholic Worker,* a penny journal addressed to the same audience as the Communist *Daily Worker,* but dedicated to a radical Christian idealism. This paper first appeared on May Day, 1933.

The Catholic Worker movement, daring, yet realistic in its views, soon caught the fancy of young clergy and lay people across the country. In Rochester, Father George E. Vogt, a professor at St. Andrew's Seminary, organized a "Catholic Worker" group in 1934 to study the papal encyclicals. Associated with this group were students from Nazareth College, St. Andrew's Seminary, and Aquinas Institute. The members not only studied together, but some of them distributed the *Catholic Worker*—even at Communist-led street rallies, to the evident displeasure of Communist organizers. John Hurley, a seminarian at St. Andrew's, also formed a "Catholic Worker Club" among a dozen of his fellow-seminarians, to teach catechism to Negro children on the West Side of town. They held classes on Sundays in a Negro home on Ford Street, and for a couple of summers conducted a summer school in a rented house on Clarissa Street. The Catholic Worker group encouraged this "Catholic Worker Club," but the Club was basically an independent venture.

The first person from the Rochester area to fall under the spell of Dorothy Day—and that, during the earliest months of the movement—was Miss Margaret Bigham of Canandaigua, who was then studying in New York. However, it was Father Benedict Ehmann who first arranged for Miss Day to speak in Rochester, around the end of 1933. She addressed a capacity crowd on that first visit. When she came a second time, on February 11, 1935, a full auditorium greeted her at the Columbus Civic Center. On this occasion she urged the establishment of houses of hospitality of the type her group operated in lower New York. The Rochester Catholic Worker unit had already been considering that course of action; and after the Day lecture it began to lay long-range plans. But by the time the program was ready to start, Archbishop Mooney had already been transferred to Detroit.

The Rochester Catholic Worker unit was authorized—in so far as that was necessary—by the Diocese, although as time went on, it came to be treated with some reserve, as veering a bit to the radical. Some of the local group did accept, at least theoretically, the pacifism and other provocative views of the *Catholic Worker.* The remaining members did not go so far. But both parties agreed in the matter of social theory and practical charity. The liturgical movement also received an early and warm welcome among them, for like the New York group they saw in the Mass a true expression of community, and, as such, an antidote to atheistic communism. It is not surprising, then, that when Father Virgil Michel, O.S.B., America's pioneer sociological liturgist, came to Rochester on February 26, 1937 to talk to the Nazareth College students on "Liturgy and Life in the Church," he should have attended with interest a meeting of the Rochester Catholic Workers.[77]

The local Catholic Worker unit was still a small, independent study group during the Mooney regime. As such, it could only merit, along with the other unofficial Catholic philanthropies, the approving nod of the Archbishop, who was himself dedicated, of course, to social justice and charity, and to their implementation among the needy of the world.

3. TOWARD WIDER HORIZONS.

During his Rochester episcopate, Edward Mooney was ever ready to follow the lead of Pope Pius XI in promoting Catholic Action, whether in the formal or the more informal sense of that term. After 1935 he worked at it on two levels, first as bishop of Rochester, second as chairman of the executive board of the National Catholic Welfare Conference, the prime agency of American Catholic Action.

As bishop of Rochester, the Archbishop often encouraged the older diocesan lay organizations to voice their protest against harmful trends. Thus the diocesan Holy Name Society, at its convention in Geneva, New York, on April 8, 1934, issued resolutions opposing both the proposed child labor amendment to the federal constitution, and current State legislation on divorce and contraception.[78] At its third annual convention, held in Canandaigua on April 28, 1935, the Diocesan Holy Name Union published further resolutions condemning American interference in Mexico, and deploring the Nazi anti-religious movement.[79]

In his keynote address to the Holy Name convention of 1934, Mooney urged support of the *Catholic Courier,* the diocesan newspaper, as a form of Catholic Action. During his regime he also brought Scouting more actively within the same apostolic perimeter. In 1934, the Diocesan Committee on Scouting listed twenty-eight Catholic Boy Scout troops in the Diocese. This represented only 24% of the diocesan parishes. An earnest effort was made during the next few months to augment the total. The effort met with some success; but an (undated) report for 1936 or 1937 indicated that of the 870 Catholic Scouts then in the Diocese, only 555 belonged to Catholic troops. The foundation and maintenance of Scouting in a parish presents many problems, and the Archbishop would not have chosen to use pressure on pastors reluctant to accept the program. Nevertheless, he gave his backing to the Diocesan Committee's work, and in 1937 approved a new Catholic ceremony for Scout investiture.[80]

Another long-standing Catholic organization that lent itself readily to apostolic efforts was the Sodality. The Rochester Parish Sodality Union, in September, 1935, opened an evening school of Catholic Action, with sessions in the Columbus Civic Center. Its director was Miss Dorothy J. Willmann of St. Louis, the executive secretary of the national Sodality union; and its purpose was to instruct diocesan sodalists in the possibilities of Catholic action that were open to them. This Rochester "Catholic Action School" was the first of its sort in New York State. Archbishop Mooney was pleased to give it his approbation.[81] The Archbishop likewise urged the need of social action in his address to the State convention of the Catholic Daughters of America in May, 1937. The Catholic Daughters, dedicated to promoting religious and social welfare, were strong in the Rochester Diocese; and it was the diocesan branches that played host at this State convention, which was held in Elmira.[82]

There were, of course, several smaller enterprises that could more or less qualify as lay apostolates: for example, the Catholic Evidence Library, the Narberth Movement, and the Catholic Theater Guild.

The Catholic Evidence Library was opened in the Columbus Civic Center on November 6, 1933, and still continues to function. Founded in order to provide Catholic reading in a day in which few Catholic books were available in the public library, the Library was brought into being (as we have already stated) by Father Benedict Ehmann; but it has always been staffed by volunteer laywomen.[83] The Narberth Movement, whose central office was at Narberth, Pennsylvania, engaged in the distribution of Catholic tracts. In 1935, Archbishop Mooney welcomed the movement's program into the Rochester Diocese.[84] The *Catholic Courier* often printed Narberth syndicated articles thereafter. It was Father John S. Randall, an assistant at St. Patrick's Cathedral, who in 1933 founded the Catholic Theatre Guild. When he was transferred to Auburn, Father Randall took over the Auburn Little Theater Players, founded earlier by Father Donald Cleary.[85] Both of these dramatic groups were short-lived, but they were succeeded later on by more ambitious theatrical organizations.

There were two national apostolates that especially engaged the interest of Archbishop Mooney: the Legion of Decency and the Confraternity of Christian Doctrine.

The American Catholic hierarchy organized the Legion of Decency in April, 1934, for the double purpose of reminding Catholics of their obligation not to patronize improper motion pictures, and producers of their obligation not to concoct them. During the Great Depression, Hollywood sought increasingly to offset its declining income by issuing films of a sensational nature. On June 21, 1934, the bishops sponsored the taking, in every Catholic Church, of a Catholic pledge not to attend motion pictures which favored immorality or violence.[86] Eight thousand Rochester diocesan Holy Name men, assembled that day in a rally held in Elmira, set an example to the Diocese by taking the Legion pledge in the presence of the Archbishop. In December, 1934, some 200,000 diocesan Catholics renewed the pledge—a practice that was repeated each December thereafter.[87]

One reason why this "grass roots" movement went off so smoothly was that pains had been taken beforehand to explain it to the people. The diocesan superintendent of education, Father John M. Duffy, alerted his teachers as early as April 22, 1934. In May, Father Leo C. Mooney spoke on the subject to the Diocesan Council of Catholic Women. And in the same month, Father Daniel Lord, S.J., of St. Louis (who had had a hand in composing the new Movie Production Code) told the Rochester diocesan Sodality Union how they could help the cause.[88] Furthermore, on May 28, 1934, the Rochester Interfaith Good Will Committee, meeting at the Columbus Civic Center, named a special committee to study the effect on the public of the plunging cinematic trend. Meanwhile, this interfaith group issued a resolution urging the Catholic, Protestant and Jewish congregations to support the decency campaign in whatever ways seemed best.[89] Having made the Legion of Decency a permanent organization, the bishops set up a central office in New York City, to publish prompt classifications of new motion pictures, arrived at by a committee of the International Federation of Catholic Alumnae. The upshot of this national effort—Catholic and intercredal—was that the film producers eventually changed their tune, and profited rather than lost by the change. As Father Lord observed, "The whole industry learned that good morals are good business."[90]

After 1934, when it was put under the direct jurisdiction of the N.C.W.C., the national Confraternity of Christian Doctrine entered into a more vigorous life, focussing its attention particularly on adult study clubs. As we have seen, Edward Mooney, while residing in Rome, had assisted Cardinal Pietro Gasparri in the compilation of a catechism. Now he took a special interest in this adult study program. He particularly commended the local phase of the project to the attention of the Diocesan Council of Catholic Women, on the occasion of their fourth annual meeting in Rochester on October 29, 1934.[91] In 1935 he set up a diocesan C.C.D. office to supervise released-time instruction, vacation schools in the City of Rochester, and parish discussion groups.[92] The adult study clubs began to meet in Lent, 1935. Advance briefing on the method of conducting them had been given to the diocesan priests by Miss Miriam Marks, executive secretary of the National C.C.D. The initial discussion text was *The Ceremonies of the Mass*.[93] In the Lent of 1936 a second round of discussions started, and the diocesan office published a count of 740 study groups in the Diocese, involving well over 5,000 people.[94] After 1936, the number fell off; but the clubs were still quite active in 1937, and the whole program was considered to have achieved a moderate success.[95]

In two other fields of social action, Edward Mooney took the initiative: the rural life movement and the labor relations movement.

The National Catholic Rural Life Conference, which came into existence in 1920 as a bureau of the National Catholic Welfare Conference, was given independent status in 1923. Through the efforts of its apostolic national director, Father (later Archbishop) Edwin V. O'Hara, the Rural Life agency dedicated itself to religious instruction in country areas, mostly by religious vacation schools; but it also took an interest in the temporal welfare of rural Catholics.

While the Diocese of Rochester has had occasional problems of rural welfare, rural catechetics has presented the most serious dilemma. The vacation school idea therefore appealed to priests stationed in smaller communities. In 1934, Father Joseph Guilfoil, pastor of St. Vincent de Paul Church in Churchville, became the first to set up a rural catechetics "school" (although as we have noted above, there were already several vacation schools in Rochester itself). Father Guilfoil inaugurated the program at his mission church, St. Fechan's, in Chili. He followed the national Rural Life syllabus, and the Sisters of Charity connected with St. Mary's Hospital were in charge.[96]

In November of the same year, Archbishop Mooney asked another country pastor, Father John M. Ball of St. Rose Church, Lima, to attend the national Rural Life convention in St. Paul, Minnesota in order to see whether any phase of its activities could be of service to the Rochester Diocese. On his return, Father Ball reported that the country cathechetical program had much to recommend it for general adoption. Archbishop Mooney thereupon invited Father Ball to coordinate all diocesan catechetics, urban as well as country, Confraternity as well as Rural Life. He replied, however, that he would rather leave the urban C.C.D. efforts to the diocesan superintendent of schools. And so it was done: Father Duffy was entrusted with the C.C.D.; Father Ball with the rural religious instruction in the Diocese. During the latter's term of office (1935-1940) the number of month-long country catechetical summer schools rose to about forty. Subsequently the two programs *were* combined, under a special C.C.D. director; and this plan continues in operation today.[97]

Father Ball's visit to St. Paul bore fruit in still another way, in that the Rural Life Conference decided to hold its 1935 convention in Rochester. The Archbishop-Bishop of Rochester played host that fall not only to the Rural Life but also to the national catechetical conference of the C.C.D. (October 27-October 31). Prelude to this joint meeting was a nationwide broadcast by Mooney, who delivered the address "Rural Life and Christian Doctrine," on the "Church of the Air" program. National radio facilities also carried subsequent addresses by Bishop Edwin V. O'Hara, the founder of Rural Life, and by Father W. Howard Bishop, the future founder of the Glenmary Home Missioners. Another radio speaker was the apostolic delegate, Archbishop Amleto G. Cicognani, whose broadcast originated in Washington. The convening bodies held their sessions in the Columbus Civic Center. Among the numerous episcopal participants were eight American archbishops and twenty American bishops, as well as several Canadian prelates. The roster of priests registered included some noted rural or catechetical specialists, for example: Fathers George W. Johnson; Joseph J. Baierl (of St. Bernard's Seminary); John LaFarge, S.J.: James Tompkins (of Antigonish, N.S.); Rudolph Bandas; Luigi Ligutti; and Joseph Collins, S.S. Among the prominent laymen present were Michael Williams; Frederick P. Kenkel; Dorothy Day; and Anne Sarachan Hooley. Visitors who came to the C.C.D. meetings had a good chance to learn firsthand about the functioning of the "Rochester Plan" of released-time instruction, now in its fifteenth year.[98]

That Archbishop Mooney should have been interested in catechetics surprised no one. Some, on the other hand, may have been puzzled by this former diplomat's active interest in labor relations. But there was nothing artificial about that interest. It sprang not only from his devotion to papal social doctrine but from his heritage as the son of a Youngstown ironworker.

Within months after his installation, Mooney demonstrated his concern for equitable labor relations. He praised the national Central Verein for its work in spreading sound social doctrine, when addressing its seventy-ninth annual convention, held in Rochester in August, 1934. In his remarks to the delegates he declared: "There is to my knowledge no society in the United States which has done so much to keep before our people the social principles of the Catholic Church."[99] Two months later, in a Columbus Day talk to an audience of Knights of Columbus and members of local Italian societies, he enumerated among the benefits of American liberty the "right to property as a human right"; the right to a living wage; and "the separate human right to organize to secure or maintain" that living wage. Men were talking much then about the "Old Deal" and the "New Deal." "What we need most of all," he said, "is the Square Deal"; and this implied a highly cultivated sense of right and wrong, in rich and poor, employer and employee.[100] On May 14, 1936, the Catholic lay organizations of Rochester sponsored a meeting in the Columbus Civic Center commemorative of the anniversary of the papal labor encyclicals, *Rerum Novarum* and *Quadragesimo Anno*. Archbishop Mooney presided. The speakers were Father Raymond A. McGowan, assistant director of the Social Action Department of the N.C.W.C., and Mr. John J. Carroll, member of the New York State Labor Department's Industrial Board.[101]

But the largest social justice conference held under Mooney was the regional meeting of the Catholic Conference on Industrial Problems, which gathered at the Columbus Civic Center on November 30-December 1, 1936. The program of the parley, arranged by the N.C.W.C. Social Action department, featured a variety of experts: priests like Rev. Dr. John A. Ryan of the Catholic University, and Rev. Dr. John P. Boland of Buffalo, Regional Director of the National Labor Relations Board; laymen like Percival de St. Aubin, General Treasurer of the State of Rhode Island, and Dr. J. E. Hagerty, Director of the School of Social Administration, Ohio State University.

As usual, Father Ryan's address (titled "A Program for the Immediate Future") was a highlight of the conference. As before, Ryan called for more effective legislation on wages, unemployment, and child labor, and for greater collaboration between capital and labor. The main provisions of the NRA, he said, should be incorporated into the law of the land. In his own speech, Archbishop Mooney was more cautious about recommending legislation. But his knowledgeable remarks were in substantial agreement with Ryan's principles. He denounced the "rugged individualism" and monopolism that had all too often characterized industrial management. Genuine cooperation between labor and capital, he held, would solve the basic problems, and would also, in his opinion, reduce the need of state intervention. At all events, a solution was urgently needed.[102]

One of the recurrent problems alluded to by Dr. Ryan, child labor legislation, became the subject of a nationwide constitutional debate in the 1920's and 1930's. In 1924, a child labor amendment had been proposed for the federal constitution, and its promoters were fighting a long battle to persuade thirty-six states (the necessary majority) to accept it. Catholics, of course, deplored abusive child labor; but they inclined to prefer that it be controlled by State rather than federal law. The issue was strongly contested in 1934-1937 before the New York State legislature, for New York was a key State in the voting. However, the Catholic bishops of the State, as members of the New York State Catholic Welfare committee, already agreed that they would oppose ratification. On March 24, 1934, Cardinal Patrick Hayes of New York telegraphed Edmund F. Gibbons, Bishop of Albany and spokesman there of the Committee, that he could count on his support. In reply, Bishop Gibbons informed the Cardinal that the Archbishop-Bishop of Rochester and all the other New York State bishops were of the same mind.[103]

Consideration of the amendment by the Legislature was postponed to a later date. Meanwhile, in early 1935, Father Walter A. Foery of Rochester, as the Rochester diocesan delegate to the N.Y.S.C.W.C., pointed out to the people of the Diocese of Rochester the reasons for the bishops' opposition. Not only were the New York State prelates of the opinion that the child labor problem should be dealt with by regional rather than federal legislation; they also held that the federal amendment would in effect nullify the New York State laws that already regulated the employment of minors. Furthermore, child labor was no longer the burning question it had once been. Statistics showed that the number of working children had declined from 26.4% in 1900 to 6.4% in 1930. The National Recovery Administration had already plugged most of the remaining holes, and it was highly likely that these reforms would be enacted into permanent federal law. The N.Y.S.C.W.C. was therefore of the opinion that what was left of the child labor problem could be better solved if each State should reach an agreed conformity in its protective laws with all the other States.[104]

The battle in New York State was finally joined on February 21, 1937. In what seems to have been a unique—and was certainly a dramatic—gesture, Bishop Gibbons of Albany personally addressed the

State Assembly on the proposed amendment. He undertook the task with no small fear of failure. He knew that Catholics themselves were divided on the issue; that President Franklin D. Roosevelt had urged ratification; that the State Senate had approved; and there was in the Assembly chamber itself a voluble claque intent upon stampeding the Assemblymen into favorable action. Nevertheless, the Bishop went on with his presentment; and it was a well-prepared document. In support of his arguments he quoted statements by Archbishop Mooney and the other New York State prelates. During the address, a public relations man engaged by the N.Y.S.C.W.C. moved about the floor, observing the reactions of the legislators. Although Bishop Gibbons had made a poor beginning by speaking too low, when he left the chamber, the observer reported to him that his plea had been well received. The outcome of the balloting confirmed this impression. Brought to a vote the amendment was defeated, 102-42.[105] The New York defeat seems to have doomed the amendment once and for all. At least no other State ratified the measure thereafter.

It must not be thought that these activities for social justice were merely theoretical and legislative, and that no effort was made to put them into practice in the Diocese. Several diocesan priests led the way in popularizing—and with practical intent—the papal labor encyclicals. Most prominent among them were Fathers George E. Vogt and Benedict Ehmann of Rochester, and Father Michael Groden (1886-1940), pastor of St. Mary's Church, Horseheads.[106] Father Ehmann's interest led him on one occasion to accept the post of mediator in a dispute between the employees and the management of the Gannett newspapers.[107] There is also a well-founded story that Archbishop Mooney himself tried, although unsuccessfully, to persuade the management of the Eastman Kodak Company to permit its employees to unionize.[108]

What gave the Archbishop an added incentive to encourage Catholic Action and social justice in the Diocese was the fact that from 1934 on he was a bishop-member of the board of the National Catholic Welfare Conference. At the bishops' meeting of November, 1934, he was elected episcopal chairman of the Conference's Social Action Department.[109] And a year later he was voted chairman of the Administrative Board of the Conference, in succession to the former Rochesterian, Archbishop Edward J. Hanna of San Francisco. This was the chief executive post of the N.C.W.C. Because of the extraordinary skill which he showed as a chairman (an effective blend of humor, cajolery, and strength) he was reelected to the position every year thereafter, two years excepted, until 1946. His elevation to the Cardinalate in the latter year disqualified him from further renomination to the chair, according to the constitution of the Conference.

The Rochester years of Archbishop Mooney's Conference chairmanship — 1935-1937 — were years that added international moral problems to the national economic worries of Americans. The fascism of Mussolini raised one such problem, especially when he invaded Ethiopia in 1935. During the same period, the Nazism of Hitler was beginning to lash out against Jews and Catholics and the whole democratic world. In July, 1936, the Spanish Civil War erupted in a welter of ideological confusion, violence and martyrdom. Even though an ocean separated them from these European and African events, American Catholics could scarcely escape emotional involvement. Radio and press furnished them with more than sufficient information (and misinformation).[110]

As N.C.W.C. chairman, it fell to the lot of the Archbishop to protest against still another oppressive regime, the anticlerical Mexican government. As early as May 1, 1935, the Administrative Committee of the Conference had criticized the silence of the federal government in the face of the renewed Mexican persecution of Mexican Catholics. Archbishop Mooney launched a crusade of prayer throughout his diocese at the beginning of the following month. Since the Mexican campaign to annihilate the clergy waxed rather than waned thereafter, Mooney, in a diocesan circular of April 23, 1936, ordered special Mass-prayers for Mexico and the parish recitation of the litany of St. Joseph.

Early in 1936, the American bishops decided to help their Mexican confreres, in a very positive way, by erecting in this country a seminary for the training of Mexican seminarians whom discriminatory laws prevented from making their studies in their own country. The committee of bishops appointed to execute this plan secured an old resort hotel at Montezuma, New Mexico, to house the school; and in the late summer, a collection was taken in every American diocese to finance the undertaking. The Archbishop-Bishop of Rochester proposed this charity to his own diocesans in a letter dated August 18, 1936. He had reason to be proud of their response. The faithful of the Diocese contributed $14,000.00—the third largest amount from any diocese in the country, and an amount in excess of that given in the archdioceses of Boston, Baltimore, or Philadelphia.[111] Early in 1937, Archbishop Leopoldo Ruiz y Flores, the Apostolic Delegate to Mexico, sent to Mooney and the other American bishops a spiritual bouquet expressing the gratitude of Mexican Catholics.[112] Mexican Catholicism has had good reason to rejoice in this enterprise that was begun in Archbishop Mooney's time as N.C.W.C. chairman and supported so generously by his own diocese. By 1965, the Montezuma Seminary had graduated 1,345 young Mexican priests. Its alumni by then constituted 25% of all Mexican priests in the forty-three Mexican dioceses; and seven of them had already been made bishops.[113]

We cannot conclude our account of Edward Mooney's Rochester days without some record of his attitude toward those of other faiths.

Diplomat though he was, he also had another trait that is basic to sound ecumenism—a natural openness and candor. The trait is well illustrated by a delightful story which dates from his pastoral days in Youngstown and has all the ring of authenticity.

One summer evening in 1922, during his brief term as parish priest, he presided over a fund-raising drive for the benefit of a new church building. The drive was held in an open field near Youngstown. Now, the Ku Klux Klan was active locally in those days, and the Klansmen of the area happened to be holding a rally the same night in the adjacent field. Roundabout, for some distance, the air was brightened by the light of their fiery crosses.

The parishioners of St. Patrick's must have smiled at the irony of the situation—that Catholic parishioners should convene so close to the "konklave" of an organization professedly dedicated not only to racism and anti-Semitism, but anti-Catholicism. However, this circumstance was not permitted to interfere with the parochial agenda. As the main speaker, Doctor Mooney addressed his people on the needs of St. Patrick's Church and urged them to make pledges to the fund. They responded readily and quickly subscribed a total of $12,000.00.

At the conclusion of the business meeting, Mooney thanked his people and then announced, to their surprise: "Now I am going over to address the meeting next door." He did just that, and requested that the Klan leaders permit him to speak. When they did so, he graciously thanked the Klansmen for helping to illuminate his own meeting with their bright lights. "My parishioners," he said, "are just about to serve ice cream and cake. We would like very much to have you as our guests."

Dazed, no doubt, by the invitation, the members of the Klan nevertheless decided to accept it. Before the party was over, good will was so well established that the St. Patrick's subscription was reopened, and the total pledged rose from $12,000.00 to $15,000.00.[114]

Bishop O'Hern, in his most outgoing mood, never did anything quite like this. As Bishop of Rochester, Edward Mooney manifested both tact and frankness when dealing with non-Catholic groups. Nevertheless, he was less sanguine than his predecessor about the real value of superficial interfaith gestures. His theological point of view, his diplomatic experience, the restrictions imposed upon him by his position as bishop, and—even more, perhaps—his position as administrative chairman of the N.C.W.C., caused him to tread circumspectly in the interfaith area.

Six months after his installation, Archbishop Mooney was invited to represent the Diocese of Rochester at a large intercredal dinner sponsored by the newly-established interfaith committee of the Rochester Centennial Celebration. Rabbi Philip Bernstein spoke to the diners for the Jews of the community, and Dr. Justin Wroe Nixon for the Protestants. There were frequent words of praise for Bishop O'Hern during the evening, and at one point all were invited to observe a minute of silent prayer in his memory.

When his turn came to talk, the Archbishop saluted his listeners: "Jews, Catholics, Protestants: I address you in chronological order." Then he delivered a candid yet graceful speech that he had obviously prepared with great care. One can gather that he believed the Rochester interfaith movement had veered somewhat into the direction of indifferentism. At any rate, he cautioned that any joint work that they undertook as Rochesterians should be based on an honest recognition of religious differences. "Do not be startled," he admonished them, "when I say that I would wish nothing quite so much as that all Jews should be Christians and all Christians Catholics, but that, as a good Catholic, I could not wish this to be brought about but by the power of personal conviction." Having made this reservation (assuredly necessary to any true ecumenism) he was happy to pledge Catholic cooperation in civic action. "It is my earnest wish and fervent hope," he concluded, "that a second century of continued civic progress may give us still more ample opportunity of working together in charity."[115]

The Archbishop struck a similar note on May 9, 1937 when he spoke at a Communion breakfast of the Newman Club of Cornell University. While he praised the Newman movement, he pointed out that the Church preferred to see Catholics attending Catholic colleges. For Catholics to attend non-Catholic institutions was, in the eyes of the Church, much like the marriage of Catholics with non-Catholics.[116]

In general, Mooney went along with intercredal activities that involved civic and social cooperation, once his principles on the matter had been made clear. However, in keeping with his executive practice, he usually delegated others—especially the Vicar General, Monsignor

William M. Hart—to represent him. Unexplored paths of interfaith dialogue he left unexplored. Like most American Catholic churchmen of his day, he saw no signs of the times to justify a different approach. Had Vatican Council II already embraced ecumenism, we may be sure that Edward Mooney would have accepted it fully. But Vatican II was still three decades away.

When Doctor Mooney stepped down from the world of papal diplomacy and assumed charge, still adorned with the title of archbishop, of the sizeable but not quite major diocese of Rochester, his new diocesans assured themselves that for him Rochester was just a way-station in an extraordinary career. But whenever he himself heard that belief voiced or implied, the Archbishop protested—and quite honestly—that he considered Rochester his home and would be perfectly happy to spend the rest of his life as its bishop. When he authorized the construction of a new crypt for bishops in Holy Sepulchre Cemetery, he was content that his remains would some day be laid to rest in one of its niches.

Of course, the conjecture of his diocesans proved to be correct, as the Archbishop himself surely realized it might be. On May 22, 1937, Pope Pius XI elevated the Diocese of Detroit to archdiocesan status, and three days later he named Edward Mooney its first archiepiscopal incumbent. The new metropolitan-elect of Detroit was probably less happy about leaving Rochester for that see than he would have been for any other. In 1937 the city of Detroit was seething with strikes in its all-important automotive industry. And the Archdiocese of Detroit was not only in acute financial straits; it was also in a painful quandary over the highly controversial radio priest, Father Charles Coughlin. Mooney remained the good soldier, however; and overruling his own misgivings, he once again accepted obediently the orders of his general, Pope Pius XI.

A last minute decision concerning the Rochester Diocese was forced upon the Archbishop before he departed for Detroit in August, 1937. Around the middle of that July, the Eastman Kodak Company, through Mr. A. F. Sulzer, asked the Diocese whether it would consider selling to Kodak the church properties adjacent to the Eastman office building on State Street. These properties were St. Patrick's Cathedral and rectory, the diocesan chancery, and St. Andrew's Seminary. Archbishop Mooney replied that the Diocese was interested in the sale. Kodak therefore offered $300,000.00 for the whole complex.

Selling so many properties, and especially a cathedral formally designated as such, required permission from the Holy See. The Archbishop therefore communicated the proposal to Archbishop Amleto G. Cicognani, the apostolic delegate, stating his own reasons for recommending its acceptance. The church property, wrote Mooney, was now all but engulfed by Kodak buildings; and his two predecessors had wanted to sell to Kodak but had failed because they had not acted quickly enough. The present offer was considered a good one, for it represented an increase over the amount originally invested in the property. Furthermore, $300,000.00 in cash would be particularly welcome to the Diocese at that moment. The Archbishop therefore requested that the Delegate ask the Holy See to permit the sale and to designate Sacred Heart Church, Rochester, as the diocesan pro-cathedral (i.e. temporary cathedral).[117]

Negotiations for the sale were protracted until early September. By that time the Archbishop had already been installed in Detroit. It therefore fell to the lot of Monsignor Hart, as Vicar Capitular of the Diocese pending the arrival of a new bishop, to carry the deal to its conclusion. When the news broke that Mooney's successor would be the Most Reverend James E. Kearney, Bishop of Salt Lake, Bishop Kearney's permission also had to be secured for the projected sale.[118] With the canonical obstacles finally cleared away, Kodak approved the contract of sale on September 8, 1937; the money was paid; the legal transfer was accomplished. Thus the venerable St. Patrick's, Rochester's first cathedral, passed over into other hands. The last Masses were offered there on September 12th, and on the 13th the owners began to dismantle the church to make way for a new Eastman building.[119]

We have already alluded to that detachment which was so characteristic of Edward Mooney. Throughout his life he preferred to stand a bit apart from the crowd. Even though this by no means meant that he was cold or uninterested—his was a warmly sympathetic detachment—the laity who had no personal contact with him probably did consider him rather austere. His priests, like all those who had been friends with him since his boyhood, found him cordial and humane; and those still more closely associated with him were ready to die for him. But his personal impact on the general public in Rochester was not strong. Hence it is easy to understand why, although he was greeted by an estimated 75,000 on his arrival in Detroit, a disappointingly small crowd had bidden him farewell when his train left the Rochester station.

To say that the faithful of the Rochester Diocese did not really know Archbishop Mooney is not to say that they did not admire him. As they followed with interest his subsequent career, they came to appreciate more fully his extraordinary talents. For he was soon able to refinance the Archdiocese; he handled, with a sure touch, the case of Father Coughlin; and he displayed his skill as a builder—which circumstances had prevented him from doing while in Rochester. His former Rochester flock were gratified by the strong leadership which he gave during World War II as administrative chairman of the N.C.W.C. They rejoiced when on February 18, 1946, Pope Pius XII gave him the red hat as Cardinal Priest of the Title of Santa Susanna: for the first time in history "one of theirs" was advanced to the cardinalate. They mourned at his sudden death in Rome on October 25, 1958. Ailing though he was, he had returned to Rome out of an urgent sense of duty, to participate in the conclave for the election of a successor to Pope Pius XII.[120]

Archbishop Mooney, while at Detroit, had not only displayed mature administrative talents; he had taken a strong interest in Catholic charities, Catholic action, and social justice. The national magazine *America,* commenting upon his career, ranked him with the "greatest sons of the American Catholic Church: educator, diplomat, administrator, civic leader, and "one of the most knowledgeable social apostles ever to wear the episcopal purple."[121]

The Catholics of the Rochester Diocese, viewing these later accomplishments, saw in them the flowering of what Edward Mooney had begun in Rochester. And this was no mere boast. In the evolution of the notable pastoral career of this quiet, brilliant prelate, the Rochester years provided an indispensable internship.

In 1959, at the annual blessing of the graves in Holy Sepulchre Cemetery, Bishop Lawrence B. Casey, auxiliary bishop of the Diocese of Rochester and former secretary to Cardinal Mooney, blessed a special marker in front of the bishops' vault bearing the bronze coats of arms of all the deceased bishops of Rochester, including Edward Mooney. Mooney had asked this favor of the then Father Casey when he left for Detroit in 1937. If the Cardinal's remains are interred in Plymouth, Michigan, rather than in the Rochester vault which he built to receive them, there is at least this modest tablet to recall the distinguished churchman who was the fourth shepherd of the Diocese of Rochester.

Underneath the tablet some other hand may one day add a phrase from Bishop Casey's own eulogy of the Cardinal: "Here was authentic greatness."[122]

CHAPTER THIRTEEN

BISHOP KEARNEY AND WORLD WAR II

T HOSE WHO lived through the apprehensive years of the late 1930's and early 1940's and the forty-five months of world-wide war that followed them, probably never dreamed that they would forget that experience. While we who are older have *not* forgotten, even for us the memory has lost its edge. Those of a younger generation do not have even that memory to remind them that we live in an imperfect world.

Let us therefore briefly recall the events that shook the world (and consequently the Diocese of Rochester) after 1937. In September, 1940, Mussolini's Fascism and Hitler's Nazism, bound themselves in an alliance with Japan's militarism. Hitler had already taken over one central European country after another; and Italy, in 1939, had invaded little Albania. On August 23, 1939, Nazism, heretofore the professed enemy of Communism, signed a non-aggression pact with Soviet Russia. which paved the way to the division of Poland.

War now seemed inevitable. Britain and France had made the Munich Pact with the Nazi-Fascist Axis in September, 1938, principally because neither of the two democratic signatories was ready for a war. But Britain had taken advantage of the succeeding months to prepare somewhat for hostilities. Franklin Delano Roosevelt meanwhile exerted himself to prevent the impending conflict. Pius XII culminated his own pleas for peace in the anguished broadcast of August 24, 1939: "Nothing is lost by peace; all may be lost by war."[1] But there was no will to heed warnings. On September 1, 1939, Germany invaded Poland. Two days later, Britain and France declared war on Germany.

World War II developed slowly, but all to the advantage of Hitler in its early phases. In several brilliantly organized moves, Hitler invaded Denmark, Norway, Belgium and Luxembourg. His underling Mussolini brought Italy into the conflict on June 10, 1940; and four days later Paris fell before the German "Blitzkrieg." Thereafter the Nazis concentrated on invading England.

The program that President Roosevelt inaugurated to prepare for our entry into the war was controversial but effective. The registration of enemy aliens, the vast outlay on defense (which finally obliterated the unemployment of the Great Depression), the draft of military defense personnel: all these were milestones on the Rooseveltian highway. New bureaus were established to take care of new situations: the Office of Price Administration; the United Service Organization (for recreational work among the armed forces). Daylight Saving Time, renamed "War Time," was imposed on the whole country as a year-round practice. And there were national drives for scrap metal. This nation took a firmer stand towards Germany, Italy and Japan; it asserted its purpose to defend the rest of the Western Hemisphere; and it adopted, on August 14, 1941, a plan for international postwar collaboration, the Atlantic Charter. At the same time, the President kept the home front united by a constant appeal to American patriotic values. Probably the most notable of all his prewar addresses was that of January 6, 1941, in which he enunciated the Four Freedoms: freedom of speech and expression, freedom of religion, freedom from want, and freedom from fear.

Then came Pearl Harbor, December 7, 1941; and with this onslaught of the Japanese on American territory, we entered the fray against the Axis. The war lasted until the summer of 1945, and postwar "reconversion" occupied the rest of the decade.

If most of this terrible conflict took place in lands and seas far removed from the Diocese of Rochester, still its smoke hovered like an atomic mushroom-cloud over the entire home front. It was in these fateful thirteen years, 1937-1950, that James Edward Kearney passed through the first trying phase of his career as bishop of Rochester.

1. Fifth Ordinary of Rochester.

A large number of bishops attended the installation of Edward Mooney as Archbishop of Detroit, on August 3, 1937. As yet there had been no news about his successor. He had been selected, however; so the apostolic delegate, Archbishop Amleto G. Cicognani, taking advantage of the presence of so many prelates, publicly announced that the fifth Bishop of Rochester stood in their very midst. He was the Most Reverend James E. Kearney, Bishop of Salt Lake, Utah.[2]

As soon as his appointment had been revealed, Bishop Kearney sent a message to his future flock.

> I am very much delighted with the appointment, with the honor and with the confidence manifested by the Holy See. My only hope is to be a worthy successor of the outstanding group of prelates who have conferred such honor upon the See. To that end, I humbly solicit the prayers of the priests, the religious, and my good people of the See of Rochester.[3]

The appointment was indeed a sign of papal approval. True, the Diocese of Salt Lake was far larger territorially than that of Rochester: it embraced the whole State of Utah. But it had a population of only 10,000 Catholics; while the "official" population of the Diocese of Rochester in 1937 was 233,600, and would rise by 1940 to 320,700. James Kearney was therefore transferred from a distinctly missionary see in the West to an eastern diocese whose see city was already "an emerging metropolis."

The newly-named Bishop of Rochester was a midwesterner by birth. The second of the three sons of William Patrick and Rosina O'Doherty Kearney, James Kearney was born in Red Oak, Iowa, on October 28, 1884. Red Oak was even then a sizeable village in the farming district of Montgomery County, which is in the southwestern part of the State. The Kearneys had crossed the Atlantic from their native County Donegal to join a number of other Irish immigrant farmers in the Red Oak neighborhood.[4]

Midwesterner though he was by birth, and westerner by his original episcopal title, Bishop Kearney was inveterately and affectionately a Manhattanite. For in 1886, when he was still an infant, his parents moved back to New York City, where William Kearney entered the business that was to occupy the rest of his bread-winning life—retail furniture sales.

In New York the William P. Kearneys lived within the boundaries of St. Agnes parish, East Forty-Third Street. St. Agnes' was still a new parish, however, and as yet had no parochial school. So James attended Public School #27, and after that, DeWitt Clinton Public High School, from which he was graduated in 1901. Despite the fact that he grew up in New York, he never acquired a New York accent. His parents had no such accent, of course; and furthermore, the family spent the year 1892-1893 back in County Donegal, Ireland. Owing to these factors, James retained a more cosmopolitan pattern of speech.

Rosina O'Doherty played an important role in setting for her three sons high standards of achievement. The Sisters of Loretto at Omagh, in Donegal, had given her a more advanced education than many future immigrant girls received. Through them, she had acquired a love of music and poetry, and she communicated this Irish love of song to her sons, especially to James. But most of all, she inspired her children by her own good sense. "Son," she once told the future bishop, "keep your mouth shut and be good to the poor." And when he confessed to her that he was thinking of studying for the priesthood, she urged him first to prepare himself for another calling, so that if he should decide to leave the seminary in mid-course, he would be ready to enter at once upon another sort of career.

Following this good advice, James signed up for the two-year course offered by the (now defunct) New York Training School for Teachers. He spent his last semester as a substitute teacher in practically all the elementary grades. Subsequently, he passed the examinations required for both the City and the State teacher's licenses.

License or no, the young graduate was more intent than ever on becoming a priest, so in the fall of 1903 he enrolled in St. Joseph's Archdiocesan Seminary at Dunwoodie, Yonkers, New York. One of the Seminary professors to whom he became particularly attached was Father Francis P. Duffy (1871-1932), who later won renown for his heroism as chaplain of the "Fighting 69th" in World War I, but who was also a talented theologian and scholar.

Having thus far made a good record at studies, James Kearney was designated in 1908 to finish the last year of his theological course at the Catholic University of America. In anticipation of this assignment, he was given an early ordination to the priesthood. The ordination took place on September 19, 1908; and the ordaining prelate was the saintly Thomas Francis Cusack (1862-1918), Titular Bishop of Themiscyra, and auxiliary bishop of New York. On arriving at the Catholic University, Father Kearney forthwith won his bachelor's degree in theology by taking a special examination. The rest of the year he devoted to canon law (in which he received a bachelor's degree) and to English literature. He also took additional courses under Father Walter Elliott, C.S.P. at the "Preachers' College."

Cardinal Farley, the Archbishop of New York, had intended to leave Father Kearney at the University for a second year. Owing to a shortage of priests, however, the Cardinal settled for the single year; and after assigning the young priest briefly to Holy Rosary Church, he appointed him assistant at St. Cecilia Church, on East 106th Street. Here he was to remain until 1928. Father James also taught for a while at Cathedral College, but gave it up because it interfered too much with his parochial duties.

In 1928, Father Kearney was commissioned to found a new parish in the Bronx. The result was the parish of St. Francis Xavier, whose church he built on Lurting Avenue and whose destinies he guided for four years. During his pastorate he also taught religion twice a week in nearby White Plains at Good Counsel College, a school conducted by the Religious of the Divine Compassion. In 1931, Cardinal Hayes gave him the additional job of superintendent of Catholic schools in the Borough of Bronx.

In 1932, Pope Pius XI chose Father Kearney to succeed another New Yorker, Most Reverend John J. Mitty, Archbishop of San Francisco, as bishop of Salt Lake. The official date of appointment was July 1st. The Bishop-elect of Salt Lake was consecrated to the episcopate in New York's St. Patrick's Cathedral on the following October 28th. Cardinal Patrick J. Hayes, the consecrator, was assisted by Archbishop Mitty and by the auxiliary bishop of New York, Most Reverend John J. Dunn. Formal installation in the Cathedral of the Madeleine, Salt Lake, took place on November 24, 1932.[5]

The Great Depression, which impeded the efforts of Archbishop Mooney during his Rochester regime, impeded even more seriously the efforts of Bishop Kearney in a Utah where Catholics were scarce and Mormonism ruled. Nevertheless, the Church in Utah made sure, if modest, progress under its fourth bishop. He was able to raise the number of his priests from 23 to 33. At Monticello, he opened St. Joseph's Chapel; at Midvale, he raised the church of St. Therese of the Child Jesus from missionary to parochial status; at Provo he dedicated the new church of St. Francis of Assisi; and at Cedar City he founded the parish of Christ the King. To finance these projects and other diocesan undertakings, the Bishop had of course to become a "beggar for Christ." The New York branch of the Society for the Propagation of the Faith, the Board of Home Missions, and a number of parishes in New York City were especially generous to his diocesan needs. He did have one drive for funds within the Diocese, in order to wipe out the debt on the Cathedral of the Madeleine. The drive was successful, so Bishop Kearney proceeded to consecrate that handsome structure on November 28, 1936. This was a red-letter day in the history of Utah Catholicism. The apostolic delegate, Archbishop Cicognani, came out from Washington to celebrate the Mass of dedication.

During the four years of his Utah episcopate, Bishop Kearney won the respect of his non-Catholic fellow citizens. His Catholic flock quickly came to love their bishop as a man who had an ear to heed them and a hand to help them.

When James Edward Kearney arrived in Rochester on November 10, 1937, he received a welcome in keeping with the finest Diocesan tradition. Seven thousand people crowded the Central Station; five thousand more milled about outside. Monsignor Hart, as Vicar Capitular of the Diocese, greeted the Bishop-designate in the name of his flock; and

Mayor Charles Stanton hailed him in the name of the Rochester community. The Bishop responded aptly; and his remarks, carried by radio station WHAM, went out to the whole Diocese. A procession then formed to conduct Bishop Kearney to the Chancery on Chestnut Street. It was led by the Fourth Degree Knights of Columbus, the Knights of St. John, and the Boy Scouts. From the Chancery, the Bishop subsequently moved on to the Bishop's House, 947 East Avenue. Here he announced his intention to continue in office the curia that had served Archbishop Mooney: Msgr. William M. Hart, Vicar General; Msgr. William F. Bergan, Chancellor; Father Lawrence B. Casey, Secretary; and the existing board of diocesan consultors.

James Edward Kearney was formally installed on the following day, November 11, 1937, by Most Reverend Stephen J. Donahue, auxiliary bishop of New York, representing Cardinal Patrick Hayes. The installation was the first to take place in the newly designated Pro-cathedral of the Sacred Heart on Flower City Park. (After the closing of St. Patrick's Cathedral on September 12th, the episcopal throne had been transferred to the remodeled sanctuary of Sacred Heart Church.) Two of Bishop Kearney's predecessors were present at his installation: Archbishop Thomas F. Hickey and Archbishop Mooney. The ranking civic officials in attendance were Governor Herbert H. Lehman and Lieutenant Governor John J. Bennett.[6]

From the start, the fifth Bishop of Rochester made a good impression. At the railroad station he pledged to follow in the footsteps of the bishops of Rochester who had gone before him, and to give open-handed cooperation to his country and to men of all religious backgrounds. At the installation luncheon he declared himself "the servant of his priests."

Asked by an interviewer for his opinion of the man who had succeeded him on the see of Rochester, Archbishop Mooney replied with a chuckle, "He's better looking than I am, younger and a far better singer." The Archbishop was right on all counts.

The new Bishop, at fifty-three, did cut a striking figure: tall, trim, and with a lively face that news photographers at once discovered to be photogenic. In becoming one of Rochester's most frequently photographed citizens, he reminded Rochesterians of Bishop O'Hern. He also resembled Bishop O'Hern in the great round of activities which he at once undertook. Seldom if ever did he decline an invitation to a Catholic or a civic function. Utah had accustomed him to long diocesan journeys, so he felt no qualms about going from one end to another of his twelve New York State counties. In the late winter after his installation he began to visit the remoter deaneries. On March 13, 1938, he was welcomed to Elmira by the Knights of Columbus, the Mayor, an Episcopal minister, and a local editor. A week later he went to Auburn to "rededicate" St. Mary's Church.[7] In the following week he paid his first visit to Corning, where he blessed a new organ at St. Patrick's Church.[8] Ithaca's turn came on May 6, 1938, when—along with the President of Cornell University, Dr. Edmund Ezra Day—he addressed a Communion breakfast of area college Catholic clubs.[9]

Wherever he went, Bishop Kearney demonstrated his ability as a speaker. His literary training revealed itself in the ease with which he composed both pastoral letters and addresses. He spoke with facility, briefly, to the point, and with an amazing inventiveness that enabled him to deliver as many as four or five different talks at different places on the same day. The content was often strongly literary; but what he said was truly pastoral in the sense that he was able to convey on each occasion an arresting spiritual thought. "Preach to the people entrusted to you," Cardinal Hayes had admonished him in the ritual formula of episcopal consecration. James E. Kearney paid special heed to that admonition. He always remained a "preaching bishop."

Bishop Kearney was also a good speaker on less formal occasions. He was an able storyteller, witty and urbane, with a delightful, crackling Irish sense of humor. Nevertheless, he could also administer a decisive corrective if at a public gathering a previous speaker had spoken amiss. His strictures on such an occasion were never offensively expressed—he was most careful never to offend—but their meaning was perfectly clear. Such incidents were few, however. The Bishop was a friendly man.

Just before the close of 1937, Bishop Kearney issued a public invitation to his clergy, laity, and diocesan organizations, to attend open house at his residence on New Year's Day, 1938. Seven hundred people accepted the invitation to this event which the *Courier* said was unique in the history of the Diocese.[10] Every year thereafter when he was able the Bishop continued the practice. It was gestures like this that marked Rochester's fifth Ordinary as more a "layman's bishop" than a "priest's bishop." Without in any way compromising his official dignity, Bishop Kearney made countless friends among layfolk and their children. Here he displayed that pastoral touch which he had acquired during his years of work in the parishes of New York City.

To say that he was a "layman's priest" does not mean that Bishop Kearney did not enjoy the affection of his priests. Towards the end of his regime he told one group of them, "I have always believed that

when I appointed a priest to a job it was because I thought him qualified for it, and therefore I should not interfere with the way he filled
it." Thus his attitude towards his priests was that of the good executive, and his priests appreciated the permissiveness it implied. They
seldom failed him.

When James E. Kearney was installed in Rochester, the nation was
still trying to scatter the smog of the Great Depression. Unemployment
declined in 1937 to 6.4 million. But it rose again to over nine million
as the result of a recession in 1938, and in 1939 the figure was still as
high as 8.7 million.

Bishop Kearney had been in Rochester for only eleven months
when he took up a lance against the Great Depression and won his
spurs as a civic leader. In October, 1938, he publicly advocated the
adoption in the city of Rochester of a "community plan" to fight the
recession: "a cooperative endeavor to remove fear and the causes of
fear from the minds of the people." He admitted that his scheme was
not original, that it had been proposed in several other communities;
but he thought that since it might prove helpful in Rochester, it deserved to be considered by the city fathers.

This, in essence, was the proposal. He recommended that the
Chamber of Commerce and similar organizations make a study of local
conditions, and on this basis formulate a master plan to stimulate sales
and promotion. The press, various groups, and individuals, should then
give full cooperation in carrying the master plan into effect. For his part
the Bishop intended to urge the Catholic laity and Catholic societies to
offer a loyal response.

On October 10, 1938, Bishop Kearney received twenty-five civic
leaders at his residence, and presented his ideas to them in a form tailored to Rochester conditions. The discussion that followed was frank,
but the discussants showed themselves well-disposed; and Mayor Lester
B. Rapp said that he, for one, preferred the Bishop's suggestion of just
"going out and buying" to the alternate recommendation, a "buying
week." A good number of congratulatory letters came to Bishop Kearney's desk after that, sent by various business and labor organizations.
The Kearney project was also newsed about through the national Catholic press by the N.C.W.C. News Service, and brought forth favorable
comments in Catholic newspapers.[11]

The Bishop struck the same energetic note in his 1938 Thanksgiving circular. He called on his people to stimulate retail activity so as to
"keep the business in our community strong." By loosening the purse

strings, he reminded them, they could provide more jobs for the unemployed. Thus they would help fulfill the aim of his campaign, to "Help people to help themselves."[12]

All this, as the editorial writer of the *Democrat and Chronicle* observed, showed "vision and good sense." How effective the Kearney Plan was, would be impossible to ascertain. But it was at least a constructive effort in the right direction, and it won for its newly-arrived proponent the esteem of the Rochester community.

While Bishop Kearney avoided personal involvement in organizations and movements dedicated to social justice, he made his own views on the subject quite clear, and gave ample permission to activists to put Catholic social doctrine into practice. Preaching at the Labor Day Mass in 1940—this was an annual practice which he inaugurated in 1938— he emphasized the need of teamwork between employers and laborers. Of course, the concept of "teamwork" summarized well the teaching of the papal labor encyclicals, which Rochester's Central Verein and Rochester's Judge Philip Donnelly were still diligently publicizing. Occasionally there was a particular opportunity to put these principles into practice. Thus in April, 1940, Monsignor John J. Lee of Elmira served on the board of arbitration in a wage dispute between the truckers and the management of the P.M.T. Lines, Inc.[13]

In 1940, the Bishop played host to a second regional Catholic Conference on Industrial Problems. Organized by the Social Action Department of the N.C.W.C., the Conference, held on September 23rd and 24th, presented several distinguished speakers to its audiences in the Columbus Civic Center. Among the clerical experts were Fathers John Cronin, S.S., of Washington; John P. Monaghan, of Staten Island; and John P. Boland, Chairman of the New York State Labor Relations Board. Lay speakers included Thomas F. Woodlock, editor of the *Wall Street Journal;* Hugh Thompson, Secretary-Treasurer of the New York State Industrial Council, C.I.O.; Francis P. Fenton, Director of Organization, A.F.L.; and Roland B. Woodward, Executive Vice-President of the Rochester Chamber of Commerce.[14]

One of the sessions addressed itself to priests. Its purpose was apparently to acquaint the diocesan clergy with what they could do along practical lines to promote social justice.

Some of the Rochester clergy had already come up with one answer to this question. In the fall of 1939, with the enthusiastic approval of the Bishop, they had opened a "Catholic Labor College" for the benefit of prospective Catholic labor leaders. Courses were given in labor ethics, labor history, and parliamentary law, with a view to equipping

Catholic workers to take a more active role in trade union locals, where leftists had too often made headway simply because they came better prepared. The "College" grew out of the study group conducted for some time, as we have seen, by Father George C. Vogt, diocesan director of the Confraternity of Christian Doctrine. Father John P. Boland of Buffalo spoke at the first class, November 12, 1939; and there were other guest speakers on later occasions. But the basic staff comprised: Father Vogt; Father Francis B. Burns, Professor of Moral Theology, St. Bernard's Seminary; Dr. Aaron I. Abell, of the department of history, Nazareth College; and Edward R. Murphy, of the staff of Niagara University School of Business, Rochester Division. Classes were held Monday evenings in St. Andrew's Seminary (which had moved in 1937 into the old St. Patrick's Parochial School building); and there was both a winter and a spring semester. Fifty signed up the first year —a number considered good in a city as ill-disposed to unionism as Rochester. Registration was lower the second year. After that, the College continued on a reduced basis in the smaller quarters whence it had sprung—the Catholic Worker House of Hospitality.[15] All in all, the "Labor College" was an unassuming enterprise of rather brief duration. While it is difficult to assess its worth, it certainly made a positive contribution. Several years later the Chairman of the New York State Labor Relations Board, the Reverend William J. Kelley, O.M.I., praised the several American bishops, including the Bishop of Rochester, for training Catholics in labor leadership during one of American labor's most critical periods.[16]

Whatever efforts Bishop Kearney may have made to rescue the community from its economic plight, the fact remained that he could not embark on a program of diocesan expansion while the Great Depression continued. And even with the return of prosperity in the early 1940's, wartime restrictions made it necessary to defer all but the most necessary construction. It was therefore not until after 1945 that the Bishop was able to catch up with the building needs of the twelve counties.

Nothing ever gratified James E. Kearney more than to be able to dedicate, as he put it, "new tabernacles to God." Between his installation and the outbreak of World War II, he established two new parishes and one new mission church.

On October 8, 1938, he elevated the Italian chapel of St. Philip Neri, in Rochester, to quasi-parochial status. At the same time, however, he closed the Italian chapel of Our Lady of Sorrows on Niagara Street. Italian Catholics had largely displaced the German Catholics in the old German parish of St. Francis Xavier, so it seemed to the Bishop wiser to abandon the frame church of Our Lady of Sorrows, to transfer its rector, Father Patrick Moffatt, to the pastorate of St. Francis, and to move the pastor of St. Francis Xavier, Father George Weinmann, to his former mission church, St. Philip. After the transfers, most of the German families of St. Francis began to attend St. Philip's. Here was a foreshadowing of the profound shifts of population that were to occur in Rochester later on, with almost inevitable conflicts between the national and ethnic groups involved.

The second new parish was brand-new: Our Lady of Lourdes, Elmira. This was cut away from St. Patrick's parish, Elmira, and included both the western part of Elmira proper and West Elmira. Bishop Kearney named Father Leo G. Schwab the founding pastor. The parish was incorporated on August 2, 1940; and the new pastor forthwith built a substantial stone church which the Bishop dedicated on October 26, 1941.[17]

The new mission established was St. Mary Magdalen, at Wolcott, in Wayne County. Permission was given in 1940 to the district pastor, Father J. Norman Margrett of Cato (Cayuga County), to build this church, principally to accommodate summer cottagers on the shores of nearby Lake Ontario. Since there were less than fifty Catholics resident in Wolcott, the little church building, 32 feet by 80 feet, was largely a do-it-yourself production. It cost only $7,000.00; but even that sum was not easy to raise. For a time the mission could not afford to buy pews, so benches were borrowed from the village park for the services! Bishop Kearney dedicated this resort chapel on October 30, 1940.[18]

The Bishop dedicated one more church before our nation entered World War II, and one mausoleum. The church was the new St. Thomas Church at Red Creek (Wayne County), blessed on November 28, 1940.[19] The mausoleum was the new little mortuary chapel for Rochester's bishops in Holy Sepulchre Cemetery. He blessed it on June 19, 1938, in connection with the annual field Mass of the Rochester Knights of St. John.[20]

Most interesting of the new prewar churches and chapels was the Chapel of St. John Bosco, in the State Reformatory at Elmira—the first Catholic chapel ever to be erected within an American penal institution.

The construction of the chapel was brought about through the efforts of the Catholic chaplain at the Reformatory, Father Francis J. Lane, who occupied that post from his appointment in 1922 by Bishop Hickey to his retirement (now with the rank of domestic prelate) in 1959. Father Lane, on undertaking the chaplaincy, became quickly convinced that rehabilitation should be the chief aim of the institution. His attitude was appreciated by the authorities, who subsequently named him a member of all three of the Reformatory's administrative committees. Father Lane's efforts won him wider recognition, too. For several terms he held the presidency of the American Prison Chaplains' Association. And his personal "follow-up" program, under which he kept contact with his "gang" once they had been released from prison, received national publicity.[21]

Chaplain Lane was nevertheless convinced that there could be no real rehabilitation without a religious emphasis. He got permission to give a course in Christian ethics to whatever inmates might want to attend. But his real dream was to have a chapel on the grounds. By dint of long persistence, he received permission from the State government in 1934 to have a Catholic chapel included in a proposed new wing, with the provision that he himself secure the funds for the construction of the chapel. Father Lane accepted this condition, and over the next few years he and his convicts, by shows, raffles, boxing matches, etc., gathered a sizeable sum, to which Archbishop Mooney added a generous donation. The total realized was far more than was necessary, so the project was enlarged to include the building of a rectory as well.

The construction of both chapel and rectory began in 1937. Two legal obstacles threatened to prevent their completion. In 1938, the labor unions in Elmira secured an injunction against the Chaplain for using the labor of the inmates. Father Lane had to carry the case to the State Supreme Court before vindicating his policy. Later on, the League for the Separation of Church and State obtained another injunction to prevent the opening of a denominational chapel on State property. Again Chaplain Lane carried the case to the State Supreme Court. In his judgment, favorable to Father Lane, the Justice declared: "The courts have universally concurred in the doctrine that the stability of our government rests upon the basis of religious belief in God."

When, therefore, Father Francis Lane offered the Mass of thanksgiving on the day of dedication, June 28, 1938, he had many reasons to be grateful. Bishop Kearney then followed him with a new "first": the first solemn pontifical Mass (it was said) ever to be celebrated in an American penal establishment. Public officials in attendance were properly impressed by the rite itself; and the Chapel of St. John Bosco, constituting a sort of "home church away from home" for the many Catholic inmates, assisted greatly their eventual rehabilitation.[22]

On James E. Kearney's arrival in Rochester, this "educator-bishop" expressed his pleasure at taking over the government of a diocese which had such a strong tradition of parochial schools.[23] That he shared the views of his Rochester predecessors on the value of Catholic schools he made abundantly clear in a pastoral letter on Catholic education which he issued on the feast of the Sacred Heart, June 12, 1942. For here he urged upon parents their grave obligation to send their children to schools which would provide for their religious needs.[24] Once more, however, the prewar and postwar conditions prevented him from increasing the number of diocesan elementary schools. One new school was opened in 1943—St. Helen's, in Rochester, staffed by the Franciscan Sisters of Allegany. But one other was closed—St. Patrick's, Rochester—when the Cathedral property was sold in 1937. So the total number of diocesan school remained the same until the end of the war.

Secondary education, enjoying as it did a higher priority, was able to advance a little more during the prewar and war years. On June 9, 1940, Bishop Kearney blessed a new wing at Nazareth Academy in Rochester; and on September 25, 1941, he dedicated a handsome annex at Mercy High School.[25] The Diocese eventually decided against allowing the Salesian Fathers to set up an industrial school. (This was a project earnestly advocated by Father Alfredo Morotti [1880-1958], an Italian-born priest of the Rochester Diocese.)[26] But the diocesan authorities gave full backing to the transfer of Nazareth College from its humble quarters on Augustine Street to a spacious new location on East Avenue in the Town of Pittsford. As we have already seen, Archbishop Mooney had disapproved of the original plan to relocate the College in close proximity to the Pittsford motherhouse of the Sisters of St. Joseph. For this reason, the Sisters had purchased another site, the Lomb estate, closer to Pittsford Village, where, for the interim, they had opened their Model School (1938-48). However, when Bishop Kearney arrived the question of location was raised again; and since the new Bishop had no objections to building the new college near the Motherhouse, the Sisters went back to their earlier plans. In the autumn of 1940, a Nazareth College building drive for $200,000.00 was conducted in the Catholic parishes.[27]

In the second semester of the school year 1941-1942, the College began to function at the new address. On the following June 7th, Bishop Kearney blessed the new buildings. Meanwhile, the Basilian Fathers took over the old College building on Augustine Street as their home. (Hitherto they had lived in the old Mercy Motherhouse on South Street). In the fall of 1942, they opened a novitiate in one wing of this building.[28]

Educational in another sense was the recreation center dedicated on May 9, 1941, in St. Francis of Assisi parish, Rochester. This Italian parish was too poor to have a school of its own, so it had a large catechetical program. Desirous of providing room for both classes and recreational facilities, the pastor, Father Joseph A. Cirrincione, started to build a large building on a very small budget. Parishioners contributed most of the labor, and the project generated wide interest in Rochester among people of all faiths. The chief speaker at the dedication dinner was Monsignor Edward J. Flanagan, a seminary schoolmate of Bishop Kearney's and the founder of the famous Boys' Town, Nebraska. There were also many other prominent church and civic leaders in the capacity audience.[29]

Charitable projects also enjoyed a prewar and wartime priority. In 1939 the Bishop gave his support to a drive for funds conducted by Mercy Hospital in Auburn. As a result of the 1938 recession, a number of those who had pledged towards the new building were unable to live up to their promises, so the Hospital was deep in debt.[30] St. Mary's Hospital in Rochester was even more sore-pressed, for the Civil War-era building was now outmoded and overcrowded. Therefore in 1941 the Sisters of Charity started to build a completely new plant just south of the original structure. A drive conducted in 1942 brought in $300,-000.00. The rest of the million dollars that the new hospital cost was collected from other sources. Bishop Kearney blessed the completed structure on January 14, 1943.[31] The historic old hospital building was razed in part in 1948; but the remaining wing was demolished only in 1959.

Since the local orphanages were directly owned by the Diocese, their amalgamation was more a diocesan affair than the building of the new St. Mary's Hospital. On October 14, 1937, the trustees of St. Joseph's orphanage voted to merge with St. Mary's Boys' Orphanage and St. Patrick's Girls' Orphanage. St. Joseph's Orphanage was therefore closed on July 1, 1938. In November, 1937, the Diocese obtained a suburban site for a single home for orphans—the Clark Farm, on Dewey Avenue in the Town of Greece. The new institution, "St. Joseph's Villa," was incorporated on March 24, 1942, and the certificate consolidating the three orphanages into one was registered on the following May 14th. Through the particular efforts of Father Gerald C. Lambert, Director of Rochester Catholic Charities, a "villa-plan" orphanage was erected, with three "cottages" or home-type residences for boys and two for girls. As we have already noted, the Rochester Board of Education had long since paid the salaries of the Sisters of St. Joseph who taught the Rochester orphans. By a letter of March 27, 1941, Mr. James M. Spinning, Rochester Superintendent of Schools, assured the diocesan authorities that even if the new Villa was outside the city boundaries, the City Schools department would continue to pay for the teaching of every city child who attended the little schoolhouse on the orphanage grounds. Bishop Kearney blessed the buildings of the pleasant new "orphans' village" on June 24, 1942.[32]

While we are speaking of diocesan Catholic charities, we should not fail to mention an interesting development in Elmira Catholic Charities. E. C. C. was, of course, a smaller unit than the Rochester organization. It did case work but had no institutions under its supervision. (The Elmira summer camp, Villa Maria, launched in 1941, made use of the Chemung County camping facilities on Harris Hill.[33]) But E. C. C. took a worthwhile step on June 16, 1940, when the Bishop received 147 local women into the Ladies of Charity, an international organization.[34] Around the same time a corresponding Men's Council of Catholic Service was established. Both the men's and the women's groups were soon busy assisting the management of the Elmira Charities office.[35]

In the days before the Second Vatican Council, American bishops were seldom faced with problems of questionable theological opinions among their diocesans. The principal doctrinal issue on which Bishop Kearney felt obliged to address his people was that of contraception. On March 19, 1941, after a number of public contraceptive clinics were opened within the Diocese, he issued the first formal pastoral letter of his Rochester career. "The Catholic," he concluded, "who would enter one of these centers, knowing the object of their existence, by that very act denies her faith, repudiates the teaching authority of Christ's Church, and sets at naught the divine law."[36]

In general, the Bishop's mode of teaching his flock was positive, especially through urging upon them the practices of Christian piety. This he did by example as well as word; for as all could clearly see, Bishop Kearney was himself a deeply pious man, strongly devoted to Our Lord, Our Lady and the saints.

The Liturgical Movement was a new and uncertain factor in the Diocese before World War II. When in August, 1938, a Liturgical Institute, featuring the Benedictine liturgical scholar Father Godfrey Diekmann, was held in Immaculate Conception Church, Rochester, the Bishop gave it his blessing.[37] But his own preference was for what he often termed "the liturgy of the heart." Thus, on the first Christmas he spent in Rochester, Bishop Kearney inaugurated a Christmas pageant in connection with the midnight Mass at the Pro-Cathedral. Even though, with the sale of St. Patrick's Cathedral, Ireland's patron was no longer the semi-official patron of the Rochester Diocese, the Bishop's tender Irish heart would never have permitted him to give up the annual pontifical Mass at St. Patrick's Church and its guest panegyric; or to decline the invitation of the Knights of Equity to their regular St. Patrick's Day banquet.[38]

Because of his special devotion to St. Francis Xavier (patron of his Bronx parish), Bishop Kearney made a point, from 1938 on, of preaching in whole or in part the annual Novena of Grace to that saint in Rochester's St. Francis Xavier Church.[39] For the legal profession of Rochester, he inaugurated in 1945 the annual practice of the "Lawyers' Mass" or "Red Mass," celebrated in St. Joseph's Church downtown.[40] Perhaps his happiest pastoral inspiration was to promote, from 1940 on, family Communion on the feast of the Holy Family. It has remained a durable tradition in the Diocese.[41] The Bishop also strongly encouraged the Laymen's Retreat League. On May 30, 1942, he offered the Mass of dedication at the League's first retreat house of its own: the handsome old Harvey mansion on the shore of Seneca Lake at Geneva. The diocesan men's retreat house, entrusted by the Bishop from the start to the care of the Redemptorist Fathers, remained on this site until June 16, 1950. Then it moved into the former Baptist Seminary on Alexander Streeet in Rochester—a large building but one farther removed from the geographical center of the Diocese.[42]

A constant refrain in the Bishop's spiritual counsel to his people was that they be strong in their devotion to the Mother of God, especially through her rosary. Bishop Kearney testified in a very special way to his reliance on the rosary when he welcomed to the Diocese a little community of cloistered Dominican Nuns of the Perpetual Rosary. Bishop O'Hern had desired to see this community establish a convent under his jurisdiction, but circumstances had prevented it. In the 1940's the nuns of the Buffalo Rosary Monastery mentioned this fact to Father Gerald C. Lambert of Rochester, who in turn referred it to the attention of the diocesan authorities. On August 16, 1944, the pioneer nuns formally set up, in Elmira, the Monastery of Mary the Queen, in a frame building that had been the clubhouse of the Elmira Country Club. Bishop Kearney donated the altar of the small original chapel. The cloister was officially established on June 8, 1945, and daily exposition of the Blessed Sacrament commenced August 3, 1945.[43]

In a sense, the Bishop's supreme tribute to Our Lady was his solemn consecration of the Rochester Diocese to the Immaculate Heart of

Mary. At his direction, parishioners in every parish pronounced the formula of consecration on Sunday, August 22, 1948—the feast of the Immaculate Heart of Mary.[44]

From the start of his regime, the fifth Bishop of Rochester supported Catholic Action, whether in the formal or the informal sense of that term for the lay apostolate. As time passed, the Confraternity of Christian Doctrine received his increasing encouragement. Its Lenten Study Clubs continued to function.[45] Vacation schools throve in Rochester and in some forty other places in the Diocese, with about 5,000 children enrolled.[46]

An important legal development in 1940 confirmed the constitutionality of granting "released time" to public school children for weekday religious instruction. There had been obscurities and inconsistencies across the State in the local interpretation of "released time." These were resolved on July 1, 1940, when new rules added to the State education law fully authorized the permissive use of "released time", for pupils in high schools as well as elementary schools.[47] The extension of the permission to high school students necessitated some rearrangement of schedules by both the Catholics and the non-Catholics who gave weekday instructions, so that they might be ready in the fall of 1941 to take advantage of the expanded program.[48]

A new and valuable apostolate was the Legion of Mary. *Praesidia* (or circles) were founded in 1931, in rapid succession, at St. John's Church, Clyde; Sacred Heart Pro-cathedral, Rochester; St. Anne's, Rochester; and St. Monica's, Rochester. These were joined together on December 14, 1939, to form a *curia,* or federation; and the federation enabled them to carry on still more efficiently their disciplined program of prayer and apostolic works. (By 1967 the number of diocesan *praesidia* had risen to 108, with 1,100 members.)[49] The Bishop encouraged these developments. Furthermore, on December 17, 1937, he gave an official mandate to the Rochester branch of the Catholic Central Verein, thus constituting it a Catholic Action group in the strict sense.[50]

Long-established organizations like the N.C.C.W., the Sodality movement and the Scouting movement could of course count on the Bishop's continuing patronage. On occasion he turned for special support to the Legion of Decency. Thus in November, 1941, he brought the moral pressure of the parish Legion units to bear against the film "Two-Faced Woman", which the Legion of Decency's national board of reviewers had classified as "condemned."[51] (On other occasions, pastors throughout the twelve counties alerted their people to protest against the local or neighborhood showing of such films. Sometimes these efforts proved very effective; sometimes they were unsuccessful.[52])

The increased circulation of pornographic material through newsstands prompted the nation's Catholic bishops in 1939 to enlist the aid of Holy Name societies in a drive against indecent literature. In April, 1939, Bishop Kearney directed the men of the diocesan Holy Name Union to undertake the local drive; and he reiterated his view on June 22nd at a rally of 15,000 diocesan Holy Name members. The strategy of the campaign was for parish Holy Name men to promise to help stem the sale of salacious material, and then through committees, to secure the cooperation of neighborhood newsdealers. The overall movement was called the National Organization for Decent Literature. In November, 1939, in the final diocesan report on the initial drive, diocesan chairman Mr. Frank E. Wolfe was able to report that the 472 diocesan campaign workers had secured pledges of cooperation from 468 stores, and had been turned down by only 33.[53]

Bishop Kearney had a part in the establishment of two activities which took place in Rochester on the First Fridays of the month. In 1940 he initiated the St. Monica Sodality for the mothers of priests and seminarians, and offered Mass for the members each first Friday in St. Patrick's Church.[54] He also encouraged Thomas H. O'Connor, Grand Knight of the Rochester K. of C. Council, to start a First Friday men's-luncheon-with-guest-speaker. This practice was becoming increasingly popular in American cities. The Bishop himself attended the first luncheon in December, 1942, at which the speaker was the Reverend Dr. John F. Dwyer, professor of moral theology at St. Bernard's Seminary.[55] First Friday luncheons have remained on the agenda of the local Knights ever since. The Elmira Council of the K. of C. began the same practice in August, 1944.[56]

Some efforts to reach the Negroes in Rochester continued during the prewar years. The St. Peter Claver Center on Rome Street still functioned, and for a time the Catholic Worker group conducted there an art class and a catechism class. In 1941, a similar center was opened at 396 Clarissa Street, to serve Negroes on the west side of town. The work of this house, called the Martin de Porres Settlement House, was mostly catechetical and service. It was undertaken under the direction of the Reverend John S. Randall, and the principal workers were the Cleary Veteran Mission Unit, made up mostly of young adults who while in high school had been members of the Catholic Students' Mission Crusade. In 1942 and 1943, the Sisters of Charity conducted a vacation school in Rochester for colored children; and the School Sisters of Notre Dame performed a similar task during the school year.[57]

The outbreak of World War II marked the beginning of a declension for these Catholic projects. The Martin de Porres House had to suspend operations after a couple of years because its personnel were called to wartime duties. In 1944, the Diocese invited Father Francis Mahon, S.V.D., to study the Negro problem in Rochester, with a view to proposing a master plan for a more official diocesan Negro apostolate. As we have already intimated, it was in anticipation of this new effort that the St. Peter Claver Center abandoned its program, sold its house, and handed over the price of the sale to the diocesan authorities for future Negro work. On the basis of his study, Father Mahon proposed a single diocesan center operated by volunteer workers. Unfortunately (as future events would prove) the diocesan consultors vetoed the recommendation.[58] Thus Rochester remained without a single Catholic institution geared to the postwar Negro population.

Two organizations did spring up, however, which to some degree carried on the work that had been discontinued. One was the Mother Cabrini Circle, an interracial Catholic committee established in 1946 to provide scholarships for deserving Negro children in the local Catholic high schools. (By 1966, the Circle was sponsoring twenty-one Negro children in eight local Catholic secondary schools.) The other organization was the fraternal order of the Knights (and Ladies Auxiliary) of Peter Claver. This Negro fraternal group, originally established in Louisiana in 1909, initiated its Rochester chapter, Bishop McQuaid Council #106, in 1948, with the sanction of Bishop Kearney. Prominent in the foundation were several Rochester Negroes who had been active in the St. Peter Claver and Martin de Porres centers, among them, Mr. Orlando J. Greene and Mrs. Harriet Schuyler.

What Catholic Rochesterians did not have themselves, they gave to the South. On September 5, 1940, Bishop Kearney bestowed mission crosses on Sister Francis Marie Keough (the superior) and four other Rochester Sisters of St. Joseph, as they left to take up teaching duties in the Negro section of Selma, Alabama. Four years later, the Rochester Sisters opened in Selma the Good Samaritan Hospital, which has since that time proved a real blessing to the Negroes of the vicinity. Both of these interracial efforts received generous support from Rochester diocesan Catholics.[59]

A Rochester Catholic theatrical society was inaugurated in 1937 with the encouragement of Bishop Kearney. This was the Rochester chapter of the Blackfriars Guild. The Blackfriars Guild was a national theatrical organization sponsored by the Dominican Fathers (traditionally called the "Black Friars" from their black cloaks). It aimed to promote amateur Catholic theatre on something above the parochial level. Thanks to the backing of Father John S. Randall of Rochester, and to the enthusiastic salesmanship of the Dominican priest-playwright Father Urban Nagle, Rochester's Catholic stagers set up a local Blackfriars unit on November 12, 1937.[60] Their first production achieved a marked success: the Emmet Lavery play, "The First Legion." Presented on February 18-19, 1938, it had a good local cast and starred Bert Lytell, the famous Broadway actor who had created the leading role in the original New York production.[61] During the following two years the Rochester Blackfriars Guild presented over a dozen shows, mostly popular Broadway plays that were both entertaining and wholesome. Unfortunately, the local Guild was obliged to suspend operations in 1941 because of declining interest.[62] Contemporary with the Rochester Blackfriars Guild was an Auburn Little Theater group, which had much the same aim as the Rochester Guild.[63]

Meanwhile, James Edward Kearney remained true to his initial commitment to interfaith good will. Five months after his installation, he was one of the speakers at an interfaith dinner held at the Rochester Chamber of Commerce; and in November, 1938, he addressed the students of Hobart and William Smith colleges, two distinguished institutions conducted by the Episcopalians at Geneva.[64] In 1940, he spoke at the Rochester Brotherhood dinner, held each year on Washington's birthday in concert with similar dinners across the nation.[65] Ever the gentleman and master of the appropriate word, Bishop Kearney was a welcome guest at such gatherings.

In general, the Bishop preferred to let others represent the Diocese on various interdenominational occasions, whether in or outside the see city.[66] Wartime activities would prove beyond cavil his willingness to collaborate with people of other faiths in civic enterprises. However, he did refrain, by policy, from endorsing any distinctly denominational appeal for funds.[67] It must also be admitted that Bishop Kearney was disturbed at the opposition taken by some Protestant spokesman to President Roosevelt's 1939 appointment of a Protestant, Mr. Myron C. Taylor, as a personal delegate to Pope Pius XII. This controversy was not without repercussions in the twelve counties of the Rochester Diocese.[68]

No public figure can agree with all men, or expect all to agree with him. Nevertheless, there is ample evidence that the fifth Bishop of Rochester quickly won and firmly retained the respect of Rochester's citizenry, whether Catholic or non-Catholic.

2. Into Global War.

Far removed though it was from the multiple fronts of World War II, the Diocese of Rochester naturally suffered from its involvement. The Great Depression had finally been conquered, but this new fear, this new pain had risen in its place.

Even the Spanish Civil War of 1936-1939, aptly termed a rehearsal of the Second World War, had its echoes in the Rochester area. This war broke out in a decade in which a current American catchword was "Be nice to Russia!" Russia's role in Spain's war seemed deliberately soft-pedaled in the American secular press. Furthermore, international Communism, firmly behind the "Loyalist" cause in Spain, promoted a strong "anti-Franco" propaganda in this country. As a result, American public opinion became so divided that to this very day United States historians find it hard to be objective in recounting the complex Spanish struggle.

The Communists, working principally through "front" organizations, made an effective appeal to the "liberal" mentality, and won from many American liberals a support which they would surely not have given had they known they were being manipulated. Like the press in most American cities, the Rochester daily press was anything but nuanced in its reporting of the war. In Rochester, too, as in most major American centers, there was a branch of the North American Committee to Aid Spanish Democracy, whose letterhead bore the names of several sincere but misled local citizens. A few Rochesterians joined the Communist-dominated Abraham Lincoln Brigade. When they returned to the city in 1939, their patrons greeted them with the clenched-fist Communist salute; and as veterans of the war they subsequently campaigned for the lifting of the American embargo that had thus far prevented the shipping of American arms to the Loyalist forces.[69]

American Catholics were too chary of Communist tactics and too unsympathetic towards doctrinaire "liberals" to become easily embroiled in the "front" tactics. Nevertheless, they, too, became divided on the Spanish issue. Some of the more pensive Rochester Catholics, influenced by the neutralist stance taken by the *Catholic Worker* and the *Commonweal*, raised the question about the practical need of taking sides.[70]

A short controversy arose in the pages of the Rochester *Catholic Courier,* between two diocesan priest-columnists, Father Benedict Ehmann and Father Owen B. McGuire.[71]

The *Courier* itself strongly supported the Insurgent cause. It printed regularly the N.C.W.C. despatches on the war, which gave antireligious sidelights usually excluded by the reportage of the daily press. It also carried the complete text of the joint pastoral of the Spanish bishops, who defended the justice of the Insurgent cause and denounced the Marxist bias of the Loyalists. The *Courier* likewise printed the Roman article by Father Mario Cordovani, O.P., the personal theologian of Pope Pius XI, decrying the attitude of neutrality in a battle in which Christianity was wrestling with Marxism for its life. The editors of the diocesan paper called on *Life* magazine to correct certain misstatements —and actually won an admission of error. Finally, the *Courier* urged diocesans to petition their congressmen to stand fast by the arms embargo.[72]

The diocesan chancery itself became somewhat entangled in the Spanish controversy. Spanish Loyalist agencies sent speakers to address Rochester audiences; and on three occasions the Chancery felt obliged to question the credentials of Loyalist spokesmen who claimed to be Catholic. Thus, on May 20, 1937, an Irish priest, Father Michael O'Flanagan, addressed a pro-Loyalist gathering in Rochester's Convention Hall. In the public eye, he appeared as a Catholic cleric in good standing, implying that the Loyalist cause deserved a sympathetic Catholic hearing. Actually, he had been suspended from his priestly functions twelve years before; and the *Courier* informed its readership of this fact.[73] Again, on April 14, 1939, José Bergamin came to the city to address a select group of teachers and other intellectuals. He was advertised as a "famed Catholic editor." In the actual lecture, he avoided making such a claim, and answered evasively questions put to him on Marxism. It seems that, as a matter of fact, he was not a Catholic but a freethinker.[74] The third controversial speaker was Father Leocadio Lobo. It was announced that this Spanish priest would deliver a lecture on April 21, 1939, for the benefit of the Spanish Refugees Relief Campaign, an organization not wholly dissociated from Communist influence. Promoters stated that Father Lobo was a priest in good standing. The Chancery, on good authority, replied that he had been suspended, and invited him to show his credentials. At a formal confrontation in the diocesan offices on the day of the speech, the Spanish cleric admitted that the Church officials were correct.[75]

Father Bergan, the diocesan chancellor, followed the Spanish issue with great concern, as is evident from the large file of clippings which he kept on the subject. His tart correspondence about Bergamin with the treasurer of the North American Committee to Aid Spanish Democracy, Rochester Chapter, provoked an irate letter from that personage. With a professor from the University of Rochester who was a far more urbane member of the same Committee, Father Bergan had a calmer exchange of opinions.[76]

Even Bishop Kearney, who did not enter personally into these controversies, was denounced in a letter to a local paper because he repudiated in one of his addresses not only the Fascist government, but the Loyalist government of Spain and the revolutionary government of Mexico. The writer of the letter wrote in the name of the Medical Bureau and North American Committee to Aid Spanish Democracy.[77] On December 11, 1938 — one day after the letter appeared—the Bishop spoke to the City Club of Rochester on "The Parochial School, Is It Necessary?" During the forum which followed, the chairman ruled out of order a question from the floor about the Spanish Civil War. But Bishop Kearney chose to answer the question. He said it was his personal conviction that democracy in Spain would be "safer in the hands of Franco than in the hands of those on the other side."[78]

The end of the Spanish war on March 29, 1939, brought a feeling of genuine relief to America as well as to Spain. American liberals who had gone along with Communist-front activities on an honest anti-Nazi basis, received a rude shock on the following August 23rd, when Germany and Soviet Russia signed a non-aggression pact.[79]

On September 1st, Germany, as a sequel to the non-aggression pact, invaded Poland and divided that luckless country with Russia. It was the initial step in World War II. This is not the place to rehearse the history of the war, either its European or its Asiatic phases. We need only mention that the Diocese of Rochester and its Bishop had not been remiss in prayers for the preservation of peace. Even the solemn Requiem Mass offered for Pius XI on February 13, 1939, in the Columbus Civic Center, was, in a sense, a prayer for peace. It was for a pope who had offered his life in that cause.[80] In concert with the new pope, Pius XII—elected March 2nd—Bishop Kearney again requested that his people pray for peace.[81] And subsequent to the invasion of Poland, he authorized the taking up of the Polish Relief collection which the American hierarchy had authorized.[82] Furthermore, throughout the years of hostilities, the Bishop of Rochester again and again asked prayers, especially prayers addressed through Mary, Queen of Peace, for the restoration of international tranquillity.[83]

This is not to say that the Bishop considered the cause of peace inconsistent with the cause of national defense. When the Army Chief of Chaplains, Monsignor William R. Arnold, issued an appeal for 1,000 more chaplains (275 Catholics) to serve our "greatest peacetime army," Bishop Kearney invited his priests to volunteer.[84] The first to do so were Fathers Edward J. Waters and Austin B. Hanna, who were given their Army Reserve commissions on October 23, 1940. When these chaplains departed, the Bishop gave them a personal send-off—a practice which he continued with each of the subsequent volunteers.[85] During the next twelve months, four more priests of the Rochester Diocese joined the Army Chaplain Corps; and two, Fathers John K. Wheaton and John Woloch, became chaplains in the Naval Reserve.[86]

To provide recreational facilities for the draftees, the United Service Organization was founded, a national association. The nationwide Catholic affiliate of the U.S.O. which the bishops established was called the National Catholic Community Services (N.C.C.S.). Mrs. Daniel Culhane, a Catholic laywoman of Rochester, was named national program director of the N.C.C.S.; and a Rochester Catholic layman, Judge James P. B. Duffy, was designated Washington representative of the U.S.O.[87]

Prayer crusades alternated that year with drives for scrap aluminum and war relief. But America still remained uncommitted to the actual conflict. All was changed on December 7, 1941, when in the midst of Japanese-American efforts to settle their differences amicably, the Japanese air force bombed our defense installations at Pearl Harbor in the Hawaiian Islands. At least one of the sailor-victims of that holocaust was from the Rochester Diocese: Robert J. Dineen, of St. Ann's parish, Hornell.[88]

After the bombing, the United States moved without delay. On December 8th, the federal government declared war upon Japan; and on December 11th, upon Germany and Italy. Nor did Bishop Kearney delay to speak for his own diocese. He instructed the faithful in each parish to make the pledge of allegiance to the flag at all the Masses on Sunday, December 14th. In the circular letter read from every pulpit that day, he expressed the following sentiments:

> The American people have been trying to adjust their affairs with Japan over the conference table. While these conferences were in progress, an unexpected and unprovoked attack was made on our defenders.
>
> Obviously, the Japanese want war. Well, they must be taught

the decencies of civilization and obviously we must do it. Our armed forces are ready to defend the American Way of Life at any cost and to punish this dastardly attack on the flag of our country.

We place at the disposal of our country all the spiritual, moral and material forces of our church. Our thoughts go out in deep sympathy to those whose sons are in that far off battle line, and day by day these men and those near and dear to them will be in our prayers at God's altar.

May God bless and protect our country![89]

On December 22nd, the nation's Catholics sent to President Roosevelt a letter pledging their cooperation. It was signed by Archbishop Mooney as chairman of the Administrative Board of the N.C.W.C.[90] So far as the Diocese of Rochester went, James E. Kearney was to give it strong patriotic leadership throughout the war years. When he registered for the draft in April, 1942, he was, of course rejected.[91] But the very act of registration symbolized his devotion to his native land.

The four years of blood and destruction which followed upon Pearl Harbor need not be described here. They solved some outstanding problems; they raised new ones, still more tormenting. Our present purpose is simply to indicate the contribution which the Catholics of the Rochester Diocese made to the cause.

Fortunately, parish lists of diocesan participants were kept during the war years; so we have a fairly exact knowledge of what the Diocese gave to the nation by way of manpower—and womanpower.[92] The total of Rochester diocesan personnel in the armed forces was 31,585. This comprised 30,771 men in the various branches; and 814 women, members of the Army and Navy nursing corps, the WAC, the WAVES, the SPARS, and the Women Marines. To the total of those in uniform we should add the eleven diocesan men and nine diocesan women who were paid employees of the American Red Cross. This makes a grand total of 31,605.

Of the service personnel, 18,271 hailed from Monroe County— 17,863 men; 408 women. The largest number of service people from any one parish in Monroe County or in the whole Diocese, was from the Italian parish of Our Lady of Mt. Carmel, Rochester: 1,263. Holy Rosary ranked next, with 983; and there were ten other Rochester parishes which could claim over 500 on their honor rolls. Outside Monroe County, the parish which held the record was St. Ann's, Hornell (606). The figure for Immaculate Conception, Ithaca, was 543; for St.

Francis de Sales, Geneva, 502. Rural parishes and missions naturally were at the lower end of the scale. The mission church of St. Rose of
Lima, at Sodus Point (Wayne County) had the smallest honor roll of
all—one name.

Diocesan servicemen and servicewomen naturally represented many
national origins—although the lines had by now often become blurred,
through the intermarriage of Irish, Germans, Franco-Belgians, Italians,
Poles, Lithuanians. Catholic families were no longer as large as in
pioneer days, but many a parent gave several boys to the nation's forces.
James O'Connell of Clifton Springs was represented by five sons; as was
Patrick Moriarty of Scipio Center.[93] The honor roll of St. Mary's, Corn-
ning, bore the names of six sons of the Speciale family and seven sons
of Mrs. Susie Sweet.[94] But Mr. and Mrs. Philip Fedele of Rochester apparently held the record. Eight of their boys wore the United States uniform.[95]

The proportion of Catholic servicemen who held officers' commissions was, of course, greater than in previous wars. One Rochester officer bore a name evocative of Civil War days: Colonel Ernst, who won
the Legion of Merit award for his service on the staff of General Douglas MacArthur. This latter-day Colonel was Joseph L. Ernst; but he was
the grandson of the Colonel Louis Ernst who clinched the victory of
Rochester's regiment at the battle of Little Roundtop.[96]

Those who reached the highest official rank were, naturally, professional soldiers. Thus Dominic Sabini, a Corningite who had entered the
army in 1913, was promoted to brigadier general in 1945.[97] Captain
Hubert W. Chanler, U.S.N., of Geneseo, was an Annapolis graduate of
the class of 1922. When he retired on April 1, 1950, it was with the
rank of rear admiral.[98] But the highest-ranking officer of Rochester
origin was the Marine aviator, Francis P. Mulcahy. He had won the
Navy Distinguished Service Medal in World War I, for "extraordinary
heroism" in pioneering food-dropping air missions. From 1942 to 1945
he was engaged in several important Pacific air commands, which earned him a second Navy D.S.M., the Army D.S.M., the Legion of Merit,
and the English O.B.E. He had been promoted brigadier general in
1942 and major general in 1944. He retired on April 1, 1946 with the
rank of lieutenant general.[99]

A representative number of diocesan servicemen were decorated
for their military accomplishments. The wounded were awarded Purple
Heart Medals; and a good many received the Bronze Star Medal.

Recipients of the Silver Star Medal were fairly numerous too. Thus,
Sergeant Francis E. Updaw of Ontario, was given the Silver Star on the

completion of fifty-three Army air missions.[100] Sergeant Anthony Maio of Corning won the award for wiping out two German machine gun nests.[101] Two Waterloo men received Silver Stars: Corporal René LeBrun and Lt. Daniel V. Lent. Lent, whose leadership in battle was termed "brilliant" by his commanding officer, earned not one but two Silver Stars, plus other decorations.[102] In some cases, of course, the Silver Star award was posthumous; for instance, Sgt. Paul I. Wegman of Rochester, killed in action in April, 1945.[103]

Posthumous, also, was the bestowal of the Navy Cross on Lt. (j.g.) Robert W. Boyle, an alumnus of St. Ambrose School, Rochester.[104] At least three men received the Distinguished Flying Cross personally. Sgt. Richard M. Hasbrouck of Rochester earned it during the African Campaign; Lt. John J. Hickey of Corning earned it as pilot of a Flying Fortress.[105] A third, and one of the most distinguished fighting pilots from the State, was Charles R. Fischette of Clyde, who downed five planes.[106] Lt. Col. Michael M. Karlene of Rochester was given the Legion of Merit decoration for his work in the 12th Air Force.[107] No diocesan serviceman won the Congressional Medal of Honor; but a few merited the second-highest combat award, the Distinguished Service Cross. The award was posthumous in the case of Pvt. Mario Pomponio of Fairport; but it was *inter vivos* in the case of the Seneca Falls physician, Captain John Setteneri.[108]

The diocesan Colonel O'Rorke of World War II was Marine Private John J. Wantuck, one of the five uniformed sons of Mr. and Mrs. Lawrence Wantuck of St. Casimir parish, Elmira. Young John died heroically on July 14, 1943, while he and one companion were holding back a force of 150 Japanese in the jungle of New Georgia Island. Not only was he awarded the Navy Cross for "extraordinary heroism"; a destroyer-type transport ship was named after him. When its finished hull slid down the ways into Boston Harbor in November, 1944, his sister Mary christened it the U.S.S. "Wantuck."[109]

Not all the commendations went to service *men*. Three service *women* received special recognition. For courageously rescuing a soldier from a pool of flame, WAC Private Margaret Helen Maloney of Rochester was given the first Soldier's Medal (for non-combat heroism) ever bestowed on a woman.[110] First Lieutenant Rose Kelly, a Genevan member of the Army Nursing Corps, received a Bronze Star Medal for meritorious work in Germany.[111] Another Army nurse-lieutenant, Marie M. Flanagan—a Hornellian by origin—spent two years at the U. S. Base

Hospital at Bar-le-Duc, France. For her good work there Nurse Flanagan was subsequently made a chevalier of the Grand-Ducal Order of the Oaken Wreath by Grand Duchess Charlotte of Luxembourg.[112]

Rochester's diocesan chaplains also established a distinguished record. Between October, 1940, and the close of the war, their number reached a total of forty-two.[113] To this number we can add the three Redemptorist Fathers and the one Basilian Father who were stationed in the Rochester Diocese when they received their chaplain's commissions. Most of these men saw foreign service; some were in the thick of the African, Italian, Normandy and Ardennes actions, or engaged in the "island-hopping" of the Pacific campaign. Father David B. Singerhoff held the record for active service: forty-one months and ten days.

Several of these priests-in-uniform were recipients of decorations. Purple Hearts went to Father John K. Wheaton (Navy), wounded in the Battle of Kula Gulf, 1943; and to Father John S. Maloney (Army), wounded in the Normandy Invasion. Eight received the Bronze Star Medal: Fathers Donald Cleary, John S. Hayes, Thomas J. Manley, Donald J. Murphy, Elmer W. Heindl, David B. Singerhoff, Francis H. Vogt, and John J. Brennan, C.SS.R. Fathers Murphy and Heindl also merited the Silver Star Medal, as did Father William J. O'Brien. Major General Sherman Miles presented the Legion of Merit to Chaplain Walter J. Donoghue; Admiral Chester W. Nimitz presented the same award to Chaplain John V. Loughlin. Two Rochester Diocesan chaplains earned the Distinguished Service Cross. Lieutenant General Omar N. Bradley conferred it on Father John S. Maloney for heroism in the D-Day Invasion. General Douglas MacArthur conferred it on Father Elmer W. Heindl for heroic action during the Luzon campaign.

None of the diocesan chaplains lost his life; but many lay diocesans in uniform suffered capture, or wounds, or death. The total of diocesan service deaths in World War II was 928. One of these was a woman: WAC Private Dorothy J. Reynolds of Corning, who was killed in a train wreck in Pennsylvania.[114] Most of the victims—516—came from Monroe County, in which the total service deaths were 1,297.

As in previous wars, the men and women who entered the armed forces from the twelve counties knew they had the unquestioning backing of those who remained to serve on the home front. Love of country was still one of the less complicated American virtues.

As usual, wartime restrictions imposed certain austerities on the nation. Food distribution was made according to tickets, so a new bureaucracy arose. Gasoline and tires were strictly rationed, and the highways were so little traveled that dogs returned to their ancestral practice of snoozing in the road. (There was a bit of a fuss in Rochester in June, 1943, when a local gas-rationing officer declared that driving to Sunday Mass was not permissible. An appeal to his superior officer led to a quick overruling of the decision.[115])

But the positive contribution of the home-front was vastly more important than its wartime austerities. Most factories were engaged in defense production through the daylight hours lengthened by War Time, and through the night shifts. Women rallied to fill the labor shortages in even the heavier industries, and showed themselves almost as adept as the men they were replacing—to the chagrin of the nation's menfolk. Some worked mainly for income; many out of strong patriotism. Take, for instance, Miss Pearl Gentile, a blind Corning girl. When her Marine-brother Lawrence died in the service, she sought some way to help the cause for which he had given his life. She got a job in the Corning Glass Works packing percolator handles. This she did very competently; and by taking the position she also freed another man to serve in the armed forces.[116]

Special dispensations were in order for such busy citizens as these. Bishop Kearney exempted his people from Lenten fast and from abstinence except on Fridays, Ash Wednesday, and Holy Saturday—an exemption which was continued until February 1946.[117] He likewise permitted defense workers on the night shift to receive Holy Communion after fasting only four hours from solid foods and one hour from liquids (alcohol excepted).[118] Afternoon Masses were also introduced at this time to serve the needs of the emergency. Father Frederick G. Straub of Auburn announced in July, 1942, that he would schedule a 5:15 P.M. Sunday Mass for war workers.[119] This seems to have been the first "evening" Mass ever scheduled in the Diocese, at least for a civilian congregation.

Red Cross work received the warm endorsement of the Bishop and the ready response of his flock. Many parishes had Red Cross units for the making of surgical dressings—a time-honored contribution of American womankind to the needs of the wounded. By March 1, 1943, the unit at St. Alphonsus Church, Auburn, had already prepared over 23,000 dressings.[120] Junior Red Cross units, like that at Nazareth Academy, Rochester, did sewing and knitting.[121] In Rochester, the executive secretary of the Red Cross was Miss Veronica Maher, a native of Ovid and a prominent Rochester executive.

Probably no Red Cross activity appealed to the citizenry quite so much as the Blood Bank. The donating of blood as a humanitarian gesture had been promoted in Rochester as early as 1937 by the popular radio announcer, Alphonse J. Sigl, of St. Joseph's parish. Following in "Al" Sigl's footsteps, the local Red Cross and the Strong Memorial Hospital opened a wartime blood bank in 1941; and this operated until May 19, 1945. One of its backers was the Catholic Sponsoring Committee, which donated 1,500 pints of blood—the gifts of laymen, priests, nuns and seminarians.[122] The Rochester Catholic Worker group made another sort of "hospital" contribution during the war years. The federal government brought in a number of Negroes from Jamaica, British West Indies, to serve as a temporary work force in Strong Memorial Hospital. For about a year the Catholic Worker provided twenty-eight of them with a residence in St. Joseph's House of Hospitality.[123]

Diocesans also responded well to the collections of "inert material." In December, 1941, parochial school children took up 32,000 lbs. of paper.[124] Bishop Kearney also urged their cooperation with the Victory Book Drive a few days later.[125] Tin cans and other salvage materials were gathered with particular abundance in Rochester in 1942, thanks to the special efforts of the head of the Rochester Salvage Department —Mr. William T. Nolan of Rochester Catholic Charities.[126] There were other drives, too: old rubber, old silk, old nylon, old clothes, old almost everything else.

Then there were the great bond drives, seven of them, run tandem throughout the war period. The Bishop stood firmly behind these campaigns, and many parishes and parish societies, as well as individual Catholics, invested funds in national bonds. The Knights of Columbus were leading solicitors. So were the children in diocesan schools, who were responsible for bringing in almost $2 million in bond funds.[127] In one early effort, De Sales High School of Geneva reported a record in bond sales of $2,172.25. The main purchaser was student Jeremiah Coughlin, who had bought bonds with all his savings—$1,275.00. He received a special commendatory message from the federal Treasury Department.[128]

The Diocese meanwhile played an active part in providing comforts and recreation for service personnel who passed through the twelve counties or were stationed in the area. The National Catholic Community Services and their district officers collaborated with Protestant and Jewish agencies in operating a U.S.O. center on Franklin Street in Rochester. It opened in January, 1943; and in April, Mrs. Robert Hartmann, a past president of the Rochester Catholic Women's Club, was named a program director.[129] By the end of a year, the Center was so overburdened that its facilities had to be expanded. The N.C.C.S. therefore opened a canteen in the Columbus Civic Center on March 12, 1944; and in May it added dormitory accommodations in the Civic Center building. During the two years that the canteen operated, various parochial groups and various Catholic-allied societies (like the Catholic Kolping Society and the Ancient Order of Hibernians), took turns serving breakfasts to military visitors.[130]

The other important U.S.O. center was in Geneva. This center was entrusted entirely to the N.C.C.S.; and Father John S. Randall, as head of the diocesan N.C.C.S. committee, had much to do with setting it up. In June, 1942, Bishop Kearney dedicated the permanent center at the corner of Geneva and Exchange Streets.[131]

Geneva was given its U.S.O. center because of the opening in 1942 of the huge Sampson Naval Training Center on the eastern slope of Seneca Lake a few miles south of Geneva. Recreational provisions were urgently needed in this normally quiet little city which suddenly became a way-station and time-off refuge of thousands of lonesome "boots." Catholic Navy chaplains were assigned to the base, of course; but their work was heavy, and they welcomed the assistance of the diocesan clergy. The Bishop kept a pastoral eye on the vast base, and presided there at many major religious ceremonies. He officiated, in October, 1942, at the dedication of the camp's Chidwick Chapel.[132] He twice administered the sacrament of confirmation to classes of servicemen.[133] Thousands attended the solemn Christmas midnight Masses which he celebrated on the base in 1942 and 1943; and the Masses he celebrated on civic holidays, especially Memorial Day and Independence Day.[134] Most memorable of all was the great Fourth-of-July Pontifical Mass of 1944. That day Bishop Kearney offered the Mass in the open air; Bishop William T. McCarty, C.SS.R., Military Delegate, preached; and 16,000 servicemen formed the congregation.[135] The announcer who covered the event on a nationwide broadcast termed this the largest religious gathering in the history of the United States Navy.

Elsewhere in the Diocese there were smaller groups of military personnel in training. For example, there were Navy V-12 units at both the University of Rochester and at Hobart College, Geneva. A good many Army and Navy men also pursued courses in Ithaca at Cornell University. A Military Police group had headquarters at Van Etten.[136] Local diocesan priests were assigned to take care of the spiritual needs of Catholics in these units. Five of the priests engaged in the task had faculties from the Catholic Military Ordinariate as auxiliary chaplains.

Eighteen priests of the Diocese, in all, held the official rank of auxiliary chaplain. Most of them worked among Italian and German prisoners of war, who in the later months of the conflict were engaged in paid labor at non-military work, principally in the canning plants of the twelve counties. Rochester was buried under the big snow of December 11-12, 1944. While America and Germany were fighting the "Battle of the Bulge" in Europe, German P.O.W.'s were helping snowbound Rochesterians to shovel out in the "Battle of the Blizzard." (A curious sidelight on the war!) War Prisoners were usually accommodated in barracks that had served the Civilian Conservation Corps. The auxiliary chaplains, most of whom had some knowledge of German or Italian, serviced camps at Cobb's Hill (Rochester), Clyde, Dansville, Fair Haven, Elmira Holding and Reconsignment Point, Geneva Branch Camp, Macedon, Hamlin Beach, Marion, Newark, Ontario, Port Byron, Romulus Depot, Rushville, Sodus Point, and perhaps elsewhere. The Italian prisoners, whose nation had been on the side of the Allies since September, 1943, were cheerful and sociable. Some of the Germans were more aloof. Bishop Kearney himself visited at least one of these camps, that at Clyde, where Italian-born Father Alfredo Morotti was diocesan chaplain of 200 Italian prisoners.

By June, 1944, the tide of war was finally turning. When Rome fell before the Allies on June 4, 1944, Rochesterians were happy to learn that their former priest, Archbishop Edward J. Hanna, who had resided in Rome since retiring from San Francisco in 1935, was still alive.[137] The D-Day invasion was launched from Britain on June 6, 1944. Rochester diocesans received the news with unprecedented prayerfulness; and Bishop Kearney, making his retreat at St. Bernard's Seminary, issued a heartening statement.[138]

But it was difficult to be of good heart. On the home front, the end of the war still seemed very remote. Those in the field were even more eager for a quicker victory. Perhaps none of them bespoke so well this bitter weariness as Chaplain William J. O'Brien, who, after slogging through the hideous Italian campaign for a year, wrote home the following lines.

> The road from Christmas 1943 to Christmas 1944 will be the one I will always remember as a ghost road. I saw Monte Cassino crumble. I've crossed the Arno on a Bailey Bridge and looked at the ruins of the Ponte Vecchio. I lived in a hole in Anzio, and I know why its story will never be told. I drove my peep ["Jeep"] to the steps of St. Peter's and said Mass there. Then I fought all

the way to the Gothic Line. I've walked the roads that saints and martyrs walked and I've buried the latest saints and martyrs. The Angels of the Passion have been with us, carrying the spear and the nails and the scourge. Blood, torn bodies, death, frustration, loneliness, bad news from home, broken spirits and terrible homesickness. But I say Mass this Christmas in Fra Angelico's country. May his golden angels clustered about Bethlehem's stable bring rest to the world.[139]

One more tragedy of the war occurred when President Franklin D. Roosevelt died on April 2, 1945. "While he did not die on the field of battle," said Bishop Kearney of the dead leader, "he surely died fighting for his country." The Bishop directed that on April 15th, prayers be offered in every parish for the repose of the President's soul.[140]

A month later, on May 8, 1945, President Harry S Truman proclaimed "V-E Day"—"Victory in Europe Day." However, because the war in the Pacific was not yet at an end, the May 8th celebration was muted. Father Charles Bruton gave the opening prayer at a public street rally in Rochester; the churches were crowded that night for thanksgiving services; and on Sunday, May 13, solemn Eucharistic exposition took place across the twelve counties.[141]

The atom-bombing of Hiroshima and Nagasaki on August 6th and 9th, 1945, added a new and appalling dimension to international relations. But Japan, already prepared to surrender, laid down its arms a week later; and at 7:00 P.M. on August 14th, President Truman announced the end of hostilities. Thirty thousand Rochesterians gathered that evening at Main and East Avenue not only to rejoice but to pray for the victims of the dreadful conflict. Throughout the twilight hours, and the following feastday, Catholics in great numbers made voluntary visits to the churches of the Diocese to express to God their relief and gratitude.[142]

During the four years of the struggle, Bishop Kearney had led his people in prayers and devotions for peace and human welfare. He recognized in V-J Day an answer from God, and he attributed peace in particular to the intercession of the Blessed Virgin. As he wrote to his armed forces chaplains:

> Well, at last we change our chant to "Deo Gratias"! Fulfilling my constant hope and sincere conviction that "In terra, pax hominibus" would ring through Our Lady and on one of her feasts, the Assumption brought us the welcome news.[143]

What had begun with Pearl Harbor on the eve of the Immaculate Conception, 1941, had indeed terminated on the eve of another Marian festival: the feast of the Assumption. During the forty-five sad intervening months, James E. Kearney had proved himself a loyal citizen and a solicitous shepherd. And his people had stood by their country amidst the anguish of the world's most frightful war.

3. RECONVERSION.

American generosity to the conquered has always been one of our more admirable national traits. We demonstrated it fully after World War II. Not only did the nation embark on such programs as the Marshall Plan, which combined politics with philanthropy. The nation's Catholics, religious groups among them, engaged in many charitable undertakings, on an organized or personal basis, for the benefit of the needy of war-torn nations.

Thus, for example, the Diocese donated 138 tons of canned food in the collection of December, 1945.[144] In 1946, Rochester diocesans contributed 46 tons of used clothing. In 1949, the American bishops made this Thanksgiving clothing drive an annual affair; and between 1949 and 1958, the Rochester Diocese turned in over 884 tons.[145] (From 1947 on, the Diocesan Council of Catholic Women was put in charge of these Thanksgiving clothing collections.[146])

Some Catholic organizations undertook particular charities. For instance, the German Catholic Kolping Society, by June, 1949, had shipped 1,000 relief packages to the German dioceses of Osnabrueck and Freiburg.[147] The Rosary Society of Holy Family parish, Rochester, up to February, 1948, had sent 200 packages to Germany.[148] The library of St. Alphonsus Church, Auburn, collected 81 boxes of books for transoceanic shipping.[149] In Geneva, one group raised $200.00 towards rebuilding St. Ann's Church in Heidelberg, Germany.[150] Religious communities also joined the march of charity: the Rochester Sisters of Mercy, for example; and the nuns of the Rochester Carmelite monastery.[151] Much of the packing and shipping of this material for the first few postwar years was voluntarily undertaken by the Will Scientific Corporation of Rochester, through the good offices of its president, Mr. Harold J. Coleman.[152]

Father John M. Baksys, pastor of St. George's Lithuanian Church, in Rochester, was meanwhile soliciting usable clothing to send to Lithuanian war victims.[153] But the greatest special drive was for war-torn Italy. The pastor of Rochester's Mt. Carmel Church, Father Charles J.

Azzi, headed the diocesan clothes-for-Italy drives of 1944 and 1945. He reported 160,000 lbs. the first year, and 70,000 lbs. the second year. The Diocese did another great favor to Italy at the time of the first national Italian elections, April 18, 1948, when it was feared that the Communists might win political control of that country. Italo-Americans of the Rochester Diocese not only prayed for the defeat of the Communists; they joined in the America-wide letterwriting campaign to their Italian kith and kin to discourage them from voting Communist. The Rochester Valguarnera Society alone sent 1,200 copies of a letter written by Miss Gina Trovato, a sixteen-year-old student at Rochester's East High School who had only recently emigrated from Italy. The result, as everybody knows, was a sweeping defeat of the Italian Communist candidates.[154]

One of the most piteous problems of the Reconversion was that of "displaced persons." The inflexibilities of our American immigration laws served for a time to exclude certain homeless refugees. In 1946 and 1947, Bishop Kearney appealed for emergency aid for DP's stranded at Ellis Island.[155] Finally, the laws were amended to permit a larger influx. In December, 1947, the N.C.W.C. set up a National Catholic Resettlement Council to take charge of the admission of Catholic immigrants. Earliest of the new arrivals in the twelve counties were fifty young Ukrainians, who had been resettled at Auburn by December, 1948. Another Ukrainian, the middle-aged Ivan Bandura, was the first DP to come to Rochester proper.[156] Although the Rochester Catholic Charities was local agent of the Resettlement Council, these Ukrainian immigrants belonged not to the Diocese of Rochester but to the Ukrainian Diocese of Philadelphia. However, a considerable number of Poles also entered the twelve-county area as DP's. The largest group was the "farming community" of 48 Poles who were established near Weedsport on June 16, 1949.[157] Most numerous of the resettled Latin-rite DP's were the Lithuanians. Of the 750 Catholic refugees welcomed into the Diocese up to 1951, 300 were Lithuanians, for whom Father John Baksys (who was largely responsible for arranging their entry and employment) was truly the Good Samaritan.[158]

With the war over, Pope Pius XII was once more free to communicate easily with his bishops around the world. On February 18, 1946, the Pope, for the first time in his regime, held a consistory for the appointment of Cardinals. He named 32 churchmen to that honor. One was Edward Mooney, Archbishop of Detroit and former Bishop of

Rochester. By special invitation, Father Lawrence B. Casey, his former Rochester secretary, went to Rome to witness the Cardinal-elect's installation.[159]

The Cardinal Priest of the Title of Santa Susanna — to give Mooney his official cardinalitial name—paid his first official visit to Rochester on October 23, 1946, to attend the meeting of the Alumni Association of St. Bernard's Seminary.[160] Two of the new non-American Cardinals also came to Rochester shortly after they received the Red Hat. Cardinal Thomas Tien, S.V.D. (1890-1967), Archbishop of Peking and the first Chinese Cardinal in history, was given a splendid reception on April 13, 1946. A similar welcome was extended on February 19, 1947 to one of the heroic prelates of Germany, Cardinal Count Conrad von Preysing, Bishop of Berlin (1880-1950).[161]

Bishop Kearney held a sort of "little consistory" himself on November 11, 1947, the tenth anniversary of his installation. Thus far he had not petitioned Roman prelatial honors for any of his clergy. Now, on his request, Pope Pius XII bestowed distinctions upon twenty-four diocesan priests. Highest rank (protonotary apostolic) went to Msgr. William M. Hart, the Vicar General; Msgr. William F. Bergan, the Chancellor; and Msgr. John F. Goggin, Rector of St. Bernard's Seminary. Three were accorded the "junior" rank—papal chamberlain. The rest were domestic prelates, and their number included several officials and pastors, among them Father Lawrence B. Casey.[162]

The Bishop made his own *ad limina* visit to Rome—the first since his coming to Rochester—in April and May, 1949, in the company of Bishop Walter A. Foery of Syracuse. The two bishops were greeted at Naples by two Rochester priests stationed in Italy. One was Msgr. Richard K. Burns, who after a year in official Vatican service had been named in 1947 to the vice-rectorship of the North American College in Rome. The other was Father Joseph J. Sullivan, American correspondent for the Press Bureau of the N.C.W.C.[163] In addition to the two diocesan priests, there were waiting at the dock fifty or sixty former Italian Prisoners of War who had served on labor brigades within the Rochester Diocese. When Bishop Kearney disembarked, this delegation presented him with a bouquet of roses. The Bishop, forewarned about the ceremony, responded with a prepared Italian speech. After a visit to Rome and an audience with Pope Pius XII on May 13th, Bishop Kearney moved westward to England, sailing for home on the "Queen Mary" on May 26th. As his predecessors had by custom been given a formal "welcome home" reception on their return from *ad limina* voyages, so the fifth Bishop of Rochester was feted by the diocesan Holy Name Union on May 30th at a large banquet held in the Sheraton Hotel.[164]

World peace did not mean an end of human conflict. The business boom in postwar America gave rise to new contests between management and labor. Thus, in May, 1946, unskilled laborers employed by the City of Rochester went on strike; and the rest of the local unionists also struck in a gesture of solidarity. The right to unionize was probably the chief factor underlying the struggle. When an agreement was worked out, it was achieved in large measure through the efforts of the Rochester Religion and Labor Institute, and particularly by three members of this committee, Dr. Justin Wroe Nixon, and Fathers John S. Randall and Patrick J. Flynn.[165] A year later, the Diocese sponsored another Industrial Conference. First-rate experts representing federal and state agencies, management and labor, were featured on the agenda. The representative of labor was Mr. Victor Reuther, educational director of United Auto Workers, who was substituting for his still more controversial brother, Walter Reuther. Some Rochester industrialists complained about the appearance of any Reuther on the Conference's agenda.[166]

With the war over and building restrictions removed, the Diocese was finally able to expand. Within two years after V-J Day, Bishop Kearney established one new mission and four new parishes. The mission was St. Isaac Jogues, at Fleming, Cayuga County (1946). Of the four parishes, two were mission churches promoted to parochial status: Annunciation, on Norton Street, Rochester, made a territorial parish in May, 1946; and St. Leo's, Hilton, Monroe County, elevated in the following month. In east Irondequoit, the Bishop set up two completely new parochial units: St. Cecilia and St. James. The positioning of all four parishes indicated that suburbia had already begun to mushroom. Bishop Kearney did not dedicate the new Irondequoit church buildings until the 1950's. However, he did bless a new chapel at the Divine Word Seminary, Conesus, N. Y., in September, 1948, and a new chapel at St. Joseph's Villa, Rochester, in June, 1949.[167]

School buildings received a special priority. When a new school structure was announced at St. Margaret Mary Church in Irondequoit in 1947, it was stated that this was "the first major diocesan school building project in eighteen years."[168] Actually, Bishop Kearney had the pleasure of blessing ten new parochial school buildings between 1947 and 1950. Most of these were in parishes which up to that time had had no parish schools. Two downtown schools had lately closed down: St. Patrick's in 1937, when the Cathedral property was sold; and Our Lady of Victory, in 1947. But the latter schoolhouse was reopened in 1951 by the Sisters of St. Joseph as the School of the Holy Childhood, a non parochial school (first established at Immaculate Conception School in 1946) for mentally retarded children and adolescents of every race and creed. This little school, which accommodated some ninety students, was supported by voluntary contributions, and quickly proved to be a notable work of educational charity.

Diocesan higher education was going to splurge even more. Aquinas Institute built a stadium to seat 21,000 spectators; and the Bishop dedicated it in October, 1949. The "Little Irish" football teams had won widespread popularity in the Rochester area. But Aquinas had also made a contribution to adult education since 1940 by its annual Christian Culture Series of lectures delivered by topnotch speakers from America and abroad.[169] Most popular of these speakers was Msgr. Fulton J. Sheen of the Catholic University of America.

Dispossessed of its home by the sale of the Cathedral property in 1937, St. Andrew's Seminary had been carrying on in the rickety old Cathedral school building. An influx of postwar students—many of them earnest war veterans—caused a rise in registration. A new building was painfully needed; so in February, 1946, the Diocese launched a drive for $500,000.00 to build it. Pledges totalled $856,000.00—a new indication of the devotion of Rochester diocesans to the cause of their seminaries. Originally the new structure was to be built on Dewey Avenue, across the open lots from St. Bernard's Seminary. By the time construction was ready to begin, however, the site had been changed to the Dowd Farm on Buffalo Road.[170]

A School of X-Ray Technology was instituted at St. James Mercy Hospital in Hornell in 1948.[171] But the major educational undertaking of the 1940's and 1950's was the foundation of St. John Fisher College.

Granted by their Aquinas contract the sole right to open a Catholic men's college in Rochester, the Basilians in 1947 purchased seventy acres on the Fairport Road for a future campus. Bishop Kearney suggested that the projected school be named after St. John Fisher, the martyred bishop of Rochester, England. A diocesan-wide campaign was initiated at the Eastman Theater on January 26, 1948, under the chairmanship of Mr. Joseph Myler, a Catholic executive of the Neisner Company. Cardinal Francis Spellman, Archbishop of New York, attended the opening and contributed a check of $20,000.00. The goal of the campaign was $1,047,336.00; the pledges amounted to $1,235,-

057.00. Delighted with the result, the Basilian Fathers laid plans for early construction. St. John Fisher College did not open, however, until the early 'fifties.[172]

Another development associated with higher education was the opening of the Newman Oratory in Ithaca in 1947. A large residence close to the Cornell Campus, the Oratory contained a chapel, quarters for the Catholic Newman chaplain and several boarding students, and facilities for meetings. The opening of this center brought into realization at least one phase of the Catholic program Bishop McQuaid had envisioned for Cornell just before his death.

The final grand project announced in the 1940's was the plan for a future drive for $2.35 millions to enlarge existing high school facilities and to build three more Catholic high schools across the Diocese. Father Charles J. Mahoney, diocesan superintendent of schools, revealed this news in 1949.[173] Clearly, the Diocese intended to make up for the building time lost during the Great Depression and World War II.

After the close of the war, Bishop Kearney also welcomed several new religious orders into the Diocese.

One of these was the Religious of the Cenacle, a community of nuns who specialize in conducting retreats for women. The Bishop had long intended to introduce the Cenacle into the Rochester Diocese. Finally, on November 21, 1946, he was in a position to extend the invitation.[174] When the offer was accepted, Bishop Kearney assigned to the Sisters the Libanus Todd mansion, on Rochester's East Avenue, as their convent and retreat house. Mrs. Libanus (Norah Conway) Todd had offered the property as the site of a new diocesan cathedral. The Bishop, preferring to have his cathedral closer to St. Bernard's Seminary, chose rather to use the Todd estate for retreat purposes. Mrs. Todd, a Catholic, deeded her home to the Diocese before her death on February 14, 1948.[175] The Cenacle religious arrived on June 12, 1948 —three choir religious and one lay sister, headed by Mother Angela Murphy. The initial retreat given in the Rochester Cenacle opened on February 11, 1949. Soon the retreats became very popular. On June 24, 1960, a new wing and the present chapel were dedicated to provide accommodations for a total of forty-five women retreatants.[176]

The Carmelite Fathers and three Franciscan orders set up houses in the twelve counties in the late 1940's. Carmelites of the Province of St. Elias (Regular Observance) opened a novitiate called Whitefriars in Auburn in 1946. Bishop Kearney dedicated their building on September 7th of that year.[177] On September 14, 1949, the Bishop blessed

St. Anthony's Minor Seminary and High School, lately set up in the buildings of the former Glen Springs Hotel above Watkins Glen. This was a foundation of the Franciscan Friars Minor of the Assumption Province (Polish-American); and its Padua High School was intended to serve not only prospective students for the priesthood but any boys interested in attending a Catholic secondary school.[178] In the adjacent village of Montour Falls, the Franciscan Friars of the Atonement had in 1948 purchased the property of the ninety-year-old Cook Academy —a private school which had started out as "People's College." The "Graymoor" Friars refurbished the property at a cost of a quarter-million dollars to serve as a minor seminary of their own order. The Bishop of Rochester dedicated it on November 30, 1949.[179]

It was also in 1948 that the Italian-American Capuchin Franciscans of the Province of the Stigmata of St. Francis bought the Italianate Nester villa at Geneva, also to serve their own seminary needs. Archbishop Amleto G. Cicognani, the apostolic delegate to the United States, presided at the dedication on October 12, 1949, Bishop Kearney delivering the sermon. On the occasion of this visit to the Rochester Diocese, Archbishop Cicognani was escorted by the Bishop on a tour of several diocesan churches and institutions.[180]

Catholic lay organizations continued to be active throughout the 1940's. One new to the postwar period was the Catholic War Veterans. Holy Rosary parish in Rochester was the first to establish a C.W.V. post—August 12, 1946. Bishop William R. Arnold, of the Military Ordinariate in New York, conferred the charter on Holy Rosary Memorial Post #942 three months later.[181] The second post inaugurated in the Diocese—and the first outside the see-city—was the C.W.V. unit at St. Alphonsus Church, Auburn.[182] In 1949, the ten posts in Monroe County underwrote a series of Catholic Information Talks for prospective converts, conducted at Hotel Seneca under the direction of Father Richard Tormey, assistant editor of the *Catholic Courier Journal*.[183]

On September 29, 1945, a diocesan sodality union was organized, and Father Joseph J. O'Connell was named its moderator.[184] Boy Scouting also received a new lease on life when a diocesan-wide lay committee on scouting was set up by Bishop Kearney on June 8, 1947, under the leadership of Mr. Louis A. Langie, Sr.[185] The Holy Name Society, enlarged by the return of the servicemen, renewed its diocesan rallies. At the first postwar candlelight assembly in Red Wing Stadium, Rochester, on October 6, 1946, the Holy Name Union paid tribute to thirty-four diocesan service chaplains who had returned to their peacetime posts. A few months before, the same diocesan union had taken a public stand against the proposed removal from office of J. Edgar Hoover, the strong and respected head of the Federal Bureau of Investigation.[186]

Largest and most active among the lay groups was the Diocesan Council of Catholic Women. This organization not only took care of the Thanksgiving Clothing drive; it also opened the Catholic Information Center in the Columbus Civic Center; launched the Pre-Cana Conferences (for engaged couples) and the Cana Conferences (for married couples); and established the Mothers' Circles. These last three programs remained under its supervision from the mid-1940's to 1958, when Father Gerald E. Dunn was put in charge of them as director of a Family Life Bureau.[187]

The presentation in Rochester of two "C-class" movies in 1946-1947, called forth a summons from Bishop Kearney to the Legion of Decency to mount a protest. In the second case, that of "Forever Amber", the Rochester Commissioner of Public Safety banned the film. Since it had already been passed by the State Board of Review, the theater people secured a judicial decision that the Rochester Commissioner had overstepped his authority. Thereupon the Catholic War Veterans picketed the theater. In the following year, the State Court of Appeals ruled that a local Commissioner can ban a film passed by the State Authority.[188]

In these film controversies, the *Catholic Courier* played a prominent role. Father John S. Randall, managing editor since 1942, and Father Patrick J. Flynn, editor from 1943 to 1958, were both (to use the title of Father Flynn's column) "On Guard"—prompt to speak out on such issues as birth control, social justice, juvenile delinquency, anti-Catholicism, and general public morals. In 1944, the diocesan paper was honored by election to the Audit Bureau of Circulation; by May, 1945, it had a paid circulation of 25,980 copies; and in 1947-1948— not without some initial difficulties—it acquired a press of its own.[189] The American Catholic press has improved greatly in techniques and expertise since 1950; but even in the 1940's the *Catholic Courier* practiced a good practical journalism, and when it was in controversy its opinions often had a strong impact on the whole Rochester community. The "Sunday Edition of the *Catholic Courier*" was the most effective of the several diocesan Catholic radio programs. This continuation of the WHAM "Catholic Hour" won a wide audience after 1947, when Father Richard Tormey, assistant editor of the newspaper, presented an able commentary on the news from a Catholic point of view. When WHAM-TV opened in 1949, the emphasis in broadcasting quickly shifted from radio to television. Since the Diocese had never been able to finance radio programs, it was all the more unable to buy television time. Hence the more recent local Catholic broadcasts have been on free radio (or occasionally free video) time. To this there has been one exception. On March 4, 1950, Father Joseph Cirrincione, pastor of St. Francis of Assisi Church, Rochester, started the Family Rosary for Peace over radio station WSAY: a half-hour recitation of the Rosary. This has continued to the present day as a paid program, supported by listeners. It is now accessible to the whole Diocese.[190]

But let us stop merely cataloguing news and views, and turn to some deceased representatives of the early Kearney era. For a diocesan history is essentially the history of the people of a diocese, however much it must dwell on the events in which those persons were engaged.

Take, for instance, Mrs. Anthony Battaglia Barone, an Italian-born parishioner of Assumption Church, Mount Morris. In 1942 she calculated that she had walked 5,000 miles to and from church in her years of daily Mass attendance.[191] Or take the stern but devoted diocesan chancellor, Msgr. William F. Bergan, whose untimely death in 1947 put an end to a life of service.[192] Another notable priest was the jolly Father Gerald Brennan (1890-1962), pastor of St. Bridget's and author of a dozen internationally known children's books.[193] Distinguished Rochester laymen included John P. Boylan (1875-1960), president of the Rochester Telephone Corporation and a Cathedral trustee[194]; and two able lawyers: Eugene Dwyer, diocesan attorney and civic leader (1873-1946); and the saintly and philanthropic James E. Cuff (1890-1948).[195] To represent Auburn, we can mention clothier John J. Leo (1879-1960), outstanding citizen and Catholic. To represent Elmira, we can choose Cornelius J. Milliken (1900-1956), model editor and father. And few could represent Waverly better than Miss Mary Muldoon, who died in 1958 after years of dedicated work as public school principal and promoter of community causes.[196]

German-born Brother Fridolin, S.V.D. (1868-1939) became well-known for the Rosary Grottoes that he crafted at St. Michael's Mission House above Hemlock Lake. A devout man who had always prayed to die on Friday in honor of Christ's passion, he was granted that wish. [197] J. John Hassett (1873-1947), a leading lawyer and financier of Elmira, combined business skill with a truly Christian family life. "No good cause," said Bishop Kearney of Hassett, "was too small to attract his attention."[198] Of another generation was Sister Lucienne St. Laurent, a novice assigned in 1941 to the Sisters of St. Joan of Arc at St. Bernard's Seminary. Aged only seventeen, she shortly contracted a fatal case of spinal meningitis; but by a special privilege she was allowed to make her religious profession on her deathbed. She died five weeks later, offering her gentle young life for the sanctification of priests. [199]

A better-known nun was Irish-born Mother Rose Miriam Smyth (1880-1963), superior general of the Rochester Sisters of St. Joseph from 1939 to 1951. We have already mentioned the particular interest Mother Rose Miriam took in Negro work and in the foundation of a mission school and hospital in Selma, Alabama.[200] Another prominent layman was Alphonse J. ("Al") Sigl (1883-1966), folksy radio commentator and benefactor of the community, who merited the title "Mr. Rochester," not only for founding the Legion of Blood Donors, but for aiding the war on cerebral palsy and multiple sclerosis, and for publishing the needs of almost every good cause or deserving person. Thus did this Catholic layman show how one can infuse true Christian charity into one's daily work.[201] And finally, we name the self-effacing William G. Wynn (1885-1943), the postal clerk who was a prime promoter of the Diocesan Retreat League and of the Nocturnal Adoration Society.[202]

We need list no more. This sampling is sufficient to show the sort of response that Bishop Kearney could receive from the faithful Catholics of his Diocese, cleric and layman, rich and poor, executive and mystic.

Contests over church-state relations were not wanting in the 1940's. In the matter of bus transportation for parochial school students, several boards of education in the twelve counties refused to cooperate until they were finally ordered to by the State Commissioner of Education.[203] The constitutionality of this New York busing law was implicitly upheld by the U.S. Supreme Court in 1947 in the Everson Case.[204] Another "auxiliary service" permitted by the New York State constitution of 1938 was "health and welfare services for all children." Moved by this apparent legal trend to give to Catholic pupils more than they had usually been granted out of government funds, the majority of the American Catholic bishops began to change their approach from one which (like McQuaid's) sought no aid because it would not be granted, to one which sought aid because there was a fighting chance they might get it.

This new strategy prompted the hierarchy, in 1949, to protest against a federal law proposed by Rep. Graham A. Barden which would have excluded parochial school children from federal educational benefits. Cardinal Spellman of New York denounced Congressman Barden as an "apostle of bigotry," and a heated controversy arose. Bishop Kearney also urged that his diocesans write their congressional representatives to oppose the bill as unfair. The bill was subsequently defeated.[205] While the Cardinal's accusation of personal bigotry was perhaps indelicate, Mr. Barden had given, in other contexts, more than one indication of his distrust of Catholicism.[206] Even more clearly anti-Catholic was the manifesto issued on January 11, 1948 by a newly formed pressure group, Protestants and Other Americans United for the Separation of Church and State—better known as the P.O.A.U. The signers were prominent Protestant ministers from across the nation— worthy men, but apparently, like one of their number, Methodist Bishop D. Bromley Oxnam, men more or less obsessed by the "menace" of Catholicism. P.O.A.U. stated a basic principle with which Catholic Americans would certainly agree: the defense of our constitutional premise of separation of church and state. But then it went on into less reasonable specifics, demanding: "the immediate discontinuance of the ambassadorship to the Papal head of the Roman Catholic Church" (as we have indicated, much ink had been spilled and many a Protestant pulpit had been pounded over this subject since 1939, when Roosevelt named the Episcopalian financier, Mr. Myron C. Taylor, as his personal representative to the pope); the revocation of any laws that sanction public funds for church schools; the reconsideration of laws granting free textbooks and bus transportation to "pupils of parochial schools," etc. Those who proclaimed the Manifesto asserted that they were not "motivated by anti-Catholic animus"; but discerning readers found its discriminatory attitude transparent. The Lutheran scholar, Dr. Jaroslav Pelikan, has called P.O.A.U. one of the "polite forms of Anti-Catholicism."[207] As such it was an updated and more genteel A.P.A.ism.

Although the Manifesto was broadcast nationally, it had particular repercussions in Rochester for the reason that the president of P.O.A.U. was the Reverend Dr. Edwin McNeill Poteat, head of the Colgate Rochester Divinity School. Bishop Kearney reacted strongly to the action, publicly lamenting that as a result of the Manifesto, "Rochester becomes a sort of national center for bigotry and religious hatred . . ." His vicar general, Msgr. William M. Hart, long chairman of Rochester's Interfaith Goodwill Committee, was likewise deeply shocked. In an editorial in the *Catholic Courier,* he grieved that Rochester, for years known as a city of interfaith good will, should "in its shame now become the city of Interfaith Bad Will." Nor would he be mollified. When asked by local ministers to discuss the issues raised by the Manifesto, he declared: "We Catholics are not fooled. We know that we have been insulted." And, indeed, the text of the Manifesto had by that time already been endorsed by the two hundred members of the Pastors' Union of Rochester, with only one dissenting vote—that of Canon Arthur R. Cowdery of the Rochester Episcopal Diocese.[208]

One of the Manifesto's signatories was Dr. Charles C. Morrison, editor of the *Christian Century*. In that magazine he rebuked Bishop Kearney, the Knights of Columbus, and other Catholic leaders, for raising an "indecent controversy." His rebuke brought forth from the *New World,* Chicago archdiocesan paper, the retort that if anybody had raised an "indecent controversy," it was Protestants and Other Americans United.[209] In Rochester, the contretemps soon subsided, thanks in no small measure to the retirement of Dr. Poteat from the Divinity School presidency in June, 1948, for reasons of ill health, and the appointment of the able and friendly Reverend Dr. Wilbour E. Saunders to succeed him. But the resolution of the Pastors' Union of Rochester apparently still stood, and Catholic advocacy of interfaith confidence was for some time considered a fruitless effort.

If the intercredal antagonism generated by this incident finally evaporated, the clouds of the international Cold War between Communism and the Democratic World would not be dissipated. In 1946, when Tito's Yugoslavia brought to trial Aloysius Stepinac, Catholic Archbishop of Zagreb, American Catholics were very disturbed, and Rochester's *Catholic Courier Journal* undertook to get the signatures of 500 editors and writers connected with the American Catholic press to a protest sent to President Harry S Truman.[210] Three years later, on February 3, 1949, Communist Hungary opened a similar trial of Cardinal Josef Mindszenty, Catholic Primate of Hungary. On that occasion, Bishop Kearney, by a circular letter, asked his Rochester diocesans to join with all American Catholics on February 6th in a special day of prayer for the imprisoned Cardinal and his country.[211] Because world Communists had long since observed May 1st as a day of protest and agitation, American Catholics decided to make May Day, 1947, a day of contrasting prayer to Our Lady for Russia. In the Rochester Diocese, the Bishop requested outdoor Marian ceremonies, including the ringing of church bells at 5:30 P.M. One thousand people gathered that day at Old St. Mary's alone; and the Bishop personally conducted the recitation of the rosary over radio station WHAM.[212] Nor was the cause of the United Nations forgotten. Bishop Kearney had prayers for its success offered in all diocesan churches on the annual "U.N. Sunday."[213]

Then came the disturbing news of September 23, 1949. President Truman made the dramatic announcement to our nation: "We have evidence that within recent weeks an atomic explosion occurred within the U.S.S.R." Before that, the United States alone had possessed the secret of manufacturing the catastrophic weapon, and that fact had given us the upper hand over the principal Communist state. Now Russia faced our country as one possessed of equal arms—arms by which the possessors could destroy each other and the whole world. No wonder the Vatican newspaper, *Osservatore Romano,* straightway begged both the U.S.A. and the U.S.S.R. to renounce all destructive use of atomic power.[214]

CHAPTER FOURTEEN

RENEWAL

A T THE moment when these lines are written, no nation but ours that possesses the atomic "secret"—and there are now several Marxist and non-Marxist nations—has ventured to use its annihilating weaponry. The period 1950-1967 was nonetheless an explosive one in several other aspects.

So far as actual conflict goes, the United States became involved in two small, agonizing and very unpopular East Asiatic wars. The Korean Conflict ran from 1950 to 1953. The Vietnam War entered its critical stage in mid-1965 and by mid-1967 seemed even farther from resolution. In both cases our national commitments obliged us to intervene to thwart further conquests by Communist China. However, the old-time, single-minded patriotism of the people which had earlier guaranteed our government popular support in its foreign wars had largely given way to a more critical and pacifist mood. On the other hand, many valorous young Americans still showed by their sweat and blood a conviction of the justice of our cause in Asia.

In neither of these latter-day contests have statistics been kept of Rochester diocesans in the armed forces. But during the Korean Conflict the *Courier Journal* reported the death in action of more than thirty local Catholic servicemen, and there were doubtless others who were never reported to the paper. Most of the casualties recorded were, of course, from metropolitan Rochester: for example, William D. Culhane, Anthony DeManno, and Joseph Mura.[1] John Fallat was the first Auburn Catholic and the first Auburnian to give his life in Korea.[2] Among the Genevan victims was Captain William J. Glunz, a West Point graduate. Among those from the Southern Tier was Lt. Commander William Bell of Watkins.[3] Several of the area Catholics merited battle awards: William Bassett, Jr., of Rochester, the Distinguished Flying Cross; Louis A. Visco of Geneva, the Silver Star Medal, William J. Flynn of Rochester, the Bronze Star Medal.[4]

Sixteen Rochester diocesan priests were in the service during the Korean period—five of them Reserve chaplains who had been recalled to duty. But only four of the sixteen were assigned to Korea itself, and of these only three were in combat. Father Bernard L. Hickey accompanied the First Marine Corps unit to land on the Korean peninsula. For his efforts there he won the Bronze Star Medal and other commendations.[5] The Bronze Star was also awarded to Army Reserve Chaplain David B. Singerhoff, who was attached to the 115th Medical Battalion.[6] A younger priest, Paratrooper Chaplain Joseph Natale, spent eleven months in Korea with the 45th Infantry Division. He subsequently became a member of the "Century Club" by completing one hundred parachute jumps.[7] Meanwhile, Navy Chaplain Joseph F. Cloonan distinguished himself in the non-combat zone by organizing charitable work for the benefit of needy Koreans.[8]

As in World War II, Bishop Kearney encouraged his diocesan soldiery in the fulfillment of their duty. But he also raised his voice in constant appeals to pray for peace, and urged his people to donate their blood to the wounded through the American Red Cross.[9]

The Vietnam War was to be even more frustrating and controversial than the Korean Conflict. Pacifists of many hues denounced American involvement and the structure of the Selective Service, sometimes with considerable noise and disorder. This was an attitude quite incomprehensible to the Bishop of Rochester. At an interfaith observance on August 16, 1956, he declared: "We need prayers for Vietnam. Last week they interfered with a train taking American boys who were willing to give their lives for their companions, to that country. We need prayers, too, for these enemies within."[10]

But the American mood towards war had without doubt altered along the years, and many earnest citizens of the less demonstrative type were ready to campaign for the abolition of all war. Catholics among them were especially inspired by the cry of anguish which Pope Paul VI uttered on October 4, 1965 before the United Nations in New York: "No more war, war never again!"[11]

The struggle in Vietnam continued to mount, nevertheless—a grievous but apparently inescapable evil, though prayers for a peaceful solution continued to be offered at the behest not only of Bishop Kearney but of President Lyndon B. Johnson.[12] Once more, the Rochester Diocese lost some of its finest young men in battle, like Marine Corpsmen John B. Tette, John L. Ehrmantraut, Jr., Robert J. Van Reypen, and Ralph Scheib.[13] Of the eleven Rochester diocesan chaplains in uniform in 1966, two were detailed to Vietnam: Father Gerard J. Gefell and Frederick W. Straub. Father Straub was in the thick of the action as a *Padre* of the "Green Berets." Seriously wounded in May, 1966, he was flown back to Walter Reed Hospital in Washington. Here President Johnson paid him a personal visit to pin on him the medal of the Purple Heart. He was later awarded the Bronze Star Medal as well.[14]

Our nation had other trying hours, too, with the hydra of international Communism. In April, 1961, there was the ill-starred invasion of the "Bay of Pigs", quickly repulsed by Cuba's Communist dictator, Fidel Castro, and in 1962, the Cuban "missile crisis." In August, 1961, came the new threat of conflict at Berlin, symbolized by East Germany's famous "Wall."

But in the midst of these unsettling events there were others of unalloyed glory. Such was the series of triumphs of the Space Age: explorations of the outer universe by the astronauts of the Mercury and the Gemini space programs. Such, too, was the brief but memorable career of the nation's first Catholic president, John Fitzgerald Kennedy. This is not the place to recount President Kennedy's regime. We shall only say that the Catholics of the Rochester Diocese, like most American Catholics, were happy to have "one of their own" elected to the office of chief executive, and even happier to see him discharge his duties with great competence. And if his tragic assassination on November 22, 1963 caused the whole world to mourn this symbol of young hope, Catholics would always be grateful for his memory. As Bishop Kearney wrote: "And the tear that we shed, though in secret it rolls, will long keep his memory green in our souls."[15] For in winning the election Kennedy had destroyed the last great taboo of nativism. An American Catholic *could* be chosen president—a Catholic, and by the same token, a deserving member of any American minority religion or race. No longer would American Catholics have any warrant for believing that they were second-class citizens who could prove their patriotism only on the field of battle.

But it was not solely in international politics that the era 1950-1967 was explosive. Explosive, too, was the growth and movement of peoples; explosive, the great social crises that arose, particularly in our country. Most unexpected of all was the explosive leaven of the Second Vatican Council, which shook the Church itself with a creative might. The renewal it sparked was accompanied by many strange phenomena, and these were to prove a disturbing factor during the final months in office of the fifth Bishop of Rochester.

1. THE QUICKENING PACE.

In 1950, the *Official Catholic Directory* reported a population of 320,700 for the Diocese of Rochester. The 1967 issue of the same book gave a figure of 361,790. But a door-to-door diocesan census taken up in the spring of 1965 resulted in a quite different tally. It indicated that in the twelve diocesan counties Catholics numbered 449,198, and thus constituted 36% of the total population.[16]

110

JAMES EDWARD KEARNEY
Fifth Bishop of Rochester
1937-1967
Died January 12, 1977

111   **BISHOP KEARNEY PONTIFICAL MASS**
Sampson Naval Training Station, July 4, 1943

112   **INVESTITURE OF MONSIGNORI, NOVEMBER 11, 1947**

(Seated): *Wm. M. Hart, P.A.; Bishop Kearney; Wm. F. Bergan, P.A.; (missing: J. F. Goggin, P.A.).* (First Row): *Jas. C. McAniff; Edward M. Lyons; Edmund A. Rawlinson; John S. Randall; Gerald C. Lambert.* (Second Row): *Wm. E. Cowen; Jos. J. Baierl; Geo. W. Eckl; Francis J. Lane; Wm. E. McPadden; F. Wm. Stauder; Adolfo F. Gabbani; Thos. F. Connors.* (Third Row): *John B. Sullivan.* (Fourth Row): *Wm. J. Brien; Jos. A. Balcerak; John Conway; Edward J. Byrne; Lawrence B. Casey; Wilfred T. Craugh; Walter J. Donoghue.*

114   BLESSING OF MOTHERS
AND BABIES
SS. Peter and Paul Church, Elmira, May 13, 1945

113   THE BISHOP
AND FRIENDS
*(with Msgri. Leslie G. Whalen
and John E. Maney)*

116
AT VATICAN COUNCIL II,
1962
*Bishop Kearney and Casey,
with Msgr. Maney and
Msgr. Richard K. Burns*

115   CONSECRATION, SACRED HEART
CATHEDRAL
*(Bishop Casey and Msgr. W. T. Craugh, M.C.)
October 25, 1961*

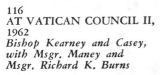

117
LAWRENCE B. CASEY
Titular Bishop of Cea and Auxiliary
Bishop of Rochester 1953-1966
Fifth Bishop of Paterson 1966-1977
Died June 15, 1977

118   ABBOT M. GERARD
McGINLEY, O.C.S.O.

119   MSGR. WILLIAM F. BERGAN
Chancellor, 1936-1947

120   FATHER LEO C. MOONEY

121   CORNELIUS J. MILLIKEN, SR.
(Elmira)

122   JOHN T. LEO   *(Auburn)*

123   "AL" SIGL

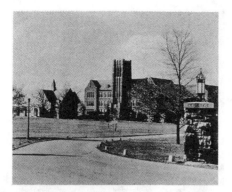

124 NAZARETH COLLEGE, 1942

125 ST. JOHN FISHER
COLLEGE, 1952

126 CATHERINE McAULEY
COLLEGE, 1959

127 BECKET HALL, 1967

128 ST. ANDREW'S
SEMINARY, 1950
(King's Preparatory, 1967)

129 DE SALES HIGH SCHOOL
Geneva, 1951

130   McQUAID JESUIT HIGH
SCHOOL, 1955

131   ST. JOSEPH'S HOSPITAL
ELMIRA

132   ST. JAMES MERCY
HOSPITAL, HORNELL
(Photo 1967)

133   ST. MARY'S HOSPITAL
(Photo 1967)

134   ST. ANN'S HOME
(1963)

135   A "COTTAGE"
St. Joseph's Villa,
1943

136   **ST. MARY'S**
of the Lake,
ONTARIO
1967

137   **ST. CHARLES BORROMEO,**
GREECE
1967

138   **ST. JOHN THE**
EVANGELIST, GREECE,
1965

139   **ST. MARGARET MARY,**
APALACHIN,
1967

While the discrepancy of 100,000 in these figures can be attributed in part to the inexactness of earlier estimates, there had without a doubt been a considerable diocesan growth since 1950. Larger families became popular again after World War II. There were also many new immigrants admitted to the country after the passage of the Refugee Relief Act of 1953. A number of people from Italy settled in the Diocese, sponsored by the Rochester Chapter of the American Committee on Italian Immigration.[17] Exiled Lithuanians to the number of four hundred were resettled in Rochester, thanks to the efforts of not only the clergy of St. George's Church, but also of the late Mr. Pranas Saladzius, a Lithuanian DP who himself had come to Rochester only in 1949.[18]

Rochester's Hungarian colony had never been large, but it increased considerably after World War II. The earliest Hungarian immigrants had arrived after World War I. A much larger group, displaced persons, joined them after the close of the second World War. Perhaps a third of the whole group were Catholics. Through the hospitality of Father Leo C. Mooney, pastor of St. Patrick's Church, the Catholic Hungarians began to gather in that church from at least 1953 on, to celebrate their national feastdays with Mass and a social program. Subsequently Hungarian-speaking priests were persuaded to offer Mass for them monthly. The first to do so were Piarist Fathers from Derby, New York; later on, a Hungarian Jesuit attached to McQuaid Jesuit High School in Rochester took care of their needs. This tided the newcomers over until they could become better acquainted with English.[19]

Then in October, 1956, the Hungarians in the homeland rose in revolt in the hope of throwing off the Communist yoke. After their tragic defeat, thousands took flight from the luckless land, many of them coming to the United States and to Rochester. A mighty sympathy had welled up in America for the valiant Hungarian freedom-fighters, so all Americans extended to them a welcoming hand. By mid-November Rochester Catholic Charities had set up an Emergency Fund for Hungarian Refugees, to which Bishop Kearney contributed $1,000.00. Working with the Hungarian Relief Committee of Rochester, the Catholic agency was soon ready to receive the first fifty refugee families.[20] Although most of the newly arrived were resettled in Monroe County, others were relocated elsewhere in the twelve counties. Thus, Istvan Toth and his family and Lazlo Vamos had jobs waiting for them in Clifton Springs.[21] Gabriel Katona and his wife went to Corning, where Katona was given employment by the Corning Glass Works.[22]

To the immigrants we must add the "in-migrants": American minority groups that moved in from elsewhere in this country. The largest of the groups was the southern Negroes. Few of these were Catholic. On the other hand, practically all the Puerto Ricans were of Catholic background. Between 1950 and 1958, the total of Puerto Rican in-migration to the continental United States rose from 301,000 to 849,-000. When the big influx from Puerto Rico began in the 1940's, most of those who fled from their impoverished island moved into the scarcely less squalid locale of Manhattan's Harlem. After the late 1940's, however, the federal government saw to it that more of the Spanish-speaking newcomers were resettled outside New York City and New York State. By January, 1959, an estimated 4,500 Puerto Ricans were living in Rochester.[23] Elsewhere in the Diocese there were only two other sizable colonies of them: about 500 at Geneva, and about 200 at Newark, New York. In more recent times, with the improvement of economic conditions in the Puerto Rican Commonwealth, a good many Puerto Rican in-migrants have returned home. Today, many who come into western New York are merely migrant workers, brought up from the Caribbean for the harvest season. Nevertheless, a large percentage of the Puerto Ricans who migrated have made upstate New York their permanent home. Since their initial incomes were low and their knowledge of English slim, they tended to congregate with their fellow *Latinos* in the poorest neighborhoods of Inner City.

However, the most potent factor in changing the recent pattern of church administration has not been the increased population but the postwar flight into suburbia. Between 1950 and 1965, Bishop Kearney established twenty-two new parishes. Only six of these were non-suburban: St. Philip Neri, Rochester (full-fledged parish, 1959); St. Catherine, Mendon (mission, 1902; parish, 1956); St. Francis Solanus, Interlaken, Seneca County (mission, 1875; parish, 1956); St. Pius X, Van Etten, Chemung County (parish, 1954); St. Mary Magdalen, Wolcott, Wayne County (mission, 1940; parish, 1954); and Holy Cross, Dryden, Tompkins County (parish, 1962, comprising "the Dryden Mission", 1950, and St. Patrick's Mission, McLean, 1851). (The Bishop entrusted the administration of the Interlaken and Van Etten churches to the Capuchin Fathers of Interlaken.)

Most of the new suburban parishes were close to Rochester. Here the people in growing numbers were migrating into the surrounding townships: Brighton, Chili, Gates, Irondequoit, Ogden, Penfield, Perinton, Pittsford and Webster, and particularly into Greece and Henrietta.[24] But there was also a tendency to fly the city even in the smaller communities within the twelve diocesan counties.

Brighton received two new parishes: St. Thomas More (1953)

and Our Lady Queen of Peace (1960). The construction of St. Thomas More Church was long delayed by a legal contest between the parish corporation and the Zoning Board of the Town of Brighton. The parish finally won in 1956 through an important judicial decision of the State's highest court.[25]

Catholics in Chili had belonged since 1854 to the rural mission of St. Fechan. In 1954, Bishop Kearney transformed this mission into a parish under the name of St. Pius X. A year later he set up Christ the King parish in Irondequoit. St. Rita parish was established in West Webster in 1950. To the south of it, and partially in Penfield, was Holy Spirit parish, established in 1965. In Perinton was St. John of Rochester, which dates from 1962. Guardian Angels, begun in 1960, was assigned the northern portion of the township of Henrietta. Four new parishes were founded in the Town of Greece: Our Lady of Mercy (1957), St. Lawrence (1959), St. Mark (1964) and Holy Name of Jesus (1964). Even the slicing off of new parochial foundations did not give much relief to some of the older suburban churches. Good Shepherd in Henrietta had to expand its facilities to take care of its own parishioners, and those of its mission, St. Joseph's, in Rush, and its mission station, St. Blaise at Ballantyne Bridge. St. John the Evangelist and Our Mother of Sorrows in Greece and St. Theodore in Gates could not build fast enough to accommodate the new families that kept moving in.

Outside Monroe County, Sacred Heart Church at Auburn (1956) was a suburban parish; so, too, was St. Catherine of Siena, at Cayuga Heights outside Ithaca (1960). Immaculate Heart of Mary parish, Painted Post (1952) was largely suburban to Corning (even as St. Mary's in Horseheads [parish, 1879, renamed St. Mary Our Mother in 1965], was largely suburban to Elmira). But the fastest-growing suburbia in the Southern Tier was in the environs of Owego. Here the people were spreading out from the highly industrial metropolitan district of the nearby "Triple Cities" of Broome County (Syracuse Diocese): Binghamton-Endicott-Johnson City. To serve the influx, the pastor of Owego, Father William J. O'Brien, set up in 1955 the mission of St. Margaret Mary in the village of Apalachin, Tioga County. In the following year the new mission was given its own little church—a remodeled churchlet of the Gospel Fellowship Association. In 1959, Bishop Kearney found it necessary to erect this young mission into a parish—the remotest of all diocesan parishes from the see city; and in 1967 the founding pastor, Father Valentine A. Jankowiak, completed a new octagonal church building seating 650.[26]

Two other missions were established during the same epoch. Under the auspices of St. Mary of the Lake parish in Watkins Glen, the mission of St. Benedict opened in a basement chapel at Odessa, Schuyler County. The completed church was dedicated in 1965. In 1963, the pastor of Cato and Red Creek converted the old Odd Fellows' building at Fair Haven (Cayuga County) into St. Jude's, a summer chapel for vacationers at the neighboring Lake Ontario beach. (A third chapel, Immaculate Heart of Mary, at Bushnell's Basin [1949] continued to be used as a shrine and chapel of ease of St. Louis Church, Pittsford, until it fell under the jurisdiction of the new parish of St. John of Rochester in 1962.)

At the same time, the Diocese of Rochester "lost" three of its parishes. St. Patrick's, Dansville, was merged with St. Mary's, Dansville, in 1959. Assumption parish in Mount Morris was amalgamated with St. Patrick's parish, Mount Morris, in 1961. And in 1966, as the result of the establishment of a Melkite Rite diocese for the United States under its own bishop, Most Reverend Justin Najmy, St. Nicholas Melkite Church in Rochester was officially withdrawn from the care of the bishop of Rochester and entrusted to the prelate of this new Greek-rite exarchy. It would take some time, however, before details of the transfer could be worked out.

Several of the new churches constructed in the Diocese during these years of postwar expansion possessed real architectural distinction. In the older vein were St. Margaret Mary, Irondequoit (1950) and St. Vincent de Paul, Corning (1955), both the work of Rochester architect Joseph P. Flynn. Architects working in the 1960's tried, but seldom with full success, to anticipate the structural directions which the Vatican Council's reform of the liturgy would presumably take. Several of the new local church buildings were thus "transitional" in layout, like the striking rural church of St. Mary's of the Lake, Ontario (Ribson and Roberts, Rochester, 1966). Bridging this transition were four notable buildings by the New York architect, J. Sanford Shanley: St. Louis, Pittsford (1958); St. Ambrose, Rochester (1960); St. Thomas the Apostle, Irondequoit (1965); and St. Charles Borromeo, Greece (completed 1967). Highly original designs by the Rochester architect James H. Johnson include the arresting, controversial, and very practical St. John the Evangelist Church in Greece (1965). Begun a little later than most of these and therefore somewhat abler to incorporate new liturgical requirements, were the following structures, unfinished by June, 1967: the quadrilateral Our Mother of Sorrows Church, Greece (Stickle International of Cleveland, architects); the octagonal and plastic-spired Church of the Annunciation, Rochester (Todd and Giroux of Rochester, architects); and the multi-domed Church of the Holy Name of Jesus, Greece (Genovese and Maddalene of New York, architects).

It was far more difficult to adapt older church buildings to the new rubrical norms and counsels initiated by the Second Vatican Council. Some pastors who had only recently spent a considerable sum to set up stone "liturgical" altars facing away from the people, suddenly found their renovations out-of-date. A case in point was Sacred Heart Church in Rochester. On June 21, 1952, the Holy See, by a special decree, constituted this "pro-cathedral" the official cathedral church of the Diocese of Rochester.[27] As a cathedral, Sacred Heart deserved finer appointments than it possessed. Hence the rector, Bishop Casey, attended to the redecoration of the interior and the erecting, in the apse, of a rich new marble altar backed by a bronze figure of the Sacred Heart.[28] This was in 1957. On October 25, 1961, he solemnly consecrated the church itself at a stirring ceremony.[29] But in 1963-1964 the revisionist liturgical decrees stemming from the Second Vatican Council made their appearance, favoring main altars constructed *closer* to the people. So Bishop Casey felt obliged to install a second altar of matching marble, table-like in its dimensions, at the front edge of the sanctuary. Most pastors contented themselves with placing a temporary wooden altar facing the people at the entrance of the chancel. Once the quick succession of decrees began to give a more definite picture of what was most desirable in sanctuary arrangement, those in charge of churches and chapels gradually began to undertake a more radical rearrangement, including the re-positioning of the tabernacle and the removal of the Communion railing.

The Diocese made great strides in the 1950's and 1960's in school expansion, at least in higher and secondary education.

Sister Teresa Marie O'Connor (1873-1952), as perennial first dean of Nazareth College, had seen that institution develop from a small seed to a flourishing tree; but she would have had difficulty imagining its expansion after her death. New buildings were erected; others, still more ambitious, were planned; and by 1967 the number of students had risen to 1,200.

St. John Fisher College was formally launched on its career on September 17, 1951. The first president, Father John F. Murphy, C.S.B., and the first dean, Father John P. O'Meara, C.S.B., aimed from the start at achieving high academic standards. The maintenance of these standards was a principal reason for the rapid growth of the student body, which by fall 1966 had reached 1,126. As early as 1962, the College announced a master plan for many additional buildings, to be completed by 1975.[30] In 1964, the Basilian Fathers opened a house of studies on the fringe of the campus to house college student aspirants to their own religious order.[31]

Unfortunately, smaller colleges like these two, whether religiously affiliated or independent, found themselves in a less advantageous position as time went on, because of the great growth of State colleges supported by public funds. This individual weakness prompted Nazareth College and St. John Fisher, already geographical neighbors, to seek strength in union by pooling their academic resources. On January 27, 1961, the presidents of the institutions, Sister Helen Daniel Malone and Father Charles J. Lavery, C.S.B., announced the conclusion of a cooperative plan by which the students of Nazareth and Fisher might take the courses and use the educational facilities of both of the colleges.[32]

Meanwhile, the Sisters of Mercy initiated, in their own motherhouse, Catherine McAuley Junior College. Oriented along the lines recommended by the new National Sister Formation Conference, McAuley offered a liberal arts education geared to prospective teachers. In May, 1954, it received a temporary "charter" from the State acknowledging it as a college of transfer status with the right to confer the degree of Associate in Arts. The absolute "charter" was granted in 1959. In 1962 the degrees privilege was augmented by the concession to grant the grade of Associate in Applied Science. At the same time, the school was permitted to call itself simply Catherine McAuley College. Lay students were first admitted on a part-time basis in the winter season of 1961, for in 1959 the Sisters had constructed a new College wing attached to the Motherhouse, at a cost of $1.35 million. The College building was especially equipped with a reading laboratory and speech clinic, and with the apparatus needed for testing and guidance. Thousands of children of the area were to be given the benefit of these clinical and laboratory services. Of course, the full-time students at Catherine McAuley are normally all members of the Mercy community, who upon the completion of the course at their own college, transfer to Nazareth or elsewhere for the remaining years required for the baccalaureate degree.[33]

In the period 1950-1960, the Diocese of Rochester became accustomed to mammoth drives for educational expansion. The campaign of 1952 sought $3 million for secondary schools, and was conducted throughout the twelve diocesan counties. The campaign of 1960, though restricted to Monroe County, aimed at a still higher figure—$4 million—also for high school construction. But the largest postwar drive, and the largest in the history of the Diocese, was the $9 million Joint College Fund—a solicitation for new buildings to be constructed for Nazareth, St. John Fisher and the Diocese. Nazareth sought an auditorium and fine-arts building; St. John Fisher needed a library, science building, and student center; and the Diocese wanted funds to build a diocesan house of studies for college-level seminarians on St. John Fisher property. The campaign, tied in with Bishop Kearney's eighty-first birthday, and ably chaired by the Rochester food merchant Mr. Robert B. Wegman, achieved an almost unexpected victory. The final tally of pledges, reported on December 1, 1965, showed a figure pledged of $10,532,960.00. Two factors had contributed immeasurably to this success. The first was the generous gifts of local industries.[34] The second was the skill of Rt. Rev. Monsignor John S. Randall, the diocesan specialist in planning. He had directed eight diocesan campaigns for funds since 1938, and this was the most difficult and therefore the most notable of all.

This "diocesan house of studies", which bore the official name of Becket Hall, requires an explanation. As we have already seen, the two seminaries of the Diocese divided between them the four years of the required college course. The freshman and sophomore years were attached to the four high school years at St. Andrew's. The junior and senior years were attached to the four final theological years at St. Bernard's. Both institutions were incorporated as St. Bernard's Seminary and College, and it was to the collegiate section that the State Regents had granted the right, by a temporary "charter," to award the degree of bachelor of arts. By 1965, however, there was a growing tendency in United States seminaries—one based largely on academic considerations—to break up this widely used "six-six" plan into a "four-four-four" arrangement, which would make a rigorous separation between high school, college, and theology departments. The college department thus detached could be set up as a separate college, or it could be attached to an already existing college in the form of a house of studies, the residents of which would qualify for degrees granted by the college of affiliation. Some dioceses chose the former course, others the latter.

St. Andrew's Seminary had occupied new quarters on Buffalo Road since 1950, and in 1958 it had enjoyed an enrollment, hitherto unequalled, of 289 students, many from dioceses other than Rochester.[35] But even in 1958 the thinking of educators was changing. In 1964, therefore, the diocesan officials and the officials of St. John Fisher College, after extensive discussion, decided to close the diocesan college department and to erect at St. John Fisher College a house of studies to be called Becket Hall (after St. Thomas Becket) for those preparing to enter St. Bernard's Seminary for theology.[36] The Reverend Joseph L. Hogan of St. Bernard's Seminary was named rector of the new student residence. When the program went into effect in September, 1965, Becket Hall was temporarily housed in the former St. Elizabeth Guild House at 1475 East Avenue. But thanks to the generous support of the faithful of the Diocese, ever loyal to their seminaries, the new Becket Hall adjacent to St. John Fisher on the Fairport Road, was soon under construction, with a view to opening in the fall of 1967.[37] Unlike the two local colleges, Becket Hall, as a clerical school, could not depend so extensively upon the many federal funds and state loans lately available to regular liberal arts colleges dedicated to training the laity.

The campaigns of 1952 and 1960 enabled the Diocese to make a Catholic high school education more widely available than ever before to the young people of the twelve-county district. The Bishop's Jubilee High School Fund Campaign of fall 1952, chaired by Mr. Robert E. Ginna of Rochester Gas and Electric, was tied in with Bishop Kearney's twentieth anniversary of consecration and fifteenth anniversary of assignment to Rochester. The total in pledges by mid-November was $4,505,158.00. Out of this was taken the cost of building McQuaid Jesuit High School in Rochester (for boys); Mount Carmel High School in Auburn (co-institutional); and Notre Dame High School in Elmira (coeducational, replacing Elmira Catholic High School). Sums from this fund were also earmarked to subsidize the construction of a new St. Agnes High School building in Rochester ($250,000.00); to liquidate the debt of DeSales High School in Geneva; and to be used as a "revolving fund" for other diocesan projects.[38]

McQuaid Jesuit High School opened under its first rector, Father James R. Barnett, S.J., in September, 1954. It temporarily occupied the old St. Patrick's School. But by the following September the new building on Clinton Avenue, South, was in readiness. Bishop Kearney dedicated it on September 25, 1955.[39] The Bishop had already dedicated the new St. Agnes High School for Girls, East River Road, on October 17, 1954. The new St. Agnes plant, still under the direction of the Sisters of St. Joseph, had cost $2.3 millions to construct.[40] Mount Carmel in Auburn was dedicated by the Bishop on September 18, 1955. This successor to Auburn Catholic High School was staffed by Carmelite Fathers and Rochester Sisters of St. Joseph, with Father Brendan Hourihan, O.Carm., as the pioneer principal.[41] Notre Dame High School in

Elmira was formally blessed by the Bishop on September 24, 1955. Its building had cost $1.6 million. The Rochester Sisters of Mercy were in charge.[42]

Rochester itself was now better provided with Catholic high school facilities, but there were still no Catholic secondary schools in the populous towns of Irondequoit and Greece. It was to take care of this remaining need that the 1960 drive was undertaken in September, 1960, with Mr. Harold F. Coleman, President of the Will Corporation, as chairman, and Mr. Carl S. Hallauer, of Bausch and Lomb, Incorporated, as head of a non-denominational Citizens' Committee. At the "Victory Rally" of the $4 million campaign, held in the War Memorial on November 30, 1960, the total pledged was reported at $5,-896,690.00. A very large segment of this came from corporate gifts: the Eastman Kodak Company, for example, contributed $250,000.00.[43]

As a result of this drive, the Diocese was able to open both Bishop Kearney High School (Irondequoit) and Cardinal Mooney High School (Greece) in September, 1962. Both of these, like Mount Carmel in Auburn, were co-institutional rather than coeducational: that is, the boys and girls had their classes apart, in separate wings of the same building. At Bishop Kearney High, the Irish Christian Brothers taught the boys, the School Sisters of Notre Dame, the girls. Brother Joseph M. Clark, C.F.C., was principal, and Sister M. Louis Whalen, S.S.N.D., was vice-principal. At Cardinal Mooney High, Brother James Madigan, C.S.C., was principal, and the Brothers of the Holy Cross to which he belonged instructed the boys; Sister M. Edwina Butler, R.S.M. was vice-principal, and the Rochester Sisters of Mercy, of which she was a member, instructed the girls. Bishop Kearney dedicated the new school named in his honor on April 28, 1963. On May 5, 1963, Bishop Casey dedicated the high school which memorialized his former mentor, Cardinal Edward Mooney.[44]

Finally, in 1966, St. Joseph's Business School, a long-established private commercial school connected with St. Joseph's Church in Rochester, and staffed by the School Sisters of Notre Dame, completed a large new building next door to the church. Since 1963, it had been giving a full four-year course of high school business training.[45]

Thus, by the end of 1966, the Rochester Diocese had thirteen diocesan or private high schools within its boundaries, with a total registration of 10,350 students. And most of this expansion dated from the last sixteen years of Bishop Kearney's regime. It was no small achievement.

While higher and secondary education in the Diocese were making such progress, diocesan elementary education entered upon days of crisis.

The crisis was certainly not the result of any administrative failure in the Diocesan Schools Office. The successive diocesan superintendents —Monsignors Charles J. Mahoney, Charles V. Boyle and William M. Roche—brought to their task a professional training and a progressive spirit. Nor was the crisis due to any slackening of educational idealism. The School of the Holy Childhood gave ample proof of that. This private school for retarded children, promoted by Msgr. Mahoney and directed by Sister M. St. Mark McMahon, S.S.J., was opened in 1952 in the former parochial schoolhouse of Our Lady of Victory Church, after six years of preliminary experimentation in Immaculate Conception School.[46] The whole community was to benefit by its efforts.

The critical school situation was least of all the product of any loss of confidence on the part of the laity in their Catholic school system. In the years that followed World War II, Bishops Kearney and Casey were kept very busy blessing new schoolhouses or school annexes. Furthermore, between 1950 and 1965, twenty-six new parochial schools were opened. All the postwar parishes founded in and around Rochester up to 1964 followed the diocesan tradition of giving priority to school projects. Now several older parishes in the metropolitan area, which had hitherto been without parish schools, likewise acquired them: St. Philip Neri; Annunciation; Most Precious Blood; St. Louis (Pittsford); St. Jerome (East Rochester); St. Joseph (Penfield); and Good Shepherd (Henrietta). Outside Monroe County parochial schools were opened at the new parish of the Sacred Heart (Auburn) and at the older parishes of St. Ann of Palmyra, St. Michael in Newark, St. Francis of Assisi in Auburn, St. Mary in Bath, St. Mary in Horseheads, Our Lady of Lourdes in Elmira, and St. James in Waverly. The total diocesan enrollment rose from 31,000 children in 1951 to 55,000 in 1959, although it was again down to 43,000 in 1966, largely as the result of the recent restriction on the number of students allowed in each grade.[47]

No, the crisis was mostly a matter of dollars and cents; and it was a nationwide rather than a purely diocesan phenomenon. Catholic schools had been able to function before because they had maintained modest facilities and depended mainly on the service of nun-teachers who, as religious with the vow of poverty, were paid only nominal salaries. Now the expanding public school system, enriched as it was by public funds, was able to afford the most expensive equipment; and the

Catholic school system found in it an ever more potent rival. Furthermore, the very increase of parochial schools made it necessary to employ a growing number of lay teachers; for vocations to the teaching sisterhoods, far from keeping up with the mounting need, tended to go into a tragic decrease. One non-diocesan order, the Franciscan Sisters of Allegany, withdrew in 1962 from their three Rochester schools, St. Margaret Mary, Good Counsel, and St. Helen.[48] Fortunately, the Sisters of St. Joseph were able to supply replacements for them at Good Counsel, and the Sisters of Mercy, at St. Helen. The School Sisters of Notre Dame also gave valuable assistance by furnishing staffs for St. Margaret Mary and St. Philip Neri. The pastor of St. Francis of Assisi School in Auburn succeeded in inducing a community new to the Diocese, the Religious of Jesus and Mary, to provide a faculty for his school children. But in none of these instances were the nuns able to furnish a complete staff. As early as June, 1952, Bishop Kearney had directed that in well-established parishes there must be one lay teacher for each eight teaching Sisters. By 1966 the proportion had risen to 592 lay teachers to 712 nuns.[49] The Diocese insisted that the lay teachers be properly qualified. For want of qualified lay teachers to assist the Sisters, the parochial school at St. George's, Rochester, and the little parish school at Perkinsville both had to close down in 1965.[50] Elsewhere, the problem was not so much that of engaging certified teachers as of paying them the proper salaries—a tremendous drain on the parish finances.

Faced by this double emergency—a decline in religious vocations which left many of the large newer convents only half-filled, and an inflated salary budget for lay parish-school instructors—the Diocese, on May 26, 1963, declared a moratorium on the opening of new parochial schools, until there were once more enough teaching Sisters to staff them.[51]

Some Catholic educators were already raising the question whether the American Catholic elementary school system should not be abolished as no longer feasible. Bishop Kearney set his face firmly against this solution. But something had to be done to shore up the tottering schools, on the one hand, and, on the other, to provide adequate religious training for children who were unable to attend parish schools.

Regarding financial matters, the hierarchy decided to press once more for as much public aid as constitutional law would permit. Especially since the 1940's, the federal government in particular had shown a greater willingness to interpret educational grants and auxiliary services as aids rather to the individual student than to the school he attended, whether public, private, or church-related. State legislators had also followed the same trend. Unfortunately, the New York State constitution was less liberal in this respect than the federal constitution, with the result that even if federal funds were made available to all New York State students, the State constitution tended to exclude those who attended church-related schools from participation. For the so-called "Blaine Amendment", inserted in the 1894 State constitution in A.P.A. days, forbade the diversion of public funds to religious schools either "directly or indirectly".[52] The word "directly" expressed the accepted (though not necessarily incontestable) interpretation of Article I of the United States Constitution. On the other hand, the word "indirectly" was so broad and vague that it had served all along as an argument against the legislating of any auxiliary services for the benefit of children of church-associated schools. As we have already seen, it took a separate State constitutional amendment to clear the way for granting bus transportation to the students of parochial schools.[53]

The straw that broke the camel's back was the State Supreme Court's decision, rendered in August, 1966, that the Free Textbook Law was unconstitutional, on the basis of the "Blaine Amendment."[54] The law was designed to furnish free non-religious textbooks to all children in the State, irrespective of the school they attended. It had promised some measure of relief to parents who sent their children to parish schools. But the adverse decision had one positive effect: it strengthened the program of the State chapter of Citizens for Educational Freedom to seek the abolition of the "Blaine Amendment." The C.E.F. was a nationwide non-profit organization largely Catholic but actually interdenominational in character, whose purpose was to unite the opponents of discriminatory educational legislation in orderly agitation for fairer laws. It declared its allegiance to the separation of church and state prescribed by the federal constitution, but not to the several inequitable laws allegedly founded upon this principle. Rallying its adherents, especially the parents of those who attended parochial schools, the State C.E.F. now projected a campaign to have the unfortunate Amendment eliminated from the State constitution in the Constitutional Convention of 1967. As the election date of November 1966 drew near, the State organization publicly solicited the views, anti-Blaine or pro-Blaine, of those running for posts in the constitutional convention. The straw vote indicated that sixty-eight per cent of the candidates who answered the C.E.F. query (126 out of 189) were favorable to repeal or alteration. C.E.F. then saw to it that voters were provided with lists of the revisionists of all parties so that they might know whom to vote into office.[55] This intelligent democratic agitation was no doubt largely responsible for the election of a majority of the candidates who advocated a constitutional change. But everybody knew that it was only the first round and not the decisive round, in a contest against powerful blocs of professional educators and of those religious and humanistic groups whose predecessors had promoted the original Blaine amendment.

The other roundabout effort of the Diocese to deal with the crisis in religious education was the expansion of its catechetical program. In June, 1947, Bishop Kearney named Father Albert H. Schnacky the first full-time director of the Confraternity of Christian Doctrine in the history of the Diocese. The magnitude of the assignment given to Monsignor Schnacky increased notably in the decades that followed. In 1950 there were 27,000 children who did not attend parish schools and were therefore enrolled in the catechetical courses. By 1967 the number had risen to 53,000. And who were to teach all these children? In the Rochester district, the seminarians of St. Bernard's were brought ever more extensively into the enterprise.[56] Seminarians of the religious orders throughout the Diocese were also asked to participate. Nun-catechists assumed a key role in this development. In 1949, there were two communities of Sister-catechists in the twelve counties: the Trinitarians, who, as we have seen, arrived in 1926, and the Religious Teachers Filippini, who opened a convent in Watkins Glen in 1936. Then in 1950, the Mission Helpers, Servants of the Sacred Heart, made a foundation in Immaculate Conception parish, Ithaca, and in 1956 a second foundation in Assumption parish, Fairport. By 1966, their Ithaca group was also catechizing at Cayuga Heights, Van Etten and Trumansburg; and their Fairport group had charge of the School of Religion at Victor. In 1955, the Franciscan Missionary Sisters of the Divine Child undertook a catechetical mission at St. Francis of Assisi Church in Rochester; and in 1963, four Franciscan Sisters of the Atonement took over catechetics at St. Mary's, Elmira. In 1966, both the Rochester Sisters of St. Joseph and the Rochester Sisters of Mercy for the first time designated some of their own to do full-time catechetical work. Two Josephite nuns were assigned to the parish of Holy Spirit, Penfield; two Mercy nuns, to the parish of Holy Name of Jesus, Greece.[57] The moratorium on opening parochial schools had smitten these two new parishes.

But seminarians and Sisters were obviously not numerous enough to teach religion to 50,000 children. Lay teachers, well trained in catechetical doctrine and methods, were absolutely necessary. The Mission Helpers of the Sacred Heart were ready to prepare these teachers. In September, 1952, they began at Immaculate Conception Church, Ithaca, the first September-to-May course for lay catechists ever offered in the Diocese. Priests instructed the candidates in doctrine, the nuns instructed them in method. In the following May, Bishop Kearney awarded certificates to the twelve members of this first class.[58] The Ithaca Sisters have repeated this program in subsequent years. For prospective lay catechists of the Rochester area, the Fairport Mission Helpers began a similar project at their School of Religion in 1956. The Bishop presented the certificates to the first year's graduates—thirty-one—in May, 1957.[59] This, too, became a continuing program. Furthermore, in the fall of 1964, the Fairport Mission Helpers took over the class of catechetical methods at St. Bernard's Seminary—the first time that nuns had ever been a member of the faculty of that august institution. In the same year, the Atonement Sisters in Elmira initiated a similar course for lay catechists. Bishop Casey presented certificates in May, 1965, to forty-five graduates.[60] By the end of 1966 there were over two thousand trained lay catechists in the Diocese, with the prospect of more and more of them becoming available each year.

Some parishes used their parochial schoolrooms for the classes in religion, some utilized other meeting-space on the church property. In many cases, however, it was wiser to secure classroom facilities nearer to the public schools (holding classes *in* the public schools, practiced fairly late in a few of the rural communities, was, of course, now ruled out by legal decisions). In the case of central schools, several parishes might join together to erect and maintain catechism centers. Probably the earliest of these was the "barracks" center set up on Mount Read Boulevard, Greece, around 1939, to serve Most Precious Blood, Holy Apostles and Holy Family churches.[61] A more recent example is the $50,000.00 structure on Wegman Road in Gates Township, sponsored jointly in 1958 by the parishes of St. Theodore, Holy Ghost, St. Helen and St. Pius X.[62] Other parishes, too, have built rather ambitious structures of their own adjacent to public schools. In some cases, the "schools of religion" were designed to be converted, if that were ever possible, into true parochial schools. Among these buildings were the centers in Watkins (1958), Victor (1958), Ontario (1960), Scottsville (1962), and East Bloomfield (1964).

The most noteworthy of all, however, was the School of Religion at Fairport, headquarters of the metropolitan apostolate of the Mission Helpers of the Sacred Heart. In this attractive building, dedicated in 1957 and enlarged in 1964, Father Leonard A. Kelly, pastor of Assumption Church, pioneered a thorough program of religious education which aimed at tying in church, school and home. In Father Kelly's view, this program was not merely a substitute for the parochial school, it was its ultimate successor. Not likely to be a popular opinion in a diocese so proud of its parish school tradition, his view was nevertheless provocative, and perhaps prescient.[63]

Teaching and catechetical orders were not the only communities of nuns that set up missions in the Rochester Diocese in the postwar years. One group of Sisters served in the domestic department of St. Bernard's Seminary from 1951 to 1958, succeeding the Sisters of St. Joan of Arc, who had left the Seminary in 1947. This group belonged to the Institute of the Blessed Virgin Mary, and its members were German and Rumanian religious who had been ousted from Rumania by the Communist government. Another order engaged in domestic work—this time at the Divine Word Seminary, Conesus, New York—was the Italian Order of St. Mary of Leuca. These nuns arrived in 1959, to replace the School Sisters of St. Francis, who had had charge of domestic arrangements at the Conesus Seminary from 1938 to 1959.

But the most notable growth of religious orders in the Diocese after World War II was in the number of communities of men.

In 1946, the Carmelite Friars (Ancient Observance) had opened Whitefriars Monastery and Scholasticate in Auburn. Their presence in Auburn suggested a Diocesan invitation to assume the direction of Mount Carmel High School when that school was being planned in the early 1950's. Then in 1958, another Carmelite group, the Discalced Carmelite friars, accepted from restaurateurs Edwin and William O'Brien of Waverly the gift of a site atop Waverly Hill. Here they constructed a monastery, which Bishop Kearney dedicated to "Our Lady of the Hill" on September 8, 1962.[64]

Another case of "twinning" was the arrival of a second Capuchin foundation. In June, 1951, Capuchin friars of the Province of St. Mary —a unit distinct from the Province of the Stigmata of St. Francis represented at Geneva—purchased the old Sheldrake property at Interlaken, Seneca County.[65] Since their advent, they have been made administrators of the parishes of Interlaken and Van Etten.

When the opening of McQuaid Jesuit High School was being planned, in 1953, Father James Barnett, S.J. was named acting rector of the future Rochester house of Jesuits.[66] Thus one of the ablest and largest of Catholic religious orders became associated with the Diocese of Rochester.

Most unusual among the new male religious foundations were the Trappist Monastery of Our Lady of the Genesee, at Piffard, in Livingston County, and the contemplative Benedictine Monastery of Mount Saviour, near Elmira in Chemung County. Both date from 1951.

The Trappist Monastery—or, more properly, the Cistercian Monastery of the Strict Observance—was set up by a company of monks from the Trappist Abbey of Gethsemani in Kentucky. The site chosen was a farm on the rich upland of the Genesee Valley. Part of the acreage was donated by Mr. Porter Chandler (of New York and Piffard); the remainder was purchased by the monks. Our Lady of the Genesee was formally established on May 26, 1951, and its charter members were soon engaged in farming and in the baking and sale of bread. In those postwar days, many young men felt a calling to the contemplative life, so the new monastery grew rather rapidly and soon became self-sufficient.[67] Consequently, Our Lady of the Genesee was raised to the rank of an abbey (or independent house) on September 1, 1953. On October 13, 1953, the monks elected their first abbot. He was the superior who had founded the monastery, Father M. Gerard McGinley, O.C.S.O. (1906-1955). In a colorful rite held in Sacred Heart Cathedral on November 9, 1953, Bishop Kearney imparted to him the solemn abbatial blessing.[68] Unfortunately, the gentle, genial Abbot Gerard died an untimely death on September 19, 1955, while attending an international Trappist conference at Dijon, France.[69] To succeed him, the Piffard Monks, on October 18, 1955, elected the novice-master of the Abbey of Gethsemani, Father M. Walter Helmstetter, O.C.S.O. It was again Bishop Kearney who solemnly blessed the abbot.[70] On April 24, 1964, following the early retirement of Abbot Walter, Father M. Jerome Burke, O.C.S.O., was elected third Abbot of Our Lady of the Genesee. This time, Bishop Kearney bestowed the abbatial blessing in the chapel of the Monastery itself.[71]

The Benedictine Monastery of Mount Saviour was begun in the spring of 1951 on a hilltop farm of 440 acres just west of Elmira.[72] Its octagonal chapel, designed by Mr. J. Sanford Shanley of New York, was dedicated on October 4, 1953. Its crypt is a shrine for Our Lady Queen of Peace, whose statue—a medieval French madonna and child—is becoming the object of much devotion.[73] After experimenting with other types of farming, the monks settled upon dairy farming as their principal means of support. Mount Saviour was unusual in status, in that it was an independent monastery, subject only to the Benedictine Abbot Primate in Rome. Its membership grew slowly, owing in no small measure to the selectivity of those in charge. Nevertheless, on November 19, 1957, the Abbot Primate granted it the status of a "conventual priory"; and on December 15, 1957, he appointed as "conventual prior" the priest who had founded the monastery—German-born Father Damasus Winzen, O.S.B.[74] In 1964, the monks finished their permanent monastery—a striking complex of buildings designed by the Elmira architect, Mr. Ronald Cassetti. The octagonal chapel was enlarged at the same time. Bishop Kearney dedicated the expanded church and the new residence.[75] Meanwhile, the monks, who in true Benedictine style cultivated sacred letters and the sacred arts, had won a wide reputation in the United States for their contribution to the liturgical and ecumenical movements.

Vocations to the diocesan priesthood did not go into any steep decline in the years which we are considering. Nevertheless, owing to the assignment of more and more priests to special non-parochial work, there were never quite enough to go around. In 1955 and again in 1963 Bishop Kearney authorized special campaigns for increased priestly and religious vocations; and in 1963 he named Father Louis J. Hohman, of St. Andrew's Seminary, Diocesan Director of Vocations. [76] The Atonement Fathers at Montour Falls and the Divine Word Fathers at Conesus made their contribution to the cause by holding weekend retreats for boys of the seventh and eighth grades.[77] The Second Vatican Council suggested a new source of assistance for parish priests: the deacon. In the mid-'sixties the Bishop began to ordain the senior class at St. Bernard's to the diaconate at the end of their third scholastic year. In 1966, he assigned eight of these men to summer pastoral tasks where they could preach, baptize, and distribute Holy Communion (as their deaconal order permitted them to do) and make themselves generally serviceable in other parochial duties.[78]

James E. Kearney made several changes in his curia during the 1950's and 1960's. In 1954, he named his chancellor, Msgr. James C. McAniff, a second vicar general, and appointed Msgr. John E. Maney to the chancellery.[79] Monsignor Maney was designated a third vicar general in 1963, but was obliged by ill health to resign that post one year later.[80] In May, 1966, after Bishop Casey's transfer to Paterson, the Bishop named as vicar general to succeed him, Msgr. Wilfred T. Craugh, P.A., who had just retired from the staff of St. Bernard's Seminary after a distinguished rectorship of eighteen years.[81] Msgr. George A. Cocuzzi had already been appointed chancellor in 1964, to succeed Msgr. Maney.[82] The Bishop employed Monsignors McAniff and Maney in still another role: since both had received the rank of protonotary apostolic, he commissioned them to confer the sacrament of Confirmation in several of the parishes, especially during the time when Bishop Casey was in Rome for the Second Vatican Council. This was a novelty in the annals of the Diocese.

As the priests who held the position of diocesan consultor yielded up that office through death or resignation, Bishop Kearney appointed others to succeed them. His appointees between 1937 and 1966 were the following: Charles J. Azzi, William F. Bergan, Charles V. Boyle, Thomas F. Connors, George W. Eckl, Robert A. Keleher, Gerald C. Lambert, John E. Maney, James C. McAniff, John E. McCafferty, Albert L. Simonetti, Leo V. Smith, F. William Stauder, John B. Sullivan, and Leslie G. Whalen. Furthermore, in April, 1954, the Bishop reorganized the diocesan deaneries and named the following deans: Fathers William J. Brien (Chemung Deanery); Lawrence W. Gannon (Steuben Deanery); John M. Ball (Livingston Deanery); Joseph M. Curtin (Wayne Deanery); John A. Conway (Cayuga Deanery); William Byrne (Tompkins Deanery); Edward K. Ball (Ontario Deanery). (When some of these died, the following were chosen to succeed them: Fathers Frederick W. Straub, dean of Cayuga, 1955; Donald Cleary, dean of Tompkins, and John F. Neary, dean of Wayne, 1961; Adelbert J. Schneider, dean of Steuben, 1962; James D. Cuffney, dean of Cayuga, 1958; Leo G. Schwab, dean of Chemung, 1958). It gradually became customary for the Bishop to request Roman prelacies for his chancery officials, Tribunal, Schools Superintendent, Charities director, Propagation of the Faith director, and Confraternity director, seminary rectors, consultors and rural deans. Sometimes he sought the same favors for some who did not come under these more official categories. Roman honors were thus bestowed on over fifty priests of the Rochester Diocese during the Kearney regime.[83]

The most important of Bishop Kearney's aides was, of course, his auxiliary bishop, the Most Reverend Lawrence B. Casey, D.D., Titular Bishop of Cea. In response to the Bishop of Rochester's request, Pope Pius XII, on February 10, 1953, named Msgr. Casey, formerly vice-chancellor of the Diocese and since 1952 rector of Sacred Heart Cathedral, to the post of assistant bishop. The news was communicated to Rochester on February 18th. On May 5, 1953, the consecration of the Bishop-elect took place in the Cathedral. Cardinal Francis Spellman was the consecrating prelate, and the co-consecrating bishops were Walter A. Foery of Syracuse and Alexander Zaleski, auxiliary bishop to Cardinal Mooney of Detroit. Bishop Kearney preached the sermon. (Cardinal Mooney put in an appearance later on in the day, to congratulate his former secretary, now raised to episcopal rank.) It was a memorable day, visually, ritually, musically and spiritually. A fortnight after the consecration, Bishop Kearney appointed Bishop Casey a vicar general, second to Monsignor William M. Hart. When the jolly, competent Monsignor Hart became incapacitated by his long, sad, terminal illness, Bishop Casey became the senior vicar general in rank as well as in fact.[84]

The Titular Bishop of Cea—the first man to hold the office of *auxiliary* bishop to any bishop of Rochester—was a native of Rochester and a Rochesterian of Rochesterians. Born September 6, 1906, to Joseph and Agnes Switzer Casey, he had been trained in St. Andrew's and St. Bernard's seminaries and retained a real fondness for these two *almae matres*. Ordained a priest on June 7, 1930, by Bishop O'Hern, he had served from 1932 to 1946 as vice-chancellor. But he had had two years of parochial work before becoming a member of the diocesan curia, and while engaged in his curial tasks he had kept his hand in pastoral activities. In 1946, Bishop Kearney named him pastor of Holy Cross parish in Charlotte; and on February 28, 1952, promoted him to the rectorship of Sacred Heart Pro-cathedral, to succeed the venerable founder of that parish, Msgr. George V. Burns.

From the start of his thirteen-year span as auxiliary bishop of Rochester, Bishop Casey gave his Ordinary valuable assistance in the conferring of the sacraments of Confirmation and Holy Orders and in the administration of the Diocese—especially in the sphere of diocesan personnel, in which he showed himself exacting yet considerate. Growing through experience into the fullness of his office, the Bishop of Cea was given an increasing share in the formulation of diocesan policy.

The moral pastoral problems that engaged Bishop Kearney's concern in the 1950's and 1960's were much the same as those of the two earlier decades. Objectionable motion pictures were in circulation, and objectionable popular literature increased in volume, so the Bishop, working in union with the rest of the hierarchy, mounted a campaign against both, especially through the organs of Catholic Action.[85] Marxist ideology presented a special problem in the Diocese in 1950. The Marxist-oriented Union of Electrical Workers was contesting with the non-Marxist International Union of Electrical Workers for the control of the employees of General Electric. A Catholic U.E.W. member who worked at the Elmira plant of General Electric wrote Bishop Kearney a personal note asking about the permissibility of Catholic membership in that Union. While the Bishop was absent in Europe, the U.E.W.

made public use of the Bishop's personal reply to this letter, claiming that Kearney had said there was nothing wrong about a Catholic holding membership in their organization. When the Bishop returned from Europe, a delegation of pastors and Catholic laymen from Elmira met him at the dock and told him about the storm that had arisen. Bishop Kearney promptly repudiated the unwarranted use of his communication. In it he had merely urged those who were already members to thwart Communist domination.[86]

Even more strictly doctrinal was the brush that Bishop Kearney had with the rigoristic teachings of the former Jesuit, Leonard Feeney. In 1949, St. Bernard's Seminary was obliged to dismiss a student who had fallen under the sway of Father Feeney, and the Bishop concurred in the action. In 1952, when Archbishop Cushing of Boston published a decree of the Holy Office in which the Vatican corrected the Feeney error, the *Courier Journal* published the full text of the decree.[87] It vindicated the decision which the Seminary and the Bishop had made in 1949.

James E. Kearney presided at the Sixth Synod of Rochester on April 6, 1954. The synodal legislation applied principally to clerics, and brought up to date the legislation of the Fifth Synod (1934).[88]

The fifth Bishop of Rochester continued as before to inculcate upon his faithful a strong devotional life. For example, he corresponded readily, as he had in the past, with the requests of the Nation's presidents for days of prayer on behalf of peace and order.[89] Then, during the Holy Year of 1950, he led a pilgrimage to Rome.[90] To commemorate the dogma of the Assumption of Our Lady, which Pope Pius XII solemnly defined as an article of faith on November 1, 1950, Bishop Kearney celebrated a pontifical Mass in Old St. Mary's Church, Rochester.[91] In this same connection, he gave his backing to Father Joseph Cirrincione of Rochester in the establishment of the Family Rosary for Peace.[92] In June, 1964, he blessed a gathering of forty-four couples who were observing the golden jubilee of their marriages.[93] In 1955 the Blessing of Babies was inaugurated in the city of Rochester. During the first two years of this practice, more than 1,500 infants were brought to Bishop Kearney at Blessed Sacrament Church or to Bishop Casey at Sacred Heart Cathedral to receive this special benediction.[94]

The Marian Year proclaimed by Pope Pius XII in 1954 to celebrate the centenary of the dogmatic definition of the Immaculate Conception naturally pleased the Bishop of Rochester, and called forth his ready response.[95] That Lent, he permitted the celebration of evening Mass at the traditional Lenten devotions.[96] Many a devout diocesan

Catholic took occasion during the Marian twelvemonth to erect a garden shrine to Mary. The *Courier Journal* gave instructions how to set up these do-it-yourself shrines, and throughout the year printed pictures of garden shrines constructed in different parts of the twelve counties.[97] Marian shrine-building received a new impetus in 1958, when there was an international commemoration of the centenary of the Blessed Mother's apparitions at Lourdes. On this occasion, the Bishop himself encouraged his people to erect garden-shrines.[98]

Happy about this concept of consecrating a year to a special devotion, James Kearney dedicated 1959 in the Diocese to the Holy Eucharist; 1960 to the Sacred Heart; 1961 to the Precious Blood; 1962 to St. Joseph; 1963 to St. John the Evangelist; 1964, a second time, to the Sacred Heart.[99] The "Year of the Holy Eucharist" probably met with the best popular response. Pope Pius XII had issued a decree on January 6, 1953, reducing the requirements for the fast before Holy Communion; and on March 19, 1957, in another decree, he liberalized the fasting rule still more. The Pope's purpose, Bishop Kearney declared on the second occasion, was to eliminate "every obstacle that has stood between the worshipper and the tabernacle."[100] With the reception of Holy Communion thus facilitated, the number of Communions received rapidly mounted. In 1954 the Communions in the Diocese rose from 675,000 to five million.[101] In the Diocesan Eucharistic Year of 1959, they rose from six million to seven million.[102]

One other devotional innovation which Bishop Kearney introduced was the cult of St. John Fisher, the martyred bishop of Rochester, England (1469-1535). In 1935, while still Bishop of Salt Lake, James E. Kearney had attended the canonization in Rome of SS. John Fisher and Thomas More. He retained a feeling of kinship with these two "modern" English-speaking saints; and when he became fifth Bishop of Rochester he gave many evidences of that sentiment. As early as 1941 he secured permission from the Sacred Congregation of Rites to celebrate in the Diocese of Rochester-in-America the feast of the erstwhile martyr-bishop of Rochester-in-England. A special Office and Mass of St. John Fisher, with the rank of a "minor double" feast, was granted to the Diocese of Rochester, to be observed each June 22nd. The Diocese thus became the only sector of the Church authorized to give liturgical honors to St. John *alone,* for elsewhere SS. John Fisher and Thomas More were commemorated together.[103] Then on June 9, 1961, Pope John XXIII, again at the instance of Bishop Kearney, appointed St. John Fisher the heavenly patron of the American Diocese of Rochester. By that very fact, the rank of feast accorded to St. John Fisher was advanced to "double of the first class."[104] Other evidences of Kearney's admiration for Fisher and More were the naming of St. John Fisher College, and of the Rochester suburban parishes of St. John of Rochester and St. Thomas More. Furthermore, Bishop Kearney took a real interest in the news that the English Catholic Diocese of Southwark was planning to erect a Church of St. John Fisher in Rochester, England— the first Catholic church in that city since the time of the Reformation. To aid this project, he authorized the taking up of a collection in his own diocese. The $30,000.00 realized was a great help to the Catholics of the English Rochester in their construction project, and Rochester-in-America was represented at the opening of the attractive little Kentish church.[105]

James Edward Kearney always felt close to Pope Pius XII. When Pius, still Cardinal Eugenio Pacelli, came to the United States in 1936, Bishop Kearney, then at the helm of the Diocese of Salt Lake, had met him; and he had of course renewed this personal acquaintance during his several visits to Rome after World War II. In 1956, the Pontiff, now in uncertain health, completed his eightieth year. The Bishop of Rochester urged his flock to offer their Communions for Pius on his birthday, March 2nd, which also happened to be the First Friday of the month.[106] When this great—though much-maligned—Vicar of Christ died on October 8, 1958, Bishop Kearney tenderly applied to him the eulogy applied to the dead Hamlet:

> Now cracks a noble heart. Good night, sweet prince,
> And flights of angels sing thee to thy rest.[107]

A year after the passing of Pope Pius XII, the time came for the Bishop of Rochester's decennial visit to Rome to give an official report on his diocese. On this last of his *ad limina* visits as head of the Diocese of Rochester, Bishop Kearney once again traveled in the company of Bishop Foery of Syracuse. They sailed from New York on April 18, 1959, and he had his formal audience with the Pope on May 2nd. It was a new (though not a young) Supreme Pontiff that greeted him— the charming Pope John XXIII.[108]

There still remain two other aspects of the latter Kearney years for us to summarize: Catholic Action and Catholic Charities.

The Diocesan Council of Catholic Women continued to be the best-organized federation of Women's Catholic organizations within the twelve counties; and in the postwar period the Council extended its efforts into immigrant resettlement, interracial, and ecumenical activities.[109] The International Federation of Catholic Alumnae (I.F.C.A.) had meanwhile become of increasing importance in its social, scholarship, and missionary programs.[110] The Rochester Diocesan Council of Catholic Nurses (an N.C.W.C. affiliate devoted to the spiritualization of the Catholic nursing profession) was established in Rochester in 1941; thereafter it gradually set up chapters in Auburn, Canandaigua, Corning, Elmira, Geneva, Ithaca and Sonyea.[111] The diocesan Legion of Mary, by 1966, had 104 *praesidia* and over 800 active members. Strongly apostolic, it was able to provide many answers to current social problems. Bishop Kearney gave it an official diocesan mandate in 1958. On the same occasion, the Bishop also mandated the Sodality juridically as a Catholic Action group.[112]

The Catholic Family Movement, a nationwide organization, was first introduced into the Rochester Diocese in 1951. The Mothers' Circles of the Diocese were first launched—as the Cana movement had been—by the D.C.C.W. In August, 1966, the Bishop named Father Gerald E. Dunn director of the Family-Life Bureau of the Diocese, and put under his supervision not only the Catholic Family Movement, the Cana Movement, and the Mothers' Circles, but also the Widowed Parents organization (founded 1963).[113]

Boy Scouting continued to progress; and 1951 saw the initiation of the annual retreat for Catholic Scouts of the Diocese.[114] Nor must we forget Girl Scouting. The Catholic Women's Club had established the first Catholic Girl Scout troop in Rochester in 1929, and had subsequently set up two more local troops. By 1966, there were 2,026 girls enrolled in Catholic-sponsored troops in Rochester, 2,461 more in suburban Rochester, and 72 in Livingston County. These figures did not indicate the total of Catholic Girl Scouts, of course, for many others in Monroe and Livingston Counties belong to troops sponsored by public schools and by other non-Catholic institutions.[115]

One rather recent organization which is harder to categorize, but has not been without its influence, is Blackfriars, Incorporated, a little-theater group in Rochester. It was founded in 1951 as Catholic Theater of Rochester with the particular aim of producing plays of a positive character.[116] In 1962, CTR changed its name to the present one. It has no direct connection with the Rochester Blackfriars Guild of 1937-1941, although it is an affiliate of the Blackfriars Theater of New York, which seems to be the only remaining unit of the original Dominican-directed national Blackfriars movement. While it is more ecumenical in its membership since 1962, Blackfriars, Inc. has won widespread commendation for its unique contribution to the semi-professional theater of Rochester.

Three new spiritual associations put in an appearance in the late 'fifties and early 'sixties: the Serra International, the Eucharistic Legion, and the Daily Mass League.

The Serra International is an invitational society of prominent Catholic laymen dedicated to the promotion of priestly vocations. The Rochester chapter was formed in the summer of 1961 and received its charter in the following November.[117]

In 1959, on the urging of Father Bartholomew O'Brien of Elmira, Bishop Kearney erected the first American branch of the Sacerdotal Union of Daily Adoration. The S.U.D.A. enrolls priests and seminarians who pledge to make a daily holy hour. On November 3, 1961, the Bishop mandated as a lay organization the Eucharistic Legion, a branch of the S.U.D.A. which strives to propagate the practice of the holy hour among Catholics other than priests. By 1965, S.U.D.A. had over one thousand names on its nationwide register. Father O'Brien remained national director of both the Sacerdotal Union and the Eucharistic Legion.[118]

Likewise interdiocesan, but of Rochester origin, was the Daily Mass League, founded in 1951. Two local lay Catholics, Mr. Harold Coleman, a manufacturing executive (1897-1970) and Mr. Theodore Houck, an insurance agent (1901-1960), won the ready backing of the Bishop when they proposed to form a guild of laymen who would pledge to attend daily Mass. Especially after 1953, when Rochester's downtown "French Church", Our Lady of Victory, was designated as the Daily Mass League Center, the League began to lengthen its membership scroll. By 1957, it counted two thousand members; and on March 14, 1957, the Holy See extended to those who would join a number of rich indulgences. On May 11, 1957, Bishop Kearney formally erected the Daily Mass League as a "pious society," thus giving it a true ecclesiastical status. By 1962, the League could count 23,085 members in forty-five States and Puerto Rico, in Canada, the Philippines, and twelve other countries. This expansion was a tribute to the zeal of its lay founders. The Holy Spirit uses many instruments![119]

A final apostolate that must be mentioned is the Newman Apostolate. In view of the rapid growth of institutes of higher education, especially State-supported colleges, within the twelve counties, the Bishop found it necessary to assign several full-time chaplains to serve the Catholic students on the various campuses. These chaplaincies were established at the University of Rochester, Ithaca College, Brockport State College, Geneseo State College, and Rochester Institute of Technology. Steps were undertaken in each place to obtain or construct a building that might serve as a student center for Catholic student activities. Even on those campuses where there was no permanent chaplain, the parish priests who were appointed part-time chaplains found the demands of their Newman work ever increasing.[120]

And what of Catholic charities? We can only summarize the newer developments.

All four Catholic hospitals in the Diocese gained professional stature and enlarged their facilities during the period 1950-1966. Holy Angels Home in Rochester added a large wing in 1959 and laid plans for further construction.[121]

Rochester Catholic Charities reincorporated in 1949 as Catholic Charities of the Diocese of Rochester, and in 1950 changed the name of its social welfare agency to "Catholic Family Center." An important new step was taken on July 15, 1958, when Catholic Charities opened the DePaul Clinic, a licensed psychiatric clinic for children who attended parochial schools in Monroe County.[122] Then, in early 1955, Catholic Charities opened an Auburn branch.[123] In May, 1966, when Miss Mary FitzGerald retired after serving thirty-six years as director of the Elmira Catholic Family Service, Bishop Kearney named as her successor the assistant secretary of Rochester's Catholic Family Service, Father Joseph F. D'Aurizio.[124]

During the diocesan Charities directorship of Msgr. Donald J. Mulcahy (appointed 1963), new buildings were constructed at St. Joseph's Villa. A residence on St. Paul Boulevard was also acquired by the Villa and entrusted to a married couple, to serve as a home-like "halfway house" for several boys who were too old to continue in residence at the Villa itself, and yet too y o u n g to start out on their own.[125] (This was much the same problem that Bishop McQuaid had once faced. As we will recall, he sought to solve it by inaugurating Excelsior Farm.)

But the biggest achievement of the Diocese in institutional Charity in the 1950's and 1960's was the building of the new St. Ann's Home for the Aged. This was accomplished during the administration of Msgr. Arthur M. Ratigan, who succeeded Msgr. Gerald C. Lambert as Catholic Charities director in 1952 and continued in office until 1963.

St. Ann's Home on Lake Avenue had earlier disposed of some of its western acreage in favor of the nearby Eastman Company which converted this meadow into a parking area. In 1958, the St. Ann's corporation sold the rest of the property to the Eastman Company, for what is said to have been a satisfactory price.[126] That fall, the Home acquired a new site, twenty-three acres in size, on Portland Avenue between Norton Street and Ridge Road East. The cost of the land was $125,000.00.[127] Here rose the magnificent new St. Ann's—a spectacular nine-story structure with attached chapel, designed to accommodate 354 guests—one hundred more than the old Home had housed. The planning had taken into account the latest data on gerontology, and from the start the new St. Ann's was affiliated with Rochester General Hospital across the Avenue. Sixteen rooms were provided for aged married couples—more or less in fulfillment (perhaps unconsciously)—of what Bishop McQuaid had intended to do at the original St. Ann's Home. The cost of this geriatric showplace was $5.76 million. The federal and State governments contributed generously towards financing it—the federal Department of Health, Education and Welfare alone to the extent of $401,000.00. Sister M. Thomasina Purcell, S.S.J., Treasurer of the Home, and Sister M. Annette Brennan, S.S.J., Assistant Treasurer, merited special praise for their role in making the dream come true. When Bishop Kearney dedicated the new St. Ann's on May 1, 1963, he might well have used the words that McQuaid had used when he officially opened the old St. Ann's:

> So may the work of considering the aged go on, century after century, for this is no flimsy structure that we have built here . . . Let us give praise to God for what he has done for us.[128]

The indebtedness of St. Ann's had been reduced by 1967 to around $900,000.00; and an important factor in its reduction was the magnificent bequests of two Rochester sisters, Mrs. Sarah McCort Ward (1867-1959) and Miss Mary (Minnie) G. McCort (1870-1954). The total amount received from their legacies prior to 1967 was $1.25 million; and St. Ann's was still due to come into the possession of a large trust fund from the same estates. Other institutions in the Rochester Diocese that were legatees of the McCort sisters (whose property was worth well over six millions of dollars) were St. Bernard's Seminary, St. John Fisher College, the Rochester monastery of the Carmelite Nuns, and Our Lady of the Genesee Trappist Abbey. Maryknoll, the Catholic University of America, the Society for the Propagation of the Faith, the American Cancer Society, the National

Foundation for Infantile Paralysis, and the American Heart Association, were also beneficiaries. So far as the Rochester Catholic benefactions went, this was the largest single gift ever given to the institutions of the Diocese. And the wills devised by Mrs. Ward and her sister were appropriately called perfect documents: perfect in their legal detail, perfect in their broad and magnificent charity.[129]

2. Days of Ferment.

Our long recitation of diocesan developments between 1950 and 1966 may have suggested that the progress of the Diocese was even and unruffled. Quite the contrary was true. Particularly during the 1960's, a great turbulence arose, not only in the social but also in the religious sphere. As these lines are written, the turbulence has not abated; and it is even too early to predict when and in what manner new stabilities will be achieved.

In speaking of social turbulence we refer especially to the ethnic problems of "inner city" neighborhoods, most notably in Rochester itself, but also, though to a lesser extent, in smaller centers like Elmira. As the citizens long ensconced in central areas began to swarm out into suburbia, the unpretentious housing that they had occupied was gradually taken over by newcomers who could afford only the least expensive residences. The newcomers were generally Puerto Ricans and Negroes, and their group arrival only accelerated the departure of the white residents. As a consequence, several centrally located parishes which had already seen a considerable intrusion of commerce into their neighborhoods, now found themselves gradually losing their old congregations and faced with new linguistic and apostolic problems. St. Patrick's, St. Bridget's, Immaculate Conception—all old "Irish" parishes—and Mount Carmel and St. Lucy, Italian national parishes, were the units most affected. But other parishes bordering on these five began to witness the same spreading phenomenon.

In Rochester proper, the number of Puerto Ricans had risen from 200 in 1952 to 4,500 in 1959.[130] By 1967, the total was close to 7,000. As we have seen, about 500 others settled at Geneva, and about 200 at Newark, New York.

Unlike earlier ethnic groups, the new arrivals were already American citizens. But their Spanish language still constituted a serious barrier. Once again the specter of ethnic nativism arose. History repeated itself: the descendants of old immigrants often showed little patience and understanding towards these latter-day pioneers. As one elderly

Italian lady of Geneva put it: "They are treating Puerto Ricans the same way they treated us when we came over." But the Puerto Rican in-migrants had come to upstate New York to better their lot; and in general they showed themselves earnest and hard-working.[131]

A certain number of these *Latinos* associated with Protestant churches, especially the pentecostal sects. The majority were Catholic by baptism, and remained so by at least a casual affiliation. As early as 1954, Rochester Catholic Charities turned its attention to the Rochester Puerto Ricans. The Catholic settlement houses extended a hand to them, and the Catholic Family Center engaged a Puerto Rican sociologist, Mrs. Gladys Zapata, as a case worker. Priests in Rochester who had had experience on the Latin American missions—among them Fathers Vincent Fullerton, C.S.B. and William Jamison, C.SS.R. —came forward to give spiritual attention and counsel to these newcomers. The Legion of Mary paid special attention to Rochester's Puerto Ricans. The praesidium of Our Lady, Spouse of St. Joseph (connected with St. Joseph's House of Hospitality) took up a census among them, saw to it that the children were sent to parochial schools —or at least to released-time instruction—and in 1954 began to sponsor a series of special Masses for them at which the sermon was preached in Spanish. Only sixty attended the first of these Masses, celebrated in St. Joseph's House of Hospitality. But when Bishop Kearney offered the seventh of the series on Palm Sunday 1955 at the Columbus Civic Center, the Puerto Ricans present numbered 200. In 1956, a new Legion of Mary praesidium, that of Our Lady of Guadalupe, was established at St. Joseph's Church, to work exclusively with the Spanish-speaking. Its spiritual director was Father Charles Schenkel, C.SS.R., formerly a missionary in Puerto Rico. He was to remain in charge of the diocesan Latin-American mission until 1967, when he was succeeded by a diocesan priest, Father Roger Baglin.[132] From 1956 on, Rochester Catholics sponsored an annual festival in honor of St. John the Baptist, patron saint of Puerto Rico. Bishop Kearney usually participated in this pleasant observance.[133]

Genevan Catholics held an old-clothing drive in the spring of 1956 for the benefit of the Puerto Ricans of that city. The response was very generous. At Christmastide in the same year, the Rosary Society of Geneva's St. Francis de Sales Church gave a Christmas party to over one hundred *Latino* children. A surprise visitor at the party was Sr. Casimiro Gonzalez Correa, Rochester-based field representative of the Commonwealth of Puerto Rico. Señor Gonzalez paid special tribute that day to Mrs. William Glunz of Geneva for her efforts on behalf of the local Puerto Ricans.[134]

In addition to the Puerto Rican seasonal workers who during the harvest were lodged in a score of migrant camps across the Diocese, there were usually a few Spanish-speaking Mexicans or Mexican-Americans as well. But in 1966 the largest *Latino* group in the Diocese apart from the Puerto Ricans was the 500-600 Cuban refugees in and around Rochester. These constituted a small fraction of the throng of over 200,000 who, particularly after 1961, fled to the United States from the Red tyranny of Fidel Castro. Most of those who took flight settled in lower Florida. In more recent times, however, the federal government has sought to distribute them elsewhere in the United States. In general, the Cuban refugees had a stronger economic and educational background than the in-migrants from Puerto Rico.

Facing up to this linguistic problem, the pastors of the neighborhoods where the *Latinos* congregated sought to obtain the help of priests who were acquainted with Spanish. St. Patrick's Church and Mount Carmel Church in Rochester were able to acquire the services of two Latin American Franciscans who were completing their graduate studies. Meanwhile, several diocesan priests and seminarians prepared themselves for Spanish work by learning the language. The pastors in Geneva and Newark, and in the smaller communities where there were migrant camps, turned to these Spanish-speaking Rochester priests, both religious or secular, to provide their *Latinos* with at least an occasional Mass at which Spanish was used in the Scripture readings, homily and eventually in the vernacular liturgy. To be sure, there was room for further development along these lines. Nevertheless, by the end of 1966 the Diocese had established a fair beachhead in its Latin-American enclave.[135]

Establishing a beachhead in the expanding Negro community presented far greater difficulties. Here the barrier was not one of language, but of the lack of social and intellectual education, of incentive, and most of all of that purely accidental but historically problematic difference—color. It must also be remembered that relatively few of the Negroes in America are of Catholic background, and the insecure family life of many non-Catholic Negroes presents serious obstacles to their easy acceptance of Catholicism.

When Bishop Kearney arrived in Rochester in 1937, the city had a total Negro population of around 3,500. In-migration brought this total up to over 7,800 by 1950; to 23,000 by 1960; to about 41,000 by the end of 1966. Elsewhere in the Diocese, too, there were many new Negro arrivals. Elmira is a case in point. The Negro groups who lived in upstate New York communities before World War II were for the most part older settlers, or the descendants of long-time residents. Although the objects of typical discrimination, the majority of them seem to have been able to achieve a considerable measure of progress and self-betterment. On the other hand, the Negroes who migrated north after World War II were mostly from the rural south, and bore witness, in their lack of education, aspiration, and family stability, to the tragic degradation that has been the lot of the American Negro in general. It was principally people of this deprived, disoriented, and almost hopeless background who now poured into the inner city and became a hard core of humanity that seemed to defy both dispersion and assimilation.

Catholic Negroes in Rochester before the 1960's were to be found in several downtown parishes, but the majority—some 150 families—lived on the west side in the Clarissa Street neighborhood, and attended Immaculate Conception parish. Some of the local Negro Catholics were of Louisiana origin and had a century of Catholic background. It is likely that the majority were descendants of more recent converts or had themselves been converted to Catholicism. White Catholics have shown themselves no more exempt from racial unsociability than non-Catholic whites. The fact remains, however, that integration presents no great problem when the non-whites concerned are in a small minority. Negro children began attending Immaculate Conception School in 1937; and were probably enrolled in other local parochial schools from the same date, if not sooner. We have already mentioned the modest but effective work of the Mother Cabrini Circle since 1946 to steer some of these Negro youngsters into Catholic high schools. Through their efforts an increasing number of boys and girls entered Aquinas, Mercy High, St. Agnes High, and Nazareth Academy. In 1957, one of these Mercy High School girls, Miss Thelma Carroll, was graduated from Nazareth College. (She was not the first Negro to receive a degree from Nazareth, however. Georgia Conner Youngblood, '48, was the pioneer; and she later wrote in praise of the College in a national magazine.) [136] A Negro alumnus of Aquinas Institute was graduated from St. John Fisher College in 1959.

Up to the end of 1966, St. Bernard's Seminary had had no Negroes as students and St. Andrew's Seminary had had only one. This was not due to discrimination, however. It was simply because qualified Negro vocations had not presented themselves. The same thing is true of the Rochester sisterhoods. The very few girls who entered as postulants prior to 1966 did not persevere. On the other hand, the Diocese, under Bishop Kearney, gave two Negro Catholic men to religious orders. The first of these was Brother Ralph J. Carpenter of St. Andrew's parish, who entered the Missionaries of the Sacred Heart in 1942. When he took his perpetual vows as a lay brother in 1951, he became the first Negro to do so in the American province of that missionary congregation.[137] The second Rochester Negro vocation was Charles Hall, a graduate of Immaculate Conception High School and of Aquinas Institute. He was ordained a priest of the Society of St. Joseph on June 4, 1960. This brilliant and beloved young priest, just launched upon a promising career as a teacher of science in the noted St. Augustine's School, New Orleans, was snatched away by an untimely death in the spring of 1967.[138]

As the underprivileged Negroes of the South began to reach the North in throngs, bearing with them old griefs and encountering new, northern Catholic citizens were faced with a problem which took practical precedence over that of winning colored converts and putting them through Catholic schools. It was the problem of seeing to it that the Negro was accorded his God-given and constitutional rights to "life, liberty and the pursuit of happiness." Forward-looking Catholics began to realize that it was a Christian duty to give priority to this campaign.

One of the oldest American organizations dedicated to Negro welfare is the interracial National Association for the Advancement of Colored People (NAACP). Rochester attorney James P. B. Duffy, long a member of this society and an official of its Rochester branch, took advantage of the columns of the *Courier Journal* as early as 1951 to urge his fellow Catholics to join the NAACP ranks.[139]

How many local Catholics heeded Judge Duffy's call, we cannot say. But on June 21, 1960, a Rochester Catholic organization dedicated to the same cause as the NAACP held its first official meeting. Elected officers of this "Catholic Interracial Council of Rochester" were: Joseph C. DeMaria, president; Dr. Nathaniel J. Hurst (a Negro physician), vice-president; Judge Duffy, treasurer; and Miss Margaret Kenny, Secretary. The initial priest-moderator was Father Harry J. Maloney, S.S.J., who was at that time serving as assistant pastor of Immaculate Conception Church. At this first meeting Father Maloney stated that the purpose of the CIC (one of a federation of such associations throughout the country) was to uphold the condemnation of racial discrimination pronounced by the American bishops in 1958, and to combat the primary cause of prejudice—white people's lack of acquaintance with the Negro and his needs. Since its foundation, the CIC has been the principal Catholic agency in local interracial affairs.[140] Father Robert G. Kreckel, who succeeded Father Maloney as assistant at Immaculate Conception in 1960, was appointed the second moderator of the Rochester CIC.

One of the programs which the CIC sponsored from 1961 on was an annual Interracial Sunday Mass and Communion Breakfast. It became customary for Bishop Kearney to celebrate the Mass and to deliver the sermon. At each of these gatherings, the Bishop stressed the role which justice and charity must play in bettering race relations. In his sermon on April 12, 1964, he reminded his listeners in ringing words: "Slow justice is no justice!"[141] One week after that sermon, the Rochester CIC promoted another educational program, "Home Visit Sunday". This nationwide program was designed to bring Negro and white together on a social level—a level at which they very seldom met.[142] The Catholic Interracial Conference also presented its own panel discussions on various phases of the race question, and was a co-sponsor of the large Rochester Conference on Religion and Race—a unique interdenominational project held in October, 1963.[143]

These efforts, however unassuming, were certainly constructive. But as the American campaign for civil rights gained momentum, the national advocacy became more and more aggressive, and in some of its phases, even violent. Not only Negroes but an increasing number of white activists lifted high the banner of "involvement," and joined in "sit-ins" and various forms of civil disobedience, in order to challenge discriminatory laws. How were these agitations to be viewed by Catholics, who were historically rather aloof from involvement in American social agitation, and who were by their training suspicious of tumult and chary about public disorder? The question was posed directly in 1960 when students in Rochester picketed the local Woolworth store in protest against the discrimination practiced by the Woolworth corporation at its lunch counters in the Deep South. Local Catholic students were not represented in the picket line at Woolworth's, and somebody asked why. The *Catholic Courier Journal* replied that Catholics had by no means absented themselves because they were in favor of discrimination. Catholics had themselves suffered from discrimination for generations. The question was rather, how effective are picket lines and boycotts? How effective had been the Catholic boycotts of indecent movies and indecent publications in the past? And how free of discrimination would today's ardent young picketers be when they grew up into business roles?[144] These were good points to make. But the editorial did not really come to grips with the problem of how much involvement Christian principles demand. It was a question which the Second Vatican Council was to pose still more insistently.

A Rochester Catholic delegation, led by Fathers Robert G. Kreckel and Robert J. Kanka, did participate in the great "Jobs and Freedom" Civil Rights March of 200,00 people which took place in Washington on August 28, 1963. Three days prior to this march, a new statement by the American bishops on racial justice had been read from all the Catholic pulpits of the nation.[145] It is not recorded that any Rochester Diocesans took part in the smaller but more perilous "march for voting rights" which the Reverend Dr. Martin Luther King led from Selma to Montgomery, Alabama, March 21-25, 1965. But the Rochester Sisters of St. Joseph stationed at Selma's Good Samaritan Hospital kept the *Courier Journal* informed of the racial bigotry current in Selma. And the Sisters won special praise from Dr. King and President Lyndon B. Johnson for the work they did in taking care of the Negroes injured by the Alabama State Police.[146]

In their conflicts with police authorities in northern cities, the Negroes were often to accuse police officers of brutality on less sure grounds. In Rochester, these allegations led the City Council to set up, in 1963, a citizens' Police Advisory Board to receive appeals involving alleged police brutality, especially in cases concerning minority groups. The Police Department naturally did not care for the Board. Public safety officials considered its very existence a slur upon the responsibility of the city police, and an intrusion. But those who approved the establishment of the Board—its authority was actually quite limited—found in the number of complaints registered sufficient warrant for such a department of appeals. Like Bishop Kearney, however, in approving of the Board, they made it clear that their approbation implied no disrespect for the local police and their work. The Catholic Interracial Council gave strong backing to the formation of this Advisory Board.

Two years later, on September 21, 1965, Bishop Kearney issued another statement to the effect that he thought the Advisory Board no longer necessary. His statement soon became the object of controversy and of political exploitation. The Catholic Interracial Council asked the Bishop to make it clear that Catholics were free to support or reject the Board. It also made a public point-blank request that he show a stronger leadership in the campaign for racial justice.[147]

This was a ticklish issue, but Bishop Kearney prevented a crisis by giving a commonsense answer. The reply took the form of a brief *Courier* editorial. It said: "In a matter of this kind, His Excellency dictates to nobody, not even his own flock, and, by the same token, nobody dictates to His Excellency. Then, why this 'tempest in a teapot'?"[148]

Regarding the request for stronger leadership, the Bishop did not see fit to change the mode of leadership he had always exercised—that of a teacher of religious principles—for a more activist role. But in a diocesan circular mailed out on November 24, 1965, he reiterated his faith in the CIC: "the Council has my full support and confidence." And in his Lenten circular of 1966 he not only reasserted the right of the Negro to equal opportunity in education, housing and employment; he also commended once again the efforts of the CIC to defend these rights.[149]

Rochester, perhaps a little too proud of her progressiveness, had long since been dubbed "Smugtown, U.S.A." The *Courier-Journal* of February 7, 1964 gave evidence of sharing this self-satisfied civic spirit. Praising the smoothness of the newly inaugurated "open enrollment" in Rochester's schools, in contrast to the disorder which school integration had caused elsewhere, the lead article flaunted the headline "ROCHESTER CALM, RIOTS ELSEWHERE."

That calm was rudely shattered in the summer of 1964. The Rochester riots of July 24-26, 1964 deflated the municipal ego as nothing else could have. Furthermore, they caused the citizens genuine fright. Although many commercial properties were damaged, fortunately church property did not suffer. The sporadic nature of the row also permitted the evacuation to more distant and safer convents of the inner-city Sisters of St. Joseph stationed at St. Bridget's, St. Francis Xavier's, and St. Lucy's, and the Trinitarian Sisters who resided next to Immaculate Conception School. St. Michael's Church, on the border of the East Side trouble area, set up a temporary parish canteen to serve the police during their long and fearful vigil. At a later date the City officials presented Father Benedict Ehmann, pastor of St. Michael's, with a citation for the thoughtful assistance he and his people had given.[150]

On June 30, 1964, the Bishop of Rochester addressed a circular to his Monroe County churches requesting prayers "for the peaceful solution of the problem of race relations which have been so upset by the tragic events of the past weekend." Pray also, he asked, for civil officials, for civil rights leaders, and for "our good Negro fellow citizens who have been so embarrassed by the recent turn of events. They know, only too well, that this is not the solution."[151]

While the riots were not strictly racial in the sense that Black was ranged versus White, they were racial in the sense that they were fundamentally a revolt of Negroes against civic order in a community which seemed unable or unwilling to heed their plight. If the stirs accomplished anything, they made Rochesterians aware of the urgency of the problem.

An important civic step towards a solution was the foundation in June, 1965, of FIGHT. FIGHT, which stands for Freedom, Integration, God, Honor, Today, was organized by Mr. Saul Alinsky, whose Industrial Areas Foundation in Chicago, likewise designed to confederate Negroes into a representative pressure group, had enjoyed a controversial success. It was the Inner-City Ministry of the Rochester Council of Churches that invited Mr. Alinsky to set up FIGHT. The Catholic Diocese of Rochester, already embarked upon its own inner-city program, played no role in this foundation. As a matter of fact, Bishop Kearney, like a number of other Rochesterians, expressed some personal reservations about Alinsky's approach.[152] But in a season when action of some sort was imperative, the experiment was certainly worth a try; and St. Bridget's parish, the CIC, and Loreto House (of which more later) soon affiliated with FIGHT's supporting organization, Friends of FIGHT.[153]

Open housing, a principal solution of the minority ghetto problem, is naturally high in priority among civic rights. In late 1964, the Rochester and Monroe County Human Relations Commission asked citizens to pledge support against discrimination in the sale and rental of residences to Negroes. The CIC gave the move its backing, and with Diocesan permission, "Open Occupancy" pledges were made available at the doors of Catholic churches. Signers declared their agreement with the following statement: "I recognize that a person's freedom in choice of residence ought not to be denied because of race, religion or national origin. I will uphold this freedom in my neighborhood." With the blank went a statement of the unpretentious aims of this campaign.[154] To the great disappointment of the promoters, only seven thousand pledges were returned — a mere third of those distributed. Even allowing for a reasonable reluctance on the part of some to sign such a statement, one could only conclude that a good many Rochesterians—Catholics among them—had not yet learned to apply social ethics to practical cases. What made matters worse was that Rochester already lagged behind most large upstate cities in its provisions for public housing.[155]

Where Rochester Catholics now began to make a solid contribution was in the public campaign launched to eradicate poverty and to raise the educational level of the deprived minorities. In 1964, ABC (Action for a Better Community, Inc.) was formed in Rochester to administer federal funds allotted by the Office of Economic Opportunity. In order to guarantee a genuine citywide effort, the governing board was made truly interdenominational, and the initial chairman chosen was Father Donald J. Mulcahy, director of Catholic Charities of the Diocese of Rochester. Catholic teaching nuns were invited to share in the educational administration. Sister M. Jamesetta Slattery, S.S.J. was appointed co-director of the "Lighted Schoolhouse"— a year-round program launched in April 1965 to provide remedial and compensatory cultural training to inner-city children of low-income families.[156] Among the twelve "Lighted Schoolhouses," five were in locations made available by Catholic groups: the parish school buildings of Immaculate Conception, St. Lucy, St. Bridget, and Mount Carmel, and the St. Martin de Porres Center. The Lighted Schoolhouse project functioned smoothly and effectively. Its discontinuance after twenty-four months (as the result of the suspension of further federal funds) was therefore all the more regrettable. Fortunately, the subsequent federal educational programs salvaged a number of the best features of the Lighted Schoolhouse program.[157]

"Operation Head Start" enjoyed a longer life. Its Rochester co-chairman was Sister M. Joanne Keefe, R.S.M., of the Rochester Sisters of Mercy. This summertime program sought to prepare pre-kindergarten and pre-school children of low-income families for their entrance into the world of the grammar school. In the summer of 1966, 1,098 children were taken care of in 31 centers. Head Start activities soon ramified into a valuable program of adult-education.[158]

The Diocese of Rochester initiated its own inner-city effort in July, 1965, allotting $21,500.00 towards its implementation. The parishes particularly involved were Immaculate Conception, Mount Carmel, St. Bridget, and St. Lucy. The planning included a "twinning" of more prosperous parishes with the poorer downtown parishes. Thus the suburban parish of St. Thomas More in Brighton was "twinned" with St. Bridget's parish. Nuns were appointed as home-visitors in the congested neighborhoods, and person-to-person action was encouraged so as to give the young people and adults of more fortunate parishes an opportunity to serve the disadvantaged. The diocesan School Office, under Father William M. Roche, likewise delegated Sister M. Cyril Smelt, S.S.J., to work out a special plan of action for inner-city parishes not only in Rochester but in Geneva and Elmira, where "inner-city" conditions existed on a smaller scale. This survey was undertaken under a federal grant accorded through the National Defense Education Act.[159] The Rochester phase of the programming included three downtown parishes which had many Negro students—a large percentage of them non-Catholic—and also St. Theresa School, farther uptown, where one-third of the students still spoke Polish. As it turned out, St. Francis de Sales School in Geneva and the schools of SS. Peter and Paul and St. Cecilia in Elmira did not require such detailed assistance, for they were already working out their own approach.[160]

In addition to the official participation of the Church in administering to these needs, there was a strong and praiseworthy movement among Catholic laymen and religious to take a personal part in the work of rehabilitation. Two lay pioneers merited special praise for their pioneering efforts: Mrs. Margaret Muchard of the St. Martin de Porres Center and Miss Isabelle Dolan of Loreto House.

Mrs. Muchard formally opened the St. Martin de Porres Center on May 28, 1963, in an old store at 537 Clinton Avenue, North. The plan was to do settlement work among the Puerto Ricans on an independent and voluntary basis, but in cooperation with Rochester Catholic Charities. Although devised especially for *Latinos,* the Center was from the start interracial.[161]

Loreto House was another personalist undertaking. Miss Dolan, a business woman and member of the Legion of Mary, opened it in 1963 in a house on Hand Street near St. Bridget's Church. Her aim was the pre-school training of Negro children in "arts, manners and morals." It was a valuable approach, although since her aim was catechetical as well as cultural she could not expect the support of public funds. By 1966 the expanding welfare programs of the neighborhood had begun to largely duplicate her efforts. She therefore called a halt to her very successful Rochester project and accepted the invitation of the Bishop of Cleveland to relocate in Cleveland, Ohio, where there was much need of a "Loreto House" apostolate.[162]

The Rochester Sisters of Mercy opened yet another social service center on November 1, 1965, on Joseph Avenue. Sister M. Concepta

Walsh was put in charge. She and her colleagues came with no pre-arranged aims. "Availability" was their principal purpose, and they set up a little convent near their center to make that purpose all the clearer. They quickly established contact with the local children through recreation and cultural activities, and through the children they began to win the friendship and trust of their parents.[163]

We must mention one other group that deserves special credit for a notable gesture of interracial charity. During its 1964-1965 season, Blackfriars, Inc., the Rochester little theater association which we have already mentioned, presented the play *A Raisin in the Sun,* by the talented Negro playwright, Lorraine Hansberry. The cast—all Negro but one—performed with professional skill and played to capacity audiences. What was most significant was that those who attended constituted perhaps the most thoroughly integrated audiences that had ever attended a Rochester theatrical event. Blackfriars had, every reason to be gratified at the success of this small but wholly intentional essay in interracial goodwill.

It is true that Catholics of the Diocese had no warrant for resting content with what they had done for the Latin and Negro problems up to 1966. But they at least knew that, both as citizens and as Catholics, they had begun to realize the gravity of the situation and started searching for answers. Meanwhile, they were in the throes of another and, in a sense, a more violent "renewal," the *aggiornamento* set in motion by the Second Vatican Council.

It is a curious fact that the pope who triggered this renovation of Catholicism was himself an aged man. When elected on October 28, 1958, Angelo Joseph Roncalli was seventy-six. Vatican II had had only one session by the time he died, now eighty-one, on June 6, 1963. But he was the most dynamic of men, as his brief pontificate amply proved. As we have already seen, Bishop Kearney met Pope John XXIII on May 2, 1959, during his official decennial visit to Rome. Like all who became acquainted with this ungainly but utterly lovable pontiff, the Bishop of Rochester was enchanted by his good humor—simple, shrewd, yet deeply spiritual. "Gentle, vibrant," were the adjectives which Bishop Kearney applied to him.[164]

The Second Ecumenical Council of the Vatican was certainly Pope John's crowning achievement. He did not conceive the role of this great congress as the condemnation of error, but rather as the updating of the Church, so as to make it more appealing to the contemporary world.[165]

At the request of the Pope, the Diocese of Rochester offered public prayer for the success of the Council at Pentecost-tide in 1959 and 1962.[166] The Council opened on October 11, 1962 for a first session which was to terminate only on December 8th. Thanks to television and a communications satellite, the whole world was able to witness the grand opening procession into St. Peter's Basilica of the more than 2,000 participating bishops. Bishop Kearney and Auxiliary Bishop Casey both took part in the official inauguration. (Bishop Kearney had designated his second Vicar General, Msgr. James C. McAniff, to administrate the Diocese during his absence.)[167] James Kearney remained in Rome for the first month of the Council. His Auxiliary Bishop stayed on, attending the Council meetings until shortly before the close of the First Session.

Bishop Kearney, now nearing his eightieth birthday, was excused from taking part in the remaining periods of the great council, which was presided over, after June 1963, by Pope Paul VI. But Bishop Casey continued to represent the Rochester Diocese at the second, third, and fourth sessions, held, respectively, in the autumntide of 1963, 1964 and 1965. For him, as for all the prelates who were "Fathers" of the Council, the task was gruelling but eminently educative. The Auxiliary of Rochester kept the Diocesans back home well informed on his activities through a series of reports he sent back for publication in the *Courier Journal*.[168] Several Rochester priests were the guests of Bishops Kearney and Casey during their Roman sojourns. Another, Msgr. Wilfred T. Craugh, the Rector of St. Bernard's Seminary, merited the gratitude not only of Bishop Casey but of many an American bishop at the Council, by translating the preliminary *schemata* of the Council's decrees from Latin into English.[169] One of the events incidental to the Council which held special interest for the Diocese of Rochester was the beatification in St. Peter's Basilica, on October 13, 1963, of John Nepomucene Neumann, C.SS.R. As we have already seen, he performed his first priestly duties in 1836 in the city of Rochester.[170]

This is not the place to discuss the full story of the Vatican Council of 1962-65. Nor has the time yet come to assay the role which the two bishops from Rochester, or, for that matter, any other participating bishop played in it. Those who read these lines in 1968 will have no difficulty in recalling the turbulent impression of the Council given by the contemporary press. Nor will they have forgotten the turbulence that accompanied the execution of the conciliar decrees, for neither the task nor the tumult is yet finished. We shall refer here only to four areas of the conciliar legislation which had an immediate bearing on the Diocese of Rochester: liturgy, the missions, ecumenism, and Catholic doctrine.

As we have already indicated, the Diocese had always fostered correct liturgical practice and a sound approach to liturgical music. It had not, however, entered actively into the profounder theories and practices of the modern Liturgical Movement. True, the dialogue Mass had been inaugurated before World War II in some of the convents, and was practiced at Nazareth College and by the Catholic students at Cornell University from 1938 and by the Rochester Catholic Worker group at least from 1943. But the first pastors to introduce it as a *parish* practice were Father Leonard Kelly of St. James the Apostle Church in Trumansburg (1946), and Father Benedict Ehmann of St. Mary of the Lake Church in Watkins Glen (1948). These same two pastors were likewise the first to introduce the then experimental revised Easter Vigil rites in 1953.[171] At St. Patrick's, Rochester, Father Leo C. Mooney, aided by his capable organist-composer Mrs. Virginia Bogdan Pados, started his congregation singing Gregorian Masses.[172] But the priests of the Diocese of Rochester had been trained in the pre-Liturgical Movement school of thought, and were not disposed to adopt spontaneously what was still distinctly a minority view. Bishop Kearney even felt it necessary to point out on occasion that the emphasis placed on public cult should not go to the extreme of restraining private worship of the Eucharist.[173]

Liturgical renewal as a "hobby" was one thing; as a Roman directive it was quite another. When Pope Pius XII began in the 1950's to authorize liturgical changes, the Diocese of Rochester responded with prompt obedience. When the Pope gave general permission in 1953 for evening Masses, Bishop Kearney was the first in the Diocese to profit by the new privilege.[174] Priests and faithful also took in stride the changes introduced in the missal, the breviary, and—now in their definitive form—the revised Holy Week services.[175]

The major breakthrough came with the Holy See's Instruction of September 3, 1958, which imposed upon the faithful an active participation in the Mass. Parishes of the Rochester Diocese began forthwith to fulfill this new ruling. By February 1959, one third of the parishes had already adopted the dialogue Mass, and others planned to do so with the beginning of Lent. The responses were, of course, still in Latin; but the faithful took to the practice quite readily, and were thus rather well prepared for the further changes introduced in 1964 and thereafter.[176] To acquaint its people more fully with the theology behind this movement, the Diocese presented, on August 22-25, 1962, its first Liturgical Week, featuring such national speakers as Bishop John J. Wright of Pittsburgh and Father Gregory Smith, O.Carm Priests, nuns, and layfolk by the hundreds attended the Masses and the general and special sessions of the institute, and studied the attractive display of liturgical arts and crafts.[177]

The most radical change authorized by the 1963 liturgical constitution of the Second Vatican Council was the vernacular liturgy. Before the new permission took effect, the only Masses celebrated in Rochester in English were those offered in St. Nicholas Church in the Melkite Rite. During 1964, the committee of American Bishops hurried to get into the hands of priests an English version of that portion of the Mass allowed in the vernacular. The first priest to make use in Rochester of this (inadequate and provisional) text was Father Benedict Ehmann, when he offered Mass for the local School Sisters of Notre Dame at their conference on October 18, 1964.[178] The vernacular Mass was introduced throughout the Diocese (as well as throughout the nation) on November 29, 1964, after the parish congregations had been given three weeks of preliminary instruction.[179] Further changes were authorized on March 7, 1965 (including the omission of the last Gospel).[180] Most of the nation's dioceses put into effect still broader vernacular concessions at the start of Lent, 1966. The Diocese of Rochester had anticipated this new permission from November 28, 1965.[181] Nor was English the only vernacular employed in the churches of the Rochester Diocese: Italian, Polish, Spanish and Lithuanian were also authorized where those tongues were prevalent. Other new rites were likewise adopted when permitted. Concelebration, for instance, was first practiced at Sacred Heart Cathedral in the new form on Holy Thursday, 1965. The "neighborhood Mass" (in parish homes) was inaugurated in Rochester during the mission in St. Ambrose parish in November, 1966.[182]

In August, 1965, Bishop Kearney appointed a diocesan Liturgical Commission, chaired by Rt. Rev. Msgr. Wilfred T. Craugh.[183] One of the Commission's roles was to supervise the construction and reconstruction of the sanctuaries of churches to fit in with the new liturgical directives. Although altars facing the people were not demanded, most pastors began to install them in their churches. In the earliest months these were mostly movable altars. Some, however, were permanent, among them the altars at St. Mary's, Auburn; St. Francis De Sales, Geneva; St. Gregory, Marion; and St. Francis Xavier, Rochester.[184] The Guidelines issued by the Commission on January 21, 1966, required that the altar be built facing the people in all new churches.

And how did the faithful of the Diocese of Rochester react to this rapid succession of changes? No doubt many sympathized with the sprightly complaint of a Hoosier priest:

> Latin's gone,
> Peace is, too:
> Singin' and shoutin'
> From every pew.[185]

The singing was perhaps the hardest thing to get used to, especially if there were no parishioners equipped to conduct the hymns. As a matter of fact, Bishop Kearney felt constrained by the murmurs of some to veto Communion-time hymns, enjoining instead a "holy silence."[186] Nevertheless, the popular reaction to the liturgical changes, especially the introduction of the vernacular, was generally favorable, as was proved by polls taken by the diocesan paper in 1964 and 1966.[187] But the acceptance of change did not necessarily imply the comprehension of its profound pastoral purpose. This could be brought about in the Diocese and in the whole Catholic world only by a vast and continuing program of pastoral re-education.

The Second Vatican Council was perhaps most emphatic in its reassertion of the obligation of every Christian, by virtue of his baptism, to be mission-minded. The Rochester Diocese had long been a leader in its support of Catholic missions, thanks in particular to the four successive diocesan directors of the Propagation of the Faith society: Fathers Leo C. Mooney, John S. Randall, George S. Wood, and John F. Duffy. One symbol of this leadership was the great national Mission Scenerama which the Diocese hosted in Rochester October 16-23, 1955. The inaugural event in the brand-new Rochester War Memorial auditorium, this missionary congress brought out thousands of people to view the many exhibits of missionary Orders, and to hear such noted prelates as China's Cardinal Thomas Tien, Bombay's Cardinal Valerian Gracias, and Trivandrum's picturesque Archbishop Benedict Mar Gregorios. But by far the most popular speaker—his two lectures on the closing day drew 20,000—was the national director of the Society for the Propagation of the Faith, Bishop Fulton J. Sheen.[188]

The Vatican Council's Constitution on the Missions asked established dioceses to give more than funds, however. It asked them also to give of their own personnel, to work in missionary lands where the laborers were few. In fulfillment of this charge, Bishop Kearney sent his priests a circular on April 4, 1966, asking for volunteers to engage in missionary service in Latin America, under the general supervision of the Maryknoll Fathers.[189] Thirty priests promptly presented themselves as candidates. From these the Bishop chose, to begin with, two priests of the class of 1964: Fathers Peter Deckman and Thomas O'Brien. On July 15, 1966, Bishop Kearney bestowed mission crosses (in the form of rosaries) on the two young missionaries-elect, and wished them Godspeed on their way to Bolivia.[190]

Some months before the Diocese sent its first priests to the Latin American missions, the Rochester Sisters of St. Joseph and the Rochester Sisters of Mercy had already blazed the trail. On August 31, 1964, Bishop Kearney presented their mission crosses to five Sisters of St. Joseph bound for the Diocese of Jatai in Brazil.[191] And on August 21, 1965, the Bishop presided at the similar departure ceremony of four Sisters of Mercy who had been assigned to undertake apostolic work in Santiago, Chile (after the orientation studies required of all new Latin American missionaries).[192]

Even more impressive, in a sense, was the increased volunteering on the part of laymen and laywomen of the Diocese for missionary work on the domestic and foreign missions. Although the Vatican Council's admonitions were bound to increase lay missionary participation, there had been lay volunteers from the Rochester area long before the promulgation of the conciliar decrees.

The local pioneer seems to have been Otto J. Scheuerman, who served as a missionary aide on the Chinese missions of the Columban Fathers from 1921 to 1943.[193] In the period after World War II, a number of diocesan lay persons volunteered to do missionary work—some on their own, some as associates of mission organizations like Extension, the Grail, the Association for International Development (AID), and the Lay Mission Helpers (Los Angeles). Not all set out alone. Sometimes it was married couples, like John and Betty Havens of Ithaca, who became catechists in Oklahoma; or the Charles V. Ehmanns of Rochester, who went to the Universidad Javeriana in Bogota, Colombia.[194] Five young men who had just graduated from Rochester Catholic high schools spent time in 1962-1963 assisting the Rochesterian missionary, Father Bernard Brown, O.M.I., at his Yukon mission above the Arctic Circle.[195] Nor should we fail to allude to the rising number of young people who responded with a true missionary spirit to President Kennedy's Peace Corps. By the spring of 1964, twelve graduates of Nazareth College alone had signed up with this international cultural project.[196]

But the local lay missioners who achieved the widest repute were those who engaged in medical work.

The pioneer among them was the Rochester dentist, Dr. Paul S. LaLonde. In 1956, Dr. LaLonde began to take annual leaves from his Rochester office in order to establish dental clinics and train dental personnel at the missions entrusted to the Medical Missionaries of Mary in Tanganyika, East Africa. In 1963, at the request of Bishop Patrick Winters, S.A.C. of Mbulu, Tanganyika (Tanzania), Pope John XXIII conferred upon Dr. LaLonde the papal medal of commendation, "Benemerenti."

Another Rochester specialist, Dr. William Caccamise, undertook a comparable program in India. Appalled by the amount of blinding eye ailments in that country, Dr. Caccamise, an ophthalmologist at St. Mary's Hospital, began in 1960 to make prolonged annual visits to Holy Family Hospital, an institution in Patna, northeast India, directed by the Medical Missionary Sisters. During each sojourn he treated thousands of patients, performed hundreds of eye operations, and instructed the nurses in the care of eye ailments. He charged nothing for his own labors, and the Rochester Eye Bank and leading American chemical firms were happy to supply all his surgical and medicinal needs.

A third medical mission enterprise was the St. Martin de Porres Clinic established in 1959 in Monterrey, Mexico, by Mr. and Mrs. Daniel Whalen of Avon. Their foundation, like those of Doctors La-Londe and Caccamise, was made in response to an obvious need. In this case it was the poverty and poor health of the Mexicans—especially the Indians—which Daniel and Margaret Whalen encountered in Monterrey. The Whalens, who had done clinical work in Rochester, contributed many hours of personal service. Food and supplies and emergency funds they begged from firms and friends in Mexico and in the United States.[197]

The laity of the Diocese have therefore shown an increasing sense of missionary responsibility. Surely the souls of David LeMoyne and the other laymen who assisted the French Jesuits in their upstate Indian missions three centuries ago, must be nodding approval from their heavenly mansions. The only curious and disturbing aspect of this post conciliar lay missionary spirit is that some who might otherwise have explored vocations to the priesthood and religious life now concluded that they could serve man more fully in one of these lay missionary careers. The good sometimes becomes the enemy of the better!

The Catholic ecumenical movement received its official commission in the Second Vatican Council's Decree on Ecumenism (1964) and its declarations on Non-Christian Religions and Religious Freedom (1965). These documents were promulgated some time after the death of Pope John XXIII, but they were infused with the spirit of reconciliation in Christ which he had radiated from the beginning of his pontificate. John's conciliatory spirit certainly hovered over the sessions of the Central Committee of the World Council of Churches, that principal agent of non-Catholic ecumenism, when its members met in late August, 1963, at the Colgate Rochester Divinity School. Catholic observers at the meetings received a cordial welcome; and the tea given by St. John Fisher College to the roster of World Council delegates was a unique and successful interdenominational gesture.[198]

In accordance with the Constitution on Ecumenism, Bishop Kearney, in July, 1965, appointed a diocesan ecumenical commission of five priests: Rt. Rev. Msgr. John E. McCafferty, chairman; Monsignors Charles V. Boyle and J. Emmett Murphy, and Fathers Joseph P. Brennan and B. Edward Zenkel.[199] On October 20, 1965, the Commission issued "Diocesan Directives on Ecumenism," which outlined acceptable modes of Catholic participation in interfaith dialogue and worship. A number of Catholic parishes and Protestant parishes now began to invite each other's members to "Open House" get-togethers. Non-Catholic and Catholic clergy likewise made a greater effort to get acquainted.[200] St. Bernard's Seminary and Colgate Rochester Divinity School made promising moves towards cooperation. The ecumenical-minded Atonement Friars at St. John's Seminary, Montour Falls, and the ecumenical-minded Benedictine Fathers at Mount Saviour Monastery, Elmira, assumed ever-stronger leadership. In August, 1966, the NIP (Neighborhood Inner City Program) began the first experimental interfaith summer school for younger children ever held in Rochester. Collaborating in this work were St. Anthony's and St. Patrick's Catholic churches, and Lake Avenue Baptist and Christ Presbyterian churches.[201]

The new ecumenical friendliness by no means melted all the icy walls that had stood so long between Catholics and non-Catholics; but the extent of the thaw was indeed marvelous and hopeful. Certainly the first great Ecumenical Day of Prayer for Christian reunion, held on March 27, 1966 in the Eastman Theater, was a splendid demonstration of the new openness of spirit. Catholics, Protestants, and Orthodox filled the large theater to sing God's praises and to pray for Christian unity. The principal speakers were Father Leonidas Contos, a Greek Orthodox scholar; Bishop George W. Barrett of the Episcopal Diocese of Rochester; and Bishop Lawrence B. Casey, Vicar General of the Catholic Diocese of Rochester.[202]

A fourth effect which the Council had on Rochester Diocesan Catholics—and on most Catholics throughout the world—was a widespread initial confusion, which spread to some extent even into the field of Catholic doctrine. The causes of the confusion were really peripheral to the aim and fulfillment of the Council. It was sparked by the racy but frequently tendentious reportage of the conciliar drama by the press—Catholic and Diocesan. It was heightened by the unresolved question of contraception. After the conclusion of the Council came the rapid succession of liturgical changes, which upset the equilibrium of age-old practice. And even such canonical alterations as the abolition of the Index and of Friday abstinence disturbed the peace of mind of many Catholics. What happened—a result tragically at variance with the great intention of the Council itself—was the rise of a widespread climate of subjectivism, which led some to discount church authority and question official teachings. Not only laymen but, perhaps still oftener, priests and religious, fell under this strange spell, even to the point of losing their sense of calling. The repeated and worried warnings of Pope Paul VI indicated that it was a phenomenon that was occurring throughout Christendom.

Some Catholic writers spoke, whether consciously or unconsciously, in terms that belittled the Blessed Virgin. Bishop Kearney, devoted as he was to our Lady, could not leave this challenge unanswered. On January 7, 1965 he addressed a pastoral circular to his flock on current theological extravagances. "We know only too well," he said, "that the 'opening of the windows,' as Pope John expressed it, has had some weird results." He recalled the lines from *The Merchant of Venice:* "In religion/ What damnèd error but some sober brow/ Will bless it and approve it with a text." Therefore, in defense of orthodox teaching, and especially in defense of the prerogatives of Mary, he announced that he was dedicating the year 1965 in his diocese to our Lady under the new title by which Paul VI had hailed her at the Council, "Mother of the Church."[203]

Much to the Bishop's gratification, his gallant statement was given wide coverage in the Catholic press. Furthermore, it received special commendation from the papal Secretary of State, Cardinal Amleto G. Cicognani and from the secretary of the Vatican's Holy Office, Cardinal Alfredo Ottaviani.[204]

Nevertheless, the "renewal" launched by Pope John held great promise. Even though its course ran through the shoals of sad perplexity, the Holy Spirit still held the tiller. The old truths and the old values would therefore never be jettisoned. You cannot *renew* what you destroy.

3. "Come Unto These Yellow Sands . . ."

James Edward Kearney rounded out twenty years as bishop of Rochester on July 31, 1957, and moved on into his third decade. He was not destined to reach the mark of twoscore years in office set by Bishop McQuaid. Nevertheless, he was to exceed by a decade the nineteen years of Bishop Hickey, and thus complete the second-longest episcopal term in the history of the Diocese.

The twentieth anniversary of Bishop Kearney was magnificently celebrated. Focussing on October 27, 1957—which was the eve of the Bishop's seventy-third birthday— the festivities commemorated the Bishop's birthday, the conclusion of his second decade in Rochester, and the silver jubilee of his episcopal consecration. That day, all the Catholics of the Diocese were invited to offer their Communions for the jubilarian's intention. That evening 12,000 people, bussed to Rochester from all over the Diocese, congregated to do him honor at a mass-meeting in Rochester's War Memorial auditorium. On the actual birthday, October 28th, the Bishop celebrated Mass in the Cathedral before a congregation of 1,200 nuns. The anniversary of installation was observed in the same place on Thursday, November 7th. Cardinal Spellman presided as Bishop Kearney offered the Mass. Bishop Casey delivered an affectionate sermon, and read a special letter of congratulations from Pope Pius XII. Some thirty bishops and abbots were among the guests. Although Cardinal Mooney did not take part in the formalities, he had already made a flying trip to Rochester on November 4th to express his best wishes to his Rochester successor.[205]

Within the next five years, James Kearney overtook two more notable anniversaries: his fiftieth as a priest and his twenty-fifth as bishop of Rochester. But these events were observed on a smaller scale.[206] Furthermore, there had been a very special reason why the

1957 celebration could never really be duplicated. Although blessed with rugged good health during his first nineteen years in Rochester, Bishop Kearney had been obliged to submit to a very serious operation on December 11, 1956. For a few days his life had hung in the balance; and even after he weathered the crisis, it took him three months to recover. When he finally put in an appearance at the consecration of the Cathedral altar on March 12, 1957, the sight of the wan prelate brought tears of grateful sympathy to the eyes of many a parishioner. He had asked the prayers of the faithful when undergoing surgery. He attributed his complete recovery to these prayers.[207] The success of the Bishop's operation had therefore given his jubilee of fall 1957 a very joyful significance.

While the Bishop was soon able to resume his usual round of episcopal duties, he relied more and more upon the valuable administrative assistance of his aides, especially Bishop Casey. But Bishop Casey was taken from his side when the Holy See, on March 9, 1966, announced that the Auxiliary Bishop of Rochester had been named Bishop of Paterson, New Jersey. James E. Kearney received the announcement with mixed feelings. "Paterson will be blessed," he said. But he added that he had hoped that the Auxiliary might have continued as his lieutenant during his declining years. He said he would miss him very much. Nor was the transfer an easy one for the new Bishop of Paterson to accept. He would find it hard to leave his native city and the Bishop with whom he had been so long associated. Nevertheless, both bishops were good soldiers, and accepted the marching orders of their superior with unquestioning faith.[208]

Lawrence Bernard Casey was installed as fifth Bishop of Paterson on May 12, 1966. His installation brought back old memories, for the Diocese of Paterson embraced that portion of the old Diocese of Newark in which Bishop McQuaid had begun his priestly career. Rochesterians gave him a fond send-off, and a large group of Rochester priests, religious and layfolk attended the induction in the crowded Cathedral of St. John.[209]

It was taken for granted, in view of Bishop Kearney's age, that the Holy See would not delay the appointment of a new auxiliary bishop of Rochester, or perhaps a coadjutor bishop with right of succession. But midsummer came and went without any such announcement. Then on August 8, 1966, Pope Paul VI issued a *motu proprio* decree, *Ecclesiae Sanctae*, as a follow-up of certain regulations laid down by the Second Vatican Council. This decree requested that all bishops who headed dioceses voluntarily offer their resignations to the pope if and when they reached their seventy-fifth birthdays. The implication was that the pope was at liberty to accept or reject the resignation, but that this provision would henceforth become a part of revised canon law.[210]

When news of the radical new directive reached the public press, a reporter of the Rochester *Democrat and Chronicle* promptly raised the question: Will Bishop Kearney, now approaching his eighty-second birthday, hand in his resignation? On the following day, September 13th, the Bishop told another reporter that he would, of course, conform with the directive. But he pointed out that the acceptance of such a resignation depended on the Holy Father.[211]

James Edward Kearney promptly sent a letter of resignation to the Holy See. Only in late October was he officially informed that the Pope had accepted it, and that he would cease to be bishop of Rochester when the name of his successor was announced. Shortly thereafter, on October 26th, Bishop Kearney was told that his successor would be the Most Reverend Fulton J. Sheen, Ph.D., Titular Bishop of Caesariana and Auxiliary to the Archbishop of New York. For the past sixteen years Bishop Sheen had been national director of the Society for the Propagation of the Faith. On the day after receipt of this news, the Diocesan Consultors convened in Rochester and elected Bishop Kearney Vicar Capitular, to preside over the Diocese until Bishop Sheen was installed. It was the eve of his eighty-second birthday.[212]

As we have already pointed out, it is the custom of the Holy See to have its bishops always attached to a diocese—if not to a functioning one at least to a titular, non-functioning one. So when Kearney's resignation took effect (October 21st) he was not simply detached from Rochester but "transferred" from the bishopric of Rochester to the titular bishopric of Tabaicara.[213] Tabaicara was a town in the old Roman province of Mauretania Caesariensis, which is embraced in the present Algeria, in northern Africa. Lying between the yellow sands of the Barbary shore and the yellow sands of the Sahara Desert, Tabaicara was important enough in the fourth or fifth century to be the seat of a diocese. But all this territory fell into the hands of the Moslems in the early Middle Ages, and Catholic church organization was eventually wiped out. The existence of a See of Tabaicara is known, but the location of Tabaicara itself has long since been forgotten.

James Kearney was highly amused by his new titular assignment in Africa. At the installation dinner of Bishop Sheen, Bishop Kearney, in his most jovial mood, commented on the papal action.

The Holy Father, he said, had transferred him from Rochester to Tabaicara in Mauretania. "So it seems that now, after thirty years as Bishop of Rochester, I am going to end up as a Sheik! God rest my poor mother. She told me that there would be days like this!"

Only the man who by resigning rends the bonds that have long lashed him to an office can describe the pains of severance. All who were associated with the fifth Bishop of Rochester did their best to ease this transition. When Bishop Sheen learned that his predecessor intended to vacate the episcopal residence and move to St. Bernard's Seminary, he informed him that he wished him to continue where he was. He also advised Bishop Kearney that he should feel free to accept any invitations that were proffered him in the Diocese to preach or to preside. Rome seconded these gracious gestures by allowing Bishop Kearney to retain certain ceremonial privileges normally enjoyed only by the head of a diocese: to wear the episcopal garments known as the *cappa magna* and *mozzetta,* and to preside from the episcopal throne. Archbishop Egidio Vagnozzi, the apostolic delegate to the United States, also informed Bishop Kearney that he did not *have* to sign himself "Titular Bishop of Tabaicara," but might use the style "Former Bishop of Rochester" (*"Olim Episcopus Roffensis"*).[214] Inconsequential trimmings, yes; but they demonstrated the thoughtful good will of the Holy Father.

In a sense, James Edward Kearney's last farewell to his Rochester episcopate was the tender Christmas greeting he sent to the priests of the Diocese in 1966. It deserves to be quoted in full:

A Merry Christmas to you!

My last official message to you on this familiar stationery combines my Christmas wishes with a word of sincere thanks for your many favors during the years. I placed the Chasuble on so many of you. I have seldom regretted doing so. The Rochester priests have been wonderful men to work with. You have never let me down, and I shall always have you in my prayers.

I shall feel at home at any gathering of my priests during my leisure days and I know I shall always be a welcome guest. It is a great feeling for me.

So, with my Christmas prayer for you this year goes a sincere prayer of thanks for your part in the beautiful chapter of my life that closed December 15.

God bless you,

Fraternally yours in Christ,
James E. Kearney

The "Former Bishop of Rochester" was quite correct in assuming that he would always be welcomed by the priests of the Diocese, and by its faithful in general. As a matter of fact, during the next few months he was invited to preside and to speak on so many occasions that he had few "leisure days." Having shed the worries of the episcopal office, he was as happy as ever to accept their invitations; and they found that his old eloquence and wit had acquired a new serenity.

On the day that James Edward Kearney stepped down from office, the local paper had summarized his regime. "Bishop Kearney has broadened the work of his Church and its faith. He has enriched higher education for all. He has won the admiration and respect and affection of the entire community."[215]

His own people would agree, of course. But if they were asked their opinion of the Bishop they might prefer to use the gentle phrase applied to him by one of his priests.

"A dear man!"

CHAPTER FIFTEEN

THE COMING OF BISHOP SHEEN

W HEN THE news was released that Fulton J. Sheen had been appointed Bishop of Rochester, the nabobs of Manhattan's communications arts were frankly displeased. Why should the Holy Father have taken America's best-known bishop away from New York, the business and communications center of the nation, and have sent him upstate to a "microscopic" see?

Rochester diocesans were a little nettled by this new evidence of downstate provincialism. They were proud of their diocese, and quite aware that statistics alone could refute the charge that it was "microscopic".

Nor did the Bishop himself share the belittling views of the Gotham journalists. He said in the hearing of a *New York Times* reporter that he had chosen to go to Rochester because of the dioceses then vacant the Rochester Diocese was "the best of all."[1] Furthermore, the critical New Yorkers had apparently forgotten that Bishop Sheen was a native, not of New York City, but of El Paso, Illinois—a village of 1,400 inhabitants. Rochesterians therefore remained calm. The new Bishop would surely not feel deserted in their city, whose population of 318,000 ranked it thirty-eighth among the cities of the nation.

The sixth bishop of Rochester was born on May 8, 1895. He was one of the four children of Newton Morris Sheen, a farmer, and Delia Fulton Sheen.[2] At baptism he was given the name Peter—an augury, perhaps, of his apostolic career. However, when his grandfather Fulton took young Peter to school on the first day, he told the teacher that the grandson's name was Fulton. Fulton it remained. The name "John" was added at confirmation.

The Sheen family moved to Peoria, a city of some 70,000 population, in 1901. Young Fulton attended St. Mary's School and the Spalding Institute, a Catholic high school—both in Peoria.

The priesthood already attracted this youthful graduate of the Spalding Institute. In fact, he could never remember a time in his life in which he did not desire to become a priest. Hence, in 1913 he entered the College and Seminary of St. Viator, at Bourbonnais, Illinois, not far from Chicago. (This institution, conducted by the Viatorian Fathers, suspended operations in 1938.) At St. Viator's, Sheen was a leader in literary and debating activities. Here he won his A.B. (1917) and his M.A. (1919). He finished his seminary course at the Seminary of St. Paul, St. Paul, Minnesota; and on September 20, 1919, he was ordained a diocesan priest in Peoria by Bishop Edmund M. Dunne, the Ordinary of the Peoria Diocese.

Ordination did not mark the end of his studies. Father Sheen did graduate work at the Catholic University of America (S.T.B., 1920; J.C.B., 1920); and at the University of Louvain, Belgium (Ph.D., 1923). He also attended the Sorbonne in Paris, and the Pontifical Athenaeum "Angelico" in Rome. The latter school awarded him a theological doctorate in 1924. Furthermore, Dr. Sheen taught dogmatic theology at St. Edmund's Seminary, Ware, England. While he was at Ware, in 1925, the University of Louvain bestowed on him the higher degree of agrégé in philosophy and the Cardinal Mercier International Philosophy Award.

Sheen returned to Peoria in 1925 and was appointed assistant pastor of St. Patrick's Church. But the year 1925-1926 was the only period in his career devoted to parish ministry. As our summary of his studies and teaching amply indicates, the young Peoria priest found the world of scholarship most congenial. His appointment in 1926 to the faculty of the Catholic University of America can therefore have caused no surprise. From 1926 to 1950 he taught philosophy of religion, rising through the ranks from instructor to full professor. On June 1, 1934, Pope Pius XI made him an honorary papal chamberlain; and on October 1, 1935, the same pope raised him to the grade of domestic prelate.

It was not his class work alone that had merited these honors. By 1935 the Professor had published twelve books of a philosophical or inspirational character, and they had reached a wide public. He had also gained a reputation as a preacher and lecturer. For he possessed not only an effective rhetorical style, but a broad knowledge, a sharp memory, a rare ability to synthesize, and a flair for the memorable illustration. It was as a lecturer, in fact, that Dr. Sheen made his first formal appearance in Rochester, thirty-eight years before he became its bishop. On February 11, 1929, he addressed the Rochester Catholic Women's Club on "The Divine Sense of Humor."[3] This was the first of a long series of public appearances in his future see-city.

Dr. Fulton Sheen gained a still wider repute as a lecturer after 1930, when he became the featured speaker of the N.B.C. Catholic Hour. He maintained his popular appeal on this radio broadcast for fifteen years. Sometimes he received as many as 10,000 letters a day from his listeners—one-third of them from non-Catholics. Throughout that "Red Decade" and afterward, he was an outspoken enemy of Communist philosophy. His staunch stand was in no small way responsible for the conversion to Catholicism of several prominent people who had earlier been bewitched by Marxism. And these were only a few of the many whom he prayed and persuaded into Catholicism.

When television arrived in the late 1940's, Monsignor Sheen found the transition to visual broadcasting easy, for his physical presence was good and he had a mastery of gesture. He conducted the first religious broadcast ever televised, and thereafter became a leading video personality, contesting prime broadcasting time with popular entertainers. At the same time, he recorded sermons for commercial distribution; he wrote a syndicated inspirational column for the secular press (including Rochester's *Democrat and Chronicle*); and he continued to produce books—over fifty in all. Thus he was able to enter into thousands of homes across the nation, through writings, radio, or television. No wonder the *Catholic Courier Journal* called him "the man everyone knows."

On September 12, 1950, Professor Sheen was given a new role. Pope Pius XII named him national secretary of the Society for the Propagation of the Faith. While the central office of this fund-collecting agency is in Rome, the American branch is the most important, in that it provides the major portion of the moneys collected throughout the world for the support of Catholic missions and missionaries. Monsignor Sheen's effectiveness as national secretary has not yet been made the object of a special study. But the general impression is that he was very effective indeed. As editor of the two mission periodicals, *World-mission,* a more scholarly journal, and *Mission,* a popular booklet, and of a weekly mission-need column syndicated in dozens of diocesan newspapers, Sheen showed an imaginative awareness of the value of public relations techniques even in sacred causes.

The new national director had been less than a year in office when the Holy Father designated him titular bishop of Caesariana and auxiliary to the Archbishop of New York. This was on May 28, 1951. Seeking a relatively quiet consecration, the Bishop-elect of Caesariana went to Rome, where the sacramental rite was performed on June 11th in the church of SS. John and Paul. The consecrating prelate, Cardinal Adeodato Piazza, O.C.D., was assisted by Archbishop Celso Costantini and by an American prelate, Bishop Martin J. O'Connor, rector of the North American College in Rome.

Bishop Sheen was chosen bishop of Rochester on October 21,

1966. After discussing the matter with officials of the Rochester Diocese, he decided on December 15th as the date of installation. He planned to come to Rochester on the 14th.[4]

Before 1966, all extern bishops named to the see of Rochester had entered the city by railroad train, accompanied by an escort of extern priests and prelates, and usually also by a group of Rochester diocesan officials who had ridden out to Buffalo or Syracuse to greet them. Thousands of well-wishers had welcomed the new prelates at the Rochester station and accompanied them in triumph to the diocesan headquarters. But things had changed by 1966. Railway travel was now anything but triumphal, and the grand old Central Station at Rochester was a shambles. Furthermore, the Second Vatican Council had created an anti-triumphal mood. In keeping, therefore, with the new trends in both transportation and ecclesiology, Bishop Sheen chose to enter his see city by airplane, unaccompanied.

But if the new Bishop thought for one moment that he could avoid an ovation that afternoon, he was seriously mistaken. Bishop Kearney, as Vicar Capitular of the Diocese, was on hand at the airport to greet him. So, too, was Mayor Frank T. Lamb of Rochester, who presented him with a key to the city. ("I can't sing a note," the Bishop responded, "so this is the only key I can carry.") A crowd estimated at 3,000 stood inside the air terminal, waiting to salute him. It took him a good while to reach the outer door, for he paused to shake many a hand, to give autographs, and even to treat a group of children to candy. Hundreds lined the roadway into town, and he stopped now here, now there, along the route to say hello. Outside the Columbus Civic Center (where an apartment had been fitted out for him and where he had to "sign in" at the Chancery), there was another throng which pressed in around him. For them, too, he had a word of greeting, and even a poem.[5]

Bishop Sheen spent the night at St. Bernard's Seminary. Though tired when he arrived there at 10:30 in the evening, he still took time to give the students a beautiful conference. He had chosen to spend his first night among them, he said, because the roots of the Diocese were in its Seminary. Up betimes the next morning, he prayed Lauds at 6:40 with the faculty and seminarians, and assisted and preached at a Mass of concelebration, offered by Bishop Ernest Primeau of Manchester and the Seminary professors. Then he had a "family" breakfast with the staff and students. It was already a memorable day for those connected with St. Bernard's, and it augured a lively future interest on the part of the new Ordinary in the work of the Rochester Seminary.

An editorial in the Rochester *Times Union* commented that it is the rare notable who lives up to his own public image. Bishop Sheen, it went on to say, had proved himself one of those rarities during his first day in Rochester.

The new Bishop's mood had indeed been one of devotion, of unassuming good will, of graciousness. The rite of "enthronement" itself was quickly accomplished: Cardinal Spellman took the Bishop's right hand, Bishop Kearney his left, and both led him to the episcopal chair. In his sermon from the chair, Bishop Sheen pledged service, and invited all to write to him any constructive suggestions that they might wish to make. "Service" was also symbolized in the various rites of the Mass that followed. And the guests of honor represented service to the community. Lieutenant Governor Malcolm Wilson headed the delegation of civic leaders. The delegation of Protestant and Jewish clergy was headed by the Right Reverend George W. Barrett, Episcopal Bishop of Rochester, who had a seat in the Cathedral sanctuary. Exceptionally good television coverage carried the ceremony in the crowded church to thousands of video spectators.

The installation luncheon at the Manger Hotel was characterized by the same simplicity. During the meal, the Bishop moved about from table to table and from room to room. When Syl Novelli's five-piece combo struck up "Hello Dolly", Bishop Sheen even "directed" the number. In his formal address, however, the Bishop was at his most earnest. As the Church is both a rock and a river, so, he declared, his administration would be. Conservatives and liberals in the Church seem to be at odds today, he said; but when God places the keystone between them, unity is achieved. The important thing is for both to realize that they share the guilt for every scandal and weakness in the Church, and each must take steps to remedy them, by penance and by action.

Installation Day concluded that evening with a public reception at the War Memorial. Bishop Kearney was on hand, as well as Bishop Casey of Paterson—one of the more than forty visiting bishops who had attended the morning ceremony. Bishop Barrett of the Episcopal Diocese of Rochester gave the invocation, and Mayor Lamb bespoke the city's welcome. Greetings were brought from the Protestants of Rochester by Mr. Robert Schellberg, President of the Rochester Area Council of Churches; and from the Jewish citizens by Mr. Leon H. Sturman, President of the Jewish Community Council. After Bishop Kearney had spoken on behalf of the diocesan Catholics, paying tribute once more to the new Bishop's devotion to Mary, Bishop Sheen responded to all three speeches of welcome. He stressed especially his interest in the

140
BISHOP SHEEN ARRIVES
December 14, 1966

141   INSTALLATION, DECEMBER 15, 1966
*Cardinal Francis Spellman and Bishop Kearney assist Bishop Sheen
to the Bishop's chair. (Rear center, Father James M. Moynihan, M.C.)*

142   A VISIT TO ST. JOSEPH'S HOUSE OF HOSPITALITY

143   AT TEMPLE B'RITH KODESH

144   BISHOP AND VICAR GENERAL
Bishop Sheen with Msgr. Dennis W. Hickey, V.G. (left)
and Msgr. John E. McCafferty, Chairman,
Diocesan Ecumenical Commission (right).

145   A PARISH COUNCIL
Officials of Holy Family Parish Council: Mrs. Robert Engel; Frank Morone;
Msgr. George A. Cocuzzi, Pastor; Richard Scriver; Edward Winterkorn.

146   **AFTER THE FIRST ORDINATION**
June 3, 1967

ecumenical movement—that true ecumenicity that is rooted in the love of God. In one of his typically arresting figures of speech, he described true ecumenicity as a sort of wheel. As the spokes of a wheel draw together the closer they get to the hub, so as men of different faiths draw together the more they concentrate on the love of God.[6]

Despite the long first day, which was surely tiring to even a vigorous man of seventy-one summers, the new Bishop was up early on December 16th and at work in his office by the time the clock struck nine.[7] His new tasks would be heavy, diversified, and in many ways novel to him. But he did not use them as an excuse to abandon wider commitments. He continued to write his syndicated column and to go to New York from time to time to pre-record his program on color television. This was no change of pace for Bishop Sheen. His pace had always been intense. Yet he combined great industry, as he always had, with a program of spiritual reading and meditation. Again and again he counselled his listeners, especially priests and seminarians, to live lives of sacrifice, and to cultivate prayer through a daily holy hour. Work-and-prayer was certainly a pattern of life appropriate to a bishop; and even when his diocesans were startled by some of his decisions, they found reassurance in the genuinely spiritual outlook of their new superior.

Once he had gone through the formalities of assuming office, the sixth bishop of Rochester began the gradual process of getting acquainted with his flock and his diocesan institutions. On December 21st, he offered the annual "Christmas Mass" for the benefit of 750 staff members and patients at the State Hospital in Rochester. It was the first invitation he had received to visit an institutional group within the Diocese, and it was the first he accepted. On Christmas itself, he offered midnight Mass at the Cathedral, a second Mass at Holy Family Church, and a third at the city jail.[8]

A bishop, he said, "should give himself mobility and accessibility to priests and people who may want to see him." As he moved about from parish to parish on a pre-announced schedule, Bishop Sheen invited the people to come and see him at the rectory. He also took time to meet and chat with them at the church door and in the church itself, on the occasion of parochial visits.[9] Nor did he restrict his calls to Catholic churches and institutions. While in Elmira in late January, 1967, he made a tour of the Arnot-Ogden Hospital and the Elmira Reformatory.[10] On his second trip to Auburn he also stopped in at the Auburn Memorial Hospital and Auburn State Prison.[11]

At the time that his assignment to Rochester was first announced, Bishop Sheen declared that his program as Ordinary would be to implement the decrees of the Second Vatican Council.[12] His new flock quickly noticed that his episcopal ring was not jeweled, but one of the simple sculptured gold rings which Pope Paul VI had given to the Fathers of the Council. The Bishop's pastoral approach to his diocesan visitation was another illustration of his policy in action; and as the weeks unfolded, those familiar with the details of the Council's legislation could see in his views on the clergy, the laity, ecumenism, the inner city, the missions, and many other subjects, a strong reflection of the thinking of the recent Council.

An early case in point was Bishop Sheen's choice of a *curia*.

It is the duty of a newly installed diocesan bishop to select counsellors to advise and assist him. Some bishops who are installed in a diocese already organized simply continue in office those who served their predecessors. Other bishops prefer to make a completely fresh start. Bishop Sheen chose the second course. And the means which he elected to find the best qualified personnel was in strong accord with what the Council had said about the collaboration of the priests of a diocese with the bishop. "They constitute one priesthood with their bishop," says the Council's constitution on the Church.[13] So the new Bishop of Rochester decided to ask his priests to inform him of those whom they considered to be the best candidates.

On December 30, 1966, Bishop Sheen addressed a letter to all his diocesan priests. He requested that after prayerful consideration they write him a signed letter enclosing the names of three priests whom he might "appoint as your leaders." He promised that he would count all the ballots personally.[14]

When the votes were in, the Bishop, true to his promise, spent fourteen hours tabulating and counting the votes.[15] On January 23, 1967, he announced that he had that day named as his vicar general the pastor of St. Theodore's Church, in suburban Gates, Rt. Rev. Msgr. Dennis W. Hickey. Monsignor Hickey, he said, had emerged from the voting as "the overwhelming favorite of the priests." The new Vicar General had never served in chancery administration as such. However, he had been secretary of the Diocesan Tribunal from 1946 to 1961.[16] On February 9th, Bishop Sheen made public two more curial appointments. He named Father James Moynihan, hitherto secretary to Bishop Kearney and vice-chancellor, to succeed Msgr. George A. Cocuzzi, who had resigned the post of chancellor.[17] For his own secretary he selected the Reverend Michael C. Hogan, assistant pastor of St. Francis de Sales Church, Geneva.[18]

Except for the way in which the Vicar General was chosen, there was nothing unusual in these appointments. The offices themselves were standard positions. Much more striking—and again in the spirit of the Vatican Council's directives—was the appointment of several priests to serve as vicars in certain fields of diocesan administration or in geographical districts.

The new Bishop named the first of these vicars even before he picked a vicar general. On January 3, 1967, he disclosed that he had chosen Father P. David Finks to be Vicar of Urban Ministry, the appointment to take effect on January 25th. Bishop Sheen had talked over the problem of Rochester's inner city with the clergy of his downtown parishes, and had concluded that the inner-city neighborhoods needed a special "cabinet post" of their own at diocesan headquarters. In his letter of appointment, of which he gave a copy to the press, the Bishop told the appointee that he should take his assignment "not only as an evidence of my own sweet impatience to serve those who are most in need, but also as a token of my own confidence in you as a worthy priest of God." Father Finks, hitherto assistant pastor of the inner-city parish of Immaculate Conception, had long been interested in the spiritual and social problems of ethnic minorities. The appointment clearly indicated the new Bishop's lively interest in current social problems. His informal meeting that same day with officials of the Rochester Negro organization, FIGHT, only confirmed this impression.[19]

The second vicar named was the Reverend Joseph W. Dailey, designated Vicar of Pastoral Planning on January 31st. In this case, also, the Bishop published a copy of the letter of appointment. It entrusted to Father Dailey not only the usual tasks of acquiring property and supervising building, but the study of urbanization, of rural conditions, of chapels in industrial, housing and shopping centers, and of mobile chapels for migrant camps. Could the Diocese be better divided? Could rural priests live together in central houses? Could parish and public schools develop an exchange program of courses by means of television? Could all diocesan departments be unified for greater efficiency? These were stimulating thoughts. They might well lead to a thorough reorientation of diocesan administration.[20]

Late in April, 1967, Bishop Sheen created a Vicar of Religious Education: Father Albert J. Shamon. Father Shamon was pastor of St. Patrick's Church, Victor. Prior to this appointment, he had had a long career of teaching in Aquinas Institute, at St. Andrew's Seminary, and at the motherhouse of the Sisters of Mercy. He was also the author of four doctrinal books and co-author of a fifth, a religious textbook. His

appointment, effective May 4th, placed him in charge of religious instruction in the parish schools and the Confraternity of Christian Doctrine classes, of adult religious education, and of the Newman Apostolate. He was also instructed to cooperate with the diocesan Ecumenical
Commission, and with those who sought to introduce objective religious
instruction into the public schools.[21] In general, the purpose of this new
vicariate was to integrate the fragmentary programs of religious education in the twelve counties. Presumably the Vicar would be given something of a normative role.

The other two vicars named were given territorial jurisdiction. On
January 25th, the Bishop informed Father Bartholomew J. O'Brien, pastor of the Church of St. Mary Our Mother, Horseheads, that he was
from that moment Episcopal Vicar of the Southern Tier. The district entrusted to him comprised Chemung, Steuben, Schuyler, Tompkins and Tioga Counties. Within this district he was given certain speci-
fied dispensing and supervisory powers that belonged to the bishop.[22]
Then in May, Bishop Sheen gave a territorial vicar to the eastern part
of the Diocese: Father Raymond J. Wahl, Pastor of Sacred Heart
Church, Auburn. The appointment became effective on May 5th. Father
Wahl was granted the same powers as Father O'Brien, within the
counties of Cayuga, Wayne, Ontario, Yates, and Seneca.[23]

Nor were laymen to be omitted from the official family of the
new Bishop of Rochester. Late in January, 1967, he added to his counsellors Mr. David H. Shearer, the diocesan attorney; Mr. John Erma-
tinger, Vice-President of the Security Trust Company; Mr. Thomas
Aspenleiter, C.P.A.; and—as diocesan comptroller—Mr. John Ritzen-
thaler, also of the Security Trust Company.[24] Here was a small and
early evidence that Bishop Sheen had pondered the Second Vatican
Council's words: ". . . the laity also have their own proper roles in
building up the Church."[25]

To emphasize still more the "shepherding" role of the episcopal
function, Bishop Sheen even changed the name of the diocesan headquarters. Canon law has always called it the Chancery. This term, he
felt, had acquired a bureaucratic, rather impersonal ring. So on May
22nd he informed the press that the Rochester Chancery would henceforth be called the "Pastoral Office."[26]

In *Christus Dominus*, Vatican II's decree on the duties of bishops,
the heads of dioceses were given some basic rules to govern the relationship between themselves and their priests. For instance, one article
dealt with the retirement of clergy who were no longer able to fulfill
their tasks adequately. Another article ordered the setting up of a "sen-

ate or council of priests" to assist the bishop; and it also recommended a pastoral council composed of clergy, religious, and lay people, which would likewise have an advisory function.[27]

On January 27, 1967, Rochester's new bishop wrote to his clergy requesting once again that they cast votes. This time they were asked to ballot for one priest in their age-groups (the clergy had been divided into twelve such groups) who would serve as a member of a proposed diocesan senate. Bishop Sheen reserved to himself the right to name other priests to this senate from his secular or religious clergy—although his nominations would never exceed eight.[28]

The priests submitted their votes. As a result, the following were chosen, in the order of their age-groups: Msgr. Frank J. Hoefen; Msgr. John M. Ball (Lima); Msgr. Robert A. Keleher; Msgr. John M. Duffy; Father Joseph F. Hogan (Corning); Father Paul Cuddy (Clyde); Msgr. John E. McCafferty; Father James J. Marvin; Father Daniel Tormey; Father Paul McCabe; Father William Donnelly.[29]

The Priests' Senate—now renamed the Priests' Council—had its first meeting on March 15, 1967. By that time the Bishop had already appointed two priests of religious orders as Council members: Very Reverend Albert P. Bartlett, S.J., Rector of McQuaid Jesuit High School; and Very Rev. Peter Etlinger, C.S.B., Superior of the Basilians of Aquinas Institute. At their initial gathering, the Councillors chose committees to set up inner-city programs, adult education programs, and priestly renewal programs. A fourth committee was instituted to draw up a constitution.[30]

Fulton J. Sheen had therefore chosen with care a large number of official aides and cooperators. Their presence reassured him as he began to deal with the problems of diocesan administration.

Late in April, 1967, Bishop Sheen set up his first new parish, St. Paul's, in West Webster. Property had been bought several years before for a parish in this growing suburb. Now the task of organizing the new congregation was entrusted to Father John T. Walsh.[31] This was the only new parochial development in the Bishop's first semester in office. But with his commendation, an increasing number of older parishes founded lay boards of education or lay advisory councils. Holy Family in Rochester even held a parish convention to study new solutions for pressing parochial problems.[32]

The two diocesan seminaries quickly engaged the attention of the sixth bishop of Rochester. In collaboration with the authorities of St. Bernard's Seminary, he advanced early plans to broaden the curriculum and scope of that institution. By the first week in April, he was ready to announce some of these plans. He had engaged the lay philosopher, Dr. Eulalio R. Baltazar, to teach a course during the school year 1967-1968 on the philosophical background of dogma. Arrangements were also under way for a closer cooperation between the diocesan seminary and the smaller seminaries conducted by several religious orders which had houses within the Diocese. Some had already agreed by that time to send their students to St. Bernard's. Nuns qualified for the theological courses might also enroll. Two new spiritual directors were to be assigned to St. Bernard's. And those students who were ordained to the diaconate were to be given pastoral work to perform under skilled professional direction.[33] A few weeks later, Bishop Sheen predicted the eventual setting up of a committee of not more than eight laymen and laywomen to serve as board of review for candidates to the priesthood.[34]

A seminary should be a center for popular religious education, as well as for the continuing education of priests. So Bishop Sheen firmly believed. In keeping with the first of these seminary roles, the Bishop approved the holding of a series of popular lectures on Holy Scripture, June 28-30, 1967. The speakers were Father Joseph Brennan, Rector of St. Bernard's, and Father Sebastian Falcone, O.F.M.Cap., Rector of Immaculate Heart of Mary Seminary, Geneva. Both were trained Scripture scholars.[35]

St. Bernard's Class of 1967 was the first group of Rochester priests ordained by the sixth Bishop of Rochester. The ordination took place on June 3rd.[36] But even as he imposed his hands affectionately on these young men, Bishop Sheen was aware that a real shortage of priestly vocations loomed on the horizon. In mid-April, he had already directed a circular to his people urging that both at church and at home families join in praying for an increase of seminarians.[37]

What set the problem in high relief was the fact that only twenty-nine boys had applied for admission to St. Andrew's Seminary in the fall of 1967. It is true that at St. Andrew's, as at most minor seminaries, the "mortality" of the student body had always been high. Between 1955 and 1964, only 25% of those who entered the first year of high school completed the course. This was a costly educational charity. St. Andrew's had been accustomed to deficits before, but the deficit for 1966 promised to be very large indeed. Could the Diocese afford to continue such an institution?

The Bishop turned once more to his priests. He asked them to write him answers to three questions: Should St. Andrew's be abandoned? If it should, what was to be done with the property? If it should not, what measures could be taken to increase vocations and make up for the deficit?[38]

Most of the diocesan clergy voted to discontinue St. Andrew's. A few defended it valiantly enough to make Bishop Sheen delay immediate suppression. On May 31, 1967, he announced an unexpected solution. The Seminary would be replaced that autumn by "King's Preparatory School," a coeducational high school operated on "an entirely new concept in religious vocational education." Its aim would not be vocation, but education—education of leaders, a "spiritual elite". The applicant would not be required to declare his or her intention of embracing the priestly or the religious life—although those who did so would be given prior consideration. King's Prep would thus provide its students with an opportunity to test their "vocation for a dedicated service to God, humanity, and the Church".[39]

It was a bold attempt to solve a question that many thought insoluble.

The new Bishop quickly evinced his concern for the spiritual progress of his people. As we have already noted, he counselled priests and seminarians in particular to adopt what had long been a devotional practice of his own—the daily "holy hour" of meditation and prayer. In keeping with the more informal mood of the Vatican Council, he showed preference for more informal liturgical practice. In his first letter on the feast of the Holy Family, he urged that families undertake a program of scriptural reading and acts of self-denial.[40] At the radio broadcast of the Family Rosary for Peace on February 11, 1967, he shared the microphone with Bishop Kearney.[41] In April he addressed a Congress for young laywomen, which held its meetings in Corpus Christi Church and the neighboring Auditorium Theater.[42] In the planning of the summer parish-to-parish mission appeals, programmed by the Missionary Cooperation Plan, he arranged to have missionary bishops from all over the world present their case personally.[43]

Within the first few weeks of his Rochester regime, Bishop Sheen announced the adoption of two new diocesan devotional practices. The first was the Cursillo movement, a program designed to develop lay spiritual leadership. The Cursillo was functioning in a number of American dioceses but had not yet been authorized in the Rochester Diocese.[44]

Still more surprising was the Bishop's declaration on February 13th that he was interested in administering the sacrament of Confirmation at a later date than usual. Adolescence, and perhaps even the year of graduation from high school would, he thought, be a better time to confer the sacrament. Then it would mark better the candidate's entrance into maturity—his initiation into the "priesthood of the laity". He admitted that such a move would not be made until the whole matter had been thoroughly studied. In the meantime, he intended to administer Confirmation in those parishes where the rite had already been scheduled.[45]

Bishop Sheen's announcement on Confirmation received wide publicity, and was the object of considerable interest and comment among other bishops and theologians.

The new Bishop had scarcely taken office when a statewide campaign was launched to enact a law permitting abortion. This was the local phase of a concerted nationwide effort. The proposed law embodied certain restrictions, but still offended Christian ethics and conceded to the State an unacceptable authority over the life of the unborn. When the law was proposed to the legislators at Albany, the Catholic bishops of the New York Province addressed a circular letter to their flocks, urging Catholics to make known to the State legislators their opposition to the proposal. Bishop Sheen composed his own circular, and it was a strong one. "A bird in the nest or out of the nest is still a bird," he said; "a child in the womb of the mother or at the breast is still a child."[46]

The abortion bill had the support of a number of non-Catholic groups. Catholics, admonished by their bishops, seem to have reacted strongly against it. At all events, when the Assembly rejected the proposed law a few days later, the Assemblyman who sponsored the bill blamed the rejection "almost entirely" on the Catholics of the State.[47] Catholics knew, however, that they had not heard the end of the matter.

As an old university man himself, Fulton J. Sheen showed an early interest in the secular institutions of learning within his twelve counties. On January 24th, he gave the centennial address at the State University in Brockport.[48] In April, he attended an ecumenical weekend at Geneseo State University, and gave his support to the project of setting up in Geneseo a university interfaith center.[49] A few days later he became the first Catholic bishop to lecture at a student assembly in the University of Rochester. His subject was "The Romance of Reason."[50]

In ecumenical matters, the new Bishop followed with interest the programs of the Diocesan Ecumenical Commission. At the second annual ecumenical evening of prayer for Christian unity, held in the Eastman Theater on Pentecost Sunday, May 14, 1967, he gave the principal talk.[51]

But Bishop Sheen's involvement spread beyond the Christian churches of the Rochester area. He was happy to be invited to a special reception of welcome tendered him on January 30th by the Rochester Community Jewish Council. The soiree was held at Temple B'Rith Kodesh. It was the first time any bishop of Rochester had delivered an address in a Rochester synagogue. It was also the first time that Bishop Sheen had stood before such an audience. In introducing the Bishop, Rabbi Herbert Bronstein told the crowd of 2,300 people that he believed one would have to go back to the fifth century, when St. Jerome consulted with the rabbis of his day, to find a parallel to that evening's event.[52]

A few days later, on February 22nd, there was a colloquium on Catholic-Jewish relationships held at St. John Fisher College. In the evening session, held at Temple B'Rith Kodesh, Bishop Sheen was again on hand, sharing the platform with Rabbi Mark Tannenbaum, the National Director of the Department of Religious Affairs of the American Jewish Committee. (Rabbi Tannenbaum had been the only rabbi to participate in the activities of the Second Vatican Council.)

The Rabbi praised the Vatican Council for pointing the way to a better understanding between Catholics and Jews. Bishop Sheen once more stressed the continuity between the faith of the Old and New Testaments, and once more spoke in terms of love, the root of all reconciliation.[53] To say that the audience was impressed by his remarks would be a gross understatement. They took him to their hearts.

As we have already seen, the earlier bishops of Rochester had demonstrated their interest in the community and its welfare. Fulton J. Sheen was in complete agreement with his predecessors. When Law Day (May 1st) was approaching, the Bishop sent a circular to his priests urging that they lead their parishes in its observance.[54] In a pastoral circular of April 26th, he urged his Catholics to support the Community Chest drive. But what engaged his attention most was the critical situation in Rochester's inner city.

Two days before he named a Vicar of Urban Ministry, the Bishop had celebrated New Year's Masses in the three principal inner-city parishes of Rochester: St. Bridget's, Immaculate Conception, and Mount Carmel.[55] As we have noted, the visits had a bearing on his institution of the new inner-city vicariate. A week later, Bishop Sheen addressed a questionnaire to the inner-city pastors asking their opinions on future planning. Would it be feasible for more prosperous parishes to lend them a hand? Should inner-city and outer-city parishes perhaps exchange places of worship? Could inner-city work in general be better integrated? By a regulating commission? By having a Youth Canteen open to all? Or a joint medical and psychiatric clinic? Or by a night school in a parochial school building? Might one inner-city church be used as a training ground for prospective workers in that field? Should priests live among the people so as to be more easily available to them? Should there be interracial visits and dialogue? Should there be fewer church buildings in the inner city, made available to various denominations? These were provocative questions, but they were advanced *as* questions, not as answers.[56]

When the Bishop's questionnaire was published, a local newspaper requested comment from some Protestant clergymen who were engaged in inner-city work. While they found some of his lines of thought more appealing than others, these clergymen praised the approach as a stimulating beginning.[57]

At the time of Bishop Sheen's installation, an unfortunate friction had arisen between the Eastman Kodak Company and the Negro promotional organization, FIGHT. FIGHT challenged the Company to hire a large number of hard-core unemployed persons from the local Negro ranks. The story of this new inner-city conflict, bruited about the nation, did anything but enhance the reputation of a Rochester that had suffered a bad press since the 1964 riots.

On January 23rd, the Bishop, as guest speaker of the Chamber of Commerce, undertook to deal with this very subject—Rochester's good name. It was a delicate issue for a newcomer to comment on. But he handled it delicately and in a positive manner that made it acceptable. Critics can be obnoxious, he said, but they have something to say and should be heeded. Rochester is a great city; and if other Americans are now looking at it critically, they are only concentrating on "a pimple on our nose." A little ointment could cure this defect: the ointment of charity. So he urged business leaders particularly to increase job opportunities, to support urban renewal, to improve housing. If this were done, then Rochester's civic problems would vanish, and her greatness would stand out. As a pledge of his own sincerity, Bishop Sheen declared that he planned to impose a graded tax on any construction undertaken in the future by Catholic parishes. A percentage of this tax would be given to the poor.[58]

In the following May, the Bishop made public the details of his tax on parochial construction. The rate was to run from $1\frac{1}{4}\%$ on construction costing from $50,000.00 to $100,000.00, to 3% on projects costing $500,000.00 or over. The purpose of the tax, he said, was not only to discourage expensive building but to make the faithful more aware of their obligation towards the needy of the world. Part of the amounts collected was to be devoted to Catholic missionary work, part to the needs of the inner city.[59]

Circumstances demand that we halt our narrative at this point: June 15, 1967—the end of the first six months of Bishop Sheen's Rochester career. The date is more convenient mathematically than logically, for it leaves much in suspense. Nevertheless, within the brief period of 180 days, the sixth Bishop of Rochester had already given a clear indication of his views and the direction of his program. The decrees of Vatican II formed his charter, and he brought into his planning an imaginative approach comparable to that of the founding bishop of the Rochester Diocese.

Of one thing in particular there could be no doubt. Fulton J. Sheen shared with Bishop McQuaid the intense desire to have the Diocese of Rochester one of the best in the world.

* * * * * * * * * *

If it is arbitrary to halt our narrative of the Sheen episcopate at the semester mark, it is even more arbitrary to conclude with this date the history of the first century of the Diocese. Human life acknowledges time, not calendars.

The reader may tax us more severely, however, for dealing too incidentally with the basic question: What has the Diocese of Rochester meant to the thousands who have belonged to its fold?

In our own defense, we shall say that we *have* given a partial answer to this question. Some references to it are specific. Much more can surely be argued from the details of diocesan expansion.

But beyond a certain point, no historian of a diocese can hope to go. Considerations of space alone make it impossible for him to set down anything more than a log of this pilgrimage of God's people. And beyond that is the still profounder fact that the pilgrimage is essentially spiritual, in the unobservable depths of the human heart.

He who would read the full story must therefore wait until eternity. Then he can find it in the Book of Life.

CHAPTER SIXTEEN

THE FIFTH QUARTER-CENTURY

WHEN WE wrote *The Diocese of Rochester 1868-1968* we were able to cover its centennial history in six hundred pages. Probably six hundred more pages would be needed to recount the events of the whole quarter century 1968-1993, an era of deep, unexpected change during which the bishops of this and other dioceses were faced with new and difficult problems of organization, discipline and doctrine. It was an exciting time as the Church tried to implement the updating program of the Second Vatican Council. It was also a distressing time that saw the disappearance of many venerable traditions.

Since we are still in the midst of this vast readjustment we are unable to view it in historical perspective, so any "Volume II" of Rochester diocesan history must be indefinitely postponed. It is crucial, nonetheless, to chronicle at least the main events of the Diocese's fifth quarter-century, 1968-1993. Three bishops have occupied the See of Rochester in that period: Fulton J. Sheen (1966-1969); Joseph L. Hogan (1969-1978); and Matthew H. Clark (1979-). To each we accord a section of this supplementary chapter.

1. "BRIGHT METEOR": BISHOP SHEEN'S LATER MONTHS

Church law since 1965 has required diocesan bishops to submit their resignations to the Holy See on reaching the age of seventy-five. Fulton J. Sheen, installed as bishop of Rochester when seventy-one, would normally have complied with this rule on his birthday, May 8, 1970. Actually, he chose to retire several months earlier. Pope Paul VI accepted his request, and on October 15, 1969, named him, in personal tribute, Titular Archbishop of Newport, Wales. Thus ended the briefest episcopate of any bishop of Rochester: two years and ten months. Why should this notable prelate, after his meteoric beginnings in Rochester, have chosen so abruptly to depart? Principally because of an unfortunate turn of events.

To understand just what Fulton Sheen tried to accomplish in Rochester and why his efforts fell short, we must study a little more the personality of this complex churchman.[1]

Sheen was a trained philosopher, a "born teacher", and a "born orator". This triple talent qualified him eminently for work on radio and television, since he had a genius for simplifying concepts and communicating them at a popular level.

Journalist William F. Buckley, Jr., once termed Professor Sheen "the greatest preacher in English". No preacher of the "electronic Gospel" has thus far equalled or replaced him; but the Bishop viewed as lectures rather than as sermons his peak TV series, "Life is Worth Living" (1952-1957). His broadcasts were more philosophical than religious, although "pre-religious" might be a better description. As a pioneer in ecumenical discourse, he chose to address his American contemporaries on moral, social, devotional, nonpolitical themes that he knew the majority accepted; yet he had a gift for infusing any talk with a spiritual significance. It was a successful recipe, and won for him a weekly audience of thirty million. The fact that he had a commercial sponsor made little difference; the listeners knew that his weekly honorariums ($26,000) went to charity. Fulton J. Sheen thus became, in the eyes of non-Catholic Americans, *the* current representative and spokesman of the Catholic Church. There can be little doubt that he did more than any other person to vindicate for American Catholicism undisputed status as one of the three great American religious bodies.

Bishop Sheen was completely devoted to his church. His one constant fear was that Catholicism would be judged by other Americans as behind the times or irrelevant. During his whole radio and television career, therefore, he made a point of offering arresting, innovative insights, calculated to reconcile the Church to the secular world in those matters in which the signs of the times revealed a spiritual need. Speaking from a point of view that was nonpartisan, cosmopolitan rather than nationalist, eternal rather than temporal, Fulton Sheen came to be regarded as a prophetic voice.

We must read this earlier outlook and technique into the actions that Sheen took after his installation in Rochester in 1966.

Enthusiastic about the principles of the Second Vatican Council, he resolved to make of his middle-sized upstate diocese a showcase of conciliar observance. In rapid succession, therefore, he undertook and publicized many reformist measures, structural, ecumenical, and socio-economical. More often than not he released his news items not to the Rochester daily press but to the national press, to the growing chagrin of local journalists. While Sheen was never adverse to making headlines, his bid for national attention seems in this instance to have been dictated precisely by his desire to present the Diocese of Rochester to the whole nation and the whole American Catholic Church as a post-conciliar model.

There is no need to list here the many advanced projects that he launched or proposed. Fulton Sheen was an "idea man", with a lively imagination. His proposals were usually thoughtful, sometimes brilliant, often farsighted. He saw himself as a catalytic agent inciting constructive planning. Unfortunately, while he was good at inventing, he was not good at following through. Bishop McQuaid had also been an "idea man", but he had a seasoned practicality and a sense of detail that enabled him to see his dreams come true. On the other hand, unless somebody volunteered to translate a Sheen concept into concrete terms, it would usually die a-borning.

As the months of his regime swept on, Bishop Sheen continued to restructure his staff and policies. On January 5, 1968, Pope Paul VI gave him two auxiliary bishops. One was his vicar general, Msgr. Dennis Walter Hickey (1914 -) named titular bishop of Rusuccuru. The other was his canonist, Msgr. John Edgar McCafferty (1920-1980), named titular bishop of Tanudaia. They were consecrated together in the Cathedral on March 14, 1968. The principal consecrator was Archbishop Luigi Raimondi, apostolic delegate to the United States; the co-consecrators were Bishop Kearney and Bishop Sheen. Able and judicious men, these two auxiliaries would serve their bishop well.

As chief priest of the diocese, Fulton J. Sheen genuinely wished to know his priests. His efforts to be sociable, however, were not very successful. Lunching with their bishop had not been a tradition among the Rochester priests; furthermore, they inevitably regarded Sheen as a celebrity, and who feels comfortable with a celebrity? But the Bishop did succeed in learning his clergy's names and he was very attentive to ailing priests. As a strong advocate of social justice, he raised a question about the adequacy of priests' salaries, and established a new diocesan pension plan for them. He also wisely initiated a priests' personnel board. When priests began in increasing numbers to consider resigning from the active ministry, Sheen did his eloquent best to dissuade them, as he frowned on laicization.

The introduction of laymen and laywomen into diocesan officialdom was one of Sheen's real breakthroughs, a forward and irreversible policy. Here, too, he was careful to guarantee the proper financial benefits to his paid diocesan personnel.

Although the Bishop accepted in theory the need of dialogue so emphasized by Vatican II, he found it difficult to put it into practice. Normally he would discuss plans with his official staff, but it was generally after he had already decided what to do. He attended the meetings of the "Priests' Senate" lately established by Bishop Kearney, but he found its debates about church business tedious: "'taxidermists talking to taxidermists," he described the sessions to one of his aides. Perhaps he had expected the membership to engage in more spiritual discourse. It was much the same with the lay committees that he himself appointed. If the views of their members differed from his, he would simply call no further meetings. This reluctance to dialogue did not spring from any ill will, but from his total background. His churchmanship was basically "old-fashioned"; he was too mercurial to seek advice readily; and his prime gift was as a monologist, not a dialogist. One does not easily unlearn lifelong or innate ways.

Fulton Sheen's earlier career had been basically academic. Even his broadcasts on social ethics and international communism were rooted in study rather than in world travel. From 1948 on, however, intensive visits to Asia, Latin America and Africa gave him a wider personal sense of both the culture and the dire needs of the Third World. Consequently, when he came to Rochester it was with the cosmopolitan and ecumenical convictions of an outstanding missionary. Ecumenical, because he had learned to seek out what was good in other religious traditions, not only in other Christian churches but in Judaism, Islam, and the various polytheistic creeds. Cosmopolitan, because he had seen at first hand the spiritual and economic poverty of so much of mankind, and had become an impassioned advocate of the world's poor.

Let us focus on two projects he fostered that involved local Catholics and Protestants. In each case, doctrine was not at issue, but the duplication of pastoral efforts in areas where cooperation seemed more sensible.

Project No. 1 was the establishment in August 1967 of the Rochester Joint Office of Urban Ministry in the city center. This was the first such diocesan office set up in the United States. Father P. David Finks represented the Diocese of Rochester; Herbert D. White, the local Council of Churches' "Board for Urban Ministry". It is true that by mid-1968 Sheen was, for several reasons, less ready to support the Joint Office. Nevertheless, he deserves credit for initially approving the experiment.

Project No. 2 was the inauguration of an "ecumenical seminary".

Academic that he was, Bishop Sheen took a genuine interest in his diocesan major seminary, St. Bernard's. He encouraged its successful efforts to obtain State authority to grant degrees in theology, and to obtain academic accreditation from the American Association of Theological Seminaries. He opened registration at the Seminary to women and lay persons. He persuaded the Precious Blood Fathers, the Italian

Capuchins, the Mercedarians, and the Basilians to enroll students at St. Bernard's. He even tried, although in vain, to fuse upstate Catholic seminaries into one. And with nothing short of bravado, he invited some of the world's prominent scholars, Protestant and Orthodox as well as Catholic, to join St. Bernard's faculty. While the most notable invitees politely declined, Sheen did succeed in recruiting several specialists to adorn the staff, laymen as well as clerics, Europeans as well as Americans.

Actually, the Seminary itself was just then beginning to experience a shortfall of vocations and funds, for all the Bishop's grandiose plans. When Father Joseph P. Brennan was installed as rector in June 1966, he soon encountered a need to renovate radically the school's aging plant. Would it not be wiser, he wondered, to sell the property and build a more modest structure elsewhere? Around the same time, Dr. Gene E. Bartlett, the enterprising president of Colgate Rochester Divinity School (a long-established institution, Baptist in background but interdenominational in program) was arranging to welcome as an affiliate Bexley Hall, a small Episcopal seminary hitherto located in Gambier, Ohio. Dr. Bartlett suggested that Father Brennan consider adding St. Bernard's to this new consortium.

When Brennan communicated the proposal to Bishop Sheen, the Bishop took a fancy to it. He had often toyed, he said, with the notion of an "ecumenical seminary". Such a school would, to say the least, avoid needless duplication of facilities and expenses. Therefore, on June 27, 1967, he authorized Father Brennan to continue conversations with President Bartlett. The Bishop's one proviso was that the ruling principle of such a consortium should be "integration with identity". In other words, St. Bernard's, like the other affiliates, would retain its own identity, its faculty, its curriculum, and, of course, its doctrinal convictions, while sharing the one locale and its academic, cultural and domestic benefits. To emphasize this independence, Sheen sought a new seminary site near, but not at, Colgate Rochester; but he warned that relocation depended on finding a purchaser for the original St. Bernard's.

A committee representing Colgate Rochester, Bexley Hall, and St. Bernard's Seminary set to work in August 1967. The end product was the "Rochester Center for Theological Studies", a membership corporation chartered on May 4, 1968. Several joint undertakings of the consortium were soon under way. However, the distance between the "South Campus" (the Divinity School) and the "North Campus" (St. Bernard's) impeded, for the nonce, fuller cross-registration and interschool activities.

In the end, efforts to find land near the Divinity School failed, so the plan to build a new St. Bernard's had to be put on hold. Also, certain occurrences at Colgate Rochester in early 1969 gave the Bishop pause.

In 1967, the 18 black students at Colgate Rochester had organized a Black Caucus. Dr. Martin Luther King was assassinated on April 4, 1968. In the midst of the nationwide racial turmoil that followed, this Caucus, on December 10, 1968, demanded that Colgate Rochester name a certain quota of blacks to the faculty, administration and Board of Directors. The Caucus promised a "lockout" if its demand was not fulfilled by March 1, 1969.

Now, the Divinity School was already working in this direction, but careful selection of the new personnel was necessarily time-consuming. Nevertheless, when the task was not complete by the deadline, Black Caucus members locked themselves into the main building on The Hill, from March 2 to March 19, excluding all others from entry. In the end the dispute was settled amicably, with no penalties imposed; still, Bishop Sheen and others found the episode disturbing. What seems to have worried the Bishop most was whether it was desirable for Catholic seminarians, whose program of training required academic peace and prayerfulness, to frequent a school where social struggle could so easily disrupt the educational schedule. Did the permissive rule of life at The Hill even threaten the Catholic "identity" that he had insisted must always balance the "integration" of the RCTS consortium?

The "lockout" was one of many troublesome events in a year that had been nationally shaken by war and violence. At length, Bishop Sheen told Dr. Bartlett on June 5, 1969, that he had decided to suspend for twelve months all discussions about closer fusion with the Rochester Center for Theological Studies. "Perhaps at that time," he wrote, "through the grace of God, calmness and sound judgment will prevail again in our nation and among our people."

Fulton Sheen's "prophetic" techniques never implied radicalism in an extremist sense. For this man trained in classic philosophy and Scholastic theology, the norm was always the "golden and virtuous mean," the middle ground. The questions he raised might be venturesome, but for him the Church and its interest always came first. Regarding the RCTS, he never revoked his moratorium. By June 5, 1970, he had already taken an early retirement from the post of bishop of Rochester, leaving to his successor the task of recommencing the study of how best to interblend St. Bernard's with Colgate Rochester, Bexley Hall, and the cluster's new associate, Crozer Theological Seminary. Had

Sheen perhaps expected this turn of events when he wrote to President Bartlett?[2]

However great his interest in the academical and the ecumenical, Fulton Sheen's great passion was to better the condition of the poor, economically as well as spiritually, internationally as well as nationally. While American director of the Society for the Propagation of the Faith, his solicitude had been mostly for the poor abroad, and while bishop of Rochester he pointedly reminded his flock that, as Vatican II had declared, every Catholic was called on by his very baptism to be world-mission minded.

At the same time he stressed the needs of the poor at home.

The "poor" within the Rochester diocese were principally the blacks (whose Catholic population was small), and the Spanish-speaking, who were Catholic at least in tradition.

Sheen had long been interested in the American blacks. Before coming to Rochester he had been a major benefactor of the first black maternity hospital in the South: the Sisters of Mercy's Martin de Porres Hospital in Mobile, Alabama (1942-1971). In Rochester he expected his Office of Urban Ministry to be the major diocesan coordinator of work among African-Americans.

The Latinos in the Diocese of Rochester trace their origin to many Latin-American countries. In the early 1960s, Puerto Ricans constituted the majority, although there were also some Mexicans and Mexican-Americans among the rural migrant workers. Redemptorist priests, veterans of the Puerto Rico missions who were now assigned to St. Joseph's Church in Rochester, had already begun to serve the local Hispanics, and a few young diocesan priests were showing an interest in that apostolate.

On June 29, 1967, Bishop Sheen chose one of the latter group, Father Roger F. Baglin, to organize efforts on behalf of the Spanish-speaking. Father Baglin was then assistant pastor of St. Bridget's parish in the inner city. Under his creative guidance, the Hispanics soon acquired a center, Concordia Hall, originally the recreational center of the fading German parish of Holy Redeemer. From this center, Baglin was able to expand the diocese's apostolic efforts.

Two groups in the program were especially notable. One was the Hermanos Catolicos (Catholic Brothers), a group of Hispanic laymen who had made the Cursillo (an intensive Spanish-American type of retreat). These became lay apostles working effectively among the Spanish-speaking seasonal migrant workers outside Rochester. The other was the Guadalupan Missionaries of the Holy Spirit, who opened a small house in Rochester in April 1968. Members of an order of sisters based in Mexico City, they would serve the Spanish-speaking in Rochester, Brockport, Geneva and Newark, N.Y., until June 1992. They did much to consolidate the area's Latinos and build up in them a sense of their religious identity.

In dealing with the Rochester blacks, Father Finks saw as the primary need the social and political organization of their minority to combat a demoralizing poverty. While Sheen did not ignore this organizational avenue, he himself favored the more traditional approach of personal charity; and "convert-maker" that he was to a superlative degree, he envisaged a certain amount of Catholic evangelization among the non-Catholic Afro-Americans.

Perhaps the very title that the Bishop gave to Father Baglin's assignment, the "Spanish *Apostolate*," was expressive of this missionary thrust. But the Hispanics, too, needed to achieve a united front in American society in order to make themselves heard. Consequently, on June 28, 1968, state approval was given to a new corporation, The Ibero-American Action League, whose stated aims were sociocultural. Father Baglin was one of the incorporating trustees and served as its interim executive director. If the Center's agenda henceforth was less explicitly religious, the League nevertheless embodied the social ideals of the Church.

In addition to providing an approach to the Afro community and the Latino community, Bishop Sheen also authorized a new program to support Rochester's seven inner-city parish schools, which, along with the whole diocesan school system, he was intent on preserving.

Shortly after naming Father Albert Shamon Vicar of Education, Sheen gave him a year to work out a plan for financing the seven schools. Father Shamon's eventual proposal was, first to divide the diocese into 14 regions. The resultant regions in Monroe County would each include some 15-20 more prosperous parishes, plus one or two impoverished inner-city parishes. The pastor of each of the poorer parishes would then approach annually the pastor of one of the better-off parishes in his region and ask for a donation (normally only about $5,000) to balance the inner-city school's budget. Bishop Sheen approved Shamon's project, and by the time of his retirement in 1969 it was beginning to function.

Although the gravest problems of poverty were concentrated in Metropolitan Rochester, Fulton J. Sheen did not overlook the needy in the more rural counties of the diocese. As early as June 29, 1967, he established an apostolate called the Secular Mission, with Father John J. Hempel as director.

The Secular Mission's assignment was to seek out isolated Catholics in the hinterlands. Father Hempel took up residence at Penn Yan and focused personally on Yates and Seneca counties. Younger priests were assigned to the two other centers: Steuben County and Tompkins-Tioga counties. Working practically on their own, the priests on the team developed plans suggested by the varying religious and socioeconomic necessities they encountered. The Secular Mission did not have time to set up permanent structures, for in July 1969 Father Hempel was called back to Rochester to head the new diocesan Office of Human Concern, which would take charge of both the urban ministry and the rural apostolate. Credit is due the Secular Mission, however, for one important achievement. It had discovered many clusters of Catholic migrant workers hitherto unknown or uncared for. They were principally Hispanics, but there were also a group of Catholic Indians from Canada and clusters of Afro migrants and "staygrants" (migrants who had become settlers). Once alerted to the presence of these ethnic groups, the Diocese began to reformulate its rural outreach coverage.

Bishop Sheen himself undertook two notable projects designed to provide the local poor with better housing. One of the projects still continues, with remarkable success. The other, more ambitious in concept, failed notoriously to get off the ground, a failure that prompted the Bishop to seek early retirement.

The first project was the Bishop Sheen Housing Foundation.

In June 1967 Sheen met a black couple with three children who were living in two squalid rooms in Rochester's Third Ward. Having inspected their flat himself, he took the mother and a real estate agent on a tour of the residential neighborhoods. When they found a house suitable to their needs, he purchased it for them out of his own pocket.

Vividly aware of the shortage of low-income living quarters, he took the occasion, sometime later, at a gathering of the Catholic Interracial Council of Immaculate Conception Church, to present a plan for collecting a housing fund. He invited 70 "disciples" to donate $10 a week for 24 weeks. This "10-24-70" club, launched on December 12, 1967, was incorporated on April 16, 1968, as the Bishop Sheen Housing Foundation, a not-for-profit organization. A number of people signed on as "disciples", but by the date of incorporation the inflow of donations had diminished, and no housing had yet been provided.

Meanwhile, several Catholic women volunteers working in the inner-city parish of St. Bridget's were concerned about housing in that area, where the Urban Renewal program had razed the ramshackle low-income residences. In the fall of 1968, one of these volunteers, Eleanor (Mrs. Jerome) Cook, a contributor to the "10-24-70" project, wrote Bishop Sheen to ask if the Housing Fund could provide a black family of 12 in the St. Bridget's neighborhood with enough money to make a down payment on an available home. The Bishop told Mrs. Cook yes, and to go ahead with arrangements. She did so with effective speed. Delighted by what she had accomplished "without fanfare", Sheen authorized her to continue the housing efforts. By the time of his retirement in late 1969, 18 low-income families with potential for property ownership had been settled in homes of their own. Bishop Sheen was happy to be called the "father" of this enterprise, but he insisted that Eleanor Cook was its "mother".

Reorganized in 1972 under Bishop Joseph L. Hogan, the BSHF continued to be operated by a loyal group, and by 1971 it had rehoused 26 families, comprising over 200 persons. Then on October 14, 1980, under Bishop Matthew H. Clark, it merged, for practical efficiency, with the Episcopal Housing Commission of the Episcopal Diocese of Rochester, and was renamed the Bishop Sheen Ecumenical Housing Foundation. The BSEHF report for 1993 indicated that in that year alone it had serviced 328 families at a cost of $1,152,874. Functioning in 13 counties of western New York, the Sheen agency has been recognized as a uniquely successful service. "It helps the poor to help themselves," and gives them a feeling of "dignity and pride." So says Mrs. Cook, now retired from active participation.

While the Housing Fund concept was being deftly developed by a group of skilled lay persons, Fulton Sheen also conceived another more grandiose but abortive plan to provide low-income residences. The idea, which occurred to him in the autumn of 1967, was to give to the federal government the property of an inner-city parish on which to erect needed housing for the poor. Such a gift, he hoped, would have an electrifying effect on the nation's bishops and inspire them to follow his example.

In framing this proposal, Sheen acted with minimal consultation. He did inform the Vatican and the Apostolic Delegate in the early stages. He also spoke of the plan in vague terms with Father Finks and his other official confidants. Their reaction was to urge him to move deliberately, but they sensed that he was not about to be dissuaded. Neither did he confer early with the Rochester Housing Authority, which supervised all local public housing. Most unfortunately of all, he did not consult with the pastor or parishioners of the parish finally selected: St. Bridget's, a small congregation of "Irish", Italians, Afro-Americans and Hispanics, but an oasis of faith, schooling and charity in a deserted neighborhood.

Having thus decided to make this striking gift, the Bishop by-passed the Rochester City officals and dealt directly with Mr. Robert V. Weaver, secretary of the federal H.U.D. (Department of Housing and Urban Development) in the cabinet of President Lyndon B. Johnson. By letter of November 8, 1967, Sheen offered Washington in gift the whole property of one inner-city Rochester church, with the sole stipulation that the federal government erect upon it housing for the poor "within the shortest possible time". Secretary Weaver accepted the offer by letter of January 29, 1968, choosing, among the possible urban parishes, St. Bridget's, whose church, school, rectory and convent were valued at $680,000. As they proceeded with the planning, Mr. Weaver accepted the Bishop's recommendation that all negotiations be kept secret, "so as to achieve the maximum effect."

Despite the agreement about dramatic secrecy, rumors of the plan leaked out, and with them rumors of a possible protest. Refusing to be deterred by "a few negative persons", Sheen announced the gift to the national press on February 28, 1968, which was Ash Wednesday. In his release he stated that while he was making this Lenten offering of a parish plant, he fully intended to provide in other ways for the church, school, and social needs of the parishioners (an assurance apparently not fully grasped by all).

The news of the property gift did indeed cause the nationwide stir that the Bishop had anticipated, but to his dismay the reaction was more unfavorable than favorable. None were more upset than the pastor and parishioners of St. Bridget's; Bishop Sheen had given away their parish plant without even asking their opinion! Inquirers now kept the telephone lines busy with calls to rectory and Pastoral Office. The mail to both places was heavy with letters of protest, some of them bitter and incredibly crude. A group of young women from Monroe Community College who had been working in the parish as volunteers gathered to picket outside the Bishop's office, carrying placards demanding "Save St. Bridget's!!"

But it was the Priests' Association of Rochester that mounted the most effective critique. This was a voluntary organization of a number of diocesan priests that had been formed in November 1966. It was patterned after the Association of Chicago Priests formed on October 24,

1966 to provide the Chicago Catholic clergy, in those days when "Speak Out" was becoming a nationwide motto, with a united front, and, if need be, a pressure group for church reforms.

The officers and some of the members of the P.A.R. met, (presumably on Thursday) with Father P. David Finks, the diocesan Vicar of Urban Ministry, and Father Francis H. Vogt, the pastor of St. Bridget's, present. They composed a strong but respectfully worded letter urging that Bishop Sheen rescind the gift of property. Loth to engage in public confrontation with the Bishop, the 22 signers sent him their communication privately, with the request that he receive at once their *ad hoc* committee of three pastors to discuss the issue. As the hours passed and others learned of the Association's action, over 100 more priests asked to add their signatures to the letter.

When Sheen had not responded by Friday evening, March 1, the Association released to the local press the news of its protest. The *Democrat and Chronicle* carried the gist of the letter the next morning.

Whether it was wise of them to go public so quickly, the priests of P.A.R. certainly hastened Bishop Sheen's response. On Saturday he sent its committee a hand-delivered reply indicating his acceptance of the Association's recommendation. Father Vogt was thus able to announce at the Masses on Sunday, March 3, that the Bishop had revoked his gift to the federal government. St. Bridget's parishioners were beside themselves with delight. Monday morning's newspaper headlined the good tidings: "ST. BRIDGET'S SPARED; JOY REIGNS." Naturally, Secretary Weaver accepted the withdrawal of the gift. The federal agency was doubtless happy to back out of so unpopular a bargain.

The P.A.R. protest had objected to the property gift chiefly because there had been no preliminary dialogue with those involved, particularly the parishioners and the priests laboring in the Inner City. Local critics and national commentators pretty much agreed with this judgment. Father Vogt was prompt to praise not only Sheen's motive but the proposal itself. Ironically, he said, if the Bishop had first asked the parishioners, they would quite likely have approved his giving away the St. Bridget plant.

Fulton Sheen's life career, up to this point, had been to all appearances, one constant success. How did he react to this major failure?

Outwardly, he simply refrained from discussing the subject. Inwardly, he probably accepted it with Christian resignation. But the wound was deep and never really healed. He had considered the whole proposal as an important gesture of Catholic charity. Shocked by his priests' apparent indifference to the needs of the poor, he concluded that he could no longer depend on their collective support in anything. This was, of course, a mistaken conclusion. Some priests who opposed the gift may have had axes to grind, but most of them had disapproved rather of his method and his failure to understand the importance of St. Bridget's as a Catholic presence in the neighborhood.

Nevertheless, according to his closest associates, from March 3, 1968, on, Fulton J. Sheen was a "changed man". He ceased thereafter to play the public catalyst, simply busying himself with the routines of his office. Finally, deciding that the cross of diocesan leadership was too heavy to bear, on a visit to Rome in early 1969 he asked permission of Pope Paul VI to resign his see a year in advance.

Sheen gave out his last "surprise" news release in late summer, 1969. He informed the press that he had submitted his resignation from the See of Rochester to the Holy Father, and it had been accepted. Named Titular Archbishop of Newport on October 15, 1969, he left Rochester for good in October, returning to New York City, the site of his earlier triumphs: not to retire, he promised, but to resume his work, as a teacher, preacher and retreat master.

In his farewell address to the Rochester priests on November 28, 1969, Archbishop Sheen pointedly asked forgiveness "for the things I left unsaid and should have said, for the times I monologued when I should have dialogued." Once back in Gotham he spent a decade full of honors, as busy as advancing age would permit. He died of a heart affliction on December 6, 1979. Burial was in St. Patrick's Cathedral, where in bygone days he had stirred thousands with "the message of the Cross".

Commentators on the Rochester career of Fulton J. Sheen agree that he could have been a more effective residential bishop if he had had more administrative and pastoral experience. He himself seems never to have appreciated the seriousness of this lack. In the brief chapter he devoted to the Rochester years in his rambling autobiography, he recalled several things that he "would like to have done but failed to do." While all of the ideas listed had some merit, they were largely unworkable.

In view of his several errors in judgment while bishop of Rochester, and the brevity of his episcopate—34 months—can we rightly speak of a "Sheen heritage"?

We can. And with the passage of time, his positive contributions to the Church of Rochester become more evident.

First, he set the Diocese off in the right postconciliar direction. Faced like the other bishops with the need to reorganize diocesan structures, he promptly made basic changes with the vigor of a much younger man. He asked the priests to nominate his counselors, as we have seen; he established a proper priests' council and a priests' personnel board, and provided a priests' pension plan. He likewise introduced lay men and women into the financial and operational departments of the Diocese, and saw to it that these salaried persons were covered by pension arrangements.

Second, he taught the Diocese by word and work its conscientious obligation to the world's poor. Three such "teaching gestures" were the appointment of a vicar of urban ministry, of a coordinator of work on behalf of the Spanish-speaking, and of a director of rural ministry. An object lesson to his priests was his imposition of a "tax" on parochial building projects, particularly rectories, the income to be used for the benefit of the poor. Finally, as noted above, he established the Bishop Sheen Housing Fund, a continuing monument to this Good Samaritan. All in all, he left us far more sensitive to our duty to the poor.

Third, he authorized the setting up of a graduate department of theology at St. Bernard's Seminary, and the Seminary's membership in the Rochester Center for Theological Studies. Although circumstances would necessitate the closing in 1981 of the Seminary's program of priestly formation, thanks to him the graduate department was able to continue, as St. Bernard's Institute, on the Colgate-Rochester campus, along with the three other member institutions of the ecumenical Rochester Center for Theological Studies.

Fourth, certain of Sheen's inspirations, which were initially ignored or not developed, were later accepted and acted on, suggesting that he was in several ways in advance of his time. The diocesan cadre of permanent deacons was established only in the 1980s, but Bishop Sheen had ordained his first permanent deacon in 1969. It was likewise he who appointed the first co-pastors of the diocese. In view of the declining number of priests, he foresaw the "clustering" of parishes, although "clusters" were officially adopted only several years later. When he proposed that Rochester's St. Mary's Hospital sponsor clinics in poor neighborhoods, his recommendation was turned down. Eventually, however, the Hospital did launch just such a project, and to good effect. Also, when the Bishop published nationally his suggestion that the age for confirmation be advanced into the teen years, he encountered differing opinions among the United States bishops; but in 1994 the Holy See officially permitted to American dioceses the Sheen option.

Even Sheen's admonitions to secular leaders, though not warmly welcomed at first, were deemed acceptable later on. Thus his early advice to the major industries of Rochester to provide more job opportunities for the local minorities was received rather coolly, but eventually implemented. The Bishop, known for decades as a staunch anticommunist, startled the country on July 30, 1967, when in a sermon delivered in Rochester, he urged President Lyndon B. Johnson to withdraw all U.S. troops from Vietnam. He spoke, he said, not as a politician but as a moralist. President Johnson did not heed the advice, of course. But in 1973, his successor, President Richard M. Nixon, put an end to America's most unpopular war.

In the chaotic and egocentric 1960s, no American bishop, even the youngest, the most vigorous, and the most pastorally experienced, had all the answers about how to chart the course of the postconciliar Church. Bishop Sheen had *some* of the answers, at least. Once implemented, these set his own diocese on a road of no return, and gave to the heads of other dioceses a nudge in the right direction.

The "Sheen heritage" in Rochester was therefore not so much a bequest of achievements as of focus. P. David Finks put it well when he wrote that the Bishop's heart was in the right place: "In a time of ambiguity, he did some good things. That is not a bad epitaph for a man, or a bishop."

The people of the Diocese of Rochester should not forget the honor that is theirs in just having had Fulton J. Sheen as their bishop, however briefly. He was certainly an outstanding figure in American Catholic history. Furthermore, he was a thoroughly good and dedicated priest. If he became a national celebrity, with all the temptations to pride that the celebrity status suggests, he countered vainglory by his humble devotion to the cross of Christ, by his daily hour before the Blessed Sacrament, by his childlike affection for the Mother of God, and by his all-embracing charity. Sheen never wanted to be anything but a priest, and a worthy one. Rochester Catholics certainly recognized him as such, and his spiritual influence here was positive.

On October 2, 1979, two months before he died, the Archbishop of Newport was presented to Pope John Paul II during the papal visit to St. Patrick's Cathedral in New York. The Holy Father embraced him and they conversed briefly. Sheen was deeply moved. Asked afterward what the Pope had said, he replied, "He told me that I had written and spoken well of the Lord Jesus, and that I was a loyal son of the Church."

No words of commendation could have been more pleasing to the sixth bishop of Rochester. To preach Christ and to serve the Church faithfully had been the sole aim of his extraordinary life.

2. "THE LONG WINTER OF RENEWAL": BISHOP JOSEPH L. HOGAN (1969-1978) [3]

To succeed Fulton Sheen in the see of Rochester, Paul VI, on October 6, 1969, designated Msgr. Joseph L. Hogan, a Rochester priest. Sheen did not hesitate to say that he himself had recommended the bishop-elect to the Holy Father.

It was a sign of the times that the Rochester Association of Catholic Laymen should have protested the appointment. As champions of a more egalitarian postconciliar Church, they complained that the process of election had been undemocratic. They hastened to add, however, that they had no objection to the man selected.

Msgr. Hogan was indeed qualified to serve as the seventh bishop of Rochester. Impressively tall (six-feet-four-and-more), and graciously good-humored, he was the very image of a diocesan bishop. At 53 he was young enough to be energetic and old enough to be sagacious. Best of all, perhaps—at least in the opinion of Rochester diocesans—he was "one of their own": the first local priest to head the diocese since John F. O'Hern (1929-1933). That meant that, unlike an extern appointee, he was well acquainted with the "tone" of the Rochester diocese and with its people, particularly the priests and religious. Of course, the very familiarity of a "home-grown" bishop can sometimes be a drawback. A well-known person like Msgr. Hogan can find popularity a snag when he is called on to make unpopular decisions.

Joseph Lloyd Hogan was born in rural Lima, New York, on March 11, 1916, second of the six offspring of Michael C. Hogan and Mary Shaw Hogan. Michael C. was a foreman at the local Porcelain Insulator Corporation. Mary, raised a Methodist, was received into the Catholic Church before her marriage. Joseph graduated with distinction from the parochial school of St. Rose parish and from Lima High School. Feeling called to the diocesan priesthood, he took the prescribed courses at the Rochester preparatory and theological seminaries of St. Andrew's and St. Bernard's. Bishop James E. Kearney ordained him a priest on June 6, 1942, in the Pro-cathedral of the Sacred Heart, Rochester.

Back at Lima High School, the bespectacled young cleric had somehow acquired the nickname "Academic": "Ack" for short. The monicker not only stuck, it became prophetic. During the first 27 years of his priestly career he would spend only four years in parish work:

assistant pastor of St. Mary's, Elmira (1942-1945) and pastor of St. Margaret Mary, Rochester (1968-1969). The rest of the years he was truly an *academic,* on one side of the desk or the other. Teacher, high school, St. Andrew's Seminary (1945-1949). M.A. candidate at Canisius College, Buffalo, with dissertation on Bishop McQuaid as educator (1948-1949). Doctoral student at the Angelicum University, Rome, Italy (1949-1951). Teacher, college department, St. Andrew's Seminary (1951-1953). Principal, De Sales High School, Geneva, New York (1953-1955). And finally—the post for which he had been trained in Rome—professor of fundamental theology (plus lecturer on papal social doctrine and academic dean) at St. Bernard's. Along the line, Dr. Hogan had also taught at summer school at Canisius College; lectured the novices of the Sisters of St. Joseph on spiritual theology; and taught theology at St. John Fisher College.

It was while dean of St. Bernard's that Hogan became active in updating the local seminary program along more professional lines. St. Andrew's Seminary had hitherto provided four years of high school and two years of college; St. Bernard's, two years of senior college and four years of theology. The "split-level" college department had been granted a State charter on April 22, 1931, but it had never sought professional academic accreditation. In 1965, however, the Diocese decided to follow the example of some other diocesan seminaries and obtain accreditation by affiliation. The "six-six" plan would yield to the "four-four-four" plan. St. Andrew's would be reduced to a high school and St. Bernard's to a theologate. Thenceforth the college-level seminarians would attend St. John Fisher College, whose degrees were accredited. For these collegians the Diocese would build a new residence across from Fisher, to bear the name "Becket Hall". Father Hogan, enthusiastic about this new venture, was happy to cooperate with Bishop Kearney in its development and promotion. Appropriately, he was named the first rector of Becket Hall (1965-1968). On January 18, 1966, Pope Paul VI, at the request of Bishop Kearney, conferred on Hogan the title of domestic prelate.

When, therefore, the same pope appointed Msgr. Hogan bishop of Rochester in 1969, he was entrusting the diocese to an experienced educator. Of course, Bishop Sheen had also been primarily an academic in his public career, but along different lines. Time alone would reveal how the seventh bishop of Rochester intended to place his scholastic experience at the service of his new pastoral duties.

The episcopal consecration and installation of Bishop Hogan took place on November 28, 1969, in Sacred Heart Cathedral. The ordaining prelate was Archbishop Luigi Raimondi, Apostolic Delegate to the United States. Official con-consecrators were Archbishop Sheen and Bishop Lawrence B. Casey.

Incidentally, for the record, a rather startling question was raised at the time of the ordination about the possible alteration of the Rochester diocesan boundaries. In a moment of private conversation, Archbishop Raimondi asked the new bishop what he thought of the current recommendation to set up new dioceses in western New York. Hogan had heard rumors of such a proposal, but he knew nothing of its details or its authority.

The gist of the plan became widely known only much later. First to broach it, in the 1960s, was Father Francis McCloskey,[4] assistant pastor at Ilion in the Albany Diocese. Noting that diocesan boundaries in New York State too often ignored district demographics, McCloskey, citing Vatican II, argued for a more logical diocesan realignment around the State's socio-economic centers. His primary focus, of course, was on the dioceses of Albany and Syracuse. He proposed that new sees be set up at Utica and Binghamton, to include at least Cayuga and Tioga counties, to be taken from the Rochester Diocese. What to do with the remaining Southern Tier counties of the Buffalo and Rochester dioceses McCloskey was less sure, but he thought two more dioceses might be created there. The proposal made sense to several priests and prominent laymen in central New York, and an unofficial committee was formed to study it.

In his impromptu reply to the Apostolic Delegate, Bishop Hogan said that whatever revisions might be under scrutiny, he believed that there was no need to disturb the existing borders of the Rochester diocese. That was apparently all Raimondi needed to know. Father McCloskey's proposal got no further. Thus the new bishop of Rochester, without fully realizing it, had helped keep his diocesan map intact. The McCloskey goal, while sound in theory, would have been complicated in practice. For example, in the four rural hill-counties of Rochester's Southern Tier, there had been relatively little increase for a century in either the general or the Catholic population, and there was still no city really qualified to situate a cathedral.

In his inaugural sermon, Bishop Joseph Hogan recognized that his chief priority was to reveal to his flock the vision of Church projected by Vatican II. "It is one thing to initiate a reform," Auxiliary Bishop John E. McCafferty observed around this time, "but it is quite another to put it into practice." The Council had projected an "updating"; but its reforms, more radical than they first appeared, were as yet little implemented. The turbulence that had already arisen in the process of implementation showed Hogan that the task could take "many winters". He did not fear the challenge, however. Having chosen as his motto, "Gladly will I spend and be spent" (2 Cor 12:15), he accepted his new office with joy, confident of the assistance of the Holy Spirit.

The brief space at our disposal permits only a summary of the bustling Hogan episcopate.

A new bishop must first gather a staff. One of Bishop Hogan's enduring aims was to correct what he termed the "Canal syndrome", a long-standing tendency of the Rochester Chancery to formulate diocesan policies without much consulting the parishes south of the Erie Canal—or, for that matter, anywhere outside of Monroe County. Nevertheless, he began to collect a *curia* that seemed to be quite bureaucratic. The staff members chosen were, of course, lay and religious as well as priests. A layman was engaged to organize the personnel. For the first time, a layman was also appointed diocesan treasurer. In setting up an office of Black Ministry (the second such in any American diocese), Bishop Hogan chose a young black priest, Fr. Jerome Robinson, O.P., as its director. The Bishop made a point of enlisting many younger people—priests, sisters, and laypersons. He was not afraid, he declared, of the so-called "new breed". He admired their zeal and generosity. Some of these appointees had special fields of interest: social, institutional and educational; and he was ready to adopt many of their forward-looking programs. Another practice that he pioneered in 1970 was the publication, for the first time, of the annual financial statement of the Diocese. As he rightly believed, this action was a prudent demonstration of the financial responsibility of the diocesan corporation, especially in a decade when its income was in perilous decline.

With the diocesan offices now assuming more corporate dimensions, more floor space was needed. The Chancery had occupied compact quarters in the downtown Columbus Civic Center since 1937. When that property was sold in 1971, the episcopal office became homeless. In 1970, however, Bishop Hogan closed Bishop Sheen's "King's Prep" (the former St. Andrew's Seminary at 1150 Buffalo Road). This building was remodeled extensively in 1971-1972; and in September 1972 its ample space was occupied, for starts, by the Pastoral Office, the financial office, the schools office, and the Tribunal.

Had the enlargement of his *curia* canceled out the Bishop's plans for a more decentralized rule? No. He and his successor would find other ways to bring the diocesan center into the regions and to associate the regions more closely with the diocesan center.

The Fathers of Vatican II had thought it best to begin their conciliar discussions with the subject of liturgical reform. Although the postconciliar revisions proposed were based on sound historical traditions, they were tediously piecemeal in execution. Only in 1974 was the complete new English Missal available. It had much to recommend it, but there had sprung up in the "experimental period" a number of hardy caprices impatient of rubrics. Bishop Hogan himself had a deep personal devotion to the Blessed Sacrament. For that very reason he accepted the renewed liturgy as an official instrument of *aggiornamento*, and was not hesitant to authorize Saturday evening Masses; lay lectors and Eucharistic ministers, male and female; Communion in the hand; and other practices then novel but eventually commonplace. Always striving to teach his people that the liturgical changes had a single aim, to remind the faithful that they celebrated the Eucharist as a sacred community, he sometimes changed the times and venues of festal Masses for further emphasis. Thus, instead of celebrating the Holy Week Mass for the Blessing of the Holy Oils always in the Cathedral, which relatively few could attend, he began to solemnize it each year in a different part of the Diocese. Likewise, since attendance at the Christmas Midnight Mass was falling off, he proposed scheduling another Mass earlier on Christmas Eve, at a time when children could attend. This Christmas Family Mass has remained very popular up to the present.

Bishop Hogan also established a new policy regarding the sacraments of Confirmation and Matrimony. Bishop Sheen, as we have seen, favored deferring Confirmation until the upper years of high school, as a sacrament of Christian maturity. His successor chose to administer it to children in grades seven through nine. Again, teen-age marriages were on the increase in the 1960s. Hogan ordered that couples aged between 18 and 21 take a special course of premarital instructions. These courses proved effective, and the Rochester plan was adopted by other dioceses. Public Anointing of the Sick also won considerable favor. Crowds of the sick and elderly flocked to receive the healing sacrament either in their home parishes or at diocesan services at which the Bishop presided.

Vatican II likewise admonished Catholic bishops and their people to "take an active and intelligent part in the work of ecumenism." Joseph Hogan readily complied. While, like most American bishops, he did not seek substantial contacts with the Eastern Orthodox Churches in the area, he did cooperate cordially with Western Christian denominations, particularly the Episcopalians and the mainline Protestant bodies. His people also rallied to the call for Catholic involvement in ecumenism, especially in joint projects of civic and social concern.

Of unusual note was Bishop Hogan's collaboration with the Episcopal Bishop of Rochester, the Rt. Rev. Robert R. Spears, in the issuance of a joint pastoral letter on September 16, 1971. The incentive was a recent prison riot at nearby Attica State Prison, violent in conception and bloodily suppressed. The letter, read from the pulpits of both the Episcopal and the Catholic dioceses, expressed sympathy for the victims of the uprising, inmates and guards alike. It urged that the embattled negotiators accept the conciliatory points of agreement already formulated, and it stressed the moral obligation to establish fairer norms of appeal applicable to prison conflicts in the future.

Most striking among the ecumenical accomplishments of the Hogan era was the formation in 1971 of the Genesee Ecumenical Ministries, better known by its acronym "GEM".

Prior to 1970, nine white Protestant denominations of Monroe County and the local Black Church Ministers' Conference had for some time been united for social cooperation in a body called the Churches of Rochester and Monroe County. After the Second Vatican Council had adopted an ecumenical stance, the Protestant association decided to change its name and invite the Diocese of Rochester to become a member. Bishop Hogan welcomed the invitation and GEM came into being in late 1971. In January 1972 the membership elected a Catholic as its first executive director. He was Father Henry A. Atwell, the pastor of St. Agnes Church, Avon, New York. As forthright editor (1958-1967) of the diocesan *Courier Journal,* Atwell had been a local pioneer in interdenominational and interfaith relations. Apparently he was the first Catholic priest in the United States to be chosen for such an office. Poor health obliged Father Atwell to resign after two years, but until his death in 1980 he remained a vibrant GEM consultant. Genesee Ecumenical Ministries continued to function until 1991, when it again reorganized as the Greater Rochester Community of Churches. It had meanwhile proved serviceable in many situations where joint social engagement between the churches was in order; such as jail ministry, the judicial process, and urban education.

Collaboration between Catholics and Jews and members of other non-Christian faiths is not technically ecumenical, but Vatican II urged Catholics to enter into discussion and collaboration with these bodies as well. Since the Muslim and Far East faiths were little represented within the Rochester Diocese in the 1970s, this rule was applicable principally to the Jewish community. Joseph Hogan was happy to work with

Rabbi Judea Miller of Rochester's largest congregation, Temple B'Rith Kodesh, on social issues of joint interest. Miller was one of the area church leaders who in the early '70s went to Washington with the Bishop to discuss American prisoners of the Vietnam War with federal legislators. In the long run, Bishop and Rabbi became good friends, and when Hogan, vested in a chasuble made of Jewish prayer shawls, formally launched the 1974-1975 diocesan Holy Year of Jubilee, Rabbi Miller graciously signalled the beginning of the Cathedral procession with a blast of the *shofar,* the ram's-horn trumpet prescribed for heralding the Old Testament years of jubilee (Lev 24:9).

In its Constitution on the Church in the Modern World, Vatican II laid the blame for a number of contemporary problems on failure to respect the rights of the human person whom God created in the divine image and likeness.

The Rochester Diocese under Bishop Hogan did much to defend these human rights to "life, liberty and the pursuit of happiness." For instance, while the Bishop Sheen Housing Foundation continued to provide low-cost housing, Catholic agencies also worked to develop housing for middle-income citizens. Sheen's other inspiration, the rural Secular Mission, united under Hogan with the Urban Vicariate as the Office of Human Development, maintained several rural centers to "assist the poor to help themselves." Out of a sense of worldwide responsibility, the Bishop also set up, in September 1976, an International Justice and Peace Commission to do what it could to break the cycle of poverty in the Third World.

Catholic social doctrine has long accepted the right to strike and boycott in nonviolent ways as a protest against social injustices. Joseph Hogan was not only aware of this teaching, he himself had taught it. During his episcopate, for example, he spoke approvingly of the efforts of Cesar Chavez to stop the exploitation of the California farm workers.

The Bishop played a leading personal role in one such labor contest, the strike initiated by the Amalgamated Clothing Workers against the Farah Corporation, a major manufacturer of pants, accused of treating unfairly the Hispanic employees in its factory in El Paso, Texas. The Amalgamated union, particularly strong in Rochester, approached Hogan to ask his support of the El Paso strike. Texas was far distant from Rochester, but the issue did have relevance to his diocese not only as a moral theme but because Farah slacks were extensively retailed in Monroe County, and many Mexican and Mexican-American migrants were employed annually on farms in the Diocese.

Before consenting to the request of the ACWA, Bishop Hogan sought full information about the controversy from Sidney Metzger, the Catholic bishop of El Paso. After five months of study and much prayer, the Rochester bishop, convinced of the justice of the cause, issued a pastoral circular on February 14, 1971, declaring his support for a boycott of Farah products. It was a bold step, and there were wide repercussions. Hogan issued a second letter on December 12, 1973, to clarify certain aspects of his point of view. Nevertheless, he received much criticism from the retail clothiers of his own diocese. Meanwhile he worked out a series of procedural norms for dealing with this sort of church intervention. Other American bishops welcomed these norms and adopted the Rochester plan for use in similar cases in their own dioceses.

The El Paso battle was long but the workers were finally victorious. After 21 months, in February 1974, Farah and ACWA reached an agreement. Bishop Metzger and his closest associate, Bishop Patrick F. Flores, the Latino auxiliary bishop of San Antonio, Texas, expressed their heartfelt thanks to the Bishop of Rochester. Subsequently the N.Y. State Religion and Labor Council gave Hogan an award for his role in the boycott and its settlement.

Vatican II had also restated the principle of the irrationality of war as the key to world peace, but it was difficult to preach reason in an America so at odds about the Vietnam War. Demonstrations in favor of our quitting the conflict reached their peak around the time of the Hogan installation, and the U.S. bishops had to beware of heaping more coals on the fire of controversy. Bishop Hogan spoke out against the further extension of the Indo-Chinese struggle, and favored amnesty for American men who registered as conscientious objectors. Cautious, however, about the trend to violent protest, he proposed a type of peace activism that would be acceptable to Catholics discomfited by noisy demonstrations. The open-air Mass for world peace held in Highland Park, Rochester, on October 11, 1970, under the auspices of the Legion of Mary, was just such an occasion. The Bishop accepted to be its principal celebrant and homilist.

President Nixon withdrew the U.S.A. from the war in 1973, and the military draft was abolished. Thus ended our nation's first war-without-victory, "not with a bang but a whimper." Four years later President Jimmy Carter pardoned most Americans who had evaded the draft. The bitterness bred by the struggle would slowly subside, but the chief casualty of the killing fields, it would seem, was traditional American patriotism.

Had the war in Vietnam also further desensitized an America already tending to favor legalizing abortion? Hitherto common law and the legislative codes of many states had branded abortion as criminal. But in June 1970, New York State passed a law decriminalizing feticide. On July 14, 1970, the Bishop of Rochester wrote a pastoral letter strongly condemning the procedure as immoral. The Catholic bishops of New York State likewise denounced it in a joint pastoral letter. Both letters had been composed after careful study. The Federal Supreme Court, however, cancelled all state laws forbidding abortion by the Roe vs. Wade decision of January 22, 1973. Henceforth, abortion was to be technically legal at any time within the nine months of pregnancy, by virtue of a "right of privacy". Now, by 1973 Catholics of the Diocese of Rochester may have been more ready than before to question certain Catholic teachings, but the majority would stand firm in defending the unborn child's right to life.

If the faithful, according to Vatican II, have a duty to protect physical human life from conception to death, they are also called on, as Christians graced by baptism, to share the gift of salvation with those still unacquainted with the Good News. Promoting this was no new idea in the Diocese of Rochester, long distinguished for its missionary awareness. As early as 1940, the Rochester Sisters of St. Joseph, backed by fellow diocesans, had undertaken black service work in Selma, Alabama. A year before the Council's decree on missionary activities, their community had undertaken a volunteer mission in Brazil. The Rochester Sisters of Mercy shouldered a similar task at Santiago, Chile, in August 1965. Then, in 1966, Bishop James E. Kearney began sending priest volunteers to Bolivia to assist the Maryknollers. The pioneer priests were Fathers Peter A. Deckman and Thomas M. O'Brien. Three years later the Rochester priests established a new parish, San Jose Obrero, in the poverty-stricken suburbs of LaPaz. Rochester diocesan identification with the parish would continue until 1974. Returning to Rochester after their Latin-American experience, the diocese's missioners were able to serve the expanding *Latino* population of their home diocese, which by 1976 had risen to 30,000.

Neither Bishops Kearney nor Sheen made a visitation of these far-flung enterprises. Bishop Hogan had the privilege and pleasure of starting that custom. In April 1970 he and his secretary, Father Michael F. Conboy, set out on the arduous circuit: four Josephite convents of sisters in rural Brazil; two Mercy convents in the shantytowns of Chile; and the copastored new parish in the windswept outskirts of sky-high LaPaz. Accompanying the two clerics was Mr. Cliff Carpenter of the local

Gannett Press. Carpenter wrote back regular reports of their exotic adventures to the Rochester *Democrat and Chronicle*, thus not only pleasing his readership but giving the missions helpful publicity. Hogan found the whole trip both informing and inspiring, and the devoted missionaries deeply appreciated his presence among them.

In 1971, Bishop Hogan paid a visit to the Sisters of St. Joseph mission in Selma, Alabama. In 1976 he made his second and last round of the South American mission centers. That same year the Diocese of Rochester also established an initial mission contact with the Mexican diocese of Tabasco.

Having made a fair start at revamping diocesan management, Joseph L. Hogan began in 1970 to plan what would be perhaps his major achievement, a diocesan pastoral council. In the documents of Vatican II, Pope Paul VI had termed such a council, representing the clergy, religious and laity of each diocese, a "desirable" institution. The Bishop believed that a local body of the sort, with members for the most part democratically chosen, would serve the diocese as an object lesson in coresponsibility. Although the membership could not possess a deliberative vote, it would have a truly consultative vote on major issues. Implicit in his vision of a pastoral council to advise him was Hogan's concept of authority in the Church as synonymous not with power but with love. Each of the faithful had gifts that could serve the Faith. The bishop's role as leader, he believed, was to marshal those gifts, and achieve in a future diocesan synod a consensus on the directions that the diocese should take. He realized that such government-in-partnership might miscarry, but he believed the risk worthwhile.

The Pope may have recommended diocesan councils, but he left it to the dioceses to draw up their design. Hogan entrusted this task to a Pastoral Council Formation Committee. Meanwhile, as necessary preliminary steps, he reorganized his Priests' Council; founded, as its parallel, a Sisters' council; and mandated that each parish organize a parish council (as no more than 50 had thus far done). Regional links would integrate the parishes of various sections of the diocese. (Regional linking would prove the hardest to achieve, partly because the "regions" were not "grass roots" entities but divisions imposed from above.) After five arduous years of discussion and an extraordinary number of meetings, the Diocesan Pastoral Council made its official debut in June, 1975. Of its 54 members, 40 were laypersons from across the diocese, six were priests, six were nuns, and one was a religious brother. Most of them were elected by their constituencies; 25 percent, appointed by the Bishop, were picked to be officers, representatives of special ministries, or spokesmen of minorities. This body was to meet with the Bishop every two months to discuss goals, ways and means, and to propose new programs in worship, education, social ministry and pastoral training, exemplifying a diocesan collegiality.

The development of the DPC was only one demanding project undertaken in the 1970s. Concurrent with it, and equally time-demanding, were the Year of Renewal; the publication of the pastoral *"You are Living Stones"*; the Advance Holy Year of Jubilee; and the Catholic observance of our nation's Bicentennial.

First off, on September 4, 1972, Bishop Hogan launched the "Year of Renewal" (later called the "Time of Renewal"). Its aim was to guide the Diocese in an "examination of conscience" about its conformity with Vatican II.

To determine just where the diocesans stood with regard to Catholic belief and practice, the Renewal Committee engaged a professional research firm to take "A Survey of Catholic Households in the Diocese of Rochester". A valuable study, this poll provided abundant, if sometimes disturbing indications of bewilderment in the local faithful: a lack of adult religious education, a deterioration in religious practice, a polarization of ecclesial opinions, and a growth of individualism; yet, for all that, a yearning for guidance. The Diocese tried to respond to some of these concerns by publishing catchy (and costly), informational articles in the local religious and secular press, but these articles seem to have gone largely unread. However, the Year of Renewal study at least identified the three Catholic groupings that needed to be addressed: the "nostalgic", the "belonging", and the "searching" members.

Secondly, Bishop Hogan's closest associates also suggested that he summarize in a formal pastoral letter the concept of diocesan governance that he had evolved inchmeal in his talks, his monthly radio broadcasts, and the weekly column, "Pastoral Perspective" that he wrote for the *Catholic Courier Journal*. He obliged with an ample pastoral letter titled *"You Are Living Stones"*, dated November 28, 1975. Well conceived and well written, the letter expressed once again his concept of the local church as a segment of the people of God that a bishop leads in the common search for solutions, not by "imperial mandate" but by loving guidance. Renewal, he frankly admitted, would be no quick win; "it is a long and painful process that will stretch beyond my lifetime and possibly beyond the lifetime of most of you." He had spoken before of this "long winter of renewal", but he was sure of eventual spring. The Holy Spirit can always "blow where he will."

"You are Living Stones" furnished much material for diocesan discussion groups to ponder. It also received widespread notice in other dioceses.

The third undertaking, the Advance Holy Year of Jubilee, was of course the scheduled Holy Year celebrated by the popes every 25 years. For centuries the bishops of Rome had invited the faithful from around the globe to make a pilgrimage to the Eternal City on these occasions, to visit its sacred shrines and to gain the Jubilee plenary indulgence called the "great pardon". Normally, during the year following the Roman Holy Year, its favors have been extended to the various dioceses for the benefit of those unable to travel to Rome. In preparing for the Holy Year 1975, Pope Paul VI reversed the procedure, authorizing the local observances to take place the year *before* the Roman celebration. The timely theme of the 1974-1975 Jubilee was "Pilgrimage of the People of God in Renewal and Reconciliation."

Bishop Hogan was glad to blend the activities of this commemoration with his diocesan renewal program. He designated a number of churches in the twelve counties as "pilgrimage churches." If the quest for the "great pardon" was no longer as ardent as in bygone years, the popular diocesan response was strong enough to indicate that its Catholics, young, as well as old, could still be touched by exercises of public devotion.

Project number four was the Diocese's participation in the celebration of our nation's bicentennial of independence.

Although the Bicentennial of 1976 was a civic festivity, the National Conference of Catholic Bishops was eager to participate in a manner that would reflect both the religious and the civic contribution of the Church to American society. The Conference therefore invited its member bishops to do two things: set up a diocesan archives if they did not have one; and take part in what might be called a national Catholic "town meeting."

The Bishop of Rochester accepted both invitations. The first invitation was easily complied with. He named the present writer as the official diocesan archivist to begin the task of organizing the diocesan records.

The bishops' second proposal was more ambitious, and became quite controversial. The National "town meeting" was the "Call to Action Conference", hosted in Detroit on October 21-23 by that city's Cardinal archbishop, John Dearden. Its aim was to air American Catholic postconciliar opinion, particularly on the broad and provocative American theme of "liberty and justice for all."

The total voluntary attendance from 152 out of then 167 U.S. dioceses was 1360: bishops, priests, religious, and laypersons. In two hectic days, its participants voted speedy approval of 182 recommendations. Most of the proposals were consonant with principles set down by Vatican II. Others, as the N.C.C.B. would later comment, were "problematical and in some cases untenable." The communications media typically publicized the more radical propositions, like the ordination of women to the priesthood, the abolition of clerical celibacy, a more democratic procedure in the naming of pastors and bishops, and elective artificial contraception.

Bishop Hogan, opting to attend the Conference, made careful preparations. He chose eight representative delegates and 12 "observers" to accompany him. He was one of some 120 bishops who participated in person.

The Bishop of Rochester would later admit that the Conference's *modus agendi* was in some respects faulty. Yet he, like many who took part, found "Call to Action" invigorating—a unique, loving expression of the concerns of the faithful, concerns that might prove unwarranted but should not be ignored. The experience would have no small impact on his own way of thinking, as he afterwards testified.

Once back home, in fact, Hogan followed up the "Call to Action" by launching a series of diocesan dialogues on 22 of the issues broached at Detroit, including some of the avant-garde proposals. While it was ill-advised to ask the laity to voice extempore opinions on questions that required extensive background knowledge, these discussions at least made Rochester diocesans aware that a rising number of American Catholics were now favoring the abolition of obligatory clerical celibacy and the opening of Holy Orders to women.

When the press asked Bishop Hogan thereafter what views he held on women's ordination and married priests, he frankly stated that he was open to both possibilities. Now, on November 15, 1976, the Vatican's doctrinal congregation issued a strong statement on the first of these subjects, the Declaration *Inter insigniores*. Of late, the persistent demand for women priests in the Anglican community of churches had won out. Many Catholic feminists and others who shared their views now urged that the Roman Catholic Church follow suit. The Roman document of 1976 replied that, in fidelity to the example of our Lord, the Church "does not consider herself authorized to admit women to priestly ordination." Bishop Hogan, asked in public how he viewed the ruling, questioned its theological underpinnings.

Each residential Catholic bishop of the Latin Rite is required to send to Rome a quinquennial report on the state of his diocese. He is also required to pay the pope an official visit every tenth year. Joseph Hogan submitted his first questionnaire in 1974. Pope Paul VI chose to advance the date for the next report and the *ad limina* visit by one year; hence the Bishop of Rochester, in company with all the other bishops of New York State, went to the Vatican in April 1978. Bishop Hogan's personal interview with the Holy Father while there, proved pleasant and constructive.

Hogan brought along, of course, his official report for the past four years. Having compiled the carefully composed statement, he decided to allow his diocesan newspaper to publish it. The publication was apparently a novel gesture in those times, but it did provide readers with an informative account of the direction the diocese had been taking.

We have already mentioned a number of these efforts at updating. The 1978 report included several others of interest. In the pastoral area it noted the popularity of the sacrament of the anointing of the sick; the provisions made for charismatic Catholic groups; the helpful work of the new Office of Family Life; the appointment of an "urban vicar" with delegated authority to solve inner-city problems; the continuing care of rural migrant workers, who now totaled 15,000 each year. Regarding religious education, it alluded to the required changes of curriculum at St. Bernard's Seminary; the continuance of the diocesan school system despite the need to close a number of the elementary schools. It called attention to the heavy calendar of the diocesan tribunal. (The cases were chiefly matrimonial, although tribunals are also courts of last appeal for due-process disputes.) Concerning financial problems in an inflationary economy, the Bishop noted the recent introduction of a new optional plan for parochial funding called "Stewardship".

Bishop Hogan placed great emphasis on the increased employment of nuns and laywomen in various ecclesiastical positions. At one point in the report he even added, "We would state that it would be desirable to have a careful examination on the role of women in the official ministries of the Church. Particularly in our society the formal recognition of the talents and the capabilities of women becomes an increasing question for the Roman Catholic Church."

Hogan did not try to cloak the problems of his diocese with a false optimism.

The Catholics of today, he reported, are too often puzzled by the meaning of "authority" in the Church. They too readily translate as "dominance" what is really "a pastoral grace, offering them light on the meaning of life and genuine wisdom in regard to moral practices." Reacting to a Church which seems to them "a bureaucratic encumbrance," they are liable to fall into the individualism that characterizes our society. Individualism dulls the sense of human sinfulness, and may explain the decline in confessions. It may also explain the diminished sense of commitment, so crucial to marriage and the religious life. In matters of a sexual nature, it seems that the faithful look for moral guidance more often to the secular media than to the Church. As for artificial contraception (Pope Paul VI's vigorous encyclical against it, *Humanae vitae*, had been published July 25, 1968), Bishop Hogan opined that "the majority of Catholic couples" did not hesitate to practice it, even though Natural Family Planning is now available and morally acceptable. On several issues, therefore, the Bishop found some polarization and some dissent. But he also sensed "a new willingness to reconcile differences in the context of the Church."

Meanwhile, continued the Bishop, the postconciliar downturn in the number of priests and sisters was becoming a major concern.

(In 1969 the *Official Catholic Directory* had reported a total of 569 priests in the Diocese of Rochester, of whom 362 were active, 38 retired or off-duty. There were also 335 [sic] upcoming seminarians. The 1979 *Directory*, listing statistics for 1978, would report a total of 513 priests, of whom 330 were active diocesans, 56 retired or off-duty. The upcoming seminarians numbered 54.)

At the moment, Hogan said, none of his churches was without a priest, but a future crisis was inevitable. More of his graying presbyters were retiring each year. Resignation from priestly service (33 during his episcopate) gave no signs of abating. What prompted such departures ? "Although many causes are alleged for those leaving the active ministry," he wrote, "celibacy and the perceived slowness of the Church to respond to modern needs seem to be the principal reasons". Furthermore, even if all the current seminarians should persevere to ordination, they would still be too few to make up for the losses.

Hogan had tried, incidentally—seminary-minded as he was—to attract vocations to the priesthood by a campaign of prayers. He had given strong support to St. Bernard's Seminary in its efforts to strengthen the spiritual, doctrinal and pastoral programs of the remaining student body. "Transitional" deacons, for instance, were now required to spend their last year of theology serving in a parish, and their first three years after priesthood ordination as interns under special supervision. He likewise appointed nuns and laypersons as "pastoral assistants" to perform parish functions that did not require priestly orders.

Furthermore, the Bishop, after a two-year preparatory study, announced on May 3. 1978, his intention to establish a permanent diaconate. Although the deacons would be unable to offer Mass or hear confessions, they would be able, by virtue of the holy order of diaconate, to preach homilies, baptize, and perform several other ministerial roles. The first class of Rochester's permanent diaconate would not be ordained during the Hogan regime, but he was the true founder of this admirable cadre of clergymen.

As the membership of the diocesan presbyterate had entered into a perilous decline, so had that of the various sisterhoods serving the diocese.

The *Catholic Directory* for 1969 had given 1502 as the total number of women religious in the diocese. By 1978 the number was down to 1095. Largest of the sisterhoods were the two Rochester-based congregations, the Sisters of Mercy and the Sisters of St. Joseph.

In 1965, the total Mercy membership had been 473, of whom 397 were professed. When Bishop Hogan was installed in office in 1969, it was down to 438, with 391 professed and 22 departures. In 1965, the Sisters of St. Joseph had counted 999 members, of whom 754 were in perpetual vows; by 1969 the total was down to 907, of whom 767 were in perpetual vows. By 1979, the Sisters of Mercy membership had further declined to 302, 291 of them professed, 11 aspirants. By the same date, the Sisters of St. Joseph were down to 662, 650 in perpetual vows, and had only four associates and no novices. Motives for voluntary departures were many and varied, but like departures from the priesthood, they created a negative impression of the religious life itself. Young women and men who might earlier have considered entering convent or seminary now often chose instead one of the many other careers that contemporary society made available to them, positive and even church-related in character, but without the requirement of celibacy.

Since most of the sisters were teachers in the diocesan parochial schools, their decrease in numbers seriously threatened the system of "Free Christian Schools" that Bishop McQuaid had established in his diocese. Not that they had been "free" in recent decades. As old schools had been enlarged and new schools founded after World War II, the diocese had run out of teaching nuns and had been obliged to employ more and more lay teachers. Ironically, the Sisters who had actualized McQuaid's dream out of their own poverty would eventually yield their schoolhouses to worthy but more justly compensated lay faculties. The pastors had to fall back on tuition to pay the salaries, but decline in enrollment and economic inflation gradually forced many parishes to close their schools. The Diocese would at length find it necessary to put the remaining schools under firmer management in order to protect McQuaid's school system from complete dissolution.

According to the *Official Catholic Directory*, the number of diocesan parish schools dropped from 99 in 1969 to 75 in 1978.

Particularly distressing was the closing of Rochester's inner-city schools in 1975. The parishes involved were grand old ethnic congregations, Irish, German and Italian, where the Sisters of St. Joseph, the Sisters of Mercy, and the School Sisters of Notre Dame had coached countless children of immigrants in the "Four R's" and the American Way. After World War II, however, when a more prosperous generation fled to the suburbs, the Hispanics and blacks who settled in the old neighborhoods were too few to fill the pews and schoolrooms and too poor to maintain the parish budgets.

The inner-city pastors, nevertheless, were dedicated to the "preferential option for the poor". Determined to keep their churches and schools in operation as long as possible, they banded together for common action in a "Council of Inner City Parishes". Each parish sent delegates to this Council's meetings, and the diocesan offices of black Ministry and the Spanish Apostolate were likewise represented. In an era when parish councils were a novelty, an interparochial council was even more creative.

Creative, but in the school issue, unavailing. The C.I.C.P. hoped that the Diocese would increase the subsidies to their individual parishes. Instead, the Diocese proposed a single subsidy of $250,000 to all seven parishes with consolidation of the schools as an alternative. Reluctantly, the Council agreed to the consolidation. On Rochester's East Side, therefore, St. Bridget and St. Francis Xavier closed their schools; Holy Redeemer and Our Lady of Mount Carmel remained open, but with only kindergarten and grades 1-6; and St. Michael's became a junior high. On the West Side, Immaculate Conception School, already integrated with St. Lucy's, continued to function.

Unfortunately, even this otherwise sensible compromise proved too costly for the seven parishes to sustain without a special appeal for funds. The Council and the Diocese discussed several possible courses of action but could not reach a consensus. Finally a motion was made to recommend that the Bishop simply close the four remaining schools, assigning the children whose parents so chose, to other parochial schools.

It was a sad day for the parents when the closures took effect. Catholic or non-Catholic (and there were many of the latter), they had appreciated the quality education given by their neighborhood parish schools.

It was a sad day for the educator Bishop. He would often refer to the whole episode later on as the most painful experience of his episcopal career.

In a lighter moment, Rochester's seventh bishop had once defined his job in terms that parodied contemporary jargon: "Executive Director of Eschatological Tension". Tension there certainly was; and he who favored terms for bishops would be obliged by physical strain to relinquish his episcopal office after only nine years.

By 1978, although still only 62, Hogan proved to have already "spent himself". After recurring bouts with pneumonia he was found to have a chronic lung ailment that the constant pressures of his office only worsened. On the advice of physicians he therefore asked permission of Pope Paul VI to resign the See of Rochester. The Holy Father kindly consented, and at the request of Bishop Hogan, set November 28, 1978, as the date of retirement. That would be the ninth anniversary of his episcopal ordination and installation. Pope Paul also designated him as the apostolic administrator of the Diocese until the inauguration of his successor.

Poor health did not prevent Hogan from fulfilling the unexacting duties of administrator. Part of his duty was to pave the way for the selection of Rochester's eighth bishop. He was much interested in this process. After the "Call to Action" conference urged that diocesans be allowed more of a part in the choice of bishops, Bishop Hogan had suggested to his Diocesan Pastoral Council that they name a "Selection of Bishops Committee". Accepting his suggestion, the D.P.C. had chosen a panel of 15 priests, sisters, and laypersons. Now, in consultation with the Apostolic Delegate, Archbishop Jean Jadot, the Administrator activated this committee.

However novel, the role undertaken by the Selection Committee was no blind concession to democratic procedure. Its members were not asked to nominate a candidate but to compose a job description of the type of priest best suited to the current needs of the Diocese. This was a highly intelligent approach, and when the name of the eighth bishop was announced in 1979, many noted how well the man chosen corresponded to the specifications of the standing committee.

After the installation of that prelate, the "Former Bishop of Rochester" continued to reside in suburban Victor, New York, where he had lived since 1970. Once his general good health had been restored, he was happy to accept, in 1979, the invitation of St. John Fisher College to rejoin its faculty. Not only was "The Academic" gratified to return to the classroom; he was pleased with the course assigned him: the Church since Vatican II. Few, if any, local scholars were better equipped than he to address that topic, and his elective course proved very popular during the three years of his adjunct professorship. Meanwhile, Bishop Hogan was serving as "assistant" in the Victor parish, St. Patrick's. From 1982 on, he undertook a personal apostolate to the sick and house-bound of Old St. Mary's parish in downtown Rochester. He likewise continued to help Bishops Clark and Hickey in conferring the sacrament of Confirmation.

Unfortunately, the Bishop fell ill again in 1995. Since he now needed more medical attention, he moved into the infirmary of the Sisters of St. Joseph Motherhouse. There he remains at the present writing, in good fettle and a ready authority on the history of his life and times.

It is obviously too early to appraise the Hogan era in Rochester diocesan history. It does seem appropriate, however, since in his efforts to update the Church he had become a rather controversial figure, to review some of the contentious issues *in their context.*

One criticism frequently made of Bishop Hogan was that he tended to be too permissive. Admittedly, his equation of authority with love, which biblical scholar John McKenzie had argued in *Authority in the Church* (1966), has scriptural foundations; but it has to be tempered with realism. It does seem that the Bishop was at times too uncritical, and too trusting.

Another tendency of Bishop Hogan that disturbed some "salt-of-the-earth" diocesans was to glorify their postconciliar future by poking fun at their preconciliar past. The diocesans were justly proud of their diocese's history and it pained them to hear anybody belittle it. I believe, however, that the flaw was in rhetoric rather than in sentiment. Joseph Hogan had a deep personal affection for his native diocese, and he yielded to none in his grief at the passing of any of its noblest institutions and traditions.

Those who censured Hogan's intervention in the Attica Prison affair and in the Farah boycott had little real grounds for their objections. The first intervention was motivated by Christian respect for human life. The second was both a defense of human economic rights and collegial response to the cry of brother bishops.

More troubling to many Catholics was the Bishop's disagreement with the Holy See on two matters of sacramental discipline. In the first place, he and some other American bishops encouraged reversing the customary scheduling of first confession before first Communion. In the second place, he and some other American bishops favored a wider use of general absolution in the sacrament of Penance as an incentive to Catholics to return to a more frequent use of the sacrament. The Holy See challenged these preferences. Fortunately, compromise solutions were reached on both issues.

Since the advocacy of a married clergy and the ordination of women were burning issues in the 1970s, the local media hastened to seek the opinion of the Bishop of Rochester whenever the question arose about the Roman Catholic Church's changing its mind on these subjects. Bishop Hogan had won a reputation as a "liberal" prelate by stating that he believed a mixed male clergy (celibates and noncelibates) and a female priesthood were at least a possibility. In the Eastern churches, even the Catholic Eastern churches, this sort of "mixed clergy" is an old tradition. The Western Church, however, has traditionally ordained only celibates to the priesthood, apart from certain exceptions. The comparative history of clerical celibacy in East and West has only lately become the subject of scholarly study. Nevertheless, the revised Western *Code of Canon Law* (issued five years after Bishop Hogan's retirement), retained its strong insistence that clergy of the Latin Rite "are obliged to observe perfect and perpetual continence for the sake of the kingdom of heaven" (277.1). Obviously, the Western rule will not be readily revoked.

As we have noted above, when the Congregation for the Doctrine of Faith issued the Declaration *Inter insigniores* in 1976, ruling that the Church "does not consider herself authorized to admit women to priestly ordination," Bishop Hogan was critical of its theological aspect. But those who commended and those who condemned his "liberal" views on women's ordination and clerical celibacy, sometimes failed to notice how he constantly qualified them. At no time did he imply that he or any other bishop could take individual action on either of these opinions. What he meant was that he considered them questions to be subjected to open debate. Any final judgment, he maintained, could be made only by the college of bishops in union with the pope. Nor were his statements on these matters, as he always pointed out, ever reproved by higher church authorities.

"To be the Church," Joseph Hogan had written in his pastoral letter "You are Living Stones," "is to join the pilgrimage of persons who have found communion with the Lord and who share a fellowship of faith, life and love for one another on the journey." Fully aware that in teaching his flock by example as well as by word, he was sowing winter wheat, he nevertheless had the joy of witnessing among his loyal faithful ample evidences of the co-responsibility and solidarity that the Vatican Council sought.

Let one practical illustration serve for all: his people's ready response to the disastrous flood that engulfed the Southern Tier counties on June 23, 1972, in the wake of Atlantic hurricane "Agnes".

This deluge evicted thousands who lived along the Chemung River, and caused millions of dollars of grimy damage. The government and many relief agencies came to the rescue, among them the Diocese of Rochester. Bishop Hogan and a group of associates, flying down by Gannett helicopter, inspected the stricken area and cried Mayday to the diocesan bureaus (including the Bishop Sheen Housing Foundation) and to diocesan volunteer laborers. Thus did a tragedy in one part of the Diocese bring together Catholics from all over in common ecumenical service to the homeless.

Bishop Joseph L. Hogan was the first of the bishops of Rochester to feel in no wise glued to the episcopal pedestal. Without sacrificing his proper dignity, he made it clear that he was a bishop of and for the people.

When he retired from office many observers commented favorably on his earnest efforts to rediscover the highway in the midst of the postconciliar fog. One of the most interesting comments came from Msgr. James C. McAniff, a former vicar general of the Rochester Diocese. Bishop Hogan, he said, "was very open to the advice given. Advice was freely given and freely received. He was very devoted to his people. He was very much interested in following all the dictates of Vatican II. He really was a good shepherd to his flock."

Msgr. McAniff's estimate was especially significant. Although thought of as a dignitary of the "old school," he was nevertheless recognized as one of the sagest senior priests to have served the Rochester Diocese.

3. A CHURCH IN DIALOGUE: BISHOP MATTHEW H. CLARK (1979 -)[5]

Bishop Hogan was finally able to announce the name of the new bishop at a press conference on Wednesday, May 2, 1979. He was Father Matthew Clark, a priest of the Diocese of Albany, serving at that moment as spiritual director at the North American College in Rome.

Hogan, who had taught the candidate at St. Bernard's, was delighted to point out that his *persona* closely resembled the sketch drawn by the Rochester diocesan committee of the ideal eighth bishop of Rochester. While not himself a Rochester priest, Clark was from upstate New York, and had spent two years in Rochester as a student at St. Bernard's Seminary. He was young: at 41 the second youngest residential bishop in the country. Too young perhaps? Rochester diocesans could scarcely think so, recalling that their founding bishop, Bernard J. McQuaid, was only 46 when named. Maturity, after all, is more a matter of wisdom than of years.

Matthew Harvey Clark was born on July 15, 1937, at Troy, New York, but his family lived in adjacent Waterford, a village of 3,000 at the confluence of the Hudson and Mohawk Rivers. That he grew up in a village was perhaps a good augury. All the earlier bishops of Rochester except McQuaid and Thomas F. Hickey had come from small towns.

Clark's father, M. Harvey Clark (1908-1977), was deputy director of the U.S. Customs Office at Albany. His mother, Grace Bills Clark (1910-1995), was by vocation a homemaker, with a vivid sense of family. The Clark couple also had a daughter, Helen, a year younger than Matthew and close to him in spirit. (In due time Helen would marry Professor James Early, one of her brother's classmates; and the five Early daughters would become a welcome part of the Clark circle, and great favorites of their "Uncle Matt".)

Matthew was baptized and confirmed at the Waterford Church of Our Lady of the Assumption, staffed by Augustinian Fathers. He also became an altar boy. Since Assumption at that time had no parish school, he attended Waterford Public School No. 1.

If a Catholic elementary school was not available, Catholic Central High in Troy, New York, was an easy bus ride away, so young Clark became one of its commuter students from 1951 to 1955. His urban classmates at C.C.H.S. at first pretended to scorn this lad from "the Sticks", but he soon won their respect as an all-round athlete. Harvey Clark, a great sports fan, had early introduced his son and daughter to the practice and love of athletics, and much of the family's table talk had been sports talk. Matt was active, however, not only in sports but in everything else as well, academics in particular. At graduation he was offered four in-State scholarships. When he chose instead to attend Holy Cross College in Worcester, Mass., it was even then on a naval R.O.T.C. academic grant.

While they were driving him back to Holy Cross for the first semester of his second year, Matthew announced to his folks that he

147

MATTHEW HARVEY CLARK
Eighth Bishop of Rochester
1979 -

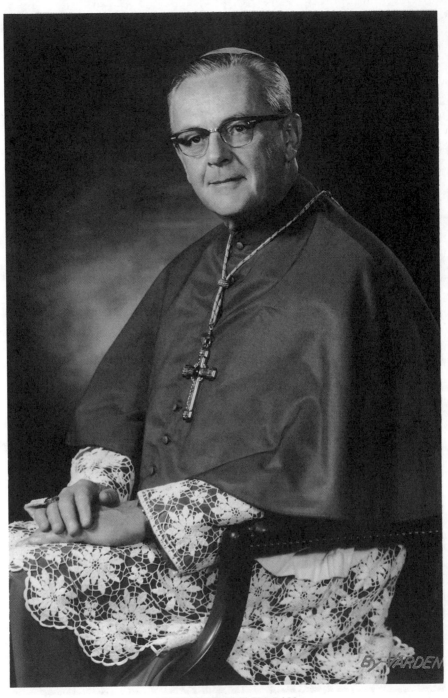

148   **JOSEPH LLOYD HOGAN**
Seventh Bishop of Rochester
1969-1978

149

DENNIS WALTER HICKEY
(1914-)
Titular Bishop of Rusuccuru
Auxiliary to the Bishop of Rochester
1968-1989

150   **JOHN EDGAR McCAFFERTY**
(1920-1980)
Titular Bishop of Tanudaia
Auxiliary to the Bishop of Rochester
1968-1980

intended to enter the seminary in January 1957. Harvey and Grace were surprised at the news, but scarcely shocked. They knew their son with the ready smile was not given to snap judgments and stuck by his decisions.

Clark spent the spring semester of 1957 at Albany's Mater Christi Seminary. Then he did his two years of "philosophy" (senior college) at St. Bernard's Seminary in Rochester. In fall 1959 the bishop of Albany, William Scully, sent him to the Pontifical North American College in Rome, Italy, to take the four-year degree course in theology at the Jesuits' Gregorian University. During the first semester of his last year, on December 19, 1962, he was ordained a priest by the rector of the American College, Most Rev. Martin J. O'Connor. At the end of the spring semester 1963, having passed the examinations at the Gregorian, he was awarded the degree of Licentiate of Sacred Theology (S.T.L.).

After the festivities of his homecoming, Father Clark was appointed assistant pastor of Our Lady of Mercy Parish in Albany, and concurrently a member of the faculty of the local Vincentian Institute. These assignments were brief. In fall 1964 Bishop Scully sent him back to Rome to the Gregorian to acquire the licentiate in canon law. That task achieved, he returned to Albany in 1966, and was named vice-chancellor of the Diocese of Albany and chaplain of the Newman Club at Albany Law School. From 1967 to 1969 he was assistant pastor of St. Ambrose Parish in Latham, New York, his longest stint as a parish priest. From 1969 to 1972 he served as chairman of the new Priests' Personnel Board of the Albany Diocese, a demanding but creative responsibility in the field of interpersonal relations.

Although Fr. Clark's first decade as a priest may have seemed piecemeal, it was not unfavorably judged. In 1972 he was called back to the North American College in Rome to become, first, assistant spiritual director of the students, and then spiritual director. To prepare himself better for that post, he undertook, again at the Gregorianum, studies for a doctorate in spiritual theology (1972-1973). He had completed the doctoral requirements apart from the dissertation when he was elected to the see of Rochester in 1979.

What motivated Pope John Paul II, himself bishop of Rome for only seven months, to assign to Rochester a priest so young in years and so limited in parochial experience?

The Evangelist, official weekly of the Diocese of Albany, asked the same question of those best acquainted with the unassuming young priest. The respondents—men and women, clerics, religious and layfolk—were prompt to affirm his merits: "deeply spiritual", "always the priest", "a gentleman", "even-tempered", "a good sense of humor", "able to laugh at himself", "caring", "people-oriented", "a great organizer", and "a born leader". But it was Howard J. Hubbard, Father Clark's schoolmate and since 1977 his bishop, who described him best: "He is a strong leader who listens, evaluates, and then embarks on a firm course of action. He will see his directions through, always respecting those who see things differently."

How, then, would these perceived talents of the Bishop-elect serve him in the thick of "the distrust, the polarization and the entrenched positions" (as Cardinal Joseph Bernardin had put it) of a typical post-conciliar American diocese?

Pope John Paul II decided to consecrate personally a large number of bishops-elect in St. Peter's Basilica on May 27, 1979. Matthew H. Clark was one of the 26 candidates, who hailed from twelve different countries. (Among the five Americans were Msgr. W. Thomas Larkin of St. Petersburg, Florida, a native of the Diocese of Rochester; and the Philadelphia-born retired U.S. Navy chief of chaplains, Msgr. John J. O'Connor, later archbishop of New York and cardinal.) A large delegation of friends represented the dioceses of Albany and Rochester, among whom Bishop Clark's mother Grace held a place of special honor. Unfortunately, Harvey Clark had not lived to witness the promotion of his son.

Bishop Clark was installed in Rochester on June 26, 1979. Since Sacred Heart Cathedral was too small to accommodate the invited congregation, the Diocese rented the Rochester Community War Memorial. (A "Rochester Catholic Action Group", in a letter addressed to the new bishop, had protested the choice of auditorium. Its 14 signers asked, in the name of peace and of the poor, whether a *War* Memorial was a fitting site for the installation of a bishop. In reply to this criticism, the *Catholic Courier Journal* would point out correctly that the chosen auditorium, erected in the 1950s, was not a memorial to war but to its victims!) No effort had been spared to make the vast hall as churchly and the liturgy as contemporary as possible. When Cardinal Terence Cooke of New York and Archbishop Jean Jadot, the Apostolic Delegate, led the newly consecrated bishop to his throne, 10,000 witnesses cheered.

The following day, June 27, 1979, was the new bishop's first work day. We have already described the earnest efforts of Bishops Sheen and Hogan to implement the ideals of the Second Vatican Council. They themselves were preconciliar priests; Matthew Clark would be our first fully postconciliar prelate. He had been in Rome during the whole

Council, and had been ordained a priest eight weeks after its opening. What he was to do in Rochester, as we shall see, was clearly inspired by the conciliar decrees, and he seems to have pondered with special fascination the Council's constitutions on the Church (*Lumen gentium*) and on the Church in the Modern World (*Gaudium et spes*). At this writing Matthew H. Clark has already occupied the See of Rochester for 19 years. We present here a summary of his regime up to 1993, which marked the 125th anniversary of the Diocese. Summary it must be, perforce; and we shall relate only what we consider the most significant aspects of an intensely busy 14 years.

The new bishop allowed the diocesan curia to remain as he found it, with Bishop Dennis W. Hickey and Bishop John E. McCafferty, the Cathedral rector, as vicars general. Sadly, Bishop McCafferty succumbed to cancer as early as April 29, 1980. Clark appreciated and praised the spirit of joy and peace that the deceased prelate had shown during his terminal illness. In due time the eighth bishop would change the personnel of his office a good deal, but he was happy to continue the policy begun by Sheen and Hogan of hiring more and more laymen and laywomen as his aides, and holding them to professional standards.

First off, however, Bishop Clark had to get acquainted with the diocese. During the next year or so, he made a systematic tour of the twelve counties, visiting churches, missions, schools and religious communities. Wherever possible he tried to meet people in a "town meeting" sort of assembly. There he would toss out a few questions, listen intently to the answers, and file them away mentally for future reference. Thus he verified from the start his reputation for being a good listener. Dialogue would indeed prove to be one of his chief methods of both acquiring knowledge and instructing others. He found inspiration for group discussion particularly in the writings of Pope Paul VI.

Clark's year of noncommittal "sampling' of the diocese was too slow for some local activists. Interviewed by the *City Newspaper* of August 5, 1980, a group of them complained that he had already shown himself too "Roman" through his failure to speak out on behalf of the poor of the Inner City, against alleged police brutality, and in favor of the burgeoning Catholic women's movement. Had they waited a bit to proclaim the "honeymoon" over, they would have heard him address bravely these subjects and many more of even broader significance.

By December 1980, the Bishop was ready to be interviewed by George Murphy of the Rochester *Democrat and Chronicle.* Murphy, looking for "news", fired the most neuralgic current church questions, like: "personalism" in marriage; the resignation of priests; the ordination of women; abortion; genetic engineering. But Bishop Clark withstood the barrage well. Speaking with poise and modesty, he gave the best answers he could, frankly and moderately. He had been deeply impressed, he said, by the diocesans he had met during his "get-acquainted" tour, not the least by the women, before whom, he said, he was "absolutely humbled". The Gannett Press was evidently pleased by the Murphy interview, for Clark was henceforth treated as an interesting local newsmaker and a welcome contributor to its "Op-Ed" pages.

Mr. Murphy's inquiry about the growing scarcity of priests focused on a nationwide, even international problem that nobody could solve easily. Not until 1987 would the Bishop find it necessary to appoint other than a priest to administer one of his parishes (Sister Julia Norton, R.S.M., to Our Lady of Mount Carmel, Rochester).[6] But as he had admitted to George Murphy, the diocesan *presbyterium* had already lost many by retirement and death and at least 75 by resignation. Even more ominous was the reduced number of seminarians. Normally these would have replaced the retired, deceased and departed; but Clark himself would ordain no more than two or three yearly during his first fourteen years, and in one year there were no candidates at all for orders. Granted, he was able to ordain the first class of permanent deacons on April 17, 1982, and by 1993 could count on a numerous diaconal corps, but the service they provided, though valuable, was necessarily limited.

Since the conclusion of the Vatican Council, the faculties of both Becket Hall and St. Bernard's Seminary had taken pains to adapt their programs for priestly formation to the altered standards set down in the conciliar documents. But the drop-off of seminarians and a spiraling inflation now posed the question of the continued existence of both institutions. Bishop Hogan had agreed with the advice to close Becket and St. Bernard's; because, however, of his deep attachment to both he decided to leave that task to his successor. Therefore on March 19, 1980, the diocese sold Becket Hall, the residence of the college-level seminarians attending St. John Fisher College, to that college. The title "Becket Hall" was transferred to the former convent of St. Boniface Parish, and a new diocesan director of vocations was assigned to supervise its handful of students.

The closure of St. Bernard's, McQuaid's proud achievement, had still wider repercussions. Bishop Clark announced it to the faculty on January 7, 1981. The program of priestly training, he said, would terminate on June 30, at the end of the spring semester. As a former student there, the Bishop was anything but happy to have to break this news.

The rest of the Seminary alumni were also saddened, as were the diocese, the City, and, indeed, the American Catholic Church, to learn of the passing of this historic 88-year-old theologate. The faculty was taken by surprise. They accepted the decision, but in doing so they expressed to Bishop Clark the hope that some way might be found to retain in Rochester something equivalent to what St. Bernard's Seminary had been, a "Catholic intellectual presence."

Thanks to St. Bernard's affiliation with Colgate Rochester Divinity School in the Rochester Center for Theological Studies, a way *was* open to maintain this "Catholic presence". The Seminary's budding graduate department was able to transfer its operations to "The Hill" under the title "St. Bernard's Institute", governed by the Seminary's amended charter of incorporation. As a matter of fact, so speedily were the library and the essential furnishings moved that summer that the Institute was able to start its classes in September 1981 with 54 registrants. Thus the name of Bernard of Clairvaux would remain on the list of Rochester schools of higher studies.

And what became of the noble buildings of the Seminary that had been designated in 1979 as a city landmark? They were sold for $2 million to Eastman Kodak on October 6, 1982. Kodak set about remodeling the structures and the terrain. In 1993, however, having changed its plans, it sold the 20 acres to two other organizations. Holy Sepulchre Cemetery bought much of the playing field as an addition to its own adjacent property. Conifer Development Associates bought the buildings and the park area, intending to use them for senior housing and activities, in collaboration with Park Ridge Hospital. When the first remodeled unit, the "North Building" (the old "Theology Hall"), was opened on August 1, 1996, as "St. Bernard's Park", its 59 attractive apartments were occupied by delighted elder citizens. The developers then proceeded with the renovation of the other major buildings, pledged to leave intact their City-landmark exteriors.

Housing the elderly was a gracious use for the venerable structures. St. Bernard's Park remains a monument to the 2300 priests and 27 bishops trained there to serve the Church on five continents.

Another heavy task that confronted the Bishop in his first years in office was the refinancing of the diocese. After soliciting the opinions of a wide range of advisers, Clark, in autumn 1981, launched the first annual drive for funds, called the "Thanks Giving Appeal". The goal that year was $2.2 million. Well organized, with the focus on parochial solicitation, the initial campaign brought in a welcome $3.2 million. By the 1990s, the Appeal, designed to replace both the *cathedraticum* (a church tax payable by parishes to the bishop) and the collection for "diocesan needs", was garnering well over four million. In 1992, the diocese would inaugurate a second appeal, called "The Miracle of Sharing". This capital campaign was initially addressed to major givers. It had four objectives: to provide for retired women religious; to support the education of lay ministers at St. Bernard's Institute and to assist needy parishes in hiring these ministers; to make Catholic elementary education more widely available, especially to the inner-city poor; and to continue support of current programs of faith development, parochial services and social ministries through the annual Thanks Giving Appeal. The "Miracle of Sharing" was professionally planned and staffed, and has proven increasingly effective as the Diocese's "developmental arm" in the secular community. The success of these appeals (over $60 million was raised) naturally redounded to the managerial credit of Rochester's eighth bishop.

On April 29, 1982, Bishop Clark, now close to three years at the helm of the Rochester Diocese, issued his first formal pastoral letter.

The letter was titled *"The Fire in the Thornbush: A Pastoral Letter on Women in the Church."* Before his appointment to Rochester, the Bishop had had no occasion to study in depth the complaints of discrimination voiced by American women in the 1970s and 1980s. Many Catholic women, especially Catholic religious, influenced not only by papal praise of womankind but even more by the writings of Catholic feminist theologians, had joined the chorus. Clark, listening attentively to the earnest concerns of local women, had come to a new understanding of the gravity of the issue. In a carefully crafted treatise on women's rights, he pointed out that baptism, according to the documents of Vatican II, confers a share of the Church's prophetic, priestly and pastoral responsibilities and rights on the whole People of God, male and female alike. Singling out Our Lady in proof, he reminded his readers that she, the perfect disciple, was not only contemplative but activist, obedient yet questioning. Let women's roles, then, he concluded, be discerned and upgraded in social and religious practice. To those who considered women equally entitled to ordination to the priesthood, the Bishop (who had come to think that in due time the Church should consider that possibility) carefully explained that the traditional "'exclusion" of women from holy orders sprang from the Catholic Church's effort to be faithful to "what it understands as a divine tradition that comes to us from the earliest days."

Apologizing to women for any bias they had experienced in the past, Clark urged them to become increasingly "a sign of charity and unity." He asked his diocesans in general to study and discuss *"Thornbush"*, focusing on 16 points. Chief of these points for reflection, prayer and action were: showing greater respect for women (particularly by using "inclusive language"); showing greater respect for their gifts within the church community; employing them as widely as possible in paid and volunteer positions in church administration; and engaging them in all liturgical offices that did not require holy orders.

"Fire in the Thornbush" was widely discussed throughout the diocese over the next several years. It proved to be a milestone in Bishop Clark's episcopal career. Initially, it seems, Matthew Clark had expected to govern the Diocese of Rochester by the trim norms of Canon Law. His "listening sessions" had shown him that disciplinary laws often need to be enforced with some delicacy. These same listening sessions, so helpful to him in reaching decisions, were also to prove an effective tool for teaching his flock. After *"Thornbush"* he would usually prescribe a broad, open-ended dialogue on any matter of importance before reaching a decision.

The publication of *"The Fire in the Thornbush"*, and its dialogistic follow-up brought the eighth bishop of Rochester into national prominence as one of the few American bishops who had devoted a formal pastoral letter to women as an overlooked minority. Henceforth he would be associated in the public mind with the several American bishops of the "more progressive" wing. It was doubtless because of his specialization in "Catholic feminism" that the National Conference of Catholic Bishops elected him in 1984 to the episcopal committee delegated to write a national pastoral letter on the Church and womankind. He was also elected, in 1989, to the chair of the NCCB Standing Committee on Women in Society and in the Church. The writing committee had no easy task. Over the years 1983-1992 they produced four drafts of a statement. When each draft was rejected, the stumbling block proved to be the ordination of women, by that time a highly politicized issue. Clark himself voted against the fourth draft of the pastoral as inadequate. The NCCB decided after that to give up the idea of a letter on women, utilizing as much as possible of the material industriously gathered for it in other public statements.

The major problem posed by Vatican II still remained unsolved. Bishop Clark summarized that problem on March 24, 1984, in an address to the Rochester Diocesan Pastoral Council. Emphasizing as it did the concept of the People of God, the ecumenical council had clearly wanted the faithful to assume more responsibility for the Church. "Let's face it," said Clark, "We come out of an age history will characterize as very structural, hierarchical, clerical. . . . How do we shift from that and still keep the essential?" (Pope John Paul II, himself a leading bishop in the Second Vatican Council, has constantly asked the same question.)

From ancient days, the Church had indeed acknowledged the centrality of the See of Peter, but the successors of Peter at Rome were in less frequent contact with the scattered bishops, who governed their own people more directly, in concert with the regional hierarchy. As time passed, however, the popes had come to exercise a more detailed control over the Western Church. The authority of bishops was thus reduced to the point that the residential bishop sometimes seemed more a papal delegate than a shepherd with true jurisdiction over his own flock. The Fathers of Vatican II aimed at restoring the balance of authority between the pope and the bishops by stressing that, somewhat like St. Peter and the Apostles, they formed a *college*. The bishops, always united with the pope, governed the whole Church, but each individual bishop deserved the title "vicar of Christ" for his own diocese, even as the pope deserved the title "vicar of Christ" for the whole Church. The Council also made it clear that the hierarchy, or ministerial priesthood, though diverse from the common priesthood conferred by baptism on all the faithful, is at the service of that common priesthood. As such, therefore, members of this common priesthood share to a certain extent not only in the priestly, but in the prophetic and kingly aspects of Christ's unique priesthood.

Vatican II, in applying the title "vicar of Christ" to both pope and bishops, did not clarify the precise future relationship of local bishops to the bishop of Rome in the exercise of authority. Clark, pleased with the concept of collegiality, evidenced a growing interest in the 1980s in this further canonical problem. He had learned by experience that the Vatican still reserved to itself authority over some matters that might be dealt with more efficiently in the local dioceses. In such cases he believed that the principle of *subsidiarity* should be invoked. (Subsidiarity, a sociological term, means, colloquially, "If you can settle a problem in Paducah, don't pass it on to Washington.") The Bishop came to consider the "Charles Curran Controversy" a case in point.

Father Charles E. Curran, a priest of the Diocese of Rochester, has been since 1991 the Elizabeth Scurlock University Professor of Human Values at Southern Methodist University, Dallas, Texas. A professional moral theologian well respected by his peers, Father Curran began to teach at the Catholic University of America in Washington, D.C., in 1965. In 1968, when Pope Paul VI issued the encyclical letter *Humanae vitae* confirming the Church's opposition to contraception, Curran, who had already become a controversial figure on this subject at Catholic University, drew up a statement detailing his reasons for thinking that Catholics could dissent, both in theory and in practice, from this papal teaching as "non-infallible"; that is, not formally defined by the pope or the whole college of bishops. Over six hundred American Catholic scholars subscribed to Curran's statement. A faculty committee at Catholic University, after conducting an inquiry, decided that the faculty members from Catholic University who had endorsed the statement had not violated thereby the professional responsibilities they owed to the pontifical (papal) university. So Father Curran continued his teaching and writing in the 1970s. In the course of further study, he came to the conclusion that several other actions traditionally considered by the Church to be wrong, in an absolute sense, could in certain circumstances be judged morally right.

On July 13, 1979, scarcely a fortnight after the installation of Bishop Clark, the Vatican Congregation for the Doctrine of the Faith informed Father Curran that his writings were being officially scrutinized. He was sent a list of "observations" that would serve as the basis of a private correspondence between the Congregation and himself about certain of these theological views. The Vatican letter to Curran noted that Bishop Clark had also been informed of the procedure. (Clark would become actively involved, however, only in the last phase of the exchange.)

On July 25, 1986, the Congregation reached its final conclusion that Curran had expressed public dissent to an unacceptable degree regarding artificial contraception and four other sex-oriented issues; also on the indissolubility of marriage and the possible justification of abortion and euthanasia in very limited conflict situations. Because of this dissent from Church teaching (the *Magisterium*), the Congregation for the Doctrine of the Faith ruled that Curran could no longer be considered "suitable nor eligible to teach Catholic theology." That implied, of course, that he forfeited his professorship at the Catholic University of America.

The Bishop of Rochester had followed the case closely. Hoping that a compromise might be reached to avert a censure, he wrote to the Congregation for the Doctrine of the Faith on March 12, 1986, and later issued a public statement. He described Curran as an exemplary priest and supported the judgment "commonly accepted in the Roman Catholic theological community that Father Curran is a moral theologian of notable competence whose work locates him very much at the center of that community and not at all on the fringe." He lamented the failure of the Congregation to consult on the case with the Church in the United States, and urged the need for particular churches (dioceses) to be allowed greater initial input in cases in which they had a vested interest.

The Congregation nevertheless announced its ruling, approved by the Pope, on July 25. Bishop Clark published a formal statement of acceptance on August 18, 1986. While stressing that Father Curran remained a priest in good standing in the Diocese of Rochester, he went on to say: "In recognition of the ultimate authority of the Holy Father, who has confirmed this decision, and in a spirit of collegiality with him, I accept the decision as the final word on this matter and urge all members of our community to accept it in a similar spirit."

In his weekly *Catholic Courier* column, "Along the Way", on May 8, 1986, the Bishop had already replied to some correspondents who had concluded from his statement of March 12, 1986, that he personally *endorsed* Father Curran's specific moral conclusions. He made clear that his remarks of March 12 were intended to be pastoral in nature and an expression of concern that the less-than-open procedures of the Congregation might have a chilling effect on scholars engaged in theological pursuits. Nowhere, he indicated, had he commented "about the positions Father Curran takes about specific questions in moral theology."

(The Sacred Congregation, in dealing with Father Charles Curran, had been following regulations drawn up in 1971. It is interesting to note that in 1997 it would adopt a somewhat altered procedure. Henceforth when a theologian comes under scrutiny, his own bishop will have a recognized role to play. The constructive criticism of prelates like the Bishop of Rochester no doubt prompted this alteration of the Congregation's rules in the direction of greater subsidiarity, if not greater publicity.)

Returning now to our thesis that the decrees and documents of Vatican II were a principal inspiration of Matthew Clark's episcopal program, let us list at random several typical conciliar themes and see how he tried to comply with them.

Liturgical reform was, of course, a notable aim of the ecumenical council. As early as January 1980, the Bishop appointed a committee to organize a handbook of sacramental guidelines. Published in 1981, "Sacramental Life in the Diocese of Rochester" treated in detail: the *Rite of Christian Initiation* (RCIA), a revival of the ancient catechumenal method of conferring baptism, confirmation and first communion on new candidates for church membership; Penance, the rites and rules of the Sacrament of Reconciliation; and Marriage, the nature of the sacrament, and the preparations necessary for this holy state. So thorough was the text of "Sacramental Life" that it has remained the basic directory ever since publication.

Liturgical reform moved ahead unevenly, halted at times by unexpected questions. Thus, communion under both forms was to be restored, but even at crowded Sunday Masses? The Diocese of Rochester was granted Sunday permission on June 9, 1985. Although Sunday *administration* was thenceforth the rule, *reception,* of course, remained optional. Then the question was raised about the English translation of the Latin Missal, notably the words of consecration for the chalice, "It will be shed for you and for all *men*." The Church in the United States was finally authorized to drop the word "men" from that phrase as of May 1981.

But the most notable Eucharistic conflict was the demonization by Catholic "traditionalists" of the revised Roman Missal promulgated by Pope Paul VI on November 29, 1969, to replace the "Tridentine" Roman Missal (1570-1962). Leading this ultraconservative and anticonciliar opposition was the French Archbishop Marcel Lefebvre (1905-1991). By temporizing with the popes, Lefebvre was able to win an extensive following in Europe and America (including Rochester) before he set up his own hierarchy by illicitly consecrating four bishops on June 30, 1988. Pope John Paul II would try to prevent further leakage to Lefebvre's "Society of St. Pius X" by permitting wider use of the Tridentine Latin Mass in its 1962 format. This first permission (Circular *Quattuor abhinc annos*, October 3, 1984), was too stringent to be serviceable. But three days after the schismatic consecration, John Paul issued the *Motu proprio, Ecclesia Dei*, facilitating occasional use of the old Missal not just to win back Lefebvrists but to recognize the "rightful aspirations" of those who loved the old Latin Mass. Having carefully studied developments, Bishop Clark announced, on May 9, 1993, that beginning June 6, a Tridentine Latin Mass would be celebrated each Sunday and holy day at St. Stanislaus Church in Rochester. The average attendance has been 200.

The Council had carefully instructed residential bishops to treat their priests "as sons and friends." Clark certainly did so. Not just because the Rochester *presbyterium* was an "endangered species", but because by character and conviction he himself deeply loved the priesthood. As early as November 1979, the Bishop appointed a priest to direct a new "Ministry to Priests". Meanwhile, he saw to the timely adjustment of the clergy's salaries and pensions. On January 1, 1989, he issued a document called "Policies for the General Welfare of the Presbyterate". Carefully worked out, this basic manual took a "holistic" approach to the needs of the individual priest. Appendices could be added, when necessary, to this standard text. One such appendix, "Sexual Abuse by Clergy" (May 20, 1993), evoked by a rash of tragic church-wide occurrences, prescribed a prompt, informed and just response to any charges of maltreatment brought against a member of the Rochester clergy. Wrongdoing by clerics would simply not be tolerated. The Bishop could and would be very strict in dealing with grave offenses.

Far more to his liking than disciplining his fellow priests was keeping them motivated. In agreement with the Council, he encouraged the clergy to constantly update their professional education. He established rules for sabbaticals that included both study and travel, and as an endorsement he himself took a five-month leave in 1988-89 to study Spanish in Mexico. He inaugurated annual convocations of all active priests, three-day away-from-work gatherings for learning and fraternization. Clark likewise collaborated with all the upstate bishops of New York State in establishing (1981) a series of week-long workshops for the benefit of priests newly named to pastorates.

Vatican II expected a bishop to have a priests' "senate or council", and when Bishop Clark arrived, he was greeted by the Priests' Council developed by his two predecessors. Finding, however, that the Council's sessions tended to become routine, in the mid-1980s he decided to reform their proceedings. "You are my advisors," he reminded the members, "and you must give me advice." He therefore named a committee of councilors to revise the rules. Henceforth Clark would actively participate in the agenda meetings of the executive committee. The new rules brought bishop and members into a more understanding and more productive relationship.

As the Rochester diocesan Curia grew in the number of its departments and personnel, and came to employ more nonclergy officials, the need arose for a coordinator of operations. Vatican II did not propose such an office, but the 1983 revision of the Code of Canon Law did: Canon 473.2 wisely recommended that each diocesan center have a "moderator of the Curia". In 1988, therefore, when Bishop Clark appointed Father John M. Mulligan a vicar general of the diocese, he likewise named him Pastoral Office Moderator. With one "ombudspriest" overseeing all activities at 1150 Buffalo Road, everything seemed to function better, human relations were kept more amiable, and the Bishop, although naturally an able delegator, was freed up further for his major responsibilities.

Canon 492.1 *prescribes* a diocesan advisory council on financial and related matters. Rochester's response was the Stewardship Council

(1989). Its membership presents a cross section of diocesan leadership, able to serve as a creative liaison between the Diocese and the business world. This secular expertise recalls the unique role that Vatican II acknowledges to lay Catholics: "to make the Church present and fruitful in those places and circumstances where it is only through them that she can become the salt of the earth" (*Lumen gentium*, 33).

What was Rochester's eighth bishop doing meanwhile to promote vocations to the priesthood, a duty that the Council recalled in its decree on bishops (*Christus Dominus*)?

Nothing would have been more pleasing to this former educator of seminarians than to add many worthy and well-trained young men to the roster of the Rochester priesthood. As we have seen, Bishop Clark had appointed one priest as diocesan director of vocations. That priest's devoted efforts had discovered several candidates of high caliber, but, alas, too few.

In 1989 the Bishop launched a "Call to Priesthood" campaign. Pastors were to request their parishioners to submit to him the names of parish young men who they thought might qualify for the diocesan priesthood. Numerically, the response was good. Clark sent to 700 "nominees" an invitation, to attend an open forum on the subject of priesthood as a life career. Some 80 accepted, and the dialogue at the forum was pleasant and positive. However, very few of those who came showed any personal interest in becoming priests. As the Bishop later revealed, most of them expressed a fear of the required celibacy and of the isolation and loneliness they presumed the priesthood necessarily implied. Clark began to think that if all the bishops could meet to discuss clerical celibacy as a grave, if subjective, deterrent to priestly vocations, they might consider the possibility of making it optional rather than obligatory for Latin Rite priests, as it was for many Eastern Rite Catholic priests. Meanwhile, he concluded, "celibacy that is God-given is a blessing for the Church". (See Clark's essay "The Priest and Celibacy", in Donald J. Goergen O.P., Ed., *Being a Priest Today*, Collegeville, MN 1992.)

In speaking of priestly vocations, we should not overlook Matthew Clark's active interest in diocesan youth programs for both sexes as at least a remote contribution to vocational recruitment. Such programs brought bishop and young people together in a more informal ambiance. There were the Scout Masses, the diocesan youth conventions, and the national youth days. At most public happenings, Bishop Clark was appropriately reserved. At youth events, however, (as observers noted), he seemed to be a teen again, relaxed and sociable. The outstanding young folks' gathering in which he participated was the World Youth Day celebrated in Colorado in 1993 with Pope John Paul II present. The Rochester diocese sent a delegation of 500. Unique, perhaps, among the American bishops who were there, the Bishop of Rochester backpacked it with his diocesan youngsters to the site of the mountain-top Mass. The junior Rochesterians were impressed by his informality and openness. As one of them said, "It brings him closer to younger people. He's someone we can trust and talk to."

Vatican II, in urging bishops of more stable dioceses to come to the aid of brother bishops of poorer dioceses, was simply asking for collegial charity. Responding to this call, Matthew Clark picked up where Bishop Hogan had left off. He visited the missions run by the Rochester Sisters of St. Joseph in Brazil and the Rochester Sisters of Mercy in Chile. He gave ready support to the "sister-diocese" affiliation of the Rochester Diocese and the Diocese of Tabasco in Mexico. From 1983 to 1989 he maintained at Tabasco a Rochester priest and missionary team to set up food cooperatives and to minister to 15 scattered communities. The Bishop of Tabasco, in turn, sent one of his priests to help with the Latinos of the Rochester Diocese and the Mexican migrant workers. In the process Bishops Matthew H. Clark and Rafael Garcia Gonzalez became the best of friends.

In its Decree on Ecumenism, the Council stated that "the concern for restoring unity involves the whole Church, faithful and clergy alike." Bishops are naturally called on to be leaders in this interdenominational thrust towards Christian unity.

Matthew Clark, as Bishop of Rochester, accepted the ecumenical and interfaith accomplishments of his two predecessors and in various ways augmented them.

He continued the diocesan affiliation with GEM, the Genesee Ecumenical Ministries. He authorized the transfer of St. Bernard's Institute to the Colgate Rochester Divinity campus. But, like Bishop Hogan, the closest association he fostered was with the Episcopal Diocese of Rochester. As early as 1980, Bishop Clark and Bishop Robert R. Spears of the Episcopal diocese agreed to merge the Bishop Sheen Housing Fund with the Episcopal Rural Mission, forming the Bishop Sheen Ecumenical Housing Foundation, Inc. It was a sensible move, for the two institutions complemented each other perfectly. Now, William G. Burrill succeeded Robert R. Spears in 1984. By then, the Episcopal Diocese of Rochester no longer had a cathedral church of its own, so Clark cordially invited Bishop-elect Burrill to use Sacred Heart Cathedral for his episcopal consecration and installation. Burrill was happy to accept the invitation. (The agreed destination of the collection that day caused some amusement. It was handed over to the Bishop Sheen Ecumenical Foundation.)

No rapprochement was undertaken between the Rochester Catholic Church and the several district parishes of its sister-churches, the Eastern Orthodox. But under Bishop Clark, relations with non-Christian bodies, also encouraged by Vatican II, would be deepened. Clark, like Sheen, was invited to address the Congregation B'Rith Kodesh. Its rabbi, Judea Miller, later said that, in his opinion, Bishop Clark's talk was even more insightful than Fulton Sheen's had been. In the years that followed, an innovative "Agreement" would be reached by the Diocese and the rabbis of the leading liberal and conservative congregations to engage in a series of nontheological colloquies.

From 1979 to 1994, the Church of Rochester was blessed to have as chairman of the Diocesan Department of Ecumenical and Interreligious Affairs, Mrs. Margery S. Nurnberg (1924-1995) of Elmira, New York. A cradle Catholic, she discharged her task with delicacy and grace. Among her creative achievements, for which she was nationally honored, were the 1987 covenant signed by the Catholic and the Episcopal dioceses of Rochester, and the Interfaith Forum. The Forum arranged for public discussions of secular subjects of interest to Catholics, Protestants, Anglicans, Jews, and *Muslims*. The Muslim community in the Rochester area had increased considerably since Vatican II. Even though the Interfaith Forum diplomatically excluded from its programs theological subject matter, it was the first Rochester diocesan project to extend the hand of welcome to Islamic fellow Americans.

Finally, the Second Vatican Council reminded bishops that they must be solicitous of the welfare not only of their own flocks but of all the rest of humankind, equally children of God. This implied speaking out on current issues involving social justice, public morals, world peace and whatever else touched on human dignity.

Social justice? Following the footsteps of Bishop Joseph Hogan, Clark, in 1980, endorsed an ongoing boycott against the J.P. Stevens Textile Company, charged with unfair treatment of its employees. In 1982 he gave vigorous backing to an international boycott against the Swiss Nestlé Corporation. Nestlé was marketing an infant food denounced by the World Health Organization as dangerous to health. The manufacturer long resisted this "interference" with scandalous insensitivity, but finally accepted the W.H.O.'s alternate formula in 1984.

When scientists first achieved the fertilization of a human egg in a laboratory dish, the Holy See condemned *"in vitro"* manipulation as an intrusion into God's domain. In 1983, the University of Rochester announced its intention to launch a series of experiments along these lines. Bishop Clark, commenting on the Catholic stance, pointed out the main objection, that the generation of a child in a petri dish dehumanizes the act of married love.

In the midst of the long-term American battle over abortion that the U.S. Supreme Court settled but did not solve in its 1973 Roe v. Wade decision, the Bishop of Rochester and the majority of his people continued to maintain that declaring abortion legal did not make it moral. Sometimes the conflict between "pro-life" and "pro-choice" people gave rise to practical social problems. In 1992, Planned Parenthood of Rochester, traditionally accepting of abortion, succeeded in acquiring a place on the list of charitable agencies supported by United Way of Rochester and Monroe County. Many Catholics urged that their bishop, according to custom an ex officio member of the United Way Board, resign the Board and take with him Catholic affiliates of the fund. While such a gesture would surely have reiterated the immorality of abortion, it was all too drastic. The Catholic Diocese had been a co-founder in 1919 of the original Rochester Community Chest, and its sudden withdrawal over a single issue would have deprived many Catholic nonprofit associations of their expected funds. Bishop Clark did *not* disaffiliate. In due time a reasonable compromise was arrived at, and United Way of Rochester continued undisturbed its valuable contribution to local civic welfare.

Among the seemingly apocalyptic disasters that befell the world in the later twentieth century, HIV infection (human immunodeficiency virus) and its customary sequel AIDS (acquired immune deficiency syndrome), condemned millions around the world to irresistible and agonizing death. When the epidemic first surfaced in America in the 1970s its victims were principally active homosexuals; but it soon spread to heterosexuals and to children through intravenous drug injection, tainted blood transfusions, and the like. The AIDS context still remained largely one of vice, but the Church, while condemning the sin, felt for the sinner. Bishop Clark, on February 29, 1988, published a pastoral instruction to his people titled "The Lord Himself Taught Me to Have Compassion". A splendid response, at once scientific, spiritual and practical, it set for the diocese a truly Christian policy: give to the stricken the most tender care, and make every effort to discover an antidote.

Around the same time, another sad practice was reported on the rise: child abuse, particularly in the form of pedophilia. Regrettably, some Catholic priests and religious in several countries were charged with this crime, by now diagnosed as a mental aberration, treatable but still traumatic in its effects. Stephen J. Rossetti, a licensed therapist, invited the Bishop of Rochester to write an article for a book he was preparing, *Slayer of the Soul: Child Sexual Abuse and the Catholic Church* (Mystic, CT, Twenty-Third Publications, 1990). Clark's essay insisted on the need to respond promptly and justly to any such charges, with no bias toward the clerical wrongdoer.

Perhaps it was the athlete in Matthew Clark that made him appreciate the teamwork aspect of collegiality. Even when he spoke out as an individual bishop, it was usually in solidarity with fellow bishops. For example, he joined the prelates of the New York Province in opposing the restoration of the death penalty.

In 1980, when crowds of Haitians were taking flight from the oppressive hand of Haitian dictator "Baby Doc" Duvalier, Bishop Clark undertook to write President Jimmy Carter urging that he grant the fugitives refugee status in the United States.

During the Cold War, just before the presidential election of 1984, the Bishop addressed cautionary open letters to the two presidential candidates, Walter Mondale and Ronald Reagan. He recommended that they promote deeper discussion with the nation's religious leaders of the moral issues that lay behind the leading political issues of the day, such as abortion; the current U.S.A.-U.S.S.R. race for nuclear superiority; and the plight of the 35.2 million Americans who lived below the poverty level. This was no presumptuous bid on the part of Clark for personal publicity. It was the reasoned, diplomatic appeal of a conscientious Catholic spokesman and patriotic citizen.

Whether President Carter or candidates Mondale and Reagan were influenced by these messages, Matthew Clark had made no mistake in proclaiming once more to national leaders the dignity of the human person.

Probably the most exciting statement that Bishop Clark made about the threat of nuclear war was the address he delivered on October 19, 1983, at the Seneca Army Depot in Romulus, New York, a federal military installation within the Rochester Diocese.

On May 3, 1983, the National Conference of Catholic Bishops had issued an impressive message on armaments and peace: "Facing the Challenge of Peace: God's Promise and Our Response". Bishop Clark was invited to address the meeting at Romulus a year later. The Depot was allegedly a storehouse for nuclear weapons, so protest meetings had already been held there, not infrequently involving acts of civil disobedience. Furthermore, among the speakers scheduled for the October gathering were politician Bella Abzug and pediatrician Dr. Benjamin Spock, both strongly pro-abortion. To complicate matters, Rochester was scheduled to host on the same day a convention of the New York State Right-to-Life movement, with pro-life leaders Congressman Henry Hyde and ex-abortionist Dr. Bernard Nathanson as featured lecturers; and the Bishop of Rochester was expected to be, and wanted to be, on that program.

Should Clark appear also at the Romulus venue? He sought advice. The Diocesan Pastoral Council thought that the risks were too many. The Priests' Council favored taking the chance.

In what was one of the busiest and surely one of the most stressful performances of his episcopal career, Matthew Clark chose to address *both* audiences that day. In the morning, as host bishop, he spoke on abortion to the 300 Right-to-Life delegates assembled in Rochester. In the afternoon, backed by prayer vigils held in 15 diocesan churches, he delivered a 15-minute talk at Romulus on "Religious Leadership in the Quest for Peace". Tactfully but frankly he even linked nuclear weaponry with abortion! Security at the Depot was tight, but the event moved along with no notable incident. Although similar protest meetings were being staged across the country that same day, the one at the Seneca Depot called forth the largest crowd, 5,000. Bishop Clark won wide praise for his forthright contribution to the event. He had indeed made a courageous decision.

On May 7-10, 1984, the Catholic bishops of Germany sponsored an ecumenical symposium on peace at Loccum, Germany. The National Conference of American Bishops, invited to send representatives, chose the Bishop of Rochester, and Joseph M. Sullivan, Auxiliary Bishop of Brooklyn and a campaigner for peace. The German hierarchy doubtless intended to recognize, by its invitation, the American hierarchy's 1983 peace pastoral.

The collapse of both the Berlin Wall and European Communism in and after 1989 marked the end of the Cold War, and lessened the immediate threat of nuclear combat. But the world had not yet learned that it is fruitless to seek peace through any sort of war. As Benjamin Franklin once shrewdly observed, "There never was a good war or a bad peace."

In 1990 Iraq invaded the oil-rich state of Kuwait on the Persian Gulf. A coalition of nations led by the United States went on armed alert. On December 7, 1990, Bishop Clark, distressed by this new sabre-rattling, joined with William G. Burrill, Episcopal Bishop of

Rochester, in a joint reminder published in the *Democrat and Chronicle*, that in our day war is not a justifiable means of settling international disputes. While the prelates condemned the Iraqi invasion of Kuwait, they urged that the concerned parties press rather for a negotiated settlement through the United Nations.

Impatient, the allied forces launched the Persian Gulf War. After aerial and missile attacks on Baghdad in January 1991, there was a brief land operation (February 24-27, 1991) that easily expelled the Iraqis from Kuwait. "Desert Storm" was then offered to the world as an example of a "tidy little war".

Actually Desert Storm was anything but tidy. Not long after the conclusion of this fragile peace, its undesirable aspects came to be better known. On December 27, 1991, the same two Rochester churchmen contributed yet another joint letter to the *Democrat and Chronicle*. Criticizing the wastefulness of the conflict and its vastly underreported casualties and deaths, Burrill and Clark urged that the world henceforth seek only the nonviolent peace of Christ. "One of the great tasks given us by God today," they wrote, "is to work for the total abolition of war as a means of settling international conflicts."

Neither bishop was Utopian about such a task. They would not really be surprised to find Iraqi President Saddam Hussein still a thorn in the side of the United Nations as the second millennium drew to a close. But meanwhile they could at least keep reminding their people that true peace is a divine gift. "In His will," wrote Dante Alighieri, "is our peace."

If Matthew Clark valiantly upheld world peace during his first 13 years in office, he did not always find peace in his own bailiwick. Several of his decisions encountered strong opposition, and a couple of times his critics called for his transfer to some other diocese.

No bishop could hope to please the people of the Rochester Diocese if he scuttled their beloved diocesan school structure. The subsidiary arrangement devised by Bishop McQuaid (each parish school remaining relatively independent) had served well enough in its day, but after the Council, it proved ever more inept. By 1989 20 parish schools had shut down across the diocese, and a careful five-year study of the problem showed that more schools would have to be closed or regrouped in the future. While this systematization might not solve the issue, it was better to try it, thought the educators, than to let the whole framework collapse because of sheer inaction. In the end, a mixed solution was adopted. Schools outside Monroe County remained for the most part under the parishes. The schools inside Monroe County were reorganized under a central management as the "Catholic Schools of Monroe County". Just which Monroe County schools would now be closed was, as the Bishop put it, the "hard choice". Although there were ample discussions in the parishes, not all the schoolhouses could win.

When the decision was announced in 1990, widespread protest was voiced in the letters section of both the diocesan and the secular press. Some claimed that Bishop Clark had no real interest in Catholic schools, and pointed to the regrettable closing of Cardinal Mooney High School in 1989 as a further proof (although the Holy Cross Brothers had arrived at that decision unilaterally). The majority of parents, however, seem to have accepted the clustering. Some chose to send their children to older Catholic private schools. One group of parents established, in the suburbs of Rochester, an independent school conducted along traditional Catholic lines. Still other couples opted to train their children at home. "Home schooling," as it was called, had of late become fairly widespread in America, and by 1998 some 60-70 Rochester diocesan families would embrace the plan. But the diocesan schools department survived. While its elementary schools section reported only 11,651 students in 1993, that figure would rise to 15,000 over the next four years. (In 1965 it had been 46,965!)

The school question was not the only issue that divided the faithful under their eighth bishop.

A good many members of the Rochester diocese were disturbed, for instance, by Bishop Clark's interpretation of certain canonical rules of divine worship. Three rules in particular were cited. (The reader will please excuse a brief detour into church law.) Canon 813.2 of the 1918 Code of Canon Law forbade women (or girls) to serve Mass. Canon 1327.2 permitted only popes, bishops, priests and other qualified *men* to preach. And Canon 968.1 said that only males could validly receive the Sacrament of Holy Orders.

Now, without going into the fact that a number of postconciliar Rochesterians were averse to these same regulations, we must remember that many of the earlier church laws still had to be studied officially in light of Vatican II for possible revision—a revision in which the college of bishops would naturally play its part. Personally, Bishop Clark favored allowing women to participate in all liturgical roles that did not require Holy Orders. Personally, indeed, he thought that the possibility of women being admitted to the orders of diaconate and priesthood should be explored.

As the postconciliar years passed, the Church addressed these and similar questions, many of them in the revised Code of Canon Law promulgated in 1983.

The new Canon 905.2, (replacing the old Canon 813.2) was officially interpreted on June 30, 1992, as permitting the *laity*, to discharge in the liturgy any role that did not require Holy Orders, simply on the basis of their baptism into the People of God. Hence girls and women were *of course* permitted to serve Mass! This interpretation was essentially the same one that Bishop Clark had been advocating for some time.

Canon 766 of the new Code, (replacing the old Canon 1327.2), allowed preaching by the laity in certain circumstances, subject to the rules set by the national conferences of bishops. However, Canon 767 reserved the preaching of the homily to priests and deacons; that is, to those in Holy Orders. Here the old law was relaxed only in part.

In the graver matter of the sex of those called to Holy Orders, Canon 1024 made no essential change in the old Canon 960. It stated: "Only a baptized male validly receives sacred ordination." Those who strongly advocated ordination for women still entertained the hope that this rule might not be final, so let us follow this issue a bit beyond our cutoff date 1993. To clarify the point, Pope John Paul II, on May 30, 1994, would state in the Apostolic Letter "On Reserving Priestly Ordination to Men Alone" (*Ordinatio Sacerdotalis*), "that the church has no authority whatsoever to confer priestly ordination on women and that this judgment is to be definitively held by all the church's faithful."

A good many Catholics, deeply disappointed, continued to consider *Ordinatio Sacerdotalis* not a constitutive but a mutable document. The Congregation for the Doctrine of the Faith issued a reply to this "doubt", approved by the Pope, on October 28, 1995. The "doubt", or question raised, was put thus: "Whether the teaching that the Church has no authority whatsoever to confer priestly ordination on women, which is presented in the Apostolic Letter *Ordination Sacerdotalis* to be held definitively, is to be understood as belonging to the deposit of the faith." The answer given was *"affirmative"* ("Yes"). In the explanation that followed, the Congregation said this teaching requires "definitive assent" because it is founded on Scripture and Tradition, and thus "has been set forth infallibly by the ordinary and universal Magisterium" of the Church. The rule was therefore not merely disciplinary and alterable, but doctrinal.

(On November 20, 1995, Bishop Clark would issue a formal statement of assent to this October 28th response of the Congregation: "I accept this teaching with respect and reverence. I ask all Catholics of the Diocese of Rochester prayerfully to invite the wisdom and understanding of the Holy Spirit to fill our hearts and guide our common life as church." The teaching, he pointed out, is not new, and in no way diminishes the dignity of women. Let women continue, therefore, to share their great gifts with the rest of the Church.

Nor was his assent strained. As he had stated in his column "Along the Way" in the *Catholic Courier* of May 8, 1985: "Let me say for the record that I do accept and affirm the teaching office of the Church and I do accept and affirm all that is taught by the ordinary magisterium of the Church."

Why, then, did many come to think that Bishop Clark's ideas were immoderate, and to subject them at times to gross misinterpretation?

Perhaps it was because, in his favored practice of group dialogue, he believed that open-ended discussion should not exclude even unconventional subjects if their review offered to shed a flicker of light on a moot question. Once a Rochester lawyer, writing to the *Democrat and Chronicle* in defense of Clark's technique, made this helpful distinction: "His writing is a call for discussion, not a call to action." Lawyers could appreciate the methodology of dialogue in the quest for truth. On the other hand, the average Catholic might find the introduction of avant-garde topics somehow disloyal and therefore objectionable.

The Diocese of Rochester was now drawing close to its 125th birthday, March 3, 1993. Bernard J. McQuaid, as its founding bishop, had established 69 parishes and built up a strong local church prepared to welcome and acclimatize thousands of European immigrants. For 100 years the McQuaidian structure had served its purpose well. During the fifth quarter-century, however, the epoch introduced by Vatican II, that structure had begun to change as the diocesan population became more fully Americanized and secularized. For all that, even when controversy over Church renewal was shrillest and most divisive, many diocesan Catholics were quietly engaged in admirable good works of which McQuaid himself would have strongly approved.

Quite apart from the wide-ranging welfare activities of the diocesan Charities were a number of new, independent service undertakings established by the religious orders, by parishes, or by lay groups, (some of them ecumenical), to meet the myriad needs of the destitute.

One thinks, for example, of the diverse programs of the local Sisters of Mercy. While their philanthropy has of late focused mainly on the care and shelter of unwed mothers, they have been as ready as their foundress, Venerable Catherine McAuley, to respond somehow to every new cry for help. Mercy Center with the Aging, for example, provides specialized aid for senior citizens *and* for those who undertake their care.

At St. Joseph's Neighborhood Center, the Rochester Sisters of St. Joseph give holistic assistance to men, women and children who are uninsured. Each year they serve over 2000 persons. Among their other enterprises are soup kitchens, the home care of patients, and foster homes both for small children who have inherited HIV or drug-addictive tendencies, and for older children who are handicapped.

Various parishes have adopted service projects of their own. Some have joined the ecumenical "Habitat for Humanity" movement, whose aim is to provide inexpensive housing for the poor by building new homes or reconditioning old ones. Among the Rochester parishes active in philanthropy, Corpus Christi certainly heads the list. There the imaginative Father James B. Callan and his team have set up 16 different welfare ministries, among them a medical center, a halfway house for offenders, a shelter for the homeless, a child-care center, a hospice for the dying (including patients with AIDS), and a full-fledged restaurant ably serviced by ex-offenders.

By the way, the first hospice ministry for the terminally ill in Rochester city was Mount Carmel House, established in 1984 by a group of Carmelite tertiaries at the urging of Deacon Fernando Ona, M.D. Since 1984 several other hospices have been opened in the Rochester district, some under Catholic auspices, others with different religious affiliation, and still others more secular in character. Mount Carmel House was initially inspired by the example of Mother Teresa of Calcutta, and has always operated according to her selfless principles.

All this unselfish service to neighbors-in-need depends in a major way on the contributed work of a host of volunteers. A baptized volunteer is one who demonstrates his or her sense of responsibility to the People of God. And was it not the aim of Vatican II to activate this responsibility?

It is good to note that many of our Catholic schools today are striving to teach upcoming generations the duty of serving others that comes with baptism. For instance, Rochester diocesan high schools now incorporate into their curriculum a certain number of hours of public service. This course in Christian altruism will surely not soon be forgotten by the young participants.

As for signs of spiritual renewal, there are many that offset in part the decline of Sunday Mass attendance. For youth there are the Teen Seminar, the family camps, and the campus ministry, all intent on developing spiritual leadership. For adults there are the prayer groups and the prayer centers conducted by the Sisters of St. Joseph and the Sisters of Mercy, and others. For couples there are Engaged Encounter, Marriage Encounter, and, on behalf of troubled spouses, *Retrouvaille-Rochester*. The Rite of Catholic Initiation for Adults (RCIA) is a prolonged catechumenate for those joining or rejoining the Church. A small but effective Rochester undertaking is the Monthly Prayer Request for Priests, a calendar that assigns to every day in the year, a living priest to be prayed for. Opportunities are available for Cursillo retreats of various types, and for Catholic Charismatic Celebrations. Pilgrimages to shrines in the United States, Canada, Latin America, Europe and the Mideast have perhaps never been so popular. One of the most heartening developments is a new awareness of the centrality of the Eucharist, as illustrated both by lay involvement in the Mass and by the popularity of several chapels for weekday and round-the-clock adoration. Volunteers, again, are largely responsible for this touching trend.

In 1986 Matthew Clark, looking for a major method of instructing his people in this responsibility for the Church, proposed to convoke a diocesan synod. The Priests' Council did not take to it then, but by 1989 they had come to view it as a fitting way to prepare for the 125th anniversary of the Diocese (1993), and the end of the second millennium (2000). After due consultation, on July 17, 1990, the Bishop convoked the Seventh Synod of the Diocese of Rochester, and named Father Joseph A. Hart of St. Bernard's Institute director of this complex three-year effort.

A synod is any assembly of church people summoned to take official action on matters pertaining to their religious community. A *diocesan* synod is one in which a local bishop, after consulting with his clergy, issues various directives and regulations considered necessary for the local church. Before Vatican II, Canon Law normally limited synodal participation to the bishop and clergy. When the Code was revised in 1983, however, the definition of diocesan synod was rewritten to reflect the decrees of the Second Vatican Council. While the bishop would remain the legislator, synodal participation was to be extended also to the religious and laity, and all subjects under consideration were to be discussed thoroughly.

Much homework went into the planning of the Seventh Synod in order to elicit from the diocesans, through their elected delegates, their views of what tack the Diocese should take in future years. The process started at the parish level and moved upward. An initial appeal for subjects to discuss brought in 20,000 responses. From these replics six themes were drawn. In the fall of 1992 the six themes were sent to the parishes for formal deliberation. Participants in these "parish synods" were first to read a brief background explanation; then to identify the current needs of the Diocese, and see how they related to Gospel and church teachings; and finally, to propose concrete recommendations. The parish delegates were then asked to forward the top recommendations to "regional synods" to be held in December 1992 and May 1993. Here the same type of discussion and recommendation was followed.

At length the General Synod took place. It was held on October 1-3, 1993, in the Rochester Riverside Convention Center. Bishop Clark presided, and 1300 delegates were in attendance. They had the task of winnowing out five recommendations from all those submitted: recommendations intended to form the background of a diocesan pastoral plan that would guide the local church into the 21st century.

Bishop Clark was the main celebrant of the concluding Mass at the Rochester Community War Memorial on Sunday, October 3, commemorating the 125th anniversary of the Diocese of Rochester. Among the guests were several bishops, ecumenical representatives and civic officials. At the end of the liturgy the Bishop disclosed the five priorities chosen by the delegates as of paramount importance: 1. Lifelong religious education; 2. Catholic moral education; 3. A consistent life ethic; 4. The role of women in the Church; 5. The establishment of "small Christian communities."

Rochester Diocesan Synod No. 7 was very well organized, and generated much interest among the participating delegates. It amply vindicated Bishop Clark's conviction that dialogue is an effective teaching tool. The delegates had learned much, not only about the subjects prioritized, but also about other subjects widely debated but of lesser priority. Furthermore, the participants were not allowed to forget that the synodal meetings were truly spiritual activities. The Bishop had asked the faithful to invoke the aid of the Holy Spirit on the General Synod, and to make Friday, October 1, a day of abstinence and prayer.

The Seventh Synod had listed what the faithful of the Diocese discerned to be their most pressing needs. But as the diocesan newssheet *Synod 1994* would observe, "The Synod isn't over—it is really just beginning!" A "Synod Implementation Commission" was set up in late 1993 to start turning dream into reality.

Would that undertaking be effective? It is obviously too early to say; furthermore, we promised to end this chapter at the Diocese's 125th birthday.

Pope John Paul II does assure us, however, that the contemporary form of diocesan synod can contribute much to clarify the Council's heavy stress on the "New People of God". In words that Matthew Clark himself might have written, the Pope says:

> I know from experience how this synodal approach responds to expectations of various groups and what it can achieve. I think of the diocesan synods which almost spontaneously got rid of the old unilateral emphasis on clergy and became *a means for expressing the responsibility of each person toward the Church.* The sense of communal responsibility toward the Church, felt especially by lay people today, is certainly a source of renewal. In view of the third millennium, this sense of responsibility will shape the image of the Church for generations to come. (*Crossing the Threshold of Hope,* 1994.)

Thus far, Vatican II has caused us much pain of adjustment, although no more perhaps than the twenty earlier councils caused the faithful of their eras. The Paraclete is always with us, but in times of crisis he musters pope and bishops and suggests necessary new directions.

Synod 1993 is the Rochester Diocese's formal response to the Twenty-first Ecumenical Council. With God's help its measures should lead us bravely into the new millennium.

Therefore, we pray: "Come, Holy Spirit! Fill the hearts of your faithful and enkindle in them the fire of divine love. Send forth your Spirit and they shall be created; and you shall renew the face of the earth."

"You shall renew the face of the earth!"

NOTES

AANY — Archives, Archdiocese of New York.

AASP — Archives, Archdiocese of St. Paul.

ACAB — *Appleton's Cyclopedia of American Biography* (New York, 1887-1899).

ACSSR — *Annales C. SS. R. Provinciae Americanae.* Joseph Wuest, C.SS.R., Ed. (Ilchester, Md., 1888-1924). (Printed annals of the American Redemptorists.)

ADA — Archives, Diocese of Albany, N.Y.

AP — *Annuario Pontificio* (Vatican City) (Official yearbook of the Holy See.)

ARD — Archives, Rochester Diocese.

CC — *Catholic Courier* (Rochester, 1932 - 1945). (See also: *CC&J, CCJ, CJ.*)

CCCJSPC — *Cathedral Calendar, Centennial Jubilee, St. Patrick's Cathedral* (Rochester, November, 1919).

CC&J — *Catholic Courier and Journal* (Rochester, 1929 - 1932). (See also: *CC, CCJ, CJ.*)

CCJ — *Catholic Courier Journal* (Rochester, 1945-). (Continuation of: *CJ, CC&J, CC.*)

CCSSR — Chronicles, Redemptorist Fathers, St. Joseph's Church, Rochester N.Y. 1857- . (A MS journal of the local Redemptorists.)

CE — *The Catholic Encyclopedia* (New York, 1907-1914).

CG — *A Century of Grace: A History of St. Mary's Roman Catholic Parish, Corning, New York, 1848-1948.* By Robert F. McNamara. (Corning, 1948).

CHR — *Catholic Historical Review* (Washington, D.C., 1915-).

CJ — *Catholic Journal* (Rochester, 1889-1929). (See also: *CC, CC&J, CCJ.*)

CJHPE — *Catholic Journal, Historical-Pictorial Edition* (Rochester, 1914). (A supplement.)

CT — *Catholic Times* (Waterloo, Rochester, 1877-1881).

DA — *Daily Advertiser* (Rochester, N.Y., 1828-1857).

DAB — *Dictionary of American Biography* (New York, 1928-).

DAm — *Democrat and American* (Rochester, 1857-1864).

DC — *Democrat and Chronicle* (Rochester, 1870-).

DCh — *Daily Chronicle* (Rochester, 1868-1870).

DCHNY — *Documents Relative to the Colonial History of the State of New York.* Edmund B. O'Callaghan, Ed. (Albany, N.Y. 1853-1883).

DD — *Daily Democrat* (Rochester, 1831-1857; 1864-1870).

DHSNY — *Documentary History of the State of New York.* Edmund B. O'Callaghan, Ed. (Albany, N.Y., 1849-1851).

DNB — *Dictionary of National Biography* (London, 1885-). (Biographies from the British Isles and colonies.)

DT — *Daily Times* (Rochester, 1859).

DU — *Daily Union* (Rochester, 1852-1856).

EE — *Evening Express* (Rochester, 1859-1882).

FJ — *Freeman's Journal and Catholic Register* (New York, 1840-1918).

HCCWNY *History of the Catholic Church in Western New York, Diocese of Buffalo.* By Thomas Donohue. (Buffalo, N.Y., 1904).

HGDR *Hundertjaehrige Geschichte der Deutschtums von Rochester.* By Hermann Pfaefflin. (Rochester, 1915).

HMC *History of Monroe County.* By W. H. McIntosh. (Philadelphia, 1877).

HRMC *History of Rochester and Monroe County.* By William F. Peck. (New York, 1908).

HRS *Historical Records and Studies,* United States Catholic Historical Society (New York, 1899-).

HTCTS *History of Tioga, Chemung, Tompkins and Schuyler Counties.* By Henry B. Pierce and D. H. Hurd. (Philadelphia, 1879).

ICCM *Immaculate Conception Church Magazine* (Rochester, Immaculate Conception parish, 1907-1921).

JR *The Jesuit Relations and Allied Documents.* Reuben G. Thwaites, Ed. (Cleveland, O., 1896-1901).

Mansi *Sacrorum Conciliorum Nova et Amplissima Collectio.* Gian D. Mansi, Ed. (Rev. ed., Paris, 1901-1924).

McQuaid *The Life and Times of Bishop McQuaid.* By Frederick J. Zwierlein. (Rochester, 1925-1927).

MCUND Manuscript Collection, University of Notre Dame.

MWNY *Missions of Western New York and Church History of the Diocese of Buffalo.* By the Bishop of Buffalo [John Timon, C.M.]. (Buffalo, 1862).

NCE *New Catholic Encyclopedia* (New York, 1967).

OHYCR "One Hundred Years of Catholicism in Rochester." By Frederick J. Zwierlein. *Centennial History of Rochester,* 4 (1934): 189-276 (Vol. 13 of *RHSPFS*).

PE *Post Express* (Rochester, 1882-1923).

RACHS *Records of the American Catholic Historical Society of Philadelphia* (Philadelphia, 1887-).

RDAm *Rochester Daily American* (Rochester, 1851-1857).

RET *Rochester Evening Times* (Rochester, 1888-1917).

RH *Rochester Herald* (Rochester, 1879-1926).

RHis *Rochester History* (Rochester Public Library, 1939-).

RHSPFS Rochester Historical Society Publication Fund Series (Rochester, 1922-1937).

RHSP Rochester Historical Society Publications. (A continuation of RHSPFS, 1937-1942.)

RR *Rochester Republican* (Rochester, 1829-1849).

SCB *Some Cross Bearers of the Finger Lakes Region.* By Bernard Heffernan. (Chicago, 1925).

SSJR *Sisters of Saint Joseph of Rochester.* By a Sister of Saint Joseph. (Rochester, 1950).

TU *Times-Union* (Rochester, 1918-).

UA *Union and Advertiser* (Rochester, 1856-1918).

WEJ *West End Journal and Orphans' Advoca*te (Rochester, 1870-1877).

WWSRRMC*World War [I] Service Record of Rochester and Monroe County.* Edward R. Foreman, Ed. (Rochester, 1924-1930).

CHAPTER ONE:

THE FIRST SOWING: 1615-1763

1. H. P. Biggar, Ed., *Works of Samuel Champlain* (Toronto, 1929), 3: 53-58, 213-224. For a summary of French contacts in upstate New York see Alexander M. Stewart, *French Pioneers in North America* (forthcoming publication of the N. Y. State Archeological Assn., Albany, N. Y.).

2. The village attacked may have been at Nichols Pond (Town of Fenner, Madison County) or on Lake Onondaga; but it was not on Canandaigua Lake. William M. Beauchamp, "Champlain and the Oneidas in 1615," *Annual Report, American Scenic and Historic Preservation Society* (1918), pp. 625-43.

3. *JR*, 41: 91-129.

4. *JR*, 42: 101-25. First Mass, *ibid.*, p. 99. LeMoyne had not celebrated Mass during his visit (*JR*, 41: 129).

5. *JR*, 13: 37-83.

6. *JR*, 43: 307-17, for Ménard's visit to the Cayugas.

7. *JR*, 44: 69.

8. *JR*, 44: 21-27, for the whole story of Chaumonot's trip to the Senecas.

9. *JR*, 44: 159-61.

10. *JR*, 47: 69, 77.

11. *JR*, 47: 185-86.

12. *JR*, 47: 191, 287.

13. *JR*, 56: 49.

14. *JR*, 54: 111. R. P. Orhand, S. J., *Un admirable inconnu* (Paris, 1890), p. 197. There is no evidence that chapels were built at St. Étienne and St. René.

15. *JR*, 52: 195. Most Seneca village sites have been located and largely excavated. But the Iroquois moved their villages every couple of decades to new or even previously-occupied locations. This complicates their exact identification and dating. Thus Gannagaro was surely on the slope of Boughton Hill in 1687 and Totiakton was surely once at Rochester Junction; but the length of time each occupied these sites is unknown. Archeologists Charles F. Wray and Harry L. Schoff, disagreeing with earlier opinions (some of which have been stated in mission-site monuments), have ventured the following sequence. *Totiakton-Sonnontouan* (La Conception) #1: Dann's Corners, Route No. 15-A west of Honeoye Falls (marked by the Order of the Alhambra missionary tablet): 1650-1675; *Totiakton-Sonnontouan* #2, Rochester Junction, 1675-1687. *Gandachiragou* (St. Jean): at Cummins Corners (York Street and Corby Road), one mile south of Honeoye Falls, from 1650 to 1675; at the Kirkwood farm, two miles west of Dann's Corners, from 1675 to 1686. *Gannagaro*, the eastern capital (St. Jacques): on the Thompson (Marsh) farm east of Holcomb (called site of Gandougarae in the marker), 1650-1675; on the summit of Boughton Hill, south of Victor, 1675-1687. *Gandougarae*, the Huron village (St. Michel): at the crossroads, Victor-Holcomb Road and Cherry Street, from 1650 to 1675; on the Beal Farm, Cherry Street, a mile west of previous site, from 1675 to 1687. See Wray and Schoff, "A Preliminary Report on the Seneca Sequence in Western New York, 1550-1687," *Pennsylvania Archaeologist*, 23 (July, 1953): ii, 53-63. Further details kindly furnished by Mr. Wray.

16. Alexander M. Stewart, "Early Voyager Priests," *CC* annual supplement VII (1935).

17. *JR*, 54: 79.

18. *JR*, 54: 81, 117.

19. *JR*, 54: 121.

20. *JR*, 52: 119-21; 53: 207-13.

21. Galinée journal, Louise P. Kellogg, Ed., *Early Narratives of the Northwest, 1634-1689* (New York, 1917), pp. 167-209.

22. Father Hennepin's *A New Discovery*,

Reuben G. Thwaites, Ed., (Chicago, 1903), pp. 80-88, 101, 326.

23. In 1673-1674, before his assignment to the Seneca mission, Father Jean Pierron traveled from Quebec to Acadia, Massachusetts and Maryland. If he returned north via the Susquehanna, he may have passed through the eastern part of the Rochester Diocese (*JR*, 59: 72-79).

The French stationed at Fort Niagara during the French and Indian War did make a missionary approach to the Delaware Indians who were then living in the Chemung Valley as guests of the Iroquois. A Jesuit Father who was currently missionary to their Algonquin relatives, the Abenakis, spoke on the excellence of religion to an invited group of Delawares. But the listeners showed no special interest. See M. Pouchot, *Memoir upon the Late War in North America . . . 1755-1760.* Franklin B. Hough, Tr. (Roxbury, Mass., 1866), 1: 92-93.

24. *JR*, 54: 117-19.

25. *JR*, 55: 91.

26. *JR*, 54: 87-93.

27. *JR*, 54: 123.

28. Orhand, *Un admirable inconnu*, pp. 222, 239; *JR*, 62: 229; *DCHNY*, 9: 229. Father Vaillant de Gueslis, at that time obliged to go away from the Mohawks, left behind a chest of interesting mission supplies which the Commissaries at Albany seized and dutifully inventoried. Among the items were: 22 bunches of black beads; 2 dozen little looking glasses for Indians; 2 little Paternoster chains; 1 priest's white surplice; 3 small bunches of copper fingerrings; 4 dozen tinder boxes with steel and flints; 2 little paintings; 5 burning glasses; 27 little books; 11 paper pictures. Also, in a tool basket, a 16-pound bell. *DHSNY*, 2: 205, 208-09. Missionaries to the Iroquois probably followed in general the

practical instructions for living among the Indians which St. Jean de Brébeuf gave to the Huron missionaries in 1637 (*JR*, 12: 117-23).

29. Reports on the expedition are: Chevalier de Baugy, in *RHSPFS*, 9 (1930): 1-56; Abbé Belmont, in *Mid-America*, 34 (1953): 115-47; Thierry Beschefer, S. J., in *JR*, 63: 269-87; Denonville, in *DCHNY*, 9: 334, 336-44, 358-69; LaHontan, in *The Historical Writings of Orsamus H. Marshall* (Albany, 1887), pp. 181-84. We are also indebted to Mr. J. Sheldon Fisher of Fisher, N.Y., for a copy of notes (1966) on the Battle of Victor by Rev. Jean Leclerc, S.J., of Quebec.

30. Claude Chauchetière, S. J., in *Katherine Tekakwitha, the Lily of the Mohawks* (New York, 1940), pp. 143-51.

31. Orhand, *Un admirable inconnu*, pp. 182-83.

32. *DCHNY*, 9: 737, 749-50, 762, 775.

33. *DCHNY*, 9: 829-30.

34. *DCHNY*, 9: 902.

35. *DHSNY*, 1: 428-39.

36. John G. Shea, *History of the Catholic Missions among the Indian Tribes . . .* (New York, n.d.), p. 265, f.n.

37. *MWNY*, pp. 202-03. Also information from the Rev. Michael K. Jacobs, S. J., of St. Regis Reservation.

38. Several men from the Rochester area deserve special credit for their efforts at discovering and marking our diocesan mission sites. They are: Rev. James Dougherty, Rev. Andrew Byrne, Rt. Rev. Msgr. Edward Byrne, Rt. Rev. Msgr. J. F. Goggin, Mr. Herman Hetzler, Rev. Mr. Alexander M. Stewart, Mr. George C. Selden. Mr. Stewart, a retired Baptist minister, wrote more than anybody else on the area's Jesuit mission history. Mr. Selden, also a Protestant and a long-time student of local French and Spanish contacts, kindly read and criticized the present chapter.

CHAPTER TWO:

SECOND SEEDTIME: 1783-1847

1. *DHSNY*, 1:377-81

2. Journal, in *The Sullivan-Clinton Campaign in 1779* (Albany, 1929), p. 205.

3. Clayton Mau, *The Development of Central and Western New York*, 2nd ed. (Dansville, N. Y., 1958), p. 85.

4. *DHSNY*, 2: facing p. 691.

5. J. H. French, *Gazetteer of the State of New York* (Syracuse, 1860), p. 496.

6. Stafford C. Cleveland, *History and Directory of Yates County* (Albany, 1873), 1:172; Orsamus Turner, *History and Pio-*

neer Settlement of the Phelps and Gorham Purchase (Rochester, 1851), pp. 138, 139, 155, 231; Frank L. Swann to present writer, Penn Yan, November, 1961. There was no priest stationed at Oswego at this time, according to the available records.

7. Turner, *Phelps and Gorham Purchase*, pp. 348-49. François, Duke de la Roche-foucauld-Liancourt, *Travels Through the United States of North America* (London, 1799), 1:158-60.

8. Turner, *Phelps and Gorham Purchase*, p. 366; *McQuaid*, 1: 1-8; Kate Mason Rowland, *The Life of Charles Carroll of Carrollton* (New York, 1898), 2:101-02, 441-42. Rochester's State Street was called Carroll Street after Major Carroll until September 13, 1831. The only other Catholic signer of the U. S. Constitution, the Philadelphian , Thomas FitzSimons (1741-1811), was briefly a landowner in the Genesee Country, although *in absentia*. In 1798, after Robert Morris went bankrupt, some of his property around Mount Morris came into FitzSimons' hands. See FitzSimons in *DAB*; James A. Farrell, "Thomas Fitzsimons . . ." *RACHS*, 39 (1928): 174-224; Martin I. J. Griffin, "Thomas Fitzsimons . . .", *ibid.*, 2 (1886-1887): 45-114.

9. Charles W. Sloane, "Charles O'Conor . . .," *United States Catholic Historical Magazine*, 4(1893): 225-68, 396-429; Joseph Walsh, "Charles O'Connor," Journal *American Irish Historical Society* 27 (1928) 285-313; *HTCTS*, p. 679; "Thomas O'Connor" and "Charles O'Conor" in *ACAB*; "Charles O'Conor" and "Francis Kernan" in *DAB, CE;* Kernan Family Collection, Collection of Regional History, Cornell University; genealogical data kindly supplied to the writer by Mr. Warnick Kernan of Utica, N. Y. Guy H. McMaster, *History of the Settlement of Steuben County, N. Y.* (Bath, 1853) pp. 81-82, 123, 178-87.

10. *SCB*, pp. 47-48.

11. The 1810 census, Town of Northampton, lists John McGuire and family, comprising one male (16-25), one female (26-45) and two boys under 10. It also lists a "Philemon" McGuire — probably Felix (Phelim), for the census often misspells names, and Felix' own name appears in other documents as "Phelix." This McGuire had in his family one female (over 45), one male (26-45), and a boy and girl under ten. See also *HMC*, pp. 204, 207; *Mother of Sorrows Herald* (Mother of Sorrows parish, Greece), Vol. 1, No. 3

(Pentecost, 1930). For James Flynn, see *HRMC*, pp. 1046-49.

12. Leo R. Ryan, *Old St. Peter's* (New York, 1935), p. 52.

13. John J. Dillon, *The Historic Story of St. Mary's, Albany, N. Y.* (New York, 1933), pp. 60-84.

14. O. J. Harvey and E. G. Smith, *History of Wilkes Barre . . .* (Wilkes Barre, 1929) 4:1967; Henry C. Bradsby, *History of Luzern County . . .* (Chicago, 1893), p. 447; data kindly supplied by the Rt. Rev. Msgr. John P. Bolen, pastor of the Basilica of the Sacred Heart, Conewago, Pa. But the story of Pellentz's trip to Wilkes Barre (and therefore to Elmira, see *Elmira Telegram*, July 16, 1922) is now considered unfounded. (Information of Rev. John P. Gallagher, Scranton, Pa.).

15. Jean Dilhet, *Beginnings of the Catholic Church in the United States* (Washington, 1922), pp. 77, 83, 84; Robert F. McNamara, "Father Jean Dilhet: His Visit to Western New York," *HRS*, 49 (1962): 77-85.

16. *HRS*, 2 pt. 1 (1900): 36-38.

17. Joel H. Monroe, *Historical Records of a Hundred Years* (Auburn, 1913), pp. 103-04; *MWNY*, p. 211; *SCB*, pp. 21-22. Timon says the Mass was in the courthouse. Auburn tradition indicates that Father O'Gorman transferred the Mass-site from the O'Connor home to the courthouse when the former place could no longer accommodate the crowd. (Unidentified clipping from the Auburn *Citizen*.)

18. *SSJR*, pp. 47-48; *Cathedral Calendar*, March, 1913 (pp. 55-56); May, 1913 (p. 95). This story is given on the authority of Elizabeth Rigney. Her father, John [Patrick?] Rigney and Patrick Buckley came to Rochester from Kings County, Ireland. Patrick's son Keron (1812-1881), while a youth, was on close terms with Col. Nathaniel Rochester's family. (*CT*, May 14, 1881). The priest summoned may have been nearer at hand than New York. But *Mother of Sorrows Herald*, I, No. 3 (Pentecost, 1930) records as the Paddy Hill tradition that Felix McGuire brought the first priest into the area to celebrate Mass. William B. McLaughlin says Felix went to Canandaigua and brought Father O'Gorman to Rochester to offer Mass. But he dates the visit in January, 1819 (McLaughlin to Thomas F. Hickey, October 9, 1916, in Zwierlein notes).

19. Oneida County courthouse, Religious Associations records, p. 37.

20. SCB, pp. 21-27, has the best sketch.

21. J. S. M. Lynch, A Page of Church History in New York (Utica, 1893), pp. 15-18; SCB, pp. 32-39.

22. Cayuga Republican, (Auburn, N.Y.), July 7, 1819; February 16, 1820; February 16, 1820; February 23, 1820.

23. Monroe County courthouse, Miscellaneous Records, 1: 3.

24. DD, January 30, 1850.

25. Cayuga County Clerk's Office, Deeds, Book W; Cayuga Republican (Auburn, N.Y.), August 9, 1820; SCB, 33-34.

26. MWNY, p. 212.

27. Monroe County courthouse, Deeds, Liber 1: 657-58. For the supposed rivalry over the lot for St. Luke's Church between Catholics and Episcopalians, see DC, April 7, 1929; OHYCR, pp. 191-92.

28. McQuaid, 1: 14; OHYCR, p. 193.

29. McQuaid, 1: 15.

30. John Talbot Smith, History of the Catholic Church in New York (New York, 1908), 1: 64, says Connolly made a visitation in 1817, "travelling as far west as Buffalo." John Gilmary Shea, History of the Catholic Church in the United States (New York, 1886-1892), 3: 182, is inclined to agree, and thinks that the bishop who, according to Timon (MWNY, p. 211), came to Buffalo around 1821, was not, as Timon thought, Henry Conwell of Philadelphia but John Connolly of New York. Father John Shanahan's "Reminiscences" state that "Bishop Connolly made [only?] one visitation of the diocese in 1822 . . ." But he names no places visited except Albany, Utica and Rome (U.S. Catholic Historical Magazine, 2, No. 5 [January, 1888]: 105). Bishop McQuaid doubted Smith's statement about the Connolly visitation to western New York. (MCUND: J. T. Smith Papers, McQuaid to Edgar Wadhams, Rochester, N.Y., March 3, 1886).

31. The poem quoted is Michael Hughes' "Knownothingism," from his MS copybook, kindly loaned by Mrs. Gertrude Hughes Furlong. For the Montezuma episode, see George W. Potter, To the Golden Door (Boston, Mass., 1960), pp. 184-85. Irish

laborers were less numerous during the earliest years of Erie Canal construction than during the period of expansion after 1830. See Ronald E. Shaw, Erie Water West (Lexington, Kentucky, 1966) pp. 90-91. For Elmira, see Winifred Kittredge Eaton, "Living in a Goldfish Bowl," Highlights of History in Chemung County, 1 (Elmira, June, 1950): 4; Ausburn Towner, Our [Chemung] County and its People (Syracuse, N.Y., 1892), pp. 187-88.

32. George Schantz, in CC, February 15, 1934; HGDR, pp. 24-25.

33. CT, February 12, 1881.

34. MS parish history, Sacred Heart Church, Perkinsville; A. O. Bunnell—F. I. Quick, Dansville . . . (Dansville, N.Y., 1902) 1: 90-91.

35. Hughes to Freeman's Journal . . . (New York), October 24, 1841, in McQuaid, 1: 93. Vital Rèche (1794-1894) subsequently moved to Rochester and is buried in Holy Sepulchre Cemetery. For Wood, see CCJ, October 23, 1947.

36. ACSSR, 3, Part 1: 135.

37. Rochester Telegraph, September 25, 1828.

38. Dubois, report to Society for the Propagation of the Faith, Rome, March 16, 1830, HRS, 5, pt. 2 (1907): 216-30. Apparently he merely stopped in Auburn en route to Buffalo (SCB, p. 5).

39. Charles S. Herbermann, "The Rt. Reverend John Dubois . . . ," HRS, 1, pt. 2 (1900): 333.

40. McQuaid, 1: 78; HRS, 2, pt. 2 (1901): 241-42.

41. John F. Byrne, C.SS.R., Centennial Souvenir, St. Joseph's Church (Rochester, 1936), pp. 16-17.

42. Hughes, in McQuaid, 1: 91-94; SCB, pp. 65-66.

43. McQuaid, 1: 96-97.

44. DA, August 15, 1844; Mullaney, Four Score Years . . . (Rochester, 1916), pp. 37-38.

45. FJ, July 26, 1845; Wilfred J. Rauber, Parish Pathways . . ., p. 19; AANY, A-23, George Quin to John McCloskey, Salubria (Watkins), (December 12, 1845); McCloskey to Quin, New York, Decem-

ber 17, 1845, in *HRS,* 9 (1916): 158-60. Donohue says McCloskey celebrated Mass in this church in 1847 (*HCCWNY,* p. 312).

46. A new source of mission funds was the donations of three new European mission-aid societies, the French Society for the Propagation of the Faith (reorganized 1822); the Austrian Leopoldine Society (est. 1829) and the Bavarian Ludwig Mission Society (est. 1838). These supplied fair sums to the New York and Buffalo dioceses and even to the Rochester Diocese. (In 1868-69 they gave to the latter, respectively, $4,000.00, $800.00 and $120.00.) Theodore Roemer, O.F.M.Cap., *Ten Decades of Alms* (St. Louis, 1942), pp. 159, 176, 168. The Austrian and Bavarian societies gave considerable assistance to the Redemptorists. A Leopoldine gift of 5000 florins ($2,500.00) made in the midst of the depression of 1837 to Father Prost, pastor of St. Joseph's, enabled him to prevent foreclosure of mortgage on both St. Joseph's and St. Patrick's churches (*McQuaid,* 1: 74-75).

47. *McQuaid,* 1: 50-52.

48. *McQuaid,* 1: 66, 98. Also, McQuaid to Edgar Wadhams, Rochester, N.Y., March 11, 1886, in *MCUND,* J. T. Smith Papers. Foley later served at Ogdensburg (1836-38) where he is buried. *HRS,* 2, pt. 1 (1900): 72-73.

49. The Holy Family Congregation occupied the old Methodist church on Chapel Street (*SCB,* pp. 54-55). Dubois gave $200.00 for the purchase of the original (and present) site of St. Francis de Sales, Geneva, and $130.00 more to the church construction fund (MS parish history, St. Francis Church, Geneva).

50. *McQuaid,* 1: 68.

51. *MWNY,* p. 220; *ARD,* St. Patrick (Mount Morris) parish questionnaire.

52. MS parish history, Sacred Heart Church, Perkinsville; Wilfred J. Rauber, *Parish Pathways* . . . (Dansville, 1945), p. 18.

53. *HCCWNY,* pp. 316-17. It was still unfinished when Timon visited there in February, 1848. *MWNY,* p. 246.

54. *AANY.* A-23, George Quin to John McCloskey, Salubria [Lake?], (December 12, 1845); McCloskey to Quin, New York, December 17, 1845, in *HRS,* 9

(1916): 158-60. Quin later removed to Utica and died a Catholic. *MWNY,* pp. 242-43.

55. *CT,* March 19, 1881; *MWNY,* 25.

56. *McQuaid,* 1: 52-53; *Mother of Sorrows Herald,* 1, No. 3 (Pentecost, 1930); *Truth Teller* (New York), November 15, 1834; obituary of Nicholas Read, *UA,* May 19, 1864.

57. *McQuaid,* 1: 70-79, and Mullaney, *Four Score Years,* pp. 12-29, for the beginnings of St. Joseph's. Prost's own account, written 1857, is in *ACSSR, Supplementum ad Vol. I, II, III,* 1, Part 1, (Ilchester, Md., 1903): 3-338, and especially 76-78, 100-08.

58. Michael J. Curley, C.SS.R., *Venerable John Neumann, C.SS.R.* . . . (New York, 1952), pp. 61-64. Neumann conducted services in St. Patrick's Church. Although he states in his diary under July 7, 1836 (MS in the Redemptorist Baltimore Provincial Archives, Brooklyn, N.Y.) that he performed his first baptism on that day, he entered the Koch baptism in St. Patrick's register on July 10th. Most likely he postdated the baptism three days through oversight. The entry reads: "Carolina filia Antonia[e] Charles et Bernardi Koch, Patrina Mariana Schweitzer baptizavi Joan. N. Neumann." For the full story of Neumann's Rochester sojourn, see in addition to the diary, his autobiographical sketch (1852, Provincial Archives), and Neumann to Herr Dechant, (Buffalo, August, 1836), *ACSSR,* 1: 254-60. Father Neumann was back in Rochester briefly in late 1838 (*ACSSR,* 1: 50, and its *Supplementum,* 1, Part 1: 103). He became the first cleric to join the American Redemptorists, in 1840. While a novice, he was officially attached to St. Joseph's, June-September, 1841 (*CCSSR,* 1: 8). As Redemptorist superior he gave a mission at St. Joseph's in 1847 and made a visitation there later in the same year. (*CSSSR,* 1: 21-22). A solemn requiem was offered for this fourth bishop of Philadelphia on January 16, 1860, seven days after his death (*CSSR,* 1: 89.) He was canonized June 19, 1977.

59. Dubois was at Salina on June 17, 1837, and planned to leave for Rochester the following day (*HRS,* 2, Part 2 [1901]: 241-42). While in Rochester he pontificated twice — most likely on Sunday, June 22nd, and on the feast of the Nativity of St. John the Baptist, June 24th. Accompanied by Prost, he went from Rochester

to Buffalo, probably on June 27th. Before the Franklin Street church was built, the Germans worshipped for about six months in St. Mary's church building, South St. Paul. It had been offered to them—apparently early in 1841 — by Catholics who had regained possession of the abandoned church. But Bishop Hughes disapproved of the arrangement, so the pastor, Father Simon Saenderl, eventually led his flock back to the Ely Street church. (Mullaney, *Four Score Years,* p. 31; *ACSSR,* 1: 87.)

60. *McQuaid,* 1: 94-97; *MWNY,* pp. 230-32; *CCSSR,* 1: 8-10.

61. J. L. Zaplotnik, "Rev. Ivo Leviz, O.F.M.," *HRS,* 9 (1916): 176-79.

62. David Craft, *History of Bradford County, Pennsylvania* (Philadelphia, 1878): p. 167; *CCJ,* October 27, 1949. On O'Flynn's earlier missionary career, see: Eris M. O'Brien, *Dawn of Catholicism in Australia* (Sydney, 1928); Henry J. Koren, C.S.Sp., *Knaves or Knights?* (Pittsburgh, 1962); Catherine Fitzgerald (his niece), "Rev. Jeremiah Francis O'Flynn . . . ," *American Catholic Historical Researches* (Philadelphia) 6 (1889): 121-127 (reliable only with regard to his Pennsylvania career).

63. *CG,* pp. 15, 215-15; *Democratic Leader* (Binghamton), October 11, 1873.

64. *HCCWNY,* p. 316.

65. Mullaney, *Four Score Years,* p. 21.

66. *ACSSR* and *CCSSR* list each year's missions.

67. *McQuaid,* 1: 85.

68. *McQuaid,* 1: 111.

69. Rauber, *Parish Pathways* . . . , 10-11, 18-19.

70. *McQuaid,* 1: 85-86; *CCCJSPC,* p. 77.

71. *McQuaid,* 1: 105-07. Zwierlein says the first house mother was a Miss Kelly, but the *Cathedral Calendar* says her name was Nilan (May, 1913: p. 95). The Orphanage was incorporated as the Roman Catholic Asylum Society of Rochester on February 9, 1845.

72. *FJ,* December 13, 1845. Sister Martha Daddisman was superior of the original band of Sisters; the other members were Sisters Patricia Butler, Sylveria O'Neill, and Andrea Corry (Sister Josephine to present writer, Emmitsburg, August 31 1962). According to the *Catholic Almanacs* for 1847 and 1848, there was also a select school for boys in those years, "under the charge of two brothers" (probably of the brotherhood founded by Timon). The Christian Brothers (Brothers of the Christian Schools) did not take over St. Patrick's school until 1857.

73. Raphael DeMartinis, *Ius Pontificium de Propaganda Fide* . . . 6, Part 2 (Rome, 1894): 24-26.

CHAPTER THREE:

BISHOP TIMON GATHERS HIS FLOCK

1. For the blight and famine, see especially C. Woodham-Smith, *The Great Hunger. Ireland 1845-1849* (New York, 1963); for the Irish immigration in general, see George W. Potter, *To the Golden Door* (New York, 1960). For the German migration, see Mack Walker, *Germany and the Emigration, 1816-1885* (Cambridge, Mass., 1964).

2. *DD,* May 22, 1847, September 28, 1847.

3. Timon to directors of Society for the Propagation of the Faith, Buffalo, November 21, 1854, in *Annals* of the Society, London, 1855, pp. 231-33.

4. See letter of complaint against the Erie Railroad, by P. W. Ryan and others, the *Pilot,* Boston, Mass., September 15, 1855.

5. A. O. Bunnell-F. I. Quick, *Dansville* (Dansville, 1902), 1: 90-91.

6. *AANY,* A-12 Timon (to John Hughes?), Buffalo, August 3, 1849, reprinted in *Union and Echo,* Buffalo, N.Y., April 11, 1947; Thomas E. Byrne, "Spanish Influenza, . . . ," *Chemung County Historical Journal* (Elmira, N.Y.), 3: 384-85 (Dec. 1957).

7. *CCSSR,* 1: 16.

8. *Manual of the Churches of Seneca County* (Seneca Falls, 1896), 138-45.

9. *McQuaid*, 1: 74-75.

10. There were some French in Brockport. *CCSSR*, 1: 102.

11. James T. Dougherty, *Golden Jubilee of St. Patrick's Church* (Dansville, 1900), p. 7.

12. *CCSSR*, 1: 70.

13. *CCSSR*, 1: 39, 50, and 43.

14. *RR*, March 23, 1830.

15. John K. Sharp, *History of the Diocese of Brooklyn, 1853-1953* (New York, 1954), 1:47-54.

16. See notice in the *Onondaga Sentinel Register* (Onondaga Valley, N.Y.), February 21, April 25, 1827.

17. *SCB*, pp. 41-45; George Paré, *The Catholic Church in Detroit* (Detroit, 1951), *passim;* Louis W. Doll, *History of St. Thomas Parish, Ann Arbor* (Ann Arbor, Mich., 1951), pp. 5-17; Peter Leo Johnson: *Stuffed Saddlebags* (Milwaukee, 1952), pp. 174-76, and *Crosier on the Frontier* (Madison, Wisc., 1959), *passim.*

18. *SCB*, pp. 52-54.

19. *MWNY*, pp. 246-47; *HRS*, 3 (1904): 299; *CT*, April 1, 1880.

20. *McQuaid*, 1: 18.

21. *Ibid.*, 1: 81-83, 93; *DA*, August 27, 1851; *DD*, September 5, 1851. The Seneca Falls Historical Society possesses a Father Mathew pledge, No. 354,302, administered in Ireland on December 30, 1839, to one Martin O'Neal.

22. *HRS*, 2, Part 2 (1901): 256.

23. *New York Tablet*, February 20, 1858; *Manual of the Churches of Seneca County*, p. 140; Aidan H. Germain, O.S.B., *Catholic Military and Naval Chaplains . . .* (Washington, D.C., 1929), pp. 59-60.

24. For Father Serge, see James T. Dougherty, *Golden Jubilee of St. Patrick's Church, Dansville, N.Y.*, pp. 10-11; Wilfred J. Rauber, *Parish Pathways* (Dansville, N.Y.), p. 24. One Sunday, two women from out-of-town who were visiting at the Dansville Sanitarium entered the church clad in the pantalooned "Turkish dress" which Amelia Bloomer had lately made popular. Father Serge ordered them to leave. He said he did not want to have any "grasshoppers" in the church. (*The International*, St. Patrick's, Dansville, 1, No. 2, August 24, 1897).

For O'Connor, see *The Yule Tide Yeast* (St. Mary's, Canandaigua), December 20, 1902; obituary of Mallory in *DAm*, September 19, 1856.

25. *ACSSR*, Supplement, pp. 109-10.

26. *McQuaid*, 1: 4.

27. *Mother of Sorrows Herald*, Town of Greece, 1, No. 3 (Pentecost, 1930); John J. Dillon, *St. Mary's, Albany*, p. 110. (But St. Mary's parish records are had only from 1830 on.)

28. *CG*, pp. 14-15.

29. *ARD*, WPA records, St. Mary's parish, Dansville.

30. *CCSSR*, 1:72; George E. Schantz, *CC*, February 15, 1934; Alphonse Klem (grandson of Bernard), interview. However, our check of the baptismal register of both St. Peter's and St. Patrick's churches in New York showed no record of the baptism (Msgr. Arthur Tommaso to present writer, New York, December, 1962). Nor could the child have been baptized at St. Anne's Church, as Herman Pfaefflin states (*HGDR*, pp. 24-25). St. Ann's was not established until much later. But the story itself seems too well vouched for to be rejected.

31. *CT*, October 10, 1878. For Mathew Hogan, see *Mother of Sorrows Herald*, Pentecost, 1930.

32. Timon, letter in the *Annales* of the Society for the Propagation of the Faith, 21 (1849): 3-37.

33. *McQuaid*, 1:115.

34. *HCCWNY*, pp. 126-27.

35. Timon, *MWNY*, pp. 236-58.

36. Letter of Timon, *Annales* of the Society for the Propagation of the Faith, 21 (1849): 34.

37. *DAm*. October 23, 1858; Timon Diary, October 24, 1858.

38. Robert F. McNamara, "Father Maurice of Greece, New York," in *RACHS*, 21 (1950): 175-76; Boston *Pilot*, September 8, 1860, October 20, 1860; *DNB*. Dr.

Cahill also visited Seneca Falls on October 5th (*Pilot,* October 5, 1860). Wherever he went in the United States this imposing — six-foot-five — and influential Irish priest thrilled and touched his fellow-Irishmen, who gave him tumultuous welcomes.

39. *McQuaid,* 1: 141. In 1855, Keely had designed St. Patrick's Academy, on Brown and Frank Street (Plymouth Avenue North), which was dedicated in 1857. (*McQuaid,* 1: 133-35.) Apparently the only other Keely building in the diocese of Rochester was the present St. Mary's, Auburn, begun 1870, dedicated 1877 (*Ibid.* 2:64; *CJHPE,* 211-13). See Francis W. Kervick, *Patrick Charles Keely, Architect* . . . (South Bend, Ind., 1953).

40. *Elmira Telegram,* July 16, 1922; Timon Diary, July 19, 1857.

41. *New York Tablet,* April 16, 1859.

42. Brother Angelus Gabriel, F.S.C., *The Christian Brothers in the United States* (New York, 1948), pp. 158-59.

43. The *Metropolitan Catholic Almanac* for 1856 and 1857 implies that the Brigidines were at St. Mary's only in 1855 and 1856. Bishop Timon presided at a profession there on February 1, 1856 (Diary). They were also at St. Bridget's School, Buffalo, 1854-1858, and St. Mary's, Medina, N.Y., 1858-1860. They moved to Titusville, Pa., in 1866. The community broke up in 1869. See James A. Hogan, *The Story of a Hundred Years. St. Mary's Church, Medina, N.Y.* (Medina, 1940), p. 35; Timon Diary, February 7, 1858. For the whole Brigidine effort, see Peter Leo Johnson, "The American Odyssey of the Irish Brigidines," *Salesianum* (Milwaukee, Wisc.), 39 (1944): 61-67; letter of Sister Gabriella Eardly, O.S.B., to Mother Josephine, Erie, Pa., June 23, 1927, *ibid.,* 48 (1953): 181-82.

44. Sister Mary Berchmans Gallavan, *The Sisters of Saint Mary of Namur,* typed MS in archives of Eastern U. S. Province, Kenmore, N.Y., *passim.*

45. Sister M. Josephine, S.C., to present writer, Emmitsburg, Md., August 31, 1961.

46. Louise Callan, R.S.C.J., *The Society of the Sacred Heart in North America* (New York, 1937), pp. 434-52; Elizabeth Madden, *A Century of Love: Academy of the Sacred Heart, 1855-1955* (Rochester, N.Y.), *passim.*

47. Parish archives, Sacred Heart Church, Perkinsville.

48. Sister M. Innocentia Fitzgerald, R.S.M., *Historical Sketch of the Sisters of Mercy in the Diocese of Buffalo, 1857-1942* (Buffalo, 1942), *passim;* historical notes, Rochester Sisters of Mercy, loaned by Sister M. Petrus Sullivan to the present writer.

49. For the Plan at St. Mary's, Corning, see *CG,* pp. 65-71. For SS. Peter and Paul School, Elmira, see Sister Mary Berchmans Gallavan, typed MS *The Sisters of St. Mary of Namur,* in archives of the Eastern U. S. Province of the Sisters, pp. 197-98; also the *Diaire* of the Sisters of St. Mary of Elmira, in the same archives, June 22, 1876, p. 74; *Elmira Daily Advertiser,* September 20, 21, 1875. For the Plan at Lima in 1875, see *McQuaid,* 2: 147-48. William H. Shannon has treated all three cases in *The Religious Garb Issue as Related to the School Question in New York State,* unpublished doctoral dissertation, University of Ottawa, 1952.

50. *McQuaid,* 1: 128-33; *CJ,* October 1, 1917.

51. James R. Bayley, *A Brief Sketch of the History of the Catholic Church on the Island of New York* (New York, 1870), p. 223.

52. *CJHPE,* p. 179.

53. Elizabeth Mary Cocks, *A History of Catholic Institutional Child Care in Rochester 1842 to 1946.* Unpublished M.A. dissertation, Fordham University, New York, 1947, pp. 28-29, 60-61.

54. *Ibid.,* pp. 21-27, 61-64.

55. Archives, St. Mary's Hospital; McQuaid, 1: 234-45; Gerald Kelly, *The Life of Mother Hieronymo,* Rochester (pamphlet, 1948).

56. Daniel F. McColgan, *A Century of Charity* (Milwaukee, 1951), 1:57-58.

57. *Ibid.,* 1: 194-97, 2: 257-64; *ARD,* Louis Janine to Bernard J. McQuaid, New York, September 20, 1870. For the Seneca Falls branch, see also Ensign and Everts' *History of Seneca County* (Philadelphia, 1876), p. 52.

58. *McQuaid,* 1: 245-51.

59. Peter Colgan, Dunkirk, N.Y., July 8, 1859, to Editor, *New York Tablet,* July 16, 1859.

60. For the legal story of trusteeism see Patrick J. Dignan, *A History of the Legal*

Incorporation of Catholic Church Property in the United States (New York, 1935).

61. *Concilia Provincialia Baltimorensia* (Baltimore, 1851), pp. 74-76.

62. *McQuaid*, 1: 18-24, 48-65.

63. *ACSSR.*, 1: 37-49.

64. *CCSSR*, 1: 8.

65. Thomas F. Meehan, "Very Rev. Johann Stephan Raffeiner, V.G.," *HRS*, 9 .(1916): 167-68.

66. Lawrence Kehoe, *Complete Works of the Most Reverend John Hughes, D.D.*, (New York, 1866), 1: 441.

67. *Ibid.*, 314-27.

68. John R. G. Hassard, *Life of the Most Reverend John Hughes, D.D. . . .* (New York, 1866), pp. 261-62.

69. *McQuaid*, 1: 101.

70. "Historia Ecclesiae Perkinsville," p. 3, archives of Sacred Heart Parish, Perkinsville.

71. *McQuaid*, 1: 96-97.

72. *Ibid.*, 197-222; additional material in parish questionnaire, *ARD.*

73. CCSSR, 1: 45; *DU*, October 28,

1853; *DD*, October 29, 1853; James F. Connelly, *The Visit of Archbishop Gaetano Bedini to the United States of America . . .* (Rome, 1960), *passim.*

74. CCSSR, 1: 54-116, *passim; UA*, November 7, 9, 12, 1863.

75. Timon Diary, April 15, 16, 1862.

76. *CCSSR*, 1: 112; Timon Diary, January 28, 1863.

77. In 1848, a group of German Catholics, apparently parishioners of St. Joseph's Church, Rochester, set up as an independent "Free German Catholic Congregation" and appealed to the American and Foreign Christian Association for a Protestant clergyman. This action was possibly a by-product of the trusteeist era. The group subsequently built Emanuel German Evangelical Reformed Church on Hamilton Street, where services were conducted in German until 1925. Since 1957 this church has been called Emanuel United Church in Christ. See *HMC*, pp. 102-03; *HGDR*, pp. 190-92; William F. Peck, *Semicentennial History of the City of Rochester* (Syracuse, 1884), p. 290; Orlo J. Price. "One Hundred Years of Protestantism in Rochester," *Centennial History of Rochester, RHSPFS*, 12 (1933): 294; *DC*, August 5, 1962, p. 6-M.

CHAPTER FOUR:

NO-POPERY, SLAVERY AND THE AMERICAN WAY

1. *McQuaid*, 1: 25-47.

2. *SCB*, p. 57.

3. *DA*, November 5, 1845.

4. *MWNY*, p. 245.

5. *RR*, March 22, 1842.

6. For the Ovid incident, see *Manual of the Churches of Seneca County*, p. 44. While pastor at Watertown and Carthage, N.Y., in 1839, Father Gilbride had won a legal battle for religious freedom in Lewis County. See *New York History* 47 (1966): 163. For the Geneseo incident, see Arthur A. Hughes, *Souvenir of the Golden Jubilee St. Mary's Church, Geneseo, New York* (Geneseo, 1904), pp. 3-4.

7. Bishop Thomas A. Hendrick's recollections, *Penn Yan Democrat*, June 20, 1902.

8. *CT*, January 17, 1878.

9. For a general account of American nativism before the Civil War, see Ray Allen Billington, *The Protestant Crusade, 1800-1860* (New York, 1938); for its political repercussions in New York State, see Louis D. Scisco, *Political Nativism in New York State* (New York, 1901).

10. Blake McKelvey, *Rochester the Water Power City, 1812-1854* (Cambridge, Mass., 1945), p. 351.

11. *McQuaid*, 1: 159-60. See the whole of Chapter VII, "Know Nothings," pp. 148-96.

12. James T. Dougherty, *Golden Jubilee of St. Patrick's Church* (Dansville, N.Y.) p. 10.

13. *CT*, September 19, 1878.

14. *Auburn Journal*, June 21, 1854.

15. *RDAm,* July 28, 29, 1854; *UA,* July 28, 29, 31, August 1, 2, 3, 1854.

16. *Ontario Times,* August 3, 1854; *Ontario Messenger,* August 9, 1854.

17. Sermon by Bishop Thomas F. Hickey, St. Mary's diamond jubilee, *CJ,* October 24, 1919.

18. Letter to editor, from "A Subscriber," Palmyra, N.Y., August 9, 1854, in Boston *Pilot,* August 19, 1854. See also *Wayne County Whig* (Lyons, N.Y.), August 11, 1854, quoting the *Wayne Sentinel.*

19. *Southern Tier Times* (Owego, N.Y.), April 5, 1855.

20. *Elmira Republican,* March 8, 1850.

21. *Ibid.,* August 16, 1853.

22. *RDAm,* August 5, 1854.

23. This parish tradition was related to the present writer by Mrs. Herman Lincoln of Holcomb, N.Y.

24. *DU,* November 21, 1855.

25. *UA,* September 28, 1859; *New York Tablet,* October 8, 1859 through November 26, 1859 (weekly); *New York Times,* October 6, 1859; *New York Daily Tribune,* October 5, 1859.

26. Louise Callan, R.S.C.J., *The Society of the Sacred Heart in North America* (New York, 1937) p. 437.

27. *Owego Times,* September 27, 1855.
28. *McQuaid,* 1: 168-77.

29. Major Wheeler C. Case, "Rochester's Citizen Soldiers," *RHSPFS,* 14 (1936): 225-57; Rear Adm. Franklin Hanford, "Visits of American and British Fleets to the Genesee River, 1809 to 1814," *RHSPFS,* 3 (1924): 37-64. For McGuire, see *Mother of Sorrows Herald,* 1930, #1, p. 3. The information about James Flynn comes from his descendant Mr. William J. Flynn of Rochester, and from Peck, *HRMC,* p. 1046.

30. Guy H. McMaster, *History of the Settlement of Steuben County, New York* (Bath, 1853), pp. 178-87; and information kindly supplied by Mr. Warnick Kernan of Utica, N.Y.

31. Obituary of McGarry, *UA,* January 27, 1868.

32. *DD,* January 7, 1847, *DA,* July 31, 1847.

33. *Dewey's Rochester City Directory,* 1857, pp. 66-68; *Rochester Daily Union Annual City Directory,* 1859, pp. 15-16.

34. *McQuaid,* 1: 256-90, treats the entire Civil War period.

35. Timon Diary, October 30, 1860.

36. *UA,* January 3, 1861, April 23, 1861, April 26, 1861, May 1, 1861, June 11, 1861; also pension records, National Archives, Washington, D.C.

37. *UA,* April 16, 18, 19, 20, 22, 23, 25, 27; May 2, 3, 1861.

38. *UA,* April 20, 1861.

39. Henry Lomb (1828-1908), captain of Co. "C" of the 13th, and well known as co-founder of Bausch and Lomb and founder of Mechanics Institute (now Rochester Institute of Technology), was baptized and raised a Catholic in Germany but did not practice his faith in this country. (Information kindly supplied by his relative Mr. Raymond F. Decker, Rochester, N.Y.)

40. *American Citizen* (Ithaca, N.Y.), May 15, 1861 (McCool); Edward B. Simpson, *History of St. Francis Church, Phelps, N.Y.* (Phelps, 1942), p. 6 (Clark); "Reminiscences of Rev. William Mulheron," the *Yule-Tide Yeast* (St. Mary's Church, Canandaigua), December 26, 1902 (Early).

41. *Seneca Falls Reveille* (Seneca Falls, N.Y.), May 4, 1861, May 25, 1861.

42. *Ibid.,* November 23, 1861.

43. Obituary note, *Sadlier's Catholic Directory* (New York, 1871), p. 43.

44. *WEJ,* May, 1870.

45. *New York Tablet,* May 4, 1861; *Auburn Morning News* (Auburn, N.Y.), obituary of Father Creedon, May 9, 1870; Henry Hall and James Hall, *Cayuga in the Field* (Auburn, 1873) p. 21.

46. Obituary, *Auburn Morning News,* May 9, 1870.

47. Elliot G. Storke and James H. Smith, *History of Cayuga County* (Syracuse, 1879), pp. 107-11.

48. Deuther, *Life and Times of the Rt. Rev. John Timon . . .,* pp. 283-86; *UA,* May 2, 1861, quoting *Buffalo Courier.*

49. Timon Diary, July 13, 1861.

50. The future Co. "G" of the 23rd Regt. was quartered at Corning: *Hornellsville Tribune*, May 16, 23, 30, 1861.

51. *DC*, May 4, 1886.

52. *UA*, July 27, 1861.

53. *UA*, August 5, 1861.

54. James T. Dougherty, *Golden Jubilee of St. Patrick's Church* (Dansville, N.Y.), p.p. 26-27.

55. Edward McCrahon obituaries, *Syracuse Journal, Syracuse Herald*, August 24, 1918, and *Post Standard* (Syracuse, N.Y.), August 25, 1918; Alexander McCrahon (otherwise McCrane): veteran papers, National Archives, Washington, D.C.; added information by Mr. John E. McCarthy, Victor, N.Y., and Mr. J. Sheldon Fisher, Fishers, N.Y.

56. Frederick Phisterer, *New York in the War of the Rebellion*, 3rd ed. (Albany, 1912), pp. 341, 2300.

57. *McQuaid*, 1: 271-73; unidentified clipping, "War Reminiscences" of the 105th, collection of Mrs. Louis Roche, Rochester, N.Y.

58. Ernst obituary in *DC*, April 4, 7, 1892; *PE*, April 4, 1892; plus information kindly provided by Col. Joseph L. Ernst.

59. Obituaries in *UA*, *PE*, December 30, 1891; *DC* and *RMH*, December 31, 1891.

60. Obituary, *DC*, June 2, 1915; Charles E. Fitch, *Memorial Encyclopedia of the State of New York* (Boston, etc., 1916), 3: 308-10; Phisterer, *New York in the War of the Rebellion*, p. 438.

61. Information kindly supplied by Misses Mae and Cecilia Hughes and Mrs. Henry Furlong of Rochester. For a fuller account, see *CCJ*, May 31, 1963.

62. George H. Washburn, *A Complete Military History and Record of the 108th Regiment New York Volunteers* (Rochester, 1894), pp. 239-42.

63. The marker of Felix McGuire Jr., in Our Mother of Sorrows Cemetery, says he died on July 10, 1864.

64. Marker, SS. Peter and Paul Cemetery, Elmira, N.Y.; Martin Purtell, "Chemung County's Irish, the Master Builders," *Chemung Historical Journal* (Elmira, N.Y.), 1 (1956): 102.

65. *SCB*, 102.

66. *Corning Journal*, May 19, 26, 1864.

67. Phisterer, *New York in the War of the Rebellion*, p. 2032.

68. *UA*, September 22, 27, 1862.

69. *UA*, July 28, August 5, 1864.

70. *UA*, March 11, 14, 18, 1864.

71. *ACAB;* Porter Farley, "Reminiscences of the 140th Regiment," in *Rochester in the Civil War, RHSP*, 22 (1944): 220-24; The Comte de Paris, *The Battle of Gettysburg* (Philadelphia, 1886), pp. 165-68; William W. Sweeney, "Colonel Patrick H. O'Rorke, U.S. Army," in *Journal of the American Irish Historical Society*, 26 (1927): 260-65. See also the present writer's account in *CCJ*, June 28, 1963.

72. *New York Tablet*, July 25, 1863.

73. Reprinted in *Union and Echo* (Buffalo, N.Y., October 3, 1947.

74. Timon Diary, August 7, 8, 10, 1863.

75. *UA*, September 8, 1862.

76. Deuther, *Life and Times of Rt. Rev. John Timon . . .*, pp. 293-94.

77. Timon Diary, September 4, 5, 1864; Clay W. Holmes, *The Elmira Prison Camp* (New York, 1912), pp. 41-42.

78. St. Mary's Hospital Archives, "Albany Report and Census Register," report for December 1, 1866. For the whole story, see the present writer's "St. Mary's During the Civil War Era," in *CCJ*, November 2, 1962. Rochester City Hospital treated 448 soldiers (*Hospital Review*, City Hospital, February 15, 1866, pp. 102-04).

79. *UA*, April 7, 10, 1865.

80. *UA*, April 25, 1865.

81. Copybook of Michael Hughes, in the possession of Mrs. Henry Furlong, Rochester.

82. *UA*, April 18, 20, 1860.

83. *UA*, April 27, 1865.

84. See Surratt's lecture, *Evening Star*, (Washington, D.C.), December 7, 1870; *Trial of John S. Surratt in Criminal Court for the District of Columbia* (Washington, 1867), *passim*; notes kindly supplied by

Mrs. Margaret McN. Kahler Bearden of Rochester, an authority on J. H. Surratt. See also the same writer's popular account in *CCJ*, April 22, 1965.

85. After the synod of 1859, Bishop Timon named three of his priests to the rank of canons of his cathedral. These were the Very Rev. Francis O'Farrell, Vicar General of the diocese; Very Reverend Francis N. Sester, Pro-Vicar General for the Germans and French; and Very Reverend Michael O'Brien, Pro-Vicar General. Father O'Brien was then pastor of St. Mary's Church, Rochester. (Boston *Pilot*, July 2, 1859; Timon Diary, May 31, 1859). The American hierarchy, generally speaking, has declined to set up chapters of canons in our cathedrals. Apparently Bishop Timon himself subsequently cancelled these unusual appointments.

86. Deuther, *Life and Times of the Rt. Rev. John Timon* . . ., p. 263.

87. *New York Tablet*, February 4, 1860.

88. *CCSSR*, 1: 89-90.

89. Buffalo *Catholic Sentinel*, March 3, 1860; Boston *Pilot*, February 25, March 17, 1860.

90. *MCUND* microfilmed archives of the Sacred Congregation de Propaganda Fide: *Scritture Riferite*, 18: 1306r, Timon to the S. Congregation, Buffalo, April 16, 1860.

91. *New York Tablet*, July 14, 1860; Deuther, *Life and Times of the Rt. Rev. John Timon*, p. 278.

92. *HCCWNY*, p. 205.

93. Buffalo *Catholic Sentinel*, March 9, 1857, quoted in the *Union and Echo* (Buffalo, N.Y.), March 14, 1947.

94. Deuther, *Life and Times of the Rt. Rev. John Timon*, pp. 262, 268; *McQuaid*, 1: 252-55; *Statuta Diocesis Buffalensis . . . A.D. 1854* . . . (Buffalo, 1854), pp. 10-11.

95. Timon Diary, August 24, 1863.

96. *CCSSR*, 1: 135.

CHAPTER FIVE:

A DIOCESE FOR ROCHESTER

1. *UA*, September 12, 1866.

2. Timon Diary, October 8, 22, 1866.

3. Cardinal Alessandro Barnabò to Martin J. Spalding, *Collectio Lacensis*, 3 (Freiburg-im-Breisgau, 1875): cols. 389-90.

4. *McQuaid*, 2: 1-11.

5. Original document in ARD. There is a somewhat inexact transcription in Raphael de Martinis, *Jus pontificium de Propaganda Fide*, 6, Part 2 (Rome, 1895): 11. When a diocese is set up the Holy See assigns it a Latin "curial" name for official purposes. From the beginning, the Roman Curia applied to the Diocese of Rochester the Latin adjective "Roffensis" ["in America"]. "Roffa" was the old curial name of the see of Rochester in England, now become an Anglican diocese. (Later documents sometimes refer to the American see as "Rostensis" or "Rossensis"; but these are misspellings or misprints.) In order to distinguish the old and new Rochester sees more carefully, the Latin noun "Rucupae" was given to Rochester, New York, instead of the "Roffa" (or "Rutupiae"), which designated the English diocese (*AP*, 1921,

p. 868). The locative of "Rucupae" is "Rucupis", and this is the form of the word used in official Latin documents dated "at Rochester." How the Roman Curia hit upon the word "Rucupae" passes understanding. It seems to share with another Rochester word, *Kodak*, the distinction of having been created out of nothing.

6. This figure is based on the statistics furnished in 1869-71 by the various parishes, (*ARD*), as analyzed by the Reverend Joseph M. Egan, S.T.D., pastor of St. Patrick's Church, Elmira.

7. Patrick Cronin, *Memorial of the Life and Labors of Rt. Rev. Stephen Vincent Ryan, D.D., C.M.* (Buffalo, N.Y., 1896).

8. For his early career, see *McQuaid*, 1: 293-354.

9. See biographical sketch "verified by the Bp." in the Francis X. Reuss Papers, Archives of the American Catholic Historical Society, St. Charles Borromeo Seminary, Overbrook, Philadelphia, Pa.

10. Arthur J. Scanlan, *St. Joseph's Seminary, Dunwoodie, New York, 1896-1921,*

U.S. Catholic Historical Society Monograph Series, VIII (New York, 1922), pp. 16-24.

11. James J. Hartley, "Some Memories of Bishop McQuaid", *CC*, November 11, 1943; *ICCM*, 10: 103-05 (September, 1918). McQuaid was in Rochester a second time in 1858 or 1859, when he came to visit his old schoolmate, Father Francis Mc-Keon (*ibid*, 2: 175, May, 1909).

12. Obituary of McQuaid in the Boston *Republic*, reprinted in St. Patrick's (Rochester) *Cathedral Calendar*, February, 1909.

13. Katherine E. Conway, "The Anecdotal Side of Bishop McQuaid," in *Extension*, (Chicago), July, 1909, p. 13.

14. Sister Mary Agnes Sharkey, *The New Jersey Sisters of Charity* (New York, 1933), 1: 10.

15. *Ibid.*, 1: 156

16. K. E. Conway, "Anecdotal Side," *Extension*, July, 1909, p. 13.

17. James J. Hartley, "Some Memories of Bishop McQuaid," *CC*, November 11, 1943.

18. De Martinis, *Jus Pontificium de Propaganda Fide* 6, Part 1: 184-85.

19. Bayley subsequently became eighth archbishop of Baltimore (1872-1877). On his father's side he was first cousin to Blessed Elizabeth Seton, foundress of the American Sisters of Charity (1774-1821). On his mother's side he was first cousin-once-removed to President Franklin Delano Roosevelt. While still an Episcopalian deacon (he entered the Catholic Church in 1842) he had spent the summer of 1840 as a temporary minister of Zion Episcopal Church in Avon, N.Y., a village now in the Rochester Catholic Diocese. Sister M. Hildegarde Yeager, C.S.C., *The Life of James Roosevelt Bayley* (Washington, D.C., 1947), pp. 22-23.

20. *McQuaid*, 1: 312-13; Yeager, *Bayley*, pp. 131-34; Joseph M. Flynn, *The Catholic Church in New Jersey* (Morristown, N.J., 1904), pp. 205-08.

21. Yeager, *Bayley*, p. 139.

22. K. E. Conway, "Anecdotal Side," p. 13; Flynn, *Catholic Church in New Jersey*, p. 204.

23. Henry G. J. Beck, *The Centennial History of the Immaculate Conception Semi-*

nary, Darlington, New Jersey, (Darlington, 1962), pp. 5-8.

24. Yeager, *Bayley*, pp. 170-79.

25. Beck, *Immaculate Conception Seminary*, p. 10.

26. Yeager, *Bayley*, pp. 235-36.

27. James J. Hartley, "Some Memories of Bishop McQuaid,", *CC*, November 11, 1943.

28. James J. Hartley, "Some Memories of Bishop McQuaid,", *CC*, November 25, 1943, December 2, 1943.

29. *McQuaid*, 1: 353-54; 2: 2-3.

30. James J. Hartley, "Some Memories of Bishop McQuaid," *CC*, November 25, 1943.

31. *SSJR*, p. 50.

32. Richard M. Quinn, *The Early Influences and Later Contributions of Hippolyte De Regge to Catholicism in Rochester, passim.* (Unpublished M. A. dissertation, Canisius College, 1949.)

33. SS. Peter and Paul parish historical report, *ARD*; Diocese of Rochester Clergy Record, Vol. 1; interview with the late Rev. J. Emil Gefell, April 13, 1958.

34. Robert F. McNamara, "Father Maurice of Greece, New York: A Footnote to the Liberian Mission," *RACHS*, 61 (1950): 155-83.

35. Obituary, *UA*, May 25, 1871.

36. *ARD*, Diocese of Rochester Clergy Record, Vol. 1; *CT*, February 9, 1879.

37. *Mother of Sorrows Herald* (Mother of Sorrows Church, Greece, N.Y.), 1, No. 3 (Pentecost, 1930): 5-6; Brother Angelus Gabriel, F.S.C., *The Christian Brothers in the United States*, 1848-1948 (New York, 1948), pp. 158-59.

38. Interview with the late Msgr. James J. Hartley, July 14, 1943.

39. *CT*, May 14, 1881.

40. For these early troubles, see *McQuaid*, 2: 1-47.

41. Cayuga County Court House, Book A, Religious Corporations, p. 250. By a circular of July 31, 1868, McQuaid announced that all church property was being

reincorporated under the N.Y. corporation aggregate law of 1863 *(ARD,* McQuaid Papers).

42. Holy Family parish corporation, Book of Minutes, p. 1.

43. *PE,* December 31, 1892. It is gratifying to be able to report that Father O'Flaherty spent his last years as pastor of St. Mary's, Genesee Township, Potter Co., Pennsylvania, (Diocese of Erie) when he died on April 25, 1895.

44. *CCSSR,* 1: 140.

45. McQuaid to Very Rev. James Early, Rome, May 1, 1870, in Henry J. Browne, Ed., "The Letters of Bishop McQuaid from the Vatican Council," *CHR,* 41 (January 1956): 429. De facto, the change was not made until fall, 1871.

46. *McQuaid,* 2: 75-118; *SSJR, Passim.*

47. Sister Mary Agnes Sharkey, *New Jersey Sisters of Charity,* 1: 122-23.

48. Sister M. Evangeline Thomas, *Footprints on the Frontier* (Westminster, Maryland, 1948), *passim.*

49. James J. Hartley, "The Beginnings of St. Bernard's Seminary," *Memorare* (mimeographed student journal, St. Bernard's Seminary, Rochester, N.Y.), February 16, 1941, pp. 4, 10.

50. McQuaid to James Early, Rome, June 30, 1870, in Browne, "Letters of Bishop McQuaid from the Vatican Council," *CHR,* 41: 438.

51. On McQuaid's part in the council, see: *McQuaid,* 2: 48-74; Henry J. Browne, Ed., "Letters of Bishop McQuaid from the Vatican Council," *CHR,* 41 (January, 1956): 408-41; James J. Hennesey, S.J., *The First Council of the Vatican: The American Experience* (New York, 1963).

52. *Mansi,* 51: cols. 391, 402, 411.

53. *Mansi,* 51: cols. 681-82.

54. *Mansi,* 51: cols. 1051-52.

55. *Mansi,* 52: cols. 444-46.

56. *ARD,* McQuaid Diary, *CCSSR,* 1: 152.

57. *Mansi,* 53: col. 1050. McQuaid had phrased his statement on infallibility somewhat differently in an address given September 18, 1870, at the laying of the cornerstone of St. Mary's Church, Auburn. "There is a wide difference between one who merely pronounces his own views and one who comes clothed with authority, speaking, not his own opinion, but divine truth. A year ago had I spoken to you, standing here, I would have given you my views, my opinion about infallibility. I would have told you that I thought the Pope and Bishops were infallible. Today I tell you, on the authority of the Church, that the Pope alone is infallible . . ." *WEJ,* October, 1870, p. 4. At first reading this seems to imply that the bishops enjoy no infallibility, even when defining in council. It is interesting to note how the Second Vatican Council's Constitution on the Church (Chapter 3) clarifies the whole issue, so troublesome to Bishop McQuaid, of the relationship between papal and episcopal doctrinal authority.

CHAPTER SIX:

"LEX SUPREMA"

1. The coat of arms which Bishop McQuaid adopted was apparently of his own design. It consisted of a gold saltire, charged with a green (?) trefoil or shamrock, all on a blue background. This was suggested by the arms of the old diocese of Rochester in England (red saltire, charged with a gold scallop shell, all on a silver background). McQuaid used only these personal arms. He never had arms devised for the Diocese itself.

2. *McQuaid,* 2: 66-69.

3. Katherine E. Conway, *Republic* obituary, *Cathedral Calendar,* February, 1909.

4. *McQuaid,* 3: 151.

5. Norman T. Lyon, *History of the Polish People in Rochester,* (Rochester, 1934), pp. 13-35.

6. *The Yule-Tide Yeast* (St. Mary's parish, Canandaigua), December 27, 1902.

7. The migratory trend of many of these Italians was doubtless a source of confusion to Bishop McQuaid. In 1888, somebody published an estimate that there were 2,900

Italians in the Rochester Diocese. McQuaid firmly denied the estimate, declaring that there were no more than three hundred, and that these were mostly transients. (*AANY*, C-16, McQuaid to Michael A. Corrigan, Rome, December 8, 1888.) The number 2,900 is indeed too high, but from the figures quoted in our text it will appear that there were quite likely 300 in Rochester alone at that date, to say nothing of the rest of the Diocese.

8. J. Van der Heyden, "Belgian and Holland Parishes in America," *American College Bulletin* (Louvain), 12 (1914): 26-31; *CC*, January 6, 1938.

9. *ARD*, McQuaid Diary. For the rite, see *UA*, November 7, 1870; for the sermon, *WEJ*, December, 1870.

10. *CJ*, December 25, 1908 (Halstrich advertisement). His last work, the stone St. Joseph, was installed in the façade of St. Joseph's Church, Rochester, on December 20, 1910, nine days after the sculptor's sudden death (*CCSSR*, 1: 522-23). For Pedevilla, see *CJ*, December 25, 1908; July 14, 1909.

11. Anon., *Golden Jubilee of the Most Holy Redeemer Church, Rochester, N.Y. 1867-1917* (Rochester, 1917), pp. 29-39.

12. *AANY*, McQuaid to Michael A. Corrigan, Rochester, April 14, 1890. *North Rochester News*, Vol. 8, No. 10, September 22, 1940. Druiding also drew the plans for the chapel at the Academy of the Sacred Heart (1891).

13. A tragedy occurred during the construction of the original St. Stanislaus Church. On August 14, 1890, the unfinished roof collapsed, killing two and injuring three more of the workmen. *DC*, August 22, 1890; *CJ*, August 23, 1890.

14. St. Michael's, Lyons, had already been a parish, 1853-1857. In 1882, St. Thomas' was made a mission of St. Patrick's, Cato (Cayuga Co.), which it remains today.

15. The Phelps church, after enjoying parochial status for about five years, again became a mission around 1862. St. Januarius, built by contributions of the Germans of Rochester, retained its first pastor, Father Mathias Hargather, only a year. After that it became a mission of one or another of the Rochester German parishes until 1897 when it was attached to Cohocton. It became a parish again in 1919.

16. Father Simon FitzSimons, pastor of St. Patrick's, Dansville (1877-1894), established the mission of St. Simon, Springwater, and first administered it. The mission's incorporation was filed at Albany on December 1, 1881. Around 1895 it was assigned to the care of the pastor of Livonia Center; and in 1897 it was made an outmission of St. Joseph Church, Wayland. The church was a small frame chapel on a hillside spur of the railroad track, two miles west of the village. It was sold around 1904 and used thereafter to store grain. (Rt. Rev. Msgr. Joseph H. Gefell; Mrs. Madge E. McIntyre to present writer, Springwater, N.Y., September 6, 1963; Rochester Diocesan Chancery papers, Dansville file.) All Saints Church, Fowlerville, filed its incorporation in Albany on January 24, 1884 (Rochester Chancery papers, Caledonia file). It was a mission of St. Mary's, Geneseo (1884-1901), and of St. Columba's, Caledonia (1904-1910). It was abandoned after 1910, and the chapel was dismantled in 1912 (Mary R. Root, *History of the Town of York, Livingston County* Caledonia, N.Y., 1940, p. 130; photo, p. 67.)

17. St. Rose was the gift of Rose Lummis (1844-1900), a convert and member of the prominent Lummis family of Philadelphia, Pa., a major landowner in the Sodus district. After becoming a Catholic, she became noted for her benefactions to the Church in the United States and Canada (Delia Gleason, *Madame Rose Lummis* [New York, 1907]).

18. *ARD*, WPA report on St. Ann's, Lummisville.

19. *McQuaid*, 2: 64-66.

20. *CT*, May 7, 1881.

21. *CT*, February 14, 21, 27, 1878; March 7, 1878.

22. Dedication article, *UA*, November 7, 1870.

23. *ARD*, James T. Wolfe, "Professor Eugene Bonn," MS, 1952.

24. *CT*, August 30, 1877; *McQuaid*, 2: 309-11, 339-44.

25. *CJ*, October 12, 1889.

26. James J. Hartley, "Beginnings of St. Bernard's Seminary," *Memorare* (St. Bernard's Seminary), October 13, 1940; Katherine E. Conway, "Anecdotal Side," *Extension*, July, 1909, p. 13.

27. *WEJ*, November, 1872, p. 5. St. Patrick's graveyard had originally been adjacent to the church. In 1839, a new St. Patrick's Cemetery was purchased in the Pinnacle Hill area on the southeast edge of town. This was used by all the "English" parishes. The German parishes of St. Joseph's, SS. Peter and Paul, Holy Family and St. Boniface had their own small parish cemeteries. *McQuaid*, 1: 86-88; 3: 349.

28. *CT*, October 8, 1881; *McQuaid*, 3: 349-57.

29. *CT*, October 15, 1881.

30. *CJ*, October 9, 1908. Folklore also attributes a pair of ghosts to Holy Sepulchre. They are an elderly couple who stand at the Lake Avenue gate and accept a ride into town but vanish by the time their driver reaches the "Four Corners" downtown. (Louis E. Jones, *Things that Go Bump in the Night* [New York, 1959], p. 171.)

31. Katherine E. Conway, "Anecdotal Side," *Extension*, July, 1909, p, 24.

32. *Cathedral Calendar*, May, 1894.

33. Daniel T. McColgan, *A Century of Charity* (Milwaukee, 1951), 1: 194-96; 2: 256-64.

34. *CJ*, December 16, 23, 1893.

35. Patricia E. Fisler, "The Depression of 1893 in Rochester," *RH*, 15, No. 3 (June, 1953): 15.

36. *WEJ*, November, 1871.

37. *ARD*, McQuaid Papers, Patrick W. Riordan to McQuaid, San Francisco, July 24, 1906.

38. *CJ*, February 2, 1891, November 28, 1891.

39. *WEJ*, June, 1872.

40. *McQuaid*, 3: 326-64.

41. The Sisters maintained the orphanage in the Saltonstall St. Convent, 1854-1873, and at the present convent, 1873-1901, after which it was discontinued. The present convent is a brick Greek revival home built in 1834 by General John A. Granger, son of Gideon Granger, Postmaster General under Presidents Thomas Jefferson and James Madison. In its parlor —a part of which is now the chapel— General John Granger entertained Henry Clay, General Winfield Scott, and Presidents Martin Van Buren and Millard Fill-more. (*The Yule-Tide Yeast*, St. Mary's parish, Canandaigua, December 31, 1902.)

42. Auburn orphanage papers, Rochester Diocesan Chancery; *ARD*, Minutes book of the orphanage corporation; *SSJR*, pp. 74, 155.

43. *McQuaid*, 3: 341-44.

44. *UA*, May 21, 1859; *Sadlier's Catholic Directory*, 1867 (New York, 1867), p. 183.

45. A Sister of Mercy, *Mercy* (Rochester, 1932), p. 28; *UA*, January 23, 1866, September 25, 1875; *McQuaid*, 3: 341; Sister M. Petrus notes.

46. *UA*, April 4, 1881; January 11, 1886.

47. *CJ*, June 4, 1892; July 18, 1896.

48. *McQuaid*, 3: 332-36.

49. Sister Hieronymo became the center of a controversy in 1870. That October, the Very Reverend Father Francis Burlando, C.M., superior of the Emmitsburg Sisters of Charity, assigned Sister Hieronymo to another mission, and replaced her at St. Mary's Hospital, Rochester, with a new superior. Father Burlando was acting quite within his rights in so doing, but perhaps did not give enough consideration to the fact that Sister Hieronymo in her thirteen years as founding head of Rochester's first hospital had become a Rochester "institution." Leading Rochester citizens, Protestant as well as Catholic, held a public meeting and sent resolutions to Father Burlando asking that Sister Hieronymo be sent back. He refused. Bishop McQuaid likewise deplored the reassignment of Sister Hieronymo as unwise. Personally, he regretted the departure of a nun who years before had nursed him through his illness in New York. He now wrote to Father Burlando informing him that he was taking St. Patrick's Orphanage in Rochester out of the hands of the Sisters of Charity who had founded it, and entrusting it to his own Josephite nuns. This was an administrative action, he assured Father Burlando, not one of retaliation. But although it was in keeping with McQuaid's scholastic policy, Rochesterians interpreted the Bishop's step as a reprisal. Adverse comment against him now became as strong as the adverse comment against Father Burlando (*CCSSR*, 1: 154-55). Burlando at this point tried to bargain, offering to return Sister Hieronymo if the Bishop would restore the orphanage to the Sisters. McQuaid refused.

Meanwhile, Sister Hieronymo had gone to her new mission, but had found it dissatisfying. She therefore decided not to renew her annual vows when the time came around, so that she might transfer to the Sisters of Charity of New Jersey. But when she passed through Rochester and called on McQuaid, he suggested that she stay and join the Rochester Sisters of St. Joseph. She accepted the suggestion and entered the Rochester community that same month, April, 1871. While it turned out well for Rochester, the incident was a bit untidy all around (*McQuaid,* 2: 76-84).

50. *McQuaid,* 3: 344-48. Subsequently several parishes set up comparable facilities for their own young men. One of the most notable was the Catholic Young Men's Association of St. Joseph's parish, Rochester. Founded in 1890, it functioned for many years, and after 1903 had its own building at 23 Ormond Street. See Thomas W. Mullaney, C.SS.R., *Fourscore Years* (Rochester 1916), pp. 125-26, 162-64. Many churches suffered from want of funds in the depression of the 1870's. But for the loyalty of the parishioners of Immaculate Conception parish, Rochester, the schoolhouse would probably have been lost. *ICCM,* 5 (February, 1912): 75-7; (February, 1914): 89.

51. *PE,* April 21, 1909. See Dr. Aaron I. Abell, "Elementary and Secondary Catholic Education in Rochester," *RHSP,*17 (1939): 133-53.

52. *UA,* January 8, 1869.

53. *McQuaid,* 2: 373-75; James E. Hartley, "Beginnings of St. Bernard's Seminary," *Memorare* (St. Bernard's Seminary), March 24, 1940.

54. Information on the location of the proposed school came from the late Father J. Emil Gefell, at one time McQuaid's acting secretary.

55. *Acta Consultationum Missionis Germanicae Americae Septentrionalis* (Canisius High School, Buffalo, N.Y.), under September 12, 1878; December 12, 1878; February 14, 1879; March 10, 1879. Extracts kindly furnished by the Reverend Edward T. Dunn, S.J.

56. John Baptist Lessmann, S.J., to Very Rev. Pierre-Jean Beckx, S.J., May 14, 1879 (Mankato, Minn.); August 14, 1879 (Buffalo, N.Y.). Archivium Romanum Societatis Jesu, Amer. S. G., i, II-9, 10. Transcription from microfilm copy, archives of Loyola Seminary, Shrub Oak, New York,

kindness of the Reverend James J. Hennesey, S. J.

57. *McQuaid,* 2: 84-86; *SSJR,* p. 55. After Nazareth Academy moved to Lake Avenue (1916), boarding facilities were available until 1939.

58. James J, Hartley, "Beginnings of St. Bernard's Seminary," *Memorare* (St. Bernard's Seminary), February 11, 1940. Regarding the dormitory, see *ARD,* McQuaid Diary, October 3, 1870.

59. *McQuaid,* 3: 367-89. Joseph L. Hogan, *A Study of Bishop McQuaid's Outstanding Contribution towards Catholic Education in the Diocese of Rochester* (unpublished M.A. dissertation, Canisius College, Buffalo, N.Y., 1949), *passim.* Aidan Gasquet, O. S. B., "Impressions of America," *Dublin Review* (London, England), 138 (1906): 96-97. James E. Hartley, "Beginnings of St. Bernard's Seminary," *Memorare* (St. Bernard's Seminary), February 11, 25, 1940; March 10, 24, 1940.

60. *ARD,* seminary pastoral of August 20, 1882. Initially the donation for a burse was $5,000.00; it was raised to $10,000.00 in 1934. The original donation for a professorship $20,000.00, was raised to $40,000.00 in 1937. (Seminary Letters of 1934 and 1937). By 1964 twelve professorships and more than forty burses had been established.

61. Most notable of these were Sister M. Delphine Kane, who was in charge from 1894 until her death on January 13, 1929, and Sister M. Solano Scherer, who took care of the laundry and the chapel from 1893 to a few months before her death on January 26, 1929 (Archives of St. Bernard's Seminary, *Liber Status Alumnorum* 2: 358). Sister M. Magdalen Lucy was cook from 1907 to 1931. These nuns performed their difficult task with utter dedication. One of the laywomen longest in service was Margaret Corcoran, who died in 1930 after more than thirty years in the bakery and kitchen (*ibid.,* 382-83).

62. *McQuaid,* 2: 390-430; *St. Bernard's Seminary, 1893-1968* (Rochester, N.Y., 1968),*passim.*

63. *McQuaid,* 2: 118. For the schools in general, see *McQuaid,* 2: 75-118.

64. Bishop McQuaid was by no means opposed to having some Catholic schools under other than parochial jurisdiction. The Religious of the Sacred Heart continu-

ed with his blessing their private Rochester academy, which taught high school as well as grammar-school subjects, and their "free school." The Sisters of Mercy also retained their select school at South Street, and Nazareth Academy kept a private grammar school department until 1940. Furthermore, with the approval of the Bishop, the Sisters of St. Joseph established in 1884 Nazareth Hall, a private school for boys. Although basically a grammar school, Nazareth Hall had a four-year high school department, 1905-1918, and a partial high school program until 1921.

H. J. Alerding in his *Diocese of Fort Wayne* (Fort Wayne, Ind., 1907) implies that McQuaid established a pioneer diocesan school board before 1879 (p. 493). Zwierlein, *McQuaid,* does not allude to such a board. However from 1888 on, there was a diocesan school board of two priests, according to the current Catholic directories.

65. K. E. Conway, *Republic* obituary, *Cathedral Calendar,* February, 1909.

66. St. Patrick's parish also had a "branch school" at West Main and Genesee Streets by 1894; three grades and seventy children (*Cathedral Calendar,* October 1894). This school, moved in 1898 to Chili Avenue, was thereafter entrusted to the new St. Augustine's parish, which used the building as both church and school. (*Ibid.,* November, 1898).

67. *CCSSR,* 1: 356-63. The Marianist Brothers of SS. Peter and Paul's school, Rochester, had departed in 1887.

68. *McQuaid,* 2: 92.

69. *McQuaid,* 2: 306-07; interviews with the late Rt. Rev. Msgr. J. F. Goggin and the late Father J. Emil Gefell.

70. *ARD,* J. R. Bayley to McQuaid, Baltimore, June 25, 1874; *AAB,* 42-E-11, McQuaid to Bayley, Rochester, June 29, 1874. Most Catholic parents seem to have gone along with the Bishop's ruling on attendance at parochial schools. No doubt there were some who objected, whether on arguable or less arguable grounds. The most notable case of conflict was that between the Bishop and Mr. William Gleason (1836-1922), prominent Rochester industrialist and founder of the Gleason Works. In the 1870's he had his boys in the public schools. Bishop McQuaid personally reminded him that according to the diocesan ruling he should transfer them to a parochial or

other Catholic school. When Gleason refused to comply, the Bishop, no respecter of persons, excluded him from the reception of the sacraments. The embittered industrialist never sought reconciliation, with the result that both he and his children drifted away from the practice of the Faith (John H. Gleason to the present writer, Rochester, July 24, 1959).

71. *American Ecclesiastical Review,* 16 (May, 1897): 461-80.

72. J. L. Hogan, *McQuaid's Outstanding Contribution . . .,* 117-20; *McQuaid,* 2: 114.

73. *WEJ,* December, 1871, February, 1872, on the first lecture. On the *DC* interview, see *McQuaid,* 2: 135-38.

74. *McQuaid,* 2: 142, 148.

75. *McQuaid,* 2: 146-48.

76. *ARD,* McQuaid Papers, copybook, McQuaid to John J. Williams, Rochester, April 3, 1886.

77. *McQuaid,* 3: 391-92.

78. *ACUA,* Denis O'Connell Papers, Edward J. Hanna to O'Connell, Rochester, November 19, 1904.

79. *McQuaid,* 2: 321-23, 391-96. John Tracy Ellis, *The Formative Years of the Catholic University of America* (Washington, 1946), *passim.* Colman J. Barry, O.S.B., *The Catholic University of America, 1903-1909* (Washington, 1950), pp. 43-58.

80. *McQuaid,* 2: 321; on the Plenary Council in general, *ibid.,* 289-344.

81. *Titulus VI,* decrees 194-207, *Acta et Decreta Concilii Plenarii Baltimorensis Tertii* (Baltimore, 1886).

82. "Public Schools and Parochial Schools," in John Ireland, *The Church and the Modern World* (2nd ed., Chicago and New York, 1887), pp. 199-214.

83. *McQuaid,* 3: 160-98. Daniel F. Reilly, O. P., *The School Controversy* (1891-1893), (Washington, 1943), *passim* (partisan but of value). James J. Moynihan, *The Life of Archbishop Ireland* (New York, 1953), pp. 79-103.

84. Archives of the American Catholic Historical Society (St. Charles Borromeo Seminary, Overbrook, Pa.), Herman J. Heuser Papers, McQuaid to Heuser, Rochester, January 28 1892.

85. *McQuaid,* 3: 191-96; Archives of the American Catholic Historical Society, Herman J. Heuser Papers, McQuaid to Heuser, Rochester, January 9, 1892, January 28, 1892, March 10, 1892, March 16, 1892.

86. *McQuaid,* 3: 203-33; Zwierlein, *Letters of Archbishop Corrigan to Bishop McQuaid and Allied Documents* (Rochester, 1946), pp. 166-88; Moynihan, *Life of Archbishop John Ireland,* pp. 262-63. Moynihan does not face the facts on this issue.

87. *ACUA,* Louis A. Lambert Papers, John Ireland to Lambert, St. Paul, December 18, 1894.

88. Donald L. Kinzer, *An Episode in Anti-Catholicism: The American Protective Association* (Seattle, 1964), pp. 134-35. The proposal was adopted that fall as Article IX, Sec. 4 of the New York Constitution. However, Article VIII, Sec. 14 did allow the payment from public funds of teachers in charitable institutions, even those conducted by religious denominations (*McQuaid,* 3: 321-33). The State constitutional convention of 1938 changed the numbering of the "Blaine Amendment" from Article IX, section 4, to Article XI, section 4.

89. *ACUA,* Lambert Papers, John Ireland to Lambert, St. Paul, December 18, 1894.

90. *McQuaid,* 3: 207-10, recollections of the late Msgr. Louis W. Edelman, who was present in the sanctuary.

91. *ACUA,* Lambert Papers, John Ireland to Lambert, St. Paul, February 3, 1895.

92. *ARD,* McQuaid Papers, Francesco Satolli to McQuaid, Washington, November 28, 1894.

93. *ARD,* McQuaid Papers, Cardinal Rampolla to McQuaid, Rome, December 17, 1894.

94. *ARD,* McQuaid Papers, Michael A. Corrigan to McQuaid, New York, January 6, 1895.

95. *McQuaid,* 3: 216-35. The consensus among Vatican officials seems to have been that McQuaid had provocation for his action but that a public attack upon an archbishop, naming names, was damaging to the dignity of both the prelate and his see. *ARD,* McQuaid Papers, Charles E. McDonnell to McQuaid, Brooklyn, September 12, 1895.

CHAPTER SEVEN:

THE MELTING POT

1. *CJ,* August 20, 1898.

2. *CG,* p. 157; Cook obituary, *New York Times,* June 21, 1962.

3. For Quigley, see: Wheeler C. Case, "Rochester's Citizen Soldiers," *RHSPFS,* 14 (1936): 277; for Clooney, *CG,* 157-58; for Kane, *CJ,* October 15, 1898; for Mills and Quinn, Patricia E. Fisler, "Rochester in the Spanish-American War," *RH,* 13, No. 2 (April, 1951). The three Ithaca boys who enlisted and made the supreme sacrifice were all from Immaculate Conception parish in Ithaca (*CJ,* May 21, 1920).

4. *CG,* p. 157. Connor belonged to the 7th Artillery.

5. Even that old soldier of fortune, Father Michael O'Dwyer, pastor of St. Mary's Church, Elmira, praised but did not positively encourage the men who volunteered from his parish. (See *Diamond Jubilee of St. Mary's Church, Elmira, New York*

[Elmira, 1948], p. 45.) There is an oral tradition that McQuaid himself was never quite convinced of the justice of the War. A few soldiers were cared for at St. Mary's Hospital, Rochester. The Irondequoit D.A.R. sponsored several volunteer nurses. One of these, Sister Mary Carroll, was a Sister of Charity. She served as an Army nurse at Jacksonville, Florida. Another, Sister Magdaline, cannot be identified. (Fisler, *loc. cit.,* pp. 10, 17; Sister Josephine, S.C., to the present writer, Emmitsburg, Md., August 3, 1964).

6. *Elmira Sunday Telegram,* article on St. Joseph's Hospital, March 13, 1932.

7. *CG, passim.*

8. *ARD,* James E. Tierney, Jr., "St. James Mercy Hospital", MS, 1958.

9. *ADA,* Michael A. Corrigan to Thomas M. A. Burke, Mt. St. Vincent, N.Y., April 20, 1896; Burke to Corrigan, Albany, April 21, 1896 (copy).

10. *AANY,* G-23, Charles E. McDonnell to Michael A. Corrigan, Brooklyn, N.Y., May 11, 1896.

11. *ARD,* McQuaid Papers, original papal brief.

12. *Cathedral Calendar,* February, 1897; *McQuaid,* 3: 10-11.

13. *AANY,* I-41, Michael A. Corrigan to Sebastiano Martinelli, New York, January 27, 1897 (copy); *ARD,* McQuaid Papers, James E. Quigley to McQuaid, Buffalo, January 22, 1897.

14. *Cathedral Calendar,* March, 1897.

15. Archbishop Quigley obituary, *CJ,* July 14, 1915. For Joseph Quigley, see *CJ,* November 13, 1908; September 16, 1927.

16. *ARD,* McQuaid Papers, James E. Quigley to McQuaid, Buffalo, January 22, 1897.

17. *Elmira Sunday Telegram,* article on St. Joseph's Hospital, March 13, 1932; *SSJR,* pp. 96-98.

18. Sister M. Berchmans Gallivan, *The Sisters of St. Mary of Namur,* MS, pp. 97-103 (Archives, Provincial House of the Eastern Province, Kenmore, N.Y.).

19. Sister M. Innocentia Fitzgerald, *The Sisters of Mercy in the Diocese of Buffalo, 1857-1942,* pp. 57-60.

20. *CG,* 116-17; *CJ,* August 3, 1901. McQuaid discharged his normal responsibilities towards the Sisters of Mercy, but he never felt he knew them well (*AANY,* G-36, McQuaid to Michael A. Corrigan, Rochester, April 22, 1902).

21. *DC,* October 16, 1963.

22. The national Catholic directories list the "Dutch Hill" mission until 1912; actually, Mass was no longer celebrated in the chapel after 1905-1906 (Frank Ketter to present writer, Elmira, August 25, 1962; November 16, 1963). The directories of 1896-1898 also state that St. John the Baptist Church had charge of a mission (church or station?) called St. Mary's, Southport. Whatever this may have been, it was not St. Mary's in south Elmira, already a full-fledged parish by that time.

23. *ARD,* Chancery records, *Southern Tier Deeds, 1897,* records the deed of a lot on Waverly Street, Van Ettenville, "for church purposes only," November 28, 1891.

24. *CG,* pp. 63, 135.

25. *CJ,* July 18, 1896; *Cathedral Calendar,* August-November, 1896; January, March, May, June, August, September, December, 1897.

26. The feast of the consecration was set on the second Sunday of October. Later Roman regulations excluded this practice, so the diocesan synod of 1914 designated October 10th as the official feast day. (*Acta Synodi Roffensis Tertiae* [Rochester, 1914], p. 109).

27. *CCCJSPC*; *CJ,* October 8, 1898; *Cathedral Calendar,* October, 1898.

28. *CG,* pp. 121-25; 247-51.

29. Sister Prudentia O'Connor *v.* Hendrick, in *Reports of Cases Decided in the Court of Appeals from February 6, to April 24, 1906,* Edwin A. Bedell, Reporter (Albany, 1906), pp. 427-30. On the whole case, see *Cases in the Court of Appeals,* Library of the Appellate Division, 2863, (1906); 15, 47, 89, 108. See also William H. Shannon, *The Religious Garb Issue as Related to the School Question in New York State,* unpublished Ph.D. dissertation, University of Ottawa, 1952, pp. 117-63. The Blaine Amendment was also invoked (but unsuccessfully) before the Appellate Division N. Y. S. Supreme Court, to justify charging St. Patrick's School, Corning, N.Y., for "free" school water (St. Patrick's Church Society *v.* Heermans, 68 Misc. 487, 24 N.Y.S. 705 [1910]).

30. *McQuaid,* 3: 228, 324-25. Sargent *v.* Board of Education (904), 177 N.Y.S. 317, 69, N.E. 722.

31. *McQuaid,* 2: 110-18; *SSJR,* pp. 86-92.

32. Albert Shamon, *The Aquinas Story,* MS, 1952, pp. 14-27.

33. Father Edward J. Hanna voiced some of these complaints in a confidential letter to Msgr. Denis J. O'Connell, November 19, 1904 (*ACUA,* Denis J. O'Connell Papers). It is probably wise to accept the criticisms with some caution, for Dr. Hanna was out of sorts at that moment.

34. *CJ,* December 2, 1889.

35. Information kindly supplied by Msgr. J. F. Goggin. McQuaid held diocesan synods in 1875 and 1887. *Acta et Statuta Synodi Diocesanae Roffensis Primae* (Roch-

ester, 1875); *Statuta Diocesana . . . in Synodo Roffensi Secunda 14th Junii A.D. 1887 Lata et Promulgata* (Rochester, 1887).

36. *McQuaid*, 2: 154-64, 367-77; *ARD*, McQuaid Papers, Peter Colgan to McQuaid, Corning, N.Y., February 18, 1890, February 20 (?), 1890, March 5, 1890.

37. *McQuaid*, 2: 193-208.

38. On Lambert's earlier career: *McQuaid*, 3: 86; *ARD*, McQuaid Papers, Peter J. Baltes to McQuaid, Belleville, Ill., July 16, 1869; Aidan H. Germain, O.S.B., *Catholic Military and Naval Chaplains, 1776-1917* (Washington, 1929), pp. 73-77.

39. *CT*, July 10, 1879; July 17, 1879.

40. On the Lambert affair in general, see *McQuaid*, 3: 84-149 and *passim*.

41. *McQuaid*, 3: 427-28.

42. *ARD*, Louis A. Lambert Papers, Francesco Satolli to Lambert, Washington, November 15, 1895 (Protocol # 2303).

43. *ARD*, McQuaid Papers, Daniel I. McDermott to McQuaid, Philadelphia, December 5, 1889; James J. Hartley, "Beginnings of St. Bernard's," *Memorare* (St. Bernard's Seminary), September 22, 1940.

44. Hartley, *ibid.*,

45. K. E. Conway, "Anecdotal Side," *Extension*, July, 1909, p. 24.

46. James J. Hartley, "Some Memories of Bishop McQuaid,", *CC*, December 2, 1943.

47. Information kindly supplied by Msgr. Thomas Connors. McQuaid had actually nominated O'Hare in 1886 as a possible candidate for the bishopric of Syracuse. Syracuse Diocesan Archives: Thomas F. O'Connor, *History of the Diocese of Syracuse*, MS, Part III, pp. 122-23.

48. *McQuaid*, 3: 362-64.

49. *CJ*, October 8, 1892.

50. *CT*, October 28, 1880.

51. *CT*, October 1, 1881; *CJ*, June 4, 1892. On Memorial Day morning, a special electric trolley, which had taken the presidential suite to Charlotte for breakfast, made an unscheduled stop on the return trip to pick up the Bishop, who was waiting at one of the trolley stations. N.Y. State Governor Roswell P. Flower greeted McQuaid and gave him his seat next to the President, where he sat chatting with Harrison for some time. Harrison, during the ride back to town, achieved every boy's dream. he was allowed to play motorman over part of the route. See also *UA*, May 30, 31, 1892; *DC*, May 30, 1892.

52. McQuaid obituary, *UA*, January 19, 1909. The Bishop was also a director of the Rochester Public Health Association. (See *ARD*, McQuaid Papers, Dr. M. J. Leary to McQuaid, Rochester, December 19, 1908, announcing the next board meeting.)

53. *UA*, December 29, 1884; *DC*, November 26, 1894.

54. *CJ*, July 24, 1908.

55. Address to the A. O. H., *UA*, June 24, 1894.

56. *CJHPE*, pp. 111-13.

57. *UA*, August 18, 1885.

58. *McQuaid*, 3: 40-44; Colman J. Barry, O.S.B., *The Catholic Church and German Americans*, (Milwaukee, 1952), *passim*.

59. *McQuaid*, 2: 209-19.

60. *ARD*, McQuaid Papers, unidentified, undated clipping, Boston *Pilot*. But Bishop McQuaid felt a strong Catholic solidarity with German-speaking European Catholics. When Prussia, and later Switzerland, began that political persecution of Catholics dubbed the *"Kulturkampf"*, McQuaid was deeply disturbed. With the aid of Father George Ruland, C.SS.R., pastor of St. Joseph's Church, he composed a letter of sympathy to be sent to the German hierarchy through Archbishop Paul Melchers of Cologne. The letter was signed by the Rochester clergy and despatched January 27, 1875. Melchers replied gratefully a few weeks later, stating that the Rochester missive had been published in the German papers. Some time afterward, McQuaid sent a similar communication to Bishop Karl Greith of Sankt Gall, Switzerland, which was received with equal gratitude (CCSSR, 1: 171-73).

61. *ARD*, McQuaid Papers, Sebastiano Martinelli to McQuaid, Washington, March 11, 1898; July 28, 1898. McQuaid to Cardinal Prefect Miecislaus Ledóchowski, April 24, 1896 (copy). Additional information kindly furnished by Msgr. Thomas F. Connors and Msgr. Louis W. Edelman. For the

McIntyre extortion case, see: *UA,* August 4, 1897; November 8, 9, 11, 12, 13, 15, 1897.

62. J. Van der Heyden, "The Association of Belgian and Holland Priests," *American College Bulletin* (Louvain, Belgium), 11 (1913): 130-37; "Belgian and Holland Parishes in America," *ibid.,* 10, (1912): 173-77; 11 (1913): 69-83; 12 (1914): 21-33. *CJ,* June 10, 1921, March 20, 1928.

63. *ET,* October 21, 1912. Also, Owen B. McGuire, "As an Old Priest Friend Knows Him," *ibid.,* December 20, 1912.

64. *ARD,* Anthony F. Calimeri, "Italians in Rochester, 1896-1900", MS.

65. *ARD,* Chancery, Clergy Record, Vol. 1; obituary, *DC,* November 17, 1916; information kindly supplied by Msgr. Joseph H. Gefell.

66. *CJ,* obituary of Father FitzSimmons, June 10, 1927. *ARD,* McQuaid Papers, McQuaid to Louis W. Edelman, Rochester, April 8, 1905; plus information kindly furnished by Msgr. Edelman.

67. We are indebted to Msgr. Paul M. Ciaccio for biographical details on Dr. Canali.

68. *CCJ,* March 30, 1951, recounts Father Cappelino's golden jubilee of priesthood, celebrated among the Dominicans in Kentucky, whose order he had entered in 1915.

69. Father Paganini was the first resident pastor of St. Bernard's Church, Scipio Center (1872-1873). Father Nuonno, a former Franciscan friar, was pastor of St. James, Trumansburg, 1872-1877. Father Eugene Pagani, also a former Franciscan (who returned to that order in his last days), entered the Diocese 1871, and served as: pastor, St. Michael's, Union Springs (1871-1877); pastor, St. Michael's, Penn Yan (1877-1892); chaplain, St. Mary's Hospital, Rochester (1892-1919). Father Lugero (a former Passionist) was pastor, Trumansburg (1877-1881); pastor, Victor (1882-1888); pastor, Penn Yan (1893-1899); professor, St. Bernard's Seminary (1901-1906); pastor, Phelps (1907-1909).

70. Abbé Félix Klein, *In the Land of the Strenuous Life* (Chicago, 1905), p. 110.

71. *ARD,* McQuaid Papers, Theophilus Szadzinski to McQuaid, December 26, 1893.

72. *ARD,* McQuaid Papers, Polish committee to McQuaid, December 11, 1899; March 30, 1900.

73. *CJ,* September 2, 1905. *UA,* August 28, 1905; and editorial "The Polish Church Troubles."

74. *ARD,* McQuaid Papers, James Gibbons to McQuaid, Baltimore, September 1, 1905.

75. *ARD,* McQuaid Papers, Josaphat Bok, O.M.C., to McQuaid, Buffalo, September 13, 1905.

76. *ARD,* McQuaid Papers, Diomede Falconio to McQuaid, Washington, March 29, 1906; April 9, 1906.

77. *ARD,* McQuaid Papers, Theophilus Szadzinski to McQuaid, October 12, 1899; June 18, 1906.

78. *DC,* July 6, 1908.

79. On the general story, see Norman T. Lyon, *History of the Polish People in Rochester,* (Rochester, 1934). The point of view of St. Casimir parishioners is presented in *The Golden Jubilee Book of the St. Casimir Polish National Catholic Church* (Rochester, 1958). The P.N.C.C. possesses what the Catholic Church would consider, at least in theory, valid but illicit priestly orders, so that those ordained priests by its bishops conceivably have true priestly powers. They celebrated Mass as in Catholic churches, but in Polish, not Latin (and increasingly in English). But their beliefs on several matters became widely divergent from Catholic teaching, and therefore unacceptable to Catholics. See Theodore Andrews, *The Polish National Catholic Church in America and Poland* (London, 1953). Incidentally, Father Szadzinski visited Leon F. Czolgosz, Polish-born assassin of President William B. McKinley at Auburn Prison prior to his execution, but apparently failed to reconcile him to the Church (*DC,* October 23, 1901).

80. On Fenianism in Hornell, for example, see *Hornellsville Tribune,* March 9, 16, 1865; April 13, 1865; August 3, 17, 1865; September 7, 1865. For Dansville Fenianism, see A. O. Bunnell—F. I. Quick, *Dansville,* 1: 121.

81. William D'Arcy, O.F.M. Conv., *The Fenian Movement in the United States, 1858-1886* (Washington, 1947), presents the best survey, referring to Owen Gavigan of Auburn on p. 146. The Rochester area's

reaction to the first campaign is given in *UA*, June 1st to July 2nd, 1866. For Sullivan, see *UA*, June 6, 1866. Connolly refers to his part in *A Complete Military History and Record of the 108th Regiment, N.Y. Vols. from 1862 to 1894* (Rochester, 1894), p. 242. For Sharpe, see *UA*, May 28, 1870. See also the general recollections of James Fee of Rochester, in *Corning Daily Journal*, April 28, 1916.

82. McQuaid to James Early, Rome, May 1, 1870, *CHR*, 41 (January, 1956): 429-30.

83. For the Rochester diocesan collection, see *CT*, March 11, 1880; for the Southern Tier collection, see *ibid.*, April 15, 1880. For Corning, see *CG*, p. 96.

84. E.g., Ithaca (*CT*, December 11, 1880); Waterloo (*CT*, December 25, 1880); East Mendon (*CT*, April 2, 1881); Chili (*CT*, April 30, 1881). On the League and the Diocese in general, see *McQuaid*, 2: 220-88; 378-436. Charles S. Parnell spoke in Rochester on January 26, 1880.

85. *McQuaid*, 2: 378-474, *passim*. See also Fergus Macdonald, C.P., *The Catholic Church and Secret Societies* (U.S. Catholic Historical Society Monograph Series XXII: New York, 1946), *passim*.

86. *CT*, October 10, 1878.

87. *ARD*, McQuaid Papers, McQuaid to Dr. Richard Curran, Rochester n.d. [May, 1872] (copy); Rochester Irish Club Committee to McQuaid, Rochester May 23, 1872; McQuaid to Committee, Rochester, May 24, 1872 (copy). In 1894, the three pastors of Elmira (still in the Buffalo diocese) denounced a lay Elmira organization, the Father Mathew Temperance Society, for "sedition and discord" (*Elmira Daily Advertiser*, October 22, 1894). A long and painful struggle followed.

88. *ARD*, Robert McFiggins, *The Foundation of the Knights of St. John*, MS, 1953.

89. *ARD*, McQuaid Papers, L.C.B.A. file. Virginia Croston, Supreme treasurer, to present writer, Erie, Pa., February 22, 1964.

90. On the chaplain at Willard Hospital, see *CJ*, August 27, 1898; October 9, 1898.

91. *ARD*, Francis J. Lane "Religious Program at Elmira Reformatory", MS, 1960. On the whole subject, see *McQuaid*, 3: 255-310.

92. *McQuaid*, 2: 436-61; Henry J. Browne, *The Catholic Church and the Knights of Labor* (Washington, 1949), *passim*.

93. This was a formula prescribed to be taken by Father Richard L. Burtsell, by Holy Office decree (#3456), of August 2, 1893, approved by Leo XIII, August 3, 1893, as described by Denis J. O'Connell to Archbishop John Ireland (*AASP*, Ireland Papers, O'Connell to Ireland, Rome, November 3, 1893).

94. *AASP*, Ireland Papers, Denis J. O'Connell to Ireland, Rome, August 3, 1892. Bishop Spalding was also puzzled that McGlynn was not even required to apologize. See David F. Sweeney, O.F.M., *The Life of John Lancaster Spalding* (New York, 1965), p. 326.

95. E.g., Father James McManus, V.G., of Geneva (*McQuaid*, 3: 50-51): Father James J. Bloomer, of Elmira (letter from "Veritas," *Elmira Daily Advertiser*, June 25, 1887). For the reaction in Corning, see *CG*, pp. 88-92.

96. *McQuaid*, 3: 63, 74. (Emphasis added.) On the whole episode, see *McQuaid*, 3: 1-83; and Zwierlein, *Letters of Archbishop Corrigan* (Rochester, 1946), pp. 90-126, 133-39. On George, see Charles A. Barker, *Henry George* (New York, 1955). Barker fails to grasp the theological issue, however. McQuaid had not wanted Rome to condemn the book *Progress and Poverty*, but only the false proposition denying landownership (*ARD*, McQuaid Papers, William H. Elder Cincinnati, to McQuaid, November 28, 1887).

97. See, for the general subject, Natalie F. Hawley, *The Labor Movement in Rochester, 1880-1898*, MS, n.d., in Local History department, Rochester Public Library.

98. Although Corning was not yet in the Rochester Diocese, we should mention the part played in the mediation of the Hawkes Glass Works strike of 1886-1887 by Father Peter Colgan, (*CG*, pp. 83-88; Browne, *Catholic Church and the Knights of Labor*, p. 230). William Purcell, Catholic editor of Rochester's *Union and Advertiser*, served on the N.Y. State Board of Mediation and Arbitration, 1886-1899. Mr. Charles Rivier, Ph.D., French-born professor of Church History at St. Bernard's Seminary (1901-1903), showed a good understanding of the ideals of the *Rerum Novarum*, in a lecture he delivered in 1903

to the Manufacturers' Club of Buffalo (*ARD*, unidentified clipping from a Buffalo paper, n.d.). See also his article "Labor Unions Once More," *Catholic Union and Times* (Buffalo), June 12, 1902.

99. When Msgr. Denis O'Connell resigned, Bishop McQuaid, who had always respected him, invited him to reside in the Rochester Diocese until he received another assignment (Robert F. McNamara, *The American College in Rome, 1855-1955* [Rochester, 1956], p. 738).

100. The New York Provincial bishops were informed by Archbishop Corrigan of his intention to send the letter, gave their approval, and received from him a summary of the letter, but did not see the actual text before it was dispatched (*ADA*, Corrigan to Thomas M. A. Burke, New York, March 8, 1899, March 11, 1899; Burke to Corrigan, Albany, March 9, 1899 [copy]; *ARD*, McQuaid Papers, Corrigan to McQuaid, New York, March 10, 1899).

101. *McQuaid*, 3: 235-51; Thomas T. McAvoy, C.S.C., *The Great Crisis in American Catholic History, 1895-1900* ["Americanism"] Chicago, 1957).

CHAPTER EIGHT:

REQUIESCAT

1. *Elmira Daily Advertiser*, October 22, 1894. In 1877, for his refusal to testify in a court case involving professional secrecy, Father Bloomer was arrested by the Elmira Police constable (*Elmira Daily Advertiser*, December 12, 13, 15, 17, 19, 21, 24, 25, 1877).

2. Brochure in honor of Father O'Hare's silver jubilee of priesthood, Immaculate Conception Church, Rochester, 1894.

3. Obituary, *Cathedral Calendar*, June, 1900. One member of the Rochester Literary Coterie was Jeremiah G. Hickey, brother of Bishop Thomas F. Hickey and subsequently a prominent clothing manufacturer (1867-1960). Too poor in his youth to go beyond grammar school, Mr. Hickey acquired notable skill as a public speaker through his association with the Coterie.

4. *ARD*, McQuaid Papers, John M. Farley to McQuaid, Washington, D.C., April 23, 1903.

5. *AAB*, 100-L-5, James Gibbons to Mariano Rampolla, Baltimore, May 6, 1903 (copy).

6. *FJ*, July 4, 1903.

7. *ARD*, Frederick J. Zwierlein, MS, *Bishop Hendrick of Cebu; The Catholic Encyclopedia and its Makers* (New York, 1917); *CJ*, December 3, 1909.

8. On the differences of opinion between Hanna and McQuaid, see: *ACUA*, Denis O'Connell Papers, Hanna to O'Connell, Rochester, November 19, 1904. For a biographical sketch of Dr. Hanna, see: Robert F. McNamara, "Archbishop Hanna, Rochesterian," *RHis*, 25, No. 2 (April, 1963), pp. 1-24; James P. Gaffey, *The Life of Patrick W. Riordan, Second Archbishop, San Francisco*, unpublished doctoral dissertation, the Catholic University of America (Washington, D.C., 1965).

9. McQuaid to Cardinal Gotti, February 2, (*sic*) 1904 (*draft*); *ARD*, McQuaid Papers, Girolamo Gotti to McQuaid, Rome, March 4, 1904. That McQuaid's original petition was dated February 29, 1904, appears from the letter of Diomede Falconio to him, Washington, D.C., September 14, 1904.

10. *ARD*, McQuaid Papers, minutes of meeting of diocesan electors; interview with Msgr. Charles F. Shay.

11. The Vatican's *Gerarchia Cattolica* (1906) gives the date January 18. The *Cathedral Calendar* (June, 1905, p. 172) says Hickey was elected on January 22nd, and his election was ratified by Pius X on February 6, 1905.

12. *RH*, May 25, 1905.

13. *St. Mary's Hospital, Jubilee Souvenir History* (1932), p. 54; *Cathedral Calendar*, June, 1899.

14. *CJ*, December 17, 1898.

15. *Cathedral Calendar*, May, 1906.

16. *McQuaid*, 2: 338-41; *CJHPE*, pp. 131-33.

17. See her obituary, *Cathedral Calendar*, August, 1903. As editor of the *Calendar*, she saw to it that the Reading Circles were given much publicity.

18. *CJ*, November 11, 1893 (Dansville); August 25, 1894 (Clyde); January 6, 1897 (Mount Morris); October 2, 1908 (Canandaigua).

19. *Cathedral Calendar, passim;* especially: June, 1894; May, 1897; October, 1897; February, 1898. See also James A. White, *The Founding of Cliff Haven* (U.S. Cath. Historical Society Monograph Series 14, New York, 1940); "Summer Schools," in *CE;* and regular reports in the *CJ* on the Reading Circles and the Summer School.

20. *CJ*, October 22, 1892.

21. *Catholic Calendar*, August, 1897.

22. *CT*, January 17, 1878; February 7, 1878.

23. *CJ*, January 14, 1927; Annette S. Driscoll, "In Memoriam—Katherine E. Conway," *Catholic World*, 126 (1927-1928): 481-87; Sister M. Eleanore, C.S.C., "The Passing of a Valiant Woman," *America*, 36 (1926-1927): 410-12. Her employer in the later years of her *Republic* career—and a man who held her in high esteem—was Mr. John F. Fitzgerald, grandfather of President John Fitzgerald Kennedy.

24. *The Story of a Little Seminary* (pamphlet, Rochester, 1904); *CJ*, September 10, 1904.

25. James J. Hartley, "Beginnings of St. Bernard's Seminary," *Memorare* (St. Bernard's Seminary), May 5, 1940.

26. *ARD*, McQuaid Papers, Miecislas Ledóchowski to McQuaid Rome, April 23, 1901; *AAB*, 98-V-4, McQuaid to James Gibbons, Rochester, May 10, 1901; *American Ecclesiastical Review*, 25 (1901): 59, 69-71. By virtue of this faculty, the Seminary granted four doctorates of theology and nine doctorates of philosophy, in addition to a larger number of baccalaureates and licentiates. However, on May 24, 1931, Pope Pius XI, in his constitution *Deus Scientiarum Dominus*, ruled that, in order to grant degrees, seminaries must have two teaching faculties, one for the ordinary, one for the degrees course. Since St. Bernard's was financially incapable of meeting this stringent requirement, the prerogative to give ecclesiastical degrees, though conceded *in perpetuum*, became *de facto* inoperable after 1932. (See *ARD*, Sacred Congregation of Seminaries to John F. O'Hern, Rome, September 30, 1932).

27. *ARD*, McQuaid Papers, Girolamo Gotti to McQuaid, May 7, 1908; June 25, 1908. Cardinal Gibbons' opinion may have influenced Rome's decision. The apostolic delegate, Archbishop Diomede Falconio, had consulted him on McQuaid's request (*AAB*, 106-D-3, Falconio to Gibbons, Washington, April 13, 1908).

28. *MCUND*. Hudson Papers, McQuaid to Daniel E. Hudson, C.S.C., Rochester, May 30, 1907.

29. *ACUA*, Keane Papers, McQuaid to John J. Keane, Rochester, February 25, 1890, cited by Patrick H. Ahern, *The Catholic University of America*, 1887-1896. *The Rectorship of John J. Keane* (Washington, 1948), p. 63. *ARD*, McQuaid Papers, Keane to McQuaid, Washington, D.C., February 22, 1890; February 26, 1890.

30. *Outlook* (New York), 75 (1903): 764-65.

31. Sharkey, *The New Jersey Sisters of Charity* (New York, 1930), 1: 228-58.

32. Information kindly furnished by Mrs. Walter A. Calihan of Rochester (Anna Messer, Cornell, '05). Mrs. Calihan says that chapel services at Cornell were not obligatory, and that, in her opinion, the Bishop overstated the other dangers.

33. Miss Virginia Croston to present writer, Erie, Pa., February 26, 1964; Mrs. Earl A. Uebel (Leah McParlin, University of Rochester, '06) to present writer, Rochester, August 12, 1964.

34. Information kindly supplied by Mrs. John J. Finucane, Rochester, N.Y. (Harriet Murphy, Smith College, '07).

35. Miss Margaret E. Flynn to present writer, Palmyra, N. Y., April 28, 1959.

36. "Catholic Students at State Universities: A Growing Problem," *American Ecclesiastical Review*, 34 (1906): 113-20. But it is quite likely that McQuaid had already been theorizing along the same line two decades before. When the Bishop of Rochester raised the question in 1906, Msgr. Denis J. O'Connell, then rector of

the Catholic University of America, wrote to Archbishop Sebastian G. Messmer of Milwaukee on January 7, 1907: "I remember very well, unless my memory fails me, that years ago, when it was question of founding a University in America, for the benefit of our Catholic laity, the Bishop of Rochester remarked that the solution was to be found elsewhere, namely, in building the Catholic Hall by the side of the non-Catholic university, and from different sources I heard recently that the venerable Bishop persevered in the same opinion." (Archives, Catholic University of America, Rector's Office, Correspondence, 1903-1909, Box 4). On the same date, O'Connell wrote much the same recollection— "if I remember aright"—to John J. Farrell of East Cambridge, Mass. (*Ibid.,* Box 2). Transcripts by courtesy of the Reverend J. Whitney Evans, of the diocese of Duluth.

37. *AAB,* 103-L-5, printed report of annual meeting of Archbishops, April 26, 1906.

38. *McQuaid,* 3: 396-405. Joseph L. Hogan, *A Historical Study of Bishop McQuaid's Outstanding Contribution towards Catholic Education in the Diocese of Rochester* (MS dissertation, 1949). Michael J. Murphy, "The Cornell Plan of Bishop McQuaid," *St. Meinrad Essays* (St. Meinrad, Indiana), 12 (1959): 76-87.

39. Anecdote kindly furnished by the late Msgr. Louis W. Edelman.

40. *CJ,* June 28, 1890.

41. James J. Hartley, "Beginnings of St. Bernard's Seminary," *Memorare* (St. Bernard's Seminary), February 16, 1941.

42. McQuaid to Sister M. Pauline Kelligar, O-Neh-Da, Hemlock Lake, July 22, 1905, in Sharkey, *New Jersey Sisters of Charity,* 1: 253. As we shall see later, the farm and vineyard were eventually sold to the Society of the Divine Word, and became the site of St. Michael's Mission Home.

43. K. E. Conway, "Anecdotal Side," *Extension,* July, 1909, p. 24. Zwierlein says (*McQuaid,* 3:414) that Williams vacationed at Hemlock Lake twenty-five summers (1882-1907). The earliest documentation on this practice dates from 1883 (*AANY,* McQuaid to Corrigan, South Livonia, August 17, 1883). McQuaid had purchased the property in 1873 or a little before.

44. *CCSSR,* 1: 366; Msgr. Louis W. Edelman; Mother B. Green, R.S.C.J., to the present writer, Rochester, August 9, 1964.

45. *MCUND,* Edwards Papers, diary, under October 10, 1902 (pp. 61-62).

46. Félix Klein, *In the Land of the Strenuous Life* (Chicago, 1905), pp. 91-105; *La route du petit Morvandiau, V, Sans arrêt* (Paris, 1949), pp. 220-01, 328-29. When the present writer wrote to Abbé Klein in January, 1951, to express the thanks of St. Bernard's Seminary for his kind reference in *Sans arrêt,* the feeble octogenarian replied: ". . . J'ai été touché de revivre, grace a vous, l'un des plus chers souvenirs de ma longue existence" (Paris, January 18, 1951).

47. *ARD,* McQuaid Papers, Ireland to McQuaid, St. Paul, June 18, 1903; June 25, 1903; January 25, 1904; July 5, 1904.

48. Francis Clement Kelley, *The Bishop Jots It Down* (New York, 1939), pp. 91-94; *McQuaid,* 3: 251; *Rochester Herald,* rotogravure, December 10, 1905 (photo of the visiting Archbishop); and details kindly furnished by Msgr. John F. Goggin.

49. The professor was Alexius M. Lépicier, as we shall note below (*ARD,* Andrew B. Meehan to John F. Goggin, Rome, December 12, 1907). Lépicier subsequently published his lectures *De stabilitate et progressu dogmatis* (Roma, Typographica Editrix Romana, 1908), in which he criticized all three of Hanna's articles, without mentioning the author's name.

For Hanna in general, see the present writer's article, "Archbishop Hanna, Rochesterian," *RHist,* 25, No. 2 (April, 1963): 1-24. For the coadjutorship in general, see James Gaffey, *The Life of Patrick W. Riordan.*

50. Sharkey, *The New Jersey Sisters of Charity* (New York, 1930), 1: 282-83. Dr. Breen had submitted the *New York Review* article with a covering letter, dated September 18, 1907, to Msgr. Nicolo Marini, a friend in the Roman curia, most likely intending that he call it to the Pope's attention through the Cardinal Secretary of State, Raffaele Merry del Val. (The letter and *Review* copies are in APF [San Francisco file] P.N. 07/78658) The Propaganda Archives copy of the *American Journal of Theology* is associated in the file (P.N. 08/80891) with a calling card of Dr. Breen. We owe this information to the kindness of Father James Gaffey, of Santa

Rosa, California. Salvatore M. Brandi, S.J. told McQuaid, in a letter of December 28, 1907, that a party other than Breen had submitted the protest on the *Catholic Encyclopedia* article (*ARD,* McQuaid Papers). Andrew Breen's action was quite likely prompted by sincere qualms about Dr. Hanna's orthodoxy. But he seems to have acted for mixed motives, one of which—perhaps unconscious—was his personal dislike for Dr. Hanna, whose urbanity contrasted with his own brusque flamboyance. He had a right to present his doubts on Hanna's doctrine to the competent church authorities, but should rather have presented the objection, at least in the first instance, to Bishop McQuaid, who was responsible for the theology taught in the Diocese. After his withdrawal, Dr. Breen served as assistant pastor of SS. Peter and Paul's Church, Rochester; and as pastor of St. Patrick's Church, Mount Morris (1909-1919). He ended his creditable, if rather stormy career as professor of Sacred Scripture in St. Francis Seminary, Milwaukee. See Benjamin J. Blied, " Rev. Andrew E. Breen, D.D., Priest, Professor, Author," *Salesianum* (Milwaukee), 48 (1953): 172-79. For the disclosure that Breen was the delator, see *Rochester Herald,* January 14, 1908; *DC,* January 13, 14, 1908; *PE,* January 14, 1908; *ARD,* McQuaid Papers, McQuaid to Breen, January 30, 1908 (copy).

51. *McQuaid,* 1: 182-85. We have discovered no correspondence between McQuaid and Newman. The Bishop was an old admirer of the Cardinal, however. While still a priest in Newark, he had donated $5.00 towards Newman's defense in the Achilli case (*MCUND,* Newman Papers, microfilm reel 106, batch 170: unidentified newspaper clipping listing American donations). According to Katherine E. Conway, McQuaid took the great writer as his model in oratory (*Republic* obituary of McQuaid, in *Cathedral Calendar,* February, 1909). The two prelates met at least once. The late Monsignor Edward J. Byrne, of St. Bernard's Seminary, so informed the present writer. The Bishop had once told Dr. Byrne of the meeting, and how much it had moved him. "I felt like kissing the hem of his garment," McQuaid said. Byrne was under the impression that this encounter took place soon after the Vatican Council. If so, there may have been another meeting when McQuaid passed through England after his grave illness in Rome in the winter of 1878-1879, for

Newman somehow knew of this illness. This meeting was probably at Birmingham, for the Bishop certainly stopped off at Liverpool (*ARD,* McQuaid Papers, Bernard O'Reilly to McQuaid, Liverpool, April 14, 1879). In late 1885 or early 1886, Roger Watts, a representative of the English stained glass window firm of John Hardman and Company, paid a visit to McQuaid in Rochester. On returning to England, he penned a letter to the Bishop to which he added this footnote: "Cardinal Newman upon whom I had the privilege of calling the other day with my wife after our travels, asked me very particularly if I had seen you in America and if you had fully recovered from the effects of your illness contracted in Rome, the incident of which his Eminence related to me with much concern." (*ARD,* McQuaid Papers, Watts to McQuaid, London, February 3, 1886).

52. *Liber Status Alumnorum,* St. Bernard's Seminary archives, 1: 174. On the 1905 trip he also went to Cuba, stopping enroute at St. Augustine (*ARD,* McQuaid Papers, St. Bernard's file: Maurice P. Foley to McQuaid, St. Augustine, January 9, 1907).

53. *CJ,* September 27, 1907.

54. Sharkey, *The New Jersey Sisters of Charity* (New York, 1930), 1: 279.

55. *MCUND.* Hudson Papers, McQuaid to Daniel E. Hudson, C.S.C., Rochester, September 3, 1907.

56. K. E. Conway, *Republic* obituary, *Cathedral Calendar,* February, 1909.

57. *Liber Status Alumnorum,* St. Bernard's Seminary Archives, 1: 255-56; *Cathedral Calendar* obituary, February, 1909; recollections of Bishop Edmund F. Gibbons of Albany, N.Y., and Msgr. John F. Goggin of Rochester.

58. McQuaid Will and documents of probation, File No. 1909-525, Surrogate Court of Monroe County.

59. This statement was made to the present writer by Msgr. John F. Goggin, who said that the meeting took place at the Cathedral rectory in the Bishop's last days. Zwierlein was under the impression that there was no reconciliation, but cited no source for his information (*McQuaid,* 3: 149).

60. For McQuaid's death and burial, see *Cathedral Calendar,* February, 1909; *CJ,* January 22, 29, 1909; and the local press, especially *UA* and *DC,* from January 18th to January 23rd. Bishop John G. O'Connor preached at the month's mind Mass on February 17, 1909 (*Rochester Herald,* February 18 1909).

61. Francis Clement Kelly, *The Bishop Jots It Down* (New York, 1939), pp. 91-94, relates this and some other charming anecdotes which we have transcribed.

62. *UA,* January 18, 1909.

63. McQuaid, in the pulpit or on the platform, delivered his well-organized and logical material slowly and in a grand, rolling, declamatory manner. He never lost the broad "A" and the quiescent "R" of his New York accent: "My de-ah peo-ple!"

64. To Mother Xavier Mehegan, Rochester, January 18, 1908, in Sharkey, *The New Jersey Sisters of Charity* (New York, 1930) 1: 281. The quotation from Father O'Neill is in *ICCM,* February, 1909.

65. "Bishop McQuaid," in *Ave Maria* (Notre Dame, Indiana), 68 (1909): 146-47.

66. McQuaid to Sister M. Pauline Kelligar, Rochester, June 17, 1907, in Sharkey, *The New Jersey Sisters of Charity* (New York, 1930). 1: 278; to Mother Xavier Mehegan, January 18, 1908, *ibid.,* p. 281

67. Cited by Father Andrew L. Morrissey, C.S.C., President of the University of Notre Dame, in an address delivered in Rochester (*Cathedral Calendar,* February, 1902).

68. *ARD,* autographed brief *Proximo Mense,* May 20, 1908.

CHAPTER NINE:

BISHOP HICKEY AND THE WAR YEARS

1. *CJ,* April 23, 1911.

2. *CJ,* July 8, 1910. Organizer of the 600 local Ruthenians was Father Leo Sembratowicz, nephew of the Ukrainian Cardinal Sylvester Sembratowicz, Archbishop of Lvov. When the growing parish moved into the former First Evangelical Church, on lower Hudson Avenue, on October 18, 1914, Bishop Ortynsky again officiated, and local Latin clergy participated. (*CJHPE,* 123-24; *CJ,* September 25, 1914, October 23, 1914; *UA,* September 28, 1914, October 17, 1914, October 19, 1914.)

3. For Hickey's early life, see Chancery Clergy Record, Vol. 1; *DC,* September 3, 1933 (St. Patrick's School centennial plans); obituaries, *DC,* December 11, 1940, *CJ,* December 12, 1940. Interviews with the late Jeremiah G. Hickey and with Mr. James P. B. Duffy. The baptismal record, St. Mary's Church, indicates that Father Daniel Moore supplied the baptismal ceremonies on February 9, 1961.

4. *ARD,* McQuaid Papers, Hickey to McQuaid, Geneva, March 24, 1886.

5. Msgr. Frank Mason, interview.

6. Jeremiah G. Hickey, interview.

7. *Cathedral Calendar,* January, 1899.

8. *Cathedral Calendar,* March, 1902; September, 1904; March, 1905; July, 1906; October, 1906. Also Albert J. Shamon, *The Aquinas Story,* unpublished MS, Rochester, 1952.

9. Instigator of the honor was the Reverend Frank A. O'Brien, LL.D., a pastor in Kalamazoo, and very influential at Notre Dame. *ARD,* McQuaid Papers, O'Brien to McQuaid, Kalamazoo, Michigan, April 30, 1903; Andrew Morrissey, C.S.C., President of Notre Dame, to McQuaid, June 9, 1903. Also, Thomas A. McAvoy, C.S.C. to present writer, Notre Dame, June 28, 1965.

10. *CJ,* April 2, 1909.

11. *PE,* February 26, 1909 (Breen). *UA,* October 21, 1912; *Rochester Herald,* December 5, 1912 (Hanna).

12. *Our Parish Register,* St. Columba Church, Caledonia, New York, November, 1910.

13. Hickey's personal coat of episcopal arms (like McQuaid, he used these alone, uncombined with a diocesan blazon) allude clearly to his predecessor. The left half of the shield reproduces the McQuaid arms. The upper right quarter contains the monogram of Mary with a silver star above it. The lower right quarter contains the silver spear of St. Thomas the Apostle. A silver horizontal bar separates the two quarters.

Both quarters have a blue ground. The motto is *"Fides et Constantia,"*: "Faith and Constancy."

14. Father Moffatt was administrator from 1920 to 1938. In 1938, the Italian population in the nearby St. Francis Xavier parish had so overwhelmingly outnumbered the original German parishioners that he was transferred to the pastorate of the latter church. The Genesee Institute, a Catholic settlement house, then moved into the former Our Lady of Sorrows chapel, where it still remains.

15. On the early problems, see *ARD*, Chancery files, St. Anthony Church: petition to McQuaid, 1908 [?]; Diomede Falconio to McQuaid, Washington, June 7, 1908.

16. *UA*, October 24, 1914.

17. *CJHPE*, p. 195; *ARD*, Chancery file, Cuylerville church: Edward W. Brown to Thomas F. Hickey, New York, September 11, 1911, and other papers. The church was dedicated December 25, 1914.

18. *New York Times*, February 8, 1957. The deed was recorded by the Livingston County clerk, May 23, 1960 (Liber 363: 204). The name "Retsof", Russian though it may sound, is actually "Foster" spelled backward. William Foster, Jr., was president of the International Salt Company. See Vince Spezzano, *A History of St. Lucy's Parish, Retsof, New York,* published by the parish, 1965. The leading pioneer of the mission was the admirable Antonio Tabacchi, trustee for thirty-three years, who died in 1944 (obituary, *CC*, March 16, 1944).

19. *DC*, June 22, 1912.

20. The Sisters of Mercy also took charge of St. Cecilia School, Elmira, after the Sisters of St. Joseph withdrew from it in 1917.

21. *Mercy*, p. 42. Notes of Sister M. Petrus Sullivan, R.S.M.

22. *CJ*, July 14, 1916.

23. The Reverend Richard A. Hart to the present writer, Geneva, New York, December, 1964.

24. *CJ*, November 7, 1913.

25. Shamon, *The Aquinas Story*, 38-40, 75-76; *CJ*, April 16, 1915.

26. *CCJ*, September 19, 1940; September 26, 1940; October 31, 1940.

27. *Cathedral Calendar*, January, 1913; February,1913; August, 1913; George W. Montgomery, Jr., *The Emergence of the Multiple Functions of the Catholic Family Center of the Catholic Charities of the Diocese of Rochester,* unpublished M.S.S. dissertation, University of Buffalo, 1950, pp. 15-22 (hereafter referred to as: Montgomery, *Catholic Family Center*). *CJ*, September 13, 1918. Interview with one of the former catechists, Miss Elvira Paolone.

28. *CJ*, June 19, 1916; *Cathedral Calendar*, July, 1916.

29. *DC*, July 12, 1917.

30. *CCSSR*, 1: 515.

31. *Acta Synodi Roffensis Tertiae*, Rochester, 1914: 316, 317, 319-28. Before the reform of St. Pius X, children were admitted to confession on reaching the age of reason, but excluded from Holy Communion until about twelve. With the promulgation of the new regulation, the pastors had to prepare about three separate first Communion classes in 1911 in order to "catch up."

32. No consistent records were kept of the increase of Communions after the papal decree on frequent Communion in 1905; but at St. Mary's Church, Corning, the number mounted from 13,500 in 1905 to 25,500 in 1912.

33. *ICCM*, November, 1910: 299; *CCSSR*, 1: 250.

34. *CJ*, October 13, 1911; October 18, 1912; October 17, 1913. *DC*, December 12, 1914.

35. *CJ*, May 19, 1916.

36. *ARD*, Francis Goodrow, "The Laymen's Retreat Movement in the Diocese of Rochester," MS, 1960. James P. B. Duffy, interview.

37. *ICCM*, 10: March, 1919: 157-71.

38. *ICCM*, 2: January, 1909: 33-49.

39. *ICCM*, 2 (1908-09) and 3 (1909-10), *passim. CJ*, February 10, 1911.

40. *CJ*, February 26, 1909; March 9, 1917.

41. *ICCM*, 6 (1913): 65-71, 97-101, 133-39 ("Socialism and Christianity"); and *ICCM*, 6 (1913): 241-45, 273-77, 301-05; and 7 (1913): 1-5 ("The State and Social Distress").

42. *The Parish Record* (Ithaca, New York), 10: October, 1916: 3-11.

43. *E.g.*: *CJ*, February 28, 1910; October 7, 1910; May 5, 1911; February 21, 1913; December 11, 1914; March 19, 1915. Interview with August M. Maier.

44. See Georgina Pell Curtis, *The American Catholic Who's Who* (St. Louis, 1911). The *CJ* refers to Mrs. Avery as "a former Rochester woman" (June 5, 1914).

45. See Sister M. Harrita Fox, *Peter E. Dietz, Labor Priest* (Notre Dame, 1953); also Aaron I. Abell, *American Catholicism and Social Action*, 1865-1950 (Garden City, 1960).

46. *CJ*, July 28, 1916; August 18, 1916; August 25, 1916.

47. *CJ*, July 5, 1945; interviews with Attorney Joseph H. Gervais, and August M. Maier.

48. Fox, *Peter E. Dietz*, pp. 43-45; Whalen obituary, *CJ*, May 19, 1913.

49. Fox, *Peter E. Dietz*, pp. 70-76.

50. *ET*, October 21, 1912.

51. Rochester *Herald*, June 18, 1910; August 8, 1910; August 9, 1910.

52. *UA*, June 24, 1912; Rochester *Herald*, June 28, 1912; November 18, 1912; November 19, 1912.

53. Daniel T. McColgan, *A Century of Charity* (Milwaukee, 1951), 2: 259, 264.

54. Catharine S. Connelly to present writer, Elmira, April 4, 1965.

55. *Cathedral Calendar*, November, 1916; *History of St. Ann's Church, Hornell, N. Y.* (1937), pp. 4-5.

56. *ARD*, James F. Baker, "A History of the Genesee Settlement House," MS, 1947.

57. *CJ*, October 9, 1915; May 21, 1909; July 26, 1912.

58. *CCJ*, special golden jubilee tabloid, on St. Joseph's Hospital, September 19, 1958.

59. *CCJ*, September 19, 1919; *ARD*, Edward C. Driscoll, "The Early History of Mercy Hospital, Auburn, N.Y.," MS, 1951. The nursing school was abandoned during World War II.

60. *ARD*, Auburn Orphanage Association book of minutes, pp. 41-47.

61. St. Joseph's Villa, records of St. Mary's and St. Patrick's Orphanages. On closing down in 1906, the orphanage at St. Mary's, Corning, had likewise sent its remaining orphans to these two Rochester asylums: *CG*, p. 232.

62. *ARD*, Chancery files, paper of agreement; *Sisters of Saint Joseph of Rochester*, p. 74.

63. *CJ*, February 5, 1915; October 22, 1915. *DC*, July 26, 1958. *CCJ*, January 24, 1958.

64. *ARD*, Jeremiah G. Hickey, Jr. "History of the Charles Settlement House," 1956, MS (copy); *UA*, November 7, 1917; *CJ*, December 7, 1917.

65. Archives, Family Service of Rochester: Records of United Charities of Rochester, 1: 2-51, and later minutes; James P. B. Duffy, interview.

66. Montgomery, *Catholic Family Center*, pp. 15-25.

67. Montgomery, *Catholic Family Center*, pp. 19-20; *ARD*, Robert J. Winterkorn, "Rev. Jacob Staub, 1865-1923," MS, 1953; article on retirement of Miss Elizabeth McSweeney after forty years as treasurer and worker with the local Catholic Charities (*CCJ*, November 30, 1951).

68. Montgomery, *Catholic Family Center*, p. 20; *CJ*, April 9, 1915, April 16, 1915.

69. On the engagement of Mr. Tobin, see Archives, New York State Catholic [Welfare] Committee, Albany, New York, File 50.5: J. A. Franklin to Nelson H. Baker, Albany, April 5, 1916; Thomas F. Hickey to Charles J. Tobin, Rochester, February 19, 1915. These and other papers of the N.Y.S.C.W.C. were kindly made available to the present writer by Mr. Charles J. Tobin, Jr., the present attorney of the Committee. On the meeting of January 25, 1917, see Archives of the Diocese of Ogdensburg, minutes of the meeting (courtesy of Very Rev. Msgr. Robert J. Giroux, Chancellor, Diocese of Ogdensburg).

70. Montgomery, *Catholic Family Center*, pp. 26-28; interview with Mr. William F. Nolan, Secretary. The law is Chapter 256, Laws of 1917.

71. Montgomery, *Catholic Family Cen-*

ter, pp. 29-31; 62-63; 152-57. Interviews with Mr. Montgomery, Mr. James P. B. Duffy, and Mr. William T. Nolan. For Miss d'Olier, see *CCJ,* May 30, 1952, October 15, 1964.

72. *CC,* November 25, 1937.

73. *CJ,* October 10 to November 16, 1917. *passim; DC,* November 13, 1917; *Rochester Herald,* November 13, 1917; *ARD,* Rochester Catholic Charities Aid Association campaign leaflet.

74. For Hickey's role in the formation of the State Council of Catholic Charities, see note 69 above; also *CJ,* February 1, 1918, February 22, 1918. On the foundation of the Council, see *New York Times,* January 31, 1918. This organization changed its name to New York State Catholic Welfare Committee at the meeting of December 5, 1933 (Committee files, 50.4: notice of meeting of that date); and to New York State Catholic Committee, on December 7, 1966. The organization has from the start remained a non-incorporated body comprising three representatives—the bishop, a priest and a layman—from each diocese. Its purpose is to protect Church interests before the State legislature and to maintain harmonious relations between the Church and State agencies.

75. *ICCM,* December, 1919: 281. For an estimate of Father O'Neill as a citizen, see the editorial on him, *Rochester Herald,* December 22, 1921.

76. Obituary and estimate by Professor Jacobstein, *CJ,* January 19, January 26, 1923. *ARD,* Robert J. Winterkorn, "Rev. Jacob F. Staub, 1865-1923."

77. *ARD,* McQuaid Papers, Hickey to McQuaid, Sligo [Ireland], April 17, 1907; *Cathedral Calendar,* April, 1907, May, 1907.

78. *Cathedral Calendar,* N o v e m b e r, 1913.

79. On Hickey's war experience, see *Cathedral Calendar,* August and September, 1914; *CJ,* July 3, 1914, August 7, 14, 21, 1914, September 11, 18, 1914; *UA,* September 14, 1914; and Geo. V. Burns, MS, "History of Sacred Heart Church," Sacred Heart Cathedral archives.

80. *CJ,* August 21, 28, 1914; *UA,* September 28, 1914.

81. Blake McKelvey, Rochester: *The Quest for Quality, 1890-1925* (Cambridge, Mass., 1956), p. 293; *CJ,* August 28, 1914; *CJ,* October 2, 1914.

82. *CJ,* October 13, 1916; *RET,* October 12, 1916; *Liber Status Alumnorum,* St. Bernard's Seminary archives, 2: 100.

83. *WWSRRMC,* 2: 1750, 1763. In 1918, the Polish Legion was encamped at Niagara-on-the-Lake, Ontario. On April 15, 1918, Prince Stanislaus August Poniatowski, coming over from the camp, addressed a mass meeting in Convention Hall, Rochester. *DC,* April 16, 1918.

84. *CJ,* March 30, 1917.

85. *CJ,* April 20, 1917.

86. *DC,* July 5, 1917.

87. *CJ,* April 26, 1918.

88. Daniel T. Roach, "War Service of the Four-Minute Men, Rochester and Monroe County," *WWSRRMC,* 3: 215-19.

89. *ICCM,* June, 1917: 334; March, 1919: 178-79; June, 1919: 216.

90. On "Liberty measles", see *DC,* April 16, 1918.

91. *CJ,* November 9, 1917.

92. John D. Lynn, "The United States Marshal's Office in the World War," *WWSRRMC,* 3: 69-120. There was also a rift, at least temporarily, in the ranks of Rochester's Lithuanians, one party accusing the other of pro-Germanism, the other stoutly denying the charge (*DC,* August 13, 15, 19, 1917).

93. For the War Council, see Michael Williams, *American Catholics in the World War* (New York, 1921), pp. 100-53. Bishop Hickey was suggested as a member of the governing board of the National Catholic War Council, but not subsequently elected (John Tracy Ellis, *Life of James Cardinal Gibbons* [Milwaukee, 1953], 2: 295).

94. *CJ,* February 8, 1918.

95. John J. McInerney, "World War Service of the Knights of Columbus," *WWSRRMC,* 3: 399-404.

96. *WWSRRMC,* 3: 153-58; *CJ,* August 2, 1918, April 10, 1908.

97. *ICCM,* September, 1918: p. 111; December, 1918: 143-44. During the war, Cornell University in Ithaca trained over 5,000 Army, Navy, Marine and Service-related personnel, not only in basic military techniques, but in aeronautics, aerial pho-

tography and mechanical skills. (*Cornell Register*, Cornell University, 1918-1919, pp. 169-172). Apparently there was no special diocesan program set up for the Catholics of this group, so presumably they were left to the care of the local pastor, Father William H. Harrington.

98. Montgomery, *Catholic Family Center*, pp. 40-41; Fred T. Harris, "The Rochester War Chest," *WWSRRMC*, 3: 263-79. Because of the Diocese's participation in the War Chest, it was not required to participate in the joint Catholic drive that took place that fall in the other New York State dioceses. At home, the Bishop named a diocesan War Council, including George Roche, Grand Knight of the Rochester K. of C.; Attorney Eugene J. Dwyer; City Assessor Joseph Fritsch; and Attorney William F. Maloney.

99. *DC*, July 17, 1917.

100. *ARD*, unidentified clipping, Rochester, 1917.

101. Capt. Wheeler C. Case, "The 108th Infantry," *WWSRRMC*, 2: 1913-21; Freeman Galpin, *Central New York, An Inland Empire* (New York, 1941), 3: 271; Burt E. Stage, "With Company L in 1918," *Chemung County Historical Journal*, 6 (1961), 824-32; "History of Co. B", *Geneva Times* (undated clipping, Scrapbook, Geneva Historical Society). There were a good.many Catholic soldiers in the 27th Regiment. Although he naturally does not indicate their religious affiliation, Harry R. Malone lists the war dead in all branches of the service for all the counties of the Diocese except Monroe and Livingston (*History of Central New York*, Indianapolis, Ind., 1932. pp. 311-23).

102. *DC*, August 27, 1917. On the draft in general, see "The Draft in Rochester and Monroe County," *WWSRRMC*, 3: 1-50.

103. F. J. Zwierlein, "One Hundred Years of Catholicism in Rochester," *RHSPFS*, 13 (1934), 255-56.

104. Clement G. Lanni, "The Italians in Rochester," *RHSPFS*, 6 (1927), 186, 196. For the other Monroe County war victims, see *WWSRRMC*, *passim*.

105. I am indebted to Mr. Howard W. Gunlocke, of Wayland, for this information about Mr. O'Connor. For Mr. Coughlin, see Heffernan, *SCB*, pp. 185-88. Two Catholic nurses from Rochester died in the service: Cecil Josephine Cochran and Catherine Rose Connelly.

106. For the Rochester chaplains see. George J. Waring, *United States Catholic Chaplains in the World War* (New York, 1924); *WWSRRMC*, *passim*. For Father LeMay: obituary, *CC*, April 7, 1955. For Abbé Flynn: *Catholic Calendar*, April, 1918; *ICCM*, June, 1918: 45-46; *CJ*, April 19, 1918; *DC*, April 16, 17, 18, 1918.

107. Thomas E. Byrne, "Spanish Influenza . . .", *Chemung County Historical Journal*, 3 (1957), 384-85.

108. *CG*, p. 169.

109. *CJ*, November 15, 1918; interviews with Messrs. George Montgomery and William T. Nolan.

110. These data are based on *Mercy* (pp. 44-45), and on notes provided by Sister M. Petrus Sullivan, R.S.M., and inquiries made among the Rochester sisterhoods.

111. *SSJR*, pp. 102-03.

112. *Cathedral Calendar*, December, 1918.

113. *DC*, November 29, 1918.

114. *ICCM*, June, 1919: 216.

CHAPTER TEN:

BISHOP HICKEY: THE LAST DECADE

1. *DC*, April 18, 1928.

2. Another eastern-rite Catholic group which established itself within the twelve counties in the early 1920's was the Ukrainian colony of around twenty families, most of them farmers, who moved into the neighborhood of Bath, Steuben County, and who now constitute the small parish of

Christ the King. (Information kindly supplied by Mr. John Gerych, Bath.) Like the other Ukrainian churches in the twelve counties, Christ the King parish belongs to the Ukrainian Rite Eparchy of Stamford rather than to the Diocese of Rochester.

3. St. Charles Borromeo Church is privileged to possess an unusual relic of its pa-

tron, Saint Charles Borromeo (1538-1584), the great reforming Cardinal and Archbishop of Milan, Italy. It is the lining of the stole which the Saint was wearing on October 26, 1569, when he was shot at by a member of a religious order that was resisting his attempts to enforce reform. Though the bullet, fired from a distance of no more than five yards, reached its kneeling target, it was prevented, apparently by a miracle, from penetrating the Saint's body. Bishop Hickey gave the relic to the church at the time of its foundation. The story is told that the contemporary Archbishop of Milan gave it to the Rochester Diocese when he heard that Hickey contemplated a church dedicated to St. Charles. But the document of authentication which accompanied the relic was signed as early as April 19, 1911 by Cardinal Andrea Ferrari, Archbishop of Milan (1894-1921).

4. The church was given its name because a Mrs. Salome Boucher donated the property. Its patron saint is St. (Mary) Salome, the mother of the Apostles James and John. St. Salome Church was then, and apparently still is, the only church in the United States to bear this unusual (and to some, puzzling) title.

5. For the episcopal residence, *CJ*, January 12, 1917 and *ARD*, parish financial accounts, 1917 and 1918. Material on the sale of the O-Neh-Da property is abundantly documented in: *CC*, October 3, 1935; Minutes of the Board of Trustees, St. Bernard's Seminary, 72-76, 81-85, 101-03; and in special Hemlock files, *ARD*, Chancery and Seminary repositories.

6. *Mercy*, pp. 49, 52-53. Architects of the school and motherhouse were J. Foster Warner and Leo J. Ribson of Rochester.

7. *SSJR*, pp. 113-17.

8. *SSJR*, pp. 110-13. Nazareth College was accredited, 1930-1931. For the act of incorporation, see *Laws of the State of New York, 148th Session, 1925*, Chap. 446, p. 764.

9. *ARD*, Hickey Papers, Hickey seminary circular of August 20, 1922.

10. *ARD*, Hickey Papers, seminary circular of September 13, 1927.

11. *DC*, February 11, 1919; *Rochester Herald*, February 11, 1919. Obscurities in the State laws regarding legacies to institutions had meanwhile worked to the disadvantage of St. Bernard's Seminary and similar institutions throughout the State. Bishop Hickey took active steps to correct this situation. The final result was a new law which abolished the restrictive elements written into the previous legislation. (*Laws of the State of New York, 1911*, Chapter 857, p. 2399.) It was a measure that benefited not only the Rochester seminary but all other institutions in the State that stood to suffer from the previous laws. *ARD*, Hickey Papers, special file on "Educational Institutions Bill."

12. *CJ*, December 31, 1920.

13. *CJ*, March 24, 1922; *Laws of the State of New York, 145th Session, 1925*, Chaper 133, p. 434.

14. *CJ*, July 27, 1923; October 19, 1923; November 23, 1923.

15. *CJ*, March 7, 1924.

16. *Rochester Evening Journal*, September 29, 1925; *CJ*, September 11, 1925, October 2, 1925.

17. Archives, Rochester Department of Public Instruction, Herbert S. Weet, circular to parents, January, 1920 (copy).

18. "Highlights of Federation History," in *After Forty Years* (brochure of The Federation of Churches of Rochester and Vicinity, Inc., 1959), p. 1, declares that Rochester was the first city in the State and the eighteenth in the nation to introduce the plan. For the spread up to 1933, see Mary Dabney Davis, *Weekday Religious Instruction* (brochure No. 36, Office of Education, U.S. Department of Interior) Washington, D.C., 1933, pp. 26-29. For Auburn's refusal on constitutional grounds, see *CJ*, January 12, 1923.

19. Archives, Rochester Department of Public Instruction, Herbert S. Weet to Rev. Cameron J. Davis, Rochester, n.d. [October-November, 1921], (copy).

20. *TU*, December 14, 1940; *CC*, December 19, 1940; Frederick J. Zwierlein, *OHYCR*, pp. 263-65; Zwierlein notes in *ARD*. Mr. James P. B. Duffy, the only Catholic member of the board at that time, recalls that Hickey played a major role in working out the details. Another Catholic who assisted was Dr. Joseph O'Hern, assistant Superintendent of the public schools. Judge Duffy's own presence on the Board surely did the cause no harm.

21. Information about the pre-official

released-time at School No. 18 was kindly furnished by one of the former catechists, Miss Elvira Paolone. A list of the paid catechists between 1919-1936 is in *ARD*, special "Italian Work" file.

On the Catholic Women's Club sponsorship, see *CJ*, July 3, 17, 1925; *ARD*, Grace I. Duffy, "The Catholic Women's Club," MS; *Catholic Women's Club Bulletin*, especially June 1929, October 1932 issues; Miss Rosemary White, B. Litt. (Oxon.), to the present writer, Rochester, August 8, 1965. Miss White, now professor-emeritus of Nazareth College, was director of the Annunciation vacation school in the late 1920's.

Director in 1924 (and later the first person to take a census of Annunciation parish) was Miss Inez Maier (1906-1944). In 1925 the mission-minded Miss Maier entered the Missionary Sisters, Servants of the Holy Ghost, as Sister Theophane, and in 1934 was sent to do hospital work on the missions of the Society of the Divine Word in New Guinea. When World War II broke out, she and her missionary companions were taken captive by the Japanese in July, 1943. On February 6, she and sixty-two other missionaries were killed when their prison ship was mistakenly strafed by Allied airmen. (See the memorial collection of her letters: *New Guinea Adventures*, by Sister Theophane, S.Sp.S., Compiled and Edited by Sister Rosalie [Maier], S.S.J., Rochester, Sisters of St. Joseph, 1945. Additional information by Sr. Rosalie and Mr. Rufus Maier.)

22. Montgomery, *Catholic Family Center*, pp. 40-41; 62-68; 110; and interview with Mr. Montgomery. In May, 1925, Bishop Hickey urged pastors in a circular to give a series of talks to their school children informing these "future wage-earners" of the value of the Chest (*CJ*, May 8, 1925).

23. Montgomery, *Catholic Family Center*, pp. 45-48; *CJ*, January 16, 1920.

24. *CJ*, March 14, 1919; May 5, 1922; September 14, 1923; May 6, 1927.

25. On the beginnings of the Club, see *CJ*, December 5, 1919; April 9, 1920. For Camp Madonna; see: *ARD*, Grace I. Duffy, "The Catholic Women's Club," MS; *CJ*, June 27, 1919, July 3, 17, 1925, June 29, 1928; and bulletins and releases of the Club.

26. *CCJ*, June 29, 1951.

27. Obituary of Father Brophy, *CJ*, February 13, 1920. Francis J. Lane, Catholic Boy Scouts, *ICCM*, 11 (December, 1920): 209-13; 12 (March, 1921): 53-55.

28. *CJ*, May 1, 1925; "Holy Sepulchre Cemetery," in Golden Jubilee Supplement, *CC*, 1939, p. 95. The Pinnacle Cemetery property was sold in 1960, pursuant to a decision of the N.Y.S. Supreme Court on January 26, 1960. A copy of the record of this case is in the archives of St. Patrick's Church, Rochester, See also *DC*, January 29, 1960.

29. *CJ*, September 27, 1918.

30. *CJ*, December 31, 1915.

31. *ARD*, Hickey Papers, pastoral of September 9, 1926.

32. *Cathedral Calendar*, February, 1918, p. 1.

33. *ARD*, Hickey Papers, Lenten pastoral, 1927.

34. *ARD*, Hickey Papers, pastoral on vocations, November 22, 1921.

35. *CJ*, October 22, 1926.

36. *ARD*, Hickey Papers. Undated pastoral (1927?).

37. *CJ*, July 7, 1922; February 8, 1924.

38. *CJ*, January 13, 1928.

39. We have already alluded to the controversial writings of Father O'Neill. In 1926, Father FitzSimons spoke out in criticism of atheistic trends at the University of Rochester (*CJ*, March 12, 1926). Dr. Zwierlein took occasion of many local controversies to set forth the views of the Church—as, for instance, the defense of artificial contraception and companionate marriage which the Colorado judge, Ben B. Lindsey, made in an address to the Rochester Club (*CJ*, March 16, 1928). Editorials in the *Catholic Journal*, a lay-published periodical, though generally routine and unaggressive, tended to be shrilly orthodox on basic matters of faith and morals: e.g., "Women Awake," *CJ*, February 22, 1924.

40. For the War Council, see *CJ*, October 11, 1918. For the proposed suppression of the N.C.W.C., see *ARD*, Hickey Papers, Archbishop John Bonzano to Hickey, Washington, D.C., March 22, 1922, covering a copy of a decree of the Sacred Consistorial Congregation, February 25,

1922 (Protocol 106/22). For Hickey's stand against suppression, see Archives of the Albany Diocese, Edmund F. Gibbons to Peter Muldoon, Albany, N.Y., telegram (copy) " . . . Rochester away from home Will sign [plea for preservation] when he returns. Consented to my request to authorize you meantime to use his name . . . "

41. *CJ*, September 4, 1914.

42. *CJ*, February 3, 1922.

43. The decrees of this synod were never published. *ARD*, Hickey Papers, has a copy of the few new paragraphs.

44. *CJ*, July 4, 1924; *ARD*, Hickey Papers, official diocesan report (copy).

45. *TU*, October 20, 1924.

46. *DC*, October 1, 1924; *CJ*, October 3, 1924.

47. On the creation of the monsignori, see *TU*, October 20, 1924. Andrew B. Meehan (1867-1932) was a pioneer member of the faculty of St. Bernard's Seminary, and its rector from 1923 until his death. Ordained in Rome on July 25, 1892 (he spent seven undergraduate years at Rome's North American College), he received his doctorate in theology at the University of Propaganda Fide in 1893. He went back to Rome 1907-1908 and won a doctorate in Canon Law. Returning to St. Bernard's he gradually acquired a wide ecclesiastical reputation, through his teaching and writing, for his wisdom and his expertise in church law and rubrics. He was made a papal chamberlain by Benedict XV on November 10, 1914. In 1918 he was named to the bishopric of Trenton by the Holy See, according to an announcement made in Rome on March 2nd. (*New York Times*, March 2, 1918; *Rochester Times*, March 2, 1918; *CJ*, March 18, 1918.) A retiring man by disposition, and one who realized his inexperience in administration, Msgr. Meehan requested his physician, Dr. Leo Simpson, to support him with a report on his chronic heart ailment, for he intended to beg off from the appointment. The Holy See accepted the plea and chose Father Thomas J. Walsh, Chancellor of the Diocese of Buffalo, in his place. See obituary, *DC*, January 30, 1932; Daniel Brent and Robert F. McNamara, "Doctor Meehan," in *The Sheaf*, St. Bernard's Seminary, 1962, pp. 8-10, 40; Owen B. McGuire, "Monsignor Meehan (Appreciation by an Old Friend)," *CCJ*, March 25, 1932.

48. Vince Spezzano, *The History of St. Lucy's Parish, Retsof, New York*, 1965, p. 11.

49. For the postwar conflicts in the shoe, clothing and building trades, see Blake McKelvey, *Rochester: The Quest For Quality, 1890-1925* (Cambridge, Mass., 1956), pp. 346-53.

50. Joseph H. Gervais to the present writer, Rochester, January 5, 1966.

51. *CJ*, January 19, 1923.

52. *CJ*, June 4, 11, 1892. Also recollections of the Reverend Edward J. Eschrich.

53. *ARD*, Special files on the Royal Development and Father Naughten.

54. Among the most active "temperance priests" were Father William Payne (1856-1925) and Father James T. Dougherty (1863-1921). Father Payne was pastor of Holy Cross, Charlotte (1895-1913) and of St. Mary's, Auburn (1913-1925); and his temperance activities were a part of his civic activities (*CJ*, April 10, 17, 1925). The same was true of Father Dougherty, pastor of St. Patrick's, Dansville (1893-1901) and of St. Mary's, Canandaigua (1901-1921) (*CJ*, February 11, 1921; and recollections of the late Msgr. John B. Sullivan of Rochester). We have already noted Father Dougherty's interest in the sites of the seventeenth century Jesuit missions, which prompted him to cause the erection of commemorative tablets at Boughton Hill, Mud Creek near Holcomb, and Great Gully Brook, Cayuga County (*CJ*, September 10, 1909; October 6, 20, 1911).

55. *AAB*. 128-E-6, Hickey to James Gibbons, Rochester, September 17, 1919.

56. *CJ*, May 28, 1920; November 6, 1925.

57. Archives, New York State Catholic [Welfare] Committee, Albany, N. Y. Miscellaneous File 170.1, contains Hickey's and related letters, nine items, from 1919 to 1925.

58. *Ibid.*, File 50.5: Hickey to Charles J. Tobin, Rochester, March 3, 1920; Tobin to Hickey, Albany, March 5, 1920 (copy).

59. On both the *Menace* and the Klan, in general, see John Higham, *Strangers in the Land: Patterns of American Nativism 1860-1925*, (New Brunswick, N. J., 1955).

60. *ICCM,* 5 (May, 1912): 163-64; interview with the late Msgr. Frank Mason.

61. Quoted by *CJ,* October 2, 1914. But the letter's extreme tone suggests that it was a political forgery.

62. Michael Williams, *The Shadow of the Pope* (New York, 1932), pp. 299-301.

63. *CJ,* October 16, 1914.

64. *CJ,* February 26, 1915.

65. *CJ,* December 8, 1922.

66. *PE,* February 26, 1913; the Reverend John P. Norris to the present writer, Industry, N. Y., January 5, 1966.

67. *CJ,* May 26, 1916; June 2, 1916.

68. *ARD,* Arthur A. Hughes Scrapbook, unidentified clipping from a Rochester newspaper, period 1914-1918.

69. *DC,* April 4, 1912; *CJ,* April 5, 1912.

70. F. J. Zwierlein, *Talks to Men and Women on the World of Today* (privately printed, Rochester, 1946), pp. xi-xii; plus further details furnished by the late Dr. Zwierlein.

One person who could not avoid unfavorable publicity during the McQuaid and Hickey regimes and afterward was the controversial priest, Father Charles E. Flaherty of Mount Morris (1856-1939). This very intelligent man and capable preacher was unfortunately tried and convicted of criminal assault in April, 1893. Appeals followed, and in 1901 the case was dismissed. He had already been suspended from the exercise of his priesthood, but continued to live in Mount Morris, still wearing clerical garb. Now he studied both medicine and law and engaged in both practices without license, so that he became embroiled with the courts time and again. In 1928 he was convicted of performing an illegal operation on a young woman of the vicinity who afterward died. Appeals failed this time, and at the age of seventy-two he entered Auburn Prison, from which he emerged. on parole, in 1931. His last years were less eventful. (*DC,* November 16, 1939). Highly respected priests who knew the story rather well, while agreeing that his career after 1901 was reprehensible, were strongly persuaded that the first charges laid against Father Flaherty were untrue, and that Bishop McQuaid had been at fault for not standing by him.

71. *CJ,* December 22, 1922; January 12, 1923.

72. Nunda, *CJ,* July 13, 1923. Henrietta and Hemlock, *CJ,* November 30, 1923.

73. For Corning, see *CG,* pp. 191-92. For Geneva, see Thomas C. Kane. *The Song of Stephen* (Geneva, St. Stephen's Church, 1954). For Penn Yan, see Arch Merrill, *DC,* April 11, 1965, p. 18-W.

74. Arch Merrill, *DC,* April 11, 1965, p. 18-W.

75. *CJ,* May 4, 1923; June 1, 1923.

76. *AANY,* Y-8, Report, "The Oregon School Defense Fund."

77. *Pierce v. Society of Sisters,* 268 U. S. 510, 45 Sup. Ct. 571, 69, L. Ed. 1070 (1925).

78. *DC,* November 25, 26, 1922.

79. *CC&J,* October 3, 1930.

80. For Vay, see obituary, *CC&J,* September 4, 1931; for Wollensak, see *CC,* January 30, 1936.

81. *CJ,* November 22, 1929 (Maloney). For Connelly, see June 7, 1929. Additional information from his daughter, Miss Catherine S. Connelly of Elmira.

82. *The Parish Record,* Immaculate Conception Church, Ithaca, April, 1916; *Ithaca Daily News,* March 24, 1916.

83. *Who Was Who in America,* Vol. 1.

84. *CC,* April 10, 1941.

85. *Who Was Who in America,* Vol. 1.

86. See Mrs. Chanler's autobiographical books, *Roman Spring* (New York, 1934), and *Autumn in the Valley* (New York, 1937). Further details come from the late Mrs. Fred (Evelyn Walsh) Quirk, of Geneseo, and Miss Blanche Jennings Thompson of Rochester, formerly of Geneseo. The papal privilege of reserving the Blessed Sacrament in St. Felicity's Chapel was first granted July 5, 1913. The chapel is still used during the summer season (Admiral Hubert W. Chanler to the present writer, Geneseo, January 7, 1966). Mrs. Chanler also largely provided the funds, about $7,000.00, to attractively redecorate St. Mary's Church, Geneseo. The architects were the well known firm of McKim, Mead and White. Stanford White's son, Lawrence, was Mrs. Chanler's son-in-law.

87. *CJ*, March 7, 21, 1919.

88. *CJ*, March 19, 1920.

89. *DC*, Jack Tucker by-line, March 17, 1965; *TU*, May 26, 1964, p. 8-A; *CJ*, December 3, 1920, December 30, 1927; obituary of Mrs. Wheelwright, *CJ*, June 17, 1932. A popular life of deValera is Mary C. Bromage, *DeValera and the March of a Nation* (New York, 1956). See also Dorothy Macardle, *The Irish Republic* (New York, 1965). Thomas Wheelwright was born December 18, 1890; professed a Redemptorist, August 2, 1911; ordained a priest, June 7, 1916; died July 22, 1946. (Information kindly furnished by Reverend Joseph C. Winiecki, C.SS.R., of St. Joseph's Church, Rochester.)

90. For instance, *CJ*, September 30, 1921; April 18, 1924.

91. Obituary of Mrs. Wheelwright, *CC&J*, June 17, 1932. For the Eucharistic Congress incident, see *CC&J*, July 1, 1932, August 5, 1932.

92. *CJ*, August 14, 1916.

93. *CC*, April 4, 1935.

94. *CJ*, October 27, 1922.

95. *ARD*, Hickey Papers, Richard E. Olds, Asst. Secretary of State, to Thomas F. Hickey, Washington, May 28, 1926.

96. For Vannutelli, see *CJ*, October 14, 1910; for the seven Cardinals, *CJ*, June 18, 1926; for Marchetti, *CJ*, October 7, 1927.

97. *CJ*, October 3, 10, 17, 1919.

98. *CJ*, March 2, 1928.

99. *CC*, May 31, 1945.

100. *Acta Apostolicae Sedis*, 17 (1925): 270; *CJ*, February 27, 1925, May 29, 1925.

101. *ARD*, Hickey Papers, Pietro Fumasoni Biondi to Thomas F. Hickey, Washington, October 29, 1928; decree of the Sacred Consistorial Congregation, protocol 678/28, October 30, 1928, accepting the resignation; papal brief *Supremi Apostolatus Officium*, October 30, 1928, conferring the titular see of Viminacium. *DC*, October 31, 1928; *CJ*, November 2, 1928. In late Roman times, Viminacium was a metropolitan see in the province of Moesia Prima in the Balkans. In the fifteenth century it fell, with the rest of Serbia, under Turkish rule. Its location was at the present Costolatz, Yugoslavia, some forty miles east of Belgrade.

102. *AANY*, Q-25, Hayes to Hickey, New York, November 5, 1928 (copy); Hickey to Hayes, Rochester, November 11, 1928.

103. *CJ*, January 16, 1929; *CJ*, May 29, 1930.

104. Floyd Anderson, *Father Baker (1843-1936)* (Milwaukee, 1960), p. 133. This founder of the Basilica of Our Lady of Victory and the adjacent charitable institutions has been mentioned as a possible candidate for canonization. He was stationed at St. Mary's, Corning, in 1881-1882. (*CG*, p. 227).

105. *CC*, August 19, 1937.

106. *DC*, March 20, 1929.

107. The Reverend Edward J. Eschrich, interview.

108. *DC*, February 18, 1941.

109. Interview with the late Jeremiah Hickey, for the stories about Stein and Brown.

110. *AANY*, Q-3, Hickey to Hayes, Rochester, July 4, 1921; Hayes to Hickey, New York, July 13, 1921 (copy).

CHAPTER ELEVEN:

JOHN FRANCIS O'HERN

1. Biographical information on the early life of Bishop O'Hern is drawn from his entry in the Rochester Clergy Record, Vol. 1, Chancery; from a series of unidentified newspaper clippings from the Olean area, kindly supplied by Fr. Irenaeus Herscher, O.F.M., Librarian, Friedsam Memorial Library, St. Bonaventure University; and from information provided by the Bishop's relatives: Mrs. Mary Baish, Miss Agnes Casey, and Colonel Charles Francis Baish, U.S.A., Ret. *The Missionary* (Washington, D. C.), Vol. 14, February, 1931, devotes a whole issue to describing and eulogizing the ca-

reer of Father Lewis O'Hern, C.S.P.

2. *Rochester Echo,* March 15, 1929, says he attended St. Mary's parochial school in Olean and Olean High School, and had a good scholastic record. But the Sisters of Mercy in charge of St. Mary of the Angels' School and the staff of Olean High School report the absence of records for the period of his attendance (Irenaeus Herscher, O.F.M., to present writer, St. Bonaventure, December 14, 1915).

3. *Rochester Echo,* March 15, 1929.

4. Transcript of scholastic record, Urban University, Rome, kindness of the Reverend Stephen Virgulin, S.T.D. The future Bishop's brief Roman diary (in *ARD*) bears ample testimony to his appreciation of Rome and its devotional aspects. Bishop McQuaid had decided by 1900 to appoint both O'Hern and his classmate, J. Francis Goggin, to the staff of St. Bernard's Seminary on their return. O'Hern was apparently scheduled to take additional studies and teach Sacred Scripture (*ARD,* McQuaid Papers, O'Hern to McQuaid, Rome, December 12, 1899, March 15, 1900; Goggin to McQuaid, Rome, December 11, 1899; McQuaid to Goggin, Rochester, May 6, 1900). But according to the records of the North American College, J. F. O'Hern, *"adversae valetudinis causa domum rediit."*

5. *CJ,* May 11, 1901; September 21, 1901.

6. *Cathedral Calendar,* April, 1909; November, 1909; January, 1910; February, 1910; September, 1911; April, 1912.

7. Records of the Rochester Society for the Prevention of Cruelty to Children, courtesy of Mrs. Roberta Roth.

8. *ARD,* Hickey Papers, Pietro Fumasoni-Biondi to Thomas F. Hickey, Washington, D. C., October 29, 1928, Protocol #1635-H.

9. O'Hern's appointment was officially published in the *Acta Apostolicae Sedis,* 21 (1929): 31. The brief naming him was printed in the consecration booklet. For the consecration, see *DC,* March 20, 1929; *CC&J,* March 22, 1929.

10. Of these "temporary" buildings during the late 1920's and early 1930's, Precious Blood is still in use at the present writing. St. Philip Neri burned down in 1967. St. Margaret Mary was moved to West Webster and remodeled into St. Rita's

Church; and St. Ann's, dismantled and removed to Greece, was transformed, after considerable reconstruction, into the parish church of St. Lawrence.

11. *CC&J,* July 3, 1931.

12. *CC&J,* June 21, 1929.

13. *CC&J,* June 6, 1930.

14. *ARD,* William Donnelly, MS, "The Origins and Early Years of Holy Family High School, Auburn, New York" (1961).

15. *ARD,* Thomas H. Wheeland, MS, "The History of the Catholic High School in Elmira" (1963). Bishop O'Hern sought to have this high school incorporated by a special act of the State Legislature. Perhaps in imitation of the Aquinas Institute arrangement, he had the bill phrased to set up "The Elmira Catholic College." This would have allowed the Diocese to expand the school's program into a collegiate one. Meanwhile, authority to conduct a high school would be implicit in a collegiate charter. The bill passed in the Senate on April 6, 1933 (*ARD,* offprint of bill 31 Rdg 1039 No. 2352); but it failed of passage in the Assembly because of the closing of the session. Archbishop Mooney, in the following November, decided to seek a simple incorporation rather than go over the heads of the Board of Regents. (Archives of New York State Catholic [Welfare] Committee, Albany, New York, Correspondence—General, file No. 50.1.6: Cornelius O'Dea to Charles J. Tobin, Elmira, April 4, 1933; Tobin to O'Hern, telegram, Albany, April 10, 1933 [copy]; Tobin to O'Dea, Albany, April 12, 1933; John M. Duffy to Tobin, Rochester, November 2, 1923; Tobin to Duffy, Albany, November 18, 1933.)

16. *CC&J,* September 26, 1930.

17. Archives of the Diocese of Ogdensburg, Thomas F. Hickey to Joseph H. Conroy, Rochester, January 17, 1927; Conroy to Hickey, Ogdensburg, January 18, 1927 (copy); same to same, February 4, 1927; *CC&J,* September 9, 1932.

18. *CC&J,* August 10, 1929; October 4, 1929; September 19, 1930.

19. *CC&J,* September 13, 1930. That year the course was extended from five to six years. In 1931 the entrants numbered 260. But the diocesan paper rejoiced prematurely: "Fifty additional future priests." *CC&J,* September 18, 1931; Msgr. Richard M. Quinn.

20. *CC&J*, May 29, 1930; May 1, 1931. Statistical information, kindness of Sisters of St. Joseph and Sisters of Mercy.

21. *CC&J*, June 20, 1930; July 18, 1930; February 13, 1931. According to the present (1966) superior, Mother Mary of the Immaculate Conception Garrity, the original nuns of the Rochester foundation were: Mother Mary of St. Agnes Zimmerman (sister of Mayor George Zimmerman of Buffalo); Sister M. of St. Anne Zenner; Sister M. Lawrence O'Neill; Sister M. Emmanuel Kearns; Sister M. of St. Joseph Friel; Sister M. of St. Andrew Zimmer; Sister M. of St. Teresa Morrissey.

22. *CC&J*, November 29, 1929; June 20, 1930; *CC*, July 18, 1935; February 2, 1939; *ARD*, William J. Gordinier, MS, "Mother Beatrix of the Holy Spirit" (1955). The original choir nuns of the Rochester foundation were: Mother Beatrix; Sister Ignatius of Jesus and Mary (née Elizabeth Town); Sister Mary of the Blessed Sacrament (Carroll). The lay nuns were Sister Anne of Jesus (Mayock) and Sister Joanna of the Cross (Mayock), who were sisters-german, natives of Ireland. The "out-sister" was Sister Elizabeth of the Trinity (Comerford), who is still portress as these lines are written.

When Mother Beatrix was stationed in Boston in the late 1880's, she suffered an attack of appendicitis and her life was despaired of. Archbishop John Williams, standing at her bedside, declared that if he had any powers to heal, he wished to exercise them at that moment. Associates of Mother Beatrix recounted that a quick, almost miraculous cure followed the Archbishop's blessing (*CC*, February 2, 1939).

23. *DC*, February 7, 8, 9, 1922; *TU*, February 20, 1922.

24. *DC*, January 21, 22, 23, 24, 28, 1932; and information given by Father Charles R. Reynolds.

25. *TU*, June 9, 1930; *CC&J*, June 6, 13, 1930; recollections of Father Charles R. Reynolds.

26. *ARD*, program of consecration, pp. 15-16. The program also describes the O'Hern episcopal coat of arms, designed by the Bishop himself, and used, as his two predecessors had used theirs, as both his personal and the diocesan blazon. In the (spectator's) upper right-hand corner, three herons (O'Hern) on a gold field; below, the "pelican in her piety" (silver, "the nest

is in natural colors") on a blue background. In the lower left the arms of McQuaid are reproduced (green shamrock on a St. Andrew cross), the cross surmounted by the monogram of Mary and the sixpointed star from the arms of Hickey, and having beneath it the lily of St. Joseph, on whose feastday the consecration took place. On the upper left is a realistic picture of the main falls of the Genesee River, mist and all, in "natural colors" on a blue ground. This complicated design was to cause anguish to many a heraldic expert and engraver in subsequent years.

27. *TU*, February 6, 1932; and Father Charles R. Reynolds.

28. *CC&J*, April 17, 1931.

29. *DC*, January 28, 1932; *CC&J*, January 29, 1932.

30. *TU*, January 13, 1927.

31. *DC*, February 19, 1931; *CC&J*, February 20, 1931; Father Charles R. Reynolds.

32. *CC&J*, September 6, 27, 1929; October 4, 1929; information provided by Rt. Rev. Msgr. Charles F. Shay; William LaVerdière, S.S.S., "The Flour City," in *Sentinel of the Blessed Sacrament* (New York, N. Y.) 40 (1937): 338-40.

33. For Auburn, Geneva, Hornell, Seneca Falls, Elmira and Ithaca, see: *CC&J*, February 26, 1932; March 11, 25, 1932; April 8, 1932; October 28, 1932.

34. *DC*, March 27, 1955.

35. *CC&J*, November 25, 1932; *CC*, January 6, 1933.

36. *CC&J*, June 12, 1932; *CC*, January 12, 1933; *CC*, June 15, 1933.

37. *CC&J*, November 4, 18, 1932; *CC*, May 11, 18, 1933.

38. *CC&J*, March 14, 1930.

39. Raphael M. Huber, O.F.M. Conv., Ed., *Our Bishops Speak* (Milwaukee, 1952), pp. 387-87.

40. Rt. Rev. Msgr. Paul Tanner to present writer, Washington, D. C., April 12, 1965. Bishop O'Hern was also elected to the Board of Governors of the Catholic Church Extension Society on November 22, 1932, but he died before he was able to take much of a part in that home mis-

sionary society's deliberations (Rt. Rev. Msgr. Joseph B. Lux to the present writer, Chicago, August 23, 1965).

41. *CC&J*, October 9, 1931; *DC*, October 13-15, 1931; *Rochester Journal*, October 15, 1931.

42. *CC*, November 13, 1931; May 20, 1932.

43. Interview with Judge Frederick J. Mix, Rochester, New York.

44. *CC&J*, April 24, 1931; June 12, 1931; July 17, 1931; October 16, 30, 1931; *DC*, October 23, 1931. See also Miss Yawman's obituary, *CCJ*, January 5, 1951.

45. *DC*, March 20, 1931; *CC&J*, February 19, 1932; December 23, 1932.

46. *CC&J*, November 28, 1930.

47. *CC&J*, April 1, 1932; June 3, 1932; *DC*, May 10, 1932.

48. *DC*, March 20, 1931.

49. *CC&J*, May 29, 1931; *DC*, May 25, 1931; *ARD*, O'Hern Papers, program of installation.

50. *CC&J*, March 4, 1932; April 8, 1932. *ARD*, O'Hern Papers, *Souvenir of the Investiture*.

51. Interviews with Mr. William A. Lang and Mr. Stephen J. Fitzgerald.

52. *CJ*, October 5, 1889; *CC&J*, March 15, 1929; Willard A. Marakle and others, "Press Progress," *CC*, Golden Jubilee Supplement, 1939, pp. 64-75; *ARD*, Bernard F. Dollen, MS, "The Founding of the Rochester Diocesan Newspaper" (1949); Judge Frederick J. Mix, interview.

53. *CC&J*, August 7, 1931.

54. A movie record of Roosevelt's visit to the centennial of Our Mother of Sorrows parish, in 1930, was later deposited in the F. D. Roosevelt Library, Hyde Park, New York. Incidentally, the Eastman Company photographed Bishop O'Hern's consecration in the film then called Kodacolor. Copies of these films were presented by Mr. Eastman to both the Bishop and Cardinal Hayes.

55. *ARD*, Francis J. Erb, MS, "Catholic Radio in Rochester," (1951).

56. *CC*, April 6, 1933.

57. *CC&J*, March 14, 1930.

58. *DC*, November 23, 1931.

59. *DC*, May 4, 1933.

60. *CC&J*, January 29, 1932.

61. *Health News* (New York State Department of Health, Albany, N.Y.), 6 (1929): No. 31.

62. *CC&J*, October 31, 1930.

63. *CC&J*, April 19, 1929.

64. *CC&J*, September 18, 1931. One of Clara Barton's earliest associates in Red Cross work in Europe and in Dansville was the Franco-Swiss painter, Miss Antoinette Margot (1843-1925), a convert to the Catholic faith, who lived with Miss Barton in Dansville for over a year, and then went to Washington with her in March, 1886. (Thomas D. Williams, *The Story of Antoinette Margot*, Baltimore, 1931.)

65. *CC&J*, March 29, 1929.

66. *CC&J*, November 7, 1930; *DC*, November 3, 1930.

67. *CC&J*, December 31, 1931.

68. *DC*, June 12, 1930.

69. *CCJ*, February 5, 1932.

70. W. W. Mendenhall, "A Quarter Century of Cooperative Religion at Cornell University," *Religious Education* (Chicago), 41 (1946): 114-19; *Ithaca Journal News* (Ithaca, N.Y.), October 29, 1930.

71. *CC&J*, April 18, 1930.

72. *CC&J*, April 26, 1929.

73. *CC&J*, April 4, 11, 1930; *DC*, April 7, 9, 1930; *TU*, April 7, 1930. The meeting, when projected, became the subject of some controversy, for two local ministers publicly refused to attend. Rev. Dr. Ralph S. Cushman, pastor of Asbury Methodist Church, said he thought it hypocritical to protest against Soviet persecution of Christians until Russian Christians, the Orthodox in particular, were ready to admit their own discriminatory policies of the past. The Unitarian minister, Dr. David Rhys Williams, said that during a recent visit to Russia he had received the impression there was no persecution; so he would oppose any protest until a representative religious committee had made a thorough investiga-

tion of the Russian situation. Father Walsh's fresh facts and figures at the meeting and Dr. Frederick J. Zwierlein's newspaper attack on "bigoted" opposition to the mass meeting adequately counterbalanced both the idealistic inhibitions of Dr. Cushman and the liberal inhibitions of Dr. Williams. The other Protestant ministers present in Convention Hall had no scruples about denouncing the current Russian mistreatment of Christians and Jews.

74. *TU*, March 30, 1933; *CC*, March 4, 1933.

75. Frank Kelly, article on St. Dominic parish, *CCJ*, July 25, 1958. On Italian unemployment, see *ARD* File on Italian Unemployment, 1930—.

76. *CC&J*, November 27, 1931.

77. *CC&J*, November 4, 1932.

78. *CC*, March 16, 23, 1933.

79. *CC*, March 23 ,1933.

80. *CC&J*, October 23, 1931.

81. *CC&J*, April 8, 29, 1932; May 13, 27, 1932; information kindly furnished by Father Geiger. For girls of a younger age, the Bishop gave approval to the introduction of the Catholic Girl Scouts in Rochester in May, 1929 (*CC&J*, May 29, 1929.) The Catholic Women's Club thereupon founded Troop #32 (Catholic Women's Club *Bulletin*, Vol. 13 [December, 1939]).

82. Montgomery, *Catholic Family Center*, pp. 76-77; 87; 114.

83. *ARD*, James F. Baker, MS, "A History of the Genesee Settlement House" (1947).

84. *CC&J*, January 24, 1930.

85. *CC&J*, July 25, 1930; February 13, 1931; Miss Mary E. FitzGerald to the present writer, Elmira, N.Y., January 24, 1966. The pastor of St. Mary's Church in Bath, N. Y., Father Edward M. Lynch (1884-1938) was also active in charities. Long a member of the Steuben County Child Welfare Board, at the 1931 Convention of the New York State Welfare Boards he was named to head a committee for the revision of the State Child Welfare Law (*DC*, October 12, 1931; *CC*, June 23, 1938.)

86. *CC&J*, April 25, 1930.

87. *ARD*, Circular letter of April 9, 1930.

88. *AANY*, X-25, O'Hern to Cardinal Patrick Hayes, Rochester, June 29, 1931, enclosing the report of the consultors' meeting on the project (April 20, 1931); Hayes to O'Hern, New York, July 2, 1931 (copy).

89. *CC&J*, August 14, 1931. The new corporation also had difficulty in meeting the mortgage payments. In 1932, Mr. Peter Tettelbach of Rochester donated to the Center corporation some $6,000.00 worth of stock in the Dome mine, a Canadian gold mine. When Father Gerald C. Lambert, in charge of the Civic Center, complained to him in 1933 that they did not have enough to pay the annual interest, Tettelbach asked, "How about that stock?" On investigating, Father Lambert found that its value had risen in a year to $18,000.00. Thus Peter Tettelbach had saved the day. After that the Center proved a good investment, self-supporting. Its value in 1966 was estimated at four or five million dollars (Monsignor Gerald C. Lambert, interview).

90. *CC&J*, December 4, 1931 (Boy Scouts). Information on the Columbus Club from Msgr. Gerald C. Lambert and Father Joseph F. D'Aurizio.

91. *CC&J*, January 3, 1930.

92. *CC&J*, July 10, 1931. Archives, New York State Catholic [Welfare] Committee, Albany, New York. General Correspondence, 1915-1935: file 50.1.6. Charles J. Tobin to Eugene J. Dwyer, Albany, December 2, 1930; same to O'Hern, Albany, December 15, 1930 (copies).

93. Rt. Rev. Msgr. Francis J. Lane to the present writer, Elmira, N. Y., August 30, 1964, September 23, 1965; and interview with Father Charles R. Reynolds. Father Lane, Catholic chaplain at Elmira Reformatory, as head of the New York State Chaplain's Association in 1932, suggested that they ask the State for a rise in salary. Each chaplain agreed to work through his own bishop, and to have each bishop request the Budget Director of the State to second the appeal. Bishop O'Hern promised his backing. This was probably in 1932. The Bishop approached all State senators and assemblymen from the twelve counties, and likewise the influential Congressman from Auburn, Mr. John Taber. When the Chaplains subsequently appeared before the State Budget Director, he told them they had a "powerful lobby" working for them. Without much opposition he granted their request, and the salaries of

the chaplains at Auburn, Elmira Reformatory, the State School at Industry, and the Craig Colony at Sonyea, were raised to $2,400.00.

94. *CC&J*, August 2, 1929; *ARD*, William H. Hickey, MS, "The Heroic Action of Catholic Priests During Riots at Auburn State Prison in 1929," (1950).

95. *CC&J*, August 15, 1930.

96. *Auburn Citizen*, December 23, 1929; *CC&J*, December 13, 1929; Hickey, "The Heroic Action . . ."

97. *CC&J*, March 21, 1930; Catharine S. Connelly, "Elmira's Edward J. Dunn," *Chemung County Historical Journal*, 9 (March, 1964): 1232-37.

98. Editorial, *TU*, March 18, 1930; *CC&J*, February 13, 1931.

99. For instance, *Elmira Daily Advertiser*, September 8, 1931; and O'Hern

scrapbook, unidentified clipping about a Communion breakfast of the Corning Knights at which the Bishop spoke.

100. *CC&J*, March 13, 1931.

101. *DC*, November 23, 1932.

102. *CC*, May 25, 1933; Charles F. Welch report, *TU*, May 23, 1933; Margaret Frawley report, *DC*, May 23, 1933; also *DC*, May 24, 25, 26, 1933; *Rochester Journal*, May 23, 1933.

103. *CC*, June 1, 1933; *TU*, May 26, 1933; *DC*, May 27, 1933.

104. *ARD*, O'Hern scrapbook: messages of condolence. Bishop O'Hern's estate amounted to $29,000.00, of which he bequeathed $6,500.00 to his brothers and sisters, and over $2,000.00 apiece to St. Bernard's Seminary, St. Ann's Home, St. Mary's, St. Patrick's and St. Joseph's Orphan Asylums (*ARD*, O'Hern will file).

CHAPTER TWELVE:

THE FUTURE CARDINAL MOONEY

1. *AANY*, X-25, Mooney to Hayes, telegram, Seattle, August 28, 1933.

2. *CC*, August 21, 1933; September 7, 1933.

3. The sponsors were Thomas and Elizabeth Reynolds. The pastor's entries in the parish baptismal register were in Latin, so he even attempted to latinize Mount Savage into "Monte Feroce." For a transcript of this record and other family data the present writer is deeply indebted to the Cardinal's niece, Mrs. Frances Byrne McFadden, of Sharon, Pa., and her son, the Reverend Bernard J. McFadden, of Tampa, Florida. The Cardinal's other name, Aloysius, was assumed at confirmation on November 24, 1895 (confirmation records, St. Columba Cathedral, Youngstown, Ohio, courtesy of the Rev. Mark Zwick). Cardinal Mooney did not care for the name Aloysius, so he seldom used it.

4. This account of the early life of the Cardinal is based on the McFadden data referred to above, and on articles (not very dependable) in the *Detroit Times* (March 3, 4, 5, 1946), and the obituary, *Michigan Catholic*, October 30, 1958.

5. So wrote H. W. Dierecke, in an (unidentified) Youngstown area paper in Febru-

ary, 1926; and the Rev. Patrick J. Kenny, in the Baltimore *Catholic Review*, around the same time. Clippings in the B. McFadden collection.

6. Obituary, *Michigan Catholic*, October 30, 1958.

7. Transcript of record, courtesy of the Rev. Stephen Virgulin, September 29, 1965; also *Who Was Who?*

8. Most Rev. Joseph P. Hurley to the present writer, St. Augustine, Florida, June 2, 1966. Archbishop Hurley was later secretary to Mooney in India and Japan.

9. Michael J. Hynes, *History of the Diocese of Cleveland* (Cleveland, 1953), p. 285; the newspaper articles and B. McFadden transcripts noted above; and Most Rev. Floyd L. Begin (one of his former students at Cathedral Latin School) to the present writer, Oakland, California, April 15, 1966.

10. *Detroit News*, March 4, 1946.

11. Robert F. McNamara, *The American College in Rome* (Rochester, N. Y., 1956), pp. 507-08.

12. *Ibid.*, p. 760.

13. Edward Mooney to Mary Mooney Moore, Rome, January 11, 1926, photocopy in the B. McFadden collection.

14. *Acta Apostolicae Sedis,* 20 (1928): 129-34: 21 (1929): 337-41.

15. *Michigan Catholic,* October 10, 1958.

16. *Acta Apostolicae Sedis,* 28 (1936): 406.

17. *CE,* Supplement II, "Korea"; London *Tablet,* 151 (1931): 401-02; *CC,* September 7, 1933.

18. *AANY,* X-25: Mooney to "Caro mio" (probably Father John J. Casey, secretary to Cardinal Hayes), Youngstown, September 26, 1933; recipient to Mooney, New York, September 27, 1933.

19. For the installation, see *CC,* October 12, 19, 1933; *DC,* October 12, 13, 1933. The coat of arms for Mooney was designed in time for the installation by the heraldic expert, Pierre de Chaignon La Rose, who also designed arms for the Diocese itself, which had hitherto lacked its own blazon. The diocesan shield had a silver ground on which was mounted a red "saltire" or "St. Andrew's cross," made "lozenged" or diamond-shaped at the crossing of the bars, so as to accommodate a silver crescent at that spot. The Archbishop's arms comprised a green holly-tree (from the Irish arms of the Mooney family) on a silver ground. But in the uppermost part of the shield, on a gold field, was the red Orsini rose— a reference to the North American College in Rome. When the two blazons, diocesan and personal, were combined to signify Mooney's position as bishop of Rochester, the Rochester arms occupied the left half of the shield, the Mooney arms, the right. Because he had the title of archbishop, the ecclesiastical hat that surmounted the shield had ten rather than six tassels; and the processional cross above it had two bars rather than the single bar of the episcopal cross.

20. *CC,* August 8, 15, 1935. Preacher at the dedication was Most Rev. Theophil Matulionis (1873-1962), one of the heroes of the Lithuanian Church. Pastor in Petrograd (now Leningrad, Russia) during the early years of the Soviet regime, he was imprisoned by the Soviets 1922-1925. When released, he was secretly consecrated a bishop in Petrograd on February 9, 1929, but soon rearrested and imprisoned 1929-1933. After his term, he went to Lithuania, where he became bishop of Kaishiadorys. But he was again imprisoned by the Russians from 1946 to 1957, and from 1958 to his death in 1962. See the *Tablet* (London), September 1, 1962.

21. This new crypt was dedicated on June 19, 1938 (*CC,* June 9, 23, 1938). Incidental details in this account, as well as many other details regarding the acts and views of Mooney were kindly furnished by Most Rev. Lawrence B. Casey.

22. The Archbishop sent some of his own men to European seminaries to become better versed in their ancestral languages. In 1936 he selected Father Alexander Stec, already ordained, to study Polish at the Jagello University in Krakow; and a seminarian, Leo J. Matuszewski, to spend his last seminary year at Posnan, Poland. (*CC,* August 20, 1936). In 1937, two other Rochester seminarians of Polish extraction were sent to finish their course at the Posnan seminary: John E. Cieslinski and Valentine A. Jankowiak. In 1935, the Archbishop had sent two Rochesterians of Italian background to finish their last theological year at the seminary of Anagni, Italy: Francis Cristantielli and Albert L. Simonetti.

23. Two of these were priests of the Diocese of Springfield, Mass.: Joseph Clifford Fenton, S.T.D., who taught Special Dogma and Patrology (1935-1938); and William F. Allen, S.T.D., who taught Moral Theology and Canon Law (1936-1940). The third was Henry Dillon, Ph.D., S.T.D., S.S.L., of Kilmore Diocese, Ireland, who taught Scripture (1935-1938).

24. *CC,* November 30, 1933; I. Frank Mogavero to the present writer, Niagara Falls, N. Y., February 25, 1966.

25. *CC,* October 3, 1935; *CC* Golden Jubilee edition supplement, 1939, p. 83; and data kindly furnished by Very Rev. Chester Nowicki, S.V.D., 1967.

26. *ARD,* Chancery files, St. John Fisher file, has a copy of the agreement.

27. *Synodus Roffensis Quinta,* Rochester, N. Y., 1935.

28. *ARD,* Mooney Papers.

29. McQuaid established a clergy fund financed by quotas levied upon individual diocesan priests and the parishes (II Synod, 1875; statute #211); but abuses forced its discontinuance in 1881 (*McQuaid,* 2: 201-

04). Hickey prescribed the quota of $15.00 in 1914 (III Synod, statute #182). For the beginnings of the Clergy Relief Society, see Joseph S. Cameron, "History of the Clergy Relief Society", typescript in the files of the Society. For additional information the present writer is indebted to the Rev. Joseph W. Dailey.

30. *CC,* June 25, 1936.

31. St. Bernard's Seminary Archives, Notebook of Msgr. James J. Hartley: Ph.D. examination of April 28, 1914; *Liber Status Alumnorum,* II:77, for S.T.L. examination of May 16, 1916.

32. For Bishop Foery's life and Rochester activities, see: *DC,* June 2, 1937; August 19, 1937; *CC,* June 3, 1937, August 19, 1937; Gerald T. Brennan, *One Hundred Years of Grace: St. Bridget's Church, Rochester,* 1954, pp. 41-43; [Lawrence Palumbos], *Golden Jubilee, Our Lady of Mt. Carmel Church,* 1959, pp. 21-26; [P. J. Flynn], *Golden Jubilee History, Holy Rosary Parish,* 1939, pp. 62-68. The other two episcopal members of the "famous Class of 1916" of St. Bernard's Seminary were: Matthew F. Brady (1893-1959), bishop of Burlington (1938-1944), and of Manchester (1944-1959); and John J. Boylan (1889-1953), bishop of Rockford (1942-1953).

33. Sister Gabriel Blasi to the present writer, Watkins Glen, July 16, 1943.

34. Aaron Abell, "Elementary and Secondary Catholic Education in Rochester," RHSP, 17 (1939): 133-53.

35. *CC,* September 10, 1936.

36. *CC,* October 11, 29, 1934; October 11, 25, 1935.

37. *Shamon, The Aquinas Story,* p. 111.

38. *ARD,* St. John Fisher file, memo.

39. *CC,* August 8, 1937.

40. Chapter 541, Laws of New York State, 1936.

41. Tobin to the bishops, Albany, June 27, 1936. N.Y.S.C.C. files, 110.5. On the subject in general, see *CC,* May 7, 14, 1936.

42. *CC,* September 3, 1936; October 22, 1936; November 5, 1936.

43. *CC,* September 3, 1936.

44. *CC,* January 28, 1937.

45. *CC,* March 18, 1937; April 22, 29, 1937; May 6, 1937.

46. Judd et al. *v.* Board of Education, Town of Hempstead, Nassau Co., 278 N. Y. 200.15 N.E. (2d S.) 576.

47. As noted above, the revised constitution renumbered the articles, so that Article IX, 4 became Article XI, 4. However, the amendment did not touch the difficult clause which forbade state assistance to denominational schools "directly or indirectly." For the amended Education Law, see Laws of New York, 1939, Chap. 465.

48. *CC,* December 26, 1935; December 31, 1936.

49. *CC,* August 15, 1935; September 26, 1935; October 3, 1935.

50. *CC,* June 11, 1936.

51. *CC,* June 14, 1934.

52. *CC,* May 30, 1937.

53. John J. Philips-Edward J. O'Heron, "Martin John Petter, 1875-1938," in *Sheaf* (St. Bernard's Seminary), 1955: pp. 3-12.

54. *CC,* May 14, 1936.

55. *CC,* January 18, 1934.

56. *CC,* March 8, 1934; July 19, 1934; August 9, 1934; August 8, 1935; September 5, 1935; August 20, 1936; September 3, 1936.

57. *CC,* March 1, 1934; July 26, 1934; August 2, 1934; January 30, 1936; February 13, 27, 1936; March 5, 1936.

58. *CC,* May 20, 27, 1937. Mr. Lang's contact with the *Courier* ran through two decades. In the 1940's he wrote a column titled "Back Talk," and another under the pseudonym "Dan Patrick." Information kindly supplied by Mr. Lang.

59. *CC,* October 18, 1934.

60. St. Bernard's Mission Society minutes, pp. 66-67.

61. *CC,* April 16, 1936.

62. *CC,* July 15, 1937.

63. *CC,* October 10, 1935. As a boy, Bishop Ford for several years spent his summers in Scottsville as the guest of

Father Louis A. Lambert, since his father, Austin B. Ford of Brooklyn, owned the *Freeman's Journal,* of which Lambert was editor, 1895-1910. Ford also returned to the Rochester area occasionally as a priest and bishop. (Interview with Miss Monica Kelly, Scottsville, N. Y.) For a popular life of Bishop Ford, see Raymond A. Lane, *Stone in the King's Highway* (New York, 1953).

64. *CC,* October 22, 1936.

65. *SSJR,* pp. 129-31.

66. The data on the Peter Claver Society comes from the following sources: *SSJR,* pp. 129-31; *CC,* February 11, 1936; March 5, 1936; May 13, 1937; June 17, 1937; August 5, 1937; and interviews with Fathers George A. Weinmann, John C. O'Donnell, Eugene H. McFarland; and Sister M. Paulette Ulton, of the Sisters of St. Joseph. When Mr. Elmo Anderson and Father LaFarge came up to address the interracial meeting of March 1, 1936, Father O'Donnell gave Mr. Anderson his own room at St. Patrick's Cathedral Rectory, since it was understood that no local hotel would accept a Negro as guest.

67. Mooney petitioned the Holy See to confer the rank of Knight of St. Gregory on Mr. Finucane. The decoration arrived only after the Archbishop's departure, and was bestowed by Bishop Kearney on April 3, 1939 (*CC,* April 6, 1939). The knighthoods of St. Sylvester with which Archbishop Mooney decorated three Rochester physicians, Drs. George C. Carroll, George M. Growney and Leo F. Simpson in 1934, had been requested by Bishop O'Hern (*CC,* November 1, 1934; and information furnished by Bishop Lawrence B. Casey).

68. *CC,* October 19, 1933.

69. *CC,* July 1, 1939. As director of charities, Father Lambert also succeeded Bishop Foery as diocesan representative on the New York State Catholic Welfare Committee; and the care of the Civilian conservation camps apostolate likewise devolved upon him.

70. *CC,* July 11, 18, 25, 1935; for the flood in Hornell, see W. H. Gottlieb, Claude O. Witze, and David N. Veit, *Flood!,* a pamphlet published by the Hornell Evening Tribune shortly after the disaster.

71. *CC,* September 21, 28, 1933.

72. *CC,* August 10, 1933.

73. *CC,* November 1, 1934.

74. On the CCC in general, see *Encyclopedia Americana,* 27:538c, and the 1943 volume, p. 164; also the *State of New York Conservation Department Annual Reports,* 1935-1942, *passim.* Diocesan details were furnished by the then coordinator of the CCC work, Father John V. Loughlin, and by the following priests who participated in the program: Stanislaus H. Bialaszewski; J. Norman Margrett; Bernard C. Newcomb; and Msgr. Leslie G. Whalen.

75. *ARD,* WPA report, December 21, 1940 (MS); Mrs. Arthur Schneider, President of the Guild, to the present writer, Rochester, May, 1966, plus interviews; *CC,* November 25, 1937. In March, 1937, the Guild and other diocesan groups of Catholic women, under the leadership of Archbishop Mooney, took part in an interdenominational educational program to save the lives of mothers and infants (*CC,* March 4, 1937). This was at least one positive Catholic effort in a field in which the Monroe County Birth Control League was persistently bidding for public support (*CC,* January 16, 23, 1936).

76. For the beginnings, see *CC,* October 25, 1934. The whole story has been told by the Reverend Lawrence A. Gross, in "Holy Family Credit Union, Rochester, New York: A Typical Central Verein Parish Credit Union", 1963 (ARD, MS).

77. The account of the Rochester Catholic Worker group is based largely on a memorandum by one of its original members, Mr. Arthur P. Farren of Rochester, supplemented by interviews with Rev. George C. Vogt, Rev. Benedict Ehmann, and Rev. Eugene H. McFarland. See also: *CC,* January 31, 1935; February 14, 1935; October 27, 1936; November 5, 1936; March 4, 1937; and *CCJ,* April 1, 1965. For the background of the movement, see: Dorothy Day, *The Long Loneliness* (New York, 1952), and *Loaves and Fishes* (New York, 1963; also, Arthur T. Sheehan, *Peter Maurin, Gay Believer* (Garden City, 1959).

78. *CC,* April 12, 1934.

79. *CC,* May 2, 1935.

80. *CC,* March 4, 1937; *ARD,* Boy Scout Committee File, 1934-1936.

81. *CC,* August 15, 1935.

82. *CC,* May 20, 1937, June 3, 1937. Special information on this matter was kindly furnished by Mrs. Irene Bauer and Mrs. Charles Schrandt of the Rochester court of the C. D. of A.

83. *CC,* October 12, 1933; November 2, 1933.

84. *CC,* June 13, 1935.

85. *CC,* October 19, 1933; March 4, 1937.

86. *Our Bishops Speak* (Milwaukee, 1952), pp. 202-05.

87. *CC,* June 21, 28, 1934; December 13, 1934.

88. *CC,* April 26, 1934; May 3, 1934.

89. *CC,* May 31, 1934; June 21, 1934.

90. Daniel A. Lord, S. J., *Played by Ear* (Chicago, 1956), p. 300.

91. *CC,* November 1, 1934.

92. *ARD,* WPA typescript report, C.C.D.

93. *CC,* January 9, 1935.

94. *CC,* March 19, 1936; June 11, 1936.

95. *CC,* February 4, 1937; Rev. Charles Mahoney, report in *Catholic Action* (Washington, D. C.), February, 1937, #2, p. 19.

96. *CC,* July 19, 1934.

97. *CC,* February 7, 1935; August 22, 1935; July 2, 13, 1936; January 21, 1937; and interview with Rt. Rev. Msgr. John M. Ball.

98. *Proceedings of the National Catholic Congress of the C.C.D.* (Paterson, N. J., 1936); reports by F. A. Walsh, O.S.B., in *Catholic Action* (Washington, D. C.), December, 1935, p. 26, and by Edgar Schmiedeler, p. 27; "The Pilgrim," column "With Scrip and Staff," in *America* (New York), 54 (1935): 111-12; (*CC,* October 17, 24, 31, 1935;) and recollections of Msgr. John M. Ball and Msgr. John M. Duffy.

99. *CC,* August 23, 1934. Cf. "An Immigrant Group's Interest," etc. *American Historical Review,* 73 (1967) 367-379.

100. *CC,* October 18, 1934.

101. *CC,* May 21, 1936.

102. *CC,* November 26, 1936; December 3, 1936; Mooney's address, "Industry's Great Need: Cooperation not Competition," was printed in *Catholic Action* (Washington, D. C.), January, 1937, pp. 9-10.

103. *AANY,* X-22: Hayes to E. Gibbons, telegram (copy), New York, March 24, 1934; Gibbons to Hayes, Albany, March 27, 1934.

104. *CC,* January 24, 1935.

105. *CC,* February 4, 11, 25, 1937; March 4, 11, 1937; interview with Bishop Gibbons, August 27, 1958. When the battle was renewed in 1938, Father Gerald C. Lambert, as diocesan representative of the N.Y.S.C.W.C. led the fight in the Diocese. *CC,* January 20, 27, 1938; February 17, 1938. The passage of the federal Fair Labor Standards Act in 1938, by regulating child labor on an interstate basis, rendered a constitutional amendment unnecessary.

106, For Father Groden, see *CC,* August 29, 1935; October 10, 1925; December 17, 1936; February 22, 1940 (obituary); February 29, 1940 (editorial).

107. Interview, February 2, 1965.

108. Interview with Msgr. Charles F. Shay, April 18, 1958.

109. *CC,* November 22, 1934.

110. Father Owen B. McGuire, a retired Rochester priest who had long lived in Spain (Majorca), wrote for the *Courier* a series of percipient articles on the Spanish conflict. In the issue of August 6, 1936, he prophesied: "When the smoke of battle lifts and the ruins can be seen, the character of the forces of anarchy and communism to which the Left Wing Republicans practically handed over the government will be revealed."

111. Protests against the Mexican oppression were being solicited from individual parishes at the end of 1934 (see *CC,* November 22, 1934), but were subsequently not sent because of new developments (so says the parish MS history of Sacred Heart Church, Perkinsville, N.Y.). For the bishops' protest of May 1, 1935, see *CC,* May 9, 1935, and *Our Bishops Speak* (Milwaukee, 1952), pp. 307-09. For the Montezuma Seminary, see *CC,* August 27, 1936; and James M. Powers, *Memoirs of the Seminary of Montezuma* (Erie, Pa., 1953), pp. 213-14.

112. *CC,* March 4, 1937.

113. *Catholic Transcript* (Hartford, Conn.), December 12, 1965.

114. *Michigan Catholic* (Detroit, Mich.), October 30, 1958.

115. *CC*, April 12, 1934.

116. *CC*, May 13, 1937; recollections of Bishop Lawrence B. Casey.

117. *ARD*, St. Patrick's Cathedral Property file: text of agreement, July 31, 1937; Sulzer to Mooney, July 27, 1937; Mooney to Cicognani, July 31, 1937.

118. *ARD*, St. Patrick's Cathedral Property File, Hart to Bishop Kearney, Rochester, August 17, 1937 (copy).

119. *ARD*, St. Patrick's Cathedral Property file, Minutes of Consultors, August 23, 1937; M. K. Robinson to Hart, September 8, 1937; photostats of checks. See also *CC*, August 12, 27, 1937, and September 2, 9, 16, 1937; *DC*, August 24, 1937, September 13, 1937. A tablet on the Platt Street-Plymouth Avenue corner of the Camera Works wing marks the site of the old cathedral. It was placed by Musa Caravan No. 25, the Rochester branch of the K. of C. social affiliate, the Order of the Alhambra. Archbishop Mooney had wanted to use Blessed Sacrament Church as the pro-cathedral, and for that purpose to extend its sanctuary back towards Rutgers Street. However, the pastor, Msgr. Thomas F. Connors, advised against it, since zoning laws protected every foot of the lots facing on Rutgers Street, and any encroachment on this strictly residential street would surely have been contested in court (Interview with the late Msgr. Connors).

120. *Detroit News*, October 25, 1958; *CC*, October 31, 1958 and November 7, 1958. See also Mooney biography in *NCE*.

121. *America* (New York), 100 (1959): 158.

122. *CCJ*, November 7, 1958.

CHAPTER THIRTEEN

BISHOP KEARNEY AND WORLD WAR II

1. Radio plea, *Un'Ora Grave*, August 24, 1939, in *Principles for Peace*, N.C.W.C. (Washington, D.C., 1943), No. 1377.

2. He was named to the see of Rochester on July 31, 1937, according to the papal bull of appointment: *CC*, October 28, 1937.

3. *CC*, October 28, 1937.

4. Details on his early life and Utah career were kindly furnished to the writer by Bishop Kearney.

5. Bishop Kearney designed his own arms, incorporating references to the Blessed Virgin and St. Francis Xavier. The upper part of the shield, with a blue ground, bears the gold monogram of Mary surmounted by a gold crown. The lower section has a black ground (the darkness of paganism) into which Xavier (a surpliced arm, in silver) brought the faith (a gold cross in his hand) and the message of hope (a silver star to the right of the cross). This was combined to form the right half of his Rochester episcopal arms. The left side, of course, bore the diocesan arms designed in 1933 by Pierre Chaignon la Rose, the background now changed from silver to gold. From the start, Bishop Kearney had as his heraldic motto "In te Domine speravi" ("In Thee have I hoped, O Lord"). It was St. Francis Xavier's dying utterance; curiously enough, these were also the dying words of St. John Fisher, whom the Holy See, at the request of Bishop Kearney, later named patron of the Diocese of Rochester.

6. On the transfer of the Cathedral appointments, see *CC*, September 16, 1937. On the installation, see: *CC*, November 11, 18, 1937; *DC*, November 10, 11, 12, 1937; *TU*, November 9, 10, 11, 1937.

7. For the Elmira visit, *CC*, March 17, 1938; for the Auburn visit, *CC*, March 24, 1938.

8. *CC*, March 24, 1938.

9. *CC*, May 12, 1938.

10. *CC*, January 6, 1938.

11. *CC*, October 6, 13, 20, 27, 1938.

12. *CC*, November 17, 1938.

13. Labor Day Mass, *CC*, September 8, 1938; Donnelly, *CC*, January 13, 1938; Msgr. John Lee, *CC*, April 25, 1940.

14. *CC,* September 5, 19, 26, 1940.

15. *CC,* November 9, 16, 1939; March 21, 1940; October 23, 1941; October 7, 1943; and recollections of Msgr. Francis B. Burns and Father George C. Vogt.

16. *CCJ,* February 14, 1946.

17. *CC,* October 23, 30, 1941.

18. *CC,* October 31, 1940; November 7, 1940.

19. *CC,* December 2, 1943.

20. *CC,* June 9, 23, 1938.

21. *CC.* August 28, 1941; for examples of national publicity, see Martin Abramson, "Priest Within Cold Prison Walls," in *Pageant,* February-March, 1948, pp. 115-19; John Gainfort, "Father Lane's Gang," in *Saturday Evening Post,* October 17, 1953, pp. 38-39+.

22. *CC,* May 9, 1940; *ARD,* Francis J. Lane, "Religious Program at Elmira Reformatory" (MS); also Francis J. Lane, *Twenty Years in a Reformatory* (Elmira, 1934).

23. *DC,* November 11, 1937.

24. *CC,* June 25, 1942.

25. *CC,* June 13, 1940; September 25, 1941.

26. William F. Kelley, S.D.B., to the present writer, New Rochelle, N.Y., January 11, 1967, on the Salesian school proposal. For Father Morotti, see his obituary, *CC,* December 12, 1958. Morotti had been a pupil of Don Rua, who succeeded St. John Bosco, the founder of the Salesian Fathers. After a successful sales career for an art and metalcraft company in South America, he fulfilled a long desire to study for the priesthood, entering St. Bernard's Seminary, Rochester, in 1935 at the age of 55, and receiving priestly ordination in 1938 from Bishop Kearney.

27. *CC,* October 3, 17, 1940; November 14, 1940; December 19, 1940.

28. *SSJR,* 136-38; *CC,* July 30, 1942.

29. Commemorative parish booklet, *A Silver Candle* (1954), pp. 14-18.

30. *CC,* April 6, 27, 1939.

31. *CC,* June 5, 1941; January 22, 1942;

February 5, 1942; January 14, 1943. *DC,* January 15, 1943.

32. Elizabeth Mary Cocks, *A History of Catholic Institutional Child Care in Rochester 1842-1946.* (unpublished M.A. dissertation, Fordham University, 1947), pp. 60-65. See also *CC,* June 25, 1943.

33. *CC,* July 31, 1941.

34. *CC,* June 13, 20, 1940.

35. *CC,* April 25, 1940.

36. *CC,* April 3, 1941. In November, 1937, Mrs. Thomas N. Hepburn, a national leader of the Birth Control movement, gave an address in Elmira in which she attacked the Catholic Church and clergy for their opposition to the cause. An area Catholic Action committee was promptly formed, and on November 26, 1937, presented a counter-lecture delivered by the Catholic scholar, Father Ignatius J. Cox, S.J. (*CC,* November 11, 1937; December 2, 1937.) The opening of public birth control clinics elsewhere in the Diocese in the ensuing years occasioned Bishop Kearney's strong pastoral letter.

37. *CC,* August 18, 1938.

38. For the Christmas pageant, see *CCJ,* December 14, 1951. During the past few decades, the annual Rochester St. Patrick's Day Banquet, traditionally attended by the bishops of Rochester, has been sponsored by the Knights of Equity (1895), whose Council #10 was established in Rochester in 1935. Associated with the Knights is their auxiliary, the Daughters of Erin, organized in 1950. (Information kindly furnished by Mr. Patrick J. Murphy and Mrs. Florence O'Connell). The older Irish-American fraternal society, the Ancient Order of Hibernians, has also presented St. Patrick's Balls in recent years. Since 1948, their organization has likewise sponsored an annual John Barry Dinner (*CCJ,* February 8, 1952; March 7, 1952).

39. *CC,* February 19, 1942, and recollections of the Rev. George A. Weinmann. The Bishop was also pleased when a Jesuit Father, bearing back from Japan to Rome the Roman relic of the arm of St. Francis Xavier (which had been taken east for the quatercentenary of Xavier's Japanese apostolate) stopped in Rochester October 27-29, 1949, and exposed the relic for veneration at St. Bernard's Seminary, St. Patrick's, and St. Francis Xavier churches (*CC,* Sep-

tember 7, 1949; October 27, 1949; November 4, 1949).

40. *CCJ*, September 29, 1950.

41. *CC*, January 4, 1940. Akin to this was his annual blessing of the babies at SS. Peter and Paul Church, Elmira (*CCJ*, April 6, 20, 1951).

42. *CC*, September 25, 1941; March 19, 1942; May 21, 1942; *CCJ*, April 21, 1950; June 23, 1950. Notre Dame Retreat opened in its handsome new buildings on Canandaigua Lake in January, 1967. Architects of the new retreat house were Ribson and Roberts of Rochester.

43. *ARD*, "Historical Sketch of the Dominican Monastery" (Elmira, New York), MS contributed by the nuns. The pioneer nuns were Mother M. Teresa of the Infant Jesus, O.P. (Florence Keleher), prioress; Mother Mary of the Blessed Sacrament, O.P. (Nora Glynn), subprioress; Mother Mary of the Assumption, O.P. (Genevieve Conrad); Sister M. Clare of the Crown of Thorns, O.P. (Eleanor Russer); Sister M. Albert of Jesus Crucified, O.P. (Loretta Hallinen); Sister Mary of the Immaculate Heart, O.P. (Agnes Russer); Sister M. Joseph of the Infant Jesus, O.P. (Mary Regan); and Sister M. Consolata of the Sorrowful Mother, O.P. (Antoinette Syracuse). Four of these nuns had originally belonged to the Rochester Diocese.

44. *ARD*, circular to Diocese, August 15, 1948; *CCJ*, August 12, 1948. On the occasion of his tenth anniversary as bishop of Rochester, Bishop Kearney had authorized First Saturday devotions in honor of Our Lady (*CCJ*, October 23, 1947).

45. *CC*, February 5, 1942.

46. *CC*, June 16, 1938; August 1, 1940; October 30, 1941.

47. McKinney's *Consolidated Laws of New York*, Sect. 625B, Article 23. The law was threatened by the U.S. Supreme Court Decision in the case of McCollum *v*. Board of Education, 333 U.S. 203 (1948); but the threat was offset by the same Court's ruling in the case of Zorach *v*. Clauson, 343 U.S. 306 (1952).

48. *CC*, April 10, 1941.

49. *ARD*, John F. Gormley, "The Legion of Mary in the Diocese of Rochester, 1939-1956", MS; also *CC*, December 14, 21, 1939; and information from Msgri.

George W. Eckl and George J. Schmitt, and from Miss Marguerite McCarthy, all of Rochester. Statistics on the Legion in 1967 were kindly furnished by Rev. James Marvin, diocesan director.

50. *CC*, December 23, 1937.

51. *CC*, November 27, 1941.

52. Cf. *CC*, December 23, 1937; May 16, 1940, regarding the protests of Holy Rosary parish, Rochester. A cooperative effort in Corning in 1938 was successful (*CC*, March 31, 1938). But an attempt made at Auburn the same year failed (*CC*, July 7, 1938).

53. *CC*, April 5, 20, 27, 1939; May 4, 1939; June 22, 1939; July 31, 1939; November 9, 1939. Father Edmund A. Rawlinson had already sponsored a similar drive, on an interfaith basis, in Corning (*CC*, April 28, 1938; May 5, 1938); and in Auburn the Holy Name Society had been alerted to the same problem.

54. *CC*, March 7, 1940.

55. *CC*, November 12, 1942; December 10, 1942.

56. *CC*. August 3, 1944. A Catholic Men's Luncheon Club had been formed in Corning even before the Rochester First Friday Luncheon Club; but the Corning meetings were apparently not connected with the First Fridays. (*CC*, January 30, 1942). A First Saturday Communion and Breakfast, in honor of the Immaculate Heart of Mary, began in Rochester in 1945 and was taken over by the D.C.C.W. as managers in 1950. (Information kindly provided by Miss Mary Hinchey.) There was also a First Saturday Club at Elmira, which most likely began a little later (*CCJ*, May 2, 1952).

57. For the Clarissa Street house, see *CC*, August 14, 1941; October 23, 1941; November 13, 1941. Further information comes from Rt. Rev. Msgr. John S. Randall.

58. On the closing of the St. Peter Claver Center, see *CC*, September 29, 1944. Additional data comes from the Rev. George A. Weinmann.

59. For the Mother Cabrini Circle, see *CCJ*, May 14, 1965; *ARD*, request circular of the Circle, 1966. For the Knights of Peter Claver, see *CCJ*, May 13, 27, 1948; January 6, 1949; February 17, 1949. For the Selma Mission, see *CC*, September 19,

1940; June 22, 1944; August 24, 31, 1944. A smaller ethnic minority in the Rochester Diocese is that of Catholic Indians. Nevertheless, a Rochester Iroquois of long Catholic antecedents became, on June 4, 1945, the second Iroquois ever ordained to the priesthood. He was Father George Michael White, O.M.I., the son of Mr. and Mrs. Peter A. White of Rochester. Preacher at his first solemn Mass at St. Patrick's Church, June 24, 1945, was Father Michael Jacobs, S.J., chaplain of the St. Regis Reservation, the first Iroquois to become a Catholic Priest (*CCJ*, June 14, 1945).

60. *CC*, October 28, 1937; November 4, 11, 18, 1937.

61. *CC*, January 27, 1938; February 24, 1938.

62. For further Blackfriars activities, see *CC*, August, 1938, through January, 1941, *passim.*

63. *CC*, April 4, 1940.

64. *CC*, March 24, 1938; November 17, 1938.

65. *CC*, February 29, 1940.

66. E. G., Auburn's first Interfaith Dinner, *CC*, May 9, 1940; and the Rotary Brotherhood commemoration at Elmira, where Father Leo G. Schwab gave an address (*CC*, February 11, 1943).

67. *ARD*, Kearney Papers, S. S. K. Yeaple to Kearney on the budget fund, Federation of Churches and Council of Church Women, Rochester, March 29, 1939; Lawrence B. Casey to S. S. K. Yeaple, Rochester, April 3, 1939 (copy).

68. The Rev. Edward Lodge Curran of Brooklyn spoke on the Taylor topic at Holy Rosary Church in 1940 (*CC*, March 7, 1940); and there was some controversy on the same point in Elmira in the following month (*CC*, April 25, 1940).

69. *DC*, January 10, 1939; February 8, 1939.

70. George N. Shuster, "Some Reflections on Spain," *Commonweal* (New York), 25, (1937): 625-27; *Catholic Worker* (New York), December 1936, etc.

71. *CC*, April 15, 22, 29, 1937.

72. For the Spanish Pastoral, see *CC*, September 2, 9, 16, 1937; the Cordovani article, *CC*, January 19, 1939; the tussle with *Life, CC*, July 15, 1937; August 12, 1937; the pro-embargo petitions, January 12, 19, 26, 1939.

73. *CC*, May 13, 20, 1937; January 26, 1939.

74. *CC*, April 21, 1938. See J. de Bivort de la Saudée, *Communism and Anti-Religion*, 1917-1937 (New York, 1937), p. 99.

75. *CC*, April 20, 27, 1939. For the Spanish Refugees Relief, see Eugene Lyons, *The Red Decade* (New York, 1941), p. 280.

76. *ARD*, Spanish Civil War file, Bergan clippings and correspondence.

77. *DC*, December 10, 1938.

78. *CC*, December 22, 1938.

79. *CC*, August 31, 1939.

80. For diocesan peace prayers, see, e.g., *CC*, September 29, 1938. For the memorial requiem, see *CC*, February 16, 1939. When Pius XI died on February 10th, Bishop Kearney sent to the Holy See an expression of Rochester diocesan sympathy. Cardinal Pacelli replied with a grateful cablegram. At the Rochester memorial Mass, Bishop Kearney used the chalice of the present writer, which Pope Pius XI had used at Mass on November 1, 1936.

81. For instance, *CC*, March 30, 1939; April 27, 1939; September 7, 1939; December 3, 1939.

82. *CC*, April 4, 1940.

83. For example, *CC*, July 4, 1940; November 11, 1940; May 1, 1941; October 2, 1941.

84. Chaplain Arnold (1881-1965) was a priest of the diocese of Fort Wayne, and a graduate of St. Bernard's Seminary, Rochester (1908). He was the first Army chaplain to attain to the rank of brigadier and major general. Just prior to his retirement, he was named Titular Bishop of Phocaea, and auxiliary to Cardinal Spellman, Military Ordinary for the U.S.A. The Cardinal consecrated him on October 11, 1945.

85. *CC*, October 31, 1940.

86. Father Walter J. Donoghue, a Rochester diocesan priest, had been a chaplain in the regular army since World War I.

87. *CC,* June 19, 1941; September 4, 1941.

88. *Evening Tribune,* Hornell, N. Y., December 13, 23, 1941. Information kindly provided by Miss Josephine FitzGerald of Hornell.

89. *CC,* December 11, 1941.

90. *Our Bishops Speak* (Milwaukee, 1952), p. 350-52.

91. *CC,* April 30, 1942.

92. These lists are preserved in *ARD.*

93. *CC,* August 3, 1944 (O'Connell); *CC,* November 12, 1942, Maryrose Barron byline (Moriarty).

94. *CC,* February 10, 1944 (Speciale); and *CG,* pp. 202-03 (Sweet).

95. *TU,* November 11, 1964, Douglas Kerr byline.

96. *CC,* October 26, 1944.

97. Information from the Sabini family.

98. Admiral Chanler to the present writer, Geneseo, N.Y., January 7, 1966.

99. Data supplied by Department of the Navy, HQ. U.S. Military Corps, Washington, D.C., July 1, 1965. See also Robert Sherrod, *History of the Marine Corps Aviation in World War II* (Washington, 1952), passim.

100. *CC,* March 9, 1944.

101. *CCJ,* July 26, 1945.

102. LeBrun: *CC,* June 29, 1944; *CCJ,* May 17, 1945. Lent: *CCJ,* May 17, 1945; December 6, 1945.

103. *CCJ,* September 6, 1945.

104. *CCJ,* November 14, 1946.

105. *CC,* July 22, 1943; February 1, 1945.

106. Information from the Fischette family; see also Raymond F. Toliver and Trevor Constable, *Fighting Aces* (New York, 1965), p. 309.

107. *CCJ,* September 16, 1945.

108. Pomponio: *DC,* May 29, 1965; Setteneri: *CCJ,* June 7, 1945.

109. *CC,* September 16, 1943; November 30, 1944.

110. *CC,* November 25, 1943.

111. *CCJ,* August 2, 1945.

112. *CCJ,* January 17, 1946. WAC Corporal Margaret Hastings of Owego became the object of national interest as one of the survivors of the wreck of an Army transport plane which in May, 1945, crashed in unexplored "Shangri-La Valley" in New Guinea. Paratroopers rescued the surviving group only fifty-seven days later. Corporal Hastings later testified that during those trying days prayer was her chief support. She was given a hero's welcome when she returned to Owego (*CCJ,* July 5, 12, 26, 1945; August 14, 1945; September 27, 1945; December 27, 1945. See also *DC* articles, July 22 to August 8, 1945).

113. The following forty-two diocesan priests were Army or Navy chaplains during the period of hostilities: John F. Albert (A); W. Darcy Bolger (A); Donald M. Cleary (A); Paul F. Cuddy (A); Walter J. Donoghue (A); Daniel W. Fraher (N); William J. Gaynor (A); Joseph G. Gefell (A); Austin B. Hanna (A); Bernard C. Hanna (N); John S. Hayes (A); Elmer Heindl (A); Raymond G. Heisel (A); Gerald G. Kelly (N); Leonard A. Kelly (N); John B. Kleintjes (N); James C. Lane (A); John V. Loughlin (N); John S. Maloney (A); Thomas J. Manley (A); Leo J. Matuszewski (A); John L. Maxwell (N); Donald J. Murphy (A); J. Emmett Murphy (A); Ralph F. Neagle (A); Bernard C. Newcomb (A); William F. Nolan (N); Michael J. O'Brien (A); William J. O'Brien (A); John P. O'Malley (A); Francis J. Pegnam (N); John A. Reddington (N); Thomas M. Reddington (N); David B. Singerhoff (A); Joseph J. Sullivan (A); Francis H. Vogt (A); Edward J. Waters (A); Francis Waterstraat (A); John S. Whalen (N); Leslie G. Whalen (N); John K. Wheaton (N); John F. Woloch (N). Religious priests from the Diocese were: John J. Brennan, C.SS.R. (A); Gerald J. Kuhn, C.SS.R. (A); Thomas W. Tobin, C.SS.R. (A); and John F. Onorato, C.S.B. (N).

114. *Evening Leader* (Corning, N.Y.), June 16, 18, 1945.

115. *CC,* May 28, 1942.

116. *CC,* May 11, 1944 (Southern Tier ed.)

117. *CCJ,* February 28, 1946.

118. *CC,* February 12, 1942.

119. *CC,* July 30, 1942.

120. *CC,* March 11, 1943.

121. *CC,* January 15, 1942.

122. *CCJ,* May 24, 1945.

123. *ARD,* Arthur P. Farren, MS sketch of Rochester Catholic Worker history.

124. *CC,* December 11, 1941.

125. *CC,* January 15, 1942.

126. *CC,* July 30, 1942; October 8, 1942.

127. *CCJ,* May 10, 1945.

128. *CC,* December 24, 1942; January 17, 1943.

129. *CC,* January 28, 1943; April 15, 1943.

130. *CC,* January 11, 1945; *CCJ,* April 4, 1946.

131. *CC,* August 6, 1942; June 24, 1943.

132. *CC,* October 14, 1943.

133. *CC,* April 6, 1944; January 11, 1945.

134. Christmas: *CC,* December 31, 1942; also Bishop Casey's recollections of Bishop Kearney, *CCJ,* October 22, 1965. Holidays: *CC,* June 1, 1944; July 8, 1943.

135. *CC,* July 6, 1944.

136. In 1943, 500 Air Cadets connected with Syracuse University were lodged in Auburn, where the local Catholics gave them a hospitable welcome (*CC,* August 26, 1943; November 4, 1943).

137. *CC,* June 15, 1944.

138. *CC,* June 8, 1944.

139. *APO #50,* January 15, 1945. This was a mimeographed news bulletin edited each month at the Chancery (50 Chestnut Street) by Father Lawrence B. Casey, and mailed to each diocesan chaplain. Usually there was a greeting in each issue from Bishop Kearney. There is a bound file in *ARD.* Several diocesan pastors sent their weekly parish bulletin to all parish servicemen.

140. *CC,* April 12, 1945.

141. *CCJ,* May 10, 1945; *APO #50,* May 15, 1945; *DC* May 8, 9, 1945.

142. *CCJ,* August 8, 16, 1945; *APO #50,* September 15, 1945; *DC,* August 15, 1945.

143. *APO #50,* September 15, 1945.

144. *CCJ,* December 6, 1945; January 10, 1946.

145. *CCJ,* November 28, 1946; January 29, 1947. Also, *ARD,* circular giving the decade's statistics on the drives, November 11, 1958.

146. *CCJ,* February 24, 1949; February 10, 1950.

147. *CCJ,* November 27, 1947; March 3, 1949; June 16, 1949. Also a MS memo, in *ARD,* by Leo P. Saeum, "40 Years of Catholic Kolping Society (Inc.) in Rochester, N.Y."

148. *CCJ,* March 11, 1948.

149. *CCJ,* June 16, 1949.

150. *CCJ,* January 20,1949.

151. Sisters of Mercy: *CCJ,* August 15, 1948. Carmelites: obituary of Mother Ignatius Town (1889-1965), *CCJ,* February 4, 1965.

152. *CCJ,* June 30, 1949.

153. *CCJ,* October 11, 1945. Meanwhile, in May, 1946, disastrous floods in the Southern Tier caused vast damage, including $350,000.00 injury in Elmira to St. Joseph's Hospital, SS. Peter and Paul Church, St. Patrick's and St. Mary's Schools. Bishop Kearney took up a diocesan-wide collection to aid those institutions (*CCJ,* June 5, 12, 1946).

154. *ARD,* report "Italian Clothing War Relief"; *CC,* May 11, 18, 1944; June 15, 1944; May 3, 1945. On the letter-writing campaign, see *CCJ,* March 25, 1948; April 1, 15, 22, 1948.

155. *CCJ,* December 11, 1947.

156. *CCJ,* December 9, 1948; January 6, 1949.

157. *CCJ,* December 2, 1948; June 16, 1949.

158. *CCJ,* October 6, 1949. From 1948 to 1951, the tailoring firm of Hickey-Freeman gave employment to some 300 DP's (especially Poles, Lithuanians, Ukrainians, Latvians and Russians) in tailoring jobs. (See "Catholic Charities Review" in *CCJ,*

April 27, 1951). In May, 1951, St. Bernard's Seminary welcomed as a domestic staff nine nuns of the Institute of the Blessed Virgin Mary (*CCJ*, May 4, 1951). Six were German, three Rumanian; all had several months before being expelled from Rumania. The Sisters remained at St. Bernard's until the summer of 1958, when circumstances obliged them to withdraw. (The Sisters of St. Joan of Arc, introduced at St. Bernard's by Bishop O'Hern, had left June 14, 1947, on the expiration of their contract. Others of these Sisters continued for a while longer in charge of the St. Andrew's Faculty House and the Bishop's House.)

159. *CCJ*, December 27, 1945; February 14, 28, 1946.

160. *CCJ*, October 24, 1946.

161. Tien: *CCJ*, April 18, 1946; Preysing: *CCJ*, February 20, 1947. One who greeted Cardinal von Preysing at the public reception was Mrs. William Meilich of Rochester, a native of Germany who had been a "flower girl" at the Cardinal's first Mass as a priest in 1912.

162. The others honored with domestic prelacies were: Thomas F. Connors; William J. Brien (Elmira); George W. Eckl; F. William Stauder; John B. Sullivan; William H. McPadden (Geneva); John A. Conway (Auburn); William E. Cowen (Auburn); Edmund A. Rawlinson (Corning); Francis J. Lane (Elmira Reformatory); Adolfo Gabbani (Auburn); Walter J. Donoghue (U.S. Army); Joseph A. Balcerak; Wilfred T. Craugh (St. Bernard's Seminary); Joseph J. Baierl (St. Bernard's Seminary); Edward J. Byrne (St. Bernard's Seminary); Edward M. Lyons (St. Andrew's Seminary). John S. Randall, James C. McAniff and Gerald C. Lambert were named papal chamberlains. (In 1948, Father John M. Duffy was made a domestic prelate: *CCJ*, May 6, 1948. And on October 28, 1949, Father Benedetto Maselli of Rochester was made a papal chamberlain at the request of Bishop Epimenio Giannico of Trivento, his native diocese, *CCJ*, December 30, 1949.)

163. Father Richard Burns was named a papal chamberlain on June 26, 1948, and a domestic prelate on October 11, 1953. Father Joseph Sullivan served as a Roman correspondent from 1947 to 1955; and was made a papal chamberlain on December 29, 1952.

164. *CCJ*, March 10, 1949; April 28, 1949; May 19, 26, 1949; June 2, 1949.

165. *DC*, May 30, 1946; June 2, 1946; *Rochester Sun*, May 30, 1946; and recollections of Msgr. John S. Randall.

166. *CCJ*, April 17, 1947; May 1, 1947; and interview with Msgr. Patrick J. Flynn.

167. *CCJ*, October 7, 1948; June 30, 1949.

168. *CCJ*, May 1, 1947.

169. *CCJ*, October 6, 1949.

170. *CCJ*, September 27, 1945; January 31, 1946; February 28, 1946; March 28, 1946; June 3, 1948. On the original proposed site, see *CCJ*, January 31, 1946.

171. Information kindly provided by St. James Mercy Hospital.

172. *CCJ*, August 28, 1947; January 28, 1948; February 26, 1948. In 1947, the President of Hobart and William Smith Colleges, two institutions federated as the University of the Senecas, and conducted at Geneva under Episcopalian auspices, proposed to Father Robert I. Gannon, S.J., the establishment in Geneva of a Jesuit College as a member of the same federation. This would not have infringed on the Basilian contract, since Geneva is forty-five miles from Rochester. But the President died before further steps could be taken, and the proposal was dropped. Robert I. Gannon, S.J., to editor, *America* (New York), 105: 298 (May 20, 1961).

173. *CCJ*, May 5, 1949.

174. *ARD*, Kearney Papers, Bishop Kearney to Mother Catherine McCloskey, Rochester, November 21, 1946 (copy).

175. *CCJ*, February 26, 1948; interview with Msgr. Thomas F. Connors.

176. *CCJ*, June 17, 1948; August 26, 1948; and information kindly furnished by the Rochester Cenacle.

177. *CCJ*, September 12, 1946.

178. *CCJ*, August 25, 1949; September 15, 1949.

179. *CCJ*, October 28, 1948; November 11, 1948; August 25, 1949; December 3, 1949; and information kindly furnished by Fr. De Sales Standerwyck, S.A. Bishop Kearney dedicated a new addition at St.

John's on October 3, 1966. Like the Watkins Friars and the other non-contemplative religious located in the Diocese, the Atonement Friars have given welcome assistance to the area clergy. The Atonement Friars have been especially active in ecumenical matters—one of their particular apostolates.

180. *CCJ*, July 22, 1948; October 13, 1949.

181. *CCJ*, August 15, 1946; October 31, 1946; November 11, 1946.

182. *CCJ*, August 22, 1946.

183. *CCJ*, February 10, 17, 1949.

184. *CCJ*, October 4, 1945.

185. Robert Magin, "Fifty Years of Scouting," *CCJ*, February 10, 1967.

186. Rally: *CCJ*, October 10, 1946; Pro-Hoover protest: *CCJ*, February 7, 1946.

187. Catholic Information Center: *CCJ*, March 3, 1949. On the Pre-Cana and Cana Conferences, see *CCJ*, October 9, 16, 1947. Further information on these and the Mothers' Circles comes from Mrs. Ronald J. Gledhill of Rochester, President; Father Gerald E. Dunn, and Father Albert J. Shamon. Father Shamon, who had introduced the first Pre-Cana Conference in Rochester proper, also launched the movement in Elmira a few months later (*CCJ*, October 9, 1947; April 6, 1948).

188. On "The Outlaw," see *CCJ*, April 25, 1946; May 23, 1946. On "Forever Amber," see *CCJ*, October 30, 1947; November 6, 27, 1947; May 27, 1948; *DC*, October 30, 1947.

189. On circulation: *CCJ*, May 3, 1945; on the ABC, *CCJ*, May 11, 1944. The name of the paper was changed to *Catholic Courier Journal* with the issue of May 3, 1945. Bishop Kearney appealed for funds to purchase the press and the building at 35-37 Scio Street: first to the faithful in general (circular of July 15, 1947, in *ARD*), then to special benefactors (circular of October 22, 1948, in *ARD*). In this connection the Christopher Press, Inc., was established, with Mr. Martin Q. Moll as general manager, to print the newspaper and do commercial printing. In 1955, Mr. Moll purchased the stock of the corporation, until then held by the Rochester Diocese. (Information kindly supplied by Mr. Moll.)

190. Information kindly provided by Msgr. Joseph A. Cirrincione, pastor of St. Francis of Assisi Church and founder of the Family Rosary for Peace. In connection with this devotion, Msgr. Cirrincione, in 1948, obtained at Fatima a carved wooden duplicate of the statue of Our Lady of Fatima venerated at the Portuguese shrine, and, taking it to Rome, had it blessed by Pope Pius XII. It was then installed in an outdoor shrine at St. Francis of Assisi Church.

191. *CC*, June 11, 1942.

192. *CCJ*, December 25, 1947.

193. *DC*, January 21, 1962; *CCJ*, January 26, 1962.

194. *CCJ*, January 21, 1960.

195. *CCJ*, June 20, 1946 (Dwyer). June 24, 1948, July 1, 1948 (Cuff).

196. Auburn *Citizen Advertiser*, September 12, 1960 (Leo): *CCJ*, January 13, 1956; Elmira *Star Gazette*, January 9, 15, 1956 (Milliken); *CCJ*, March 21, 1958 (Southern Tier ed.) (Miss Muldoon).

197. *CC*, November 2, 1939.

198. *CCJ*, October 23, 1947.

199. *CC*, August 28, 1944.

200. *CCJ*, September 20, 1963.

201. *TU*, August 10, 1966; *DC*, August 11, 1966; *CCJ*, August 19, 1966.

202. *CC*, January 14, 1943.

203. For the Hornby Case, see *CC*, September 21, 1939; the Penn Yan Case, *CC*, October 5, 1939; the Town of Parma Case, *CC*, January 4, 1940; the Town of Ogden Case, *CC*, August 15, 1940. The latter two towns are in Monroe County.

204. Everson *v.* Board of Education, 330, U.S. 1 (1947); *CCJ*, February 13, 1947.

205. *CCJ*, June 23, 1949; July 28, 1949; August 4, 11, 1949; September 1, 1949. For Bishop Kearney's role, see *CCJ*, June 30, 1949.

206. *The Register* (Denver, Colorado), November 13, 1949.

207. *New York Times*, January 12, 1948. For Pelikan, see *The Register* (Denver, Colorado), August 21, 1966.

208. *CCJ*, January 15, 22, 28, 1948; *DC*, January 16, 27, 1948.

209. *CCJ*, February 26, 1948.

210. *CCJ*, October 10, 17, 1946.

211. *CCJ*, February 3, 1949.

212. *CCJ*, April 10, 1947; *DC*, May 2, 1947.

213. *CCJ*, October 17, 1946; *ARD*, Kearney circulars of October 18, 1948; October 22, 1950.

214. *CCJ*, September 29, 1949.

CHAPTER FOURTEEN:

RENEWAL

1. *CCJ*, January 8, 1954; November 14, 1952; March 2, 1951.

2. *CCJ*, October 5, 1951.

3. *CCJ*, January 15, 1954. Southern Tier edition.

4. *CCJ*, May 18, 1951; September 14, 1951; July 6, 1951.

5. *CCJ*, September 29, 1950; May 11, 1951; June 15, 1951 August 12, 1951; March 14, 1952.

6. Obituary, *CCJ*, October 14, 1960; Korean diary, kindness of Msgr. J. Emmett Murphy.

7. *CCJ*, January 14, 1955; February 14, 1958; August 23, 1963.

8. *CCJ*, January 22, 1954. One of the most prominent priest-victims of the Korean Conflict was Most Rev. Patrick Byrne, M.M. (1888-1950). Apostolic Visitor to Korea at the outbreak of the war, he was taken captive by the North Korean communists and died of ill treatment at Hachangri, North Korea, on November 25, 1950. Bishop Byrne spent most of his boyhood in Auburn, New York, where he was graduated from Holy Family parochial school and attended Auburn High School.

9. *CCJ*, June 1, 1951.

10. *DC*, August 17, 1965.

11. *CCJ*, October 8, 1965.

12. *CCJ*, December 26, 1965.

13. *DC*, August 21, 1965; *TU*, May 5, 1965; *TU*, April 11, 1966; *DC*, April 25, 1967.

14. Gefell: *CCJ*, October 28, 1966; Straub: *CCJ*, July 29, 1966, December 30, 1966; *DC*, May 13, 1966. Between the two wars, on August 24, 1961, a Rochester diocesan Army chaplain was killed in a Greenland helicopter crash while engaged in his official duties. Father Paul J. Lynch (1925-1961) thus became the first Rochester diocesan chaplain to die in the service. Cardinal Francis Spellman attended his funeral at Canandaigua, Father Lynch's boyhood parish. (*CCJ*, September 1, 8, 1961.)

15. *CCJ*, December 6, 1963. On Kennedy see also: *CCJ*, November 11, 1960; January 20, 1961; November 29, 1963. On Thanksgiving, November 29, 1963, Bishop Kearney offered the official memorial Mass for the deceased president.

16. *CCJ*, April 15, 29, 1965; April 22, 1966. Among the interesting data of the census were the following: 86% of the 7-17 age group attended church regularly, and 73% of the age group 18 and upward (many of whom were shut-ins). The average diocesan family, according to the figures, had 2.7 children. Of the children, 79.7% attended Catholic schools or religious instruction. Of those under 18, 98.1% were baptized; of those over 18, 98.3% were baptized.

17. Founder of the Rochester chapter of ACIM was insurance agent Louis A. Valenza (*CCJ*, January 5, 1962). Judge Charles P. Lambiase was active in the work of this federation of Italian societies. By appointment of Bishop Kearney, Father Albert L. Simonetti and Father Gennaro Ventura served successively as priest consultants (*CCJ*, April 6, 1956; August 31, 1962).

18. Obituary, *TU*, July 13, 1965.

19. *CCJ*, August 21, 1953, August 19, 1955; also information kindly provided by Mrs. Virginia Bogdan Pados, Dr. Eugene Horvath, and Mr. Louis Lote.

20. *CCJ*, November 20, 1956.

21. *CCJ*, February 22, 1957.

22. *CCJ*, May 31, 1957.

23. See the January 1959 publication of the Migration Division, Department of Labor, Commonwealth of Puerto Rico, *A Summary of Facts and Figures: 1. In Puerto Rico. 2. Puerto Rican Immigration.*

24. See *Annual Survey of New Construction in Monroe County (Rochester Metropolitan Area)*, published since 1948 by the First Federal Savings and Loan Association of Rochester.

25. Both the Planning Board of the Town of Brighton and its board of appeal, the Brighton Town Board, rejected the re-

quest for permission to erect a church and school on the Drescher estate, on exclusive East Avenue. When the Diocese took the matter to N. Y. State Supreme Court, it lost its appeal both before the Supreme Court proper and before its Appellate Division (1955). Attorneys David Shearer and Porter Chandler then renewed the appeal before the State's highest judicature, the Court of Appeals. In this instance, however, they revised their approach, claiming that the rejection of the zoning variance was an unconstitutional restriction of religious freedom. The American Jewish Congress and the N. Y. State Catholic Welfare Committee filed *amicus curiae* briefs. The seven justices who sat at the hearing voted 6-1 that the action of the Brighton Planning Board was unconstitutional; and the decision, read on July 1, 1956, reversed the previous decisions. On this last appeal, see: Matter of Diocese of Rochester *v.* Planning Board of Brighton, 1956 NY 2nd 508. See also *CCJ*, September 17, 1954; December 3, 1954; March 18, 1955; September 2, 1965; November 18, 1955; January 6, 13, 1956; April 27, 1956; July 13, 1956.

26. In June, 1960, the pastor of St. Patrick's, Owego, Father William J. O'Brien, rented the Lackawanna Railroad Station at Nichols, nine miles southwest of Owego, to serve as a chapel of ease to St. Patrick's. One Mass is offered each Sunday at this "Catholic Chapel," for the convenience of the 100-200 people who live there—a large proportion of them employees of I.B.M. in the Binghamton area.

27. *CCJ*, October 10, 1952.

28. *CCJ*, March 15, 1957; October 20, 27, 1961. A new 54-rank organ, built by Wicks, was ceremoniously dedicated on January 16, 1966. It replaced the organ which had been moved in 1937 from St. Patrick's Cathedral to Sacred Heart. (*CCJ*, January 21, 1966.)

29. *CCJ*, September 21, 1951; and special dedication tabloid, October 10, 1952.

30. *CCJ*, May 18, 1962. The new gymnasium and dormitory buildings were dedicated on January 12, 1964 by Archbishop Egidio Vagnozzi, Apostolic Delegate to the United States. The College conferred an honorary degree upon the Delegate on the occasion of his visit. (*CCJ*, January 17, 1964.)

31. *CCJ*, April 9, 1964.

32. *CCJ*, January 27, 1961.

33. *CCJ*, May 28, 1954; November 3, 1959; February 5, 1960; February 3, 1961; and information kindly supplied by the College.

34. *CCJ*, February 18, 1965; March 4, 1965; October 29, 1965; November 5, 1965; December 3, 1965.

35. *CCJ*, September 12, 1958. For the dedication, see *CCJ*, November 24, 1950; December 1, 1950.

36. *CCJ*, September 3, 1964.

37. *CCJ*, February 1, 1965; March 18, 1965; June 25, 1965; July 16, 1965.

38. *CCJ*, October 3, 17, 24, 31, 1952; November 7, 14, 1952.

39. *CCJ*, September 9, 30, 1955. On earlier stages, see *CCJ*, January 2, 1953; March 2, 1953; June 26, 1953; February 12, 1954.

40. *CCJ*, October 15, 17, 1954.

41. *CCJ*, September 16, 23, 1955.

42. *CCJ*, September 23, 30, 1955.

43. *CCJ*, September 16, 23, 1960; November 14, 18, 1960.

44. *CCJ*, April 26, 1963; May 3, 10, 1963. Holy Cross Fathers were assigned as chaplains to the Holy Cross brothers.

45. Intormation kindly provided by the faculty.

46. *CCJ*, April 15, 1951, May 11, 1951; *ARD*, Timothy G. Weider, "History of the School of the Holy Childhood: Beginnings, 1946-1953," MS, 1964; Sister M. St. Mark, S.S.J., "The Rochester Program for Exceptional Children," *Catholic Charities Review*, (Washington, D. C.), 38 (1954): 142-44.

47. *CCJ*, September 11, 1959.

48. *CCJ*, May 25, 1962.

49. *ARD*, Kearney Papers. Draft of a letter from the Bishop to pastors, June 24, 1952. For 1966, Diocesan School Office data.

50. *CCJ*, May 14, 1965 (Perkinsville). Inner-City changes had already led to the closing of the parish school at Old St. Mary's, Rochester, in 1950.

51. Data kindly furnished by the Diocesan School Office.

52. The "Blaine" article, renumbered XI, 4 in 1938, was again renumbered XI, 3 in 1962.

53. *CCJ*, May 6, 1960; February 16, 1962; April 13, 1962; July 6, 1962.

54. *CCJ*, August 16, 1966.

55. *CCJ*, February 11, 1966; August 16, 1966; September 2, 9, 16, 23, 31, 1966; November 4, 1966. For C.E.F. see *CCJ*, August 6, 1965 and August 5, 1966.

56. After 1955, seminarians were trained in sign language by Father John B. Gallagher, C.SS.R., who as we have seen had charge of the Diocesan work with the deaf. After his death in 1960, certain seminarians continued to cathechize at the Rochester School for the Deaf, under the guidance of one of Father Gallagher's former pupils, Father Thomas Erdle, a Rochester diocesan priest. Bishop Kearney had entrusted the whole diocesan apostolate of the deaf to Father Erdle in succession to Father Gallagher.

57. *CCJ*, October 28, 1966.

58. *CCJ*, January 30, 1953; May 29, 1953.

59. *CCJ*, February 8, 1957; May 24, 1957.

60. *CCJ*, May 14, 1965; and information kindly supplied by the Atonement Sisters.

61. *CCJ*, August 27, 1954.

62. *CCJ*, May 23, 1958.

63. *CCJ*, November 4, 1955; December 21, 1956; March 22, 1957. See also Leo R. Ward, C.S.C., The Living Parish (Notre Dame, Ind., 1959), pp. 84-90. The Fairport School of Religion was featured on the national Catholic Television broadcast, "New Directions, '64" (*CCJ*, February 21, 1964).

64. *CCJ*, March 28, 1958, September 14, 1962; data kindly furnished by the Reverend Walter Nash, O.C.D.; and *ARD*, Gerald T. O'Connor, "Our Lady of the Hill Monastery," 1963.

65. *CCJ*, July 27, 1951, February 15, 1952; and data kindly supplied by the Interlaken friars.

66. The Basilian novitiate, St. Basil's, which occupied a wing of the Basilian residence on Augustine Street, moved to a newly erected house in Pontiac, Michigan, on June 19, 1959 (*CCJ*, February 4, 1955; June 6, 1958; June 26, 1959). On the other hand, the Precious Blood Fathers opened a small minor seminary in a residence at 65 Highland Avenue, Rochester, in 1962. The first rector was Very Rev. Matthew Quaranta, C.PP.S. The students took classes at St. Andrew's Seminary. Bishop Kearney blessed this Precious Blood Seminary on February 23, 1962 (*CC*, March 1, 1963).

67. *CCJ*, December 22, 1950; May 4, 1951; October 5, 1951.

68. *CCJ*, November 13, 1953.

69. *CCJ*, September 23, 1965. See also: M. Gerard McGinley, O.C.S.O., A Trappist Writes Home (Milwaukee, 1960).

70. *CCJ*, October 14, 1955; November 11, 18, 1955; February 5, 12, 1956.

71. See *Our Lady of the Genesee*, published by the Monastery, 1953; also *ARD*, David J. Walker, "The Founding of Our Lady of the Genesee Abbey," MS, 1956.

72. *CCJ*, January 12, 1951; *ARD*, Winfried Kellner, "The Foundation of Mount Saviour Monastery," MS, 1960.

73. *CCJ*, August 21, 1953; October 19, 1953.

74. *CCJ*, January 10, 1958.

75. *CCJ*, September 17, 1964.

76. *CCJ*, February 25, 1965; March 4, 1955; September 13, 1963.

77. *CCJ*, April 30, 1964; June 18, 1964; September 3, 1964.

78. *CCJ*, June 24, 1966.

79. *CCJ*, July 2, 1954.

80. *CCJ*, October 1, 1963; August 27, 1964.

81. *CCJ*, May 20, 1966.

82. *CCJ*, August 27, 1964.

83. The following were recipients of these honors (PC=papal chamberlain; DP = domestic prelate; PA = protonotary apostolic): Charles J. Azzi, consultor

(DP); Edward K. Ball, dean (DP); John M. Ball, dean (DP); Charles V. Boyle, schools superintendent (DP); Francis B. Burns, seminary professor (DP); William Byrne, dean (DP); Joseph A. Cirrincione, Radio Rosary for Peace (PC); Donald M. Cleary, dean (PC,DP); George A. Cocuzzi, chancellor (PC,DP); Maynard A. Connell, rector, St. Andrew's Seminary (DP); Wilfred T. Craugh, rector, St. Bernard's Seminary (DP,PA); James D. Cuffney, dean (PC,DP); Joseph V. Curtin, dean (DP); John F. Duffy, Propagation of the Faith director (DP); D. Gregory Dugan, Auburn prison chaplain (PC); Louis W. Edelman, pastor (DP); Arthur F. Florack, pastor (DP); Patrick J. Flynn, *Courier* editor (PC); Lawrence W. Gannon, dean (DP); Joseph Gefell, pastor (DP); Dennis W. Hickey, Tribunal (PC,DP); Frank J. Hoefen, pastor (DP); Joseph L. Hogan, Rector, Becket Hall (DP); Robert A. Keleher, consultor (DP); Gerald Krieg, Tribunal (PC); Michael Krieg, pastor (DP); Gerald C. Lambert, charities director (PC,DP); Francis W. Luddy, pastor (DP); Charles J. Mahoney, schools superintendent (DP); John E. Maney, chancellor, vicar-general (PC,DP,PA); Frank W. Mason, pastor (DP); Edward J. McAniff, vice-chancellor (PC); James C. McAniff, chancellor, vicar - general (PC,DP,PA); John E. McCafferty, Tribunal (PC,DP); Philip E. McGhan, hospital chaplain (DP); Patrick Moffatt, pastor (DP); Donald J. Mulcahy, charities director (DP); J. Emmett Murphy, Tribunal (PC); William J. Naughton, pastor (DP); John F. Neary, dean (DP); George V. Predmore, pastor (DP); Richard M. Quinn, rector, St. Andrew's Seminary (PC,DP); John S. Randall, diocesan planning and public relations (PC,DP); Arthur M. Ratigan, charities director (DP); George J. Schmitt, pastor (DP); William M. Roche, schools superintendent (DP); Albert H. Schnacky, C.C.D. director (DP); Adelbert J. Schneider, dean (DP); Leo G. Schwab, dean (DP); William H. Shannon, professor (DP); Albert L. Simonetti, consultor (DP); Leo V. Smith, consultor (DP); Frederick L. Straub, dean (DP).

84. *CCJ*, February 20, 1953; May 1, 8, 23, 1953.

85. On *The Miracle*, see CCJ, January 21, 1951 and March 9, 1951 (S. Tier ed.); on *Baby Doll*, see CCJ, December 29, 1956. On the anti - smut drive, see *CCJ* March 12, 1954 (S. Tier ed.); June 25, 1954.

86. *CCJ*, May 26, 1950.

87. *TU*, November 16, 1949; *CCJ*, September 12, 1952.

88. *Synodus Roffensis Sexta*, published by the Diocese in 1954. *ARD*, circulars by Bishop Kearney of January 1, 1957, March 2, 1959, promulgating extra-synodal legislation.

89. *CCJ*, October 2, 1959; September 8, 1961; April 27, 1962.

90. *CCJ*, April 21, 1950; May 12, 26, 1950.

91. *CCJ*, November 5, 1950.

92. *ARD*, Francis J. Erb, "Catholic Radio in Rochester," MS, 1951; Thomas F. Bennett, "The Family Rosary for Peace," MS, 1965.

93. *CCJ*, June 18, 1964.

94. *CCJ*, April 15, 29, 1955; April 6, 28, 1956.

95. *CCJ*, December 4, 1953; December 11, 1954; May 28, 1954; July 2, 1954; November 5, 1954.

96. *CCJ*, February 26, 1954.

97. *CCJ*, July 9, 1954.

98 *CCI*, February 7, 14, 1958.

99. *CCJ*, October 28, 1958; December 25, 1959; November 25, 1960; December 29, 1961; January 3, 1964.

100 *CCJ*, January 23, 1953; March 29, 1957; April 5, 1957.

101. *CCJ*, January 7, 1955.

102. *CCJ*, January 15, 1960. These figures are based on the number of communion breads distributed by the nuns at Holy Angels Home and the nuns at the Josephite Motherhouse, purveyors to most of the parishes of the Diocese.

103. *CCJ*, May 29, 1941; June 5, 19, 1941.

104. *CCJ*, June 9, 1961.

105. *CCJ*, May 23, 30, 1952; June 6, 1952; July 4, 18, 1952; August 1, 8, 15, 1952; May 7, 28, 1954; June 4, 1954.

106. *CCJ*, February 24, 1956. To commemorate the Pope's birthday, Cardinal Francis Spellman of New York presented

him the "Papal Cup," a hand-wrought and hand-engraved glass vessel made to order by the Steuben Glass factory in Corning, New York. This cup was pictured in *Life* magazine, March 12, 1956, p. 48. For a photo of the vessel and its engraver, Mr. Roger Keagle, see *CCJ*, February 9, 1956. A copy of this handsome creation is on exhibit at the Steuben Glass Center in Corning.

107. *CCJ*, October 10, 1958.

108. *CCJ*, April 17, 24, 1959; May 15, 22, 1959.

109. Information kindly provided by Mrs. Catherine Gledhill, President of the Diocesan Council of Catholic Women.

110. *CCJ*, April 29, 1955; August 26, 1955; November 18, 1955.

111. Information kindly furnished by Mrs. Eugene Eckert, President, Diocesan Council of Catholic Nurses.

112. *CCJ*, May 27, 1966. For the mandates given to the Legion and the Sodality, see *CCJ*, May 23, 1958.

113. Information kindly furnished by Father Dunn.

114. Article on Scouting, Robert G. Magin, *CCJ*, February 10, 1967.

115. Information kindly furnished by Miss Grace I. Duffy and the Rev. Robert G. Magin. Unfortunately, we have been unable to secure data on Catholic Girl Scouting in the other ten counties of the Diocese where it is likewise flourishing.

116. *CCJ*, December 7, 1951 and later issues.

117. *CCJ*, November 10, 1961, editorial.

118. *CCJ*, November 17, 1961; brochure, "Sacerdotal Union of Daily Adoration." The present address of the Union is 816 West Broad Street, Horseheads, New York, 14845.

119. *ARD*, John M. Mulligan, "An International Lay Apostolate — The Daily Mass League of Rochester, New York," MS, 1962.

120. Sister M. Alexander Gray, O.S.F., "Development of the Newman Club Movement, 1893-1961," *RACHS*, 7 (1963): 70-128. By 1967 there were also full-time chaplains at the following public institu-

tions: Monroe County Home; Strong Memorial Hospital; Rochester State Hospital; Newark State Hospital (Newark, N. Y.); Craig Colony (Sonyea, N. Y.); Willard State Hospital (Willard, N. Y.); Elmira Reformatory; Elmira Reception Center (Penal); the State Agricultural and Industrial School at Industry, N. Y.; Auburn Prison; the Bath Veterans Administration Center; and the Canandaigua U. S. Veterans Hospital.

121. *CCJ*, March 16, 1959.

122. Montgomery, *Catholic Family Center;* also, interview with Mr. Montgomery.

123. *CCJ*, February 4, 11, 1955.

124. *CCJ*, May 13, 1966.

125. *CCJ*, June 3, 1966; also, interview with Mr. Montgomery.

126. *CCJ*, May 23, 1958; *TU*, September 22, 1958.

127. *CCJ*, September 12, 1958. The Home subsequently purchased the adjacent remainder of the old Hooker Estate for $80,000.00.

128. *UA*, January 6, 1906. For the General Hospital pact, see *CCJ*, August 23, 1962. See also, in general, *ARD*, Daniel Weeks, "The History of St. Ann's Home," MS, 1963.

129. Information kindly furnished by Mr. David H. Shearer, Diocesan attorney. See also *Brighton-Pittsford Post* (Pittsford, N. Y.), March 24, 1960.

130. See *A Summary of Facts and Figures: 1. In Puerto Rico. 2. Puerto Rican Immigration,* the January 1959 publication of the Migration Division, Department of Labor, Commonwealth of Puerto Rico.

131. See the series of articles by Pat Brasley and Kurt Rohde, *DC*, January 12-16, 1955.

132. *CCJ*, April 8, 29, 1955; April 20, 1956.

133. *CCJ*, June 30, 1961; June 8, 29, 1962. An early local Puerto Rican leader was Alejandro Velez Mendoza, who died an untimely death on August 5, 1966, aged thirty-six. After moving into the Rochester area in 1952, he helped found the Puerto Rican Affairs Committee and to establish in Rochester an office of the Puerto Rican

Department of Labor. He was tireless in his service as an interpreter, in youth work and in resettlement efforts. (Obituary in *CCJ*, September 2, 1966.)

134. *CCJ*, May 4, 1956; December 21, 1956.

135. Information kindly supplied by Father Roger Baglin.

136. *CCJ*, February 1, 1957; October 4, 1957; Georgia Youngblood Conner, "Plea for Love," *Catholic Digest*, 21 (1957): 3-5.

137. *CCJ*, March 16, 1951; April 15, 1955.

138. *CCJ*, May 27, 1960; October 27, 1965; March 31, 1967.

139. *CCJ*, February 25, 1951.

140. *CCJ*, June 17, 1960.

141. *CCJ*, February 9, 23, 1962; February 22, 1963; April 9, 16, 1964.

142. *CCJ*, April 3, 1964.

143. *CCJ*, October 11, 1963; November 1, 22, 1963.

144. *CCJ*, March 18, 1960.

145. *CCJ*, September 6, 1963.

146. *CCJ*, February 11, 18, 1965; March 11, 18, 1965; May 1, 1965.

147. *CCJ*, March 15, 1963, editorial. *CCJ*, *DC*, September 23, 26, 1965; *TU*, September 27, 1965; October 2, 1965.

148. *CCJ*, October 1, 1965.

149. *CCJ*, November 26, 1965; March 4, 1966.

150. *CCJ*, October 8, 1964.

151. *CCJ*, July 30, 1964; *DC*, July 25, 26, 1964; *TU*, July 25, 1964, August 20, 1964.

152. *CCJ*, August 27, 1965.

153. *CCJ*, June 1, 1965.

154. The CIC circular was sent to priests November 23, 1964. See also *CCJ*, December 10, 1964.

155. *CCJ*, June 18, 1965.

156. *CCJ*, August 9, 1965.

157. Data kindly furnished by Sister Jamesetta; also *CCJ*, May 28, 1965; June 18, 1965; July 2, 1965; August 6, 1965; August 19, 1966.

158. Data kindly furnished by Sister Joanne; and by Rev. Mother A. McDonell, R.S.C.J., superior of the Academy of the Sacred Heart, which entered actively into the program in 1966. See also *CCJ*, August 12, 1966.

159. *CCJ*, July 2, 1965.

160. *CCJ*, February 11, 1966; also data kindly furnished by Sister Cyril.

161. *CCJ*, May 31, 1963; June 18, 1965; April 29, 1966; May 6, 1966; also *ARD*, Calogero LaVerde, "The Formative Period of St. Martin de Porres Center," MS, 1965; and Thomas J. Murphy, "Continued Growth of the St. Martin de Porres Center," MS, 1966.

162. *CCJ*, February 25, 1965; April 29, 1965; July 23, 1965; October 22, 1965; March 11, 1966.

163. *CCJ*, June 26, 1965; December 24, 1965; December 16, 1966. The fact that the Rochester Sisters of Mercy changed to a more convenient religious habit on December 28, 1965, was of assistance to them in this inner-city work. Of the other pioneer orders of nuns in the Diocese, the School Sisters of Notre Dame had changed their habits on March 25, 1963; the Sisters of Charity gave up their picturesque linen "cornettes" and adopted a new habit on September 20, 1964; and the Religious of the Sacred Heart donned their new garb on January 1, 1967. The Sisters of St. Joseph, at the present writing, are still engaged in step-by-step experimentation. However, the Rochester Josephite Sisters (and also the Rochester Mercy Sisters) missioned to South America were allowed from the start to use a very modified dress.

164. *CCJ*, April 17, 24, 1959; May 15, 22, 1959.

165. See the apostolic constitution *Humanae Salutis* (December 25, 1961), and Pope John's opening address (October 11, 1962), in *Documents of Vatican II* (New York, 1966), pp. 703-19.

166. *CCJ*, May 1, 1959; May 25, 1962.

167. *CCJ*, September 28, 1962; October 5, 12, 19, 26, 1962; November 9, 23, 30, 1962; December 7, 1962.

168. Session II: *CCJ*, September 13, 1963; October 4, 25, 1963; November 8, 1963; December 6, 13, 1963. Session III: *CCJ*, September 10, 1964; October 8, 15, 1964; November 5, 12, 18, 27, 1964; December 3, 10, 1964. Session IV: *CCJ*, September 10, 1965; October 8, 22, 1965; December 3, 17, 1965.

169. *CCJ*, September 10, 1965.

170. *CCJ*, October 11, 18, 1963.

171. *CCJ*, March 27, 1953. Further information comes from Sister M. Paulette Ulton, S.S.J.; Msgr. Donald Cleary; Mrs. Arthur Farren; and Fathers Benedict Ehmann and Leonard A. Kelly. For the parish liturgical programs of the latter two, see also Leo R. Ward, *The Living Parish* (Notre Dame, Indiana, 1959), p. 187-90.

172. *CCJ*, November 30, 1951.

173. *CCJ*, April 5, 1947.

174. *CCJ*, April 3, 1953; May 8, 1953.

175. *CCJ*, May 6, 1955; December 2, 1955; March 23, 30, 1966.

176. *CCJ*, October 5, 1958; February 13, 1959.

177. *CCJ*, July 12, 26, 1962; August 2, 16, 1962.

178. *CCJ*, October 22, 1964.

179. *CCJ*, November 5, 12, 19, 26, 1964.

180. *CCJ*, March 4, 1965.

181. *CCJ*, November 12, 1965.

182. *CCJ*, April 22, 1965; October 21, 1966.

183. *CCJ*, August 13, 1965. Members of the original commission were: Msgr. Craugh, Msgr. George A. Cocuzzi, Fathers Benedict Ehmann, Robert F. McNamara, William H. Shannon, Gerard J. McMahon, Peter Sheehan, C.S.B., and Thomas G. Lenhard. In 1966 the Commission published a *Vigil Service for a Deceased Priest:* a vernacular scripture service for congregational participation to replace the Office of the Dead hitherto used at the church-wakes of the clergy.

184. *CCJ*, April 1, 22, 1966. St. Francis Xavier effectively utilized the marble altar installed in St. Patrick's Cathedral in 1898,

removed to Sacred Heart Cathedral in 1937, and dismantled in 1957. (*CCJ*, March 11, 1966.)

185. The Reverend Paul Courtney, Indianapolis, Indiana.

186. *CCJ*, June 25, 1966.

187. *CCJ*, December 31, 1964; August 5, 1966.

188. *CCJ*, October 14, 1955.

189. *ARD*, Kearney Papers, circular to priests; *CCJ*, April 8, 1966.

190. *CCJ*, May 27, 1966; July 15, 1966.

191. *CCJ*, December 13, 1963; January 17, 1964; August 6, 20, 1964; July 30, 1965; August 6, 27, 1965; September 27, 1965. On their plans for expansion, see *CCJ*, November 5, 1966.

192. *CCJ*, April 8, 1965; August 20, 27, 1965.

193. *CC*, November 18, 1943.

194. *CCJ*, February 2, 1964; June 24, 1964.

195. *CCJ*, January 16, 1962; September 26, 1962; February 1, 1963; March 15, 1963; July 12, 1963.

196. *CCJ*, April 30, 1964.

197. For Dr. LaLonde, see *CCJ*, August 2, 1957; July 4, 1958; July 6, 1962; March 15, 1963. For Dr. Caccamise, see: *CCJ*, February 9, 1962; May 26, 1962; *DC*, April 22, 1962; *Medical Missionary* (Philadelphia, Pa.), Vol. 36 (1962), Vol. 37 (1963), Vol. 38 (1963). For the Whalens, see *CCJ*, May 26, 1962, November 9, 1962.

198. *DC*, August 28, 29, 1963, September 2, 1963; *TU*, August 28, 29, 1963, September 3, 1963; *CCJ*, August 30, 1963; September 6, 1963.

199. *CCJ*, July 23, 1965. In May, 1966, Bishop Kearney added the following: Msgr. James D. Cuffney (Auburn); Father Joseph F. Hogan (Corning); Father Jude Taran, S.A. (Montour Falls); Sister M. Lourdes MacCarthy, S.S.J.; Sister M. Beatrice Curran, R.S.M.; Mr. Harold Hacker; Mr. Louis Martin; Mrs. David Springett. (*CCJ*, May 27, 1966).

200. *CCJ*, January 14, 1966.

201. *CCJ*, August 19, 1966.

202. *CCJ*, March 25, 1966; April 11, 1966; *TU*, March 28, 1966.

203. *CCJ*, January 7, 1965.

204. Bishop Kearney personal papers: Egidio Vagnozzi to James E. Kearney, Washington, D. C., February 2, 1965 (Protocol 130/58); Alfredo Ottaviani to James E. Kearney, Vatican City, February 24, 1965 (Protocol 183/64).

205. *CCJ*, October 25, 1957, plus special tabloid; November 1, 8, 1957.

206. *CCJ*, September 19, 26, 1958; November 9, 16, 1962. There were also commemorations of the Bishop's eightieth and eighty-first birthdays (*CCJ*, October 23, 30, 1965; October 22, 1965).

207. For the request for prayers, see *ARD*, Kearney Papers, circular from Msgr. John E. Maney to clergy, Rochester, December 7, 1956. For the recovery, see Bishop Casey's memoir, *CCJ*, October 22, 1965; and Bishop Kearney's address, April 5, 1957.

208. *CCJ*, March 11, 18, 1966. See also special supplement of *CCJ*, March 25, 1966, Anne Buckley byline.

209. *CCJ*, May 13, 20, 1966. Bishop Casey thus became the fourth native priest of the present Diocese of Rochester to become a bishop of another diocese. The others were Bishop Thomas A. Hendrick of Cebu, P.I.; Archbishop Edward J. Hanna of San Francisco, and Bishop Walter A. Foery of Syracuse. A native of Corning but never a priest of the Rochester Diocese is Bishop Francis J. Green of Tucson, Arizona (1906-   ). A native of Rochester, but by adoption a Baltimorean and by vocation a Franciscan, is Bishop Nicholas D'Antonio, O.F.M., (1916-   ), head of the Prelature of Olancho, Honduras (*CCJ*, July 29, 1966).

210. *AAS*, 58 (1966): See article #11, p. 763. Translation in *Catholic Mind*, 64 (1966): November, pp. 50-64; December, pp. 49-59. See also *CCJ*, September 23, 1966.

211. *DC*, September 12, 1966, Mary McKee byline; *TU*, September 13, 1966, Desmond Stone byline.

212. *CCJ*, October 28, 1966; also data kindly provided by Msgr. George A. Cocuzzi, Chancellor.

213. *AAS*, 58 (1966): 1189.

214. *ARD*, Kearney Papers, Egidio Vagnozzi to James E. Kearney, Washington, D. C., November 23, 1966 (Protocol 4075/66).

215. *TU*, December 15, 1966.

EPILOGUE:

THE COMING OF BISHOP SHEEN

1. *New York Times*, December 15, 1966, Paul Hoffman byline.

2. *CCJ*, October 28, 1966; Joseph B. Code, *Dictionary of the American Hierarchy* (New York, 1964).

3. Interview with Mrs. Gerald M. Luke of Rochester.

4. *CCJ*, October 28, 1966; November 4, 1966. Bishop-designate Sheen chose to use his own coat of arms by itself, instead of combining it with the diocesan arms. This represents a silver dove bearing a green olive branch, and flying to the spectator's left. It hovers over a gold orb representing the world, surmounted by a silver cross. Previous to his appointment, the Bishop had a Latin cross crowning the orb. To commemorate his coming to Rochester, he replaced the Latin cross with a St. Andrew's cross taken from the Rochester diocesan arms. The background of the shield is blue; but this is surrounded by a wide band of gold. The motto is "Da per Matrem me venire", taken from the Marian hymn, *Stabat Mater:* "Let me come to You through Your Mother."

5. *CCJ*, December 16, 1966, and the special supplement honoring the installation. See also *DC*, December 15, 1966, George Murphy byline; and *New York Times*, December 15, 1966, Paul Hoffman byline.

6. *CCJ*, December 16, 23, 1966; *DC*, December 12, 16, 1966; *TU*, December 15, 16, 1966.

7. *TU*, December 16, 1966.

8. *CCJ*, December 30, 1966.

9. *CCJ*, February 10, 1967.

10. *CCJ*, January 20, 1967, February 3, 1967.

11. *CCJ*, May 8, 1967.

12. *CCJ*, November 18, 1966.

13. *Lumen Gentium*, 28.

14. *CCJ*, January 3, 1967.

15. *CCJ*, February 3, 1967.

16. *CCJ*, January 27, 1967; *DC*, January 24, 1967.

17. *DC*, February 3, 1967.

18. *DC*, February 10, 1967.

19. *CCJ*, January 6, 1967; *DC*, March 4, 1967; *TU*, March 4, 1967.

20. *CCJ*, February 3, 1967; *DC*, February 1, 1967.

21. *CCJ*, April 28, 1967.

22. *CCJ*, February 3, 1967.

23. *CCJ*, May 5, 1967.

24. *CCJ*, January 27, 1967.

25. *Apostolicam Actuositatem*, Decree on the Apostolate of the Laity, 25.

26. *CCJ*, May 26, 1967; *New York Times*, May 23, 1967.

27. *Christus Dominus*, 27.

28. *ARD*, Bishop Sheen to priests, circular of January 27, 1967; *CCJ*, February 3, 1967.

29. *CCJ*, March 3, 1967.

30. *CCJ*, March 10, 17, 1967.

31. *CCJ*, April 28, 1967; May 5, 19, 1967.

32. *CCJ*, April 7, 21, 1967.

33. *CCJ*, April 7, 1967.

34. *CCJ*, May 19, 1967.

35. *CCJ*, June 9, 1967.

36. *CCJ*, June 9, 1967.

37. *CCJ*, April 14, 1967.

38. *ARD*, circular of March 1, 1967.

39. *CCJ*, June 2, 1967.

40. *ARD*, circular of December 30, 1966.

41. *CCJ*, February 10, 1967.

42. *CCJ*, March 31, 1967.

43. *CCJ*, May 26, 1967.

44. *CCJ*, February 10, 1967.

45. *ARD*, James M. Moynihan, circular to priests, covering Sheen memorandum, March 31, 1967.

46. *CCJ*, February 17, 1967; *TU*, February 13, 15, 1967.

47. *CCJ*, February 24, 1967.

48. *CCJ*, January 13, 1967; February 3, 1967.

49. *CCJ*, April 14, 1967.

50. *CCJ*, April 28, 1967.

51. *CCJ*, May 19, 1967.

52. *CCJ*, February 3, 1967; *DC*, January 31, 1967.

53. *CCJ*, March 3, 1967; *DC*, February 23, 1967, Mary McKee byline.

54. *ARD*, Law Day circular to priests, April 20, 1967.

55. *CCJ*, January 6, 1967.

56. *CCJ*, January 13, 1967.

57. *TU*, January 10, 1967.

58. *CCJ*, January 27, 1967; *DC*, January 24, 1967.

59. *CCJ*, May 26, 1967. At the same time the Bishop directed that the Christmas collection, hitherto a gift of the parish to the pastor, be made a part of the parish funds. A revision of clergy salaries, unchanged for over two decades, was also intimated.

CHAPTER SIXTEEN

THE FIFTH-QUARTER CENTURY

1. Sheen awaits a formal biographer. The present account depends much on the excellent Ph.D. dissertation of Kathleen Riley Fields, "Bishop Fulton J. Sheen: An American Catholic response to the twentieth century" (University of Notre Dame, 1988); and on *Treasure in Clay. The Autobiography of Fulton J. Sheen* (Garden City, N.Y., 1980). Also helpful was the Ph.D. dissertation of P. David Finks, "Crisis in Smugtown: a study of conflict, churches and citizen organization in Rochester, New York, 1964-1969" (Union Graduate School, 1975). Other miscellaneous written sources have been supplemented by interviews with persons associated with Sheen in his Rochester years.

2. For fuller treatment of the Rochester Center story, see Robert F. McNamara, "Ecumenism and the Rochester Center for Theological Studies," *Rochester History* (Rochester Public Library), Vol. LII, No. 4 (Fall, 1990).

3. This section is based chiefly on interviews, news reports, official papers of Bishop Hogan, and the Bishop's memoirs, recorded and edited by Professor Nathan Kollar of St. John Fisher College.

4. I am indebted for this information to Father McCloskey, now of Copake Falls, N.Y.

5. In compiling this section I was fortunate to have the indispensable assistance of Mr. James F. Johnston.

6. Naturally the postconciliar bishops founded few new parishes during their tenure. Sheen established St. Paul, West Webster (1967); St. Christopher, North Chili (1968); and St. Jude the Apostle (1968). Hogan established the Church of the Resurrection, Fairport (1973). Clark established Emmanuel Church of the Deaf (1981); St. Elizabeth Ann Seton, Hamlin (1983); and the Church of the Transfiguration, Pittsford (1983).

INDEX*

* Chap. 16, although not annotated, is included in this index.

"dialogistic" get-acquainted tour of diocese, 577; *Democrat & Chronicle* interview and women's issue, December 1980, 577-78; shortage of priests, 578; ordains first class of permanent deacons, 578; diocese sells Becket Hall (1980), 578; diocese sells St. Bernard's Seminary (1981-82), 578-79; St. Bernard's Institute created, 579; St. Bernard's Park, residential, opened (1996), 579; initiates annual ThanksGiving Appeal (1981), 579; initiates capital campaign "The Miracle of Sharing" (1992), 580; publishes "The Fire in the Thornbush: a Pastoral Letter on Women in the Church" (1982), 580-81; appointed to NCCB committee writing national pastoral on women (1984), 581; elected chair of NCCB Standing Committee on Women in Society and in the Church (1989), 581; concern about implementation of collegiality, subsidiarity in the Church, 581-82; subsidiarity and the "Charles Curran Controversy," 582-84; Diocesan liturgical norms, 584-85; grants permission for "Tridentine" Latin Mass (1993), 585; sets norms for priestly welfare, discipline, 585-86; sets rules for priests' sabbaticals, annual convocation, new pastors' workshops, 586; tries to promote religious vocations, 587-88; visits Rochester missions in Brazil, Chile, 588; supports diocesan exchange with Diocese of Tabasco, Mexico, 588; ecumenically active: continues GEM affiliation, authorizes move of St. Bernard's Institute to Colgate-Rochester campus, agrees to merger of Bishop Sheen Housing Fund with Episcopal Rural Mission to form Bishop Sheen Ecumenical Housing Foundation, 588; offers Sacred Heart Cathedral for episcopal consecration of Bishop William G. Burrill of the Rochester Episcopal Diocese, (1984), 589; addresses Jewish Congregation B'Rith Kodesh, 589; signs covenant with Rochester Episcopal Diocese (1987), 589; approves Interfaith Forum to discuss non-theological subjects: Catholics, Protestants, Anglicans, Jews and Muslims, 589; endorses boycott of J.P. Stevens Textile Co. (1980), 589; backs boycott of Swiss Nestlé Corporation over dangerous infant formula (1982-84), 589; states Catholic objection to *in vitro* fertilization (1983), 589-90; declines to disaffiliate from United Way over Planned Parenthood proposal (1992), 590; issues pastoral instruction on AIDS (1988), 590; adopts firm policy on pedophilia (1990), 592; writes President Jimmy Carter, candidates Walter Mondale and Ronald Reagan urging moral aspects of political issues, 591; addresses 5,000

against nuclear warfare, Seneca Army Depot, Romulus, N.Y. (1983), 591-92; attends by delegation world peace symposium, Loccum, Germany (1989), 592; protests Persian Gulf War in joint letters with Bishop Burrill to *D&C* (1990, 1991), 592-93; carries through contested reorganization of parochial schools (1990), 594; Rome decides some disputed matters, e.g. altar girls and women preachers, 594-95; Pope rules priestly ordination of women doctrinally forbidden (1983-95), 595-96; the Bishop favors discussion of pros and cons of even sensitive issues, 596; heartening good works, spiritual developments in diocese after Vatican II, 596-98; Bishop convokes Seventh Synod of Diocese (1990-1993), 598-600; promulgates its aims on 125th anniversary of diocese, (December, 1993), 599; John Paul II considers diocesan synods helpful in updating Church, 600

Cleary, Rev. Donald M., 347, 374, 409
Cocuzzi, Rev. George A., chancellor, 487-88, 528
Coleman, Harold J., 455, 479, 494
Colgan, Rev. Peter, 68-69, 563
Columbus Civic Center, 311, 372
Comes, John T., architect, 303
Connelly, Catherine C., 309
Connelly, John, 328
Connolly, Alexander, 99-100
Connolly, James C., 268
Connolly, Bishop John, O.P. (New York), 30-35
Connors, Rev. Thomas F., 275, 292, 294, 317
Conroy, Bishop Joseph H. (Ogdensburg), 255, 332-333
Consultors, Diocesan, 488
Conway, Rev. John, 347
Conway, Katherine Eleanor, 228-30, 245
Cook, Eleanor (Mrs. Jerome), 547
Corcoran, Margaret, 558
Cornell University, 232-37, 428
Corpus Christi Welfare Ministries, 597
Corrigan, Archbishop Michael A. (New York), 173, 177, 214-17, 219-20
Cowen, Rev. William E., 280-81
Coxe, Bishop Arthur C. (Episcopal), 130-31, 138
Craugh, Rev. Wilfred T., vicar general, 363, 487, 509, 511
Creedon, Rev. Michael, 95-96, 102
Cristantielli, Rev. Francis, 645
Cronin, Rev. James T., 366
Crowley, Rev. John B., 310
Cubans; *see* Ethnic groups
Cuff, James E., 402, 463
Culhane, Mrs. Daniel, 445
Cunningham, Augustine J., 361

Simonetti, Rev. Albert L., 645
Simpson, Dr. Leo F., 246, 403
Sinclair, Rev. Francis, 129
Smyth, Mother Rose Miriam, S.S.J., 402-03, 464
Socialism, 269-70
Social Justice conferences, 413, 430-31
Society for the Prevention of Cruelty to Children (Rochester), 343
Sonnontouan (Seneca Indian country); *see* Iroquois Indians
Spalding, Archbishop John L., (Peoria), 250
Spanish-speaking; *see* Ethnic groups
Spellman, Cardinal Francis (New York), 459, 488, 526
State militia, Catholic membership, 91-92
Statistics, Diocese of Rochester, 127, 179, 181-83, 222, 254, 301, 344, 389-90, 424, 446-47, 449, 470-71, 657
Staub, Rev. Jacob, 277-78, 280-82, 310, 319
Stauder, Rev. F. William, 354, 357
Stec, Rev. Alexander, 645
Steele, Joseph, 88-89
Stepinac, Bl. Aloysius (Zagreb), 466
Stevens, Mother Georgia, R.S.C.J., 398
Stewardship Council, 586-87
Stewart, Rev. Alexander M., 604
Stickle International, architects, 474
Stoecklein, Joseph, 370
Straub, Rev. Frederick J., 373-74, 450
Sullivan Expedition (1779), 22
Sullivan, Rev. Joseph J., 457, 655
Summer camps: Camp Madonna, 311-12; Camp Stella Maris, 312; Camp Villa Maria, 436
Surratt, John Harrison, 104
Survey of Catholic Households in the Diocese of Rochester, 563
Synods of the Diocese of Rochester: First and Second Synods (1875, 1887), 622-23; Third Synod (1914), 282-83; Fourth Synod (1924), 316-17; Fifth Synod (1935), 391-92; Sixth Synod (1954), 490; Seventh Synod (1993), 598-600
Szadzinski, Rev. Theophilus, 203-06, 624
Szupa, Rev. Stanislaus, 375

— T —

Tabacchi, Antonio, 631
Teachers' Institutes, 165-66
Tehoronhiongo, François, Huron, 16, 20
Temperance Societies, 54
Tettelbach, Peter, 361, 643
Tien, Cardinal Thomas, S.V.D. (Peking), 457, 512
Timon, Bishop John, C.M. (first Bishop of Buffalo): named to Buffalo, 46; early visitations of Diocese, 57-60; and anti-Catholic discrimination, 90-91; and Catholic schools, 63-66; and charities, 66-68; and the Civil War, 93, 96, 101-04;

and the Diocese of Rochester, 110; and popular funeral customs, 107; and the Holy See, 106; and pastoral legislation, 105, 107-08; and rural Catholic colonies, 68-69; and temperance, 107; personal traits, 105, 107-09
Tindell, Mother Sylvester, S.S.J., 305
Tiohero (St. Etienne), Cayuga Indian village, 13
Todd, Norah Conway (Mrs. Libanus), 460
Todd and Giroux, architects, 475
Tonty, Henri de, 17
Tormey, Rev. Richard, 461-62
Totiakton (La Conception), west Seneca Indian village, 14
Truman, Harry S., 454, 467
Trusteeism, 69-77
Tyrone (Steuben-Schuyler Counties), Irish colony at, 27-28

— U —

Utica, St. John's Church, 32

— V —

Vagnozzi, Archbishop Egidio, apostolic delegate, 658
Vaillant de Gueslis, Rev. François, S.J., 17-18
Vannutelli, Cardinal Vincenzo, 333
Vatican Council II, and *aggiornamento*, 509-17
Vay, Peter A., 328
Velez Mendoza, Alejandro, 661-62
Vogt, Rev. Francis, 549
Vogt, Rev. George E., 407, 415, 431
Vogt, Rev. Joseph E., 404

— W —

Wahl, Rev. Raymond J., 530
Wall, Rev. Michael C., 370
Walsh, Bishop Emmett J., (Charleston), 376-77
Wantuck, Pvt. John J., 448
Ward, Hugh, 28, 33
Ward, Sara McCort (Mrs. Charles), 496-97
Warde, Mother M. Xavier, R.S.M., 65
Warner, Andrew J., architect, 188
Warner, J. Foster, architect, 307
Wars:
 War of 1812, 91; Mexican War, 92
 Civil War: 92-105; and conscription, 101-02; area Catholic heroes, 93-94, 97, 99-102; Catholic soldiers and regiments, 94-99
 Spanish-American War, 180-81
 World War I: 283-98; area service personnel, 291-98; Diocesan chaplains, 294-95; area Catholic heroes, 293-95; War Chest, 290-91
 Spanish Civil War, 442-44
 World War II: 444-45; Diocesan service chaplains, 445, 449; auxiliary chap-

CANADA

LAKE ONTARIO

CANADA

OSW

NIAGARA

ORLEANS

MONROE

WAYNE

ONOND

ERIE

GENESEE

ROCHESTER

CANADA

SYRA

BUFFALO

WYOMING

ONTARIO

LIVINGSTON

SENECA

CAYUGA

LAKE ERIE

YATES

CORT

TOMPKINS

STEUBEN

SCHUYLER

CATTARAUGUS

ALLEGANY

CHEMUNG

TIOGA

CHAUTAUQUA

PENNSYLVANIA

State & Ecclesiastical Province
of New York

Diocese

Archdiocese

Counties added to
Rochester Diocese
1896